The Biodemography of Subsistence Farming

Population, Food and Family

Viewing the subsistence farm as primarily a "demographic enterprise" to create and support a family, this book offers an integrated view of the demography and ecology of preindustrial farming. Taking an interdisciplinary perspective, it examines how traditional farming practices interact with demographic processes such as childbearing, death and family formation. It includes topics such as household nutrition, physiological work capacity, health and resistance to infectious diseases, as well as reproductive performance and mortality. The book argues that the farming household is the most informative scale at which to study the biodemography and physiological ecology of preindustrial, noncommercial agriculture. It offers a balanced appraisal of the farming system, considering its strengths and limitations, as well as the implications of viewing it as a "demographic enterprise" rather than an economic one. A valuable resource for graduate students and researchers in biological and physical anthropology, cultural anthropology, natural resource management, agriculture and ecology.

James W. Wood is Emeritus Professor of Anthropology and Demography at Pennsylvania State University and a Senior Scientist in Penn State's Graduate Program on Human Dimensions of Natural Resources and the Environment, USA. His previous book, *The Dynamics of Human Reproduction: Biology, Biometry, Demography* (1994) won the 1995 W. W. Howells Prize for best book in biological anthropology awarded by the American Anthropological Association. He conducted several years' worth of fieldwork on the demography and ecology of subsistence farming in highland New Guinea and in the northern Orkney Islands of Scotland, and retired in 2017.

Cambridge Studies in Biological and Evolutionary Anthropology

Also available in the series

53. *Technique and Application in Dental Anthropology* Joel D. Irish and Greg C. Nelson (eds.) 978 0 521 87061 0

54. *Western Diseases: An Evolutionary Perspective* Tessa M. Pollard 978 0 521 61737 6

55. *Spider Monkeys: The Biology, Behavior and Ecology of the Genus Ateles* Christina J. Campbell 978 0 521 86750 4

56. *Between Biology and Culture* Holger Schutkowski (ed.) 978 0 521 85936 3

57. *Primate Parasite Ecology: The Dynamics and Study of Host-Parasite Relationships* Michael A. Huffman and Colin A. Chapman (eds.) 978 0 521 87246 1

58. *The Evolutionary Biology of Human Body Fatness: Thrift and Control* Jonathan C. K. Wells 978 0 521 88420 4

59. *Reproduction and Adaptation: Topics in Human Reproductive Ecology* C. G. Nicholas Mascie-Taylor and Lyliane Rosetta (eds.) 978 0 521 50963 3

60. *Monkeys on the Edge: Ecology and Management of Long-Tailed Macaques and their Interface with Humans* Michael D. Gumert, Agustín Fuentes and Lisa Jones-Engel (eds.) 978 0 521 76433 9

61. *The Monkeys of Stormy Mountain: 60 Years of Primatological Research on the Japanese Macaques of Arashiyama* Jean-Baptiste Leca, Michael A. Huffman and Paul L. Vasey (eds.) 978 0 521 76185 7

62. *African Genesis: Perspectives on Hominin Evolution* Sally C. Reynolds and Andrew Gallagher (eds.) 978 1 107 01995 9

63. *Consanguinity in Context* Alan H. Bittles 978 0 521 78186 2

64. *Evolving Human Nutrition: Implications for Public Health* Stanley Ulijaszek, Neil Mann and Sarah Elton (eds.) 978 0 521 86916 4

65. *Evolutionary Biology and Conservation of Titis, Sakis and Uacaris* Liza M. Veiga, Adrian A. Barnett, Stephen F. Ferrari and Marilyn A. Norconk (eds.) 978 0 521 88158 6

66. *Anthropological Perspectives on Tooth Morphology: Genetics, Evolution, Variation* G. Richard Scott and Joel D. Irish (eds.) 978 1 107 01145 8

67. *Bioarchaeological and Forensic Perspectives on Violence: How Violent Death is Interpreted from Skeletal Remains* Debra L. Martin and Cheryl P. Anderson (eds.) 978 1 107 04544 6

The Biodemography of Subsistence Farming

Population, Food and Family

JAMES W. WOOD

Pennsylvania State University

CAMBRIDGE
UNIVERSITY PRESS

University Printing House, Cambridge CB2 8BS, United Kingdom

One Liberty Plaza, 20th Floor, New York, NY 10006, USA

477 Williamstown Road, Port Melbourne, VIC 3207, Australia

314–321, 3rd Floor, Plot 3, Splendor Forum, Jasola District Centre, New Delhi – 110025, India

79 Anson Road, #06–04/06, Singapore 079906

Cambridge University Press is part of the University of Cambridge.

It furthers the University's mission by disseminating knowledge in the pursuit of education, learning, and research at the highest international levels of excellence.

www.cambridge.org
Information on this title: www.cambridge.org/9781107033412
DOI: 10.1017/9781139519700

First published 2020

Printed in the United Kingdom by TJ International Ltd, Padstow Cornwall

A catalogue record for this publication is available from the British Library.

Library of Congress Cataloging-in-Publication Data
Names: Wood, James W., 1949– author.
Title: The biodemography of subsistence farming : population, food and family / James W. Wood.
Description: 1 Edition. | New York : Cambridge University Press, 2020. | Includes bibliographical references and index.
Identifiers: LCCN 2019038862 (print) | LCCN 2019038863 (ebook) | ISBN 9781107033412 (hardback) | ISBN 9781139519700 (epub)
Subjects: LCSH: Population–Economic aspects. | Subsistence farming. | Food supply–Economic aspects. | Birth intervals. | Human reproduction.
Classification: LCC HB849.41 .W66 2020 (print) | LCC HB849.41 (ebook) | DDC 338.1–dc23
LC record available at https://lccn.loc.gov/2019038862
LC ebook record available at https://lccn.loc.gov/2019038863

ISBN 978-1-107-03341-2 Hardback

The author and publisher have acknowledged the sources of copyright material where possible and are grateful for the permissions granted. While every effort has been made, it has not always been possible to identify the sources of all the material used, or to trace all copyright holders. We would appreciate any omissions being brought to our attention.

With love, once again, for

PLJ

"We have all of us been told that grace is to be found in this world. But in our human foolishness and short-sightedness we imagine grace to be finite. For this reason we tremble... We tremble before making our choice in life, and after having made it again tremble in fear of having chosen wrong. But the moment comes when our eyes are opened, and we see that grace is infinite. ... Grace, brothers, makes no conditions and singles out none of us in particular; grace takes us all to its bosom and proclaims general amnesty. See! that which we have chosen is given us, and that which we have refused is, also and at the same time, granted us. Aye, that which we have rejected is poured upon us abundantly. For mercy and truth have met together, and righteousness and bliss have kissed one another."   – Isak Dinesen (Karen Blixen, *Babette's Feast*)

Contents

Preface

At the end of the seventeenth century [in rural France], the life of the average family head, who had married for the first time at age 27, could be summarized as follows:

He was born into a family of five children, only half of whom reached the age of 15. Like his father, he too had five children, of whom again only two or three were still alive when he died. This man lived to an average age of 52 – which placed him among the venerable elderly, for only 205 out of every thousand males born reached 52 years. Just within the circle of his own immediate family, he outlived an average of nine persons: one of his grandparents (the other three having died before he was born), both of his parents, three of his siblings, and three of his own children. He had lived through two or three famines as well as three or four periods of high-priced grain, which were tied to the poor harvests that on average recurred every ten years. Moreover, he had witnessed serious illnesses in his parents, his brothers and sisters, his wife (or wives if he had been widowed and remarried), and his children. And he had experienced several such illnesses himself, having survived two or three epidemics as well as more or less endemic whooping cough, scarlet fever, diphtheria, and so on, which each year claimed their victims. He had often suffered from physical ailments such as toothache and wounds that took a long time to heal. Poverty, disabilities, and suffering were constantly before his eyes.

Death was at the center of life, just as the church cemetery was at the center of the village. A child's average age when the first of his parents died was 14 years. Men of 25 to 30 – already scarred by harsh experience and motivated much more by enduring family needs than by the superficial attractions of physical beauty or a pleasant personality – contracted marriages that, though broken only by death, lasted on average less than twenty years.   – J. Fourastié (1959), translated by W. Petersen (1972)

This book is about traditional, preindustrial farming and how it interacts with demographic processes and events like those mentioned in the passage above. Population size and composition (and changes in those variables) are matters of interest, as are demographic events such as births, deaths, marriages and shifts in residence or migration. The primary link between traditional farming and demography is, of course, food – and the ecology of food production and its implications for the nutrition, health, demography and behavior of preindustrial farmers are all central to this book. Another central issue has to do with identifying the most informative scale at which to study all these phenomena. I take a strong position on this particular question, arguing that the traditional farming household, its members and its farm are the right place to ground (but not necessarily to end) our analyses. If the farming household in question is not just traditional but largely subsistence-oriented, then I would (and do) argue that the household is essentially a *demographic enterprise* – its fundamental goal is to produce and support a family – and not strictly an economic one, as has generally been assumed in the past. Finally,

I argue that traditional farming cannot be understood if the members of the farming household are not viewed as conscious agents and decision-makers (albeit not omniscient, omnipotent or omnicompetent ones). A large part of the book involves an exploration of the many implications that follow from adopting this perspective.

By convention, the academic study of traditional farming falls mostly within the bailiwicks of cultural and social anthropology, archaeology, cultural geography and a few other social sciences. I draw upon all these fields and more. But I want to make it clear at the outset that I am a *biological* anthropologist – and a trained demographer/population biologist. Those biographical facts by themselves mean that this book is rather different from other available treatments of traditional farming. Most fundamentally, I am primarily interested in the *biodemography* and *physiological ecology* of farming households – encompassing things such as household nutritional status, physiological work capacity, immune function and resistance to infectious diseases, other aspects of health and morbidity, reproductive performance and mortality, especially mortality among young children, often the most vulnerable members of the household. These things are all, as I hope to show, profoundly important to the success or failure of the household demographic enterprise. Farming behavior (and its social and cultural determinants) is also important to the book, but my approach is perhaps less akin to that of a conventional social scientist and closer to that of a behavioral ecologist, cultural evolutionist or niche constructionist.[1] I have also included a certain amount of relevant crop physiology, ecology and genetics, though written for the broad-minded social or anthropological scientist rather than for experts in those particular areas of agronomy.

Even though I am a biological anthropologist and my concerns are primarily biological, my book draws heavily on what is known as the *ethnographic record*, especially the many reports, written mostly by cultural and social anthropologists, that have been produced over the past century or so on small-scale, kin-based, geographically isolated, traditional ("unacculturated") farming communities. The ethnographic record is one of the most significant contributions of anthropology to human knowledge. To me, it is just as important as, say, the archaeological record or the fossil evidence for human evolution. But the older ethnographic literature is now in danger of being lost – not because of fire or decay but owing to a lack of interest. Almost every week I come across yet another academic library that has deaccessioned a classic ethnographic account or has moved it to deep storage because no one has checked it out in years. Fewer and fewer students of anthropology are reading the ethnographic literature. More and more anthropologists, including senior scholars who should know better, are willing to make sweeping statements about the ecology and evolution of human behavior that fly in the face of what we have known for

---

[1] See Kennett and Winterhalder (2006), Boyd *et al.* (2011) and Kendal *et al.* (2011). I consider the still-youthful fields of behavioral ecology, cultural evolution and niche construction to be very promising as potential sources of ideas for the study of traditional farming practices. But I also think that theoreticians in those fields are still in the process of working out the fundamentals (see, for example, Claidière and André, 2012). Their main impact is likely to be in the future.

decades from ethnographic research. This problem is especially troubling because the opportunity to study relatively "undisturbed" traditional societies is rapidly being lost – perhaps has already been lost – to the forces of globalization, the breakdown of geographical isolation, the influence of powerful metropoles, anthropogenic climate change and so forth. True, ethnographic field research continues, but increasingly it is forced to deal with all the external economic and political influences that constrain the actions and choices of local people. The study of "primitive man" (a term with more than one unfortunate connotation) was once considered the very heart and soul of anthropology. That time has passed, and mostly we should be glad of it, but so has "primitive man" himself, or, more accurately and less offensively, the relatively autonomous traditional communities of subsistence farmers, herders, and hunter-gatherers who needed to adapt above all else to their local environments and their local neighbors rather than the global market. It would be a shame if the existing works describing such communities were also lost out of mere inadvertence or a snobbish attitude that such works are old-fashioned. As detailed in the Appendix to this volume, I have read numerous ethnographic accounts of traditional farming in preparing to write the book, some of them quite old. If, by doing so, I have helped save them from oblivion, I will consider the effort well worthwhile.

I do not, however, pretend to have summarized the ethnographic literature (or the historical or geographical or any other literature) in all its rich empirical detail. Rather, I have focused my attention on that literature by viewing it through the lenses provided by various theoretical *models* – simplified conceptual schemes that can be used (and then discarded) to help us tease apart and understand the complex ethnographic and historical reality. My own approach to modeling follows in the tradition of the early nineteenth-century economic geographer Johann Heinrich von Thünen, whose work is discussed at the end of Chapter 1. (Like von Thünen's, my models will be graphical and verbal and only very rarely mathematical. Mathophobes need not panic.) Three model-inspired simplifications will appear again and again in this book: (i) a focus on subsistence farming rather than production for the market or some larger social/economic/political system, (ii) an assumption that individual subsistence farms are largely autonomous when it comes to food production and consumption, and (iii) the notion, already mentioned, that the subsistence farming household is at heart a demographic enterprise. None of these three simplifications provides an altogether true or complete picture of reality, as is acknowledged throughout the book, but all are useful in helping to narrow my enquiry into what would otherwise be a vast and untamable subject.

This book was written with a broad, but mostly professional audience in mind. I have used the material in it (including drafts of chapters) in a graduate-level course to which I admit a few, selected upper-class undergraduates. They all seem to be able to handle – I would even say enjoy – the book. Graduate students and postgraduate scholars in anthropology, archaeology, geography, economics, demography, population ecology, agronomy, economic and agrarian history, nutritional science, epidemiology and related fields should be able to find much of interest in the book, much to disagree with and (I would hope) much to learn from it. Technical material inevitably pops up, but I try to make my treatment of it as self-contained and self-explanatory as possible. I am a great believer in clarity as a principal goal of scientific writing, and I would be disappointed to learn that I have failed to reach that goal in this book. So far, my various readers seem to think I'm doing all right.

Writing this book has often lured me beyond the boundaries of my everyday professional expertise. That's fine: I like to think that all my work is inter-disciplinary in character, and besides I've learned a lot from the exercise. But it means that I've been sorely dependent on colleagues whose research overlaps only partially (if at all) with my own to read and critique the manuscript as it has evolved. Pat Johnson has carefully read everything.[2] Anne Buchanan has carefully read *almost* everything, and Sarah McClure and Tim Murtha only slightly less. I am grateful for (and more than a little humbled by) their critical comments – though I plot my revenge for the amount of rethinking and rewriting they forced me to do. Selected chapters have been vetted by Julia Jennings, Daniel Parker, David Webster and Ken Hirth. Over the years, I've benefited from discussions with George Milner, Jesper Boldsen, Darryl Holman, Sharon DeWitte, Rebecca Ferrell, Tim Gage, Lee Newsom, Carrie Hritz, Shinsuke Tomita, Ken Weiss, Rob Griffin, Craig Gerlach, Paul Gepts and Glenn Stone, as well as the eight colleagues already mentioned. In addition, I owe a lot to my students in Anthropology 575 ("Population, Food and Traditional Agriculture") at Penn State for their feedback, insights, requests for clarification and occasional gripes, especially Heath Anderson, Gina Buckley, Aurelio Lopez Corral, Anne Delessio-Parson, Lily Doershuk, Eric Dyrdahl, Richard George, Sara Getz, Sam Goodley, Heather Hilson, Sean Hixon, Nadia Johnson, Emily Kate, Saige Kelmelis, Alex Kinyck, Logan Kistler, Kendall McGill, Montira Mahinchai, Michael Marin, Andres Mejia-Ramon, Laura-marie Pope, Casana Popp, Andrew Purrington, Aliza Richman, Dominica Stricklin, Simone Sukhdeo, Anna Tremblay, Ashish Tyagi, Lindsay Usher, Mark Van Horn, Ziyu (Raining) Wang, Martin Welker and John Wheatley, whose backgrounds span cultural and biological anthropology, archaeology, paleoethnobotany, demography, agricultural economics, rural sociology, even leisure studies (the latter were great on the energetics of farm work). Many thanks as well to Ellen Weiss and Tara Mazurczyk for getting the figures ready for publication, and to Emily Kate for laying the groundwork for the permission letters. Special thanks go to Anna Tremblay, who did most of the arduous task of getting permissions for the figures, who compiled the index, and who saw the manuscript through until it was in the publisher's hands. I also thank the life sciences editors at Cambridge, Martin Griffiths, Lynette Talbot, Ilaria Tassistro, Victoria Parrin and Jenny van der Meijden, for believing in this project from an early stage and guiding its production with unfailing cheerfulness. Looking back over my career, I realize that I owe old and profound debts to the late Skip Rappaport, who introduced me to the ecology of traditional farming (although he would probably have disagreed with most of what's in this book), and the late Frank Livingstone, who provided me with my first exposure to population science

---

[2] Professor Johnson has asked me to add the following statement: "All that I am, or hope to be, I owe to my angel wife." Frankly, I think this is damning her with faint praise.

(although he would probably have pretended to disagree with everything in this book just to keep me on my toes). I also want to thank my friend Douglas Leslie, a farmer on the peedie isle of Westray in Scotland's northern Orkney Islands, for innumerable winter-time discussions about the ways of farming (he is just too busy during the summer). Douglas's expertise was perhaps more useful than anyone else's – he taught me at least a wee bit about how to *think* like a farmer, not to mention about the cosmic importance of muck. Finally, I owe quite tangible debts to the National Science Foundation (specifically the Physical Anthropology panel and the program on Human Dimensions of Global Change), the National Institutes of Health (especially the National Institute for Child Health and Human Development and the National Institute on Aging) and the Andrew W. Mellon Foundation for supporting my research over the years on topics related to this book. But please note: I steadfastly maintain my right and ability to make my own stupid mistakes. Therefore, I cannot in good conscience blame any of these people or agencies for the numerous errors that doubtless remain in the book. I own up to all of them. All I ask is that any readers who spot them please let me know at jww3@psu.edu.

A brief comment on notation. Except when quoting other authors, I try to be consistent in using metric (SI) units of measurement – with one exception. Instead of using joules for energy, I use the more familiar calorie or, more accurately, the kilocalorie or "food calorie" (1 kcal = 1000 cal). I avoid the old convention of writing Calories for kilocalories and calories for "small" calories (what the heck do you do when the word begins a sentence?). For those wishing to convert everything to SI units, one kilocalorie is roughly 4200 joules or 4.2 kJ.

Finally, an aesthetic point. I am not the sort of anthropologist who views pre-industrial people as bloodless Others who spend most of their everyday lives performing rituals, enacting tropes or topoi, or expressing deep cultural themes or symbols. I prefer to think of them as sentient creatures (like ourselves) who sweat and lust, who dig in the dirt and muck out byres and stables, who experience pain, hunger, fear, grief and love, who piss, shit, bleed and do all manner of other nonliterary things. To me, muck is richer than metaphor. In writing this book, I did not set out deliberately to express this aesthetic preference – but deep down I hope I've managed to do so anyway.

Part I

Introductory Concepts

1 Thinking about Population and Traditional Farmers

Food and [millet] beer are without doubt the most exciting and interesting topics of native conversation [among the Bemba of Northern Rhodesia]... Any one who can follow the ordinary gossip of a Bemba village will be struck at once by the endless talk shouted from hut to hut as to what is about to be eaten, what has already been eaten, and what lies in store for the future, and this with an animation and a wealth of detail which would be thought quite unusual in this country [Great Britain]. It is, of course, natural in an area where the supply is never constant from day to day that the daily meal should be a subject of vivid interest. For those who are accustomed to buy food ready prepared, it is difficult to realize the emotional attitudes to foodstuffs among peoples who are directly dependent on their environment for their diet. Most of their food the Bemba grow, and hence they view their fields and gardens concretely in terms of their future prospects of food and drink. These they constantly discuss. I timed two old women talking over an hour on the single topic of the probable order of ripening of the pumpkins in three gardens, and the way in which they were likely to be distributed. The question evidently dominated their imagination...

These casual observations of native life are significant. For us it requires a real effort of imagination to visualize a state of society in which food matters so much and from so many points of view, but this effort is necessary if we are to understand the emotional background of Bemba ideas as to diet.   – A. I. Richards (1939: 44–6)

Traditional farming – farming in the absence of fossil fuels, electricity, commercial seed, tractors and combines and other industrial inputs such as inorganic fertilizers, pesticides and herbicides – has sustained much of the human species for ten millennia. And not just sustained: the global emergence of farming led to a thousand-fold increase in the size of the human population by the beginning of the Industrial Revolution in the late eighteenth century (Cohen, 1995: 96). Traditional farming provided the foundation for early civilizations, cities and states, all of which evolved along with it. By some estimates, traditional farming or something very like it was still feeding a third of the world's people in the second half of the twentieth century (Haswell, 1973).

In preindustrial societies, even those with towns and cities, almost everyone belonged to a farming household. In sixteenth-century England, for example, when London and several other urban areas were already flourishing, an estimated 80 percent of households were rural and more or less directly involved in farming (Wrigley, 1988: 12–13). No matter how surviving written records may distort the reality, human history since the origins of agriculture has, until quite recently, been predominantly the history of traditional farmers and the food they produced, and only secondarily the nonfarming people who ate some of it. Elizabeth I, Cardinal Riche-lieu, Moctezuma and the Mughal Emperors could only ever have been two or three degrees of separation from a poor dirt farmer, and a few weeks away from starvation.

Throughout most of its history, traditional farming has yielded what present-day agricultural scientists would regard as pitifully small quantities of food each year.[1] Most of that food was eaten locally – indeed most of it was eaten by the family that produced it. In other words, traditional farming has often operated near the margin of subsistence. This has been true even where farmers were able, in a good year, to set aside some produce for sale at the local market. The fact that past agrarian societies were made up overwhelmingly of farming families is an indication of the inability of traditional farming to generate a sufficiently large and reliable surplus of food to support a substantial nonagricultural population. Life near the margin meant that even small changes in the food supply could translate into comparatively large changes in health, survival, productive capacity and the ability to raise a family. Thus, the demographic fate of our farming ancestors was hostage to food systems that many people today would consider obsolete and worthy only of "development." That is no reason to fault traditional farmers – they did what they could, with very limited resources at their disposal, against an environment that could be by turns both obdurate and capricious. Their efforts might even be viewed as heroic.

This book is about the manifold linkages between farming and human population in the preindustrial world. It draws upon evidence, recent and historical, from all parts of the world where traditional agriculture has existed in recent centuries – and in some places still exists, if only in modified form. It continues and enlarges a debate (discussed in the next section) originally framed by Thomas Robert Malthus more than two centuries ago, at about the time that modern farming was taking its first fumbling steps. Malthus bequeathed the debate to classical economics, where it played a central role until it was pushed aside by the rise of new economic doctrines late in the nineteenth century. Malthus also injected the debate into the new field of population science, although it remained a secondary concern at a time when purely methodological advances necessarily dominated the discipline. (But recall that one important population scientist, Charles Darwin, was by his own account deeply swayed by Malthus's theoretical arguments.) In the mid-twentieth century the debate caught fire again, largely under the influence of the economist Ester Boserup, who aimed to stand Malthus on his head. Boserup's ideas provided the basis for innumerable writings in anthropology, especially archaeology, placing the interaction of

---

[1] In traditional European cereal cultivation, only three or four grains of wheat, rye, barley or oats (all C_3 plants) were harvested for each seed sown (Slicher van Bath, 1963a; Titow, 1972). This startlingly low grain to seed ratio does not imply that each plant set only three or four seeds; rather it reflects everything that lowered yield, including failure of germination, losses to pests, harvest losses, etc. In such a system, fully a quarter to a third of each year's harvest would need to be set aside for next year's sowing, leaving little to buffer against fluctuations in yield. In the right environment, C_4 plants, such as maize, millet or sorghum, did better under preindustrial cultivation, but came nowhere near the standards of modern agriculture. (For the distinction between C_3 and C_4 plants and its importance for crop yields, see Hay and Porter, 2006: 99–104.)

population and traditional agriculture at the center of arguments concerning not only the evolution of farming systems but also that of preindustrial economies and political systems in general. And the fire was stoked (often to the point of over-heating) by ecologists concerned with the "population bomb," some of whom formu-lated a kind of *über*-neomalthusianism that had little to do with what Malthus actually believed. Although the debate has lost some of its fervor in recent years, it remains important in such fields as economic demography, historical demography, economic anthropology, agricultural economics and geography, development economics and human ecology.

The Classic Debate

The details of the classic debate over population and agriculture will be presented in Chapters 5 and 6, and we need only sketch a brief outline of it here. Malthus believed that the size of a population, and its tendency to grow or decline, was determined by its food supply. Therefore, any increase in food supply resulting from improvements in agricultural practice would inevitably (in the absence of deliberate "preventive checks" on fertility) lead to population growth, which in the short term could be quite rapid.[2] This rapid increase in the number of people to be fed would quickly consume any temporary surplus generated by the new methods of farming, and population size would equilibrate at the level just allowed by the new farming system and the population's minimal nutritional requirements for sustaining itself. In this scheme, the food supply is the "independent variable" or driving force for demographic change. For Boserup, in contrast, food supply is quite elastic under any form of farming, and changes in population size or density are the primary force determining the level of food production: "population growth is here regarded as the independent variable which in its turn is a major factor determining agricultural developments" (Boserup, 1965: 11). Although Boserup recognized that there were many different ways preindustrial farmers could increase their food supply in response to population growth, she emphasized only one of them: how long arable land was allowed to lie fallow after a continuous period of cultivation. It is important to note that Boserup explicitly treated population size or density as an exogenous variable and was not much interested in why it might change. It just does – or doesn't, as the case may be. All this, in Boserup's own opinion, made her an anti-Malthusian.

Not surprisingly, the actual debate turns out to be more complicated, especially once the contributions of other, more recent writers are taken into account (see Chapter 6). But most participants still adopt a position that is recognizably either "Malthusian" or "Boserupian." Only fairly recently have several authors suggested that Malthus and Boserup may not be as incompatible as we have thought (see Pryor and Maurer, 1982; Lee, 1986; Turner and Ali, 1996; Wood, 1998).

---

[2] Malthus believed that human populations could double in size in as little as 25 years when conditions were favorable. Many of his contemporaries found this claim absurd. In fact, we now know of well-documented cases in which human populations have grown even more rapidly.

As I say, the debate has lost some of its fervor – but not because it has been settled. Instead, I will argue that the debate has languished mainly because it has been dominated by inappropriate or incomplete methods, models and scales of analysis, not because we know which side won. To go even further, the very fact that the debate has crystallized into two diametrically opposed "sides" has itself impeded understanding of the underlying issues. In later chapters, I will provide a detailed discussion of the classic debate as it stood at the beginning of the twenty-first century, but most of this book will involve an attempt to transcend the limitations of the debate or at least to reframe its basic terms so that we can better understand what the important questions are.

An Empirical Example

To convey something of the current state of the debate – and some of the problems with the way it has been structured – it is useful to look at some empirical results from a major survey of traditional farming in the southwest Pacific nation of Papua New Guinea (Bourke *et al.*, 1998; Allen, 2001; Bourke, 2001). I choose this example, not because it is egregious and thus an easy target, but precisely because it represents one of the best empirical studies done to date on this subject. Between 1990 and 1995 a group of geographers at the Australian National University developed a geographical information database known as the Mapping Agricultural Systems in Papua New Guinea Project (MASP). Local agricultural "systems" (the basic map units) were defined based on field data concerning six variables (Allen, 2001: 239):

- the type of fallow vegetation established on fields just before clearing for cultivation
- the length of the fallow period
- the number of years staple crops are grown before fallowing
- the principal staple crops
- the spatial arrangement of crops within and between cultivated fields
- techniques other than fallowing used to maintain soil fertility.

These data were linked in a GIS to demographic information from the 1980 national census and to other data sources (for technical details, see Bourke *et al.*, 1998). A total of 274 local systems were mapped, a remarkable achievement under trying field conditions.

Results from the MASP project that are most pertinent to the classic debate about population and agriculture are shown in Figure 1.1, which plots Boserup's preferred measure of agricultural "intensity" (intended to reflect the magnitude of nonland inputs into the farming system) against local population density for all 274 mapped locations. Despite considerable scatter in the data, Allen (2001) concludes that there is a significant, nonlinear relationship between the two. Since population density is plotted on the x-axis, the implication is that population density is the independent variable driving differences in agricultural intensity, just as Boserup believed. So much for Malthus.

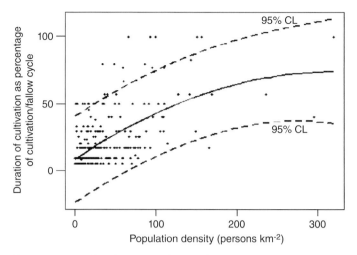

Figure 1.1 Agricultural intensity by population density, 274 local farming systems in Papua New Guinea, *c.* 1990–5. Agricultural intensity is estimated as the number of years the average field is continuously cropped as a percentage of the length of the total cropping/fallow cycle. Solid curve is a quadratic equation fit by OLS regression. CL, confidence limit. From Allen (2001: 241), with permission of John Wiley & Sons, Inc.

There are various problems of a purely statistical nature with this analysis, which its author readily acknowledges.[3] But there are deeper conceptual problems that are at least as important. First, do the two variables actually measure what they are supposed to measure? Population density is notoriously difficult to interpret. The quantity used here appears to be "gross" population density, the ratio of standing population to the area of all land that "belongs" to the farming community in question. As such, the denominator includes not only active and potential arable, but areas uncultivable because of high slopes, poor soils, waterlogging, rocky outcrops and so forth – or because they are taken up by house sites, ceremonial grounds or other nonagricultural features. Surely the different locales vary in the proportion of their territory consisting of such nonarable land. Population density is presumably intended as a proxy measure of what Boserup called "population pressure," itself a slippery concept discussed in Chapter 3. But surely the amount of "pressure" that a population exerts upon the land that feeds it is influenced in profound ways by elements of the physical environment (elevation, rainfall, temperature, slopes, soils, etc.). Rich environments can arguably support more people without undue "pressure" than poor ones. Despite the fact that Papua New Guinea encompasses an enormous range of local environments, there is no statistical adjustment for that variation in

---

[3] Briefly, the bivariate relationship appears to "explain" only a small fraction of the variation in the data, although no R^2 value is reported. The apparent relationship may also be disproportionately influenced by a small number of outliers in the NE quadrant of the plot. And no test of nonlinearity is provided. Allen (2001: 241) himself points out that "the data do not satisfy many of the requirements of regression analysis" and thus the results should be interpreted with caution.

Figure 1.1. And it is likely that there are many other unobserved variables whose potential confounding effects have not been controlled.

Similarly, cropping frequency is a problematic measurement of "agricultural intensity" (another slippery concept). The meaning of agricultural intensity will receive considerable attention in later chapters. For now it is enough to say that it reflects the magnitude of nonland inputs (labor or capital) into food production designed to increase or at least maintain crop yields per hectare of cultivable land. Cropping frequency at best tells us something about the amount of potentially cultivable land that is actively devoted to farming in a given year, but nothing about other possible inputs such as mulching, manuring, irrigation, drainage, soil preparation, weeding and other widespread traditional farming practices.[4] And note that the measure of intensity used in Figure 1.1 cannot exceed 100 percent, corresponding to permanent cultivation; it therefore cannot distinguish farming systems in which each field yields one crop per year from more intensive multicropping systems.

There is an even deeper problem with this analysis. Even if the data were sufficient to convince us of a close causal relationship between population density and agricultural intensity, they tell us nothing about the *direction* of causation. If we were to switch the x- and y-axes in Figure 1.1, we might conclude that the level of agricultural intensity determines population density – that is, that the food supply is the main factor determining population size or density, just as Malthus believed. So much for Boserup.

There are other conceptual problems. Both Malthus and Boserup talk of changes over time *within* populations. Their predictions are thus inherently dynamic and should be tested against longitudinal data. As remarkable as the MASP dataset is, it is still a cross-sectional snapshot of the situation in Papua New Guinea as it existed in the early 1990s. It is at least imaginable that (for example) the one farming system represented by the point at $x > 300$ and $y = 100$ could have, if followed prospectively for several decades, headed toward the southeast, contrary to both Malthus and Boserup. Given the lack of control for environmental variation and non-fallow methods of intensification, any number of single-system dynamic trajectories could have been observed, some consistent with existing theory, some not.

The foregoing difficulty points to the final problem with this analysis, something statisticians call the *ecological fallacy*. The ecological fallacy can occur whenever we try to draw causal inferences from data reported at a level of spatial aggregation higher than the level at which the actual causal processes are occurring – as when we try to understand the behavior of individuals by analyzing the behavior of crowds. The classic example of an ecological fallacy was a study of the epidemiology of tuberculosis conducted in the 1930s using data aggregated at the level of US states

---

[4] In fairness, I hasten to point out that this very point has been made by the members of the MASP project (Allen, 2001). The MASP data suggest that nonfallow soil conservation practices also vary by population density and cropping frequency (see Bourke, 2001, and Chapter 5 below for further discussion of these practices in Papua New Guinea).

(Cowles and Chapman, 1935). Each state's mortality rate from tuberculosis was analyzed in terms of several purported explanatory variables, all of which were statewide characteristics or averages. One finding considered especially important at the time was that the state's average altitude and hours of sunshine each year were negatively correlated with statewide tuberculosis death rates, suggesting that patients ought to be moved to mountainous regions in sunny climes. Unfortunately for people who rushed to build sanatoriums in the "right" locales, when the study was redone years later using data on individual patients the apparent beneficial effects of altitude and sunshine disappeared (Morgenstern, 1982). The state as a whole, it turns out, is just too far above the pathologic processes operating in the infected individual for meaningful results to be derived.[5]

The data in Figure 1.1 are presented and analyzed at the level of the "farming system" (Allen, 2001). We are not told how big a "system" is, but it seems to be a regional community sharing a fairly homogeneous set of farming practices. But regions aren't cropped and then allowed to lie fallow – individual fields are. And in the absence of a clearer understanding of what we mean by "population pressure," it difficult to know whether its effects play out at the regional level or at the level of the individual farm. How do we decide at which scale to pitch our analysis? In the absence of a clear answer, it's almost always best to disaggregate. We can always reaggregate our observations later if we wish to.

Rethinking the Relationship between Human Population and Traditional Agriculture

What kinds of questions do we want to ask about the relationship between a system of agriculture and the characteristics of the population it feeds – the population's size, density, growth rate, age structure, fertility and mortality levels, migration patterns and so forth? If the goal is to move beyond the conventional debate, the following questions would seem to need answering first.

---

[5] Another example is more germane to the subject of this book. In one of my demography classes I discuss the wide disparities that have been observed among countries in their average length of life. I ask my students what variables might be useful for predicting a country's average life span, and they suggest plausible possibilities such as per capita GDP, mean household income, and access to modern medical care. I then suggest that quite a good predictor might be the fraction of the country's citizens who are morbidly obese: the higher the fraction, the longer the average life span. At first they are puzzled by what they take to be an assumption on my part that obesity is good for you. But then they get it – they have fallen for the ecological fallacy. Rich countries have good medical care and public health facilities. As a result they experience very few deaths among infants and other young children – the primary determinant worldwide of variation in average life span. They also have abundant and reliable sources of food and very few jobs requiring heavy physical work, a prescription for obesity. Thus, at the country level, lots of obesity is positively associated with comparatively long life. If the data were reanalyzed at the *individual* level, where health, fatness and life span are determined, they would no doubt provide plenty of evidence that extreme obesity is strongly predictive of early death. At the aggregate level, obesity may be positively correlated with long life, but that does not mean it *causes* it.

Is the Relationship Simple or Complicated?

Despite their disagreements, both Malthus and Boserup (and their respective supporters) make the linkage sound simple and straightforward. But there may in fact be multiple linkages at many different spatial and temporal scales, not all of which linkages operate in the same direction or with the same intensity. One problem in reframing the issue is to identify all the important linkages, while recognizing that there may be a practically unlimited number of unimportant ones – a nice sense of judgment is needed. One failure of the current debate on population and traditional farming is, I would argue, that some of the important linkages have been ignored.

Is the Relationship Unidirectional or Reciprocal?

Food supply and population size may be positively correlated, but does food supply determine population size, or does an increase in population size induce increases in food supply – or both? Malthus and Boserup preferred unidirectional linkages.[6] I can think of no *a priori* reason to reject reciprocal relationships. Could Malthus and Boserup *both* have been right?

What are the Precise Mechanisms Underlying the Relationship?

This is the crucial question. If food supply is to influence population, it must do so through at least one of the basic "forces" of population change – fertility, mortality or migration.[7] It is startling, then, to realize the extent to which these essential demographic processes have been ignored in the recent debate regarding the linkage between population and agriculture. A population can be growing at a certain rate (for example) because it has low mortality and modestly high fertility *or* because it has high mortality and very high fertility, two scenarios that imply rather different things about dietary sufficiency and its effects on mortality or fertility. By the same token, if population is to influence agriculture, it must do so through at least one of the physical, temporal or spatial components of the agricultural process – the allocation of land, labor and other scarce resources, the use of manures, soil tillage, the choice of crops, the scheduling of sowing and so on (see Chapter 2). Again, the classic debate has mostly ignored all details of agricultural practice except the one emphasized by Boserup: the length of time a particular piece of land is actively and continuously cropped relative to the time it lies fallow. But there may be no predictable relationship between population density and the length of the cropping/fallow cycle if all fields are well manured. By identifying and linking specific demographic and agricultural mechanisms, we stand to gain greater insight into the relationship between population and farming.

---

[6] This is not quite correct. In various editions of his *Essay on the Principle of Population*, Malthus allowed for reciprocal interactions between population and agriculture that in many ways sound downright Boserupian (Wood, 1998). Chapter 5 presents some of the details.

[7] As a demographic force, migration should be differentiated into immigration and emigration. To spare the modern reader (and me!) the need to remember the difference, I will adopt the inelegant practice of referring to *in-migration* and *out-migration*.

At what Scale or Scales do the Mechanisms Operate?

This question, too, is crucial. As far as spatial scale is concerned, most discussions of the relationship have been restricted to quite aggregated levels of analysis – chiefly the level of an entire population, community or region, however defined. Only more recently have population scientists investigated less aggregated scales – e.g. the individual farmer, the household, the group of kinfolk who regularly combine to share food and work. There is, of course, no one universally correct scale for all analyses – it depends on the question being asked. Questions about environmental degradation may best be studied at a regional scale, those concerning agricultural decision-making at the household scale. The same holds true of temporal scale. The relationship between population and agriculture can be studied over months, years, decades, centuries or millennia, and indeed has been studied profitably at all these scales. But we cannot hope to cover all scales, spatial or temporal, in a book of reasonable length. Careful decisions must be made.

At high levels of spatial aggregation the risk of committing the ecological fallacy becomes great, especially if the most important causal linkages are operating at lower scales of aggregation. For this reason, the whole debate needs to be disaggregated. Throughout this book, I will emphasize *the farming household and its farm* as the most important (but not the only) scale at which both food production and consumption are managed and demographic decisions and outcomes occur.[8] But we need to be careful here, for no household in the preindustrial world is absolutely autonomous when it comes to food. For example, extra-household work groups are ubiquitous in traditional farming, although they tend to be small, transitory and focused on specific tasks (see Chapter 12). They also tend to be made up of people who are closely related to (and living near) whatever household is organizing them. And, of course, food-sharing networks that span multiple households are also universal (Chapter 12). In addition, households are not internally undifferentiated. Peter Laslett (1984: 353) has famously called the household "a knot of individual interests." Insofar as the household members have a stake in the success of the household, they have overlapping interests. But in general they do not have *identical* interests – a point emphasized in the recent literature on the behavioral ecology of the family (Mock, 2004; Forbes, 2005). Not all members are treated the same: females are often at a disadvantage when it comes to food distribution, sons preferred over daughters, and elder sons preferred over younger ones (Barlett, 1980c; Wilk, 1989a, b). As Maclachlan has observed in rural south India, the management of household labor may sometimes involve an element of coercion (1983: 108 *ff.*) – especially when it comes to getting adolescent and unmarried adult sons to do their customary share of the work. Nonetheless, it has been acknowledged by researchers in a wide variety of disciplines that, in every known traditional agrarian society, the household has a

---

[8] The emphasis on households and their members also influences my choice of temporal scale: I will deal mostly with the "agrarian" scale (hours to a whole farming year) and the "demographic" scale (months to a couple of generations).

unique status as the most important unit within which farm management decisions are made, day-to-day farm work organized and food resources pooled (Netting, 1993: *ad passim*; see also Hill, 1982; Fricke, 1984; Netting *et al.*, 1984; Haswell and Hunt, 1991; Wilk, 1991; Ellis, 1993, among many other possible references). The historical demographer John Hajnal (1982) has even suggested that household membership in the rural preindustrial world can be *defined* in terms of regularly shared food – *a une vino e uno pane*, as one medieval Tuscan tax roll put it (Klapisch and Demonet, 1972).

I suggest, then, that the traditional farming household, along with the farm it runs, is the most salient scale – I am tempted to say the most *natural* scale – at which to begin investigating the interactions of demography and food production. This does not mean that other scales are irrelevant; they are not. But the most localized scale would seem to be the right place to *start* identifying causal mechanisms.

In order to understand the current debate over population and farming (if only to loosen its conceptual grip), we will need to spend some time at the aggregate-, macro-demographic- or population-level of analysis; this we shall do in Chapters 4–6. But most of the rest of the book will be devoted to investigating how the questions change – along with the possible answers – when the scale of analysis is shifted to the household, its members and its farm. In the final chapter we will return to levels above the household, albeit not very far above the household.

Why Study Traditional Farmers?

At this stage an impertinent question may have occurred to some readers: if the debate about the relationship between agriculture and demography is a *general* one, why focus on traditional farming, which appears to be headed for extinction? Why not devote our attention solely to modern, industrialized farming, so utterly different in scale and productivity from preindustrial systems, so obviously (for better or worse) the way of the future? One honest answer that satisfies me but will not move many readers is that I have studied the demography and population biology of traditional, preindustrial farmers for the past 40 years, in both the field and the archive, and I think I have something to say about them. But there are at least three more general (and perhaps more generally satisfying) answers.

First, modern farming – depending of course on how you define it – has existed for, at most, about two centuries. Truly *industrialized* farming is even newer: a convenient starting date might be 1909, when Fritz Haber first demonstrated his method of fixing atmospheric nitrogen as ammonia for use in inorganic fertilizers.[9] In profound contrast, traditional agriculture has survived for more than ten thousand

---

[9] Vaclav Smil (2001: xiii) has called this "the single most important technical invention of the twentieth century" because "the single most important change affecting the world's population – its expansion from 1.6 billion people in 1900 to today's 6 [now more than 7] billion – would not have been possible without the [industrial] synthesis of ammonia." To place Haber's demonstration on a human time scale, I note that it occurred during my own father's infancy.

years in some parts of the world (Barker, 2006), an accomplishment that should not be gainsaid. If one wishes to understand the demographic dynamics of historical populations (and many prehistoric ones as well), traditional farming is the right place to start.

Second, if you are interested in economic development and wish to help transform the remaining vestiges of traditional agriculture, you need to know something about the initial conditions of the whole transformation (see, e.g., Schultz, 1964; Wharton, 1969). This is precisely why Boserup first became interested in traditional agriculture.

Third – and, I would argue, most importantly from a theoretical point of view – if you want to understand the general linkages between agriculture and population processes, traditional farming is a good place to start because, in comparison to what is found in modern, industrial farming, those linkages are simple, strong and direct. As will be emphasized later in this chapter, traditional farming depends almost entirely on local, biological sources of nonsolar energy (i.e. humans and sometimes animals), fertilizers (animal manures, green manures, etc.) and genetic resources (so-called *landraces* or local varieties of crops and livestock). Modern commercial farming, in contrast, is subsidized by vast, mostly nonlocal, industrial operations fed by fossil fuels. The physical and spatial limits of these two types of production could scarcely be more different. Modern agriculture relies upon the whole national economy and much of the rest of the world; traditional agriculture does not – indeed, *cannot*, for long-distance transport of food is too energetically costly and its infra-structure too under-developed to be economical (see below). As archaeologists can attest, longer-distance trade in the past mostly involved small, lightweight, imperishable items of high value – perhaps jade carvings or ceremonial bronze axe heads – not staple foods.

Because of high bulk transport costs – as well as the limited capacity to preserve food in the absence of refrigerated transport – food distribution is almost always extremely localized under preindustrial conditions. As a consequence, it is easier to link a traditional farming system to the population it feeds than is the case in modern commercial agriculture. Today it is possible for an orange grown in the Levant to be eaten by someone in Nova Scotia, even though the grower and the eater are very unlikely to have any other form of relationship. The "population" served by the Levantine orange grower is, potentially, the entire world. Food produced by many traditional farming systems, in stark contrast, may not go beyond the farm itself and, if it does, will rarely go far, and it will be conveyed mostly by an intimate network of kinsmen and neighbors (Richards, 1939: 154–71; Sillitoe, 1983: 256–8).

In addition, many of the potential linkages between agriculture and demography have to do with the influence of dietary inadequacy on fertility or mortality (see Chapter 8). In most modern farming systems, those linkages have been loosened or even severed by the widespread use of effective contraceptives and the comparatively easy availability of modern medical care and public health services. Thus, many of the potential causal mechanisms linking demography and food supply are too attenuated to be studied easily in modern industrial populations.

Can Traditional Farmers Save the World?

It has been suggested that there is another reason to study traditional farmers – to save ourselves (see, for example, Altieri, 1990). In recent years, many researchers in the agricultural sciences have argued that one of the surest ways to promote sustainability (whatever that means) in our own farming industry is to adopt methods used in traditional farming, which, by virtue of the fact that it has been around for thousands of years, *must* be sustainable. And even if traditional systems are not literally sustainable, it is clear that they generally do less damage to local ecosystems than modern farming does, precisely because (the supporters of this point of view argue) traditional farmers have ecologically minded practices and spiritual beliefs that discourage such damage. This line of reasoning has inspired some fine recent studies of traditional farming (for useful reviews, see Brookfield, 2001a; Cairns, 2007; Gliessman, 2007; Scherr and McNeely, 2007). But it is, I believe, based on questionable assumptions – even setting aside the likelihood that traditional farming practices would never be able to feed a global population that has now exceeded seven billion people. If it is in fact the case that many preindustrial farming communities are environmentally nondestructive (and clearly some are, at least compared to industrial farming), we have to ask whether it is because of their specific agricultural practices and beliefs, or because they are *unable* to be destructive. As the anthropologist Allen Johnson once remarked:

Ironically enough, although my own field experience convinces me that in many ways the Machiguenga [shifting cultivators living on the eastern Amazonian slope of the Andes in Peru] do feel a 'oneness with nature,' hold a 'mystical world view,' and by virtue of their materially simple life are less 'alienated' (in some sense; I agree the term is vague) than we affluent moderns, I nonetheless find the Machiguenga to be more alike than distinct from us when it comes to resource management. Their relatively small destructive impact on the environment results less from an ideology of protective oneness than from a low population density [c. 0.3 persons km^{-2}], a scattered population, and an individualistic, family-centered technology that makes it impossible for them to devastate any particular resources. Since their population density is low relative to resources mainly for historical reasons related to the depopulation of native Americans following contact with conquering Europeans, I will argue that it is essentially an historical accident that they have not yet expanded their population and methods of exploitation to produce either severe environmental degradation or a cultural emphasis on the protective management of resources to prevent such degradation. (Johnson, 1989: 214)

Whether or not one believes that post-Columbian depopulation is the cause of the Machiguenga's *current* low population density, Johnson's point is a good one: many preindustrial populations live in rough balance with nature because they do not have the strength to upset the balance. I recall, the first time I did fieldwork in a (then) remote part of highland Papua New Guinea (PNG), being rather shocked at the proposals of a group of local men who were debating the best way to become rich. As it happens one of the men had been to Port Moresby, the nation's capital city. Port Moresby is located in PNG's only pocket of savanna grassland and has comparatively few trees; Port Moresby is also, by my local informants' standards, almost unimaginably wealthy – it has paved roads, lots of motor vehicles, multistory buildings, and markets with wondrous manufactured goods that were not available locally. To the man who had seen Port Moresby, the surest path to wealth was obvious: they needed to chop down all their trees so the local environment would be more like Port Moresby's. No one in the group suggested that this was inherently a bad idea, but there was general agreement, and considerable regret, that they would never be able to muster enough manpower to effect the desired deforestation.

My own view of the advisability of emulating traditional farmers is captured rather nicely by Gene Wilken, an agricultural geographer with years of experience with, and great respect for, the traditional farmers of Mesoamerica:

> Some traditional systems have enviable resource conservation records, others do not. But those that have maintained or enhanced the resource base over time merit examination. These successful experiments by generations of farmers in particular places constitute valuable lessons that should not be ignored or lost.
>
> But before our enthusiasm for centuries-old systems outruns the record, we should note the failures. It is also condescending to view traditional farmers as sagacious husbandmen, imbued with infallible folk wisdom, in mystic harmony with the environment. In fact, they share with their industrialized counterparts the human propensities to respond to short-term opportunities while disregarding long-term costs, to misinterpret the durability and flexibility of agroecosystems, and generally to err. The many past and present examples of depleted resources and degraded landscapes attest to the potential for traditional mismanagement. But *failure is part of the agricultural experience* and has as much to teach, in its own way, as success. (Wilken, 1987: 268; emphasis added)

In this book I shall not make the assumption that traditional farming practices are *necessarily* environmentally friendly and geared toward long-term sustainability or resource conservation. To do so would bias our enquiry from the outset by taking for granted a demographic stability that may or may not exist in any particular case. Certainly, traditional farmers manage their resources – a fact that will be emphasized in Chapter 2 – but do they do so with an eye on long-term sustainability and conservation or on short-term economic advantage? I would argue that traditional farmers are usually short-termers, even if their practices do end up having (unintended) consequences for the longer term. I would also argue that some degree of environmental degradation is common under traditional farming and may even act as an important driver of both agricultural and demographic change (see Chapters 3 and 6).

Some Important Differences between Traditional and Industrial Farming

Obviously traditional and modern farming differ in a myriad of ways. There is, of course, an historical continuum linking the two, but on the time scale of farming in general it was brief, perhaps 200 years out of ten millennia or so.[10] In this section

---

[10] Some historians put the beginnings of the so-called modern agricultural revolution in southeastern England and the Low Countries as far back as the sixteenth century or earlier (Chambers and Mingray, 1966; Overton, 1996). But the earliest stages were extremely limited in geographic extent and had little effect on the region's overall food supply.

I ignore the continuum and contrast preindustrial farming with its fully developed modern industrial counterpart in order to identify the differences that are most consequential for the rest of this book.

One obvious difference has already been noted: industrial farming is underwritten by bank loans, cheap fossil fuel (much of it from other countries) and an enormous manufacturing sector providing tractors, harvesters and other tools and machinery, fertilizers of whatever chemical composition is required, carefully targeted herbicides and pesticides and seed bred according to Mendelian principles or produced through genetic engineering. The only local resources of any importance are water, soil and human labor – and the water may be pumped in from elsewhere, the soil heavily modified by industrial fertilizer and mechanized tillage and the input of human labor laughably small by preindustrial standards (if appalling by our own). Traditional farming, in stark contrast, depends upon "natural" sources of energy that are produced locally, usually on the farm that uses them. Thus, both human workers and draft animals (if the latter are used) are mostly raised and fed on the farm where they work. Other inputs, such as manure and seed stock, are also local and themselves usually come from the farm that applies them.[11] Tools are simple and are manufactured either by the farmers themselves or by a local blacksmith, if such a person exists.

There are several important implications of these differences. First, there are major differences between industrial and preindustrial farmers in the sheer amount of energy they can channel into food production (not counting, of course, solar energy, converted into storable chemical energy by photosynthesis).

Power in traditional farming comes mostly from humans and animals fueled by foods produced on the farm or in the local community... Compared with even small fossil fuel devices, human and animal power appears puny indeed... The limited power of individual humans or animals is often insufficient for tasks that involve substantial mass transfers or tight schedules. (Wilken, 1987: 15–17)

As we shall see in later chapters, this "puniness" is of profound importance in understanding the biological constraints on the household labor force, the need to allocate labor judiciously, the inability of the household to undertake large bulk transfers of soil or other materials on its own and the need for inter-household cooperation on tasks that must be done quickly. Above all, it accounts for the common observation that subsistence farmers try to invest energy efficiently and rest at every opportunity (see Chapter 9). To put the energy limits in more quantitative terms:

---

[11] In traditional rain-fed farming, water too is "local", if that's the right word for something transported hundreds of kilometers in the form of clouds. But in other traditional farming systems, liquid water may be brought in some distance by irrigation. See, for example, the Marakwet irrigation system in the Kerio Valley, Kenya (Watson *et al.*, 1998; Östberg, 2004), where water flows up to 14 km (and drops in altitude as much as 1200 m) in furrows built and maintained by local farmers without any higher-order supervision or administration.

Human work is slow because the body has poor energetic performance. The human body can convert around 25% of dietary energy to mechanical energy as physical work and most humans can continuously sustain a maximum power output of 75 W [18 cal s^{-1}]. Many laboring tasks in agriculture, such as digging, lifting, and carrying, require work rates of 300–600 W (Stout *et al.*, 1979) and so must be interspersed with substantial rest periods.

In most tasks, rates of effective work are considerably less than 75 W. In harvesting, for example, 75% of muscular effort is expended in lifting our bodies, tools, and containers, and just 25% in getting the harvest into storage. When manual harvesting operations are expended over a 10 h work day that includes [necessary] rest periods, work rate is only 22 W. Animals are superior to humans because they are bigger and stronger, not because they are intrinsically more efficient. A horse, for example, can sustain 750 W (1 HP) and over a 10 h day can deliver 27 MJ, but once again only around 6% of that is converted to useful work. In contrast, moderate-size tractors can continuously deliver 35 to 50 kW [i.e. 35,000– 50,000 W], converting (non-dietary) fossil fuel to useful work at efficiencies around 35% at the crankshaft, and 25% at the drawbar under average soil conditions. (Connor *et al.*, 2011: 413–14)

On *all* preindustrial farms, even where draft animals are used, most labor is human labor. On many subsistence farms, *all* labor is human labor.[12] And whether human or animal, the energy that fuels the labor is produced on the farm by that same labor. The farm (unlike the factory) recycles part of its manufactured goods (food) into the production process, which reduces the quantity of goods that can be used for other purposes, such as feeding children who are too young to work the farm. To most economists, a subsistence farm must seem a bit like a lunatic wooden-toy factory that burns a large fraction of the toys it makes to fuel the production of more toys.

If the energy inputs into subsistence farming are severely limited (by modern standards), so too are the energy outputs in the form of food. Figure 1.2, for example, shows perhaps the two best centuries-long time series of data on staple grain yields spanning part of the preindustrial period, the period of the industrial revolution and the period of modern, industrialized farming. The two countries shown, England and Japan, were (and are) located in two of the most intensive farming regions in the world. From the eighth century to the mid-nineteenth century, rice yields in Japan were nearly stagnant and barely more than a seventh of modern values. By the thirteenth century, English wheat yields were only about 5 percent of modern yields, although there was steady improvement over the late medieval and early modern periods. Both regions took off dramatically around 1850 with the adoption of "scientific" farming. These differences in yield between preindustrial and modern grain production can be taken, at least approximately, as exemplifying the general differences in productivity between traditional and industrial farming. They also illustrate how brief the transition between the two was.

All these points are illustrated in Table 1.1, which contrasts three recent rice-farming operations in terms of direct on-farm energy inputs, indirect inputs including those of a commercial, industrial or otherwise off-farm nature and yields

---

[12] And, of course, there are examples in which water and wind power are employed, though usually on a small scale.

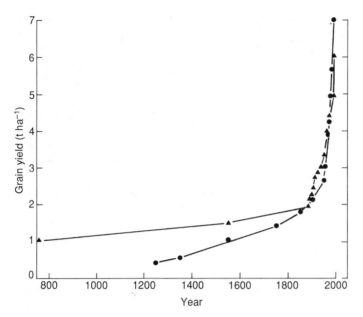

Figure 1.2 Long-term historical trends in wheat yields in England (●) and rice yields in Japan (▲). Redrawn from Evans (1993: 2), based on data from Gavin (1951), Matsuo (1959), Borrie (1970) and Stanhill (1976), with permission of Cambridge University Press.

expressed in energy units.[13] Also shown is the energy efficiency of rice production, i.e. the ratio of harvested energy to the sum of energy inputs. The average Iban subsistence farmer, wholly dependent on shifting cultivation, is almost five times more efficient than modern rice growers in California – but then modern rice growers can afford to be extravagant with energy, subsistence farmers cannot. The efficiency of subsistence farming, widely praised by agroecologists, is purchased at the price of low productivity and a situation in which every household must often work hard just to meet its own needs.

One corollary of this low productivity is that the available workforce in traditional farming communities must be dedicated almost exclusively to food production (Table 1.1). In the West African example shown in Figure 1.3, the only villagers not directly involved in farming are young children and a tiny handful of merchants, teachers, imams, government officials and elders (Haswell, 1985).

Another way in which the absence of nonhuman, nonanimal energy profoundly affected the lives of most traditional farmers was by impeding transport. Preindustrial methods of transport were energetically costly (Table 1.2), in part because most haulage was done by humans or animals that had to be fed for their efforts, and because infrastructure for transport (tracks, roads, bridges, canals, ports) was primitive well into the early modern period (Albert, 1972; Chaloner and Ratcliffe, 1977;

---

[13] These three cases do not represent any kind of random sample of traditional and modern farming systems and should be taken purely as illustrations. And beware the ecological fallacy! All three systems, however, practice monocropping of rice, which facilitates the comparison.

Table 1.1 Nonsolar energy inputs and outputs (1000 kcal ha^{-1}), energy efficiency (ratio of output to the sum of inputs) and percentage of adult population involved in agriculture, for three rice-growing systems: a subsistence farming community (the Iban of Sarawak, Borneo), a labor-intensive, partially mechanized farming system (rural Japan) and a highly mechanized system, including sowing by airplane (California). From Tivy (1990: 6). Reprinted from *Agricultural Ecology*, J. Tivy, London: Longman, copyright 1990, with permission from Elsevier.

	Iban	Japan	California
Inputs			
Direct energy:			
Labor	0.642	0.804	0.008
Machinery	–	0.189	0.360
Fossil fuels	–	0.901	4.275
Indirect energy:			
Nitrogen	–	2.088	4.116
Phosphorus	–	0.225	0.201
Seeds	0.392*	0.813	1.140
Irrigation	–	0.910	1.299
Insecticides	–	0.348	0.191
Herbicides	–	0.699	1.119
Electricity	–	0.007	1.597
Transport (nonhuman)	–	0.051	0.121
Output (rice yield)	7.318	17.598	22.370
Energy efficiency	7.08	2.45	1.55
Percentage workforce involved in agriculture	> 95	c. 20	≤ 5

* Seeds used by the Iban are included under indirect energy not because they are produced off-farm, but because they were produced in the previous farming year, not the current one.

Fenton and Stell, 1984; Hindle, 2002).[14] As the great French geographer Pierre Gourou noted with reference to China before 1940:

The transport of merchandise required large amounts of human labour, for there were almost no roads accessible to carts or motorized vehicles; and it must be remembered that draught animals were in competition with human porters for the consumption of cereals. In Szechwan, in 1938, the cost of coal transport in panniers suspended from a yoke doubled the pithead price after a journey of only 20 km. In the whole of China, in 1938, the price of a tonne-kilometre of human porterage was about 0.62 Chinese dollars, or 6 or 7 French francs of that period [approximately 21¢ US at the 1934 exchange rate]. The human porter was poorly paid, for he only earned the equivalent of 5 French francs for carrying 40 kg over 30 km in a day. However, even at these very low rates the cost of transport was crippling, being ten or twenty times higher than by modern methods. It was impossible, under such conditions, to carry heavy loads for long distances; 100 km was about the limit. When shortages or actual famine affected

[14] In late medieval London, almost all the food marketed and eaten in the city was grown within 50–60 km of its center, even during periods of rapid urban expansion (Galloway and Murphy, 1991; Campbell *et al.*, 1992).

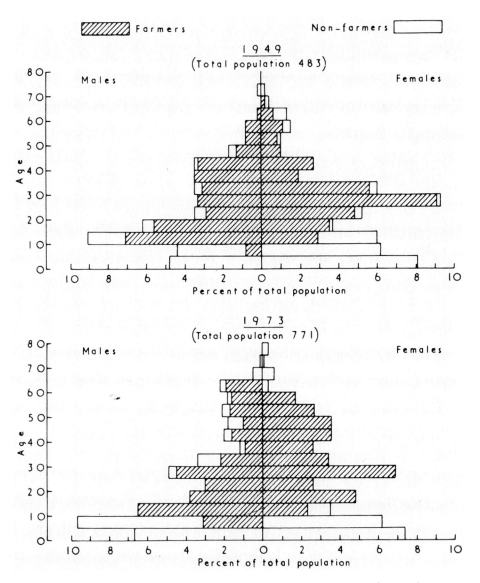

Figure 1.3 Participation of the village population in farming by sex and age (in years), Genieri Village, Gambia, 1949. From Haswell (1985: 55), with permission of Macmillan Press.

large areas, creating a huge demand for the movement of foodstuffs, it was impossible to supply the needs without water transport. (Gourou, 1975:130–1)

Clark and Haswell (1967: 178–99), who have closely examined this problem, estimate that the energetic costs of hauling a tonne of grain over moderately hilly country on the backs of humans or animals and in the absence of well-developed roads were so high that no one could move it more than about 20 km without consuming the

Table 1.2 Transport costs in the rural developing world: a summary of several studies. Note that costs have been converted to a single energetic currency based on contemporary market values. From Clark and Haswell (1967: 189).

Form of transport	Transport cost (kg grain equivalent tonne^{-1} km^{-1})		
	Minimum	Median	Maximum
Human porterage	2.0 (China 1938)	9.0	37.2 (Malawi 1968)
Pack animals	1.7 (Near East, camel)	4.6	11.8 (East Africa, donkey)
Wagons	1.2 (China eleventh century)	3.4	16.4 (England 1864)
Traditional boats	0.2 (China eleventh century)	0.9	5.8 (Ghana 1900)
Motor vehicles	0.2 (Thailand 1960)	1.0	13.9 (China 1928)
Railways	0.1 (China 1937)	0.5	4.1 (China 1928)

equivalent of more than half its energy content. No wonder people seized every opportunity to use water transport wherever it was available.[15]

High transport costs, combined with all the risks and fears associated with straying too far from home, meant that traditional farming communities were characterized by a degree of localization that most of us would find oppressive. As Joe Pierce once wrote of a traditional Anatolian farming community:

Almost everyone born in the valley lived and died there. In [the village] he would marry someone who had also been born and reared there. Hence, such things as international politics or even national politics did not concern him much. (Pierce, 1964: vii)

It is practically impossible to monitor life-time migration patterns prospectively for individuals from preindustrial populations, so various proxy measures are used in population research. For example, it is comparatively easy in a cross-sectional survey to ascertain the birthplaces of a husband and wife and later determine the map distance between those locations. The average or distribution of such "marriage distances" can then be used as a proxy measure of the spatial extent of an individual's social network. For example, Figure 1.4 shows temporal trends in the average marriage distance in the English farming community of Charlton-on-Otmoor from the late seventeenth century to the mid-twentieth century. For at least 150 years the average distance remained fairly constant at about 10 km, but then shot up dramatically after 1860, increasing by

---

[15] What may be a record for the movement of food under preindustrial conditions has been observed in the Southern Massim Islands off the eastern tip of Papua New Guinea, where in the early twentieth century outriggers regularly carried sago starch and yams to islands up to 200 km away (Macintyre and Allen, 1990: 130). An early observer speaks of "tons" of food being transported by canoe (Seligman, 1910: 526–8), and one missionary mentions five separate voyages between 1918 and 1924 when 80–100 large baskets of yams were delivered. (For comparison, one tonne of grain is about 37 bushel baskets.) But sago and yams were ceremonial foods, and their economic value was much greater than their nutritional composition would suggest. The other items traded were small valuables such as pig tusks, stone axes and fancy baskets.

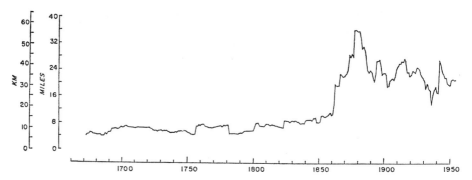

Figure 1.4 Marriage distances, Charlton-on-Otmoor Parish, Oxfordshire, England. Changes in mean marriage distance (excluding endogamous marriages) from *c*. 1670–1950. The rapid increase in marital distance *c*. 1860 reflects the railroad reaching the area. From Boyce *et al.* (1967), with permission of John Wiley & Sons, Inc.

some 300 percent.[16] Since the abrupt increase coincides with the arrival of railroads in the area, Figure 1.4 can be taken as a graphic illustration of one of the effects of industrialization on customary patterns of movement.

The lives of our preindustrial farming ancestors were thus spent in a world that was tiny compared with our own. The places known to them were known with an intimacy we can only guess at. But their knowledge may not have been worth much 20 km away. In a traditional farming village in Colombia, we are told,

[m]ost people move only between their houses and their fields. Year after year they use only a certain trail and when asked about trails in another direction they are often ignorant or uncertain of them. They may know a few neighboring trails, those used by villagers who have their fields in the same general direction, but a man who owns a field on the slopes west of the village does not necessarily know how the slopes to the east of it can be reached. And there is little interest in knowing. (Reichel-Dolmatoff and Reichel-Dolmatoff, 1961: 26)

One demographically important consequence of this extreme spatial circumscription is that populations in the rural preindustrial world tended to be extremely vulnerable to year-to-year fluctuations in local conditions. Today, at least when there are reasonably well-developed transport facilities and stable political systems, food can be airlifted thousands of kilometers to communities affected by famine. In the past it could scarcely be headloaded 20 kilometers and then only in small batches.

Subsistence Farming as the Most Basic Form of Traditional Farming

I have suggested that a focus on traditional farming allows us to simplify the conceptual and analytical problems involved in studying the connection between

---

[16] Note that these figures *overestimate* the average marriage distance because they exclude endogamous marriages, i.e. marriages within the same local parish. We are not told how the fraction of endogamous marriages changed over time.

population and agriculture. To simplify things even more, I will be concerned in this book primarily with *subsistence farming*, which can be regarded as a special kind of traditional farming. "Subsistence" has at least two distinct meanings, and we must be careful to keep them separate. In the first meaning, the unit of production – in this case, a farming household – produces primarily for its own use. This can be called the subsistence *form* of production – what Sahlins (1972) labels the domestic mode of production. The second meaning is what might be called the subsistence *level* of production, which implies that the production unit is able to produce food at a level just sufficient to meet its needs and no more. When I speak of *subsistence farming*, I am using the first of these two meanings. It is a separate question – though theoretically quite an interesting one – whether the subsistence *form* of farming usually operates at or near the subsistence *level* of production. I suspect it often does, but that is an empirical question, not a definitional one.

Mainstream economists have sometimes had a hard time dealing with the subsistence form of farming even as a theoretical concept. During the 1960s, for example, students of economic development started to realize that poor, non-industrialized countries could not be transformed overnight by investments in industry alone without prior improvements in the agricultural sector (which, of course, made up by far the greater part of the economies in question). This posed an analytical problem for economists, precisely because the agricultural sector was typically dominated by subsistence-oriented farms run by family-based households. Economists knew how to model factories, but traditional family farms were a different matter:

The theory of the family farm is essentially the theory of what may be called the "household firm"... There are two characteristics of this conceptual creature which are crucial for economic theorizing: first, that a part of the output goes to the household; and second, that a part of the input comes from the household. The "pure" firm "purchases" almost all its inputs and "sells" almost all its outputs in the market at market prices against money payments. But the household firm simply *transfers in kind* a part of the household input potential to the firm and a part of its output to the household. The consequence of this institutional hybridization is that the models of the household firm have also to be hybrids of the theory of the productive firm and the theory of the consumer household. (Krishna, 1969: 185)

To speak of things as "hybrids" would seem to suggest that they are (slightly unnatural?) products of the marriage of pure forms that already exist. In reality, of course, the family farm predates the capitalist firm by thousands of years. How do we meld established models of purely productive firms and purely consuming households to deal with this strange "conceptual creature" that does both? Or should we even try to meld them? I suggest that the primary point of confusion here is that many economists have mistakenly assumed that the real purpose of the subsistence-oriented family farm is to grow and eat food, but in reality it does those things only to attain its *real* goal. Even back in the 1960s, some economists understood this point:

With the introduction of the capitalist system labor became a commodity, like any other commodity to be purchased or dispensed with, hired or sacked, according to the needs of the firm and the state of the market. For the peasant *chef d'entreprise* such freedom of action can never exist. His labor force consists mainly of his kith and kin; his wife, his children and their dependents, his elderly parents. To hire and fire them according to the dictates of some external regulatory mechanism would be at once, inhuman, impractical, and irrational. Inhuman because only in exceptional circumstances are alternative employment opportunities ever generally available. Impractical because members of the labour force, as members of the family are entitled to a share in the ownership of the mean of production; because historically the enterprise is the sum of the labours of the generations. Irrational because *the objectives of the enterprise are primarily genealogical and only secondarily economic. . .* (Franklin, 1969: 1; emphasis added)

The objectives of the enterprise are primarily genealogical or (more or less equivalently) demographic and only secondarily economic – precisely so. The real purpose of a subsistence farm is to create and sustain a family. Food is essential for meeting that goal, but it is not the goal *per se*.

The Subsistence-Oriented Farming Household as a Demographic Enterprise

This, then, is the central principle guiding this book: *the subsistence farming household is essentially a demographic enterprise.* I will argue that, if accepted, this principle has the potential to transform the whole debate about population and traditional farming. But why call it an *enterprise*, which sounds a bit mercenary? According to the *Shorter Oxford English Dictionary*, the primary definition of an enterprise is "A piece of work taken in hand, an undertaking; *esp.* one that is bold, hazardous, or arduous" (Brown, 1993: 828). As later chapters will show, subsistence farming is certainly hazardous and arduous. Failure is not only a possibility but a reality for many households. And subsistence farming is plainly an *undertaking* – that is, it is initiated consciously and deliberately to meet a specific goal. Like any other enterprise, farming involves human agency, consciousness and purpose, plus a lot of hard work. Then why a *demographic* enterprise? As argued in the previous section, the goal of the enterprise is to create and raise a family, and the three basic forces of demography – fertility, mortality, migration – are the determinants of whether that goal is met or not.[17]

There are several important implications of viewing the subsistence farming household as a demographic enterprise. First, and perhaps most importantly for the population/agriculture debate, it means that "population" and "subsistence agriculture" are not separate things acting on each other from a remove – they are in fact the same thing. Thus, it may not be strictly correct to speak of "linkages" between demography and subsistence farming, as do Malthus, Boserup and more

---

[17] Fertility and mortality are obviously important to the success or failure of the family-based farming enterprise. Perhaps less obvious is the role of migration: people move into the household (e.g. as in-marrying spouses) and leave the household, perhaps to establish their own independent household. In sum, a household can be thought of as a tiny population subject to all the forces of demographic change (see Chapter 7).

recent writers. Instead, it may be better to regard them, at the household level, as a single, integrated set of processes. The whole *raison d'être* of subsistence farming is demography.

Second, when the principal unit of production corresponds to the principal unit of consumption, as it does by definition in subsistence farming, "production" and "consumption" become part of a single overarching process – no market mechanism intervenes to separate them. Of course production and consumption can still be distinguished empirically and measured separately. But the "agricultural" sphere, the purely productive part of the enterprise, is no longer separate from the "domestic" sphere – the domain of economic activity most oriented toward family food consumption. The two are linked as source and sink, and, as often happens in physiology, the sink can drive the source. Thus, the theory of subsistence farming should cover everything from food production to food consumption and beyond – including field preparation, tillage, sowing, weeding, manuring, reaping and transport, but also food processing, storage, distribution, haulage of fuel and water, cooking, eating, carry-over of seed and (importantly) the care and feeding of children. In subsistence farming, there is no gap between the agricultural and the domestic – both are essential parts of the household demographic enterprise. As shown in Chapters 9 and 10, this insight has important implications for how we think about household energy budgets and the allocation of household labor.

Third, any attempt to understand subsistence farming as a demographic enterprise must allow for human agency. Now, "agency" has become a terrifying bugbear in the social sciences, one that seems to inspire a lot of incomprehensible quotes from Continental philosophers. There will be no such quotes in this book. The view of human agency adopted here is simple, utilitarian and I dare say reductive. I begin, quite shamelessly, by assuming a reasonably constant human nature among all farmers, ancient and modern, as neatly captured by the archaeologist Peter Bellwood:

The range of individual human behavior patterns can be treated as relatively uniform during the time span of agriculture... Given the modern biological unity of mankind, individual human behavior patterns of 10,000 years ago were probably essentially similar in their range to those of today. Thus, desires for economic and reproductive success, peer-recognition, [and] freedom from fear and disease, plus capacities for calculated altruism and morality, have presumably always characterized anatomically modern humans like ourselves. So too have abilities to be acquisitive and destructive. There is no evidence to suggest otherwise, although this opinion is impossible to justify with complete certainty. It is maintained as a working hypothesis underpinned by uniformitarian principles. (Bellwood, 2005: 9)

Next I assume that subsistence farmers *qua* farmers are usually rational decision-makers and managers.[18] This may appear to be the same musty assumption made by classical economists – not to mention a challenge to the fascination present-day economists seem to have for the irrational in human behavior – but it is not, or at least not quite. No doubt subsistence farmers have production goals in mind at the

---

[18] I do not pretend to understand subsistence farmers *qua*, for example, performers of religious rituals.

outset of the agricultural year, and they try to manage their limited resources in an attempt to meet them. But their goals are usually modest and are not aimed at maximizing profit. Rather *the yearly economic goal of the subsistence farmer is to produce enough food to keep his or her family alive and to plant next year's crop, and perhaps a bit more to act as a buffer against unanticipated shortfalls.* To fall back on some old but useful jargon, subsistence farmers are *satisficers*, not *maximizers*.[19] Yet, no matter how modest their economic aspirations, their ultimate goal is of profound demographic importance: to produce new children who will survive to adulthood, the very process that keeps the population as a whole going (even if that is not the immediate concern of the farmers themselves). And besides, even their modest goals can be frustrated by environmental uncertainty, incomplete information, under-capitalization, institutional barriers, stupidity and sheer pigheadedness. To use a modern economic phrase, I think subsistence farmers, like everyone else, are characterized by *bounded* rationality (Kahneman, 2003). Subsistence farmers are quite as capable as we are of making foolish decisions. But the consequences of their foolishness – including perhaps the starvation of their children – are direr than the consequences of ours.

Salient Features of (a Model of?) the Subsistence Farming Household

In theory, then, this book is about demographic processes inherent to the subsistence form of traditional, family-based farming. When marshalling empirical evidence, however, I will sometimes be forced to deal with traditional farming behavior that transcends pure subsistence – for example, the activities of traditional farmers who market some of their produce. How much error do I introduce by doing so? Suffice it to say I will try to avoid discussing systems that stray very far from the subsistence ideal (or at least to point it out whenever I do). How many traditional farming systems will I exclude by doing so? Fewer than might be expected. Many traditional farming households, it is true, produce food for nonhousehold consumption – e.g. to take to the market or to meet social or political obligations (rents, taxes, tributes, etc.). But in many cases these households can be viewed as fairly straightforward extensions of the pure subsistence ideal. In those cases, some large fraction of the food produced, often well over 50 percent, may still be consumed by the household that grows it. In addition, most cash earned in marketing may itself be spent on food for the household. In fact, agricultural economists often use the fraction of a household's monetary income spent on food as an indicator of how integrated the household is in the cash economy – if the fraction is large then the household cannot be considered a truly commercial enterprise, but something still close to subsistence. The earliest stages of the farming household's involvement in the cash economy might even be considered "subsistence by other means." In my opinion, this sort of "impure" or near-subsistence farming was once widespread and is still quite common

---

[19] "Satisfice" is a neologism originally coined by Herbert Simon (1957), combining "satisfy" and "suffice."

today. The important thing about it is that food production is still dominated by a subsistence *logic* rather than a commercial one.

Subsistence farming (traditional farming without wide distribution of food beyond the household) is, like traditional farming itself (farming without industrial inputs), defined as a negative and therefore runs the risk of being a junk category. I do not think it is: despite the tremendous diversity of practices that fall under the heading of subsistence or near-subsistence farming, subsistence farming communities all share certain important characteristics and can be studied together profitably. But rather than trying to distill those characteristics into a short dictionary definition, I think it would be more useful to list the shared attributes. What follows, then, is a catalog of features that are shared widely by the farming systems discussed in this book, and that will be explored in detail in later chapters. Since several of the features have already been mentioned, this list can serve as a summary of the present chapter as well as a pointer to things to come.

(1) *The primary unit of food production – the farming household – is also the primary unit of food consumption.* Most food grown by a household is eaten by that same household. Most food eaten by a household is grown by that same household. Note the judicious use of "most." No subsistence farming household is or ever was truly isolated when it comes to food.

(2) *Supra-household work groups do exist and are important, but are small, localized and evanescent.* Mobilized to perform a few specific tasks during particular parts of the agricultural year, such groups break up into their constituent households during the rest of the year. The tasks involving larger work groups are typically those that must be done quickly and that can be expedited by a division of labor (field clearance, plowing and harvesting are important examples).

(3) *Farming households are farming families.* They are typically made up of a core of closely related kin – usually within a single degree of relatedness – plus their spouses.

(4) *The objective of the subsistence-oriented farming household is to create and feed a family, not to make a profit.* Demographic processes (fertility, mortality, migration) are an inherent part of meeting that goal. Thus, the subsistence household is a demographic enterprise, not strictly an economic one.

(5) *Most farm management decisions originate within the household.* In most cases decision-making is dominated by the male head of household, albeit under the influence of other household members (and some nonmembers). Larger groups are likely to be involved in decisions about common-use resources.

(6) *Exclusive access to arable land and disposition of its produce are (at least temporarily) vested in the household.* Under usufruct, these forms of control may last only while a plot is cultivated. Even when control is more permanent, it may not be heritable. Permanent alienation of land may be controlled by a larger group such as a lineage.

(7) *Subsistence farms are small operations.* Households themselves are small in size, usually falling between one and twelve members, with a mean of about five to seven. The area of arable land allotted to the household is also small, often much

less than ten hectares. Both household size and household land area vary in important ways, and at least some fraction of that variation is likely to be stochastic (random).

(8) *Farming households are dynamic.* Households change over time – they can even be said to have a built-in demographic life cycle. The changeability of households often makes them difficult to define, especially in prospective studies. But the changeability cannot be ignored. Household dynamics are an important element of the household's ability to adapt to changing circumstances, and yet those same dynamics can sometimes create problems to which the household in turn must adapt.

(9) *The demographic composition of the household is the single most important determinant of both production goals and availability of household labor in subsistence farming.* If the household demographic enterprise is to succeed, then agricultural yields must meet the household's joint nutritional requirements. These requirements vary by age and sex, as well as by workload and health status (which also vary by age and sex). It follows, then, that the food needs of the household as a whole are determined in large part by the age and sex composition of its members, as well as its absolute size. Insofar as household members constitute the usual labor force for farming, the total physiological work capacity of the household members is a major limiting factor in how much labor can be invested in the family farm. As detailed in Chapter 9, physiological work capacity also varies by age and sex as well as by health status.

(10) *In most years, agricultural production is likely to be slightly more than needed to meet immediate subsistence requirements.* Given the unpredictability of the agricultural environment, meeting subsistence goals *reliably* may require some excess production during normal or good years – the so-called "normal surplus" (Allan, 1965: 38–48) – as a hedge against the possibility of production shortfalls during bad years (but see Chapter 2 for a different risk-avoidance strategy that does not involve a normal surplus).

(11) *Beyond the normal surplus, there is little incentive to produce in excess of the household's own needs (including enough plant material to sow next year).* Food storage and transport facilities are poorly developed. It is difficult to carry over even the normal surplus for future consumption or to disperse it beyond the local neighborhood. There is little if anything to be gained by producing much above the subsistence level, except perhaps to meet highly localized social obligations.

(12) *Agriculture is the primary occupation of every household in the community.* Most adult workers (and many children) are directly or indirectly involved in food production. Indirect involvement might include the making of agricultural tools, milling grain, building farm structures and so on; such work is usually done by semispecialists who are directly involved in food production for most of the year. Many subsistence farmers also do a certain amount of hunting and collecting of wild foods (Wilken, 1970; Delang, 2006; Tucker, 2006), and these contributions need to be included in the household budget.

* * *

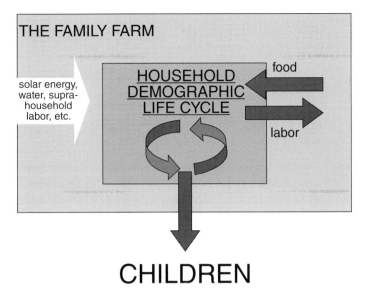

Figure 1.5 The model of subsistence farming that will guide this book.

For the moment, it might be best to think of this portrait of subsistence farming not as an exact representation of something to be found in the real world, but as a *model* – that is, an ideal, stylized picture that may provide a useful, deliberately simplified starting point for analysis and (more importantly) understanding. The basic elements of this model of subsistence farming are summarized in Figure 1.5, which will reappear throughout this book.

Raymond Firth (1969: 24) once called subsistence farming "an almost pure economic concept" – note "concept," not "phenomenon" – that excludes just about everything of interest to the anthropologist. Be that as it may, the cautious modeler always begins with the simplest possible case and adds "realistic" complications later, and only if they promise to enlighten. What this implies, however strange it may seem, is that even if subsistence farming does not exist and has never existed, it is still worth devoting a book to it.

A Digression on the Use of Abstract Models in Thinking about Subsistence Farming

Subsistence farming is an important subject for a book even if it doesn't exist? Sensible people might well regard this assertion as a sign of mental weakness on the part of the author. But that would miss the whole point of scientific modeling. As the population biologist Joel Cohen once remarked (1995: 429), models are "cartoons" of reality. What he meant by this is that a scientific model, one intended for use in empirical studies, is expected to share certain points of similarity with some delimited piece of reality, but only in a very simplified, schematic way. Like a cartoon, a model leaves out most of reality – and quite deliberately so. What it includes, the modeler dearly hopes, are the most fundamental and general elements needed to understand a set of real-world processes (note that I say "understand" not "perfectly predict the behavior of"). A model never *is* reality, it is only a tool for thinking about reality – a point all too many modelers lose sight of. A wise modeler never mistakes her model for the real world.

The logic of scientific modeling was captured admirably by counter-example in a short story by Jorge Luis Borges (1970: 141) called "Of Exactitude in Science" and purportedly taken from a manuscript of 1658. Here it is in its entirety:

. . .In that Empire, the craft of Cartography attained such Perfection that the Map of a Single province covered the space of an entire City, and the Map of the Empire itself an entire Province. In the course of Time, these Extensive maps were found somewhat wanting, and so the College of Cartographers evolved a Map of the Empire that was of the same scale as the Empire and that coincided with it point for point. Less attentive to the Study of Cartography, succeeding Generations came to judge a map of such Magnitude cumbersome, and, not without Irreverence, they abandoned it to the Rigors of Sun and Rain. In the western Deserts, tattered Fragments of the Map are still to be found, Sheltering an occasional Beast or beggar; in the whole Nation, no other relic is left of the Discipline of Geography. From *Travels of Praiseworthy Men* (1658) by J. A. Suárez Miranda

Some five decades ago, an anonymous editor of the *Journal of the American Medical Association* made the same point with considerably less irony:

A model like a map cannot show everything. If it did it would not be a model but a duplicate. Thus the classic definition of art as the purgation of superfluities also applies to models, and the model-maker's problem is to distinguish between the superfluous and the essential. (Anonymous, 1960: 407)

As George Orwell might have said – but didn't – all models are lies, but some models are more *useful* lies than others.

In a scientific context, "model" is often taken to mean an explicitly mathematical formulation – a *mathematical* model. Now, mathematical models have their virtues: they are precise and make quite focused predictions about the real world; they are also unambiguous, if only for those who are fluent in the arcane language in which they are couched. But mathematics is not necessary for doing modeling. Models can be graphical or even verbal – just pictures and words, not equations – and still fulfill all the useful functions of models. Mathematical models do have a certain cachet in some circles, but after long experience I have come to believe that they are often premature, misleading and over-sold. Certainly mathematical models of any complexity are difficult to communicate to anything but a specialist audience, and for that reason alone are of limited use to the scientific community as a whole. Almost all the models presented in this book will be graphical or verbal, and whenever an equation appears I will do my best to explain it in pictures and words.

Whatever form a scientific model takes, its underlying logic is always the same. That logic can perhaps best be conveyed by an example. The particular example I've chosen is one of the earliest models to be developed and applied in a thoroughly modern way. Happily for us, it is a model of preindustrial agriculture (although it has also been applied successfully to modern industrialized farms). While not explicitly a model of the relationship between *population* and farming, it provides important insights into the spatial distribution of farming populations and will crop up repeatedly in later chapters. Although it sometimes finds modern expression in complicated mathematical or computer models (Blaikie, 1971; Sasaki and Box, 2003), the original version was purely verbal and graphical – which is exactly the version most researchers still use and understand today. It is, in my opinion, a very pretty model.

The model was invented by the German mathematician (and farmer) Johann Heinrich von Thünen (1783–1850), who presented it in a book titled *The Isolated State*, published in 1826. At that stage in his career, von Thünen had partially retired from academia and had purchased a large farm in the northern plains of Germany. In thinking how best to organize his farm, von Thünen started with the following scenario:

Imagine a very large town at the center of a fertile plain that is crossed by no navigable river or canal. Throughout the plain the soil is capable of cultivation and is everywhere of the same fertility. Far from the town, the plain turns into an uncultivated wilderness that cuts off all communication between this State and the outside world.

There are no other towns on the plain. The central town must therefore supply the rural areas with all manufactured products, and in return will obtain all its provisions from the surrounding countryside...

The problem we want to solve is this: what pattern of cultivation will take shape in these conditions? And how will the farming system of the various districts be affected by their distance from the town? We assume throughout that farming is conducted absolutely rationally. (von Thünen, 1966 [orig. 1826]: 7–8)

We would now call these *model assumptions*. They are not intended to be particularly realistic (although the flat loess plains of northern Europe where von Thünen's farm was located meet the assumptions about as well as any other part of the Earth's surface); rather, they are intended to simplify the situation so that the effects of one particular variable can stand out unobscured. Spatial analysts would now call the uniform, featureless plain posited by von Thünen an "isotropic" plain – the same in all directions.

So we are to plunk a town down in the middle of an isotropic plain and start up a market for agricultural produce in its center. How would farming come to be organized in the countryside around the town? Well, the only thing that can possibly differentiate one farm site from another on an otherwise uniform landscape is its distance from the market. Since the plain is flat and has no feature to impede or facilitate movement, there is a perfect correlation between distance and transport costs. This means that the cost of getting a particular crop to market increases linearly with distance from the market, and thus the *net* income (or effective yield) for the farmer after subtracting the cost of transporting the crop, goes down linearly with distance (Figure 1.6). Ultimately there will be a distance from the town so great that transport costs cannot be even partly offset by the market value of the produce

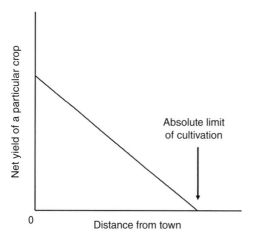

Figure 1.6 Yield of a single crop net of transport costs as a function of distance from von Thünen's town.

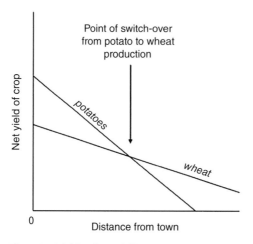

Figure 1.7 Yields of two different crops net of transport costs as a function of distance from von Thünen's town.

(Figure 1.6, arrow). If we rotate our net yield line around the center point provided by the town, we will find that the town is surrounded by a circle of finite radius, beyond which the crop will not be grown for the market – assuming, as von Thünen does, that farmers are economically rational. The town cannot expect to get the crop from outside this circle unless it coerces it.

Now imagine that two crops are available for cultivation – for example, wheat and potatoes. Potatoes yield more than wheat in northern Europe, but are bulky and heavy because of their higher water content and are thus more expensive to transport than wheat. Therefore, as shown in Figure 1.7, the line of net yield starts higher for potatoes than for wheat (reflecting higher gross yield), but declines more rapidly as distance from the town increases (reflecting higher transport costs). Under these circumstances, it will often be the case that the two net yield lines cross (Figure 1.7, arrow). Beyond that crossing point, potatoes will provide a lower net yield or income than wheat, and we would expect to see a fairly sharp boundary at the crossover point separating an area near the town given over to potato cultivation and a more distant area under wheat. And if more crop choices are available?

It is on the whole obvious that near the town will be grown those products that are heavy or bulky in relation to their value and that are consequently so expensive to transport that the remoter districts are unable to supply them. Here also we find the highly perishable products, which must be used very quickly. With increasing distance from the town, the land will progressively be given up to products cheap to transport in relation to their value.

For this reason alone, fairly sharply differentiated concentric rings or belts will form around the town, each with its own particular staple product.

From ring to ring the staple product, and with it the entire farming system, will change; and in the various rings we shall find completely different farming systems. (von Thünen, 1966 [orig. 1826]: 8)

These predictions are illustrated in the upper portion of Figure 1.8. Note that the particular form of land use within each concentric ring in this figure reflects the market values and transport costs prevailing for particular kinds of produce in northern Germany in the 1820s. The more general prediction is that zones of land use will array themselves in roughly concentric circles around their primary market, with transport costs and perishability being the main factors determining in which circle each crop or system of land use will appear. Of course, perfect concentric circles will form only under the imaginary condition of perfect isotropy; but even when isotropy is violated to some degree (Figure 1.8, lower portion), the same underlying logic can still be discerned on the ground.

von Thünen's original model was based on a centralized market system handling crops with fixed cash values. Can it possibly be applied to subsistence agriculture in which nothing is marketed and no urban centers exist? In the early 1960s, the geographer Michael Chisholm generalized von Thünen's logic beyond its commercial base (1962: 21–75). This he did first by calculating costs and income in energetic terms, not in cash value. Next he assumed that the settlement at the center of the whole system was not a large market town, but a single farmstead or a small village or hamlet with its fields arrayed around it; transport costs then involved movement of farmers from their houses to their fields and back again, sometimes lugging produce, sometimes not. He also combined the costs of bringing in the harvest with other travel costs associated with movement between house and field. For example, a farmer might head- or back-load some quantity of manure to a field well before it is ready to be harvested (Figure 1.9). The energetic costs of doing so must be included in the farm's (i.e. household's) energy budget. Since the "domestic" is not separate from the "agricultural" in subsistence farming, activities such as hauling fuel for cooking also incur transport costs (Figure 1.10), which influences the farmstead's location relative to the natural sources of fuel. Most fundamentally, if the farmer must visit a field frequently for weeding, thinning, manuring or any other tender care, it is better

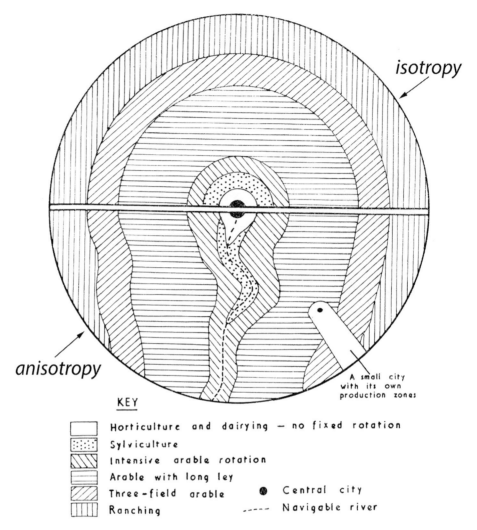

isotropy

anisotropy

A small city
with its own
production zones

KEY

Horticulture and dairying — no fixed rotation

Sylviculture

Intensive arable rotation

Arable with long ley

Three-field arable   ● Central city

Ranching   ----- Navigable river

Figure 1.8 von Thünen's system of agricultural land use. In this figure, "horticulture" refers to intensive market-gardening, not shifting cultivation. After Chisholm (1962: 29), with permission of the Hutchinson University Library.

if the field is close so that the cost of the frequent visits is minimized. For that reason, fields that are cultivated intensively are expected to lie closer to the farmer's domicile than fields that do not require everyday care. Thus, according to Chisholm, farming should become less intensive as we move from the inner to the outer rings of the farm-based land-use system.

Chisholm's extension of von Thünen's logic to non-commercial, subsistence-oriented farming was itself an important accomplishment, and numerous studies have demonstrated its usefulness for understanding the spatial organization of traditional agriculture (see Blaikie, 1971, for an especially good example). Some examples from sub-Saharan Africa are shown in Figure 1.11.

Figure 1.9 Father and children hauling cultivated green manure to house garden, Japan *c.* 1900. Note daughter carrying kettle for tea. From King (1911: 210).

Although not explicitly concerned with population and farming, von Thünen's model has played a part in the debate over population and agricultural intensification. Figure 1.12, for example, shows the distribution of distances between the birthplaces of spouses for two preindustrial farming communities: shifting cultivators from the rainforests of the Congo Basin, and intensive grain farmers in northern Italy. In both cases, the most common marriage distance is less than 5 km, and the median is less than 20 km. But the distribution for the shifting cultivators has a longer upper tail (note the difference in the right-hand portion of the scale), implying greater mobility over a larger area than is typical of northern Italian farmers. Cavalli-Sforza and Bodmer make much of this difference, taking it as showing in general that, as food production intensifies or population density increases, preindustrial communities become even more localized. Perhaps, but of course these two cases alone do not prove the assertion. Stone (1996), however, has provided a more general model by drawing on von Thünen and Chisholm's ideas about the spatial organization of farming. His model predicts that *intensification of food production* was often accompanied by spatial *concentration of food production* in the pre-modern era of high transport costs (indeed, he uses the two italicized terms interchangeably). As intensification increases, the need to visit fields frequently (to thin, to weed, to manure, to irrigate) increases as well. As a result, the travel and haulage costs to more distant fields become prohibitive. At the same time, the yield of nearby fields becomes high enough to justify abandoning more distant fields. The net result is a greater concentration of farming around the settlement or farmstead

Figure 1.10 A farm woman carrying peats for fuel, Isle of Lewis, Scotland, *c.* 1900. The peats are carried in a wickerwork basket (*cliabh* in Gaelic). Note the woman's attempt to reduce the opportunity costs of haulage: she is knitting stockings while walking with her load. From an old postcard, reproduced by Fenton (1984: 108), with permission of John Donald Publishers, Ltd.

(Figure 1.13). Perhaps, then, Cavalli-Sforza and Bodmer were justified in generalizing from the data in Figure 1.12 to claim that, as a general rule, more intensive food production implies lower mobility under preindustrial conditions. Note that we are more inclined to accept this conclusion, not because of additional data, but from the existence of a coherent model.

But recall that we are interested in von Thünen here less for his specific model and its predictions and more for what he tells us about the *logic* of modeling. Here is what he has to say on that subject:

I hope the reader who is willing to spend some time and attention on my work will not take exception to the imaginary assumptions [e.g. isotropy] I make at the beginning because they do not correspond to conditions in reality, and that he will not reject these assumptions as arbitrary and pointless. They are a necessary part of my argument, allowing me to establish the operation of a single factor, a factor whose operation we see but dimly in reality, where it is in incessant conflict with others of its kind.

This method of analysis has illuminated – and solved – so many problems in my life, and appears to me to be capable of such widespread application, that I regard it as the most important matter contained in all my work. (von Thünen, 1966 [orig. 1826]: vi–vii)

A

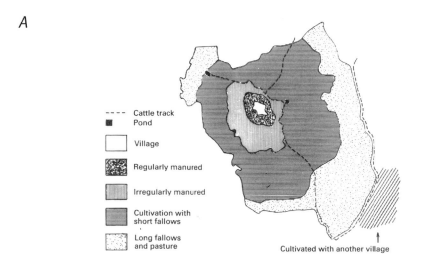

- - - - Cattle track
■ Pond
☐ Village
▨ Regularly manured
▥ Irregularly manured
▨ Cultivation with short fallows
▨ Long fallows and pasture

↑
Cultivated with another village

B

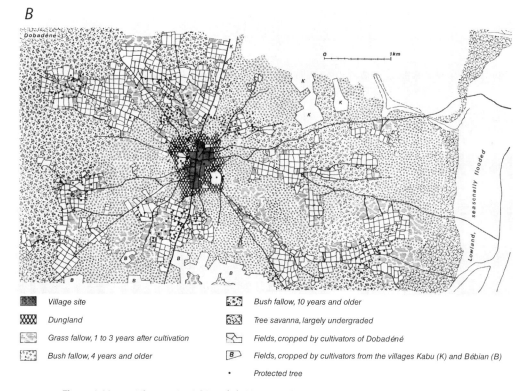

▨ Village site
▨ Dungland
▨ Grass fallow, 1 to 3 years after cultivation
▨ Bush fallow, 4 years and older

▨ Bush fallow, 10 years and older
▨ Tree savanna, largely undergraded
▱ Fields, cropped by cultivators of Dobadéné
⬡ Fields, cropped by cultivators from the villages Kabu (K) and Bébian (B)
• Protected tree

Figure 1.11 von Thünen in Africa. (A) Observed land-use pattern around a dryland village, Gourjae, eastern Niger. From Grégoire (1980) as modified by Mortimore (1998: 43), with permission of the Université de Bourdeaux. (B) Observed land-use pattern around a semiarid savanna village, Dobadéné, Chad; "dungland" is the most intensively cropped area. From Gilg (1970) as redrawn by Ruthenberg (1971: 78), with permission of EHESS, Inc.

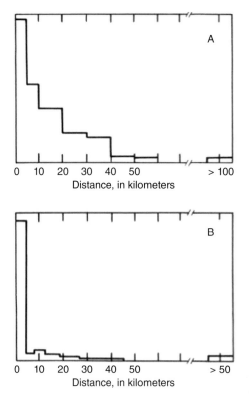

Figure 1.12 Distributions of distances between birthplaces of spouses in two preindustrial farming populations. (A) Issongo shifting cultivators, Central African Republic, c. 1965 (population density 1–2 km^{-2}, mean village size 100, 20 percent village endogamy). (B) Intensive farmers in the Upper Parma Valley, northern Italy, c. 1950 (population density 50 km^{-2}, mean village size 300, 55 percent village endogamy). From Cavalli-Sforza and Bodmer (1971: 434), with permission of W. H. Freeman Press.

So far as I know, this passage was the first clear expression of a general logic of modeling that is still widely used in the physical, biological and social sciences. The logic, involving holding everything constant in a model while allowing one factor to vary, has come to be called *partial equilibrium analysis*, *sensitivity analysis* or *the method of ceteris paribus* ("all other things being equal"). It allows for something rather like an experiment to be conducted on a schematic representation of reality.

The second half of this book, starting with Chapter 7, constitutes, in effect, a series of partial equilibrium analyses. I present a general, deliberately simplified model of the traditional farming household (a version of which was introduced in this chapter), and I proceed to ignore most of the innumerable variables falling outside the model, just as von Thünen ignored the entire world lying outside his isolated state. Throughout the book I make extensive use of three model-inspired simplifications: (i) I focus on subsistence farming rather than production for the market or compelled by elites, (ii) I assume that individual subsistence farms are largely autonomous when it comes

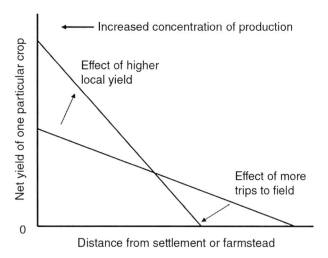

Figure 1.13 Increasing spatial concentration of production with increasing intensification of farming (i.e. increasing investments of labor and capital in arable fields), based on the logic of Stone (1996: 29–32).

to food production and consumption, and (iii) I pursue the notion that the subsistence farming household is at heart a demographic enterprise. None of these three simplifications provides an absolutely true or complete picture of reality, as is acknowledged throughout the book. But they have all been useful in focusing the enquiry and aiding model development, and they all can be modified or even discarded in future research (in fact, Chapter 12 modifies the second of my three simplifying assumptions).

One particular suite of things that I have chosen to ignore might be sorely missed by some readers – the processes and factors that are often placed under the rubric *political economy* or *political ecology*. I have little to say about voracious landlords, oppressive leaders, taxes, tributes, rents, corvée labor, marauding armies, global financiers, even markets for local produce. I choose to ignore these things, not because I think they are never important to traditional farmers. Of course they are important: often enough their effects can dominate the ecology of a farming community. But even those who most strongly argue for the primacy of sociopolitical factors in the origin, evolution and ecology of traditional farming usually acknowledge that population processes are ever-present and important, either as cause or consequence. Thus, my whole intention is to isolate and study what I regard as a universal, if not always completely determinative, set of variables – just as von Thünen highlighted the universal variables distance and transport costs without ever suggesting that these were the only or even the primary factors affecting land use. I want to turn a microscope, so to speak, on the linkages between population and traditional farming even as others train a "macroscope" on the larger social and political context. I am bold enough to suggest that the microscopic view might actually inform and enrich the macroscopic view. It certainly doesn't replace it.

Having constructed my model, I examine specific features or dimensions of it one at a time while holding the rest of its components constant. I then contemplate how each such partial analysis illuminates the reality of traditional farming in general. The confrontation with reality is, of course, an essential part of the whole modeling strategy. But we should never expect the model to fit the data perfectly – the model is too simplified to do that.[20] We should hope, however, that the model will help us interpret and make sense of the data. Insofar as it does so, it is a *useful* model – and that is the sole criterion of the model's success.[21] But, no matter how useful a model may be, never forget that it is, at bottom, a lie.

---

[20] What this means in statistical practice is that we will often need to include certain "control" variables in our analyses that we are not directly interested in but whose obscuring effects we need to adjust for in order to reveal the operation of factors that we *are* interested in. This is standard practice in statistics.

[21] There are other kinds of models, often called *statistical* models, for which a close fit to data *is* a basic criterion of model success. Regression models are a common example. Paradoxically, such models, even when they fit well, may tell us next to nothing about the real-world processes giving rise to the data.

2 Farmers, Farms and Farming Resources

Small farmers are vastly more knowledgeable than most of us can imagine. In fact, despite their lack of schooling, small farmers too are professionals. They have to be in order to survive! Through a lengthy apprenticeship which begins in childhood, small farmers are taught to use a very complex manual technology. They learn to make and use their own work implements. They learn to "read" the soil, the weather, and the heavens. They learn to study their crops for disease, insect and rodent damage, and water requirements – often on a plant-by-plant basis. They learn to follow a specialized farm task calendar, meet sequential task deadlines, and keep careful count of the passing days. They learn to build irrigation structures which are adjusted to soil quality, slope of the land, crop requirements, and water availability. They learn to make maximum use of their entire property, allow no part of their harvest to be wasted, and even collect weeds and stalk residue to feed to their animals or to use as fuel. They learn to salvage all they can when their crops are destroyed by rain, floods, droughts, wind, insects, and other calamities. . . The very durability of such methods, and of the people who have survived terrible adversity using them, is reason alone to treat them with a great deal of respect.

– J. K. Hatch (1974: 7–8)

Neither tribe [Pima or Papago] had any ritual for irrigation. One Papago informant said getting water on the fields was not a matter of ceremony but of brain work.

– E. F. Castetter and W. H. Bell (1942: 172)

Before we can investigate the role of demographic processes in subsistence farming, we need to explore some of the basic features of such farming. As argued in the previous chapter, we can understand the impact of demography only if we can link it to specific mechanisms operating in such farming regimes – which means we need to identify what the relevant mechanisms are from real-world field observations. Most of the empirical evidence concerning subsistence farmers and their farms comes from in-depth studies of living communities in the farther reaches of the rural developing world, studies conducted by anthropologists, geographers, economists, ethnobotanists, ecologists, agricultural scientists and others. Most of this field research has post-dated 1950, which means that many of these purportedly traditional farming operations had already been "contaminated" to some degree by the modern world – by the penetration of markets, the commercialization of food, the rise of wage labor, the exhortations of agricultural extension officers. In this book, I have drawn as far as possible on studies in which the contamination is limited and to some extent "correctable." Often this has required examining older literature – scarcely a hardship since the older material is often of very high quality. The studies I draw upon are extremely diverse, but the majority are either cross-sectional or of short duration (a few years at most) – a fact that often limits our ability to observe and understand the inherently dynamic nature of farming. Sometimes archaeological and historical reconstructions can provide greater time depth, but they are unable to recover many of the fine details of farming behavior. Even restricting attention to studies of living farmers (living, that is, at the time of study), we find little standardization of research methods, not surprising given the long time span over which these studies were done and the diverse professional backgrounds of the authors involved. The literature is huge, and I do not attempt to review it all; in this chapter I emphasize topics that are important for later chapters. In the appendix to this book, however, there is a bibliographical essay that provides pointers to the larger literature.

How can we summarize a phenomenon as diverse as subsistence farming? The truth is that all subsistence farming regions – indeed, all subsistence farms and farmers and farming years – are unique. Every farm differs from every other farm in prevailing soil types, topography, access to water and a host of other physical characteristics; every farmer differs in intelligence, know-how, temperament and willingness to work. Yet, from another perspective, all subsistence farmers are the same. How do we capture both the diversity and the commonality? One fundamental feature shared by all subsistence farmers has already been discussed in Chapter 1: all subsistence farmers have a common goal – to feed and support their families, this year and next year and beyond. Another thing held in common by all subsistence farmers (indeed, by farmers of every stripe) is that they are faced with the same set of basic resource management problems – water, soils, time, space, household labor, crop genetic resources, etc. The specifics of the problems vary widely from place to place and even from farm to farm in the same locality, as do the particular practices adopted to deal with them, but the basic problems are always and everywhere the same.

Before exploring the resource management problems faced by subsistence farmers, we need to discuss a conventional but historically important approach to the diversity of traditional, subsistence-oriented farming practices – the construction of *typologies* of traditional farming "systems." The typological approach, which is still common in anthropology and geography, has, I believe, been a source of some misunderstanding when applied to the debate on population and agriculture, and I introduce it mainly to exorcise it.

Typological Approaches to the Diversity of Subsistence Farming Practices

The classic way to try to capture the diversity of traditional farming is to force it into a typology, i.e. a small number of stereotypic agricultural "systems" (see, for example, Dumont, 1957; Duckham and Masefield, 1969; Ruthenberg, 1971; Grigg, 1974; Norman, 1979; Turner and Brush, 1987). Typologies can be useful as a first way to organize a large body of empirical observations, but they can also distort reality to such an extent that they hinder rather than help understanding. Some typologies are "natural" in that the barriers between "types" are real. At least at the species level, biological taxonomies are an obvious example owing to the reproductive isolation separating most species, especially among animals (plants and microbes are altogether more promiscuous). At higher taxonomic levels biological classifications are more arbitrary, but at least they are constructed with some care to reflect the inferred evolutionary history of the taxa involved. Other typologies may be more problematic insofar as they create an impression that a given type is a more or less homogeneous group that can be differentiated sharply and predictably from other types. Such types ought not to overlap or blend into each other or to exist in mixed form – all of which subsistence farming systems do.

Two standard typologies of tropical agriculture, including most surviving cases of subsistence farming, are shown in Table 2.1. The authors (Ruthenberg, 1971; Norman, 1979) identify five and seven types of tropical farming, respectively, and devote at least one book chapter to each.[1] Various subtypes are discussed in the text, but the distinctions are mostly submerged in the larger categories. Are these types natural, like biological species? To pick just one example, "irrigated cropping systems" or "arable irrigation farming" covers a wide variety of scales and arrangements, from tiny spring-seepage systems (Figure 2.1) to elaborate irrigated terraces (Figure 2.2). Mechanisms for distributing water vary widely (Hatch, 1974; Wilken, 1977, 1987; Wilkinson, 1977; Coward, 1980; Adams, 1986; Mitchell and Guillet, 1994; Watson et al., 1998). Some irrigation systems are purely gravity fed (e.g. paddy irrigation, canal irrigation, underground irrigation by qanat or puquio), some require water lifting (by shadouf, water-wheel, handheld pot or Archimedes screw) and some (most notably in the Nile Valley and the interior delta of the Niger River) rely on floodwater-recession or *decrué* irrigation (Harlan and Pasquereau, 1969; Thom and Wells, 1987). Some irrigation systems are liable to salinization, others are not. No one believes that all forms of irrigation are historically related, although some of the subtypes may be.[2] It is not at all clear what we gain in understanding by lumping all these different, historically distinct systems together in a single category. All farmers have to manage water resources. Sometimes they drain waterlogged soils (though we never speak of "arable ditch farming"). Sometimes they use methods we would call irrigation. But treating irrigation farming as if it were a distinct species separated from other forms of traditional farming does violence to the facts, as does treating all varieties of irrigation farming as if they were somehow fundamentally the same.

[1] I feel honor-bound to note that, even though I criticize their typological approach, I think that both of these books are very good (see the bibliographical appendix at the end of the present book).

[2] Or maybe not. Qanats and puquios both involve underground tunnels that bring water from higher altitude aquifers down to the farming area, often over long distances (Cressey, 1950; Beaumont et al., 1989; Schreiber and Rojas, 2003). Although qanats and puquios are similar in form and construction, the evidence shows that they developed entirely independently. Qanats (fogarras, karez) were first developed in ancient Persia or the southern Caucasus and later spread throughout the Near East, Northern Africa, and Moorish Spain. They persisted in Spain after the *Reconquista* and were imported to Mesoamerica in post-Columbian times. Puquios, on the other hand, first appeared in the arid lowlands of western Peru long before Columbus and spread almost not at all beyond that area.

Table 2.1 Two typologies of tropical farming. Lines indicate corresponding types. From Ruthenberg (1971) and Norman (1979). Reprinted, with permission, from M. J. T. Norman (1979) *Annual Cropping Systems in the Tropics*. Gainesville, FL: University Presses of Florida.

Norman	Ruthenberg
Shifting cultivation ————————————	Shifting cultivation
Semi-intensive and intensive rainfed ——————	Short fallow systems
cultivation	Permanent upland cultivation
Irrigated cropping systems —————————	Arable irrigation farming
Mixed systems of annual and —————————	Systems with perennial crops
perennial crops	Grazing systems
Cropping systems with livestock ———————	Ley systems and dairy systems*

* Leys are temporary grassland fallows used for pasturage or meadow.

Figure 2.3 shows a similar typology of farming, but with an added historical dimension. This scheme is, in effect, a phylogeny of farming, or more precisely of the various Eurasian and African farming systems that purportedly descended directly from the first domestication of plants and animals in the Near East (Mazoyer and Roudart, 2006: 127). (Whether such neat lines of descent can be traced is one of many questions raised by this figure.) According to this scenario, farming began in the wooded Mediterranean areas of the Near East, and the earliest examples took the form of shifting cultivation (or "slash and burn cultivation" as these authors call it).[3] As farming spread and evolved, two processes intervened. First, shifting cultivation led to the deforestation of the ancient heartland of Near Eastern farming, and farming spread into regions that were not particularly suited to shifting cultivation. As a consequence of both processes, shifting cultivation evolved into the wide variety of farming systems attested to archaeologically, historically and ethnographically. According to this scheme, shifting cultivation was not only the Ur-form of all western Asian, European and African farming, but it was the *immediate* ancestor of all types of farming ever found in those regions. Primitive scratch plows (ards) were added in late prehistoric Europe, and more developed heavy plows in early medieval Europe. Shifting cultivation persisted in certain parts of the world, especially equatorial Africa and the heavily forested areas of Scandinavia (on shifting cultivation and fire clearance in early twentieth-century Finland, see Mead, 1953: 44–50; Sarmela, 1987).

---

[3] Shifting cultivation is another conventional "type" of farming and is just as problematic as irrigation farming. Since shifting cultivation has played a special role in the history of the population/agriculture debate, it will receive detailed attention in Chapter 6.

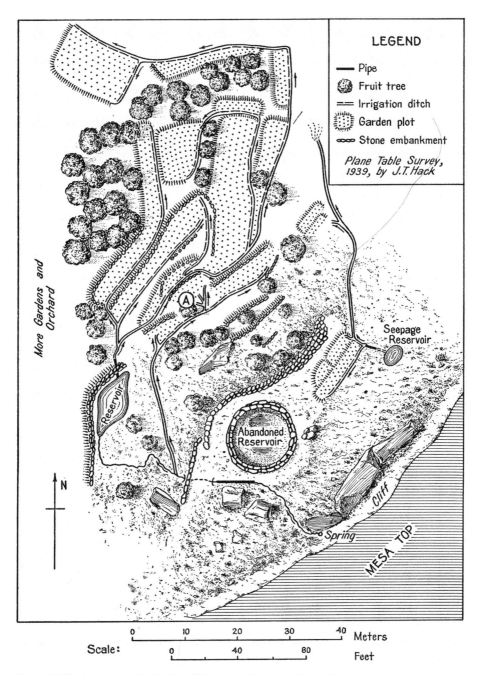

Figure 2.1 Hopi spring-fed irrigation, Tallahogan Canyon, Black Mesa District, Arizona, 1939.
Reprinted by permission from John T. Hack, The Changing Physical Environment of the Hopi Indians of
Arizona, papers of the Peabody Museum of American Archaeology and Ethnology, Harvard University,
vol. 35: 1 (Cambridge, Mass.), p. 35 (1942).

Figure 2.2 A mixed system of irrigated rice terraces, permanent rain-fed fields, shifting fields at higher elevations where the drainage system is too short for irrigation and intensively cultivated house gardens adjacent to residences, Central Madagascar. From Ruthenberg (1971: plate 16), by permission of Oxford University Press.

Figure 2.3 assumes a great deal more about reality than the simpler descriptive typologies of Norman and Ruthenberg (Table 2.1). It possesses all the normal vices of a typology while committing additional sins regarding historical patterns and processes. The historical dimension of this figure, in actual fact, represents almost pure guesswork and fantasy. Many archaeologists now agree, for example, that the earliest evidence of farming in the Near East and elsewhere indicates more permanent forms of farming and settlement than shifting cultivation (see Rowley-Conwy, 1981; Barker, 1985: 141–3; Moore *et al.*, 2000; Fisher, 2007; Bogaard *et al.*, 2013).

Another basic problem with the typological approach is that it diminishes the importance of "mixed" farming systems – systems that combine multiple types of land use, such as shifting cultivation and permanent irrigation agriculture (as in Figure 2.2). But mixed systems may be the rule rather than the exception. Benneh (1973) has pointed out that so-called shifting cultivators in Ghana devote up to 40 percent of their arable to permanent, intensive farming. Almost all forms of shifting cultivation are mixed in that they include small "house gardens" next to the farmers' domiciles, where a variety of green vegetables, medicinal and psycho-tropic plants, herbaceous perennials such as bananas and sugar cane and even rapidly maturing woody fruit trees are intensively cultivated using weeding, mulch-ing and composting (Landauer and Brazil, 1990; Padoch and de Jong, 1991). In highland New Guinea the Wola practice a form of shifting cultivation that grades almost imperceptibly into semipermanent farming with short grass fallows and

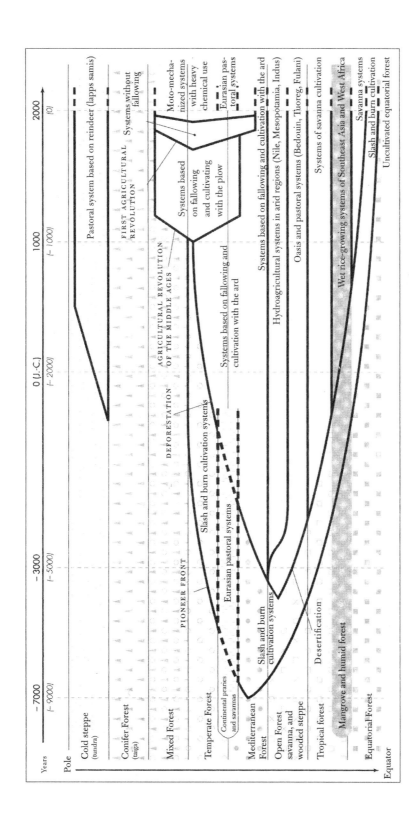

Figure 2.3 An evolutionary typology of farming. From Mazoyer and Roudart (2006: 127), by permission of the Monthly Review Press.

elaborate tillage, including mounding and ditching (Sillitoe, 1998). Similarly, Conklin (1980) has shown that the Ifugao of the northern Philippines, renowned for their elaborately terraced wet-rice fields, practice shifting cultivation at the outer, unirrigable margins of their terrace complexes (see Viên *et al.*, 2009, for a similar mixture in upland Vietnam).

Despite this evidence, Boserup (1965: 57–9) has argued that any farming system that looks, in a cross-sectional study, as if it contains multiple forms of land use is merely a transitional stage in the long-term replacement of less intensive farming with more intensive practices under the influence of population pressure. She would not, therefore, consider the "mix" to be a stable collection of differing approaches to, say, different local environments – a possibility she explicitly rejects (see Chapter 5). Yet even in the absence of local environmental variation – as on an isotropic plain – von Thünen's 1826 model would lead us to expect that the mixture could well be a stable equilibrium solution to the differential effects of distance. To treat these mixed systems as mere transitional forms is to underestimate their importance as common, stable arrangements.[4]

The larger point here is that typologies are a poor way to capture the messy realities of subsistence farming. Nonetheless, it remains true that we need some kind of an intellectual scheme to help us work our way through the thicket of empirical evidence on such farming. To say that all farms and all farmers are unique is at once true and not very helpful. In the rest of this chapter I present an alternative scheme that breaks things down, not by type of farming "system", but rather by a set of resource-management problems that trouble the sleep of all farmers, whether traditional or modern.

Farming as Resource Management

If typologies often hide more than they reveal, how else might we begin to make sense of subsistence farming in a way that acknowledges both its diversity and its shared characteristics? First I suggest, as I did in Chapter 1, that we take as our fundamental unit of analysis not the "farming system" but the family-based farming household and its farm as a living, functioning demographic enterprise operated by intelligent, rational, goal-oriented agents. Each farm can be viewed both as a collection of inter-related physical elements and as a demographic and social unit (Table 2.2). If its personnel are to farm at all, they need access to a minimal set of resources, most obviously physical resources such as land and water, but also less tangible resources such as the time it takes to accomplish the necessary farming tasks. And they must protect and allocate those resources to meet their production goals, however modest these may be.

A focus on the management of household resources by traditional farmers is by no means new, and I am far from the first person to advocate it. The foundation for a parallel approach, so-called farming systems research (FSR), was laid by the agronomist David Norman in 1977. Later developments in FSR are summarized by Dewalt

---

[4] This is not to say, however, that mixed systems are *never* unstable or transitional (see Padoch *et al.*, 1998).

Table 2.2 Salient features of the farm, farmstead and farming household as fundamental units of analysis, including rules that govern the size and composition of the household and its access to land. (Note that the existence of cultural rules is never sufficient to ensure that everyone obeys them!)

Household (as a demographic unit):
- size – by age and sex
- composition – consumer/producer ratio, kin structure
- vital events – births, deaths, migration

Farm (as a physical unit):
- house – as a functional shelter
- outbuildings – e.g. barns, livestock enclosures, etc.
- cooking areas
- food storage facilities
- household equipment – e.g. pots, utensils, mats
- farming tools
- water sources
- irrigation channels, terraces, drainage ditches
- middens, garbage dumps, muck piles
- human waste disposal areas
- house gardens
- fields, including fallow
- livestock
- pasturage, meadows, rough grazing
- fences, dikes, boundary markers

Cultural norms or expectations concerning:
- land tenure and land inheritance
- the formation and dissolution of households
- household extension and postmarital residence

(1985), Norman and Baker (1986), Meertens *et al.* (1995) and Collinson (2000). FSR is an outgrowth of development economics and has its critics as well as its admirers (see, for example, Mutsaers, 2007). But whatever its successes or failures in transforming developing-world economies, the FSR approach is to be lauded for its encouragement of on-farm research related to practical farm management activities. Another approach coming out of development economics is the "farmer first" approach (Richards, 1985, 1986, 1995; Chambers *et al.*, 1989), which shifts the focus of development policy from advances in the national economy (rather an abstract entity) to improvements in the day-to-day lives of farmers and their families.[5]

---

[5] See also the "ecology of practice" school, which is anthropological in origin (Nyerges, 1997). Other useful treatments of traditional resource management that grow out of anthropology and geography include –

Two basic assumptions of this book are (i) that subsistence farmers are rational, if not always adequately informed or wise, and (ii) that they *try* to allocate and organize their resources as efficiently as needed to provide the net output of energy and other nutrients required by their households. If local conditions, including demographic ones, are such that the necessary output is easily attained, subsistence farmers will not work hard. If not, they may work very hard indeed. But allocating resources more efficiently is one possible way to increase net yields without necessarily increasing human labor. In subsistence farming, I would argue, resources are generally managed about as efficiently as they need to be – subject, of course, to insurmountable environmental constraints, which are discussed in Chapter 3.

Resources that Require Management

Table 2.3 lists the principal resources that farmers need to manage.[6] In this section I will review all these management problems and make at least a few comments about each of them. Some (most notably space, soils and water) I will discuss at greater length, mainly because they are profoundly important but do not come up very often in subsequent chapters.

Labor

The household provides most of the manpower, womanpower, childpower – and sometimes *beast* power – for running its own farm. Work in traditional farming is a matter of muscle pulling against bone, and in a real sense it is the number and size of the living skeletons plus the total mass of muscles attached to them that determine what the household can accomplish. The deployment of the available household labor force (including draft animals) is absolutely critical to the success of the household's demographic enterprise. At the same time, the demographic enterprise is the main *source* of the household's available human labor force. Labor availability and management are, therefore, fundamental parts of the household demographic enterprise – in fact, I would argue that they are among the most important points of contact between demographic processes and subsistence farming. Accordingly, they will be discussed in several subsequent chapters, and there is little further that needs to be said about them here. Supra-household labor is also important, but is not strictly a *household* resource since it can only be cajoled, not controlled or managed by the household head (see Chapter 12).

---

among many, many others – de Ortiz (1973), Barlett (1980a,b, 1982), Wilken (1987), Netting (1974a, 1993), Nazarea-Sandoval (1995) and Stone (1996).

[6] Some authors speak of "risk management" as if risk were a resource (e.g. Browman, 1987; Halstead and O'Shea, 1989; Goland, 1993a,b). Every entry in Table 2.3 involves an element of risk, uncertainty, unpredictability based on past experience, and trying to avoid or minimize it is a part of all resource management (see Hegmon, 1989; Winterhalder, 1990; Lee *et al.*, 2006).

Table 2.3 What traditional farmers can (try to) manage.

Allocation of labor (human and, if available, animal)
Time
Space
Soil and soil nutrients
Water
Field surface, slope, aspect and microclimate
Crop genetic resources (species, landraces)
Cropping regimes (combinations, sequences, rotations)
Fallow regimes
Weeds, pests, diseases
Postharvest processing
Storage
Livestock
Fuel
Materials to build farm infrastructure
Access to land

Time

As a resource, time is notable mainly for its absolute scarcity and irreplaceability. It is the ultimate nonrenewable resource – hence the concern among economists over *opportunity costs*, the idea that time devoted to one task usually cannot be devoted to another (but see Figure 1.10). Some of the most important management decisions of subsistence households have to do with how time is allocated.

As an example of the nonrenewability of time, Figure 2.4 shows the yield of groundnuts (*Arachis hypogaea*), a major leguminous crop in Sub-Saharan Africa, as a function of the calendar date of sowing, adjusted relative to the sowing date that produced the maximum yield for that particular year. Both early and late sowing reduce yields substantially. To plant only a week before the maximum lowers yield by almost 20 percent. Late sowing has an effect of similar magnitude, but tardiness can extend much further into the growing season. To sow a month too late reduces the yield of groundnuts by about 75 percent. But here is the catch: one can only determine the best sowing date retrospectively. It is too variable from year to year to be knowable in advance of sowing. Sowing (along with any clearance and tillage that immediately precede it) also involves a large investment of labor – it is potentially one of the major seasonal *bottlenecks* in the allocation of labor over the farming year. It is easy to get the timing wrong, and the consequences can be disastrous.

Space

Space is another critical resource, especially insofar as it determines the time and energy that need to be spent in transport and travel. Since it does not receive any

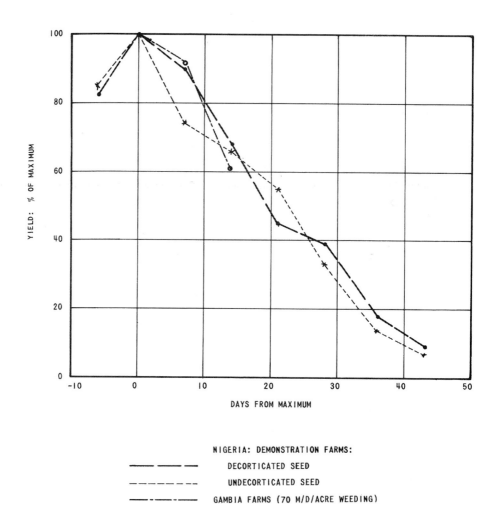

Figure 2.4 Time as a scarce resource. Fall in mean yield of groundnuts with early and late planting, Gambia 1949 and Nigeria 1952 (different line types indicate different locations and years). From Cleave (1974: 233), by permission of Praeger Press.

chapters of its own in this book, it seems appropriate to spend some extra time (and space!) on it here.

Like time, space is by its nature a limited resource. In Chapter 1, we saw that von Thünen posited a distance from the farmstead beyond which cultivation was uneconomical because of the costs of getting there and coming back (see Figure 1.6). According to this logic, the effective farm would be spatially circumscribed even if the household had control of an infinite amount of land. But, given an infinite of

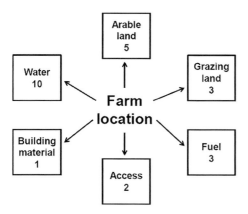

Figure 2.5 The basic locational problem in choosing a site for a new farm: how to compromise among distances to several essential resources to minimize travel costs. Numbers represent subjective weights in locational decision-making (the particular values shown are hypothetical). For solutions, see Table 2.4. Modified from Chisholm (1962: 115), by permission of the Hutchinson University Press.

land or even just a small piece of it, how would you decide where to put your domicile and your surrounding fields in the first place? This question, often called the basic locational problem in agriculture, has been discussed in great depth by Chisholm (1962) and other agricultural geographers. If the area is an isotropic plain, then you can choose a location at random. But no real landscape is an isotropic plain, so how do you decide? Figure 2.5, taken from Chisholm, illustrates the basic problem in highly schematic form. A farming household requires access to a variety of resources that are scattered across the landscape. The most efficient place to put your home with respect to any *one* resource is obviously right next to an ample supply of it. But that will usually be impossible if you require access to *multiple* resources. How do you compromise among them? Should you find the point equidistant from all necessary resources? Or do some resources carry more weight (in some subjective sense) than others, pulling your house site closer to them?

Chisholm (1962) suggested that the subjective weight or locational value placed on any one resource is determined by its mass (i.e. its literal physical weight), its necessity for life and the frequency of trips that need to be made to and from its source. The resource's mass determines the energetic cost of transporting it per trip, its necessity determines your ability to forego a trip when it runs low and the frequency of fetching it in the course of a day determines how much you have to multiply the cost of a *single* trip to compute the total daily cost. Water almost always scores high on all counts: it is essential for life, it is surprisingly heavy, and its frequent use for drinking, cooking and washing means that the household's immediate supply of it often needs to be replenished several times in the course of a single day. Thus, as in Figure 2.5, the farmer places a high subjective weight on access to a reliable source of water. Arable land is also fairly highly rated, especially if it requires frequent visits, which generally means that the weight placed on its location is higher

Table 2.4 Choosing between two possible settlement sites (*X* and *Y*) based on their distances from important resources. Subjective locational weights are taken from Figure 2.5. Site *Y* is the better choice because of its lower total cost (26.9 vs. 34.8). Modified from Chisholm (1962: 116).

Resource	Locational weight	Distance from site (km)		Cost (wt × dist)	
		X	*Y*	*X*	*Y*
Water	10	0.1	0.5	1.0	5.0
Arable land	5	2.0	1.0	10.0	5.0
Grazing land	3	2.5	1.5	7.5	4.5
Fuel	3	2.5	2.0	7.5	6.0
Access	2	2.9	2.1	5.8	4.2
Building material	1	3.0	2.2	3.0	2.2
			Σ of costs =	34.8	26.9

in more intensive farming systems than in less intensive ones. Grazing land can be further away because animals can transport themselves to it and can even be left there for entire seasons if the land is fenced. Fuel may also have a low weight if more than the daily requirement can be collected on a single trip. Building material can be heavy (think stone), but may have a low subjective weight if it is needed only rarely or can be "cannibalized" from nearby existing structures. Access (that is, access of the farmstead to the outside world) is more equivocal. If the household is involved in a market system, for example, access is likely to have a positive weight placed on it, but if the household is trying to keep away from mortal enemies, it may have a negative weight. Hard-to-reach preindustrial farming settlements, such as those located on top of steep hills, are almost always placed where they are for defensive purposes.

Given the particular weights shown in Figure 2.5, how might farmers use them to determine the best place to put the center of their farmsteads? Table 2.4, again taken from Chisholm, shows the basic logic, if not exactly the real-world process. The subjective weight associated with a particular resource is multiplied by the distance of each potential farmhouse location (*X* or *Y* in the table) to the nearest source of that resource, in order to determine the effective transport and travel cost associated with that potential site. The costs are then added across different resources. For a rational farmer, the potential house site with the lowest total cost is to be preferred.

Which is all very well and good in theory. But is there any ethnographic evidence that traditional farmers go through anything like this logical exercise? To quote Kefa Mwale, headman (as of c. 1985) and original founder (c. 1942) of Kefa village in Zambia, East Africa:

When we first came to the area that was to become Kefa village, we walked about and carefully studied the vegetation and the water sources. In this way we decided that here was where we wanted to be. The same was the case when we chose our gardens. We watched the way trees, bushes, plants, and even the grass grew, in order to pick the most fertile soil for our new fields. During the rainy season we planted a special grass that tells us where the water remains under the surface when the soil dries up. Thus we determined where to dig our waterhole, and it is from there that the women draw water for us. (Quoted by Skjønsberg, 1989: 16)

This is one of few qualitative accounts in the ethnographic literature concerning the founding of a new settlement, since such events are rare and almost never observed during the course of fieldwork. (Oral histories like the ones recorded by Skjønsberg, however, could easily be collected.) But quantitative evidence shows the primacy of water as a locational factor. In his first round of fieldwork among the Kofyar of central Nigeria, Robert Netting (1968) was lucky enough to arrive soon after a major wave of colonization and founding of new farming settlements on the Namu Plains, just south of the Kofyar's traditional homeland on the southern edge of the Jos Plateau.[7] He was able to map 140 of the new settlements and measure their distances from the nearest water source (Figure 2.6, open triangles). The distribution of observed distances was, unsurprisingly, far from random (closed circles): new settlements were tightly clustered within about seven-tenths of a kilometer of a water source, with a mode at just under 0.4 km and fully 13 percent of settlements located immediately adjacent to water. One of Netting's students, Glenn Stone, happened to do his first fieldwork among the Kofyar right after a *second* wave of migration from the Jos Plateau to the Namu Plains in the 1980s (Stone, 1996). After collecting spatial data comparable to Netting's, Stone found that the distribution of distances between settlements and water sources resulting from this second wave, while still strikingly nonrandom, had only a small fraction of settlements right next to water, a mode at somewhat greater distance, and a much longer upper tail than observed for the first wave (Figure 2.6, open circles). The obvious interpretation is that the first migrants got the best choice of settlement sites, at least with respect to water, while the next group of migrants got second best. It would be interesting to see the analogous distributions with respect to the location of other resources.[8]

Once the basic locational problem has been solved, how do farmers organize the land around their house sites? Here is where von Thünen comes into play. Since I have already discussed von Thünen is some detail, there is no reason to dwell on him here. But I do want to point to one very common feature of traditional farming, even of the most extensive kind, that conforms well to von Thünen's logic – the so-called house garden, home garden or kitchen garden (Figure 2.7). House or home gardens get their names from the fact that they are almost always right next to the domicile, and for two von-Thünenish reasons: (i) they are intensively cultivated and thus need to be tended frequently, and (ii) they often include leafy vegetables and

---

[7] In earlier years, the Kofyar had been excluded from the Namu Plains by attacks from Hausa and Fulani warriors and slave-traders (Netting: 1968: 45–6, 227). Their retreat onto the Jos Plateau was essentially defensive. By the 1960s, the Namu Plains had been brought under the control of the central government and pacified.

[8] And this whole discussion is not meant to exclude any number of additional factors that may influence locational choices. For example, the siting of houses and fields can be influenced by prevailing winds or by nearby slopes, which may encourage the drainage of cold, heavy air from higher elevations onto arable land.

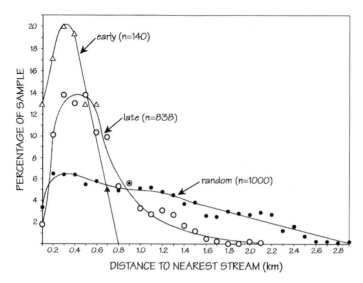

Figure 2.6 Distribution of distances to nearest water source, newly established settlements resulting from two waves of colonization, early (1960s) and late (1980s), among Kofyar farmers, Namu Plains south of the Jos Plateau, Nigeria. Note that the second wave produced settlements that were further on average from water, presumably because the first settlers took all the best sites near water sources. But both waves were drawn much closer to water than are randomly distributed points scattered across the landscape (closed circles). From *Settlement Ecology: The Social and Spatial Organization of Kofyar Agriculture,* by Glenn Davis Stone (1996), p. 161, © The Arizona Board of Regents, reprinted by permission of the University of Arizona Press.

fruits that are highly perishable and easily damaged, and thus must be harvested on the day of use and not transported any great distance. House gardens can provide important nutritional supplements to staple crops and can promote biodiversity (Imminck, 1990; Padoch and de Jong, 1991; Millat-e Mustafa *et al.*, 1996; Ali, 2005) and even provide a safe arena for experimentation with new crop varieties (see below).

There are, however, other locational considerations that sometimes override von Thünen's logic and obscure its influence on the ground. Mostly these reflect the fact that the farm is never located on an isotropic plain. For example, soils are never uniformly or even randomly distributed across the landscape but rather form a *catena* ("chain" in Latin) – a predictable sequence of soils strung along a cross-section of the landscape, especially along a hill- or mountainside. Different portions of the catena may be suited to different land uses, and it is very common to find traditional farms lying parallel to the catena in order to increase the farm's access to a range of soil types (Figure 2.8). A modern farmer would be more likely to try to obliterate the different elements of the catena using capital inputs, or avoid farming on hillsides too steep for the use of heavy machinery. A subsistence farmer, in contrast, must work with the catena.

In one respect, the farm shown in Figure 2.8 is atypical of many subsistence farms in that it is a single, compact, and continuous spatial unit. It may be more common

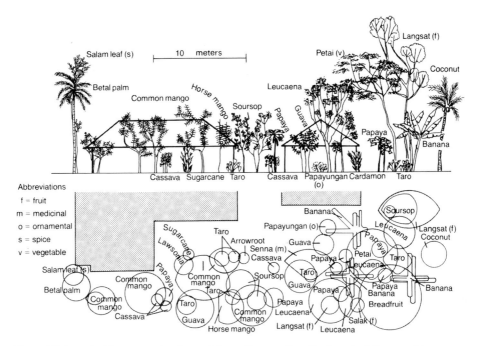

Figure 2.7 A typical house garden in west Java. Surrounding the farm buildings and house garden are intensively cultivated rice paddies. From Christanty *et al.* (1986: 144), by permission of the Westview Press.

for the fields belonging to a single farm to be subdivided into several small, discrete parcels scattered across the landscape and intermingled with the fields of other farms (Figures 2.9 and 2.10). This pattern is often referred to as "land fragmentation":

The word "fragmentation" is used in two senses: in the first place, to mean the process whereby agricultural holdings become smaller and smaller as generation succeeds generation owing to the subdivision of the inheritance on the death of each holder; in the second place, to mean the process whereby the holdings of each successive generation come to be divided into a more and more scattered collection of separate parcels. To avoid confusion, the first process will be called "subdivision" and the second, for present purposes, "scattering" (the horrible word "parcellization" will be eschewed). The two processes are related, indeed they often go hand in hand...

   In some quarters it has become axiomatic to regard fragmentation in general, and irrespective of the crop grown, as the blackest of evils, to be prevented by legislative action as one would attempt to prevent prostitution or blackmail... (Farmer, 1960)

The evils of fragmentation are in fact easy to identify. Some are restricted to particular circumstances. Thus, fragmented fields may limit the efficient application of certain technologies – for example, small, irregularly shaped plots, as in Figure 2.9, may be difficult to plow. Land fragmentation in an open-field situation (Figure 2.10) may make it impossible to apply controlled plant breeding or prevent the spread of crop diseases (Naylor, 1961). But, whatever the circumstances, one evil is *always* present. If more than one field is visited in a single day, travel costs between fields or

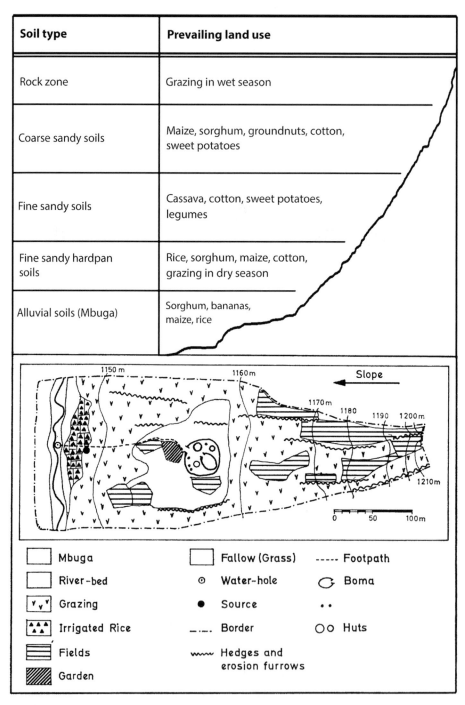

Soil type	Prevailing land use
Rock zone	Grazing in wet season
Coarse sandy soils	Maize, sorghum, groundnuts, cotton, sweet potatoes
Fine sandy soils	Cassava, cotton, sweet potatoes, legumes
Fine sandy hardpan soils	Rice, sorghum, maize, cotton, grazing in dry season
Alluvial soils (Mbuga)	Sorghum, bananas, maize, rice

Figure 2.8 Soil catena and traditional farm organization in Sukumaland, Tanzania. (Top) Generalized catena and principal land use patterns across a topographic cross-section from high to low elevation (with considerable vertical exaggeration). (Bottom) One farm holding at Nyashishi, northern Sukumaland, just south of Lake Victoria. The holding is oriented parallel to the generalized catena. Note the house garden adjacent to the residential compound (*boma*). Redrawn from von Rotenham (1968: 58–9).

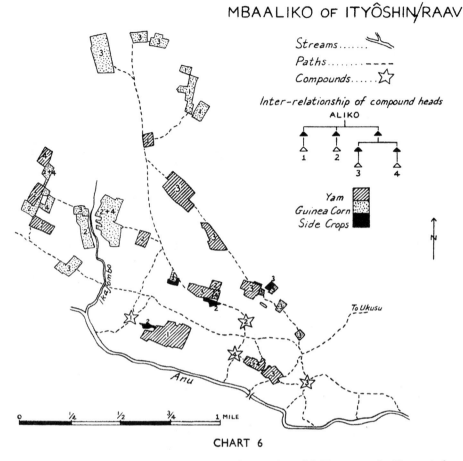

CHART 6

Figure 2.9 Land fragmentation: subdivision and scattering of fields among the Tiv, central Nigeria, 1949. Numbers indicate polygynous households (compounds) with rights to the fields. From Bohannan (1954: 68), by permission of Her Majesty's Stationery Office.

between field and domicile, including both energetic and opportunity costs, are multiplied. Fragmentation would seem to mock the logic of von Thünen.

But if fragmentation is wholly disadvantageous for the farmer – if it always increases travel and transport costs without providing any compensating benefits – then why is it so common? The standard explanation among agronomists and development economists is that it is the unfortunate result of partible inheritance (in which every child, or at least every son, gets a portion of the household's land when the father dies) combined with population growth (T. L. Smith, 1959; Igbozurike, 1970; King and Burton, 1982). In a population that is not growing in size, each family has on average only one son who survives to adulthood, limiting the subdivision needed to accommodate multiple male heirs. (The number of adult sons will of course vary from household to household even under zero population growth, so some degree of subdivision resulting from partible inheritance may be inevitable – but rapid population growth will greatly exacerbate the problem.) There are three

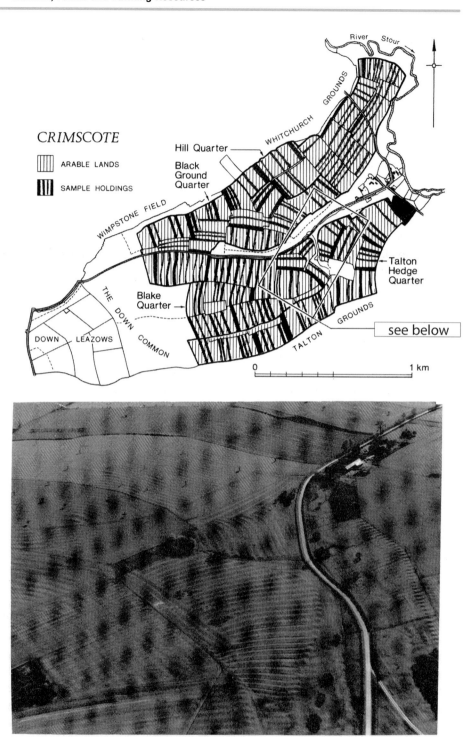

Figure 2.10 The classic form of land fragmentation in preindustrial Europe: the open field system of Crimscote, Warwickshire. (Top) 1844 plan of individual fields showing scattered

major arguments against this explanation, as pointed out by Pryor (1982), Bentley (1987), McCloskey (1991), and Goland (1993a,b): (i) worldwide, land fragmentation is not correlated with either partible inheritance or population growth, (ii) if partible inheritance is one of the culprits, land subdivision should be an ongoing process, inconsistent with reports of *stable* levels of fragmentation (Heston and Kumar, 1983), and (iii) there is abundant evidence that traditional farmers routinely ignore formal rules of inheritance and resort to other forms of land acquisition and alienation in order to counter fragmentation – when they want to (T. L. Smith, 1959; Bentley, 1992; Goland, 1993a,b).

Are there advantages to fragmentation that offset its evils? Are subdivision and scattering rational ways to organize space? Commonly cited benefits include providing the farmer with access to multiple habitats and thus a wider range of resources, and reducing potential risk from microenvironmental perturbations (e.g. frost, flooding or pests) by spreading a farmer's fields over multiple microclimates – diversifying the farmer's portfolio, as one economist has put it (Townsend, 1993: 6–8). It has also been suggested that fragmentation offers the farmer better control over the allocation of household labor. For example, fields at different elevations can be sown and harvested at different times, thus spreading out the work associated with what might otherwise be crippling bottlenecks in the farming year. For the moment, however, it is fair to say that the suggested benefits of fragmentation are mostly hypothetical, while the disadvantages (especially increased travel and transport costs) are well documented and widespread.

Perhaps the most widely accepted explanation for the wide occurrence of land fragmentation is that it is a strategy for reducing the risk associated with microhabitat-level variation in the environment (McCloskey, 1976; Winterhalder, 1990). Figure 2.11 summarizes the logic. The broken curve shows year-to-year variability in total net farm yield when the farm's fields are consolidated into a single bloc. The average net yield is fairly high, owing to low transport costs, but the variability is also high since all fields are located in a single microhabitat, which may perform poorly in any given year. The solid curve, in contrast, is the distribution of net yields when fields are fragmented: the average is lower than in the consolidated case, reflecting the costs of moving among widely scattered fields, but the variability is also low because fields are distributed across many microhabitats, few of which are likely to do badly in any one year. If "disaster" (severe food shortage) occurs whenever the annual net yield falls below point D in Figure 2.11, then the fragmented field system has a lower risk of disaster (area P) than does the consolidated one (area Q). There is, in this scheme, a trade-off between high yield and low risk; in

holdings of one household. (Bottom) Oblique air photo showing the ridge and furrow pattern of the medieval landscape. It is generally accepted that the long, thin holdings of any one household reflect the difficulty of turning a heavy plow pulled by up to eight oxen; wider, shorter fields would require more turns. It is widely if not universally accepted that the scattering of fields represents a form of risk minimization. From Astill (1988: 65, 72), by permission of Basil Blackwell Ltd.

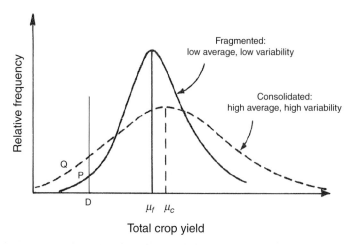

Figure 2.11 Reducing the probability of disaster (i.e. yields falling below threshold D) by reducing variability at the cost of a reduced average yield (μ_f versus μ_c). Modified from McCloskey (1976: 131), by permission of Emerald Publishing.

such a situation, we would not expect to observe the "normal surplus" that William Allan (1965: 38–48) argued should be a common feature of subsistence farming (see Chapter 1).

One of the best empirical studies of land fragmentation as a way to reduce risk in subsistence farming was conducted by Carol Goland (1993a,b) in Cuyo Cuyo District located on the eastern Andean escarpment in southern Peru. Farms in this area have a large number (range 14–18) of very small fields (about a quarter of a hectare on average). Plots are scattered over a wide altitudinal range, about 3470 to 4100 m. Goland estimates that travel costs to scattered fields reduce the net energy yield of potatoes by an average of about 7.5 percent, which is far from trivial. Although she makes a strong case that scattering does on balance reduce the risk of failing to meet the household's minimal nutritional requirements, whether that benefit is big enough to offset the reduction in net yield caused by travel is impossible to say.

Soils and Soil Nutrients

"Man, despite his artistic pretensions, his sophistication and many accomplishments, owes his existence to a six-inch layer of topsoil and the fact that it rains" (anonymous, cited by Murphy, 2007: 20). What goes on in that six-inch layer of topsoil, including how it mediates the relationship between the rain and the plants that need it, is deeply complex – too complex to review adequately here. Considerable attention has been paid by students of traditional farming to the myriad ways in which farmers manage soil to maintain its mineral content – the macronutrients nitrogen, phosphorus, potassium, sulfur, calcium, iron and magnesium, the micronutrients copper, manganese, zinc, molybdenum, chlorine, nickel and boron, and the beneficial (but not necessarily essential) elements sodium, silicon, selenium and cobalt – but also other physical properties such as pore structure, aeration, humus content, drainability and pH, the latter of which influences the ability of roots to absorb whatever mineral nutrients are present (Sillitoe, 1998; Harris, 1999). Subsistence farmers examine soils carefully for color, texture, crumb structure, dampness, smell and even taste (Wilhusen and Stone, 1990; Bellon and Taylor, 1993; Zimmerer, 1994; author's personal field observations), qualities that have long been used in the field by soil scientists in order to provide an off-the-cuff, nonlaboratory evaluation of soil quality (Plaster, 2003). On the basis of such properties, subsistence farmers make decisions about whether the soil is fit for cultivation, whether it needs to be irrigated or drained, what sort of tillage ought to be done, whether mulching or mounding of the soil is advisable, what crop varieties it is suitable for, whether it is so acidic that it needs a dressing of slaked lime, crushed bone meal or shell sand, whether manures and other amendments are needed and whether it might be a good idea to plant a crop of legumes on it (legumes are, of course, of special importance for soils because they possess root nodules that harbor nitrogen-fixing bacteria, mostly from the genus *Rhizobium*). Subsistence farmers also take active steps to counter soil erosion (Hudson, 1992). Such practices have been endlessly documented (for reviews, see Allan, 1965; Norman, 1979: chapters 4, 7, 11, 15; Norman *et al.*, 1995; Reij *et al.*, 1996; Gliessman, 2007). But surprisingly little research has been done on the fundamental question of whether or not the practices actually *work*. There is plenty of anecdotal evidence to suggest that they seem to work in the short term (which, from the farmer's perspective, may be long enough), but systematic, long-term research on the bio- and geochemical effects of traditional soil-management practices is much less common.

As it happens, one exceedingly long-term set of experiments on soil management, including certain preindustrial techniques, has been carried out for the last century and a half at the Rothamsted Experimental Agricultural Station in Hertfordshire, southern England. Ultimate credit for the Rothamsted experiments is owed to Sir John Bennet Lawes (1814–1900), who donated a large portion of his ancestral estate for the purpose in 1843 (Hall, 1905: xxi–xl). Under the direction of Dr. Henry Gilbert – and with the enthusiastic backseat participation of Sir John – Rothamsted became one of the premier centers of soil science in the western world. The aim of the experiments at Rothamsted was to compare the performance of new soil-management practices with those that were already available *c.* 1850, and in so doing they provided a considerable amount of information on traditional practices that were already becoming obsolete. The great bulk of their findings supports the belief that traditional methods work well, often as well as (and occasionally better than) newer practices. They were the first to demonstrate, for example, that most plants cannot directly assimilate atmospheric nitrogen, thus resolving a major scientific debate of the early nineteenth century; after nitrogen fixation by rhizobial symbionts of legumes was discovered by the German chemists Helreigel and Wilfarth, the Rothamsted finding was recognized in retrospect as validating the ancient habit of planting legumes in rotation or in combination with other crops

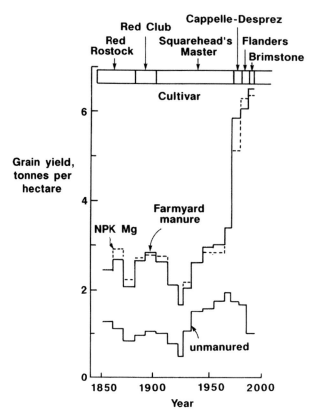

Figure 2.12 Long-term wheat yields on three plots under different fertilizer regimes, Rothamsted Experimental Agricultural Station, Hertfordshire, England, 1852–1992. The chemical composition of industrial fertilizers is indicated by: N, nitrogen; P, phosphorus; K, potassium; Mg, magnesium. Note that different strains of wheat (top) were introduced at varying times. The decline in yield during World War I and the 1920s reflected difficulties in securing enough labor to control weeds. Hand-hoeing was done until 1925, when bare fallowing was introduced to control weeds. Since 1957 herbicides have been applied. From Catt (1994: 121), by permission of the Scottish Cultural Press.

(Dyke, 1993). The Rothamsted experiments verified the usefulness of applying lime and bone to treat acidic soils. Perhaps most importantly, they showed that good old-fashioned barnyard manure, used by farmers in the Old World for millennia, maintained soil quality just as well as the new-fangled industrial fertilizers (Figures 2.12 and 2.13). Of course, not all traditional farming practices were tested at Rothamsted, but the ones that were came out looking pretty good. Other experimental stations have been established more recently in the rural developing world (e.g. the Yambo Experimental Station in South Sudan, the International Crops Research Institute for the Semi-Arid Tropics in Kenya and Niger and the International Rice Research Institute in the Philippines), and by and large they too have substantiated the virtues claimed for traditional soil management practices. Still, much more pedological research on traditional farming practices is needed.

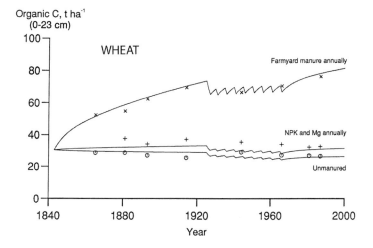

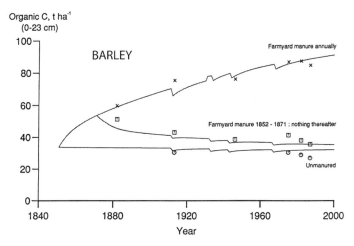

Figure 2.13 Changes in the organic carbon content of topsoil (0–23 cm depth) in plots of wheat and barley, Rothamsted Experimental Agricultural Station, Hertfordshire, England, 1845–2000. Points are measured values, lines are predictions based on a mathematical model for turnover of soil organic matter. From Catt (1994: 122), by permission of the Scottish Cultural Press.

Water

As hardly needs repeating, water is essential for all life – including that of farmers and their families, livestock and crops. But too much water can waterlog soils, depriving crop roots of oxygen and rotting the hooves of cattle. Flooding can provide much-needed run-off irrigation and rich silt, or it can destroy low-lying fields. All too often, there is either too little water or too much of it. Earlier in this chapter, we emphasized the diversity of irrigation methods; a similar point can be made about methods for *draining* wet soils (Wilken, 1969; Siemens, 1983; Cook and Williamson, 1999; Ballard, 2001; Sillitoe *et al.*, 2002).

Two further comments about irrigation ought to be made. First, wet-rice or paddy cultivation, a form of irrigation that is of profound importance in East, South and Southeast Asia, has its own unique management problem. After the rice is planted in paddies (perhaps after a spell of germination and early growth in special nursery beds), the depth of water on the field must be kept high enough to cover most of the stems but low enough not to drown the leaves and panicles (heads). This requires not only exquisite daily control over the amount of in- and out-flowing water, but also a field surface that is as close to being absolutely flat as human labor can make it (Taylor, 1981). In some areas, "deepwater" or "floating" varieties of rice, with stems up to 6 m long, are planted to circumvent this problem (Kende *et al.*, 1998); these varieties constantly adjust their stem elongation to keep leaves and panicles above water.

The second point is that water in irrigation systems is typically a common-use resource. That is, the same ultimate source of water must serve the fields of several client households, except for water lifted from a household's own well. The supply of common-use resources is everywhere vulnerable to depredation by unscrupulous individuals – the so-called Tragedy of the Commons (Hardin, 1968) – and water thievery is a universal feature of irrigation systems, traditional or modern (see Vandermeer, 1971, for a review). Tough sanctions of some sort may be necessary to prevent such abuse. It is also the case that farms at different levels in the chain of irrigation are not equivalent when it comes to opportunities for water theft: upstream farms can steal water before downstream farms ever receive it, downstream farms can only get water after some of it has been diverted (legitimately or not) to upstream farms. Thus, there are inherently asymmetrical relations between farmers depending upon their relative positions in the irrigation system. Karl Wittfogel (1964) famously extrapolated from this simple fact to the conclusion that irrigated farming tends by its very nature to produce complex, near-totalitarian political arrangements – "oriental despotism" he called it, borrowing a term from Marx. The ethnographic record makes hash of this assertion: it is filled with accounts of irrigated farming systems with very simple forms of administrative control, ranging from agreements between neighbors, decisions by ritual leaders, inclusive councils of (male) elders or democratically elected officials (whose terms are usually limited so that their positions do not become permanent or heritable); sometimes access is guaranteed by small-scale but enduring patron–client relationships, which involve different political statuses but hardly represent despotism or even benevolent state control (Gray, 1963; Leach, 1968; Fernea, 1970; Taylor, 1981; Adams, 1986; Hunt, 1988; Grove, 1993; Adams *et al.*, 1994; Watson *et al.*, 1998; Gunasena, 2001; Unami *et al.*, 2005; Chakravarty *et al.*, 2006; Wilkinson, 2006).

A final critical, if obvious, point to be made about water is that people and livestock need reliable sources of it to drink. If nothing else is available, people will make do with stagnant, filthy, polluted water – and livestock may positively revel in it. But some kind of water is necessary for more than a few days of life, depending on ambient temperature and humidity, and on the amount of physical work being done (see White *et al.*, 1972, for an excellent overview). Of course dirty water may also carry infectious diseases, including such common killers as amoebiasis, schistosomiasis, cholera, typhoid, infection by pathogenic strains of *E. coli*, and shigellosis (Hunter, 1997). As discussed in Chapter 8, infectious diseases, including waterborne diseases, are supremely important in the demography of traditional farming households.

Field Surface, Slope, Aspect and Microclimate

Except perhaps in the very most extensive agricultural systems, subsistence farmers modify the surface of their fields to encourage plant growth, control erosion and modify the microclimate immediately above ground level.[9] Modification of the field surface in preparation for sowing is called *tillage*, and entire books have been devoted to it (see Hudson, 1992; El Titi, 2003). Perhaps the most common tool used for tillage among subsistence farmers worldwide is the hoe, but the topsoil can also be tilled with something as simple as a digging stick or as complex as a plow (Kramer, 1966; Wilken, 1979). The usual purpose of tillage is to break up soil crust and loosen soil texture to improve aeration and drainage and to make it easier for tender seedlings to sprout; in addition, deep plowing can bring nutrients that have leached into the subsoil back up to the surface. To stop erosion, logs are sometimes laid parallel to the contour lines in the field, as are stone walls that, given enough time, may evolve into terraces as eroding soil accumulates behind them (see Ludwig, 1968). Terraces can facilitate plowing and other farm tasks by leveling the actual field surface even when it is located on a steep slope. Mounds, ridges, tie ridges and other modifications of the field surface are often built to retain soil moisture or aid soil drainage (Wilken, 1969, 1979, 1987; Sillitoe *et al.*, 2002). Terracing and other complicated forms of soil preparation were once thought to have been confined almost exclusively to the Old World, but an enormous amount of more recent archaeological research has shown such practices to have been widespread in pre-Columbian America (see Donkin, 1979; Doolittle, 2000; Denevan, 2001; Whitmore and Turner, 2001; Murtha, 2009).

There is little traditional farmers can do about the weather in general (short of magic and ritual), but they are able to modify the so-called microclimate of their fields, i.e. the physical characteristics of the atmosphere within a few centimeters or a meter or two of the soil surface. Windbreaks, either planted or constructed, are common. In northern Scotland, a spectacularly windy region, small enclosures known as "planticrues" were once built out of stone or turf to protect green vegetables from wind damage (Fenton, 1978: 101–15). One odd feature of old, abandoned planticrues is that gaps are sometimes left in their walls, which might seem to defeat their purpose. But, as it turns out, "[s]emipermiable windbreaks produce less violent eddies before and behind the screens and are probably more effective than solid walls" (Wilken 1972: 557; see also Gleissman, 2007: 92). The amount of sunlight

---

[9] Even hunter-gatherers sometimes modify the soil surface to facilitate the growth of useful wild plants (Harlan, 1992: 22–3).

reaching and being absorbed by the soil is often carefully controlled, either by clearing overhanging leafy vegetation to let the sunlight through, or by planting such vegetation among crops that prefer shade. Sunlight can also be regulated by choosing fields with the right slope and aspect (Wilken, 1979). The albedo of the soil surface – the extent to which it diffusely reflects sunlight and thus lowers soil temperature – can be modified by tillage or mulching (Wilken, 1972). Temperature control can also be achieved by planting crops near stone or earthen walls that absorb heat from sunlight and reradiate it to the surrounding air during the night.

Crop Genetic Resources

Not so long ago, it would have been deemed sufficient to summarize a subsistence farming community's crop inventory with phrases such as "The X cultivate maize, beans and squash..." or "The staple crops of the Y are barley and oats...," perhaps with a small table of subsidiary crop species and their Latin names. We now know that things are not so simple. Each crop species, whether staple or supplementary, is likely to be represented in a single location by several or many *landraces* (traditional local varieties) that are different enough genetically to have visibly distinct pheno-types (Tesfaye *et al.*, 1991; Salick *et al.*, 1997; Zeven, 1998; Xu *et al.*, 2001; Perales *et al.*, 2003b; Brush, 2004). Local farmers recognize and name the phenotypes. And, at least in the few places where the question has been studied, there appears to be a reasonably high concordance between traditional farmers' classifications of their landraces and the relationships revealed by molecular genetics – though the trad-itional classifications tend to under-count different genetic variants, even those with fairly distinguishable phenotypes (Bellon *et al.*, 1998; Sambatti *et al.*, 2001; Soleri and Cleveland, 2001). Variation in the performance of landraces – in terms of yield, water requirements, maturation rate, disease and pest tolerance, seed size, storability and a host of other variables – is recognized and exploited by traditional farmers (Teshome *et al.*, 1999b; Soleri and Cleveland, 2001; Wilson and Dufour, 2002). Indeed, farmers may consciously select for such traits, often on the basis of visible characteristics such as seed or tuber color that are tightly linked to one or another of the performance genes (Boster, 1985; Alvarez *et al.*, 2005; Paul Gepts, personal communication). Most researchers now accept the idea that farmers carefully allocate different landraces to the fields where they are likely to grow best, distributing them nonrandomly with respect to soil type, altitude, temperature and other microenvironmental factors (Bellon 1991; Perales *et al.*, 2003a,b; Alvarez *et al.*, 2005; Brush, 2004). In line with the argument concerning land fragmentation and risk avoidance, it has even been suggested that a wide diversity of landraces may help stabilize fluctuations in the farm's overall annual yield (Clawson, 1985; Ceccar-elli *et al.*, 1991; Zimmerer, 1991, 1996). This idea is largely untested, but it might explain the observation that some traditional farmers seem actively to promote and select for crop diversity in its own right (Shigeta, 1990; Bellon, 1991; Teshome *et al.*, 1999a). The discovery that indigenous crop species are genetically heterogeneous, and that local farmers exploit the heterogeneity, is one of the most exciting recent advances in the ecological study of traditional farming.

One other type of plant management (if not necessarily *crop* management) is important in subsistence farming – the promotion, retention and even cultivation of so-called famine foods or scarcity foods (King, 1869; Bhandari, 1974; Miyagawa, 2002; Muller and Almedom, 2008). These are foods that are usually considered unpalatable or otherwise inferior, but that do well under adverse conditions. The Iban of Sarawak, for example, loathe the taste of sago – and I can't say I blame them – but they cultivate sago palms (*Metroxylon sagu*) along the edges of their rice fields because when the rice crop fails sago palms may still yield abundant calories, if not much else (Freeman, 1955: 61, 105). Often famine foods are wild, tasty and reasonably nutritious in their own right, but still consumed exclusively during periods of dearth (Sena *et al.*, 1998; Lockett *et al.*, 2000). Only fairly recently have researchers begun to examine the selection, use and management of famine foods in the kind of detail needed for scientific evaluation. There is much left to learn.

Cropping Regimes

Crop species and landraces are used not only for their own particular qualities, but also for their functional interactions with other crops. Inter-cropping, or mixed cropping, is common in subsistence farming (if not as universal as some authors have claimed), and a wide variety of crop combinations, sequences, rotations and "pseudorotations" (see de Schlippe, 1956: 204–16) has been observed (Figure 2.14). Various benefits from these diverse cropping regimes have been hypothesized over the years, including efficient partitioning of fine-grained differences in soil and sunlight across the field, optimal use of a limited growing season by planting a combination of plants with different maturation rates, competitive control of weeds and minimization of the risk of failure associated with any one crop species (Vandermeer, 1989). Some of these benefits have received experimental support (Innis, 1997), others are plausible but have not yet been tested. In this connection, however, it is important to bear in mind that mixed cropping can potentially *lower* yields, depending upon how the crops interact with each other (Figure 2.15). As far as I know, no one has ever studied these interactions in traditional cropping regimes.

Fallow Regimes

The management of fallows in the context of shifting cultivation will be discussed in detail in Chapter 6. All that needs to be said here is that complex fallow regimes are widespread and important (Denevan and Padoch, 1987; Cairns, 2007). The simplest way to exploit fallow is to continue harvesting perennial crops such as manioc and bananas after ending the planting of annuals and biennials. But much more elaborate management techniques are also widely used to increase food supply, improve soil fertility and mitigate erosion. For example, it is a common practice in parts of highland New Guinea to plant seedling casuarina trees (*Casuarina oligodon*) in new

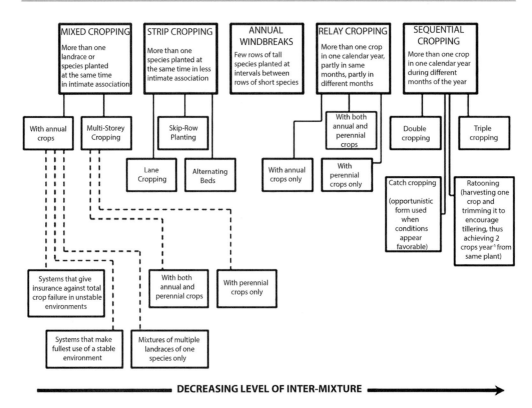

Figure 2.14 Definitions of the principal multiple cropping regimes. After Beets (1982: 5), by permission of Westview Press.

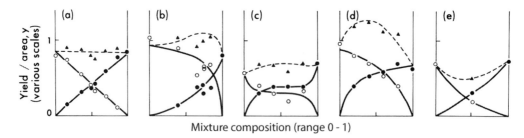

Figure 2.15 Typical patterns of two-crop interactions under mixed cropping. Circles and triangles are experimental results with legumes and grasses; circles represent yield for each crop separately, triangles yield for mixture. Mixture composition is the proportion of the initial seed represented by crop A (solid circles). (a) No interaction. (b) Crop B (open circles) more aggressive. (c) Rarer crop more aggressive. (d) Positive interaction (facilitation). (e) Negative interaction (competition). Adapted from Trenbath (1976: 151), by permission of The Alliance Crop, Soil, and Environmental Science Societies.

fallow (Bourke, 2007; author's field observations). Casuarina grows rapidly on disturbed soils, out-competes weeds (including persistent and pernicious *Imperata* grasses), is useful for firewood and for house and fence construction and is a reliable "indicator species" showing that fallowed land may be ready for recultivation. Many species of casuarina are known to be actinorhizal trees, i.e. trees that have root nodules containing symbiotic nitrogen-fixing actinomycetes, in this case from the genus *Frankia*. While *C. oligodon* has not yet been shown definitively to be actinorhizal, it almost certainly is (Bourke, 2007), and traditional farmers in New Guinea have long thought that it does something to "strengthen" the soil. Another, even more elaborate example is the management of the Asian alder tree (*Alnus nepalensis*) in fallows by the Naga of northeastern India (Cairns *et al.*, 2007). Many of the alder trees left standing in fields are very old and have been through multiple rounds of cropping and fallowing. They are even pollarded, just like trees in intensively managed European woodlots. They have all the established virtues of *C. oligodon* and are definitely known to be actinorhizal.

Managed fallow is an extremely common feature of shifting cultivation (Denevan and Padoch, 1987; Nyerges, 1989; Cairns, 2007). In addition, managed fallows of short duration are common even in so-called permanent cultivation (Orlove and Godoy, 1986; Pestalozzi, 2000). In early modern Europe, for example, grasses and legumes such as ryegrass and clover were often sown on such "ley" fallows, providing fodder or pasturage for animals and building up the soil's store of nitrogen (Shiel, 1991; Evans, 1998).

Weeds, Pests and Diseases

These are not, of course, resources *per se*, but "anti-resources," things from which real resources, crops and livestock, need to be protected. Subsistence farmers either abandon their fields when weeds and pests become intolerable, or else they weed regularly, cull any plants harboring destructive pests or diseases or pick caterpillars off their crop plants one by one – all labor-intensive jobs. Some farmers even weed *fallow* to keep it clean for the next crop (Amanor, 1991). According to many writers, the principal way to block the spread of infectious diseases is to isolate different crop or livestock enclosures by scattering them widely across the landscape (see above). But diseases can still be spread inadvertently by the farmers themselves as they move from field to field. The remarkable thing is just how much potential human food is lost each year to insect damage, diseases and competition from weeds, even when modern herbicides and pesticides are applied (Table 2.5). The losses must have been much higher under preindustrial conditions. The basic problem with all these spoilers is that they are strongly encouraged by natural selection to do precisely what farmers do not want them to do (Braiser, 2001; Booth *et al.*, 2003). Traditional farmers can counter-select for resistance genes in crop plants and (much less easily) in livestock, but the enemy can usually catch up without much difficulty.

Postharvest Processing

Once food crops have been harvested, they often require a certain amount of processing before they can be eaten or stored. This is especially true of grain crops; some root crops can be dug up at the time of use and otherwise left in the ground for "storage". A grain crop such as rice, wheat, barley, oats, rye, millet, sorghum or

Table 2.5 Estimated global preharvest food losses (percent), *c.* 1965. From Cramer (1967: 137).

Crop	Insects	Diseases	Weeds	Total
Wheat	5.0	9.1	9.8	23.9
Rice	26.7	8.9	10.8	46.4
Maize	12.4	9.4	13.0	34.8
Millet, sorghum	9.6	10.6	17.8	38.0
Sugar cane	20.1	19.2	15.7	55.0
Potatoes	6.5	21.8	4.0	32.3
Peanuts	17.1	11.5	11.8	40.4
All	13.8	11.6	9.5	34.9

Table 2.6 Estimated postharvest rice losses in Southeast Asia, 1997. From FAO (1997).

Activity	Estimated range of losses (percent)
Harvest	1–3
Handling	2–7
Threshing	2–6
Drying	1–5
Storage	2–6
Transport	2–10
Total	10–37

quinoa may be stored temporarily on the stem in a stack or rick, but eventually will need to be threshed (flailed, trampled or sledged to knock the grain off the stalk and to loosen the glumes) and winnowed (tossed up in a breeze to separate the grain from the chaff). In wet areas of northern Europe, the loose grain was often dried in a "corn kiln" to make it easier to mill or, in the case of barley used for brewing ale, to kill the sprout after it was malted; similarly, in South Asia, rice is often parched or parboiled at low temperature to prepare it for storage and milling. Finally, research in Africa has shown that traditional methods of cooking can result in substantial losses of plant nutrients (Lyimo *et al.*, 1991). The important point here is that substantial losses of grain and other foods can occur at each stage of processing (Table 2.6), and the prudent farmer will try to manage the processing to minimize such losses.

Food Storage

Food storage is, in effect, another way to manage time (Brenton, 1989). In grain-producing communities, there is usually a lag of many months between one harvest season and the next, and enough grain must be harvested, processed and stored each year to tide the family over. This is often hard to do owing to losses during storage to

Table 2.7 Food spoilage categories. From Bates (1986: 242).

	Durable	Semiperishable	Perishable
Example	cereals, oilseeds	roots, tubers	fruit and green vegetables
Stabilizing features	low moisture, protective hull	low metabolic rate	low temperature
Deterioration agents	insects, vermin, mold	injury, metabolic imbalance, vermin, mold	microbial, enzymatic
Storage life	months–years	days–months	hours–days

rodents, insects, mold and even enzymatic self-digestion (Table 2.7). Roots, tubers and corms are even more perishable during storage, but some species can be left in the ground until needed; fruits and green vegetables, on the other hand, are so perishable that they must be consumed more or less immediately after picking (Table 2.7). Caught between the twin difficulties of producing enough food to store and keeping it from being lost during storage, many subsistence farming families experience a "hungry season" almost every year, when stored supplies are running out and the next harvest is still weeks or months away (Chen *et al.*, 1979; Simondon *et al.*, 1993; Becker, 1994; S. Devereux *et al.*, 2008; F. Devereux *et al.*, 2012). The hungry season can be a serious impediment to the household demographic enterprise, principally by increasing the risk of early childhood death (McGregor *et al.*, 1970; Chambers *et al.*, 1981; Simondon *et al.*, 1993). Despite the fact that it has received comparatively little theoretical attention from the scientific community, protecting stored food is one of the most important responsibilities of traditional farming households. And of course seed stock stored for next year's sowing must also be protected and (if the household can avoid it) left uneaten.

Traditional storage facilities take many forms (Sigaut, 1988, 1989; Proctor, 1994). Often special structures are built, including underground chambers, in-house clay or basketry containers, and elaborate, free-standing house-like structures (Figure 2.16). Grain may sometimes be stored in the form of flour. Maize, for example, is rarely eaten green (as we usually eat it) or, if it is, is eaten immediately after being picked; more typically it is allowed to reach maturity and dried (the way we feed it to cattle) so that it can eventually be ground into cornmeal for making *tortillas* or mush or, in the case of some varieties, used as popcorn. Intact dried ears can be stored in the open air on racks or in bunches hanging from trees; alternatively, flour made from dried maize can be stored in clay vessels, baskets or wooden boxes.

Livestock

In traditional farming, large animals are often kept for manure, traction and fuel (in the form of dried dung) rather than as sources of food (Odend'hal, 1972; Winterhalder *et al.*, 1974; Hoffpauir, 1978; Shiel, 1991; Wrigley, 1991a; McIntire *et al.*, 1992; Harris, 1999; Krausmann, 2004). Large domesticated animals are too valuable to

Figure 2.16 Traditional grain storage facility in Burkina Faso. Image credit: Guenter Fischer / Getty Images.

slaughter for mere meat, although milk and blood may be harvested regularly from them. Typically, large beasts will be butchered and eaten only if they die for some other reason, are too old to produce offspring and milk or are too debilitated to pull a plow or perform other useful work. Meat is more commonly supplied by wild game or by small stock such as goats, sheep, pigs and poultry (young bullocks are often slaughtered in order to keep the sex ratio of the cattle herd at an optimum, and these are typically eaten). The availability of large livestock for traction can have an important effect on a household's ability to allocate time and labor efficiently (Weil, 1970; Wrigley, 1991a; Krausman, 2004), and the use of animal dung as fertilizer is a common way to intensify food production (Shiel, 1991). For the latter two reasons, domesticated animals will rear their shaggy heads in several later chapters. It should be noted here, however, that livestock can also play an important part in the management of space, because they can sometimes be left on rough pasturage lying beyond arable land or even driven many miles each summer to high-altitude pastures that are effectively off-limits for other uses, a venerable practice in the mountains of Europe and the circum-Mediterranean known as *transhumance* (Carrier, 1932; Matley, 1968; Bil, 1990; Viazzo, 1989; McNeil, 1992).

It is also important to note in passing that the New World historically had no domesticated stock (discounting dogs) other than turkeys, Muscovy ducks, guinea pigs, and camelids (llamas and alpacas) – and most parts of America, North and South, did not have even this limited set of animal domesticates. It is an enduring (and, in my opinion, still largely unanswered) question just how much difference all this made in the ecology of subsistence farming in the New World versus the Old World.

Fuel and Building Materials

An active farm occasionally needs material for building infrastructure (houses, barns, stables, fences, terraces, etc.), and the "domestic" side of the enterprise requires a daily supply of fuel (firewood, dried peat, dried dung) for cooking and heating. Access to these materials is generally part of the basic locational problem, and haulage of fuel in particular can involve considerable energetic and opportunity costs, especially for women in the household. Both fuel and building material may be provided by agroforestry, e.g. by pollarding or coppicing suitable trees in a managed woodlot, but most often must be scrounged on an *ad hoc*, opportunistic basis. Beyond that, there is little to say about these resources that is not reasonably obvious.

Access to Land

As the economist Nadia Cuffaro (2001: 3) has noted, "Property rights on land are the most important population-related *institution* in agriculture" (emphasis added). This is true for several reasons. For example, "over-population" – whatever else it may mean (see Chapter 3) – can sometimes refer to a situation in which the *average* farming family lacks the land to meet its most basic nutritional needs. But any *one* family may lack adequate land, not because of an absolute shortage of land affecting the entire community, but because that particular family does not have a secure entitlement to sufficient land under the prevailing system of land tenure and inheritance (Sen, 1981).

Subsistence farmers are acutely aware of the importance of institutionalized access to land:

My field study of the Tiv [of central Nigeria] was not undertaken primarily – or even secondarily – to investigate land tenure among them. But, Tiv are vitally interested in their farms. In order for us to live in Tiv communities for nineteen months as we did, it was necessary for us to become interested in their farms. When I had advanced far enough with the Tiv language to begin to pick out words and phrases that I didn't understand, I found that a dozen or so of the key words I heard most often were words which had to do with land in one way or another. As I began systematically to master these words and phrases, and in so doing to become familiar with more and more aspects of them, I began to realize – rather with surprise – that I was getting a great deal of "land tenure material". (Bohannan, 1954: 1)

Never is land divided equally among households. This is true in all traditional farming communities, including "egalitarian" systems without sharp social, economic or political divisions (Netting, 1982). The variation in size of households' landholdings reflects many factors, not just how much land the households need. As the previous discussion of partible inheritance suggested, land inheritance rules may play some part in generating this variation, but so can stochastic fluctuations in household demography – what Don Attwood (personal communication) calls "demographic roulette" (see Chapters 10 and 12). Indeed, a household's current holding may partly reflect several past generations of ancestral experience, including bad luck and fecklessness. Whatever its source, variation in the size of holdings almost always has important economic and demographic consequences (Vanden Driesen, 1971; Netting, 1982; Soltow, 1990). These will be explored further in Chapter 12.

It is important to consider not only the size and quality of the holding, but also the *security* with which it is held. Someone farming under a system of usufruct, in which this year's field will revert to a common pool within a year or two, cannot be expected to invest in permanent improvements on the land (such as the construction of terraces), which may not repay the costs of building for many years. It is a common observation that secure ownership of land by individual farmers tends to increase as agricultural production intensifies (Boserup, 1965); indeed, usufruct is commonly associated with the least intensive forms of shifting cultivation. There is an interesting chicken-and-egg problem here: do farmers intensify *because* they have secure tenure, or do farmers demand secure tenure once they have started to intensify? I suspect the causation works both ways.

This last observation concerning increases in the security of land tenure that often accompany agricultural intensification raises an important *general* point relevant to the whole population/agriculture debate. Despite her remarks about land tenure, Boserup focused almost exclusively on the shortening of fallow periods as a way to intensify farm production in response to population-related pressures (see Chapter 5). But, as discussed above, management of fallow regimes (which is already more complicated than Boserup allowed for) is only one of a whole array of management practices – and *each and every one of those management practices can change in response to demographic or other pressures calling for an increase in crop yield* (Chapter 6). This is precisely what I meant in Chapter 1 when I argued that much more attention should be focused on the specific mechanisms linking population to traditional farming. And it is precisely my motivation for spending so much time discussing traditional farm management practices in this chapter.

Is Subsistence Agriculture Under-Capitalized?

In classical economics, factors of agricultural production are grouped into three broad categories – land, labor and capital – and an enduring question is the extent to which these factor categories can be substituted for each other. In the debate over population and traditional agriculture, participants have raised this same question but often with the proviso that capital is of relatively little importance in preindustrial farming and thus plays no great role in the intensification of such farming. Hence, it is argued, the only real consideration is the substitutability of land and labor: by working harder, can you live off less land? As we will see in Chapters 5 and 6, this argument has limited the terms of the debate in a way that may be misleading. Certain kinds of capital, and decisions about how to invest them, are, I would argue, integral to subsistence farming.

The problem with the view that capital is unimportant in subsistence farming is that it is based on too narrow a definition of capital. When modern economists think of farm capital, they tend to think in terms of large outlays of money or of things that farmers must go into debt to purchase; an obvious example would be a modern

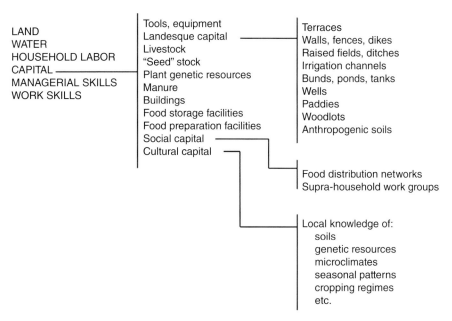

Figure 2.17 The factors of subsistence production. "Seed" stock refers to roots, shoots and other plantable material in addition to literal seeds.

combine harvester, which can cost more than a quarter of a million dollars. In subsistence farming, such things do not exist. But traditional tools are a kind of capital investment, even when they are homemade and extremely simple (see below). Seed is not purchased, but even if grown on the farm represents a form of capital (i.e. it is neither land nor labor). In fact, traditional farmers make a wide range of capital investments, even if most are too small to capture the attention of a modern economist. Figure 2.17 represents my attempt to broaden the conventional scheme of "land, labor, capital" in a way that makes it more obviously applicable to preindustrial farming, mostly by expanding the specification of capital.

Most of the items in Figure 2.17 are self-explanatory, but a few need some explication. "Landesque capital" is a term often attributed to Harold Brookfield, but apparently first used by the economist Amartya Sen (Widgren, 2007). Whoever is responsible for coining it, the term refers to permanent or semipermanent human modifications of the landscape, often by people of previous generations, that just need year to year maintenance to continue functioning. Common examples of traditional landesque capital include terraces, irrigation canals, wells, fences and paddies, but also managed woodlots and fertile anthropogenic soils such as the *terra preta dos indios* ("dark earths of the Indians") still exploited by farmers in Amazonia (Lehmann *et al.*, 2004).[10] Landesque capital, which will play an important part in later chapters, is discussed further by Widgren (2007).

---

[10] Paddy soils are also anthropogenic, profoundly "unnatural" and extraordinarily fertile (Kawaguchi and Kyuma, 1977; Barnes, 1990).

"Social capital" and "cultural capital" are also profoundly important in traditional farming. Social capital represents ties of consanguinity, affinity and affect linking different households, ties that can be called upon to bring material resources and energy (in the form of labor) into the household from off-farm. Such ties require continuous encouragement and reciprocation. Cultural capital consists of practical knowledge regarding farming practices and the environment that is usually (but not exclusively) passed from generation to generation within the family. Social capital is discussed in Chapter 12, while cultural capital is examined further in the next section of the present chapter.

In many older schemes, tools and equipment were viewed as the most important forms of capital used by the traditional farmer, so much so that they were taken to define types or levels of preindustrial food production. Curwin and Hatt (1953), for example, envisioned an evolutionary sequence from digging-stick agriculture to hoe agriculture and finally to plow agriculture. The logic of this scheme was described by Boserup (who, it should be said, rejected it):

The digging stick is the most primitive of the main agricultural tools and the peoples who use digging sticks are among the most primitive among the primitive agricultural tribes living today. By contrast, the highest levels of pre-industrial civilization have usually been reached by peoples with plough cultivation. It was natural, therefore, to view agricultural development as determined by a process of gradual change to better and better tools, whereby output per man-hour in food production was increased and part of the population made available for non-agricultural activities. (Boserup, 1965: 23)

In this view, the substitution of technology (as narrowly defined) in place of human labor was the dominant trend in the evolution of agriculture. Boserup, in contrast, argues that changes in tools actually played a rather limited role in farm evolution, and I agree with her. (As detailed in Chapters 5 and 6, however, I disagree with her argument that the substitution of labor for land was the *only* important trend in traditional agriculture.) Most preindustrial farming is based on a limited set of tools, and many of the same tool types appear again and again throughout the world. In fact, Figures 2.18 and 2.19 pretty much bracket the range of variation in the tools used by traditional farmers. (Yang, 1945: 251–7, described the full set of traditional Chinese farming tools, perhaps the most elaborate toolkit in any preindustrial farming economy.) Tools do, of course, represent capital investments, but they do little to explain the enormous diversity of subsistence farming systems. It is remarkable what can be done with a hoe or a digging stick.[11]

---

[11] None of this is meant to imply that things such as plows and harrows were not important innovations. They certainly increased the efficiency of human labor in tilling and sowing, and increased the amount of land that could be cultivated by a single household, assuming it had access to extra land. But a major part of the significance of plows and harrows resided in the fact that they required large livestock in order to be used effectively – historically mostly oxen or water buffalo (horse harnesses adapted for pulling plows, harrows and other farming equipment were a fairly late development; see Langdon, 1986). Bovids, including buffalo, are prodigious producers of manure, and draft animals in general can greatly alter a household's energy budget (Weil, 1970; Wrigley, 1991a; Krausman, 2004). Jack Goody (1976) has conjectured that adoption of the plow caused profound changes in the division of household

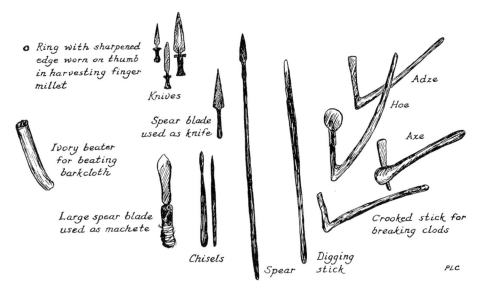

Figure 2.18 Zande farming implements, Southern Sudan, c. 1950. From de Schlippe (1956: plates 11–12), redrawn by Miracle (1967: 92), by permission of Routledge and Kegan Paul Publishers.

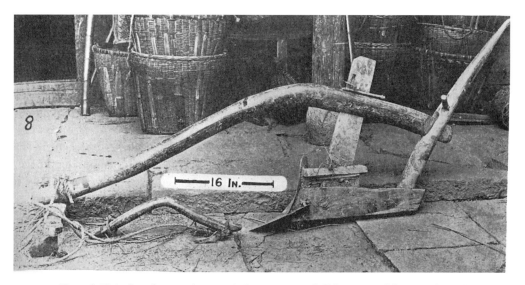

Figure 2.19 A plow from early twentieth-century rural China, one of the most intensive preindustrial farming systems known. From Hommel (1937: 43).

labor and in family relations – and perhaps he is right. Some authors have suggested that plows are so complicated that they could only have been invented once (White, 1962; Pryor, 1985). But plows are basically hoes – and harrows are basically rakes – turned backwards and attached to animals (in fact, they may originally have been pulled by humans). I can imagine multiple, independent inventions in the Old World.

Perhaps more important than tools *per se* is expertise in handling the tools and in performing other farm tasks. Farming is a skilled occupation, and training is involved in all traditional farming behaviors. If the training is successful, it presumably results in greater efficiency of production – less wastage, more work accomplished per unit time, less energy expended in a given task. For example, when the Iban plant their rice gardens, a man and women (usually husband and wife) work as a team, the man jabbing holes in the ground with a simple digging or dibbling stick, the woman following and sprinkling rice seeds into each hole.

Sowing (*menih*) is a much more onerous task than dibbling. Ranging on ahead a man thrusts in his dibbling-stick as he chooses, and the more or less regular pattern of holes which he produces is largely fortuitous, and not the outcome of any carefully premeditated plan. A woman, on the other hand, must seek out these dibble-holes one by one, and cast into each its quota of seed. On broken ground and in areas cluttered with unburnt logs and boughs, the holes are often difficult to detect; and whereas a man can jab in the *tugal* from a distance of five feet and more, the woman must clamber much closer before she can eject the seed from her hand. (Freeman, 1955: 50)

Sowing is skilled work, and women vary in how well they do it. The main desiderata are to keep up a fairly regular pace and, more importantly, to control the number of seeds per hole. Too many seeds are a waste, too few result in a suboptimal number of rice plants (Freeman reckons that 8–10 seeds per hole are probably close to the optimum). Table 2.8 characterizes the sowing performance of six Iban women ranging in age from 27 to 60 years. The average number of seeds per dibble-hole varies from 9.5 to 16.0, with the oldest woman having a number that appears to correspond most closely to the optimum. The oldest woman also has a comparatively narrow range of seeds bracketing the optimum, and she does not have to hold her hand as close to the dibble-hole as the younger, presumably less experienced, women do. (The rate of sowing, on the other hand, appears to differ little among women.) The implication is that the oldest woman is the best trained and most efficient as a result of many years of experience.

Table 2.8 Rice sowing performance of six Iban women (based on grain counts for 192 dibble-holes selected at random). From Freeman (1955: 50).

| | Names and ages of women | | | | | |
| | Ja | Limau | Gering | Nantai | Limau | Lintu |
	(60 yrs)	(28 yrs)	(27 yrs)	(33 yrs)	(38 yrs)	(31 yrs)
Mean no. seeds per hole	9.5	10.2	11.8	12.3	15.0	16.0
Range in no. seeds per hole	5–13	5–21	5–21	10–15	11–24	8–35
Mean no. holes sown min^{-1}	55	58	62	60	46	50
Distance of seed-holding hand from hole (inches)	12–18	9–12	9–12	9–12	6–12	3–9

The Importance of Cultural Capital

Now let's take a mental holiday: Imagine being parachuted without supplies or training into a vast area of uninhabited tropical rainforest, an environment you have never been exposed to before. How long would it be before you starved to death or died from eating some delicious-looking poisonous plant? What combination of edible plants (assuming you have managed to identify some without killing yourself) would add up to a life-sustaining diet? What soil would be best for cultivating each kind of edible plant? How might you make the soil even better? How would you make fire to cook the harvest? To get some animal protein, would you strike lucky like Andrew Selkirk, the real-life prototype for Robinson Crusoe, and find a herd of feral goats to run down? Or would you have to hunt large game without knowing how to make any effective weapons? If you came across a patch of bitter manioc, would you know how to process it to get rid of its potentially lethal cyanogenic glucosides? How long could you possibly survive? You might, in your despondency, take encouragement from the fact that many human populations have inhabited this same sort of environment and managed to survive for countless generations. But there is one important difference between you and them: they know what they're doing, you don't.

Subsistence farmers who have been living in an area for more than a short time have accumulated an enormous body of lore regarding plants, soils and cultivation methods and a host of other kinds of knowledge about local resources, conditions and practices. If this lore is practical and not merely symbolic or ritualistic, then at some point it must have been subjected by somebody to a process of trial-and-error – in effect, an experiment. But trial-and-error is time-consuming and not guaranteed of success, and, if the trial fails, it may even end in death. A farmer who relies completely on trial-and-error is no better off than our naïve reader parachuted into the jungle. Fortunately, humans are social creatures and are happy to learn from the experiments, successes and failures of other people (Boyd and Richerson, 1985: 133–57; Boyd *et al.*, 2011). Once someone has shown by trial-and-error that a new bit of knowledge or practice is useful, it is added to the grab bag of traditional lore and passed on to others – especially to one's own children and other close relatives (Lozado *et al.*, 2006; McDade *et al.*, 2007) – by cultural transmission. Each generation need not rediscover all the useful things in life by trial-and-error, with its attendant risks and wastage. Boyd and Richerson (1985: 135) call this nonrandom tendency to adopt and transmit *useful* knowledge the "direct bias" in cultural transmission, and it operates alongside an "indirect bias" whereby we tend to ape our social betters without necessarily knowing which particular bits of knowledge or practice led to their betterment. Both these biases ensure that the material preserved as local culture is, more often than not, helpful in (or at least not harmful to) the family's demographic enterprise (McDade *et al.*, 2007).

Anthropologists have long studied local knowledge under the rubric of *ethnoscience*. In the past the field has been dominated by what is sometimes called the "intellectualist" approach, wherein native taxonomies of plants, birds, frogs, whatever, are analyzed for what they may tell us about general patterns of human cognition. But some areas of ethnoscience have adopted a more "utilitarianist" approach to local knowledge, one that not only catalogs the knowledge but tests to see if it is adapted to local circumstances (Johnson, 1974b). Ethnobotanists, for example, have long studied plant use and management as well as plant classifications (Denevan and Padoch, 1987; Posey and Balée, 1989; Cotton, 1996; Bennett *et al.*, 2001). Another emerging subdiscipline, ethnopedology, maps traditional classifications of soils onto features that would tell a modern agronomist something about a soil's suitability for growing crops (Wilhusen and Stone, 1990; Bellon and Taylor, 1993; Zimmerer, 1994). Many of the findings from utilitarianist ethnoscience have been unexpected but satisfying. It has long been known, for example, that wet rice farmers in East Asia hold wild aquatic ferns of the genus *Azolla* in high regard, being careful to preserve them when preparing paddy for planting, and singling them out for use as green manures. Is this behavior quixotic or irrational? Is *Azolla* mainly of ritual or symbolic value? Well, it turns out that *Azolla* species harbor a symbiotic cyanobacterium (*Anabaena azollae*) that fixes atmospheric nitrogen and releases it into the surrounding water and soil (Newton and Cavins, 1976; D. J. Hill, 1977). The presence of *Azolla* and its symbiont in rice paddies can increase yields by as much as 60 percent (Lumpkin and Plucknett, 1980). Presumably, most of the farmers who encourage water ferns in rice paddies know little or nothing about cyanobacteria or nitrogen fixation, but that may not stop them from concocting their own "magical" explanations for why water ferns are beneficial. By the same token, subsistence farmers in highland New Guinea who plant casuarina trees in new fallow (see above) traditionally knew nothing about actinorhizal symbioses but believed (as our informants told us) that casuarina trees excrete something into the soil akin to pig fat, considered the most strengthening of human foods. The theory may be wrong, but the practical effects are perceived, appreciated and exploited. And that is what matters.[12]

It would be a mistake, however, to think that this kind of useful knowledge about the local environment is shared equally by all members of a farming community – in fact, it tends to run in families (Lozada *et al.*, 2006; McDade *et al.*, 2007) – or that it is absolutely determinative of farming behavior. Shared (or partly shared) local knowledge does not mean that farmers act in zombie-like lockstep with their neighbors. Referring to a classic ethnography on the Chakchiquel Maya of Panajachel, Guatemala, Allen Johnson (1972: 151) notes that:

[Sol] Tax (1953) writes... as though all farmers behaved alike, yet gives direct evidence of such individual differences in hillside plots as to the length of fallowing (p. 48), the spacing of corn plants (p. 49), the kinds of seed used (p. 52), the carefulness of the farmer (p. 56), and the amount of seed per acre (p. 109).

---

[12] For in-depth applications of utilitarianist ethnoscience to subsistence farming, see Johnson (1974b, 1983, 1989) and Sillitoe (1983, 1996).

He goes on to say,

The observations I have made among swidden agriculturalists in Northeastern Brazil are unequivocal: these farmers differ from one another to the point that every household's configuration of land types, and the crop mix within them, is unique to that household... There it is useful to distinguish at least three different kinds of individual variation in agricultural practice: first, the variation which inevitably follows from ecological differences such as soil type, degree of slope, aspect of slope, and so on; second, variation which results from differences in the qualities and capabilities of the individual producing unit, such as amount of food stored from the previous harvest or available household labor; and, finally, those differences which result from disagreement among individuals over the facts of the case or their meaning, such as whether certain crop mixes are superior to others. (Johnson, 1972: 152)

Variation can also result from disagreements among individual farmers about how best to gamble in the face of environmental unpredictability. Writing about the Motupe of lowland northwestern Peru, Hatch (1974) shows in detail how all these factors can lead to variation in cultivation techniques among farmers who presumably share the same local culture. Shared culture does not result in perfectly uniform behavior, and no subsistence farmer can afford to act like an automaton.

Local knowledge is perhaps best thought of as a rattle-bag of tricks to be used as deemed necessary by the individual farmer on his or her particular farm, which will differ in myriad ways from neighboring farms. Local knowledge is critically import-ant, but it is never applied unthinkingly.

Experimentation in Subsistence Farming

In 1964, a very different view of traditional farm lore was put forward by the economist Theodore Schultz. Even while contemplating how best to transform subsistence agriculture, Schultz (1964: 36–52) acknowledged the practical wisdom of traditional farmers and accepted that culturally sanctioned practices often result in the efficient allocation of what are usually meager resources. But Schultz also believed that the efficiency of production based on native principles was bought at the expense of flexibility in the face of changing circumstances. Local knowledge may have worked well in the past, in his view, but it is an impediment to future economic development. Once traditional lore has accumulated to a certain point, the farming system becomes, in effect, frozen in its time-honored ways and unable to respond to new opportunities. Tradition is tradition, and no one can break its hold without outside help.[13]

There was a time when I agreed with this view, although for somewhat different reasons (Wood, 1998). My arguments were (i) that, under preindustrial conditions, useful innovations are rare, and (ii) that traditional farmers are too near the

---

[13] Schultz (1964) acknowledges that this view assumes a degree of cultural continuity and stability that may not hold for a given case.

subsistence level of food production to be able to afford the risks of experimenting with novelties. But, after many years of reading ethnographies about traditional farmers and reflecting on my own fieldwork experiences, I have come to think that my former view is wrong on both counts. In some respects, subsistence farmers are avid experimentalists – just so long as they can contain the damage from failed experiments (Johnson, 1972; Richards, 1985, 1986, 1995). Perhaps the most widespread form of damage control is to try out new techniques or new genetic resources on small plots in house gardens (Conklin, 1957: 48; Ali, 2005). Care of these plots is often turned over to the elderly and the very young, who contribute little to the cultivation of staple crops and tend to spend a lot of time near the house anyway. Thus, other household members are spared even the opportunity costs of experimentation. As Izikowitz (1951: 259–60) wrote of house gardens among the Lamet shifting cultivators of what is now Laos,

These gardens have to some extent the function of serving as "fields of experimentation." One old man in my village was extremely interested in new plants. He had obtained a number from Lamet boys who had been away in other parts, and when I came to Mokala Panghay [the local village] and laid out a garden, he showed a decided interest and begged seeds and plants of me which he immediately set in his own garden. There he had a number of experimental plants, and if these were successful, he intended to plant them on a larger scale out on his swidden.

As this account suggests, subsistence farmers are especially keen to try out new plant genetic resources, both new landraces of traditional crops and completely new crop species (Rappaport, 1967: 91; Johnson, 1972; Richards, 1985). Historical accounts tell us that the Iroquois, when raiding enemy villages, often collected ears from unfamiliar varieties of maize before destroying their enemies' fields (Dean Snow, personal communication).[14] When first working in highland New Guinea, we brought along commercial vegetable seeds for our own use, none of them from species native to our field site. Local people were fascinated by them and often asked for a few to try out on their own. (It was galling that they consistently did better with the seeds than we did!) Derek Freeman (1955: 53) has written,

All Iban take the greatest interest in new or uncommon varieties of *padi* [rice], and I encountered a number of cases of men having collected seed on their travels... Kubu, [a] man of Rumak Nyala, went in 1948 on a trading expedition to the Penihing people of the Upper Mahakam River. He returned...with small quantities of three different kinds of *padi* seed, having purchased two of them, and purloined the third. In 1949 all of this seed was planted and the resulting crop stored away so that larger areas could be sown in 1950. The purloined variety, of which Kubu was more than proud, had exceptional characteristics: the length of the rachis [panicle] was about 14 inches, with some 27 branches, carrying between 530 and 560 grains. This inter-change of *padi* seed, both sanctioned and unsanctioned, among the hill tribes of Borneo shows every sign of being a long-established custom.

---

[14] It is likely that the semiisolated villages and dispersed fields often associated with subsistence farming (and warfare) encouraged the spatial microdifferentiation of crop genes over fairly short distances (Alvarez *et al.*, 2005). Traditional farming areas are often viewed as treasure houses of crop biodiversity (Brush, 1986, 2004; Zimmerer, 1996; Kaihura and Stocking, 2003).

In addition to acquiring new genetic resources from other areas, subsistence farmers often select favorable new crop phenotypes that appear spontaneously in their own fields, setting aside a few seeds or cuttings for experimentation the following year (Wilson, 1917: 47–8; Brush and Meng, 1998; Rice *et al.*, 1998; Cleveland and Soleri, 2007). Thus, the artificial selection that originally played a decisive role in plant domestication (Gepts, 2004; Murphy, 2007) has continued among traditional farmers right up to the present. (For an excellent review of conscious, methodical selection of crop genes in traditional farming, see Brush, 2004: 127–52.) All this, of course, makes subsistence farmers even more interesting as conscious agents.

A Summary View

What general lessons have we learned about subsistence farming from this and the previous chapter? I would highlight the following points. Subsistence farmers are smart, well-trained and practical-minded. Their resources are limited, but they know how to make the most of them – or, rather, how to make *enough* of them to feed their families (there being little point in trying to do much more). Subsistence farmers organize things, not perfectly, but well enough – most of the time. But local conditions fluctuate from year to year, often in ways that no one, no matter how smart and well-informed, can predict. And their local knowledge is indeed *local*: their general logic may be universal, but all their cultural capital may avail for little in some other environmental setting.

By modern standards, all subsistence farms are low-input, low-output operations. Their material resources, while allocated efficiently, are extremely limited in quantity and often poor in quality. The farm's labor pool is small and subject to both random and systematic fluctuations in size and age/sex composition. The surrounding environment is always unpredictable, albeit to a degree that varies widely from one place to another. The means of importing food to offset local shortfalls are usually ill developed. The farmer does have a bag of proven tricks to draw from, but must use the tricks intelligently and with full knowledge that this year they may not work. Risk is everywhere, failure an ever-present possibility. In sum, the world of subsistence farming is a world of narrow limits and frequent catastrophes. No wonder Michael Mortimore, a geographer with decades of experience studying dryland farming in the African Sahel, calls hope "the spiritual diet of farmers" (Mortimore, 1998: xv).

3 Limits

The main peculiarity which distinguishes man from other animals, in the means of his support, is the power which he possesses of very greatly increasing these means. But this power is obviously limited... – T. R. Malthus (1830)

There are no miracles in agricultural production. – Attributed to Norman Borlaug

Two themes ran through the previous chapters. One was that subsistence farmers are intelligent, well-trained, inventive and practical-minded, and have numerous tricks for increasing net crop production; the other that their farms provide very low yields and are subject to severe physical constraints, reflecting environments that are finite, risky and indifferent to farmers' needs. Some readers may find these two themes contradictory: if subsistence farmers are so skillful, why can't they overcome environmental limits as well as modern farmers do? The answer, explored in detail in this chapter, is that the limits are built into the basic biology of food production. In fact, they can only be overcome, even partially and temporarily, with the massive, costly and energetically inefficient inputs provided to modern farmers by the industrial sector.

Before turning to what I regard as the most fruitful approach to those limits, however, I want to spend some time examining one way of thinking about resource limitation that has played an important and recurring role in the population/agriculture debate but that has, in my opinion, very weak scientific credentials: the concept of *carrying capacity*.

Does Carrying Capacity Exist?

The idea of carrying capacity is an old one that originated in range ecology and wildlife management. It was originally intended to mean something like "the number of individuals of a given species that can be supported each year by a particular, well-defined environment (with or without human intervention)." If we know enough about the physical environment and about the physiology and ecology of the species in question, we can come up with a crude but plausible estimate of carrying capacity that is good enough for many short-term practical applications, such as deciding how many cattle to stock on a given area of rangeland this year or how many quail to release on game land (Dijkman, 1999). Its application to humans, however, including in the population/agriculture debate, is altogether more problematic (Kessler, 1994).

The definition of carrying capacity that has become standard in human ecology was first put forward by the agronomist William Allan during the 1940s as a result of agricultural research he was conducting in what was then Northern Rhodesia (now Zambia). It is important to understand the practical problem that Allan faced before examining his definition. It had long been the policy of the British colonial government of Northern Rhodesia to move native Africans onto reserves where they would be "free" to practice their traditional methods of farming if they so desired. Allan had nothing to do with the formulation or implementation of this policy; he was merely asked by the government to evaluate its practical consequences after it had been operating for some years. In particular, it was becoming obvious that some of the reserves were suffering serious soil loss under traditional farming practices, presumably owing to human population densities on many of the reserves that were far higher than on the original home territories. Allan's charge was to estimate a reasonable ceiling for human population on the various native reserves, one that would allow for long-term environmental sustainability (as we would now call it), thus enabling the reserves to become permanent homelands. In an important 1949 paper entitled "How much land does a man require?" Allan laid out his definition of carrying capacity:

It must be obvious that any area of land will support in perpetuity only a limited number of people. An *absolute* limit is imposed by soil and climatic factors in so far as these are beyond human control, and a *practical* limit is set by the way in which land is used.

If the practical limit of population is exceeded, without a compensating change in the system of land usage, then a cycle of degenerative changes is set in motion which must result in deterioration or destruction of the land and ultimately in hunger and reduction of the population. The term 'erosion,' in its widest sense, is sometimes used for this cycle of destruction, but the word as it is generally understood has too limited a connotation to describe a process which results in radical changes in the whole character of the land: loss of mineral plant foods, oxidation and disappearance of organic matter, breakdown of soil structure, degeneration of vegetation, and the setting up of a new train of land and water relationships. The whole complex process of destruction is best referred to as *land degeneration*.

For every area of land to which a given system of land usage is applied, there is a population limit which cannot be exceeded without setting in motion the process of land degradation. This limit may be termed the *critical population* or *carrying capacity* for that system of land usage. Any estimate of land carrying capacity is, of course, meaningless unless the area to which the calculation applies and the system of land usage upon which it is based, are clearly defined. (Allan, 1949: 1)

There are several points worth emphasizing here.

- A population at carrying capacity is as large as it can be while remaining consistent with long-term demographic stationarity (no growth or decline in numbers) and the absence of land degradation. Note Allan's use of "in perpetuity," which implies a very long term indeed.
- Carrying capacity (at least the "practical" limit) is set by *both* environmental factors and the prevailing farming system in its entirety.

- Consistent with modern usage, Allan's use of the term "over-population" implies a population in excess of carrying capacity, with the attendant evils of "deterioration or destruction of the land and ultimately ... hunger and reduction of the population." A population in excess of carrying capacity, therefore, *necessarily* entails environmental degradation and a reduction in human material well-being, especially a decrease in dietary quality or sufficiency ("hunger"). Since Allan's brief was to determine the maximum population consistent with no environmental damage, it is perhaps inevitable that such damage should be an integral element of his view of over-population.
- Carrying capacity represents a sharp threshold, which "cannot be exceeded without setting in motion the process of land degradation." For all intents and purposes, Allan treats the carrying capacity of a given system of land usage as a constant – once estimated, known for perpetuity (or at least as long as the current system of land usage lasts). There is no mention of environmental change caused by *exogenous* factors (e.g. changing climate) in Allan's discussion.
- Over-population can be relieved by "a compensating change in the system of land usage." In other words, the *practical* limit to population is partly a function of human behavior and decision-making and is therefore changeable, at least until the *absolute* limit is reached.
- Allan does not hint that traditional communities, left to themselves, exhibit any tendency either to remain below carrying capacity, or to grow up to carrying capacity, or to exceed carrying capacity. The issue was not pertinent to Allan's remit, which was merely to determine whether current population had been forced above carrying capacity by government policy. Yet he provides a passing suggestion that over-population will result in "reduction of the population," which would seem to imply some kind of homeostatic response to over-population, albeit one that may return the population to a lower carrying capacity reflecting irreversible environmental damage. Note that both land degradation and hunger are necessary parts of that homeostatic response. Note too that Allan never says whether "the reduction of the population" is caused by an increase in mortality or a decrease in fertility, or perhaps both, or indeed by an increase in net out-migration. Whichever it is, it is presumably sparked by hunger.

Allan based these ideas on 20 years' worth of field experience, and his view of population limitation was in some ways quite advanced for his time. But it is subject to many criticisms, both theoretical and practical. The most obvious practical question is how these ideas are to be applied empirically, i.e. to estimate the carrying capacity of an actual population – which was, after all, Allan's job. It is worth examining Allan's method of estimation in some detail because it raises many of the problems associated with the general concept of carrying capacity.

Allan envisioned five necessary steps for estimating carrying capacity. The first, and in many ways the most difficult, is to identify, characterize and map relevant environmental zones in the area of interest – more precisely, to identify discrete patches that can be classified into a manageable number of categories based on the combination of soil and vegetation found on them. The assumption is that each type of patch has distinctive characteristics when it comes to agricultural productivity (this assumption should, of course, be tested by the soil scientists and agronomists on the project). The resulting vegetation/soil categories must be easy enough for fieldworkers to recognize so as to form the basis for rapid surveying and mapping at a fairly large scale (Figure 3.1). Fortunately for Allan, the necessary field surveys for Northern Rhodesia had already been conducted during the 1930s and early 1940s under the direction of the government ecologist Colin Trapnell (Smith, 2002).

The next step is to estimate the *cultivable* fraction of each vegetation/soil type by excluding rock outcrops, steep slopes, swamps, streams, seasonally inundated lowlands, gravels, thin soils, etc. (Table 3.1). This step, in itself, requires some fine-grained mapping and can be very time-consuming (bear in mind that Allan and his associates had neither GPS, GIS nor satellite imagery at their disposal).

At the end of these first two steps, we have a patchwork quilt of discrete, nonoverlapping units reflecting soil quality and natural vegetation cover, and

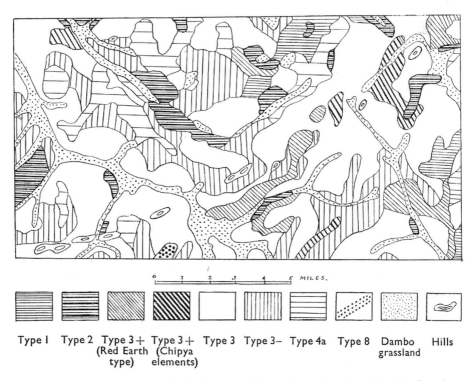

Figure 3.1 Distribution of vegetation/soil types in Ndola District, Northern Rhodesia (based on 1937 traverse survey on a 1 × 2 mile grid, plus aerial photography). From Allan (1949: 3), by permission of Oxford University Press, USA.

Table 3.1 The estimated cultivable acreage for various soil/vegetation types in Northern Rhodesia (Allan, 1949: 12). Reprinted from W. Allan, How much land does a man require? In *Studies in African Land Usage in Northern Rhodesia*, Rhodes-Livingstone Paper 15 (1949), pp. 1–23, by permission of Oxford University Press.

Vegetation/soil type	Area (acres)		Cultivable percentage	
	Total	Cultivable	Mean	Range
Th	11 090	3 500	31.8	
Th/Tr	109 450	34 580	31.6	27–32
Tr	33 430	8 598	25.7	20–34
Bl/Tr/Th	63 070	13 875	22.0	19–23
Bl/Tr	76 855	13 670	17.8	13–22
Bl	62 570	4 520	7.2	5–11
Total	356 375	78 743	22.1	5–34

we know how much cultivable land is available in each and every unit. All subsequent steps in Allan's method use the different vegetation/soil types as (in statistical parlance) strata for sampling and estimation. This kind of detailed attention to the environment is a hallmark of the fieldwork of Allan and his colleagues, especially Trapnell, and is rarely matched by more recent researchers who otherwise follow Allan's basic approach. Assuming that the discrete units capture most of the near-continuous variability in soils and plant cover, Allan's method is, up to this point, not only unobjectionable but laudable. Figure 3.2, adapted from Allan's later book *The African Husbandman*, shows just how much impact the different vegetation/soil types can have on agricultural productivity.

The third step, however, is less creditable. Now that we know the total amount of *potentially* cultivable land, we need to determine the proportion *actually* cultivated during an average year. In principle, this requires us to estimate the mean length (in years) of the active cultivation period as well as that of the fallow period – and we have to do so for each vegetation/soil type separately since those periods are likely to vary across types, as suggested by Figure 3.2. There are two major problems that crop up at this step, one practical and the other logical. The practical problem has to do with the sheer difficulty of estimating cultivation and fallow periods. Ideally, we need prospective data collected over a time interval commensurate with the periods to be estimated; and, even with such high-quality data, we still need to make life-table corrections for right-censored observations – that is, observations on fields that are still lying fallow at the end of the study period. Fortunately for Allan, he had access to data from a long-term study of the Lamba people of the Copperbelt region of Northern Rhodesia conducted by Trapnell (1943), who followed both cropping periods and fallows by vegetation/soil type for several years (although he did not correct for right-censoring). In view of the inherent difficulty of conducting such a study, Allan made an understandable if unconvincing assumption that Trapnell's data were

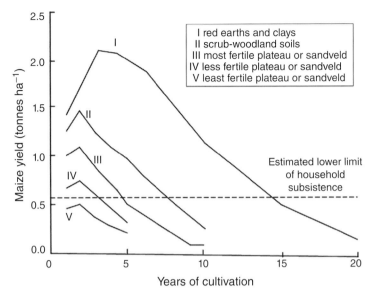

Figure 3.2 Maize yields by year of continuous cultivation without manure or other fertilizers, various vegetation/soil types, Northern Rhodesia. The increase during the first couple of years may reflect recovery of mycorrhizal symbioses after initial clearing and burning of slash. From Allan (1965: 95), by permission of Oliver and Boyd Publishing.

representative of the corresponding vegetation/soil types throughout all of Northern Rhodesia.[1]

The second problem, first identified by Street (1969), is deeper and points to a logical fallacy in virtually all estimates of carrying capacity. If you are going to estimate the mean periods of cropping and fallowing from empirical data *in order* to estimate carrying capacity, then you are tacitly assuming that those periods are, at the time of study, just what is required for the population to be at carrying capacity. Alternatively, a "given" system of land usage would seem to imply fixed periods of cropping and fallowing, at least on average. Ester Boserup (1965), in contrast, argues that the fallow period (and secondarily the cropping period) is extremely variable in traditional agriculture, and empirical studies generally show that she is right (Sirén, 2007).

The fourth step in Allan's method does nothing to calm our rising anxieties. The goal now is to estimate the amount of active garden land needed on each vegetation/soil type to support one person for a year. Allan proposes an unnecessarily roundabout way to compute this quantity. He starts by defining a "garden family":

---

[1] Modern authors who attempt to estimate carrying capacity do not go even this far. Rather, they simply compare the land being cultivated at the time of study with the land judged to be potentially cultivable. Such cross-sectional or "current-status" data are subject to severe estimation bias if not analyzed properly (Wood *et al.*, 1992a). In addition, as Allan (1949: 14) points out, some forms of shifting cultivation use different periods of cropping or fallowing at different phases of a larger cycle, a fact that would be missed in cross-sectional data (see the endnote to Table 3.4).

Table 3.2 The size of a single "garden family" for a year, Mazabuka District, Northern Rhodesia, 1944. The table refers to one particular household and is not intended to be representative of other households. Indeed the male head of this particular household is a Tongan chief who is almost certainly unrepresentative, as reflected in the size of the garden family, the large number of his wives and children and the two dependent families. Person units are not weighted by age or sex (Allan, 1949: 8). Reprinted from W. Allan, How much land does a man require? In *Studies in African Land Usage in Northern Rhodesia*, Rhodes-Livingstone Paper 15 (1949), pp. 1–23, by permission of Oxford University Press.

Household's dependents	Person units
Fed from household head's garden:	
Son, daughter-in-law and their four dependent children obtained ¼ of their requirements for 6 months	0.75
Second son, his wife and one child obtained ½ of their requirements for the whole year	1.50
Fed from household head's wives' gardens:	
One man (head of household)	1.00
His 3 wives	3.00
Nine young or adolescent children of household head and his wives	9.00
Dependent family obtained ¼ of their requirements for 6 months	0.75
Dependent family fed for 6 months	1.50
Married adult daughter (husband away at work) and child fed for 6 months	1.00
Elderly sister and husband fed for the whole year	2.00
Niece (abandoned by husband) fed for the whole year	1.00
Son-in-law (abandoned by wife) fed for 4 months	0.33
Total	21.83

This is a measure of the number of people obtaining their food supply from a family [household] land holding, and it is estimated by allowing one unit for each person, irrespective of age [or sex], obtaining the whole of his or her food supply from the holding, and an appropriate fraction for each person obtaining part of his or her supply. (Allan, 1949: 7)

Table 3.2 shows, purely as an example, the computations required for the household of a village headman or chief among the Tonga. One shortcoming of this method is that the values accorded to the various members of the garden family are not weighted by age, sex, body mass, workload or anything else. Thus, in effect, the nutritional needs of, say, a newborn baby confined to a sling are assumed to be equivalent to those of a hardworking adult. This problem could in theory be solved by introducing an appropriate set of age- and sex-specific weights within Allan's larger approach – although, as discussed in Chapter 10, valid estimation of such weights is not easy.

At any rate, this procedure is repeated on many garden families until an adequate sample is obtained, at which point the garden families in one community can be summed and compared to the total area of food-producing land available to that community as in Table 3.3, which suggests that, on average, each person requires the cultivation of about one acre of farmland per year for sustenance (with a range across

Table 3.3 Garden families and garden acreage in three Lamba villages, Mushiri District, Northern Rhodesia, *c.* 1945 (Allan, 1949: 8). Reprinted from W. Allan, How much land does a man require? In *Studies in African Land Usage in Northern Rhodesia*, Rhodes-Livingstone Paper 15 (1949), pp. 1–23, by permission of Oxford University Press.

Village	No. of garden families	Total population	Area of main gardens (acres)	Area of main gardens per unit of population
A	23	127	120.4	0.95
B	8	40	44.0	1.10
C	18	87	93.6	1.07
Total	49	254	258.0	1.01

the entire survey area of *c.* 0.7–1.5 acres). The figures in Table 3.3 show immediately why I characterized the garden-family method as "unnecessarily roundabout." Since each person, regardless of age or sex or whatever, is counted as one "person-unit", the acreage required per person could have been estimated by simply counting the number of people in each community or sample and comparing it to the total active farmland in the community or sample; the complicated rigmarole of characterizing each garden family in detail is unnecessary – though it may well have produced some interesting data on household composition, which could still be sitting on a shelf somewhere in Zambia.

But there is another logical problem here. What Allan is trying to do with the garden-family method is to estimate the amount of land (of a given vegetation/soil type) needed to support one person for a year at a barely adequate level of subsistence, i.e. at carrying capacity. But conditions at the time of survey may be radically different from those expected at carrying capacity. Indeed, the study population may be well over carrying capacity, in which case the land available per person may entail serious under-nutrition and perhaps even extensive environmental damage. Or the population may be well *under* carrying capacity, in which case the average amount of farm land available to each person may be enough to keep him or her fat and happy. In other words, the garden-family method implies that the study population is *at* carrying capacity at the time of the study, and that the amount of land currently farmed per person is the *minimal* amount needed to support a person. Alternatively, an unmentioned assumption would seem to be that, in a *given* system of land usage, the same amount of land is always farmed per person. In other words, the amount of land farmed per person seems to be a defining element of the system of land use, not a variable quantity within it.

Setting aside these difficulties, the fifth and final step in the method is to put everything together to compute carrying capacity or "critical population size" (N_c):

$$N_c = \sum_i \frac{T_i P_i}{C_i L_i},$$

Table 3.4 Some estimates of carrying capacity by vegetation/soil type, 379 m^2 area south of Ndola and the Copperbelt surveyed in 1944. Values of A and B are taken from an earlier study of the sorghum-cultivating Lamba (Trapnell, 1943). L_i is assumed to equal one acre, similar to what Trapnell estimated for the Lamba (Allan, 1949: 15). Reprinted from W. Allan, How much land does a man require? In *Studies in African Land Usage in Northern Rhodesia*, Rhodes-Livingstone Paper 15 (1949), pp. 1–23, by permission of Oxford University Press.

P_i = proportion of vegetation/soil type i that is cultivable.

$C_i = \frac{cultivation\ period + fallow\ period}{cultivation\ period}$ on vegetation/soil type i.

| Veg./ soil type (i) | Total area (acres) | Years of cultivation (A) and rest (B) | | P_i (%) | C_i | Area required per capita (acres) | Total carrying capacity (persons) |
		A	B				
1	4 380	recultivation[a]	33–34	3	9	487
2+	1 160	recultivation[a]	25	3	12	97
2	12 983	6–12	6–12	33–34	2	6	2 164
2-	1 650	recultivation[a]	25	3	12	137
3+	15 435	recultivation[a]	25–30	4	15	1 029
3	125 898	3	21	25	8	32	3 934
3-	43 615	2–3	22–28	15–25	11	55	793
4a	22 447	2	22–28	8–12	13	130	173
4a-	11 380	2	22–28	5	13	260	44
							8 858

[a] Recultivation involves land cultivated for a fairly long period, followed by a short rest under "scrub fallow" and a second cultivation, after which a long fallow is usually provided. The initial cultivation period of these soils is typically 6–8 yr followed by a scrub fallow of similar length, a further period of cultivation and a longer period of rest: for example, 6 yr cultivation, 6 yr scrub fallow, 6 yr recultivation, 12+ yr fallow, with the cycle repeatedly indefinitely.

where

i = land (vegetation/soil) type

$\sum_i$ = summation over all land types

T_i = total acreage of land type i

P_i = proportion of land type i cultivable

$C_i = \frac{cultivation\ period + fallow\ period}{cultivation\ period}$ in land type i (what Allen calls the "cultivation factor")

L_i = mean acreage needed to support one individual on land type i for one year.

The algebra in this equation is unexceptionable; it is the real meaning and estimability of some of the variables themselves that is worrisome.

Nonetheless, sample calculations from Allan's work are given in Table 3.4, while Table 3.5 provides more regional estimates of carrying capacity and "critical population density" (carrying capacity divided by square miles of cultivable lands of all types). On balance Allan reckons that a density of about 25 people per square mile of cultivable land is pretty generally the upper limit of human settlement

Table 3.5 Some results from the Eastern Province survey, Fort Jameson District, Northern Rhodesia, assuming Ngoni-Chewa methods of maize cultivation (Allan, 1949: 16). Reprinted from W. Allan, How much land does a man require? In *Studies in African Land Usage in Northern Rhodesia*, Rhodes-Livingstone Paper 15 (1949), pp. 1–23, by permission of Oxford University Press.

Area surveyed (acres)	Estimated carrying capacity (persons)	Estimated critical density (persons mi^{-2})
97 550	4 600	30.4
143 660	5 565	25.0
40 900	1 350	21.1
46 800	2 480	33.3
19 600	1 135	37.0
110 300	3 970	23.0
79 100	1 860	15.0
19 500	500	16.4
54 200	2 440	28.8
————	————	————
611 610	23 900	25.0

consistent with long-term sustainability of the environment in rural Northern Rhodesia. He then goes on to draw the following conclusions: (i) Most of Northern Rhodesia is well below the overall mean critical population density of 25 mile^{-2}. (ii) However, population is very patchily distributed, with some local high-density areas and other areas that are virtually uninhabited. (iii) In many of the densely settled areas, local populations reach densities (> 100 mile^{-2}) that exceed the local critical densities by substantial amounts. (iv) In those areas, land degradation has already begun or is likely to begin soon (how does he know?), or the local population is trying to increase their land at the expense of neighboring groups. (v) Most of the densely settled areas are the result of forced resettlement of native groups by the colonial government. With these conclusions, Allan partly redeems himself. Despite the spurious precision of some of his calculations, he ends up using rounded figures, broad generalizations and differences in densities (>100 mile^{-2} vs. 25 mile^{-2}) that are large enough to accommodate a considerable amount of error.

We can now summarize the methodological and theoretical criticisms of this general approach. Some of these criticisms have already been discussed and can be summarized briefly. Among the *methodological* criticisms, the following would seem to be the most important.

- The observed mean periods of cropping and fallowing, even if estimated properly, are not necessarily those that would be found at carrying capacity.
- Similarly, the current amount of land used to feed a person is not the same thing as the minimal amount of land *needed* to feed a person, which could be higher or lower. Implicitly this means that the level of food consumption practiced at the time of

study is assumed to be precisely at the bare subsistence level, which in turn removes the rate of resource consumption as a variable determining carrying capacity.

- The estimated nutritional needs of the average person are not weighted by age, sex or any other characteristic, the distributions of which could all vary over time or across populations.
- There is a tacit assumption that the fallow period does not contribute to anyone's diet, whereas, as we saw in Chapter 2, fallow is often managed and exploited in various ways, including for food.
- The method makes no allowance for intensive, multicropping systems in which more than one crop is grown on a particular field each year. The assumption seems to be that all the communities of interest practice some form of shifting cultivation or, at most, annual cropping.
- Allan's approach does not take water supply into account. As Allan himself admits, this omission could be critical in a semiarid environment such as Zambia's (Allan, 1949: 18). Nor does it consider fuel supply, livestock or (as pointed out by Brush, 1975) resources traded in from the outside – or traded out from the inside.

Many estimates of the carrying capacities of traditional farming systems based on logic similar to Allan's have been published in more recent years. Have the authors provided methodological refinements that are significant improvements over his method? During the 1960s and 1970s, most attempts to estimate carrying capacity were based on Allan's logic but used *less* reliable methods (for reviews and critiques, see Street, 1969; Brush, 1975). Today, many researchers rely on remote sensing to assess the environment (Allan and Trapnell did use aerial photography but not, of course, satellite imagery), but there is great variation in the degree to which they "ground truth" their assessments. Some econometricians have formalized the models and estimation procedures (e.g. Komatsu *et al.*, 2005), and Monte Carlo simulation is sometimes used to allow for random variability over time (e.g. Haraldsson and Olafsdottir, 2006). Are the estimates produced using these methods more believable than those of Allan? The fact is, we do not know, for there is no available "gold standard" for evaluating the validity of the estimates.

What's more, the problems of estimating carrying capacity are only partly methodological – there are also deeper *theoretical* problems that call the entire concept of carrying capacity into question. The following seem to me to be the most telling.

- If carrying capacity is, say, 8858, then what happens when there are 8859 people present? This question is less silly than it might appear. The real issue is: how sharp is the threshold associated with carrying capacity? In Allan's conceptualization, presumably some degree of land degradation and hunger begins with the 8859th person. But both nutritional status and environmental condition can vary continuously, and both may be influenced by other factors that may or may not be related to the size of the population (for example, nutritional status can be greatly influenced by infectious disease or workload, which may be partly, but only partly, dependent upon population size). If carrying capacity is *not* a sharp threshold, how can it be represented by a single number such as 8858?

- According to Allan, over-population leads to environmental degradation (unless remedial actions are taken). By implication, so long as the population is below carrying capacity, no environmental damage takes place. But Allen Johnson has argued that

  "environmental degradation"... begins at the moment of pioneering residence and rises steadily thereafter. There is no threshold ... beyond which degradation begins, but rather a consistent [continuously worsening?] process of degradation. (Johnson, 1974a)

  Johnson goes on to point out that, if degradation really does begin with the very first settler, then, by Allan's definition, all real-world populations are over carrying capacity! This latter point aside, I think Johnson is fundamentally right. As argued later in this chapter, farming *by its very nature* involves environmental disturbance and disequilibrium, creating the conditions for environmental damage no matter how low the human population density or how nonintensive or remedial the farming practices. If you expose a square meter of soil in the process of clearing forest for planting and it rains before crops have grown up to protect the soil, then some degree of environmental degradation in the form of droplet erosion will inevitably occur unless you immediately mulch the exposed patch. Of course, the amount of environmental degradation involved may be negligible for all practical purposes: the question is not when or if environmental degradation occurs, but when it becomes worth worrying about. If land degradation worth worrying about will not appear for 200 years, why should any farmer today even care about it? If it occurs tomorrow, that's a different matter.

- Allan is careful to emphasize that an estimate of carrying capacity applies strictly to the "system of land usage upon which it was based." But what does "a *system* of land usage" mean anyway? As argued in Chapter 2, every individual farmer is faced with a range of farm-management decisions that need to be made each farming year. No two farmers will be faced with exactly the same on-farm conditions in a given year, and no two farmers will arrive at exactly the same decisions. Similarly, any *one* farmer is likely to make different decisions from one year to the next as conditions change, however subtly. As Street (1969: 104) has put it, the idea of a *given* system of land usage presumably implies "unvarying technology and crop patterns" as well as "qualitatively and quantitatively constant per capita food consumption," adding "the assumptions of technological and gastronomic stagnation ... depart so markedly from reality as to seriously diminish the utility of the computed [critical] population densities." No system of land usage is fixed in any absolute sense. Are the factors affecting carrying capacity (both natural and agronomic) so elastic that there is no single enduring number for it? Must carrying capacity be computed separately for each individual farm? Might today's carrying capacity be irrelevant next year? Maybe there is a temporal autocorrelation between carrying capacities from year to year, but surely not an absolutely fixed number. Joel Cohen (1995) explores this issue at length.[2]

---

[2] He points out that the observed variance in estimates of the world's carrying capacity has increased over time and continues to increase, quite contrary to what has happened to estimates of real physical constants such as the speed of light or the gravitational constant.

- Under most definitions, including Allan's, an assessment of current carrying capacity is, in effect, a prediction about the future – a claim that the population can remain "in perpetuity" at or below that number without damaging the environment. But how could we possibly know short of monitoring the environment in perpetuity? We can only guess at the future, even if we want to estimate carrying capacity right now. This predictive element of carrying capacity as defined by Allan and more recent writers is particularly nettlesome. If taken too seriously, it means that carrying capacity and over-population can, at best, be assessed only in retrospect after a lapse of many, many years.

As Healey (1990: 28) put it, "Practical and theoretical difficulties associated with the concept of carrying capacity render any attempt to specify population limits superfluous." (I would have said "bootless" instead of "superfluous", but the point is clear enough.) Insofar as the concept of over-population hinges on an evaluation of carrying capacity, as it usually does, it too is subject to precisely the same difficulties. Perhaps it is time to jettison both concepts.

And yet – we are left with an ill-formed feeling that the terms carrying capacity and over-population have *some* meaning, corresponding in some vague, poorly specified way to things that happen in the real world. Even as he blasts the very idea of carrying capacity, Bob Dewar (1984: 601) acknowledges the plausibility of "the commonsense notion that a limit on resources implies a limit on the number of consumers." In the next section, I want to introduce a potentially more fruitful approach to the whole question of resource limitation and its demographic effects, an approach that circumvents many of the shortcomings associated with the classic concept of carrying capacity. If applied at the level of the individual farming household and its physical farm, it can, I believe, provide a useful basis for thinking about most of what we would like to know regarding limits on population growth.

The Ecology and Economics of Resource Limitation

The material in this section can be considered a modernized version of Malthus's basic position on the real but limited plasticity of agricultural production (in Chapter 5, I will examine other aspects of Malthus's thinking.) When viewed from a broad perspective, Malthus was espousing a *philosophy of limits*, which is why he was so deeply offensive to many utopian and idealist thinkers.[3] Today, with our growing awareness of environmental constraints, perhaps it is time to reevaluate Malthus's

---

[3] Marx called Malthus's work "a very model of intellectual imbecility" (Marx, 1954: 138). Engels referred to it as "this vile and infamous doctrine, this hideous blasphemy against man and nature" (Engels, 1954:59–60). William Hazlett quipped that Malthus could not be satisfied until he had contrived to starve someone (Hazlitt, 1807: 314). James Bonar claimed that he "defended small-pox, slavery and child-murder" (Bonar, 1885: 2) – he did not; Malthus was, among other things, passionately anti-slavery. (He was also an early supporter of women's rights.) But Bonar did say one indubitably true thing: Malthus was "the best-abused man of the age" (Bonar, 1885: 1). Hardin (1998) has suggested that the abuse was mainly inspired by a single passage in the second edition of the *Essay on the Principle of Population* – comparing life to a grand banquet to which not everyone holds a ticket – a passage conspicuously dropped from later editions.

philosophy. As it turns out, many of Malthus's basic ideas about resource limitation are remarkably prescient and consistent with the findings of modern agricultural science.

A Scottish Interlude

Since much of the following discussion of resource limitation under preindustrial farming will be somewhat abstract, I will introduce the basic concepts using a concrete (if semifictional) example. Imagine that you are a small-scale tenant farmer in the far north of Scotland (where I write these words, in the midst of a howling gale) round about the year AD 1750. As a tenant you must pay nominal rents in kind each year to the laird – some meal, butter or cheese, eggs, dried fish, a fleece or two, perhaps some woolen goods such as hand-knit stockings – but your efforts will mainly be aimed at feeding your family: you will, in other words, be practicing what I have called *near-subsistence* farming (see Chapter 1). In return for rent, you will be allocated some cultivable land, say two hectares (five acres) in area. On this land you will mostly plant bere (an old landrace of barley) and black oats, your two staple grains. You are also likely to have a small, enclosed *kailyard* (house garden) where you can grow a limited range of green vegetables – mostly, as the name implies, hardy brassicas like kale and cabbage (both varieties of the single species *Brassica oleracea*) – and perhaps some *neeps* (rutabaga) and *tatties* (potatoes), although neeps and tatties would still be fairly uncommon in much of northern Scotland in 1750. As a tenant, you are entitled to use rough, unimproved grazing land, shared in common with other tenants, on the hillsides well away from arable land; you will probably run some sheep and a few head of cattle there, both of traditional (small, not very productive) breeds. Your sheep are hardy enough to remain on rough pasture all year round with minimal care except during lambing and plucking.[4] But your cattle will have to be brought in and sheltered in a *byre* (cattle shed) and hand-fed from late October to mid-March. (Fodder will have to be cut with a scythe on semicultivated meadowland, competing with crops for your meager allotment of arable and your limited time.) Stalling, mowing hay and hand-feeding are hard work, but they allow you to collect manure for fertilizer by mucking out the byre up to three times a day – also hard work but worth it. The manure is collected in a muck pile just outside the byre; you may well supplement it by tossing on hand-collected seaweed (if you're near the ocean), ash from the hearth, old urine-soaked animal bedding (usually hay or turf), old roof thatch (enriched with cook-fire grease, rodent droppings and insect corpses), food scraps if you don't have a pig and pig dung if you do, dog and cat carcasses and the waste produced by household members. Whatever its composition, the muck pile is one of your most precious agricultural assets: permanent farming of

---

[4] Traditional sheep breeds of northern Scotland, especially Shetland, Orkney and the Hebrides, underwent an annual molt. At the right time of the year, their fleece could be harvested by plucking or *rooing* without the use of shears (Fenton, 1978).

your arable would be impossible without it.[5] But, following von Thünen (who, of course, has not yet been born but whose logic your ancestors worked out long ago), you will only spread muck on an *infield* close to your house, byre and muck pile; the *outfield* further away will be farmed less intensively, lying fallow every few years or used periodically as pasturage for your beasts – a labor-saving way to fertilize it. If you are lucky, you will own a crude wooden moldboard plow and a pair of oxen to pull it. If you are not, you will beg a neighbor for the loan or hire of a plow and beasts, or you will laboriously turn the soil using a *cas chrom* or foot plow, a spade-like implement strikingly similar to the traditional foot plows still used in parts of the Andes (compare Cook, 1920; Fenton, 1974; Gade and Rios, 1974). You are sure to own a few other tools – rakes, pitchforks, sickles, scythes, peat-cutting spades – some of which may even be fancy enough to have bits of iron tacked onto their working edges.

In this cloudy, drizzly setting, water is unlikely to be a limiting resource, but sunlight may well be, especially in view of the shortness of the season available for growing crops. Being partly waterlogged, the soils on your land are likely to be acidic or even peaty (peat can be cut and dried for fuel, but it is terrible for growing food). If you are close to a beach, you may be able to haul carbonate-rich shell sand to put on your infields in order to neutralize the acidic soils. You may have a pony to help haul the sand to the fields in straw baskets, but you are more likely to haul it on your own back or the backs of your close kin, just as you haul manure, fuel, the harvest and pretty much everything else. As one eighteenth-century visitor to the Outer Hebrides put it, "Here everything is done by rude strength and perseverance" (Heron, 1794: 89).

These, then, are the resources you have to work with: some sour, stony arable land; meadow and common grazing; plenty of rain; not so much sunlight; seed for sowing staple grains; seeds, cuttings or tubers for planting nonstaple vegetables; a limited range of farm implements; some farm buildings such as the byre and a barn where grain is processed and stored; a muck pile that is as rich as you can make it; perhaps a source of seaweed and shell sand; a peat bog where you can cut fuel; perhaps a few beasts of burden; and the arms, shoulders, backs, hands and legs of every able-bodied member of your household. You cannot do much about the rain and sunshine, and you must work with a fixed allotment of land, but you are free to apply the other resources as you see fit. Normally your goal is to harvest enough plant food to feed yourself, your immediate family (perhaps four or five people) and your beasts, with seed stock left

[5] An indication of the economic value of muck is provided by written leases preserved from the late nineteenth century, by which time rents in kind had mostly been commuted into cash payments. For example, an 1896 lease for the croft of Muslandale on the island of Westray in Orkney, Scotland, states, "The Tenants shall at no time during their leases sell, gift, or dispose of any Straw or Fodder raised upon their Farms..., or any Dung made thereon, but shall consume said Fodder and lay the whole of said Dung on their Farms; and whatever Dung is unused at the expiry of their leases shall belong to the Trustees [the effective proprietors] or incoming tenant without their paying any value therefor" (document in the Westray Heritage Centre, Pierowall, Orkney). Such clauses were standard. The significance of straw or other fodder in this connection was that it would eventually be turned into dung.

over for next year and enough material to pay your rent. But could you, if necessary, support a hundred people from your farm? What a nonsensical suggestion! Then what precisely is it that limits the number of people you *can* support?

Suppose that immediately after each harvest we measure your yield of grain and sum across all harvests and all fields cultivated this year to estimate your total annual yield (adding in a bit more to cover nonstaple crops). And let us say your total yield was about a tonne, or some 500 kg ha^{-1}. Now tell us this: what was it that produced that tonne? (What an odd question!) Well, the amount of soil that was tilled and seed that was sown, obviously, and the rain and the sunlight, and the fertilizer and shell sand, and don't forget all the labor expended in the fields, plus the hay fed to the kye so that they could produce manure, and a myriad of other things – the tonne of grain came from each and every one of these "inputs" (an ugly word you would not have recognized) acting in concert. How can we judge the contribution of any *single* factor?

Permit us to appropriate your land next year for an experiment. You will farm the land as you normally would, but with one exception. We will split all your land into a large number of small plots – at least notionally, i.e. on a map. For most plots, we will randomly select one particular input to manipulate on each. For example, there will be several plots for which muck is the selected input, and we will instruct you to apply different amounts of muck to each plot so selected – all the while holding the other inputs at the level you would choose in a normal year. And we do the same thing with every other customary input – all done to a statistical nicety we needn't bother you with (trust us, we're experts). Now, if we measure the yield from each plot, we can examine yield as a function of one factor at a time. On some plots we'll vary factors two at a time in order to estimate two-way interactions between factors, on others we'll vary factors three at a time and so forth. When we're finally done we'll cart away all our data and return to our dry, comfortable, well-fed lives, leaving you to curse us for disrupting a perfectly good farming year. Why, you wonder, do we need all that information? After all, you could have told us plainly what works and what doesn't.

Agricultural Production Functions

The ideas in the previous section can be generalized in the form of a so-called *agricultural production function*. A production function is a model (usually mathematical or computer-based) of a production process that takes a given set of inputs and predicts the output of material goods expected from them. A generic agricultural production function would take the form

$$Y_i = \Phi(X_{i1}, X_{i2}, \ldots, X_{ik}),\tag{3.1}$$

where Y_i is the total gross annual yield of crops in year i (shall we say in 1750?) and the Xs are a series of k inputs into the system of food production (perhaps manure, shell sand, a certain number of person-hours of work per annum, a particular volume of seed sown). Φ just denotes some specific mathematical function relating the Xs to Y,

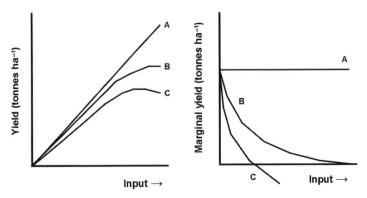

Figure 3.3 Some generic agricultural production functions and their associated curves of marginal productivity. The input might be hours of labor, tonnage of fertilizer, amount of seed planted, the tools used, etc. Marginal productivity or marginal yield is the increase in yield produced by a unit increase in the input.

such that, if we plug in specific numbers for the Xs, we can compute a specific *expected* value of Y, the crop yield. The math need not concern us here, just the idea that such an equation exists.[6] The model is, we hope, a reasonably accurate reflection of the actual physical processes involved. Once we have settled on what we consider the "right" form of the equation and satisfied ourselves that it provides reliable estimates of yield, we can then play with the model and perform thought experiments similar in logic to the obnoxiously invasive one contemplated in the previous section. We can, for example, vary one input at a time while leaving the rest fixed in order to isolate the effect of that one factor on agricultural yields (and that is the type of experiment explored in the rest of this chapter). If we get lucky, we may even be able to identify one or more factors that most severely limit the total amount of food that can be produced on the farm and thus the number of people who could be supported by it – the most important limiting factors for the farming family. To validate our model predictions, we can test them against crop yields observed in experimental plots on an agricultural research station. To proper economists, there will be something rather quaint about using production functions, but they suit our present purpose admirably. As Paul Samuelson once remarked, "Until the laws of thermodynamics are repealed, I shall continue to relate outputs to inputs – i.e. to believe in production functions" (Samuelson, 1972: 174).

Figure 3.3 (left-hand panel) shows some possible outcomes of a generic agricultural production function obtained by varying one particular input, say how much of a specific type of fertilizer is applied. Line A represents a never-ending linear increase

---

[6] For the econometrically-minded, Heady and Dillon (1961) provide a comprehensive review of standard agricultural production functions and methods for estimating them. By way of illustration, Tung and Rasmussen (2005) apply formal production-function analysis to several near-subsistence farming systems in Vietnam.

in food yield as the input increases: the more fertilizer the better the crop yield, without reversal or limitation. In various editions of his *Principle of Population*, Malthus called such a trend "the very utmost that we can conceive" (1798: 22), "probably a greater increase than could with reason be expected" (1803: 11) and even "certainly far beyond the truth" (1798: 22). In his "Summary View" of 1830, written for the *Encyclopedia Britannica* just four years before his death, Malthus wrote,

The main peculiarity which distinguishes man from other animals, in the means of his support, is the power which he possesses of very greatly increasing these means. But this power is obviously limited by the scarcity of land ... and by the *decreasing proportion of produce* which must *necessarily* be obtained from the continual additions of capital applied to land already under cultivation. (Malthus, 1830, reprinted in Flew, 1970: 225; emphasis added.)

Elsewhere in the same publication, he wrote,

the rate of increase of food [under the most favorable conditions] would certainly have a greater resemblance to a decreasing geometrical ratio than an increasing one. The yearly increment of food would, at any rate, have a constant tendency to diminish, and the amount of the increase of each successive ten years would probably be less than that of the preceding. (Reprinted in Flew, 1970: 230.)

In other words, Malthus believed in production functions B and C in Figure 3.3, not A.

With few exceptions, most economists accept that curve B is a more reasonable expectation for an agricultural production function than curve A. And for some inputs, they might well argue that curve C is more realistic: too much fertilizer "burns" the roots of crop plants, over-sowing leads to competition among crop plants that reduces total yield, too many laborers trample the crops. In the nineteenth century, the economist/philosopher John Stuart Mill enshrined curve B as "the law of diminishing returns," and the "law" has been widely accepted as a valid empirical generalization ever since.

Another way to visualize the results of an agricultural production process is in terms of its *marginal productivity* or *marginal yield* (Figure 3.3, right-hand panel, in which each curve is labeled to match the corresponding production function on the left-hand side of the figure). The marginal productivity associated with a given input is the change in yield obtained by a unit increase in the quantity of the input – for example, an additional hundred-weight of manure.[7] If the yield increases linearly with increasing input, then the marginal product is a flat line (A on the right-hand side of Figure 3.3): every unit increase in the input generates a fixed amount of *additional* yield, without limit. Curves B and C show declining marginal productivity,

---

[7] Or at least that is the simple, nonmathematical version. In formal analysis, marginal productivity is defined as $\partial Y_i / \partial X_{ij}$ for the *j*th input in year *i*. But the nonmathematical version will do fine for our purposes.

which is synonymous with diminishing returns. In curve B the marginal product goes to zero, beyond which point the production function is absolutely flat. Curve C is even more stringent: it actually becomes negative at higher inputs. That is, yields actually *decline* as we invest more in the land. For many purposes, whether in form B or C, the curve of declining marginal productivity neatly captures the practical limits of agricultural production. It is not necessarily the case that you cannot work a plot of land harder or invest more capital in it, but even if you can the land will not reward you for it beyond some limit.

The standard economic explanation for declining marginal productivity is that, if we do the thought experiment of varying a single input into a production process while holding the rest constant, we will eventually come up against a limit set by one of the *other* inputs. For example, if we have a fixed number of widget-producing machines, we can produce more widgets by adding more workers *until* workers start competing with each other for physical access to the machines. Queuing workers are not productive workers. This idea makes declining marginal productivity sound like a mere by-product of the thought experiment itself, since in real life several inputs can be varied simultaneously – perhaps we can afford more workers *and* more machines. Certainly interacting inputs are important in farming, and one goal of the farmer is to find the right combination or compromise among them. But the "law" of diminishing returns is, I would argue, built into the very biology of agricultural production in ways that are unique to farming as a productive enterprise. In that arena, perhaps it even deserves to be called a law.

The Biology of Declining Marginal Productivity in Traditional Farming

Agriculture is a set of tricks for harnessing photosynthesis to human purposes. In the leaves of any crop plant (or other green plant), the substance chlorophyll, aided by a mind-numbing array of other compounds, takes one molecule of carbon dioxide and one molecule of water and bombards them with eight photons (tiny packets of solar energy) to produce one molecule of carbohydrate and one of oxygen: $CO_2 + H_2O + 8$ photons $\rightarrow CH_2O + O_2$. This reaction is one of life's greatest achievements; photosynthesis is as indispensible to you as your own DNA. Sunlight provides the energy to drive the reaction, and if it is repeated billions of times the plant will pile up a fair amount of carbohydrate to store in its seeds, roots, leaves or stems (each crop species has its own specialized depots for storing starches or sugars, usually grossly enlarged by artificial selection). We derive our energy by extracting this "fixed sunlight" either directly from the plants or indirectly from domesticated animals that feed on the plants. The ultimate factor limiting the rate of photosynthesis is the *flux* of sunlight – the amount hitting the plant per unit time – although water and carbon dioxide may sometimes be more immediately limiting.

It comes as something of a surprise to learn just how restricted the amount of sunlight hitting the surface of the Earth is, and just how badly plants manage to use it. Figure 3.4 shows data from the Rothamsted Agricultural Research Station (mentioned in Chapter 2) on the energy content of sunlight striking a horizontal surface in southern England. The intensity of solar flux varies, as you would expect, by season

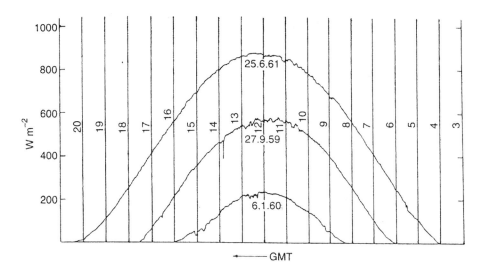

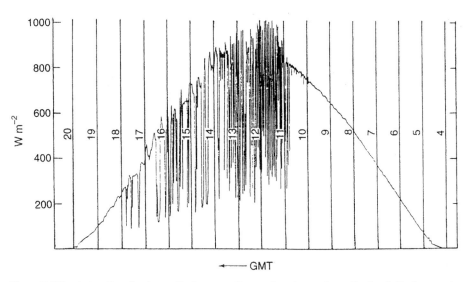

Figure 3.4 The intensity of solar radiation on a flat surface in southern England, Rothamsted Research Station. GMT = Greenwich Mean Time (in hours) running right to left. (Top) Mean solar radiant flux density (W m^{-2}) for *cloudless* days in June, September and December. (Bottom) Solar radiant density for one June day of broken cloud. From Alexander (1999: 4), by permission of Oxford University Press, USA.

and by time of day (Figure 3.4, top panel).[8] In conjunction with the *phenology* – the growth and maturation rate – of whatever crop is in question, both diurnal and seasonal variation determines whether the effective growing season is long enough

---

[8] Near the equator, the solar flux hitting the upper reaches of the atmosphere varies negligibly with season (see Chapter 11). In the humid tropics, however, the amount of sunlight hitting the *surface* of the Earth, where crops are grown, declines during the rainy season, often substantially, because of cloud cover.

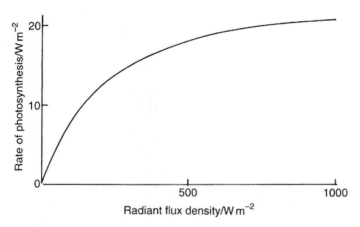

Figure 3.5 The efficiency of the photosynthetic reaction according to the flux of solar radiation. In this example the peak efficiency is only about 2 percent; 3–4 percent would be considered exceptional. Thus, more than 95 percent of incident solar energy is lost. From Alexander (1999: 10), by permission of Oxford University Press, USA.

to meet the crop's needs – or, rather, the needs of the people growing the crop. As shown in the bottom panel of Figure 3.4, cloud cover greatly reduces the incident sunlight. And here we are confronted by a basic biochemical trade-off: photosynthesis requires water as well as sunlight. You can't have a lot of sunlight and a lot of clouds and rain simultaneously. They compete. And the balance of the competition in your particular locale is part of what sets the limits on your agricultural productivity – unless you bring water in from elsewhere via long irrigation canals.

But it's worse than that. As beautiful a process as photosynthesis is, it is shockingly inefficient, as shown in Figure 3.5, which is itself a kind of production function. The photosynthetic response to sunlight exhibits diminishing returns, and even at its peak the response uses only about 2 percent of incident solar radiation (a typical result for C_3 plants; C_4 plants do better, but still reach efficiencies of only 3 or 4 percent). Thus, green plants, including crop plants, squander almost all the solar energy that strikes them. Sharply declining marginal productivity is built into the plant's very chloroplasts, the tiny intra-cellular organelles where photosynthesis takes place. You can increase the other inputs (CO_2 and H_2O) all you want, but you still cannot achieve a limitless increase in the rate of photosynthesis from a fixed area of leaf surface.

If the photosynthetic efficiency of a given area of leaf surface is so low, shouldn't plants evolve large leaves to intercept more sunlight and to hold more chloroplasts? Shouldn't farmers artificially select for big leaves? The problem with that solution, illustrated by the production functions in Figure 3.6, is obvious: the larger a plant's leaves (relative to its overall size) and the more sunlight each one can potentially intercept, the more likely they are to shade out lower-lying leaves, either their own or those of other crops in the same field. Grassy crop species, such as wheat, have long, thin leaves arrayed so that neighboring leaves alternate from side to side to minimize self-shading, but even grass leaves cast shadows. Crop plants that have opted for the

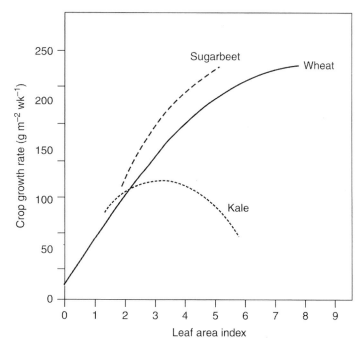

Figure 3.6 Growth rate of three crop species as a function of each species' leaf area index (LAI). The LAI is the ratio of the total upper leaf surface area of an individual plant to the surface area of the small patch of ground on which it grows. From Sinclair and Gardner (1998: 65), by permission of CAB International.

strategy of large leaves, for instance kale, actually suffer negative marginal productivity as their leaf area increases (Figure 3.6). Thus, we have another unavoidable trade-off: the more leaf area to capture sunlight, the more shading to prevent the capture of sunlight. An individual plant may delight in its big leaves, caring not a whit if it interferes with its neighbors. But the farmer needs to care about the yield of the whole field, not any one plant in isolation, and so artificial selection must often counteract natural selection for increased leaf area.[9] This, incidentally, illustrates a general principle: domesticated plants are artificially selected to be less "anti-social" than their wild counterparts (Gepts, 2004).

A similar relationship links crop yield with sowing density, or the number of seeds sown and allowed to germinate per square meter of cultivated land. As shown by the production functions in Figure 3.7, the intense competition among densely sown plants sharply limits the total yield that can be achieved. In part this competition has to do with shading, but it is also a matter of competition among root systems for water and nutrients. You don't get a lot more food by sowing a lot more seed. On the other hand, you may get a lot less food by sowing a lot less seed. The right balance needs to be found.

---

[9] Large-leafed crops such as aroids (*Colocasia* or *Xanthosoma* spp.) often have their leaves on a single level and arranged radially to minimize self-shading. They still have to be planted a meter or two apart.

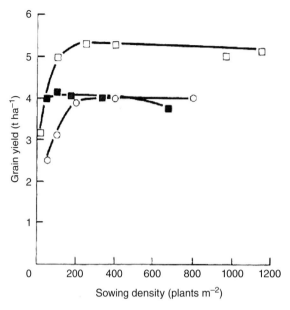

Figure 3.7 Sowing density and grain yield in barley (■, □) and wheat (○). From Evans (1993: 181), by permission of Cambridge University Press.

As already noted, water is necessary for photosynthesis but it is also important for the transport of materials within the plant and to prevent wilting, which greatly reduces the area of leaf exposed to sunlight. Plants continually lose water through transpiration, the "pump" driving fluid transport, and, unless they have an array of specialized devices to protect against desiccation, crop plants are always more or less vulnerable to water stress. But there is such a thing as too much water, even in as water-loving a crop as irrigated rice (Figure 3.8). Simultaneous application of fertilizer can boost overall yield, but note that all three production functions in Figure 3.8 start exhibiting declining marginal productivity at about the same intensity of irrigation. Since the roots and lower stems of wet rice cannot absorb the oxygen needed for respiration from water, it is vital that the water level not cover any of the aerial leaves or the panicle of the plant.

In our Scottish example, we emphasized the critical role of fertilizer (muck) in allowing permanent cultivation. Application of organic fertilizers – dung or green manures – is widespread in traditional farming, especially of the more intensive kind. But increasing the application of fertilizer cannot push up yields indefinitely. Although it involves an inorganic commercial fertilizer, Figure 3.9 shows the typical pattern of declining marginal productivity associated with the application of most fertilizers, including organic ones. With some fertilizers, most notably nitrogen, an excess can even damage plant tissues and lead to negative marginal productivity. Figure 3.10 makes an interesting point in this connection. Traditional landraces of rice and wheat seem liable to damage at levels of nitrogen application that a modern farmer would consider moderate or even modest, but new commercial varieties of the same crops have been bred specifically not only to tolerate, but to thrive under high

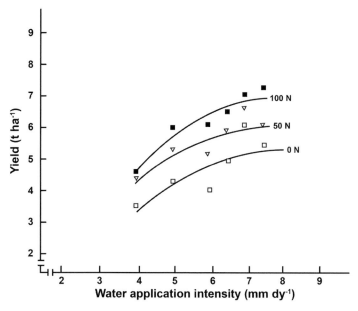

Figure 3.8 Irrigation intensity and rice yields in the Philippines at three levels of inorganic nitrogen fertilization. From Reyes (1973: 50), by permission of the International Rice Research Institute.

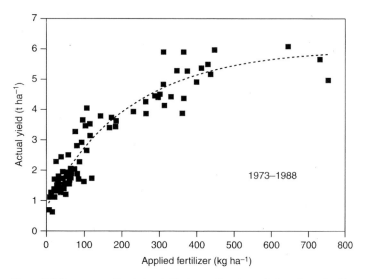

Figure 3.9 Response of potato yields to application of phosphate fertilizer. From Payton *et al.* (1989), by permission of The Alliance Crop, Soil, and Environmental Science Societies.

doses of inorganic nitrogen. A farmer possessing a good supply of nitrogenous fertilizer might well be tempted to abandon the old landraces and adopt new nitrogen-tolerant varieties. But – and it is an important but – even the new varieties eventually exhibit declining marginal productivity as more and more nitrogen is applied, albeit at much higher yields than the traditional landraces. Figure 3.10

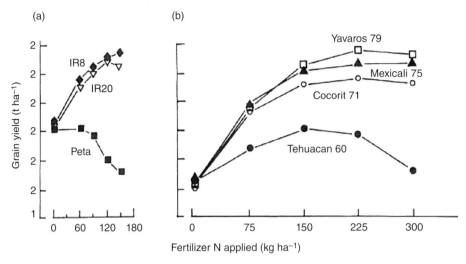

Figure 3.10 Grain yield as a function of inorganic nitrogen (N) applied to old landraces (Peta, Tehuacan) and new "Green Revolution" varieties of (left) rice in the Philippines and (right) durum wheat in Mexico. From Evans (1993: 326), by permission of Cambridge University Press.

illustrates a principle of fundamental importance for understanding innovation in traditional farming: the farmer may be able to increase crop yields in the short term by adopting new practices or new genetic resources, but cannot escape *eventual* declines in marginal productivity. The ultimate limits are still built into the biology.

At the risk of trying the reader's patience, I want to examine one more set of production functions for nitrogenous fertilizers in order to illustrate two more dimensions of the problem. Figure 3.11 graphs both the mean and the inter-plot standard deviation of barley yields according to how much inorganic nitrogen is applied, both with and without simultaneous application of a commercial fungicide. The first important lesson is one frequently observed in agricultural experiments: as average yield rises, so does the year-to-year or plot-to-plot variability of yields, as indicated by the standard deviation. This scaling phenomenon reflects a simple arithmetic fact: if you increase each data point by a constant, you increase the standard deviation by the same constant. The bigger the quantity, so to speak, the more "room" it has to fluctuate. This effect should be kept in mind when thinking about the consequences of agricultural intensification – increasing average crop yields may simultaneously *reduce* the predictability of the yields. The second lesson of Figure 3.11 is about how factors of production can interact. With the application of fungicide, the production function for barley against nitrogen reaches a plateau like Curve B in Figure 3.3. But if fungicide is omitted, the production function drops, displaying negative marginal productivity like Curve C in Figure 3.3. Why? Parasitic fungi need nitrogen just as much as the plants they parasitize. By applying nitrogen without fungicide, we are encouraging the growth of fungal species that feed on crop plants; eventually we reach a point at which we are helping the parasites more than

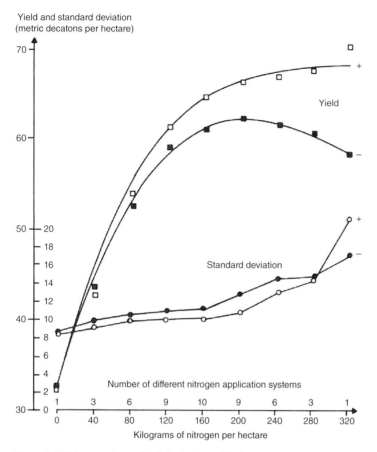

Figure 3.11 Mean and standard deviation of barley yields as a function of inorganic nitrogen application, with (+) or without (–) fungicide treatment. The standard deviation is given by the inner scale on the y-axis. From Hanus and Schoop (1989), by permission of the Johns Hopkins University Press.

we are the crops. The biologically ineluctable outcome is negative declining marginal productivity of crop yield.

I trust that these experimental results, chosen from thousands of possible examples in the agronomic literature, are sufficient to show fairly convincingly that the "laws" of diminishing returns and declining marginal productivity are indeed rather law-like when it comes to agricultural production. Malthus (1803: 11) was apparently right to think that Curve A in Figure 3.3 was "probably a greater increase than could with reason be expected" from the farming of his day and of earlier ages – and perhaps, in the long-run, even of today.

But we have still to consider one particular factor of production that is of special significance to the population/agriculture debate: human labor. As suggested in the previous chapter, human farm work is one of the principal factors linking preindustrial farming to demographic processes. It is, therefore, important to ask whether human labor inputs exhibit declining marginal productivity on preindustrial farms.

According to older data collated by Clark and Haswell (1967) and shown in Figure 3.12, it would seem so. Now it is important to note that these data do not come from formal experiments or even tightly controlled nonexperimental studies. In no case are we looking at a single farm as it increases its input of labor; instead we are examining many different farms within a larger region (e.g. northern Greece) with farming practices that are broadly similar but not necessarily identical. For these reasons, the ecological fallacy is a real risk. On the other hand, all these examples are drawn from what can legitimately be called traditional, nonmechanized farming (if sometimes done for commercial purposes). And in almost every case, the marginal productivity of labor consistently seems to decline. The one partial exception is from Gambia, where the marginal yield increases at lower labor inputs and declines only at somewhat higher inputs (the corresponding production function would be S-shaped; I leave it as an exercise for the reader to figure out why). It would be wonderful if these results were tested on experimental plots that mimic traditional farming. But for now this is the best we can do, and the data do show a consistent pattern of declining marginal productivity and thus diminishing returns as farmers work harder.

The response of yields to increasing labor inputs provides a good illustration of how diminishing returns act to limit the food supply, the ability to support population growth and the scope for agricultural intensification – i.e. an increase in yield achieved by increasing one or more nonland inputs, including labor. Consider the hypothetical examples shown in Figure 3.13, which measure work and yield in the same energetic units. In the left-hand panel (A), an increase in work effort from point 1 to point 2 results in an appreciable increase in the amount of food produced; thus, the additional expenditure of energy in food production (ΔX_{12}) is substantially though not fully repaid by the resulting increase in yield (ΔY_{12}).[10] But *precisely the same* increase in work from point 2 to point 3 results in very little increase in yield (ΔY_{23}). Since $\Delta Y_{23} << \Delta X_{23}$, the additional investment in work actually entails a large net loss of energy. It may be useful to increase your work load at lower labor inputs, but a waste of time and energy at higher ones. If your farm is already operating near point 3, you cannot add workers to your household and expect to feed them. That's the bad news. The good news is that, after a certain point, laziness becomes an economic virtue: there is no point expending more human energy on a subsistence farm if you cannot squeeze out enough extra food to repay it.

The right-hand panel of Figure 3.13 (B) makes a different point. Now labor inputs are broken down into two separate tasks: labor involved in irrigating crops versus labor involved in plowing fields. At low labor inputs, an increase in the frequency of plowing (say from no plowing to plowing once) is handsomely rewarded, more so than a low-labor investment in irrigation (point 1). But plowing more than once (cross-plowing) may add little to the yield. If, however, the same energy required by cross-plowing

---

[10] With steadily ("monotonically") declining marginal productivity, *no* increase in labor investment can completely repay itself in purely energetic terms. For an increase in labor to be worthwhile, either there must be other, nonenergetic pay-offs, or the production function must have a more complicated shape (e.g. the S-shaped curve implied for Gambia).

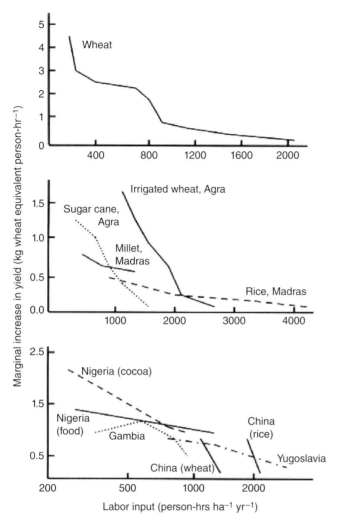

Figure 3.12 Declining marginal returns on labor in traditional farming. From Clark and Haswell (1967: 94, 99, 160), by permission of Routledge and Kegan Paul Publishers.

were put into work on the irrigation system instead (point 2), food yield could still be boosted, perhaps by enough to offset the added energy costs. Increasing labor inputs to point 3, on the other hand, gains you very little if anything, no matter which way you invest the effort. Thus, increased workloads, which Boserup (1965) considered an ever-present feature of agricultural intensification (see Chapter 5), may or may not actually intensify agricultural production depending on where you are on the production function and what kind of extra work you perform.

The yields in Figures 3.12 and 3.13, real and imaginary, are plotted as functions of labor input *per hectare*. You might think that one surefire way to increase your farm's *total* yield is to increase the number of hectares you're farming – that is, get a bigger farm. As it turns out, that strategy cannot work without limit under nonmechanized

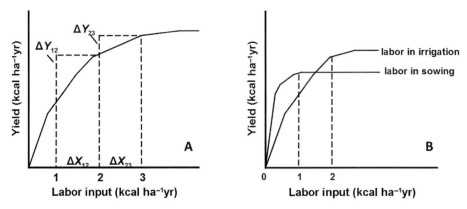

Figure 3.13 The production functions linking farm work and crop yields. All display declining marginal productivity of the sort suggested by Figure 3.12. Panel A, the production function for human labor of all types; panel B, production functions for two specific tasks. See text for details.

family farming. Figure 3.14 shows yield per hectare as a function of farm size from 34 smallholdings in Tanzania – and lo and behold it shows declining marginal productivity. There are two good reasons to think this finding ought to be common under traditional farming. First, more land requires more people to work it, and household-based farms have very limited numbers of laborers. Second, as the area of the farm increases, the energy needed to move around the farm increases. Following von Thünen, there ought to be an upper limit to farm size where haulage costs become prohibitive. As suggested by Figure 3.14, cattle help in both regards (quite aside from their generous bestowal of dung): if they pull a plow, they increase the amount of land one person can cultivate in a day; if they pull a cart or a wagon, they reduce human transport costs. But still it is remarkable how quickly diminishing returns from expanded farm size come into play in Figure 3.14, even with cattle to help out.

In sum, many forces inherent in traditional farming ultimately limit food production by deflecting the production function downward, either toward a plateau or toward an actual reduction in yield. Modern farmers can overcome these limits, but only temporarily (diminishing returns still kick in over the long run) and only at the cost of enormous expenditures of energy, mainly in the form of fossil fuels, including the energy consumed by the industrial operations needed to manufacture modern farm supplies and equipment. Traditional farmers cannot hope to marshal anything like the energy consumed as a matter of routine by modern farmers. On the other hand, traditional farmers do tend to use their meager energy supplies with great efficiency (see Table 1.1). Indeed, they cannot afford to do otherwise.

Traditional Farming and Environmental Degradation

If an agricultural production function shows negative marginal productivity (curve C in Figure 3.3), then it must be the case that the input of interest ultimately damages the plant itself *or* its environment, either its immediate environment in the field or the wider environment of the whole farm. In theory, then, any environmental

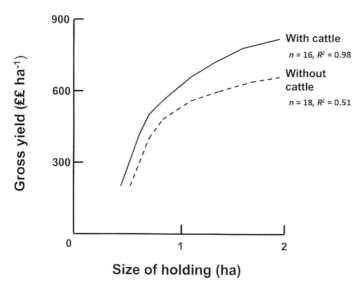

Figure 3.14 Agricultural yields (in Tanzanian pound-equivalents) versus size of farm, Bukoba, Tanzania, 1964–5. Note that cattle were kept mainly for manure and traction, not milk or meat. Redrawn from Friedrich (1968: 204).

damage associated with farming can further reduce the effective availability of food. As noted in Chapter 1, it is an article of faith these days among many agronomists that traditional farming is much more protective of the environment than is modern farming (see, e.g., Altieri, 1990; Reij *et al.*, 1996; Gliessman, 2007; Scheer and McNeely, 2007) – but it is little more than an article of faith. As I argued in the first chapter, traditional farmers differ from their modern counterparts not so much in their tenderness toward nature as in their sheer physical inability to cause environmental damage on a grand scale. But all farming, by its nature, inflicts ecological disturbance on the local environment (no field or garden has ever sprung up spontaneously) and creates an ecological disequilibrium that may be transitory (as under shifting cultivation) or long-lived (as under permanent cultivation – in which case the disequilibrium needs to be renewed on a regular basis). Farmers divert plant tissue that would otherwise nourish the land into their haystacks, their granaries, their bellies and the bellies of their animals. By sowing a range of species that is almost always much narrower than the natural vegetation that would have grown up in the farm's absence, farmers are apt to deplete whatever soil nutrients happen to be used heavily by their particular crops. In addition, clearing and tillage are themselves a kind of environmental damage.

The question is not whether environmental degradation occurs under traditional farming – it most certainly does – but whether processes of regeneration, natural or human, can keep up with it. As Blaikie and Brookfield (1987: 7) expressed it,

net environmental degradation =
(natural degradation + human damage) − (natural regeneration+

restorative management).

Table 3.6 A classification of environmental degradation often associated with traditional farming.

Soil properties	Erosional losses
Chemical changes	Raindrop
nitrogen (N)	Sheet
phosphorus (P)	Gully
potassium (K)	Mass movement (landslips, landslides)
other macro- and micronutrients	
(sulfur, calcium, magnesium,	Vegetational changes
copper, etc.)	
pH	Deforestation
organic material	Desertification
accumulation of iron oxides (ferrisols)	Establishment of disclimax vegetation
salinization	Invasion by weedy or non-native species
Structural changes	
distribution of particle size (sand vs.	Changes in water supply
silt vs. clay)	
crumb structure	Microbial contamination
porosity and aeration	Eutrophication
compaction and pan formation	Changes in level of water table
puddling and waterlogging	Salinization
Biological changes	Changes in pH
damage to soil micro- and macro	
flora/fauna	

At any one time, the condition of the land is a dynamic (and readily changeable) equilibrium among these forces (see Dejene *et al.*, 1997). Although traditional farmers have devised countless ways to ameliorate environmental degradation, there is no doubt that such farmers are capable of damaging the environment, at least locally, and sometimes incapable of putting things right again. Table 3.6 lists the main kinds of environmental damage that have been observed in association with traditional farming in various parts of the world (for reviews, see Blaikie and Brookfield, 1987; Simmons, 1987; Redman, 1999; Montgomery, 2007; Millington and Jepson, 2008). Of these forms of damage, soil loss through erosion has undoubtedly been the most common, as evidenced by numerous archaeological and paleoenvironmental studies of increased sedimentation rates under prehistoric farming (e.g. Brown and Barber, 1985; Dearing *et al.*, 1987; Hughes *et al.*, 1991; O'Hara *et al.*, 1993; McAuliffe *et al.*, 2001; Heine, 2003; Lang, 2003; Mäckel *et al.*, 2003; Zolitschka *et al.*, 2003; Fuchs *et al.*, 2004; Beach *et al.*, 2006). A couple of examples of erosional damage culled from the ethnographic literature will drive the point home.

Figure 3.15 shows some extreme environmental effects of farming in the Upper Chimbu Valley of highland Papua New Guinea, including disclimax vegetation (left) and massive gully erosion (right). This sort of damage is known to have predated contact with the outside world in the 1930s (Brookfield and Brown, 1963; Smith, 1977; Allen and Crittenden, 1987). The Chimbu are medium-intensity farmers,

Figure 3.15 Environmental damage from medium-intensity traditional farming at an elevation of about 2800–3200 m msl (mean sea level), Upper Chimbu Valley, Papua New Guinea. (Left) Disclimax mosaic of imperata grass and tree ferns. (Right) Severe gully erosion. From J. M. B. Smith (1977: 194, 200), by permission of Academic Press.

combining long-fallow shifting cultivation with semipermanent fields where mounding and ditching are practiced – and apparently have been for many centuries (Golson, 2007). The photographs were taken at elevations, about 2800–3200 m, that are at the upper reaches of the Chimbu's territory, but significant environmental change has been thoroughly documented at lower, more typical farming altitudes as well (Brookfield and Brown, 1963, provide numerous photographs and descriptions). The Chimbu population appears to have been growing slowly during the late pre-contact and early postcontact periods.

Another example from Papua New Guinea, one whose demography has been studied in detail (Wood, 1980, 1987; Wood and Smouse, 1982; Wood et al., 1985a, b,c), concerns the Gainj of the Upper Takwi Valley, on the northern fringes of the central highlands. The Gainj are long-fallow shifting cultivators. Their crude population density at the time of study was about 24 km^{-2}, and several lines of evidence suggest that their growth rate had long been close to zero (Wood, 1980). And yet their environment was still a complex mosaic of small stands of natural rainforest and much larger areas of anthropogenic vegetation such as secondary forest, tree ferns, fallow and grassland (Figure 3.16). The widespread landscape changes associated with shifting cultivation in the Gainj area partly reflect the extreme slopes they are forced to cultivate because almost nothing else is available (Figure 3.17). In this land of high rainfall, saturated soils, steep slopes and frequent earthquakes, mass erosional movements such as landslips are common on cleared fields, and the Gainj are powerless to prevent them (an incipient landslip is visible in Figure 3.17).

I am not claiming that either of these examples is at all representative, only that net environmental degradation *can* occur under traditional farming (Blaikie and Brookfield, 1987; Simmons, 1987; Redman, 1999). Much of it is, of course, far more subtle than that illustrated here (see, for example, Freedman, 1955; Marten and

Figure 3.16 A mosaic of anthropogenic and natural vegetation zones, Upper Takwi Valley, Papua New Guinea. The valley is farmed by Gainj shifting cultivators living at a crude population density of about 24 km^{-2}. The Gainj would normally be classified as low-intensity farmers since they cultivate a typical plot of land for one to two years and then leave it fallow for (as near as we can estimate) something like 20 to 25 years. (Author's photograph.)

Vityakon, 1986; Lawrence and Schlesinger, 2001), but sometimes it is as bad or worse (Hack, 1942; Bradfield, 1971; Watters, 1971; FAO, 1974; Metzner, 1982).

From the perspective of this book, the more important question is whether such damage is *generally* associated in the preindustrial world with rapid population growth, high population density or intensive farming practices. Our answer to this question must be provisional. There is a huge literature on the subject, but most of the evidence it marshals is anecdotal or circumstantial. Certainly some extreme examples of environmental degradation are found in areas that once supported large, state-organized populations – one thinks of deforestation, desertification and salinization in Mesopotamia – but correlation, as the mantra goes, does not prove causation. Comparative analyses are difficult to interpret because of the possibility of the ecological fallacy and because many published assessments of environmental degradation are qualitative and subjective. The comparisons shown in Figure 3.18 reduce, but certainly do not eliminate, the possibility of committing the ecological fallacy by restricting attention to a single (if enormous) part of the world, sub-Saharan Africa; they are also based on quantitative measurement of one particular environmental variable, soil nitrogen balance (see Drechsel and Pennin de Vries, 2001, for technical details). From cross-national data (Figure 3.18A), there seems to be a fairly strong negative linear relationship between nitrogen balance and the crude density of each country's rural population.[11] On a more local scale and controlling for land quality (Figure 3.18B), there appears to be a curvilinear but positive relationship between nitrogen balance

[11] Crude population density in this instance is the ratio of each nation's rural population (whether involved in farming or not) to its total nonurban land area.

Figure 3.17 A newly planted Gainj garden on an extreme slope. Note the fissure opening up just inside the upper line of fencing (arrows), indicating an incipient landslip. About a week after this photograph was taken, the entire garden was piled up at the bottom of the slope. (Author's photograph.)

and percentage of arable land under fallow at the time of study – which suggests a negative relationship between nitrogen balance and at least one dimension of agricultural intensity. And, finally, Figure 3.18C suggests a nonlinear relationship between nitrogen balance and the area of potentially cultivable land per capita – although the relationship is flat over a wide range of per capita land areas and nitrogen depletion seems to occur only at the lower extremes. Unfortunately, none of these comparisons controls for the application of commercial, inorganic nitrogen. Nonetheless, despite the paucity of well-designed empirical studies of the subject, the huge anecdotal literature does, to my mind, add up to a reasonably compelling *prima facie* case that there is likely to be a relationship between environmental degradation and either demographic or agricultural variables under traditional farming. The relationship may sometimes be weak and obscured by a fog of confounding variables, but I am fairly convinced that it exists and is potentially important.

Conclusion

Even if the concept of carrying capacity is too problematic to be useful, several strands of evidence support our intuition that limits to population growth must exist under traditional farming. The same evidence, however, suggests that those limits are

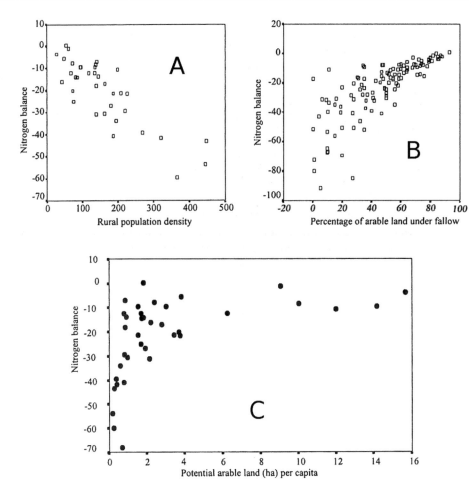

Figure 3.18 Soil nitrogen (N) balance in relation to demographic and agricultural variables, sub-Saharan Africa. Panel A shows N balance (kg ha^{-1} yr^{-1}) against rural population density (persons km^{-2}), 36 nations. Panel B shows N balance (kg ha^{-1} yr^{-1}) against percent of arable land under fallow in any year, 115 FAO land-class categories. Panel C shows N depletion (kg ha^{-1}) against potential arable land per capita of rural population, 37 nations. From Drechsel and Pennin de Vries (2001: 59–61), by permission of Scientific Publishers, Inc.

malleable and depend in part on the behavior of the farmers themselves. Thinking of the limits in terms of agricultural production functions is, I would argue, helpful in several ways. First, it implies that the limits are multidimensional and related to a variety of *specific* farming practices. Second, it suggests that the limits are unlikely to involve sharp threshold effects but rather more gradual, continuous deterioration in the population's per capita food supply, nutritional status and environmental conditions – and ultimately, as discussed in the following chapter, in its mortality, fertility and migration rates. Third, and perhaps most profoundly, it relates farming behavior to the status of the population *this year* rather than in some abstract "perpetuity." The declining marginal productivity of human labor in farming is of particular significance from a demographic point of view, at least for communities in which the large majority of households are involved in farming, for it limits the extent to which the environment and prevailing land-use practices can absorb more people. If farmers increase one or more inputs into the production system in an attempt to increase yields and thereby support more people, the attempt is unlikely to succeed indefinitely and may even result in significant net environmental degradation – even if such degradation is a more gradual and continuous process than implied by the concept of carrying capacity.

In Chapter 2, I argued that subsistence farmers are efficient at investing their resources in food production. In view of the ubiquity of diminishing returns, one important aspect of prudent investment is not to *over*-invest resources past the critical point of declining marginal productivity. Even if, for some reason, you want to produce a huge surplus of food, the production function won't necessarily let you, and you'll only end up wasting resources (including, in all likelihood, your own energetically valuable labor). In later chapters, I will argue that it is especially helpful to think of these limits on production as operating primarily at the level of the individual farming household. In the next chapter, however, I will spend some time examining the effects of the relevant limits at the aggregate, macrodemographic level.

Part II

Macrodemographic Approaches to Population and Subsistence Farming

4   A Modicum of Demography

Our central thesis is that population growth rate is the unifying variable linking the various facets of population ecology; thus analyses of population regulation, density dependence, resource and interference competition and the effects of environmental stress are all best undertaken with population growth rate as the response variable.   – R. M. Sibly and J. Hone
(2003: 40)

To the woman he said:
    'I shall give you great pain in childbearing;
    with suffering shall you bring forth children.
    . . .'
And to the man he said:
    '. . .Curséd is the ground on your account;
    in sorrow will you eat of it all the days of your life.
    It will bring forth thorns and thistles,
    though you would reap its grain.
    Only by the sweat of your face shall you eat bread
    until you return to the earth:
    for from it you were taken.
    Dirt you are, and unto dirt shall you return.'
    – *Genesis* 3: 16–19 (free translation, final redaction *c.* BC 450–500)

In Chapter 1, I made the point that very few participants in the debate over population and agriculture have provided any detailed consideration of the actual demographic processes underlying changes in population and have therefore failed to link those processes to the fruits, demands and limitations of agricultural production. To correct for what I regard as a fundamental omission, I want to use this chapter to lay out some of the basic facts of demography – using "facts" in the sense proposed in a classic paper by the preeminent demographer Nathan Keyfitz (1975). Keyfitz suggested that few of the most firmly established facts of demography are based on observations alone – reality is far too messy for that. Instead, it is the interplay of theoretical models and observations that underpins what we know about population – and sometimes it is theory alone that provides the most reliable pointers to the nature of reality. As Keyfitz famously put it, "no model, no understanding" – perhaps the most fundamental of all the facts of demography.

This chapter will provide several illustrations of Keyfitz's dictum. My presentation will be extremely narrow, focused on a few simple ideas and findings that are important for subsequent chapters. I shall focus on *bio*demography (the biological factors underlying population processes), which means that I will scarcely touch upon the vast literature on demography as a *social* science. Much of the presentation will be devoted to examining the relationship between demography and food supply, a subject necessarily at the core of any debate over population and agriculture (see Chapter 8 for more details about this relationship). Following up on Chapter 3, I shall be especially concerned to relate preindustrial agricultural production functions, with their built-in diminishing returns, to limits on population growth. Broader treatments of demographic methods and data are provided by Hinde (1998) and Preston *et al.* (2000); an encyclopedic overview can be found in Siegel and Swanson (2004).[1]

The Fundamental Forces of Population Change

We begin by identifying the basic, most immediate causes of changes in overall population size. These can be summarized in a simple algebraic expression:

$$N_{t+1}=N_t+B_t-D_t+I_t-O_t, \tag{4.1}$$

where

N_t = the size of the population *at the beginning* of year t

N_{t+1} = the size of the population exactly one year later, i.e. *at the beginning* of year $t +$ 1

B_t = the number of births that occur in the population *during* year t

D_t = the number of deaths that occur *during* year t

I_t = the number of "in-migration events" that occur *during* year t, i.e. the number of people who move into the population from the outside

O_t = the number of "out-migration events," people leaving the population to live outside it, in year t.

Equation (4.1) is sometimes called the fundamental law of population change. What it says is quite simple: the population next year is equal in size to the population this year *plus* the gains (newborns and in-migrants) during the intervening 12 months *minus* the losses (the deceased and out-migrants) during the same interval. This equation has to be true: there is no other way to get into or out of a population with a well-defined (if arbitrary) boundary. In other words, the only processes that can change the size of a well-defined population are fertility, mortality and migration, an inescapable fact that narrows the scope of our enquiry enormously. Mind you, we

---

[1] I gloss over one basic but unfortunate fact of demography: a "population" can never be defined without a degree of arbitrariness. The problem of defining a population is partly a matter of scale (one study's population may be another study's subpopulation or larger regional context) and partly a matter of boundedness (and no human populations, even remote island populations, are entirely isolated). In anthropology, populations usually correspond to topographic units (e.g. a valley), settlement units (a village), or linguistic units (a small, self-identified language or dialect group). In formal demography they usually correspond to officially bounded groups such as counties, districts or nations. Alas, humans have an unruly habit of ignoring all such boundaries.

still have to think about what determines the numbers of births, deaths and movements into and out of the local population, however defined. In this book we are, of course, concerned primarily with how those numbers are influenced by the food supply in subsistence-oriented farming communities. I return to that topic later in this chapter.

Note that all the quantities in equation (4.1) are expressed in whole numbers – specifically, numbers of individuals and demographic "events" (births, deaths, movements of people into and out of the population). Demographers generally prefer to work with rates instead of whole numbers, because the whole numbers confound the "intensity" of fertility, mortality and migration with whatever size the population happens to be at any one time. To convert the terms in equation (4.1) into rates, we begin by rearranging it as

$$\Delta_t N = N_{t+1} - N_t = B_t - D_t + I_t - O_t, \tag{4.2}$$

where $\Delta_t N$ is the absolute change in population size during year t (note that $\Delta_t N$ will be negative if the population is shrinking or zero if it is not changing in size). To find the *per capita* rate of change in year t, we just divide both sides of equation (4.2) by N_t:

$$\frac{\Delta_t N}{N_t} = \frac{B_t}{N_t} - \frac{D_t}{N_t} + \frac{I_t}{N_t} - \frac{O_t}{N_t}.$$

We can make this ugly expression a bit prettier by rewriting it as

$$r_t = b_t - d_t + i_t - o_t, \tag{4.3}$$

where

$r_t = \Delta_t N/N_t$ = the per capita annual rate of population growth or decline during year t
$b_t = B_t/N_t$ = the per capita annual birth rate during year t
$d_t = D_t/N_t$ = the per capita annual death rate during year t
$i_t = I_t/N_t$ = the per capita annual in-migration rate during year t
$o_t = O_t/N_t$ = the per capita annual out-migration rate during year t.

The rates b_t, d_t, i_t, and o_t are often referred to as *vital rates*.[2] By definition, all vital rates must be greater than or equal to zero, whereas in theory the population growth rate r_t can vary between $-\infty$ and $+\infty$ (although in reality its range of variation is quite narrow). If $r_t > 0$, then the population grows during year t, if $r_t < 0$ it declines, and if $r_t = 0$ then it remains exactly the same from the beginning of year t to that of year $t + 1$. But there is nothing in equation (4.3) that tells us what the value of r_t is likely to be if we don't already know something about the rates on the right-hand side of the equation or about N_t and N_{t+1}.

---

[2] Formal demographers will complain that I have used the population at the beginning of the year, N_t, instead of the mid-year population, which is approximately $\frac{1}{2}(N_t + N_{t+1})$, as the denominator for my vital rates. In fact, I am about to perform a mathematical trick that will make this problem vanish.

The vital rates b_t, d_t, i_t and o_t are often called *crude* rates because they provide a crude or inexact specification of the actual individuals in the population who are "exposed to the risk" of experiencing the demographic event under consideration. This is because their computation involves the whole, undifferentiated population. In the case of b_t, for example, we divide the total number of births in the population as a whole by the total number of people in the population as a whole – as if two-year-old boys (for example) and married women between 20 and 25 years of age were equally "at risk" of producing a newborn baby sometime during the year. Standard demography texts (e.g. Preston *et al.*, 2000) quite rightly devote a lot of attention to the computation of age- and sex-specific rates for which the population at risk is defined more narrowly and appropriately.[3] For the purpose of examining overall population growth, however, crude rates are good enough.

Equation (4.1) was true by necessity. All subsequent manipulations of it were either true by definition or the result of incontestable algebra. So, by extension, equation (4.3) is also true. But what does equation (4.3) imply about any particular pattern of population growth or decline such as we might observe in the real world? Absolutely nothing, precisely because it *is* always true. That is, equation (4.3) is compatible with every possible pattern of change in population size – we just have to plug in the right values of b_t, d_t, i_t and o_t. To make more interesting use of the model, we need to make some assumptions about how our vital rates behave.

The Exponential Growth Model

For example, let's assume that our birth, death and migration rates are eternally fixed and unchanging – which immediately implies that r_t is fixed and unchanging. If this assumption were correct, we would be dealing with completely unrestricted, limitless population growth. I hasten to add that I am not arguing that this is a *realistic* assumption about population growth – Chapter 3 amounts to an extended argument that it is not. But it is one that allows us to explore the *implications* of unlimited growth (or decline) *if such were to exist.* (Think of von Thünen's isotropic plain.) Under the assumption of fixed rates, it is pointless to index any particular rate in equation (4.3) with a subscript t since its value is always the same no matter what year we are referring to. Thus we can write equation (4.3) as

$$r = b - d + i - o. \tag{4.4}$$

Now permit me to perform a trick that is likely to seem magical to anyone who does not know elementary calculus. To this point we have thought about changes to population size and numbers of vital events occurring over a complete year – time is, in effect, discontinuous and jumps in one-year increments. But what if we want to model population change over a month – or even a day or indeed a fraction of a

---

[3] For age-specific fertility rates, see Wood (1994a). Comparative data on age-specific mortality are presented in Chapter 8, illustrating just how much difference age can make in explaining variation in the risk of death. The same, of course, could be said of fertility and migration.

second? Then we need to let the time interval in equation (4.4) get smaller and smaller. But if we can examine, say, a half-second, why not a nano-second or even a pico-second? Using calculus we can allow the time interval to approach zero, i.e. allow time to change instantaneously and continuously, so that all the rates in equation (4.4) become *instantaneous* rates. For example, r becomes the instantaneous rate of population growth. I do this trick partly to solve the "population at risk" problem mentioned in footnote 2 of this chapter but also, I have to admit, to make the next few equations more elegant looking and easier to calculate. The math involved in the trick is bog standard.

Next, let me pose the following question. If you know how big the village you live in is today and how rapidly it is currently growing, then how big will it be in t years *if* it continues to grow at its current rate? (Again, I am not claiming that it *will* continue to grow at its current rate, but only asking what would happen if it *did* grow at that rate.) We are talking about a period of time that begins now and lasts exactly t years.[4] Accordingly, let us call the current population size N_0 (since today is the zero point of an interval lasting t years) and its size in t years N_t, consistent with the notation we have been using up to this point. A bit of boring calculus tells us that, under our assumptions of continuous time and a constant growth rate r,

$$N_t = N_0 e^{rt}, \tag{4.5}$$

where e is a numerical constant that happens to equal something like 2.718282...To return to our question, suppose your village is today a bosky haven of 100 souls that is growing at an annual rate of 0.025, a figure within the known range of human population growth rates. How big will it be in, say, a decade if it continues to grow at that rate? To find the answer we substitute 100 for N_0 (the initial village size), 0.025 for r, and 10 for t, and solve for N_t:

$$N_{10} = 100 e^{0.025 \times 10} = 100 e^{0.25} = 100 \times 1.2840254 = 128 \text{ approximately.}$$

So over the next decade your village would have grown by something like a quarter to a third if the current growth rate persists. That may not be enough to alarm your local council's planning committee, but remember that, under our assumption of constant growth, your village will continue to expand at an annual rate of 0.025 forever. In 20 years it would be 165, in 50 years 349, and in 100 years 1218, a community large enough to require all sorts of additional services. Figure 4.1 graphs the growth of your village over a century. Even though the growth rate is constant, the absolute increment in village size per year gets bigger and bigger over time because the population exposed to the growth rate is itself getting bigger and bigger. By the end of the century the village seems to be galloping headlong for infinity, and it will keep galloping faster and faster without end. This sort of *exponential growth curve* is, in fact, the universal outcome of constant population growth whenever $r >$ 0. This in itself was an important discovery since, before Malthus introduced

---

[4] Note that, even though time is changing continuously, we still have to specify the unit in which we are measuring it.

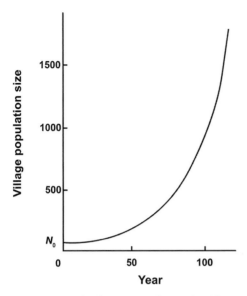

Figure 4.1 Graph of exponential growth with $r = 0.025$ and $N_0 = 100$.

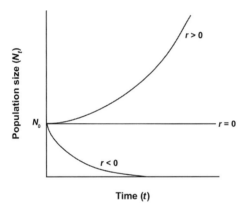

Figure 4.2 General behavior of the exponential model depending upon the value of r.

equation (4.5) – or rather its equivalent in noncontinuous time, the geometric growth model – to population science, many writers assumed that constant positive growth would produce a linear increase in population size.

Equation (4.5) is known as the *exponential model of population growth*, and it is arguably the starting point for all theoretical demography. Its precise behavior depends upon the exact value of r, but it can be summarized by the simple graph in Figure 4.2. If r is positive, then given enough time the population will explode; if it is negative, the population will go extinct.[5] Only if r is exactly zero will one or the

---

[5] More precisely it will approach zero asymptotically – i.e. it will get closer and closer to zero without ever arriving there. But in short order the population's size will become less than one person, at which point we can consider it extinct for all practical purposes.

Table 4.1 Population doubling time (τ) as a function of the annual population growth rate (r) under the exponential growth model. Only nonnegative growth rates spanning the range observed in human populations are shown.

r	τ (years)
0	∞
0.001	693
0.005	139
0.010	69
0.020	35
0.030	23

other of these fates be avoided. What does it imply to say that r equals zero? Glancing back at equation (4.4), it is obvious that r will equal zero only if the rate at which people are lost from the population ($d + o$) is exactly offset by the rate of gain ($b + i$). If the population is closed to migration – no one moves in or out – then $r = 0$ means that $b = d$, i.e. births and deaths exactly balance. But it is important to reiterate that there is nothing in the exponential model itself to cause us to believe that zero is a more likely value for r than any other.

If r is greater than zero, population size can grow quite rapidly under exponential growth. This is perhaps most easily seen by using equation (4.5) to answer the *doubling-time question*: how long does it take a population growing at positive rate r to double in size? In other words, at what value of t does $N_t = 2N_0$? Using the Greek letter τ to denote the doubling-time in years, we can write

$$2N_0 = N_0 e^{r\tau}.$$

Dividing both sides by N_0,

$$2 = e^{r\tau} \quad \text{which means} \quad \ln 2 = r\tau,$$

where ln denotes the "natural" logarithm or the logarithm to base e. Now ln 2 is just a number, and it happens to equal about 0.69315. Thus, if we know r, the doubling-time can always be found by solving

$$\tau = \frac{0.69315}{r} \quad \text{for } r > 0.$$

The right-hand side of this expression involves only one unknown, r. It contains no mention of current or future population size. For a given value of r, then, the doubling-time is always the same, no matter how large or small the population is at the outset (Table 4.1). Your village, incidentally, will double in size once every 27.7 years so long as r remains 0.025.

There is another interesting historical sidebar here. In his 1798 *Essay on the Principle of Population*, Malthus suggested that, under unusually favorable conditions, human populations could double every 25 years and thus rapidly catch up with any increase in food supply. This suggestion was rejected as an absurd exaggeration by every contemporary author to address the issue. If, however, we rearrange the previous equation and plug in $\tau = 25$, we get an r of 0.028. This value is on the high side of the range for well-studied human populations, but it is by no means the highest ever recorded. In fact, just a few years ago, the entire human species was growing at a rate not far below 0.025 (Cohen, 1995). Clearly Malthus's claim that human populations could double in 25 years – not in the typical case but *under unusually favorable conditions* – was not absurd.

Is the exponential growth model realistic? Not in the literal sense that any real-world population can grow forever without any limits coming into play. Inspired by Malthus, Charles Darwin performed a thought experiment that is pertinent here:

The elephant is reckoned to be the slowest breeder of all known animals [some whales are probably slower], and I have taken some pain to estimate its probable minimum rate of natural increase: it will be under the mark to assume that it breeds when 30 years old, and goes on breeding till ninety years old, bringing forth three pairs of young [three males, three females] in this interval; if this be so, at the end of the fifth century there would be alive fifteen million elephants, descended from the first pair. (Darwin, 1859: 64)

Soon after *The Origin of Species* was first published, William Thomson (Lord Kelvin) pointed out that Darwin had made a mistake in his arithmetic: after 500 years, there would be about 15 thousand elephants, not 15 million. But Darwin's more general point is still valid. In fact, after a little less than 6900 years (115 elephant generations by Darwin's reckoning) we would have 4.9×10^{54} living elephants. Assuming that the average elephant is five cubic meters in volume, then our population would have a total volume of 2.5×10^{55} cubic meters or about 2.3×10^{34} times the volume of the Earth. If our elephants were herded into a compact spherical mass (not a job I would volunteer for), it would have a diameter of 380 light-years and would be expanding at the speed of light. That's a lot of pachyderm flesh.

Darwin's point, of course, was that after a surprisingly short time exponential population growth will lead to numbers that are literally incredible, even if r is small (as long as it is positive). The exponential model is, paradoxically, important and useful precisely because it is, as a description of reality, so obviously wrong. In the long-run, there are *always* limiting factors that impede population growth – an important and incontestable fact of demography.

But can human populations grow exponentially for a shorter time, perhaps a few decades or centuries? Several modelers have pointed that long-term trends in human population growth can be mimicked by a series of exponential models with differing values of r (Lee, 1988; Cohen, 1995; Hanson, 2000), suggesting that human groups always grow exponentially but at varying rates, including negative rates. But that is not surprising (or very revealing) since all sorts of complicated trends can be approximated as a "piecewise" exponential model. An interesting but ultimately not very convincing attempt to characterize long-term patterns of growth based on archaeological evidence was made by Whitmore *et al.* (1993).[6] These authors collated archaeological estimates of

---

[6] This attempt was occasioned by earlier claims that there is an inherent biological tendency for human populations to grow, an assertion made most commonly by archaeologists who viewed population

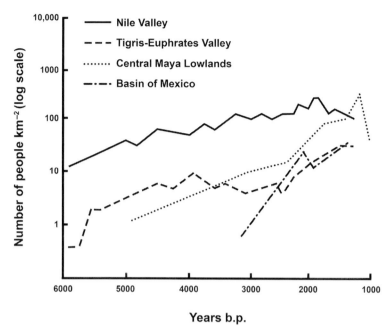

Figure 4.3 Long-term population growth patterns in humans, as reconstructed from archaeological evidence (b.p., before present). The y-axis shows the log of crude population density; since the area for each archaeological region is fixed, density has a one-to-one correspondence with population size. Were the population growing exponentially, log density would change over time as a straight line. Modified from Whitmore *et al.* (1993: 29, 33), by permission of Cambridge University Press.

changing population size over several millennia from four closely studied parts of the world: the Nile Valley in Egypt, the Tigris-Euphrates Valley mostly in Iraq, the Basin of Mexico in that country's central highlands, and the Maya Lowlands of southern Mexico and Central America. Figure 4.3 shows their results – but before we can make sense of them, we need to do a little more algebra. In the figure, population density is plotted on a logarithmic scale. But how does the exponential model behave on a log scale? If we take natural logs of both sides of equation (4.5) we get

$$\ln N_t = \ln (N_0 e^{rt}) = \ln N_0 + \ln (e^{rt}) = \ln N_0 + rt.$$

growth as a "prime mover" of economic and social change (for a review and critique of this idea, see Cowgill, 1975). Some authors falsely ascribed this view to Ester Boserup, who clearly did not believe it (see Chapter 5). When asked why such a biological tendency should exist, the reply was usually something like "natural selection leads to increased fertility and survival and therefore fosters population growth." This claim was refuted years ago when the population geneticist Bruce Wallace introduced the distinction between "hard" and "soft" natural selection (Wallace, 1968). For a clear, up-to-date discussion of this distinction and its relevance to population dynamics, see Saccheri and Hanski (2006). As both theory and experimentation show, it is perfectly possible for natural selection to operate without elevating fertility, reducing mortality or increasing population size.

Since $\ln N_0$ and r are constants, this is a linear equation in t. Thus, if a population is growing or declining exponentially, the log of N_t should follow a straight line, going up or down according to whether r is positive or negative. If we are talking about an area of fixed extent, then the log of population *density* ought to behave similarly. Returning to Figure 4.3, we see that roughly linear increases in density occurred in the Nile Valley right up to the peak population size at c. 2000 years before present (b.p.), from c. 5500–4500 years b.p. and again from c. 2500–1500 years b.p. in the Tigris-Euphrates Valley, c. 500–1200 years b.p. in the Maya lowlands (after which came the "Maya collapse"), and c. 3200–2100 years b.p. in the Basin of Mexico.[7] So, yes, at least to a first approximation, human populations can indeed grow exponentially over finite but fairly long stretches of time.

It would be a mistake, however, to take the patterns in Figure 4.3 as representative of population growth in the human species as a whole. The first question to ask is why these particular areas were chosen for such detailed archaeological scrutiny. The answer, of course, is pyramids – or, more specifically, the fact that all these locations ended up producing conspicuous, archaeologically attractive urban or semiurban architecture, much of it visible above ground even before any excavation took place. In other words, these locations were not randomly selected from all parts of the Earth's surface: they were selected precisely *because* it was already known that large population centers existed there. For example, Hiram Bingham (1948) writes of how he wandered the Peruvian Andes looking for the rare, big and impressive sites and deliberately ignoring countless tiny sites, thereby discovering Machu Picchu. Assuming that large population centers do not drop ready-made from heaven, it is almost necessarily the case that the cultural peaks we are most interested in were the final culmination of a more or less prolonged period of population growth. It would be lovely (from my point of view) if archaeologists chose their sites at random from a vast list of randomly placed points all around the globe, but it would also be idiotic (from the archaeologist's point of view) since a large fraction of those points were probably never inhabited by humans, at least never for long enough or at high enough density to leave clear archaeological traces of their occupation. (Would anyone remember Hiram Bingham today if he only dug at tiny sites or at places where there were no sites at all?) Selectivity bias is built into the archaeological record, and probably always will be.

Some Long-Term Population Growth Patterns, Mostly Not in Humans

So how did preindustrial human populations grow in the long term? The unfortunate fact is, it is hard to say. Archaeological evidence, as we have just seen, is selective;

---

[7] We must be careful when examining Figure 4.3 to look at overall trends and not just the individual line segments linking adjacent data points, which *must* be linear no matter what growth pattern separated those points. Each line segment is completely uninformative about patterns of population growth during the time spanned by its length; it is mostly informative about the fineness of resolution of the archaeologist's time scale.

moreover, archaeological estimates of population size are indirect and unverifiable (Chamberlain, 2006: 126--32), and the time intervals between archaeological horizons are usually too long to provide the necessary demographic detail. Ethnographies are not much help, even when they focus on demography: the samples are too small, the time series too short, and the populations themselves too likely to have suffered postcontact demographic disruption before they were studied. Not surprisingly, the actual estimates of r from ethnographic studies show no consistent pattern.[8] Historical records can help, but most of the *reliable* historical documents concerning demography come from northwest Europe and date from after AD 1540, thus spanning one of the strangest and least representative periods in the history of human population growth – the so-called *demographic transition* or *modern rise of population*. During this period, mortality fell sharply, fertility remained high, population grew with unprecedented speed, and fertility itself finally fell, driving growth rates down toward (sometimes even below) zero (Figure 4.4). The fact that our best historical data come from what is probably the least representative period in human population history amounts to a kind of Uncertainty Principle for historical demography.

In view of these difficulties, permit me to leave the world of (human) demographic fact and briefly enter the world of biological fact in order to ask the following question: do *nonhuman* species share a common pattern of population growth that might serve as a partial clue about what preindustrial growth may have looked like? Not that preindustrial folk were especially animalistic, but at least they and other species had in common an absence of modern medical care, effective contraceptives and an industrialized food supply to influence their population dynamics. Figure 4.5 shows observations on population growth in several nonhuman species, mostly animals, but also yeast (*Saccharomyces cerevisiae*), which are eukaryotic microorganisms belonging to the Kingdom Fungi. The yeast example (Figure 4.5A) has the great virtue of simplicity, largely because it took place in an extremely well-controlled environment known as a *chemostat*. A chemostat is just a piece of laboratory apparatus for growing all kinds of microorganisms under conditions that can be manipulated at will by the experimenter. In the chemostat experiment that

---

[8] The Yanomama Indians of southern Venezuela, whose demography was studied in some detail back in the 1960s and 1970s, used to be portrayed as having been largely unaffected by contact with the wider world at the time of study (Neel and Chagnon, 1968). As it happens, the Yanomama population appeared to have been growing at a modest rate at the time, with r estimated to be in the range 0.005 to 0.01 (Neel and Weiss, 1975). This finding was, almost inevitably, seized upon by some authors to show that "Tribal Man" was always subject to rapid population increase. But the Yanomama story turns out to be more complicated. While it was true that the Yanomama themselves were relatively isolated and unacculturated at the time of first study (Neel, 1972), several surrounding indigenous groups had been decimated c. 1900 by new infectious diseases, apparently introduced into the area by *mestizo* rubber tappers. Roughly the same period witnessed the introduction of the cooking banana, which rapidly became a major starchy staple for the Yanomama. When first studied, then, the Yanomama population may have been undergoing a recent, modest and transitory growth phase prompted by a new staple crop and the opportunity to expand into what was effectively an ecological vacuum (Neel and Weiss, 1975). The circumstances of the Yanomama were particular, not universal.

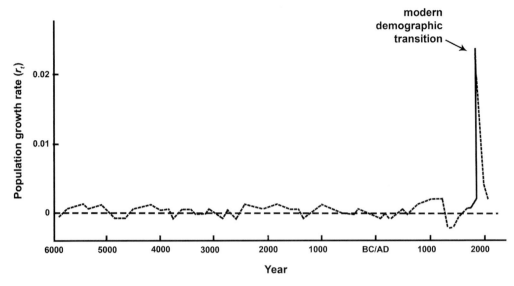

Figure 4.4 Hypothetical long-term patterns of population growth in the entire human species. Note that what is plotted on the y-axis is the population growth rate r, not population size itself. Broken lines are mostly sheer speculation on the author's part, occasionally rising to the level of semieducated guess, as in the period of the early medieval temperature optimum and the fourteenth-century Black Death. The most reliable estimates (solid lines) coincide with the modern demographic transition, when species-wide growth rates were arguably higher than they had ever been before.

provided the yeast data in Figure 4.5A, nutrients and air were fed into the system at a constant rate and removed at exactly the same rate. Therefore, the net quantity of nutrient and oxygen in the main chamber where the organisms were growing was absolutely constant.[9] Rotor blades mixed the medium thoroughly and continuously so that the environment of the chamber was the same throughout. This, then, is about as simple an environment as can be imagined: unchanging, uncomplicated, unpartitioned in space, with (in this experiment) only one living species present. Such a chemostat experiment is, in effect, the physical realization of a theoretical model – a steady-state, homogeneous environment.

If we start with a sterile (lifeless) chemostat and inject a small number of yeast cells into it, the colony starts to grow rapidly, at first following what looks like an exponential increase (and in fact is sometimes called the *exponential phase of growth*, which is not quite correct since r is not actually constant). As time goes on, the growth rate moderates, although it is still positive. Eventually the growth curve reaches a plateau and stays there until the end of the experiment (Figure 4.5A). As long as nutrients and oxygen are continuously renewed at a fixed rate, the level of yeast cells remains constant. If, however, we increase the influx of nutrients so the

---

[9] Yeast are capable of growing in the absence of oxygen, but their metabolism switches to fermentation and their growth patterns are altered.

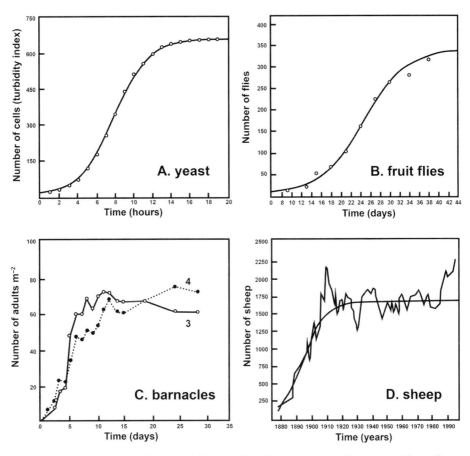

Figure 4.5 Long-term population growth in several nonhuman species, all starting with small initial numbers. (A) Yeast (*Saccharomyces cerevisiae*) grown in a chemostat. (B) Fruit flies (*Drosophila melanogaster*) grown in glass laboratory flasks (i.e. pint milk bottles). (C) Larvae of barnacle (*Balanus balanoides*) colonizing bare rock. (D) Domestic sheep (*Ovis aries*) after first introduction into Tasmania in 1818. The y-axis in panel A is not the absolute number of yeast cells, but rather a turbidity index proportional to (but much smaller than) the actual number of cells. Nos. 3 and 4 in the barnacle case are two rocks of roughly the same size, denuded of barnacles at the beginning of the observation period and kept free of predators thereafter. Original data for yeast from Carlson (1913) by permission of Springer Publishing; for fruit flies, Pearl (1927), by permission of Knopf Doubleday. Publishing Group; for sheep, Davidson (1938), by permission of The Taylor Francis Group; for barnacles, Connell (1961), by permission of John Wiley & Sons, Inc.

chamber becomes more nutrient-rich (not shown in the figure), the yeast colony resumes growth until it reaches a new, higher plateau. Since the food supply in any one experiment is constant and the population growing, at least initially, it is presumably an intensification of intra-specific competition for food that ultimately limits population growth: all other necessities of yeast life are present in abundance.

Fruit flies (Figure 4.5B) are grown in the lab under somewhat less well-controlled conditions, although the amount of food can still be fixed. Their growth follows a

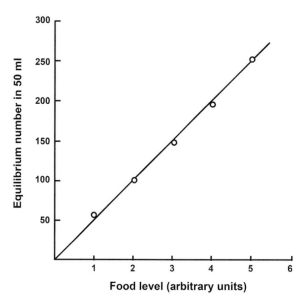

Figure 4.6 Relationship of the upper limit of population size to level of food in five experiments on the water flea *Daphnia obtusa*. Note that the demographic equilibrium or plateau is directly proportional to the food supply. From Slobodkin (1954), by permission of John Wiley & Sons, Inc.

curve that is similar to that of yeast in being *sigmoid* (S-shaped) and reaching a plateau. As in yeast, the plateau appears to be determined by food supply – you can alter the growth curve at will by adding or subtracting nutrients (Ayala, 1966; Mueller, 1997). In fact, a strong, proportional relationship between the upper limit of population growth and the size of the food supply seems to be a general feature of experiments on simple organisms in which other potential influences are held constant (Figure 4.6). Additional experiments, however, show that other factors can mediate the relationship between population and food. For example, Figure 4.7 shows that, in fruit flies, the genetic composition of the population can influence population growth: artificial populations homozygous (in the case of autosomal genes or sex-linked genes in females) or hemizygous (at sex-linked genes in males) for a variety of harmful, radiation-induced recessive mutations do follow a sigmoid curve, but grow more slowly and reach a lower plateau than "wild type" flies grown on the same amount of medium. Indeed, in these particular experiments, "bad" genes reduce population growth by almost as much as halving the food supply.[10] To cite another set of experiments, Figure 4.8 shows that the growth of water flea

---

[10] It is important to emphasize that the particular deleterious genes involved in Figure 4.7 (curve b) are so harmful that they would never be observed at such high frequencies in nature. But more subtle effects of genetic variation, perhaps involving genes that affect food metabolism, may be fairly common. The important point here is that food alone does not determine the growth curve: the interaction of genotype and food is at least theoretically important.

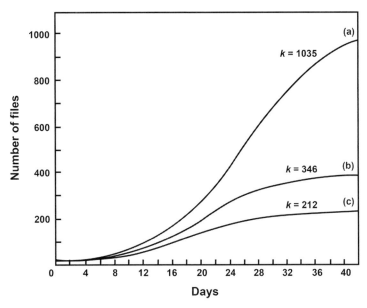

Figure 4.7 Growth of laboratory populations of the fruit fly *Drosophila melanogaster* of varying genetic composition: (a) wild type in a pint bottle, (b) stock homozygous or hemizygous for five deleterious recessive traits (e.g. vestigial wing) in a pint bottle, (c) wild type in a half-pint bottle. *K*, estimated population size at final plateau. From Hutchinson (1978: 25), by permission of Yale University Press. Data from Pearl (1925: 35, 37, 40).

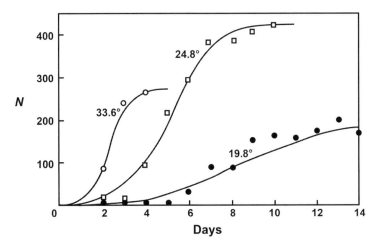

Figure 4.8 Growth of laboratory populations of the water flea *Moina macrocopa* at three different temperatures (°C). The food supply is held constant in all three cases, and the genetic composition is similar since the three subsamples were derived directly from the same wild type stock. From Hutchinson (1978: 26), by permission of Yale University Press. Data from Terao and Tanaka (1928).

populations can vary by ambient temperature even when the food supply is held constant. In these nonhomeothermic ("cold-blooded") creatures, temperature presumably affects the rate of food metabolism. Interestingly, the water fleas seem to thrive best (if attaining a higher plateau is the standard of success) at intermediate temperatures, doing less well at the thermal extremes, both hot and cold. The message of all these experiments is that food is important but that other factors can interact, significantly altering the relationship between population size and food. If this same logic applies to humans, those "other factors" would presumably include a host of behavioral, economic, social and cultural variables.

Returning to Figure 4.5, panels A and B are similar, not only in being laboratory-based, but also in that all the individuals in the experiment are direct descendants of the original colonizers: after the first inoculation, the population is closed to new in-migrants. Panel C, in contrast, shows population growth in the wild (a tidal zone off the coast of southern California) that is entirely attributable to in-migration. This panel shows colonization of two bare rocks by free-living larvae of the barnacle *Balanus balanoides*; once the larvae settle, they adhere to the rock, start to secrete a shell, and become easy to count. In this quasi-experiment, predators have been kept away from the young barnacles. Since barnacles filter their food from the surrounding, turbulent seawater, their numbers are probably not limited by food *per se* but rather by competition for space on the rock face, which allows them to continue filter-feeding as adults (Connell, 1961). But they *are* limited, and the barnacle colonies grow in roughly sigmoid fashion.

Panel D of Figure 4.5 shows our mammalian cousin the domesticated sheep (*Ovis aries*) after its introduction to the island of Tasmania in the early nineteenth century – and here we have moved very far indeed from the laboratory and much closer to the human species. I will discuss this example in more detail later; for the moment it is enough to point out that, through a scrim of obscuring complexities, the pattern of early rapid growth and eventual plateau can still be discerned.

If I may be allowed one more example that brings us even closer to humans, Figure 4.9 shows a 30-year run of data on the size of a troop of semiwild monkeys living on Koshima Island, Japan, as food-provisioning regimes changed. An artificial increase in food supply coincided with (and in this nonexperiment it cannot be put more strongly than that) a period of rapid population growth, which was reversed when the food supply was later restricted. Detailed prospective observations on these animals showed that changes in both fertility and mortality were involved in this pattern of variable population growth (Sugiyama and Ohsawa, 1982). On this evidence, then, primate populations seem to respond to changes in their food supply in ways that are not altogether dissimilar to what is observed in other species.

As a general rule, then, wild, captive and laboratory populations of a variety of nonhuman species, including primates, seem to show an ability to grow rapidly when at sizes or densities that are low relative to available food or space, but their growth rates tend to fall as the population increases, leading eventually to a demographic

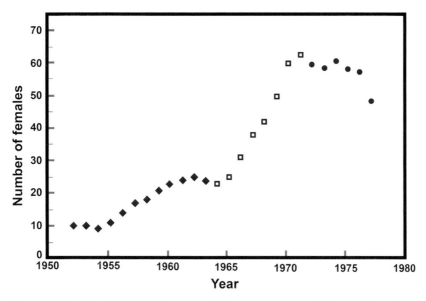

Figure 4.9 The size of the Koshima troop of Japanese macaques (*Macaca fuscata*) grew rapidly when they were provisioned intensively (□) and then dropped when provisioning was restricted (●). From Sugiyama and Ohsawa (1982), by permission of Karger Medical and Scientific Publishers.

plateau.[11] The exponential model cannot mimic this behavior. Is there an alternative model that can? As the next section shows, there is – the so-called *logistic growth model* – and while it is still too simple to replicate human population growth patterns in detail, it can still teach us a thing or two about the *theory* of population growth or its absence.

The Logistic Growth Model

The key assumption behind the exponential model is that r is constant; the key assumption behind the logistic model is that r varies in a predictable way with population size. Since the population growth rate changes over time as N_t changes,

---

[11] I do not want to leave my readers with the impression that population growth in *all* nonhuman species follows the kind of sigmoid curve discussed in this section. Some animals, conventionally called "r-selected" species, remain in a state of perpetual disequilibrium, with numbers that rise and fall spectacularly from season to season. Others, especially insects, display occasional population "eruptions," transient, irregular, but sometimes quite large, increases in population size. Yet others undergo regular fluctuations in numbers associated with complex life cycles (e.g. larval, pupal and reproductive stages). And multi-species communities (such as predator–prey associations) can display regular, multi-year oscillations or even chaotic behavior. (See Turchin 2003: 163*ff.* for numerous empirical examples of all these phenomena.) Human populations are not known to experience any of these particular complications, but they can certainly deviate from the simple sigmoid curve for a variety of reasons discussed below.

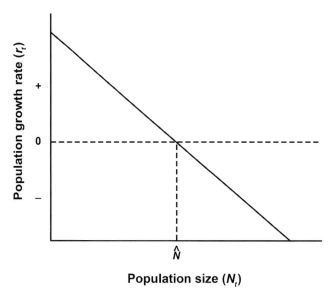

Population size (N_t)

Figure 4.10 The relationship between r_t and N_t in the logistic model. $\hat{N}$ is the equilibrium population size, where N is neither growing nor declining.

we have to go back to writing it as r_t. The relationship between r_t and N_t in the standard logistic model is the simplest one possible:

$$r_t = \alpha - \beta N_t, \tag{4.6}$$

where α and β are just positive numerical constants whose values we either estimate from data or choose for some theoretical reason. Equation (4.6) describes a *linear* or straight-line relationship. Owing to the minus sign on the right-hand side of the equation – and the fact that β itself is always positive – this is a negative linear relationship: r_t goes down as N_t goes up (Figure 4.10). This is, in effect, a kind of negative feedback relationship – what modelers would call a *first-order* feedback (i.e. operating instantaneously, without any time lag between the change in N_t and the response in r_t) as opposed to the *zero-order* feedback (no feedback at all) of the exponential model or the *second-order* feedbacks of other, more complicated models that involve time-lagged effects (more on that later). It is important to note that the line shown in Figure 4.10 passes through $r_t = 0$. At that exact point, the population is not changing in size: it is *stationary* or *at equilibrium*. Following established convention in dynamic modeling I will call the equilibrium population size $\hat{N}$ (pronounced "N-hat"). Note that $\hat{N}$ does not have a subscript t – it doesn't need one, because once N_t reaches its equilibrium it stays there for eternity unless something from outside the system knocks it away.

So population size stays at equilibrium *if* in fact it ever reaches equilibrium. But is there any built-in tendency for N_t to go toward $\hat{N}$? Or is it just as likely that N_t will go spiraling away from $\hat{N}$ toward population explosion or extinction? To answer these questions, examine Figure 4.10 again as we perform a simple thought experiment on

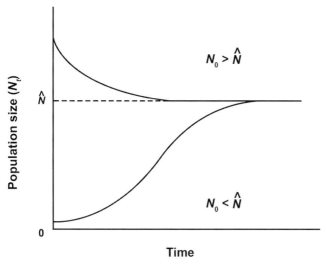

Figure 4.11 The behavior of the logistic model.

it. Let us say that the population is right at its equilibrium value $\hat{N}$. If we left the poor system alone, it would stay there forever. But, no, we can't help meddling, so we reach down our God-like finger and give the population a flick (playing God is one of the keenest pleasures of abstract modeling). Suppose we flick population size to the left, so that it is below $\hat{N}$. What happens? Well, now N_t is in a part of the figure in which r_t is positive, and the population grows back up toward $\hat{N}$. On the other hand, if we flick the population rightward, above $\hat{N}$, then r_t is negative and the population drops back to $\hat{N}$. In other words, whenever the population is forced to depart from equilibrium, whether above or below it, it automatically returns to equilibrium. The equilibrium is, as we say, *stable*. Note that we could only demonstrate that the equilibrium is stable by perturbing the system away from equilibrium; indeed this kind of meddlesome thought experiment is often called a *perturbation experiment*.

If we want to plot the trajectory of N_t over time under the logistic model, we need to solve equation (4.6) to get it into a form that looks more like equation (4.5). For this we need a bit more calculus, which I shall not belabor you with. What we end up with is, horrifyingly enough,

$$N_t = \frac{\hat{N}}{1 + \left(\dfrac{\hat{N}}{N_0} - 1\right)e^{-\alpha t}}, \tag{4.7}$$

where, as before, N_0 is the initial population size. If we set r_t to zero in equation (4.6), we find that $\hat{N}$ is equal to α/β, a fact of some importance that I will return to in a moment. Equation (4.7) is what we usually mean by *the* logistic equation, and its behavior is illustrated in Figure 4.11. When N_0 is well below $\hat{N}$, the population grows rapidly, looking at first rather like an exponential increase; but r_t declines steadily as N_t increases and so population growth moderates and eventually drops toward zero as population size approaches $\hat{N}$. The resulting trajectory of N_t is a symmetrical sigmoid curve. If, however, N_0 is *greater* than $\hat{N}$, the population declines, following what looks superficially like a negative exponential curve, until it approaches $\hat{N}$. The approaches to $\hat{N}$ are, in theory, both asymptotic, but eventually the difference between N_t and $\hat{N}$ becomes too tiny (a fraction of a person) to worry about.

$\hat{N}$ is often called the carrying capacity of the logistic model, but that is, I think, a serious mischaracterization. Recall that $\hat{N} = \alpha/\beta$, the two coefficients that specify the general relationship between r_t and N_t. If we examine that relationship in Figure 4.10, we see that nothing special happens at $\hat{N}$ except that the line passes through $r_t = 0$. The defining feature of the system, the negative linear relationship between r_t and N_t, does not suddenly change in the vicinity of $\hat{N}$ – environmental degradation does not set in, hunger does not suddenly worsen. The model is arguably more consistent with Allen Johnson's view, mentioned in the previous chapter, that environmental degradation starts with the very first settler (Johnson, 1974a). That is, r_t responds negatively to increases in N_t even when N_t is still well below the equilibrium point. There is a continuously intensifying process – of hunger? environmental damage? – as N_t increases, not a sharp threshold right at $\hat{N}$.

Equation (4.7) often fits quite well to data on small organisms grown in the lab; indeed, the smooth curves fit to yeast cells (Figure 4.5A), fruit flies (Figures 4.5B and 4.8), and water fleas (Figure 4.9) are all logistic functions. For more complex organisms in less well-controlled environments, the fit is worse but still not bad as a first approximation. Figure 4.5D, for example, shows a logistic curve fit to the data on sheep in Tasmania. Here several complications are evident. For example, since the number of sheep is much smaller than the number of yeast cells, purely random year-to-year fluctuations in births and deaths have a readily discernable effect on the population's size. At the same time, Tasmania is no chemostat, and environmental fluctuations are likely to account for some of the changes in numbers – perhaps including the two sharp but temporary downturns during the 1840s. But at least three more interesting departures from the logistic are apparent. First, the population appears to over-shoot the ultimate equilibrium point on its first pass. There are several reasons this could have occurred, including a "generational" effect reflecting the fact that sheep populations (unlike yeast populations) have *age structure*, i.e. the presence at the same time of young, prereproductive-age lambs, reproductively active sheep and in some cases older ewes no longer being put to the ram and thus effectively postreproductive. A large cohort of, say, reproductive-age sheep, born back when the population was well below the equilibrium and still growing rapidly, may continue to swell population size even as their juvenile offspring are beginning to experience strong negative feedback on their own growth – feedback caused in part by their own teeming parents. However, the over-shoot seems to last too long to be a pure generational effect, and perhaps is more likely to reflect a high turnover of sheep compared to the growth of pasture, such that a temporary excess of sheep led to some degradation of their food supply. Second, the population seems to cycle semiregularly around the equilibrium, which, again, might be a generational effect or echoes of the initial over-shoot. Finally, after about 1930, there seems to be a fairly sustained if subexponential increase in sheep numbers, which may reflect artificial improvement of pasture or changes in international wool or mutton markets, serving to remind us that the sheep production system of Tasmania is neither steady state nor completely cut off from the rest of the world. The logistic model is not designed to handle such complexities. Nonetheless, there is a sense in which the logistic model, over-simplified as it is, captures one important element of the population dynamics of Tasmanian sheep – the approach to and attainment of an equilibrium, at least a temporary and inexact one. It certainly fits much better than the exponential model would.

All in all, humans are more like sheep than they are like yeast cells, fruit flies or water fleas (although none of the comparisons is particularly flattering). Human populations, like sheep populations, have age structure and respond to changes in economic conditions. But they also have deep histories – deep, that is, compared to Tasmanian sheep – so we rarely get to witness the rapid growth phase that follows initial colonization.[12] Nonetheless, one prominent population scientist of the early twentieth century, Raymond Pearl (1925; 1927; Pearl and Reed, 1920), thought that human population growth followed the predictions of the logistic equation so closely that the model represented a *law* of human population dynamics. Figure 4.12 summarizes some of the data on which he based that claim. As he himself admitted, the population figures for France, Sweden and the world do not cover a long enough span to show the entire logistic curve: France only captures the upper part, Sweden the lower part, the world the middle. And none of them shows the existence of a prolonged equilibrium. But for Pearl the Algerian curve (Figure 4.12D) clinched the argument – it shows the whole sigmoid pattern. That curve, however, is a bit of a cheat since Pearl ignored the early data points that do not fit the logistic well. In addition, Pearl could not argue from the Algerian data he had in hand that the population stayed at its purported upper asymptote for any great length of time. We, on the other hand, *can* test that prediction in retrospect because all four "experiments" have continued to the present day. As it happens, in all four cases, the populations continued growing right past their predicted equilibrium points, although the European cases have apparently begun to level off in recent years, at least if we ignore in-migration from the developing world. In general, extrapolation from Pearl's fitted curves does a poor job of predicting more recent observations (Figure 4.13).

It is doubtful that anyone today would claim that the logistic model *or any other mathematical model* is an immutable law of human population growth. No, the virtues of the logistic model for understanding human population dynamics have little to do with how well the model fits human data. Rather, it is a useful model because it provides new tools for *thinking* about human population dynamics. More particularly, it gives us a way to conceptualize the role of what is sometimes called

---

[12] As discussed in Chapter 5, Malthus believed that the European-derived population of North America was in the midst of such a transitory rapid growth phase in the late eighteenth century.

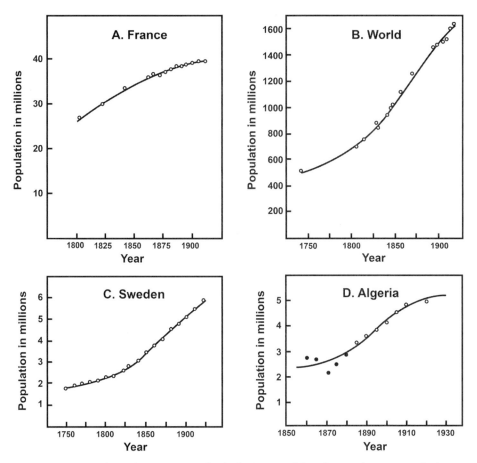

Figure 4.12 Raymond Pearl's attempts to fit the logistic model to data on human populations. (A) France 1800–1920. (B) The whole world 1740–1920. (C) Sweden 1750–1924. (D) The non-European population of Algeria 1856–1921. The data points for the world as a whole are rough estimates; the remainder are based on actual census returns. From Raymond Pearl (1927) The growth of populations. *Quarterly Review of Biology*, 2, 532–48, by permission of The University of Chicago Press.

population regulation in human demographic history – and it opens up a new set of questions and problems, one important function of any good model.

Population Regulation and Food Limitation

During the late 1960s and early 1970s, a particular approach to "cultural ecology" became dominant in human ecology, cultural anthropology and cultural geography.[13] This was during the first wave of modern publications addressing the

---

[13] To be sure, not all self-styled cultural ecologists accepted the theoretical stance I am about to describe (see, for example, Baker and Sanders, 1972), and even fewer do today.

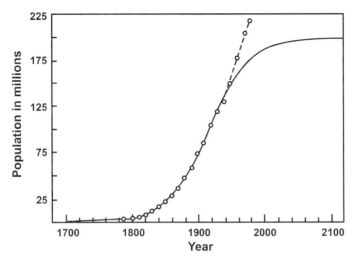

Figure 4.13 Logistic curve (solid line) fit by Raymond Pearl to the population of the United States up to and including the 1940 census, with points added from post-1940 censuses (following the broken line). If the model fit so brilliantly up to 1940, why did it fit so execrably thereafter? From Hutchinson (1978: 22), by permission of Yale University Press. Solid line and data up to and including 1940 taken from Pearl *et al.* (1940).

economic and environmental dangers of rapid population growth and over-population, exemplified most unambiguously by Paul Ehrlich's *The Population Bomb* (1968). Concerns about human population growth were, therefore, in the air. And rapid population growth seemed to many observers to be a uniquely human problem. At the same time, anthropologists suggested that rapid population growth was mostly a problem in the *developing* world, a realm thrown out of joint by contact with the industrialized nations, not the pristine world of truly traditional societies. It must follow (or so it was argued) that traditional societies *regulate* their fertility, whether deliberately or via unconscious social behaviors and norms, precisely to avoid the population-wide calamity of over-population (Abernethy, 1979). How do we know this? Because traditional societies, especially hunter-gatherers and shifting cultivators, are routinely found to be below carrying capacity (a figure of 25 percent of carrying capacity was widely cited). And why do these population-regulation mechanisms evolve and persist? Through the process of *group selection*, whereby improvident groups (populations) that outstrip their food resources face a high risk of extinction compared to groups showing reproductive self-restraint, which *for that reason* persist. After all, the British zoologist Vero Copner Wynne-Edwards (1962) had shown just a few years previously that group selection and population regulation are widespread among nonhuman animal species.

In sum, this theoretical model posited *self-restraint* (not necessarily conscious) acting primarily on fertility (or, in the case of infanticide, on neonatal mortality) in order to prevent group extinction through over-population. In other words, couples in traditional societies altruistically restrained their own fertility for the good of the population as a whole, an outcome that could only have evolved through group selection.

The criticisms of this model are so familiar that they need only brief mention here (for the classic critiques, see Maynard Smith, 1964; Williams, 1972). Most fundamentally, a large majority of population biologists have concluded that group selection cannot succeed against countervailing individual-level selection – or at best can succeed only under very strict conditions that are not often found in nature (Wade, 1977; Goodnight and Stevens, 1997). To over-simplify a bit, even if a population did somehow evolve reproductive self-restraint, it would be vulnerable to "invasion" (perhaps through local mutation) by unrestrained "cheaters" who would be favored by individual selection, which works on a shorter time scale than the differential extinction of groups; thus, self-restraint is at best an unstable equilibrium.[14]

A second criticism is that the "evidence" for the population self-regulation model rested entirely on estimates of carrying capacity. We can only know that a community is at, say, 25 percent of carrying capacity if we know what its carrying capacity is. I hope Chapter 3 conveyed the difficulty of ever knowing carrying capacity, even if such a thing exists. As an added point, many of the groups studied by the early cultural ecologists had already suffered some degree of postcontact depopulation, mainly because of introduced infectious diseases, so that, even if carrying capacity could be computed accurately, the finding that a population was below that level would tell us little about its precontact circumstances.

By the mid-1970s the old cultural–ecological model of population self-regulation was looking pretty tattered. By about 1980 (as I can attest) even to speak of "population regulation" was to be branded as naïve and out of touch with the latest theoretical models. But I argued then (Wood, 1980; Wood and Smouse, 1982) and I still argue today that the basic idea of population regulation is legitimate – *if* we can free it from its purported grounding in group-selection theory. (This view is hardly original or restricted to me; see Charlesworth, 1980; Dewar, 1984; Murdoch, 1994; Turchin, 1995, 2003; Sibly and Hone, 2003; Berryman, 2004, among many others.) The group-selectionists viewed population regulation as an evolved adaptation. I would argue, on the contrary, that population regulation is not self-regulation, but something imposed on the population by resource limitation – not an adaptation but, in effect, a failure of adaptation in the face of limited resources and an unpredictable environment.

Expanding on the example of the logistic model, we can define population regulation in purely dynamic terms without any recourse to ideas about carrying capacity, group selection or self-restraint by altruistic actors:

---

[14] The theoretical debate over group selection is considerably more complex and nuanced than this brief summary suggests. For useful overviews see O'Gorman *et al.* (2008) and Wilson and Wilson (2008). And group selection models are by no means dead (Wilson, 1987; Sober, 1994). Boyd and Richerson (2002, 2009) have even suggested that group selection can operate on cultural variation in a way it cannot on genetic variation. But it is still, I believe, a fair generalization to say that most population biologists accord group selection, at most, a minor role in evolution.

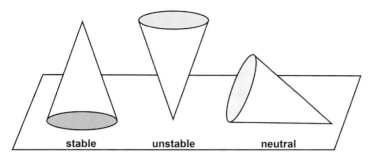

stable   unstable   neutral

Figure 4.14 The three types of equilibria. Note that even the stable example is not *globally* stable: push it far enough and it too will fall over. It is, however, *locally* stable.

Population regulation can be said to exist whenever there is a stable equilibrium for population size (assuming, of course, that the equilibrium is greater than zero).

We have already seen that a nontrivial (i.e. positive, nonzero) stable equilibrium, $\hat{N}$, exists for the logistic model: by my definition, then, the logistic model is a model of population regulation. But it is not the only possible one. To understand this, we need to spend a bit more time discussing equilibria and stability.

The existence of an equilibrium just means that there is a value where some variable of interest stays indefinitely once it has been placed there. Stability, on the other hand, has to do with how the variable acts around the equilibrium once it is displaced from it. There are three possibilities, as illustrated by the cones in Figure 4.14. All three cones are at equilibrium; if we leave them alone they will all stay put. The first cone is at a *stable equilibrium*: if we tip it a bit, it returns to the equilibrium, albeit after a series of ever-diminishing wobbles. (That's fine: the return to equilibrium need not be simple or direct.) The second cone, balanced precariously on its tip, is at an *unstable equilibrium*: if we tip it slightly it falls over – it most definitely does *not* spring back into its former balancing act. (Once it has landed on its side and settled, it is at another equilibrium, but, critically, not the same one as before.) Finally, the third cone is at a *neutral equilibrium*: if we give it a push, it will roll around until it stops at a position very unlikely to be the one it was in formerly. Wherever it stops is a new equilibrium.

Only the first cone is at a stable equilibrium, but even that equilibrium is not stable in the face of all possible perturbations. If we push the cone hard enough, it too will fall over on its side. We say that the first cone is *locally stable* but not *globally stable*: it returns to equilibrium after small perturbations, but not after large ones (what "small" and "large" mean will vary from case to case).

Figure 4.15 translates these concepts into demographic terms. The variable of interest now is total population size. In each case we start at equilibrium and perturb the system to see how it responds. Each scenario implies something different about the relationship between r_t and N_t (Figure 4.16). For a locally stable system, the relationship is negative in the immediate vicinity or *neighborhood* of $\hat{N}$. Global stability implies that the relationship is negative at all possible values of N_t. An unstable equilibrium implies r_t and N_t are positively related in the neighborhood of

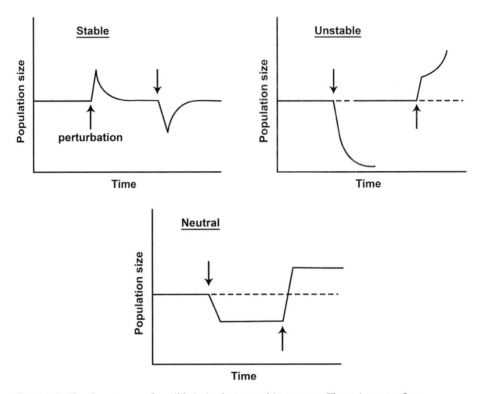

Figure 4.15 The three types of equilibria in demographic context. The existence of an equilibrium simply means that there is some value of a variable of interest (in this case, population size) such that, if the variable takes on that value, it will not change over time unless something outside the system disturbs it. Testing for stability requires briefly perturbing the system (arrows) and watching its subsequent behavior.

$\hat{N}$. In neither of these first two cases, stable or unstable, does the relationship between r_t and N_t necessarily have to be linear, although in the logistic model it is (the equilibrium is also globally stable in the logistic model for $N_t > 0$). In the case of a neutral equilibrium r_t is *always* equal to zero, no matter what the population size is. You should spend a minute or two doing the kind of mental perturbation experiment we did with Figure 4.10 to satisfy yourself that each of the relationships in Figure 4.16 does in fact give rise to the corresponding type of equilibrium in Figure 4.15.

Now we are in a position to expand on our definition of population regulation by laying down the necessary and sufficient condition for the existence of a stable equilibrium for population size:

A stable equilibrium for population size exists if and only if the population growth rate declines as population size increases, at least in the neighborhood of $r_t = 0$.

A mathematical proof is provided by Brian Charlesworth (1980: 51–2). In ecology, the negative relationship between r_t and N_t that gives rise to population regulation is known as *negative density-dependence*, even though it is usually expressed in terms

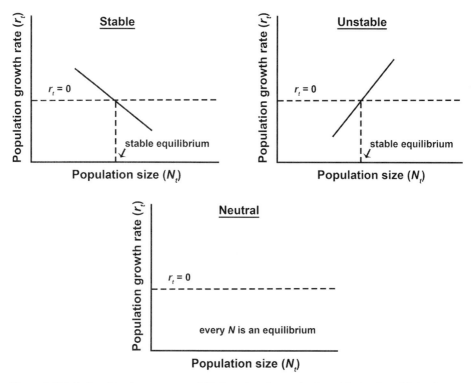

Figure 4.16 Relationships between r_t and N_t that give rise to the three kinds of equilibria shown in Figure 4.15. The sloping lines in the two top panels need not be straight; they could be curved or even more complicated lines, so long as the direction of the slope in the vicinity of $r_t = 0$ is as shown.

of absolute population size, not density. Real populations are certainly subject to density-*in*dependent shocks as well – spells of bad weather, passing epidemics, swarms of locusts – but as long as the density-dependent signal is strong enough, population regulation will prevail.

If negative density-dependence is widespread, so is population regulation. But is there any reason to expect negative density-dependence to be especially common? Recall that $r_t = b_t - d_t + i_t - o_t$, or to put it differently the rate of population growth is the difference between the rate of *demographic inflow* ($b_t + i_t$) and *demographic outflow* ($d_t + o_t$). If r_t is to decrease as N_t increases, then inflow must decline and/or outflow increase (Figure 4.17). We can give our brains a bit of a break if we restrict attention for a moment to a closed population, with no in- or out-migration. Then $r_t = b_t - d_t$ and negative density-dependence requires b_t to go down or d_t to go up (or both) as N_t grows.[15] Is either of these changes plausible?

---

[15] To be more precise, the condition for negative density-dependence in a closed population is that $\partial d_t / \partial N_t > \partial b_t / \partial N_t$, but never mind.

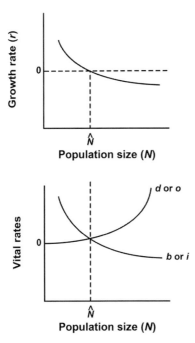

Figure 4.17 Density-dependent vital rates: some relationships between population size (*N*) and birth rates (*b*), death rates (*d*) or migration rates (*o* and *i*) that will produce a stable equilibrium. $\hat{N}$, equilibrium population size.

Ron Lee (1987) reviews several studies showing that fertility often declines as population increases in both preindustrial humans and in non-human species (Figure 4.18), while Peter Smouse and I have found strong evidence from a traditional agrarian society in highland New Guinea that age-specific mortality increases as population grows, especially among the very young and the very old (Wood and Smouse, 1982). But is there any general, theoretical reason to expect density-dependent fertility or mortality to be widespread in humans and other creatures?

The View from Physiological Ecology

In thinking about this question, it will be helpful to refer to some basic ideas from the field of physiological ecology (see, for example, McNab, 2002, 2012; Karasov and Martínez del Rio, 2007). Figure 4.19 shows all the ways a homeothermic ("warm-blooded") animal such as a human being can expend the food energy it eats, including energy lost to the inefficiencies that are an inevitable part of any form of energy transformation. From a physiological perspective this account is comprehensive, realistic (if lacking in molecular detail) and uncontroversial. It encapsulates, one way or another, much of what we want to know about the biological limits to population growth. But it doesn't give up its biodemographic secrets readily. Therefore, I have rearranged and simplified it in Figure 4.20. Together, these two figures tell us almost everything we need to know about bioenergetics for the purposes of

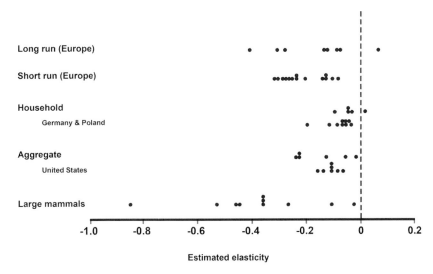

Figure 4.18 Estimated elasticities for the regression of crude birth rates (b_t) on population size (N_t), various studies. Elasticity, which is calculated from the regression coefficients, expresses the proportional change in the outcome variable relative to the predictor variable. For example, an elasticity of –0.2 in the figure means that, for every 1 percent increase in population size, the crude birth rate declines by 0.2 percent. From Lee (1987), by permission of Springer Publishing.

this book (other implications will be drawn out in Chapter 9). When an organism eats, some fraction of the energy ingested – perhaps as much as 30–40 percent – is lost through defecation. The remainder is digested and thus becomes available to fuel the creature's various metabolic processes. This metabolically available energy can be invested in one or more of several basic physiological functions: maintenance, somatic growth, reproduction, external work and storage in the form of body fat.[16] Maintenance includes everything related to the organism's survival *right now*: basal metabolism, the energetic costs of food digestion and absorption itself (which can be surprisingly large), maintenance of body temperature, tissue repair, the immune system, etc. Somatic growth involves an increase in body size, reproduction the whole rigmarole of producing offspring – including lactation in humans and other mammals. External work includes such things as locomotion and food procurement, the very activities that determine how much food is available to the organism; in humans external work would also include childcare. Any digested food energy left over from these functions can be put into storage for future use. But the food coming in is *always* finite, so unless it is sufficient to cover all these functions, they compete with each other for priority. There is an enormous literature on how this competition might be minimized or mitigated by natural selection (for reviews, see McNab, 2002;

[16] This partitioning is purely theoretical. In reality, the physiological mechanisms involved are often intertwined and difficult to separate.

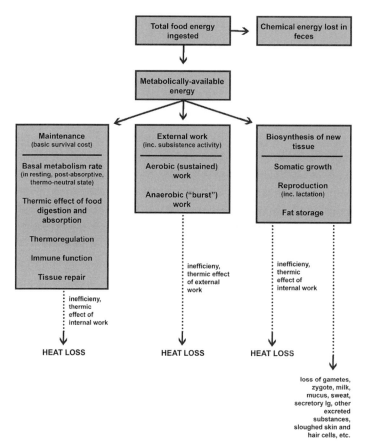

Figure 4.19 A comprehensive account of the potential energy expenditure of an individual homeotherm – e.g. a human being. Basal metabolism rate (BMR) mostly reflects the rate at which adenosine triphosphate (ATP, the primary biological molecule for effecting the transfer of chemical energy in living tissue) is used to (i) replace proteins that break down, (ii) create ion gradients across cellular membranes and (iii) synthesize nitrogenous waste materials. The BMR is therefore essential for supporting critical vital functions such as heart contractions, neural activity, the continuous replacement of dying blood cells, urine production, etc. The postabsorptive ("fasting") state occurs after the thermogenic effect of food digestion and absorption have dissipated. The thermo-neutral state occurs when the organism is at thermal equilibrium with an external environment of moderate temperature, such that no energy is being lost to active heat production or dissipation. The distinction between aerobic (oxygen-consuming) and anaerobic work is discussed in Chapter 9. Adapted from Hill *et al.* (2008: 146, 161), Snodgrass (2012: 326), by permission of Oxford University Press, USA.

Karasov and Martínez del Rio, 2007). An obvious example, found in virtually all mammals, is that the period of rapid somatic growth is almost completely separated from the segment of the life course devoted to reproduction – especially important in females, who bear almost the whole metabolic burden of reproduction, including lactation. (Physical growth and reproduction in humans can overlap during the adolescent years, but teenage pregnancy in humans is often associated with poor

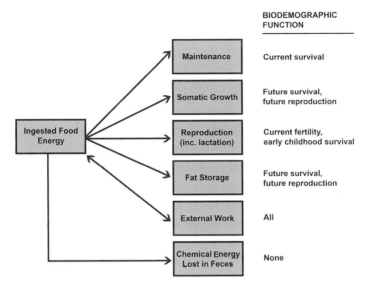

BIODEMOGRAPHIC FUNCTION

Maintenance	Current survival
Somatic Growth	Future survival, future reproduction
Reproduction (inc. lactation)	Current fertility, early childhood survival
Fat Storage	Future survival, future reproduction
External Work	All
Chemical Energy Lost in Feces	None

Ingested Food Energy

Figure 4.20 The functional partitioning of the food energy metabolically available to an organism, with its biodemographic implications. Adapted from Sibly and Calow (1986).

reproductive outcomes such as low birth weight.) Stored energy is a bit of a luxury and can always be brought back into active metabolic use when food is short. Maintenance, however, is important at every age and can never be compromised unduly without dire results including, at the extreme, death. If food is scarce, somatic growth may shut down in small children and fat stores dwindle in people of all ages; in severe famines, reproduction may be curtailed in women (see Chapter 8). These responses to food shortage serve to channel more food energy into maintenance, although defecation still takes its share (indeed, if the source of food stress involves diarrheal disease, defecation may well increase its share). Maintenance is always the top physiological priority: if you don't survive today, there's not much point in worrying about anything else.

Each of these physiological functions has its biodemographic implications (Figure 4.20). Most obviously, maintenance is closely linked to the organism's current risk of death, and active reproduction is synonymous with its current fertility. Somatic growth, similar to fat stores, is in essence an investment in the future – it is a way of turning a tiny, helpless newborn into something large enough and mature enough to have better prospects of successful reproduction and of surviving on its own. Thus, if *the average per capita food intake* in a population is low enough, it is entirely plausible that fertility and survival, now and in the future, will be compromised. At the level of the whole population, then, fertility might be expected to go down and mortality to go up as average per capita food supply decreases, as appears to be the case in many nonhuman wildlife populations (Bayliss and Choquenot, 2003; Hone and Sibly, 2003).

But, given the capacity of farmers to modify their food supply by changing their behavior and practices, is it to be expected that average per capita food intake will always go down as *human* population size increases? If *rapid* population growth intensifies intra-specific competition for food by increasing the number of mouths to feed relative to a *less-rapidly* increasing food supply, then, yes, it is. The latter is admittedly a *big* "if", but not a theoretically implausible one. It is an "if" that lies hidden at the heart of the population/agriculture debate.[17]

Population Regulation and Agricultural Production Functions

The analytical framework introduced in Chapter 3, based on preindustrial agricultural production functions, provides us with a way to approach this fundamental "if". What the "law" of diminishing returns tells us, in general, is that the food supply cannot be increased at will without limits. More particularly, we can assume that, sooner or later, increases in the food supply achieved by increasing inputs of *human labor* in a preindustrial farming system run up against declining marginal productivity, as suggested by Figure 3.13 in Chapter 3. At the aggregate level, labor inputs are partly a reflection of how long and hard each laborer works, but they are also influenced importantly by the sheer number of laborers residing in the local area. Insofar as the traditional division of farm labor is everywhere structured by age and sex – and in roughly similar ways (see Chapter 9) – there ought to be a reasonably strong positive correlation between total population size and the size of the labor force, just as Malthus (1986: 486) believed. For simplicity we can assume that the relationship is proportional: the larger the population, the larger the (potential) labor force, and by a constant multiplicative factor. This assumption is, of course, an over-simplification, but not an egregious one. In addition to the sexual division of labor, labor expectations and actual performance are strongly influenced by age: the very young and the very old contribute little or nothing to food production. In conventional demographic analysis, the potential labor force is sometimes assumed to include everyone between the exact ages of 15 and 65 years (this is often a poor assumption in preindustrial farming systems, but for the moment we will let it stand). As a matter of empirical fact, the fraction of the population that falls between these two ages is surprisingly constant across a wide range of age structures at about 60–65 percent (Cipolla, 1993: 54–8).[18] At the *macro*demographic level, then, the assumption that the size of the labor force is always proportional to total population size is not a bad one.[19] We can make the assumption even more general by allowing

---

[17] Since no natural population is truly closed, it is worth pointing out that migration could just as plausibly be density-dependent. If, for example, the local per-capita food supply diminishes as a result of population growth, members of the population could opt to leave and move somewhere more promising. It is certainly the case that, in recent food shortages, out-migration has increased (Findley, 1994; Findley and Salif, 1998) – although it is unclear how common that response could have been in the preindustrial past when movement was more limited (see Chapter 8).

[18] The most conspicuous difference between preindustrial and modern industrialized populations in this respect is in the proportion of nonlaborers who are juvenile rather than elderly.

[19] Later in this book, I will argue that the very same assumption *is* a bad one at the microdemographic or household level, where changes in proportionality are a fundamental fact of the domestic life cycle.

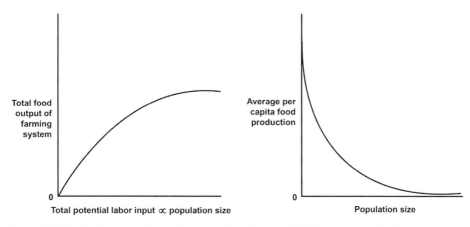

Figure 4.21 Agricultural yield as a function of total potential labor force, which is approximately proportional to total population size (see text). (Left) total yield, (right) marginal yield. If total population size is the input variable for this production function, marginal yield is equivalent to average per capita yield.

the constant of proportionality to vary from one society to another, reflecting (among other things) culturally defined differences in the division of labor. It makes no difference to the argument, which is strictly about relationships within a single population.

In subsistence farming, almost the entire potential labor force is devoted in one way or another to food production (see Chapter 1). Under subsistence conditions, then, we can treat total population size as an input into a system of agricultural production (if only as a proxy for the size of the labor force) and compute the resulting production function (Figure 4.21). If the function exhibits diminishing returns as expected (Figure 4.21, left), it is necessarily the case that the marginal yield of food declines as population size increases (Figure 4.21, right). But when population size is the input variable in the production function, the marginal food yield is equivalent to the average *per capita* yield of food. In other words, the average per capita food intake is expected to decline as population size increases. Malthus certainly thought so, and perhaps he was right.

If population regulation is common in preindustrial societies, as I believe it is, then is it usually a result of competition for *food* as implied by this argument? The evidence on yeast, fruit flies, *Daphnia* and monkeys (Figures 4.5, 4.6 and 4.9) suggests that competition for food is important in other species, although the experiments on barnacles (Figure 4.5C), *Moina* and fruit flies (Figures 4.7 and 4.8) show that other factors can also play a role. But what about humans? Historical demographic studies on early modern Europe suggest that population growth or vital processes (fertility, marriage, survival) are often negatively correlated with grain prices, sometimes after a time lag (Wrigley and Schofield, 1981: 356–401). The price of grain is treated in these studies as an inverse proxy measure of food availability: if food is scarce, farmers withhold it from the market for their own sustenance, driving grain prices upward. But the question of food limitation in humans is difficult to answer as a general matter; much of the rest of this book will be dedicated to it in one way or another. Another important question is whether population is regulated mainly by fertility, mortality or migration – or by all three forces acting together. My own view, which I examine more closely in later chapters, is that most subsistence farming communities are indeed limited by food (and sometimes water, which can of course limit the food supply) and that the resulting population regulation mostly involves early childhood mortality, which, in its turn, is caused mainly by infectious diseases taking advantage of young immune systems that have been impaired by under-nutrition – compromised maintenance, if you will. Other forces are certainly at work, but this, I believe, is the most general mechanism regulating the size of subsistence farming communities. Not surprisingly, I also believe that this mechanism mostly operates at the level of the individual farming household (see Chapter 8).

Some Complications

Humans are not simple creatures like yeast cells, and it is not surprising that a simple model such as the logistic does not fit them very well. What kinds of complications are worth considering if we are to understand preindustrial population dynamics? Perhaps the most obvious one was identified long ago by Malthus himself:

The main peculiarity which distinguishes man from other animals, in the means of his support, is the power which he possesses of very greatly increasing these means. (Malthus, 1830, reprinted in Flew, 1970: 225.)

This idea will be a major focus of Chapters 5 and 6. Among other complications, we should certainly include *stochastic* (random) variation in vital events. The logistic model is a *deterministic* model – that is, it admits of no randomness. But in the real world, births, deaths and migration events are subject to such a welter of unexpected vicissitudes that their occurrence appears stochastic. A birth rate, for example, can be calculated after the fact, but it cannot tell us when or even if a particular birth will take place. While our one explicit model of population regulation (the logistic) does not include random variation, the *idea* of population regulation is important in understanding how populations respond to random variation. Figure 4.22 explains what I mean by this: it shows the results of two computer simulations performed by Ken Wachter (1987a) in which random perturbations ("shocks") are administered to two populations, one regulated by negative density-dependence and the other unregulated but with r always equal to zero on average. (By using the same seed for his random number generator in both simulations, Wachter guaranteed that both populations experienced exactly the same series of shocks.) Both simulations start out at population size 100, which is the stable equilibrium point for the regulated population. Whenever the regulated population is randomly perturbed away from its equilibrium, it tends to move back toward it – the essence of population regulation. Thus, while the population fluctuates unpredictably, it never strays very far away from the equilibrium. In the unregulated population, the same fluctuations are not

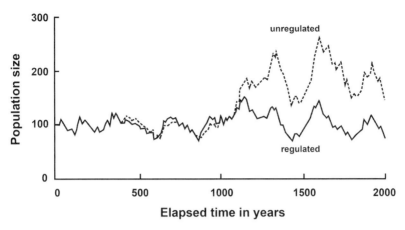

Figure 4.22 The effects of random fluctuations in births and deaths in two computer simulations, one with density-dependent population regulation around $\hat{N} = 100$, and the other without regulation but with an average r_t of zero. In the absence of density-dependent feedback, random fluctuations in births and deaths cause the population to drift away from the initial value of 100. Note that the same seed was used for generating pseudorandom numbers in both runs to ensure that the same sequence of random "shocks" is being compared. From Wachter (1987a) by permission of the Institute of International Studies, University of California at Berkeley.

countered by any tendency to move back toward the initial value – the population stays wherever the fluctuation happens to leave it (this, then, is a case of neutral equilibrium). As a result the population will drift away from its initial value over time, although occasionally it may drift by chance back toward the initial value. Indeed, some complicated mathematics (Bartlett, 1960: 18–25; Pielou, 1977: 18–19) shows that the unregulated population will eventually drift to extinction with probability one, although it may take an exceedingly long time for it to do so. Thus, ironically, the group-selectionists were right that population regulation protects the population from extinction, but not for the reasons they put forward.

Another complication ignored by the logistic model is that the physical environment is never constant (outside of the chemostat) but itself fluctuates at random and sometimes undergoes sustained, nonrandom change in one direction or another (you may think of ice ages and global warming, but more subtle changes may be important in the short term). At each point in an environment's history there may be a population size that would be a stable equilibrium *if the environment stopped changing from that point forward*. By definition it must be the case that population growth is negatively density-dependent at that instant, but the equilibrium population size changes as the environment changes – or, to say the same thing, the relationship between r_t and N_t changes (but remains negative) as the environment changes. Under such a model the population tracks the changes in the environment, possibly with some time lag as it strives to catch up (Figure 4.23). If environmental change is rapid relative to population growth, population size may never actually reach its moving target. Population size is by no means at a steady state under this

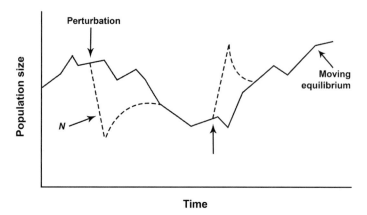

Figure 4.23 A regulated population chasing a moving demographic target.

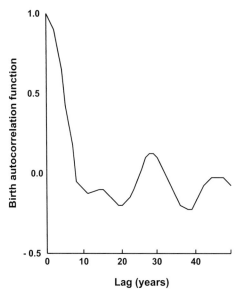

Figure 4.24 Empirical correlogram of the detrended number of baptisms in a rural French parish, Tourouvre-au-Perche, 1590–1800. The autocorrelation function correlates the number of baptisms each year (a proxy measure of the annual number of births) *with itself* at varying time lags. (At a lag of zero, the autocorrelation must equal one.) The dominant 29-year cycle is a "generational" cycle, reinforced by a weaker 15-year cycle, which may reflect cyclical changes in grain prices (Charbonneau, 1970). The overall pattern is consistent with some degree of density-dependent population regulation. From Lee (1974), by permission of Springer Publishing. Data from Charbonneau (1970).

scenario, but it can still be said to be regulated. And, given a long time-series of demographic and environmental data, it would be perfectly possible to detect the regulation statistically.

Another important complication has to do with second-order (time-lagged) feedbacks, age structure and long-term cycles in population size. In the logistic model,

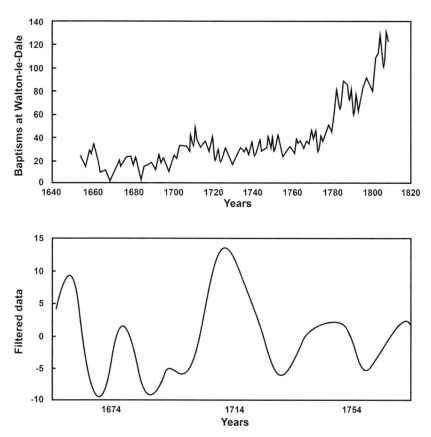

Figure 4.25 Baptisms at the village of Walton-le-Dale, England, 1640–1816. (Top) Raw counts of the number of baptisms each year. The increase in baptisms after 1780 is a reflection of population growth, not a change in fertility. (Bottom) The same data detrended and filtered to remove cycles with wavelengths below 20 and above 50 years; as a result of this data filtering, the substantial 30- and 40-year cycles become obvious. From Scott and Duncan (1999), by permission of Local Population Studies.

the feedback of N_t on r_t is instantaneous: a change in N_t affects r_t immediately, not after a lag of some weeks, months or years. But lagged effects are common in human demography. An act of sexual intercourse cannot affect a woman's fertility for nine months or so. And there is growing epidemiological evidence, some of it summarized by Barker (2002), that adverse conditions during early childhood can influence an individual's risk of death many decades later. In addition, the logistic model treats the population as a single, indistinguishable mass; it deals strictly with the size of the population as a whole, not as a collection of heterogeneous subgroups. But humans are not all identical, interchangeable units. Even if we ignore other distinguishing characteristics, humans differ from each other by age and sex, two fundamental dimensions of demographic variability. The existence of age structure – the presence in the population of individuals of widely differing ages and overlapping gener-ations – introduces the possibility of another kind of second-order feedback: for example, a large number of young adults competing for food may compromise the survival of young children or the elderly (Wood and Smouse, 1983). Models that try to incorporate lagged feedbacks, age/sex structure and other forms of intra-population heterogeneity become mathematically very complicated very quickly. But one prediction is almost universal: such complications often induce a compli-cated series of cycles in population size even when there are no cyclical changes in the environment itself (Lee, 1974; Wood and Smouse, 1983; Caswell, 2006; Turchin, 2009). Figures 4.24 and 4.25 show two examples from preindustrial farming villages, one French, the other English, of cyclical fluctuations in the number of births – fluctuations that probably do not reflect changes in fertility rates *per se*, but rather in the size of the population at risk.

In sum, populations in the real world, whether of humans or other complex organisms, should never be expected to follow the pretty sigmoid curve of the logistic model. That does not necessarily mean that population regulation is not occurring; it just means that the density-dependent feedbacks doing the regulating are more complicated than the simple, instantaneous straight line of the logistic equation. More complicated kinds of models and analyses are needed to detect such population regulation (see Berryman, 1994; Lande *et al.*, 2002).

5 Malthus and Boserup

That poverty was the lot of the large majority of people in all or almost all societies before the industrial revolution is widely recognized. Poverty is a general and rather abstract concept. Its reality was bitter and particular: a hungry child, apathetic from lack of food; a shivering family unable to buy fuel in a harsh winter; the irritation of parasites in dirty clothing and the accompanying sores and stench. The extent and severity of poverty in the past is difficult to express in quantitative terms for lack of relevant data in most cases, but that the poor were very numerous and that they suffered greatly at times in most societies is an assertion unlikely to be widely challenged. When St Matthew reports Jesus as saying, 'ye have the poor always with you' [Matthew 26:11], the context suggests that the remark was not controversial.

In industrialized countries today poor people may still be found. Their poverty is, however, now taken to be problematic in a way that used not to be the case, because it is widely believed that the continued existence of poverty reflects not the intrinsic nature of the human condition but the failure of the social system or the political regime. The capacity to produce on a scale to provide acceptable minimum conditions for all patently exists [in modern industrialized economies], and it is therefore natural to argue that poverty can be overcome by an act of will, by a suitable piece of social engineering. Looking back from a vantage point in the late twentieth century, it may be tempting to suppose that the same was true of earlier times, that the misery of the masses could have been alleviated by deliberate policy or institutional change. [But there were] *constraints common to all traditional societies* which meant that the ambition to achieve a general escape from poverty belonged to the realm of pipedreams rather than policy.   – E. A. Wrigley (1991b: 91), emphasis added

The Bemba seem to have learnt from the Lungu and other tribes to the west, that it is possible to get a second crop of millet from the one garden, and now this custom is almost invariably followed. 'Hunger taught us' is the expression usually used.   – A. I. Richards (1939: 317)

We turn at last to the "classic" debate (as I've called it) on population and agriculture in the preindustrial world. In this and the following chapter I summarize the debate as it had evolved through the 1990s. To do justice to the authors whose views I summarize, I need to lay out the logic of the debate as *they* have understood it. But that poses something of a problem for me, since I think that logic has been to some degree misdirected and confused – on both sides. In particular, there has been little explicit attention paid to what scale of analysis is likely to be most productive in moving the debate forward (see Chapters 1 and 2). Choice of scale is one of the most important decisions involved in designing any empirical research, but the population/agriculture debate has bounced back and forth between scales rather heedlessly. As a crude generality, it might be said that empirical studies have been conducted mostly at the microdemographic scale (that of individual farmers and their farms), whereas theoretical models have been formulated primarily at the macrodemographic scale (the whole population or farming system). Little thought has been given to how this disjunction might confound the comparison of empirical findings and theoretical expectations. I would guess that many empirical researchers have chosen the micro-level of study not for principled reasons but because a single fieldworker or a small team of fieldworkers cannot survey a wide area or a large number of people. Intellectually, the debate has been framed mostly at the macrodemographic level – again not deliberately but merely because that was the level at which the original framers conceived it.

Far and away the most important and influential framer of the *recent* debate has been the economist Ester Boserup, active during the second half of the twentieth century; but her views are best understood as a reaction to the much earlier writings of Thomas Robert Malthus. Whatever else they may or may not have had in common, both Malthus and Boserup approached their subjects almost exclusively at the macrodemographic level, and both can be criticized on that basis.

Boserup changed the terms of the Malthusian argument primarily by refocusing it on the issue of *agricultural intensification*. Before turning to Malthus and Boserup's actual ideas, it is necessary to clarify what we mean by this key concept.

What is Agricultural Intensification?

It is not too much to say that the post-Boserup debate on population and agriculture has actually been a debate about agricultural intensification, a much narrower topic. Intensification is defined as an increase in total crop yield *per unit cultivable land* (including land lying fallow) achieved by changing at least one of the nonland factors of production – i.e. labor, farm organization, or capital (including tools, fertilizer, farm infrastructure, skills, etc.). As the great agricultural geographer Harold Brookfield expressed it,

[Agricultural] intensification must be measured by inputs only of labour, capital, and skills against constant land. The primary purpose of intensification is the substitution of these inputs for land, so as to gain more production from a given area, use it more frequently, and hence make possible a greater [spatial] concentration of production.

It must be emphasised that we are not concerned only with labour inputs, although the relative ease with which these can be quantified and set against measured area and yield has led to an undue concentration on labour intensification in the literature. Systems which are as radically different as mounding in permanent fields on the one hand, and simple slash-and-burn cultivation on the other, may have similar labour inputs per unit area, measured by [the investment of] time. Skills indexing the technologies applied to current production are in many ways the more significant variable, especially interesting in the Pacific where so wide a range of skills has been employed by people having only a limited range of tools. Some skills are applied to the creation of "[landesque] capital", in the sense of permanent improvements to land, whether these be simply a patch of cleared forest easier to rework than the virgin growth, a fence which lasts perhaps four years, or an irrigation complex which, with proper maintenance, may endure for centuries.

Nor does agricultural intensification involve only agronomic practices. If farmers are to fit more people and more production on to constant land, it follows that they must also fit the pieces of the farming system together more closely, organise the system to take maximum advantage of resource differentials, and so structure the ground plan of the farm as to minimise costs of separation from residence to the more intensively-used sections. Organisation of the farm itself, and of the methods used to allocate land, are thus important aspects of intensification. Good organisation may achieve substantial improvements in the absence of any agronomic elaboration. (Brookfield, 1972: 31–2)

This statement is brimming with insights, many of which will be explored in the next chapter. In the present chapter, I want to introduce and discuss Malthus and Boserup, the two original framers of the debate over population and agriculture. In essence, Malthus was primarily interested in the effects of agricultural intensification, Boserup in its causes.

Thomas Robert Malthus

The Reverend Robert Malthus (Figure 5.1) was born in Surrey, England, in 1766.[1] In 1784 he entered Jesus College of Cambridge University where he mainly studied mathematics, in which field he won honors as Ninth Wrangler. Upon graduation, he was elected a fellow of Jesus College.[2] He eventually became the world's first holder of the title Professor of Political Economy, awarded to him by the East India Company's college in Haileybury, Hertfordshire, where he spent most of his professional life. In about 1796 he famously had a fireside debate with his father Daniel at the old family home. Daniel Malthus was a great fan of the French Enlightenment and a proponent of the thought of Jean-Jacques Rousseau and the Marquis de Condorcet, two of the leading utopian writers of the late eighteenth century. Both Frenchmen argued that humans can be improved without limit, and that scientific progress would someday make humans effectively immortal and (at least according to M. de Condorcet) would thereby lead to the dying away of the sex drive. The younger Malthus was skeptical about these claims, and saw immediately that if humans did not become deathless and sexless, then the utopian vision had a fatal flaw: its realization would always be thwarted by population growth. He immediately set to writing. In 1798 he published an anonymous pamphlet (he was soon revealed as the author) entitled *An Essay on the Principle of Population, as it affects the*

---

[1] The definitive biography of Malthus is Petersen (1979). From his private correspondence, it is clear that Malthus used Robert as his first name throughout his adult life. Despite this fact, most modern writers refer to him as Thomas. I would rather accede to his own preference.

[2] To accept this position, he had to qualify as a curate in the Church of England – hence the title "Reverend". Later he was awarded the benefice of Albury parish in Surrey, but a vicar was soon hired to stand in for him. Although Marx and other critics have given Malthus considerable abuse for being a prelate and hence of necessity a "bought advocate" of the aristocracy (Marx, 1954: 123), he spent almost no time as an active curate, and the position never seems to have meant much to him. His writings were consistently secular, except for two chapters on natural theology and theodicy in later editions of his *Essay on the Principle of Population*. The whole motivation of those two chapters was Malthus's recognition that the principle of population was a pretty lousy thing for God to inflict on the poor.

Figure 5.1 The Reverend Thomas Robert Malthus (1766–1834). Portrait by John Linnell c. 1820, by permission of the National Portrait Gallery, London.

Future Improvement of Society with remarks on the Speculations of Mr. Godwin, M. Condorcet, and Other Writers.[3] This "essay" was in fact a strongly worded polemic – and virtually the only thing Malthus ever wrote that is still read (or even published) today.[4] This first edition of the *Essay* laid out what might be called "the simple argument" concerning population and food supply (see below). The book was a slim thing, with very little in it that could legitimately be called demography or even empirical evidence. But in 1803 he published (under his own name this time) a second edition entitled *An Essay on the Principle of Population; or, a View of its Past and Present Effects on Human Happiness; with an enquiry into our Prospects respecting the Future Removal or Mitigation of the Evils which it occasions.* Malthus himself considered this book a completely new work, and it was certainly much larger than the slender original (my personal copy of the fourth edition [1807], which is little changed from the second, runs to 1064 pages in two substantial volumes). Its subtitle points to the book's transformation from an anti-utopian tract to a more sober scientific work. For this edition, Malthus drew upon his own studies of the United Kingdom and continental Europe and official publications from various

---

[3] William Godwin was an English utopianist. He was also the father of Mary Godwin Shelley, author of *Frankenstein*, which can be read as a challenge to her father's faith in the infinite perfectibility of humankind through science.

[4] The best, most readily available modern editions are Flew (1970), Winch (1992) and Gilbert (2008). A seventh, posthumous edition, not published until 1872, is available in facsimile from Augustus M. Kelley's Reprints of Economic Classic series (Malthus, 1986). James (1989) has produced a useful variorum text of the second through sixth (1826) editions.

countries, along with travelers' accounts and other anecdotal material. It is brimming with evidence and argument, and can be regarded as the publication that created the field of demography. The second and subsequent editions of the *Essay* set out what I shall call "the complex argument" concerning population and food supply. Many people today know the simple argument, very few know the complex one.

The Simple Argument

Before we lay out the simpler of Malthus's two arguments, I need to make certain we are not tripped up by a potential confusion of terminology. As a trained mathematician, Malthus certainly knew about continuous-time models (which date from the seventeenth century), and he was aware of Euler's discovery of the exponential model. But he chose to present only discrete-time models, presumably to appeal to a wider audience. Thus, Malthus spoke of an arithmetical increase (e.g. 1, 2, 3, 4, 5, ...), which today we would call a linear increase and treat as continuous. He also spoke of the geometrical increase (e.g. 1, 2, 4, 8, 16, ...), which is the discrete-time version of the exponential model. Given the background presented in the previous chapter, I assume I can substitute the labels linear and exponential without causing undue confusion or doing damage to Malthus's argument.

Malthus started with two axioms that today may seem too obvious to mention, but neither of which could be taken for granted during the heyday of utopian writing.

- *Humans must eat to live and in the absence of sufficient food will sicken and die.*
- *The strength of the sex drive in humans has been more or less constant (on average) over all periods of history and will remain so for the foreseeable future.*

This second axiom is obviously a denial of the utopianist claim that sexuality would wither away once humans became immortal. The first axiom is a dismissal of the prospects for immortality itself. Malthus then makes two assumptions that should be examined with some care, because they are often believed (erroneously) to constitute the whole of his argument, so that if either or both are negated the entire argument collapses.

- *Innovations in food production can <u>at best</u> achieve a linear increase in the food supply over the long run.*
- *Under extremely favorable conditions, when resources are not (yet) limiting, human population can grow exponentially and can double in as little as 25 years.*

First, the linear increase in food. Malthus nowhere claimed that food always or spontaneously increases linearly. Rather he was arguing that the agricultural advances that were occurring during his lifetime, of which he was well aware, would *at most* achieve a linear increase in food supply over the long run. As we saw in Chapter 3, he did not actually believe that such an increase was at all likely but was "the very utmost that we can conceive" (1798: 22) and "probably a greater increase than could with reason be expected" (1803: 11). The first edition of the *Essay* implies – and later editions make clear – that he believed that continuing innovations

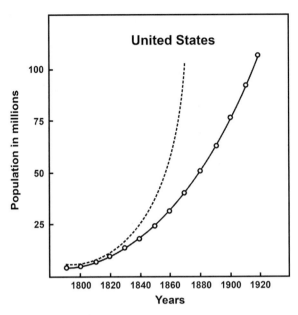

Figure 5.2 Growth of the white population of the United States from its founding to 1920 (circles and solid line). (Broken line) Exponential increase starting at the same value and doubling every 25 years. Note that during Malthus's lifetime (he died in 1834) the two curves scarcely deviated from each other. US data from Pearl (1927).

would eventually face declining marginal yields. But he adopted the linear increase, "the very utmost that we can conceive," for the sake of argument: even if we assume a food supply that grows linearly *and without limit*, we'll still end up in a pickle.

And that pickle takes the form of population growth. Malthus's second assumption is that, when the number of people is below the ceiling set by the food supply, human populations can grow rapidly and more or less exponentially. He did not, by any stretch of the imagination, claim that populations *always* grow exponentially – or that they therefore *always* outstrip their resources and end up in famine. In fact he argued, based on the writings of Benjamin Franklin, that the early decades of the United States witnessed the only real-world example of *approximate* exponential growth that he knew of, and that it could not possibly go on much longer. He was right on both counts (Figure 5.2). He argued that the US population in the 1790s was doubling about every 25 years, a claim that met with two objections: (i) that such a rate of increase is impossible in humans (as we saw in Chapter 4, it is not), and (ii) that if the growth of the US population was rapid it was only because of the great masses of British and other Europeans who were rushing there to take advantage of its many opportunities – in-migration, not "natural increase" (an excess of births over deaths). In later editions of the *Essay*, Malthus presented data from shipping manifests that indicated that migration to North America had dropped off substantially by the 1780s, and in his *Summary View of the Principle of Population*, which

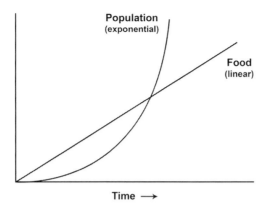

Figure 5.3 The tortoise of food versus the hare of population.

appeared in 1830, he argued that the age composition of the US population in the censuses of 1790, 1800, 1810, and 1820 could best be explained by *in situ* trends in fertility and mortality and was inconsistent with large influxes of migrants.[5] Modern scholarship has verified that migration to North America had in fact greatly declined by the second half of the eighteenth century (Bailyn, 1986: 90–104).[6]

Thus, Malthus maintained that human population could *theoretically* grow as an approximate exponential function, and do so through sheer natural increase, as long as conditions were unusually favorable – as they were in the land-rich USA once the native population had been pushed aside. And the evidence suggests that he was more or less right. The specific doubling time or growth rate is immaterial to the rest of his argument – but, in the case of the USA, Malthus was more or less right about that as well.

What happens when a linear increase in food supply is combined with an exponential increase in population? Even if the population starts out well below what its expanding food supply could support, given enough time it will always catch up (Figure 5.3). If Malthus's assumptions are correct, this conclusion is a matter of mathematical necessity: population increases each year by *multiplying* the current population by a fixed quantity (e^r), whereas food increases each year by *adding* a fixed quantity to its current level. In the long run, the "hare" of population (to borrow Malthus's own metaphor) will always outrace the "tortoise" of food – unless "we can persuade the hare to go to sleep" (Malthus 1986 [orig. 1872: 407]). That is, unless population growth is purposefully restrained, given enough time population will always reach and then keep up with the maximum allowed by its food supply, no

---

[5] It should be of interest to technical demographers that, in making this argument, Malthus anticipated some aspects of A. J. Lotka's stable population theory by seven decades.

[6] In the period leading up to the American Revolution, the number of people embarking from all countries to the 13 colonies with the intention of settling permanently was less than 3500 a year (Bailyn, 1986: 92). Most of these were British, and their numbers declined precipitously during and after the Revolution.

matter how rapidly the latter is growing.[7] Agricultural innovations may indeed improve the human condition for a while, but eventually population growth will eat up any surplus food and drive the average person back down to the margin of subsistence with all its attendant miseries. Unless population growth is deliberately restrained, permanent improvements in the material conditions of humankind (never mind utopia) are unattainable.

Since Malthus's death, most writers have assumed that his simple argument has been comprehensively disproven, either because its assumptions have been shown to be absurd or because it has done a poor job of predicting the future. When read aright, Malthus's assumptions are not absurd *as model assumptions*, just as von Thünen's isotropic plain is not absurd as a model assumption, as opposed to a description of reality. Besides, how many economists or demographers have ever been able to foresee the future with anything approaching accuracy? Based on his more *complex* argument, to which I turn next, a small body of demographers, economists and historians has been reevaluating Malthus over the past few decades and now largely accepts his ideas, at least as a useful *model* of preindustrial farming and demography (e.g. Dupâquier, 1983; von Tunzelmann, 1986; Wrigley, 1986, 1991b; Fogel, 1994, 2004). But most of them still think he was wrong about the future – that he was unable to predict the ultimate consequences of the modern industrial and agricultural revolutions. Close study of Figure 5.4 will shed light on this claim. To me it looks as if the hare has done a pretty good job of keeping up with the tortoise, just as Malthus predicted.

The Complex Argument

In all later editions of the *Essay* and in his "Summary View" of 1830 (the most mature expression of his thinking about population), Malthus retained the simple argument because of its heuristic value. Indeed, when he spoke of the *principle* of population, it was always the contrast between exponential and linear growth that he had in mind. But, beginning with the second edition, Malthus supplemented his four-page presentation of the simple argument with a 400+ page exposition of an argument of far greater complexity and nuance. Sadly, almost no one reads the longer version anymore, and so Malthus is remembered today mainly for the simple argument, not the more interesting complex one. I will now try to sketch the complex argument, albeit in modern garb, drawing out some implications not discussed by Malthus himself (for similar presentations, see Lee, 1986; Wood, 1998; Cuffaro, 2001).

First, let's jettison the idea of an unlimited linear increase in the food supply and reinstate what Malthus truly believed in: declining marginal yields. More specifically,

---

[7] Malthus's tortoise and hare metaphor is a bit misleading in that it implies that population will grow beyond what its food supply can support: the hare will *outrace* the tortoise. Elsewhere Malthus states clearly that, sufficient food being essential for human life, no population can ever truly outgrow its food supply, except during occasional, brief food shortages, when the population will tend to contract anyway (Malthus, 1807:60). Malthus's hare doesn't outrace the tortoise, but it effortlessly keeps up with it and falls back whenever the tortoise lags behind.

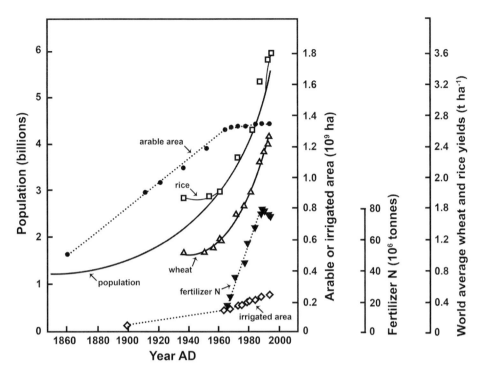

Figure 5.4 Was Malthus right? Increases in world population and various aspects of food production, 1860–2000. Note different scales for different variables. Most of the variables pertaining to food production have grown more or less linearly, and two (quantity of arable land and application of inorganic nitrogen fertilizer) seem to have slowed or stopped growing in recent years. World population, in contrast, has grown not quite exponentially, but rapidly enough to keep up with the advances in agriculture. From Evans (1998: 91), by permission of Cambridge University Press.

Malthus believed that, sooner or later, any expansion in the food supply achieved by increasing investments of *human labor* in preindustrial farming would run up against declining marginal productivity, a belief supported by the evidence presented back in Figure 3.12. In Chapter 4, I made the argument that the ultimate limit on labor inputs in any one preindustrial farming community was the size of the population itself, or at least the segment of it directly involved in day-to-day food production (which in most traditional societies would be virtually all able-bodied adults plus a fair number of children and oldsters). I also argued that, given documented cross-cultural regularities in the division of labor by age and sex and in the age–sex structure of human populations, that the total labor force was everywhere more or less proportional to total population size, at least as a first approximation. According to this argument, then, population size can stand in as a proxy measure for total potential labor input. Thus, we can think of agricultural yields as displaying diminishing returns and declining marginal productivity as a function of population size (Figure 5.5). But when total population size is the input into an agricultural production function, then marginal productivity is equivalent to the *per capita* availability of food. In other

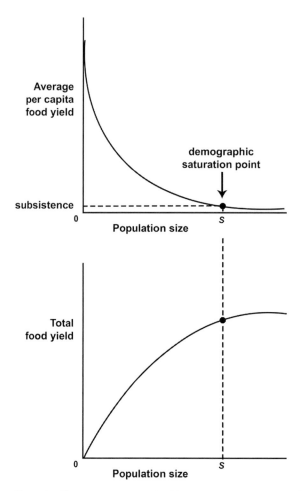

Figure 5.5 The same curves as in Figure 4.21 rearranged to show the relationship between demographic saturation (*S*) and the subsistence level of food production as defined here (see text).

words, as population size increases, according to Malthus, the effective food supply (per individual) dwindles in a subsistence-oriented rural economy, even if the total food supply is still increasing to some degree.

Now, Malthus took it as axiomatic that without sufficient food an individual would sicken and die. If the average per capita availability of food consistently declines with increasing population size, then it must follow that a point will be reached sooner or later at which the amount of extra food wrested from the system by the addition of a single laborer will be just enough to feed a single additional laborer and no more. If food intake in the preindustrial world was an important determinant of an individual's ability to survive and/or reproduce (and, as discussed in Chapter 8, the evidence on survival at least seems unequivocal), then there must be a level of per capita food intake at which the average individual's nutritional condition is just

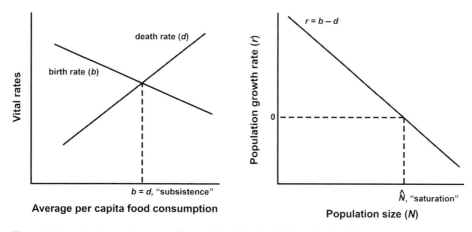

Figure 5.6 Density-dependent mortality and fertility in Malthus. The link between the two panels in this figure is the assumption that average per capita food availability in a fixed system of production goes down as population size goes up, as in Figure 5.5. Malthus believed that, in the absence of density-dependent fertility, an increase in mortality was inevitable. Density-dependent fertility, on the other hand, he considered to be partly the result of human agency.

barely enough to allow for exact *demographic replacement*, at which point $r = 0$. We can speak of the level of average per capita food intake that provides just the average rate of survival and/or fertility to allow replacement as the *subsistence level* of food consumption, and the population size that yields that level of consumption the *demographic saturation point* for that particular farming system (Figure 5.5). Beyond the saturation point the system cannot support further population growth.[8]

When we bring the idea of demographic replacement into the model, we imply that the forces of demographic change (fertility, mortality and migration) respond in a predictable way to average per capita food consumption. Now, Malthus did discuss migration, especially in the later editions of the *Essay*, but he mostly wrote about fertility and mortality; for the present discussion we will follow his example and ignore migration. His treatment of fertility differed from that of mortality in that he believed reproduction has (or ought to have) a conscious and deliberate side to it. We will set this latter complication aside until the next section. At any rate, Malthus clearly believed that mortality rates went up as food consumption went down, and he adduced various reasons (including deliberate actions) why fertility might be expected to go down with decreasing food consumption (Figure 5.6, left). Given his belief that average per capita food consumption would generally go down with

---

[8] We have hinted in previous chapters that it can be difficult to know what a "system" of food production actually is or whether the term has any meaning at all. Based on Figure 5.5, in which population size is treated as an input into a production function and is allowed to vary while all the other nonlabor inputs are held constant at their "typical" values, then that presumably is what the "system" is: the production function with everything fixed except for the size of the labor pool. It should be clear what an abstraction this concept is. In this and the next chapter, whenever I speak of a "fixed system of production," that abstraction is what I have in mind, not something actually found in nature.

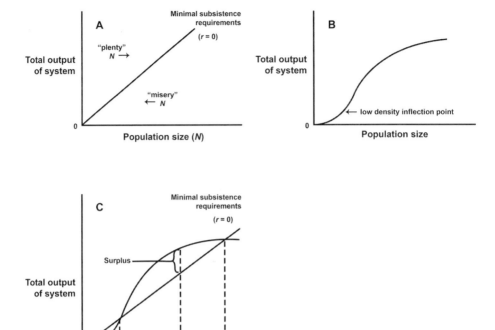

Figure 5.7 The Malthusian argument in three simple graphs (see text for details). From Wood (1998: 107, 112) after Lee (1986), by permission of Basil Blackwell Ltd.

increasing population size, his model was *ipso facto* a model of negative density-dependent population regulation (Figure 5.6, right), apparently the first ever constructed. In other words, the demographic saturation point of the farming system is a stable equilibrium: if the population is below saturation it will grow up to it, if above it will decline to it. At the equilibrium the average member of the population will be right at the level of subsistence.

The economic demographer Ron Lee (1986) has devised a useful graphical representation of Malthus's complex argument that is worth reproducing here (Figure 5.7). To start with, imagine a purely abstract space showing every conceivable combination of population size and total food yield without any consideration of whether the combination is sustainable or even achievable (Figure 5.7A). Some subset of points – those falling along the diagonal line – will represent combinations of population and per capita food supply that will just support subsistence in the sense defined here; thus, any actual combination of population and food that falls on the diagonal line will represent an equilibrium where the average member of the population has access to just enough food to support population replacement, i.e. where $r = 0$. The diagonal line splits the entire state space into a region of what Malthus would call "plenty", where per capita food availability is above the subsistence level and therefore the population grows, and a region of "misery" (also Malthus's term) where per capita food availability cannot support demographic replacement and therefore the population declines. Note that both the growth and the decline push the population toward the diagonal line.

To determine how population behaves under a particular system of farming, we need to impose that system's agricultural production function onto the abstract space of Figure 5.7A. Panel B of the figure shows one possibility: a production function that exhibits diminishing returns at higher population sizes (as we would expect) but slightly more complicated dynamics at lower sizes, dynamics of a sort we have not yet seen (actually we have, but tarry a moment). At very low population sizes, marginal productivity actually *increases* as the population grows, at least up to the low density inflection point (Figure 5.7B). The implication is that small populations may lose out on certain economies of scale – for example, they may be unable to muster enough laborers to clear land efficiently, to keep irrigation channels from silting up or leaking, or to complete the harvest before the first frost. Under these circumstances, population growth can be advantageous when the population is small, something that Malthus acknowledged. At the inflection point the economies of scale have all been realized and declining marginal productivity comes into play. And, in fact, we *have* seen this phenomenon before: the attentive reader may remember the case of Gambia from Chapter 3 (Figure 3.12, bottom panel). Following Lee's example, I am including the phenomenon here because it helps draw out additional features of his reworking of the Malthusian model.

If we overlay this production function on our abstract space defining plenty and misery, we end up with the situation shown in panel C of Figure 5.7. The production function touches the diagonal line at three points, including $N = 0$. All three *must* correspond to equilibrium population sizes. However, the point marked "minimum population" is an unstable equilibrium: if we perturb the population so that its size is just below the equilibrium, we push the system into misery, and the population declines to zero (which is a locally stable equilibrium).[9] By the same token, if we push the population above the unstable equilibrium we are in the region of plenty, and the population grows up to the "maximum population" size. Between the minimum and maximum the system enjoys a surplus of food – that is, per capita food availability is above the subsistence level – and at some point that surplus will be as large as it ever can be under this particular production function. The population size associated with this maximum possible surplus might be called the "optimal" population size – a term that was once used widely by population scientists but that has fallen out of fashion in more recent years. But there is nothing sacred about this optimum in Malthus's scheme: the population grows right past it on its way to the maximum population size, where the surplus vanishes at the edge of scarcity.

---

[9] Many modelers would call $N = 0$ a "trivial" equilibrium on the supposition that a population consisting of no members is not very interesting. But from a demographic or ecological point of view *extinction* is very interesting indeed and population dynamics in its neighborhood are profoundly important. For example, the possible existence of a low density inflection point means that it may be very difficult for a small group of people to colonize a habitat if the group tries to practice certain labor-intensive forms of farming.

Because it lies on the diagonal, the maximum population is an equilibrium – but what sort of equilibrium? Following the logic we applied to the minimum population, if we perturb the population so that its size is below the maximum, we push it into plenty and it responds by growing back up to the maximum – and conversely if we perturb it so that it is above the maximum. In other words, the maximum population is a stable equilibrium; it is, in fact, the demographic saturation point of the system, the point at which population regulation can be said to occur.

At this stable equilibrium, the population hangs precariously on the margin of misery, vulnerable to the malign effects of fluctuations in its food supply. As Malthus (1807: 60–1) put it, immediately following a passage on epidemics,

Of the other great scourge of mankind, famine, it may be observed that it is not in the nature of things that the increase of population should absolutely produce one. This increase, though rapid, is necessarily gradual [i.e. it occurs in small, if frequent, increments]; and as the human frame cannot be supported, even for a very short time without food, it is evident that no more human beings can grow up than there is provision to maintain. But though the principle of population cannot absolutely produce a famine, it prepares the way for one in the most complete manner; and by obliging all the lower classes of people to subsist nearly on the smallest quantity of food that will support life, turns even a slight deficiency from the failure of the seasons into a severe dearth; and may be fairly said therefore, to be one of the principal causes of famine.

Demographic saturation, in other words, is not inevitably associated with famine, but it leaves the population indisputably famine-*prone* in the face of environmental fluctuations ("the failure of the seasons"). The tempo and magnitude (and thus the demographic effects) of such fluctuations will, of course, vary from one part of the world to another reflecting (among other things) the natural variability of the environment.

What determines the demographic saturation point in the real world? The answer is: all the variables (other than labor supply or population size) that go into the production function but that are fixed when we examine the effects of changing population size – for example:

- climatological variables (e.g. annual cycles of rainfall, temperature, photoperiod)
- the amount and quality of available land
- the prevailing farming system
- the spatial and temporal organization of farming
- labor *allocation* (but not supply, the one variable allowed to "float")
- allocation of available genetic resources
- allocation of other available resources (e.g. animal dung, green manure, tools).

Now, these are the kinds of things that have gone into standard definitions of carrying capacity (see Chapter 3). Is the "demographic saturation point" therefore just another name for carrying capacity? I suggest not, mainly because the idea that these variables are fixed is never treated as anything more than a theoretical possibility. Most of the variables can change over time even in the absence of major changes in the basic mode of farming or the availability or quality of land. In addition, demographic saturation can apply to a single farm, not just a farming system or environment. Thus, a farm that allocates its resources badly has a lower saturation point than does an otherwise identical farm (with identical resources) that allocates them well. Demographic saturation is, to my mind, an altogether more fluid concept than carrying capacity.

The Positive and Preventive Checks

An important feature of Malthus's writings on population is that he paid considerable attention to the actual forces or mechanisms of population change, especially fertility and mortality. He argued that, as long as population was below the maximum size permitted by the food supply, fertility would exceed mortality and the population would grow; but as the population approached the maximum, certain *checks to population growth* would come into play. The "court of last resort" (Watkins and van de Walle, 1983) for checking population growth was a density-dependent increase in mortality – what Malthus called the *positive check*.[10] Malthus clearly believed that the positive check would usually involve hunger but not necessarily outright famine. Wars and plagues might also be involved, but again not necessarily so. The only workable way to improve human happiness over the long-term, according to Malthus, was to avoid the positive checks insofar as possible.

Malthus referred to any density-dependent decrease in fertility as the *preventive check* – that is, something that would prevent new members of the population from being born and thus becoming subject to the positive check. But the preventive check lacks the air of inevitably that ultimately clings to the positive check. In the absence of the preventive check, the positive check *will* have its day, to the woe of the many (especially the poor); but the preventive check *may or may not* occur – indeed Malthus was troubled by the apparent ability of couples to have many children even in the face of extreme scarcity. Such children, he feared, would end up being especially vulnerable to the positive check. To minimize childhood mortality, Malthus argued, the production of children must be coupled to *prudence*, so that couples do not begin their families until they have accumulated the resources needed to support them. The best way to instill a prudential spirit is through education,[11] and the most effective way to realize prudence is through late marriage (along with premarital abstinence) taking place only when the couple is in a position to establish an economically independent household.[12] Malthus was opposed to contraception,

---

[10] Some of his critics have claimed (disingenuously?) that Malthus meant "positive" in the sense of "good", i.e. that he truly favored death as a way to cull a population's members – especially the poor. But even the most superficial reading of Malthus makes it clear that he intended "positive" to mean "active", i.e. something that would carry away *already existing population* in the absence of other checks to population growth.

[11] Malthus was a lifelong advocate of free education, including (unusually for his times) for females.

[12] Historical demographers working with material from northwestern Europe, including the British Isles, during the early modern period (c. 1500–1800) have made a strong case that late marriage and

Figure 5.8 Ester Boserup (1910–99). Photograph by Mogens Boserup, India 1958.

but mainly because he believed that it threatened to undermine the status of young, unmarried women and turn them, in effect, into concubines dependent for their survival upon a company of uncaring wastrels. Malthus was by no means a modern thinker, but he was certainly a more nuanced one than he is generally given credit for.

Ester Boserup

We now turn from Robert Malthus to the self-proclaimed "anti-Malthus," Ester Boserup (Figure 5.8). Born Ester Børgesen in Copenhagen in 1910, Boserup received a degree in economics from the University of Copenhagen in 1935, having studied development economics, agricultural policy and sociology. During World War II she and her husband Mogens actively participated in the armed resistance to the Nazi occupation of Denmark. She spent much of the next two decades as a civil servant, first with the Danish government and then with the United Nations (UN). While affiliated with the UN she spent several years working in India and Senegal, and later travelled extensively in Africa and Southeast Asia. The remainder of her career was spent as an independent agricultural consultant and researcher. She seems to have taken a certain amount of pride in never having held an academic appointment.[13]

The book that launched the modern debate over population and agriculture was *The Conditions of Agricultural Growth: The Economics of Agrarian Change under Population Pressure*, published by Boserup in 1965. The main goal of that book was to identify the conditions under which agricultural "modernization" was most likely to occur in the present-day developing world; she did not attempt at that time to deal with agricultural change over long stretches of the preindustrial past, except in passing. But Boserup later generalized her argument to make such change a central focus of her 1981 book *Population and Technological Change: A Study of Long-Term*

---

neolocality operated exactly the way Malthus thought they should to reduce levels of childhood mortality below what is observed in most preindustrial populations (see Chapter 7).

[13] Her definitive professional biography is a memoir published in her eighty-ninth year, a few months before she died (Boserup, 1999).

Trends.[14] Her 1965 book was something of a sensation (her 1981 book rather less so), especially in the disciplines of geography, anthropology and demography, and it had wide influence during the late 1960s and throughout the 1970s. When I was a young graduate student in demographic anthropology, it was one of the few books I was told I *had* to read (it was still quite new and fresh back then). I'm glad I did read it, for it has continued to exercise my brain at an age when it needs all the exercise it can get.

An important if under-appreciated fact about the *timing* of Boserup's career is that *The Conditions of Agricultural Growth* was written soon after the modern "discovery" of shifting cultivation by anthropologists and geographers.[15] According to the understanding of shifting cultivation that prevailed at that time, it was the most primitive, least intensive and most ancient of all agricultural systems – in effect, the Ur-system of farming for the whole world. Moreover, the distinction between fallow and actively cultivated fields was considered absolute and unambiguous, and the length of the fallow period relative to the preceding period of cultivation was viewed as the primary (perhaps *only*) variable affecting the long-term productivity and sustainability of the farming system (Figure 5.9). As of the mid-1960s, then, the ratio of the duration of cropping to fallowing was considered the single most important parameter characterizing a system of shifting cultivation, and shortening the fallow period was the most obvious method for increasing the food supply in "primitive" agriculture. Moreover, it was a method that would sooner or later require deliberate countermeasures to mitigate the long-term deleterious effects of shortened fallows on soil fertility – e.g. a relengthening of fallows (thereby driving the food supply back down) or new, labor-intensive soil-management practices. As discussed in Chapter 6, many of these ideas about shifting cultivation have been called into question in recent years. But Boserup absorbed what was then cutting-edge thinking on the topic and incorporated it into her own work. It is only a slight exaggeration to say that, for Boserup, agricultural intensification was more or less synonymous with shortened fallows and, ultimately, with more work. (That this is a narrow view of intensification can be seen by referring back to the passage from Harold Brookfield quoted near the beginning of this chapter.) Indeed she developed an entire typology of preindustrial agriculture based on the relative lengths of fallow and cropping periods (Boserup, 1965: 15–16). Her agricultural types, named for the kind of

---

[14] A foretaste of that book appeared in Boserup (1976). For a useful collection of her other essays on demography and economic change, see Boserup (1990).

[15] Shifting cultivation was first described professionally by Orator Cook in the 1920s, in the form of *milpa* farming on the Yucatan Peninsula, and some 15 years later by Derwent Whittlesey, taking a more global perspective (Cook, 1921; Whittlesey, 1937a,b). Pelzer surveyed its southeast Asian varieties in 1945; van Beukering (1947) did work on the *ladang* form of shifting cultivation in the Dutch East Indies (Indonesia) during the 1930s but his findings were not published until after the war. Extended ethnographic studies of shifting cultivation began, however, only in the 1950s (Izikowitz, 1951; Freeman, 1955; de Schlippe, 1956; Conklin, 1957). Hal Conklin published the first major review of the growing ethnographic material on shifting cultivation in 1961, just four years before Boserup's first book appeared (Conklin, 1961). In Chapter 6, I review some important ways in which our understanding of shifting cultivation has evolved since the early 1960s.

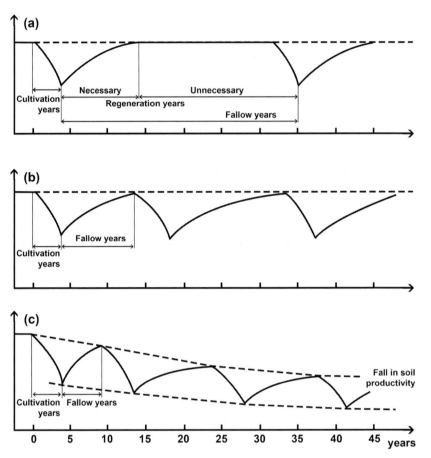

Figure 5.9 The theoretical relationships between soil fertility (y-axis) and length of cropping plus fallow (x-axis) as conceptualized c. 1955–65. (a) Stable long-term soil fertility in an extensive system in which fallows are longer than strictly necessary. (b) Stable long-term soil fertility in a somewhat more intensive system in which fallows are just long enough. (c) Declining long-term soil fertility in a short fallow system. Note in panel b that fallows must lengthen over time if soil fertility is to be maintained. Redrawn from Ruthenberg (1971: 47) from Guillemin (1956), by permission of the Institut de Recherches Agronomiques Tropicales et des Cultures Vivrières.

standing vegetation likely to be found on a field at the end of the normal fallow period, are summarized in Table 5.1, which also includes a measure of what might be called "Boserupian intensity" developed by Hans Ruthenberg (1971: 3–4) and still widely used:

$$R = \frac{mean\ length\ of\ cultivation}{(mean\ length\ of\ cultivation) + (mean\ length\ of\ fallow)} \times 100,$$

where R measures the percentage of the entire crop–fallow cycle that is devoted to cropping. The durations of cultivation and fallowing are counted in the same units (years); R is therefore a scale-free statistic that varies between zero and 100, with numbers close to zero signifying low intensity, long-fallow systems and numbers close to 100 signifying high intensity, near-permanent cultivation. For Boserup and many of her followers, R captures the single most important dimension of agricultural intensification.

It was generally assumed (and in a few cases actually known) that farming systems with high values of R were usually preceded by, and indeed historically derived from, systems with lower R values. It was also accepted (albeit based initially on rather weak and anecdotal evidence) that there was, worldwide, a positive correlation between a population's crude density and its farming system's R value, both estimated at the macrodemographic level. As discussed in Chapter 1 (see Figure 1.1 and associated discussion) this correlation may in fact be weak and difficult to interpret for many reasons, including the well-known dictum that correlation is not necessarily an indicator of causation. Nonetheless, showing that the positive correlation exists or does not exist has been the principal empirical goal of much of the post-Boserup debate over population and agriculture. And Boserup herself accepted this correlation as both the fundamental empirical phenomenon she wanted to explain and (rather circularly) the primary evidence in support of her explanation.

Before examining Boserup's explanation, it is important to mention some of the assumptions that underpinned it. First, and perhaps most importantly, she argued *contra* Malthus that the food supply had little if any determinative influence on population growth:

The neo-Malthusian school has resuscitated the old idea that population growth must be regarded as a variable dependent mainly on agricultural output... [But] few observers would like to suggest that the tremendous increase in rates of population growth witnessed throughout the underdeveloped world in the two post-war decades could be explained as the result of changes in the conditions for food production. It is reasonably clear that the [modern] population explosion is a change in basic conditions which must be regarded as autonomous, in the sense that the explanation is to be sought, not in improved conditions of food production, but in medical invention and some other factors which the student of agricultural development would regard as independent variables...

I have reached the conclusion...that in many cases the output from a given area of land responds far more generously to an additional input of labour than assumed by neo-Malthusian authors. If this is true, the low rates of population growth found (until recently) in pre-industrial communities cannot be explained as the result of insufficient food supplies due to overpopulation, and we must leave more room for other factors in the explanation of demographic trends. It is outside the scope of the present study, however, to discuss these other factors – medical, biological, political, etc. – which may help to explain why the rate of growth of population in primitive communities was what it was. Throughout, our inquiry is concerned with the effects of population changes on agriculture and not with the causes of these population changes. (Boserup, 1965: 11–14; the order of paragraphs is reversed from the original)

In other words, population grows – or does not grow – as a result of factors that are not really relevant to the agricultural economist. Incidentally, this passage shows

Table 5.1 Boserup's typology of agricultural land use. Data from Ruthenberg (1971: 3–4). Reproduced with permission of Oxford Publishing Limited from Ruthenberg, H. (1971) *Farming Systems in the Tropics*, 2nd edn, Oxford: Clarendon Press. Reproduced with permission of the Licensor through PLSclear.

Types of land use	Length of cultivation (years)	Length of fallow (years)	R	Population density
Forest-fallow cultivation	1–2	20+	< 10	LOW
Bush-fallow cultivation	2+	6–20	10–60	↓
Grass-fallow cultivation	2+	1–2	60–90	↓
Annual cropping (1 crop yr^{-1})	"continuous"	occasional	90–100	↓
Multicropping (> 1 crop yr^{-1})	"continuous"	rare	> 100? (not strictly possible)	HIGH

clearly that Boserup did not believe that rapid population growth has been a constant "push" factor throughout human history, but rather that before the modern era population growth was slow when it happened at all.

The second of Boserup's assumptions was that the natural environment was not an important consideration when trying to explain agricultural intensification:

> We have found that it is unrealistic to regard agricultural cultivation systems as adaptations to different natural conditions, and that cultivation systems can be more plausibly explained as the results of differences in population density... (Boserup, 1965: 117)

It is unclear why this should be an either/or question, why environment and population density cannot interact. Nonetheless, the assumption is fundamental to Boserup's argument.

Finally, Boserup assumed that the types of farming systems listed in Table 5.1 were in fact proper *types*, and that any overlap between them could only be transitory and unstable (Boserup, 1965: 56–8). Thus, a farming system that looks, in a cross-sectional survey, as if it contains multiple forms of land use (e.g. permanent irrigated fields and shifting cultivation) is merely a transitional stage in the long-term replacement of less intensive practices with more intensive ones under the influence of external pressure (external, that is, to the farming system as narrowly defined). According to Boserup, the "mix" should never be considered a stable complex of different approaches to, say, different local microenvironments or differing distances of fields from domicile.

I think all these assumptions are wrong – and not just wrong but *egregiously* wrong. Like any theoretician Boserup is free to make whatever assumptions she wants. But she has a habit of positing such things, not as assumptions, but as valid descriptions of the real world. As such, they are assertions that, in my opinion, tend to close down avenues of inquiry rather than to open them up. If in fact she had presented them as model assumptions – as in "variation in the natural environment is of course important in reality, but for simplicity I am going to ignore it in my model" – I would have no objection. After all, we can always relax assumptions in later versions of the model. But we cannot relax statements accepted *tout court* as factual.

Boserup's Basic Argument

The cornerstone of Boserup's argument is her belief that agricultural intensification always comes at a cost. According to Boserup, the adoption of agricultural innovations that provide a higher *total* yield (kg ha^{-1} yr^{-1}) almost always involves a decline in the productivity of labor (kg person-hr^{-1}). In other words, traditional farmers can adopt new practices to increase yield beyond the margin of the existing system, but they generally end up working harder for each extra unit of yield. To put this idea into terms that Boserup herself never used, *all* increases in agricultural yield in preindustrial farming, regardless of what particular inputs achieved them, are affected by the declining marginal productivity of labor.[16] Thus, farmers are expected to resist intensification unless "pressured" to adopt it, a quite reasonable reluctance to work harder that might be called "Boserupian inertia." The most general form of pressure acting to overcome Boserupian inertia in the preindustrial world was, according to Boserup, the declining per capita food supply caused by population growth in long-fallow systems – when and if population growth occurs. Thus, population growth can actually be a positive force in promoting agricultural change.

This logic is diagrammed in Figure 5.10, which also shows another important element in Boserup's thinking. "Population pressure," which is otherwise ill defined in Boserup's writings, begins not at the margin of subsistence, but whenever the average per capita food availability falls below the level needed to support the population at its minimal *acceptable* standard of living, which will often be higher than the subsistence level. Thus, consumption norms play a more explicit part in Boserup's scheme than in Malthus's. The subsistence level still exists (implicitly) in Boserup, but so long as the minimally acceptable standard of living is above the standard ordained by subsistence, the pressure to innovate will begin whenever population size exceeds N^*, the value associated with the minimally acceptable standard (Figure 5.10). Whenever $N^* < \hat{N}$ we can speak of "Boserupian pressure",

---

[16] If agricultural intensification always takes the form of shortened fallows, this assertion makes some sense because laborious remedial measures may be necessary to maintain soil quality. But several authors (e.g. Brookfield, 1984, 2001a,b; Padoch, 1985; Hunt, 2000; Nielsen *et al.*, 2006) have suggested that, first, shortening fallows in shifting cultivation does not necessarily compromise labor productivity and, second, other kinds of intensification, for example adopting new genetic resources or creating landesque capital such as terraces or irrigation canals, may actually *increase* labor productivity in the long run. In other words, there may truly be such things as labor-saving practices. These ideas will be explored further in Chapter 6.

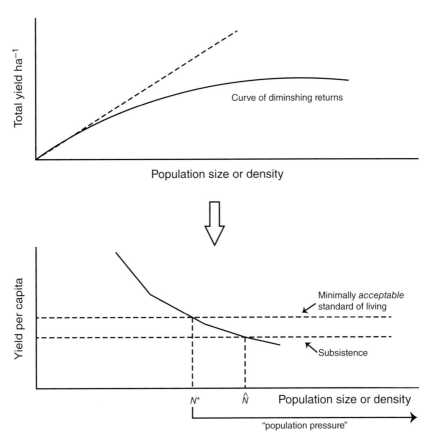

Figure 5.10 Boserup's basic argument. Under a fixed system of production (including a fixed value of R) agricultural yield exhibits diminishing returns as population size or density increases. As a result, the marginal yield (yield per capita) declines until the physical standard of living drops below some culturally acceptable minimum. As the population continues to grow, its members experience "population pressure," presumably growing dissatisfaction with their declining standard of living or even outright physical misery. In Boserup's view, the population size that produces the minimally acceptable standard of living (N^*) is usually well below that associated with the subsistence level of food consumption ($\hat{N}$).

which, if it is strong enough, can overcome Boserupian inertia before the population is driven to the subsistence level.

Figure 5.11 draws out a further point not emphasized by Boserup. When population size exceeds N^*, people will be motivated to adopt any new system of production that promises to yield more food per capita, even if it must be paid for by more labor. At the time of adoption, then, the production function of the new system will presumably be higher than that of the old system (Figure 5.11, top panel). But, if the population continues to grow (and Boserup provides no reason to believe that it will or will not), the new system itself will eventually be subject to declining marginal productivity, albeit at a higher population size. In other words, the new system will, sooner or later, be driven down once again to the minimally acceptable standard of

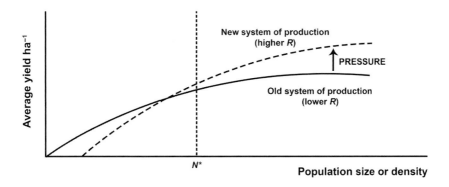

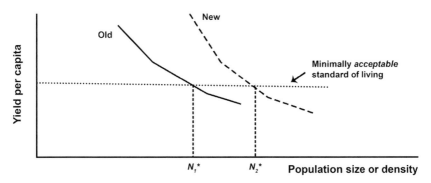

Figure 5.11 (Top panel) Boserupian pressure, starting at N^* and worsening thereafter, to adopt a new system of food production that provides a higher average and marginal yield. (Bottom panel) The newly adopted system of food production itself eventually undergoes declining marginal productivity and thus reaches a new point at which the average member is at the minimally acceptable standard of living (N_2^*). At N_2^* the average member of the community has exactly the same standard of living as at N_1^*, but at a higher overall population size.

living (Figure 5.11, bottom panel), and population pressure will be renewed. Unless innovation occurs again to relieve the pressure, agricultural "growth" will have achieved nothing in the long run but a bigger, perhaps harder-working, population – what Geertz (1963) called "agricultural involution" (see Chapter 6).

By focusing on agricultural change, Boserup reopens the issues of experimentation and innovation in the preindustrial world discussed in Chapter 2. If effective innovations are rare and hard to come by, then population growth may push the farming system all the way down to the subsistence level, where it will presumably stay, no matter how much pressure is felt, until another innovation happens to come along. This was, for example, Lynn White's view of agricultural change in the Middle Ages (White, 1962). If, on the other hand, traditional farmers are constantly experimenting with new practices or genetic resources (as I have argued), innovations may be readily available "off the shelf" in the way that Boserup seemed to have assumed – and that probably seemed natural to a development economist interested in motivating people to adopt modern methods of farming, which did not need to be reinvented *de novo* on the spot. A related question has to do with the magnitude of the improvement in yield achieved by the usual sort of innovation adopted under preindustrial conditions. A new-found landrace of rice, for instance, may boost production, but surely not by several hundred percent (even the modern Green Revolution did not achieve such an increase). One of my favorite examples of preindustrial agricultural innovation is described by Grith Lerche (1994) in her wonderful treatise on the Danish wheeled plow. The heavy wheeled plow itself was unquestionably an important innovation in early medieval northern Europe, allowing fertile but heavy clay soils on bottomlands to be cultivated much more easily than had previously been the case. But it was one of those big, rare, Lynn-Whitish sorts of innovation. Lerche points to what may have been more typical: pebble-studded moldboards. The moldboard, the piece of the plow that turns the soil, was originally made of wood and subjected to enormous frictional forces and wear. Every so often it would break or become so worn that it no longer engaged the soil deeply enough, and it would have to be replaced. Now, it was not horrendously costly to cut and shape a new moldboard – having one break was an annoyance, not a catastrophe – but it did divert some time and energy from actual food production. Then one day (we know not when or where) a peasant, no doubt kicking his newly broken moldboard out of frustration, had an inspiration: if you made a new mold-board and hammered dozens of small pebbles into its working surface, the friction and wear would be borne by the pebbles, which could withstand them much longer than the wood.[17] Voilà, an innovation! – but probably one that improved the allocation of time and energy so negligibly as to be practically impossible to measure in terms of increased yield per plowman-hour of work.

I suspect that most preindustrial agricultural innovations were of this minor variety rather than anything on the scale of the twentieth-century Green Revolution – but their cumulative effects on yield over many centuries could have been significant. Of course, Boserup was mainly interested in one kind of "innovation" – the shortening of fallow periods – which might achieve immediate and substantial (if short-lived) gains in total crop yield before requiring more labor to offset soil deterioration. Shortening fallows must have been a rather obvious option that did not require much real inventiveness. It must, says Boserup, have been the most common response in the face of population growth, unlike other less obvious means of relieving population pressure.

Over the years, Boserup's model has been criticized on several grounds. The following criticisms seem to me to be among the most telling (other important criticisms will be discussed in the following chapter).

---

[17] Surviving scraps of such moldboards, with badly worn pebbles but unworn wood, can be seen in the National Museum of Denmark in Copenhagen.

- In Boserup's theory, population growth is an *exogenous variable* – it has an effect on variables included in the model, but nothing in the model affects it in turn. Thus, the theory leaves population growth – or its absence – unexplained, except that it is not generally attributable to a change in the food supply.
- Long-fallow shifting cultivation may not have been the Ur-system from which all other varieties of farming evolved. In some parts of the world, there is archaeological evidence that permanent dryland farming and even simple forms of irrigation appeared very early in the local history of agriculture (see Rowley-Conwy, 1981; Barker, 1985: 141–3; Moore *et al.*, 2000; Fisher, 2007; Bogaard *et al.*, 2013). Since Boserup's argument is almost exclusively about changes in shifting cultivation, it is less general than it purports to be.
- Cropping frequency (as captured by R) is not the only dimension of agricultural intensification. I ask the reader to turn again to Figure 1.1 in Chapter 1 and note that the y-axis is really just R, even if it is not labeled as such. The bivariate relationship between R and population density shown in Figure 1.1 is apparently positive but also pretty weak. Now examine Table 5.2, which includes exactly the same 274 Papua New Guinean communities as Figure 1.1. In this table (which I admit is not easy to read), all 274 local farming "systems" are first classified into five agricultural intensity classes (from very low to very high) based on their estimated values of R. Then, under each intensity class, farming practices used by a certain percentage of systems *within that class* (left-most column) are tabulated, including practices used by none of the systems ("not present").[18] For example, out of all the systems that are grouped into Class 1 (very low intensity systems), 21–40 percent construct fences and 6–20 percent build small mounds or use some method of soil retention (most commonly simple logs laid parallel to the field's contours). None of the systems in the very low intensity class ever practices composting, building of large mounds or square planting beds, releasing of pigs onto fields that have already been harvested, or short fallows.[19] The point I am trying to make by including this complicated table is that there seem to be positive associations among R, population density, and *other* methods of intensification. It may be that a multivariate analysis of R and population density *plus these other methods of intensification* would have made the apparent (if weak) bivariate relationship between R and population density disappear entirely. In statistical jargon, the positive relationship in Figure 1.1 might be spurious. On the other hand, there might well turn out to be a close positive relationship between population density and the other methods of intensification, perhaps reflecting

---

[18] Actually, what is tabulated are the practices that are used *significantly* by each percentage of systems within a particular intensity class. Nowhere in the published report of these data are we told exactly what "significantly" means.

[19] It may seem tautological to include short fallows in this table since R is already defined in terms of average fallow length relative to the average period of cultivation. But it is not, at least not entirely. For example, 21–40 percent of systems classified as moderate (Class 3) use short fallow periods "significantly" but apparently not often enough to push up their R values, which reflect community-level averages, not the practices of individual farmers.

Table 5.2 Percentage of farming systems "significantly" using selected farming techniques within each of five agricultural intensity classes defined on the basis of *R*. Included are 274 local farming systems in Papua New Guinea mapped by the MASP Project, *c.* 1990–5 (see Chapter 1). Modified from Allen (2001). Reproduced with permission of John Wiley & Sons, Inc, from B. J. Allen (2001) Boserup and Brookfield and the association between population density and agricultural intensity in Papua New Guinea. *Asia Pacific Viewpoint*, 42, 237–54.

Percentage of systems within each intensity class	Agricultural intensity class				
	(1) Very low (R < 11)	(2) Low (R = 11–33)	(3) Moderate (R = 33–65)	(4) High (R = 66–79)	(5) Very high (R = 80–100)
81–100				Short fallows Fences Drains Long beds Small mounds Tillage	Short fallows Composting Fences
61–80					
41–60					
21–40	Fences	Small mounds	Drains Short fallows Small mounds Tillage	Composting Legume rotations Mounds	Large mounds Mounds
6–20	Small mounds Soil retention	Fences Mounds Short fallows Soil retention Tillage	Composting Fences Mounds Large mounds Legume rotations Square beds	Large mounds	Drains Pigs in fields[a] Legume rotations Long beds Small mounds Square beds Tillage

1–5	Drains Long beds Mounds Planted fallows[b] Tillage	Composting Drains Long beds Pigs in fields[a] Planted fallows[b] Square beds	Pigs in fields[a] Soil retention		
Not present	Composting Large mounds Square beds Pigs in fields[a] Short fallows	Large mounds Legume rotations	Planted fallows[b]	Pigs in fields[a] Planted fallows[b] Square beds Soil retention	Planted fallows[b] Soil retention

[a] Domesticated pigs released onto fields that have been completely harvested so that their rooting will grub up weeds and insect pests and their dung will manure the soil.

[b] New fallows planted with casuarina tree seedlings (*Casuarina oligodon*) as described in Chapter 2; typical of long-fallow systems.

theoretically important effects of population pressure on a wide variety of farming practices, not just the length of fallows. But if R is the only outcome variable analyzed, these potentially important effects will be missed.

- If indeed there are several dimensions or avenues of intensification, there is unlikely to be a single, universal trajectory of agricultural change of the sort suggested by Table 5.1. It may be the case that population pressure is a frequent cause of *all* forms of intensification, but the specific direction of intensification may be less predictable than Boserup supposes.

- Intensification may not always entail an increase in labor for every increase in marginal yield: some technological innovations may be genuinely labor-saving. Thus, Boserupian inertia may not be a universal brake on agricultural change, always and everywhere requiring pressure to overcome it. On the other hand, alternative forms of inertia may be operating, as discussed in the next chapter.

- Mixed farming systems may not be unstable transitional states. Boserup's conviction that mixed systems should never be regarded as adaptations to different microenvironments is simply implausible. After all, von Thünen showed that mixed systems could be stable equilibria even on an environmentally homogeneous plain. Mixed farming systems might be expected to have more potential avenues of intensification than do "pure" systems.

- Boserup's model is about longitudinal changes within single populations, and yet the data marshaled to test it are almost always (even in Boserup's case) cross-sectional and comparative across multiple populations. The ecological fallacy stalks the whole debate.

These criticisms are important, but in the final analysis none of them is fatal to the basic argument that demographic "pressure" can be *one* important motivator of agricultural change. As we shall see in the next chapter, several of Boserup's defenders have addressed these criticisms, often by modifying her original model in ways that I consider helpful. I suspect that no one today who claims to be a Boserupian really believes all the tenets and assertions of her 1965 book – just as no self-styled Darwinist today believes in pangenesis.

Can Malthus and Boserup be Reconciled?

Looking over the preceding sections of this chapter, I see that I have been harder on Boserup than I have on Malthus. In part, this is because Boserup continues to exert far more influence than Malthus, at least in my own field of anthropology where Malthus is often judged to be not just wrong but downright evil. But the fact that Malthus has been treated unfairly by others does not justify unfair treatment of Boserup. Therefore, I want to make it clear that I think both authors are vulnerable to criticism *and* that both authors had some really good ideas. What I do not accept is Boserup's life-long insistence that her argument can never be reconciled with Malthus's – that you can believe one or the other, but not both. Elsewhere (Wood, 1998) I have shown that there are numerous intimations of Boserupian thought in

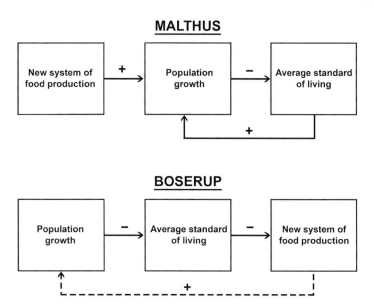

Figure 5.12 Malthus and Boserup schematized and contrasted. The plus and minus signs denote the correlations between variables taken two at a time. The *broken line* represents a causal connection sometimes implied and sometimes explicitly denied by Boserup.

Malthus's *Essay on the Principle of Population*. While it would be too much to call Malthus the original Boserupian, there is enough in the *Essay* for us to squirm whenever Boserup characterizes herself as staunchly anti-Malthusian.

My two most fundamental criticisms apply equally to Malthus *and* Boserup: (i) both theorize almost exclusively at the macrodemographic level, and (ii) both present models that are incomplete insofar as they treat important variables as exogenous and thus leave their behavior unexplained. Much of the remainder of this book is devoted, one way or another, to the first of these two criticisms. In what is left of this chapter, I will concentrate on the second. For Malthus the exogenous variable is agricultural improvement, for Boserup it is population growth. Can a combination of Malthus and Boserup provide a more complete model?

Figure 5.12 reduces both Malthus and Boserup to boxes and arrows, a gross but tactically useful over-simplification of each of them. The arrows and the plus and minus signs indicate the direction of the causal linkages between any two boxes considered in isolation; thus, a high average standard of living promotes population growth (top panel) but discourages the adoption of new farming practices (bottom panel). In the Boserupian portion of the figure, I have included a causal arrow (broken line) that Boserup herself might not have approved of: a new, improved system of food production leads to more population growth. In the 1965 *Conditions of Agricultural Growth*, Boserup bluntly asserted that population growth had little if anything to do with improvements in food supply. In her 1981 book on *Population and Technological Change*, however, she seems to accept that increases in food production might encourage continuing population growth, whatever its original cause.

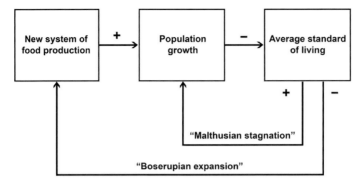

Figure 5.13 The Malthus-and-Boserup (MaB) ratchet.

If the broken line is included, then Boserup's scheme in Figure 5.12 constitutes a positive feedback loop.[20] By itself, this loop would lead to an unending cycle of population growth and economic expansion – "Boserupian expansion" as it were. The Malthusian scheme, in contrast, contains a negative feedback loop leading, again by itself, to a stable equilibrium – "Malthusian stagnation" we might call it. But the point I want to make here is that the three boxes are identical in both schemes and, whenever the arrows are shared in common, the signs are always the same (especially if my broken arrow is allowed). As I mentioned near the beginning of this chapter, Boserup was concerned with the causes of intensification, Malthus with its effects – so they were really addressing separate if related questions and their models need not compete with each other. I have also argued that Malthus himself was comfortable with the idea that population growth may sometimes lead to agrarian change instead of stagnation at the subsistence level, similar in certain respects to Boserup (Wood, 1998). All this emboldens me to suggest that the two can in fact be combined quite easily, as diagrammed in Figure 5.13. I have called my own attempt to construct a formal model combining Malthusian and Boserupian components *the MaB (Malthus-and-Boserup) ratchet* (Wood, 1998) for reasons that should become clear presently. Other attempts to reconcile Malthus and Boserup can be found in Pryor and Mauer (1982), Lee (1986), Turner and Ali (1996), and Richerson and Boyd (1998).

For a purely graphical treatment of the MaB ratchet we can start with Lee's version of Malthus's complex argument shown back in Figure 5.7. We left that figure stranded at the maximum population size, right at the subsistence level of food consumption – i.e. at Malthusian stagnation. In Figure 5.14, that initial stable equilibrium is marked A ("Old curve of production"). An interesting implication of Boserup's argument is that, whenever N^* (the population size that yields the minimally acceptable standard of living) is less than $\hat{N}$ (the stable demographic saturation point) then population pressure should become positive even before point A is

---

[20] The sign of the overall feedback loop can be found by multiplying the signs of all the arrows contained in the loop. In the case of the Boserupian loop, we have minus × minus × plus = plus.

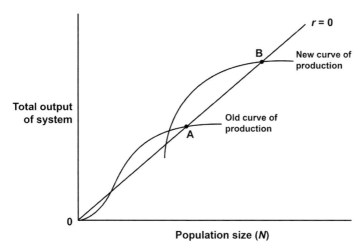

Figure 5.14 The MaB ratchet at work. A transient Boserupian expansion (resulting from a newly adopted system of food production) lifts the population's members above the subsistence level for a while, but because of the resulting population growth the system is driven back down to Malthusian stagnation. Points A and B are the stable equilibria associated with the old and new systems of production respectively. At B the average standard of living is at the edge of misery, just as it was at A. However, the population size is greater. From James W. Wood (1998) A theory of preindustrial population dynamics: Demography, economy, and well-being in Malthusian systems. *Current Anthropology*, 39, 99–135, by permission of The University of Chicago Press.

reached. Thus, *the system tends toward a stable equilibrium at which there is positive pressure to _alter_ the system itself.* If any alternative system is available that has a higher production function at the population size corresponding to point A, the community will be motivated to adopt it (assuming, of course, that they recognize the advantages of the new system and do not foresee any risks or excessive costs in adopting it), initiating a phase of Boserupian expansion. As yields increase under the new system, population pressure will be relieved and an average standard of living above the subsistence level will be attained (Figure 5.14, "New curve of production") – but only temporarily. Eventually the new production function will exhibit declining marginal productivity, and the system will reach a new stable equilibrium at point B. At that point, the standard of living will be the same (on average) as at point A, but at a higher population size. (That is precisely why I call the MaB ratchet a ratchet: it jacks up population size via a transient, cyclical turn of the "jack handle" of per capita food production.) And Boserupian population pressure at B will be just as severe as it was at A. If another innovation comes along, a new round of Boserupian expansion is expected to occur; otherwise, the system will stay mired in Malthusian stagnation.

The most important exogenous variable in *this* scheme has to do with the availability of useful innovations at any given time or, to put it differently, the factors that determine whether the system stays in a state of Malthusian stagnation or switches over to Boserupian expansion. The model as it exists now is silent on this question.

It is also silent on the related questions of whether Boserupian expansions are large or small, and are short-lived or long-lasting. It would take long and systematic study of the history of agricultural improvement over many centuries to answer such questions. The MaB ratchet is arguably more complete than is Malthus or Boserup considered separately, but it still leaves important variables unexplained.

Now, when I first formulated the MaB ratchet I thought it was terribly original – a veritable intellectual Boserupian expansion. It was bad enough to discover that several *recent* authors have formulated similar models, but it was much worse to go back and discover that Malthus seemed to have had something close to the MaB ratchet in mind over two centuries ago, starting in the very first edition of his *Essay*. I quote the relevant passage at length here, interpolating in square brackets pointers to what I think are parallels to the MaB ratchet. I leave it to others to decide if my interpolations are fair and accurate.

We will suppose the means of subsistence [sustenance or per capita food availability, not "subsistence" as we have used it here] in any country just equal to the easy support of its inhabitants [the minimally acceptable standard of living?]. The constant effort towards population [population growth] ... increases the number of people before the means of subsistence are increased. The food therefore which before supported seven millions must now be divided among seven millions and a half or eight millions. The poor consequently must live much worse, and many of them will be reduced to severe distress [misery]. The number of labourers also being above the proportion of the work in the market, the price of labour must tend toward a decrease, while the price of provisions would tend to rise [population pressure]. The labourer must therefore work harder to earn the same as he did before [declining marginal productivity of labor]. During this season of distress, the discouragements to marriage, and the difficulty of rearing a family are so great that population is at a stand [demographic saturation or Malthusian stagnation]. In the mean time the cheapness of labour, the plenty of labourers, and the necessity of increased industry amongst them [population pressure yet again] encourage cultivators to employ more labour upon their land, to turn up fresh soil [shortening of fallows?], and to manure and improve more completely what is already in tillage [generally speaking, agricultural intensification], till ultimately the means of subsistence become in the same proportion to the population as at the period from which we set out [Boserupian expansion]. The situation of the labourer being then again tolerably comfortable [relief of population pressure], the restraints to population are in some degree loosened, and the same retrograde and progressive movements with respect to happiness are repeated [the MaB ratchet!]. (Malthus, 1798: 29–31)

One important implication of the MaB ratchet, already apparent in Malthus's annoyingly prescient formulation of it, is that – *contra* Boserup and her supporters – neither absolute population size nor crude population density is a very informative measure of population pressure. A low-density population with a nonintensive form of food production may be far more pressed for food than a high-density one with a complex system of farming. As Malthus (1807: 546) put it, "This unfavorable proportion [between population and food supply] has no necessary connection with the quantity of population which a country may contain. On the contrary, it is more frequently found in countries which are very thinly peopled than in those which are populous." The capacity to support a large population is built up gradually by a more or less prolonged history of MaB ratcheting. Most low-density populations are at low density precisely because they have not (yet?) created that capacity. Consequently, population size or density is a poor measure of population pressure. This idea goes a long way toward explaining why cross-population comparisons such as those in Figure 1.1 so rarely find strong associations between population density and agricultural intensification or indeed any other interesting human behavior. To cite one example, Keeley (1996: 117–21) found no convincing correlation between population density and the frequency of warfare in preindustrial, pre-state societies. This negative finding surprised him not at all:

The type of population pressure that Malthus [and Boserup for that matter] envisioned cannot be measured by simple density... The quantity of food produced from a given piece of ground by farmers who possess the technology to deep plow, fertilize with [inorganic] chemicals or manures, and irrigate exceeds that produced by dibble-stick, long-fallow, dry farming. Primitive farmers experienced land shortages and famines at far lower population densities than do their modern counterparts. Because so many factors – latitude, rainfall, soils, forest cover, biodiversity, energy input, and general technology – must be considered, making comparisons on the basis of "equivalent" population densities is extremely difficult. (Keeley, 1996: 118–19)

In 2009, as it happens, Rwanda and Belgium had precisely the same population density (341 persons km^{-2}), but surely no one would claim that their material conditions were even remotely similar. Differences between the two countries in history, economy, environment and who knows what other factors are so profound as to render any comparison based solely on population density meaningless. Population density, as Malthus but not Boserup would have argued, is a poor measure of population pressure or much of anything else.

A related implication of the MaB ratchet is that population growth *per se* is not a sign of population pressure. On the contrary, population growth only occurs in robust, healthy communities that are below their demographic saturation points, just as Malthus thought. It is at the stable equilibrium, where population growth has ceased, that pressure is likely to be felt most keenly, especially during transient food shortages that push the stagnant population further into misery. The very fact that a population is *not* growing may be evidence that it is at saturation and therefore feeling the bite of what Le Roy Ladurie (1976) once called the "Malthusian scissors," the closing gap between food and mouths to feed.

Variation in Material Conditions under the MaB Ratchet

For me, the most difficult part of constructing a mathematical model of the MaB ratchet was to derive the expected distribution of material *well-being* among individuals as the population undergoes successive rounds of Boserupian expansion and Malthusian stagnation (Wood, 1998: 114–17). Technically, what I call well-being includes any aspect of an individual's physical condition that is positively associated with higher survival and/or fertility; it is thus analogous to Darwinian fitness but makes no claim about any genetic determination of the suite of traits influencing well-being. Nor does this definition require us to determine how to *measure* well-being on individuals, although this will be a critical task for any future empirical applications of the MaB ratchet.[21] In this simple version of the model, variation arises purely from random fluctuations in the incidence of births and deaths within households; it is thus a model of demographic stochasticity, not of systematic differences across household environments. Still, the model does take the first, tentative steps toward a more focused scale of analysis – individuals and households, not whole farming populations (the *distribution* of well-being is what links things going on at the individual and household level to the dynamics of the population as a whole). Figure 5.15 shows the model results in highly schematic form. In brief, Malthusian stagnation is associated with a stationary distribution of well-being centered on the average level ("subsistence") just consistent with population replacement – which is why $r = 0$ at the equilibrium we're calling stagnation. This prediction contravenes one of Malthus's own beliefs, namely that variation in household material conditions ought to be at a maximum at Malthusian stagnation, as poorer households bear the brunt of the marginal situation. According to the MaB ratchet, the variance in well-being is expected to be at its *minimum* at Malthusian stagnation, although it is important to note that that minimum is still well above zero. During Boserupian expansion, both the mean and variance of well-being increase, owing mostly to expansion of the upper portions of the distribution (the lower tail of the distribution, representing poor households, does not change nearly as much). The rich get richer, but the poor stay about the same, partly because, if their well-being got much worse, they would die: truncation selection always works at the lower tail of the distribution. But, as we have seen, any round of Boserupian expansion ends right back in Malthusian stagnation as a higher stable equilibrium population size is attained – and at that new "higher" state of stagnation, the distribution of well-being falls back to precisely what it was before the expansion. The community as a whole is just as bad off as it was before – even though it is larger and producing more food. And variation in material well-being among members of the community persists. As Jesus and St. Matthew purportedly claimed, our farming ancestors had the poor always with them.

Do the empirical distributions of well-being in subsistence or near-subsistence farming communities bear any similarity whatsoever to the predictions shown in Figure 5.15? And if they do, are they closer to the predictions that the MaB ratchet makes for a state of Malthusian stagnation or to those for Boserupian expansion? In short, do subsistence and near-subsistence farming populations appear, based on their distributions of well-being, to spend most of their time stagnating as Malthus believed or expanding as in Boserup's model? Does change or stasis predominate in the rural preindustrial world? The honest answer is that we do not know – and *cannot* know until we figure out how to measure well-being in the real world. But we can

---

[21] As will be discussed in Chapter 8, I suspect that nutritional status and immunocompetence were two of the most important measurable dimensions of individual-level well-being in preindustrial societies.

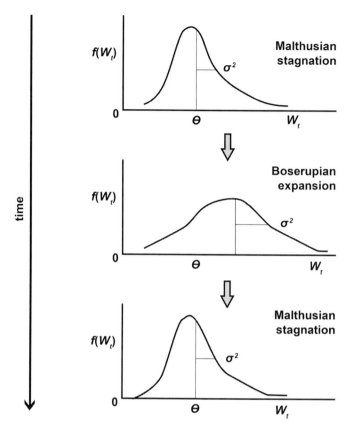

Figure 5.15 Changes in the distribution of physical *well-being* (any phenotypic trait that influences an individual's ability to survive and/or reproduce successfully) as the population cycles from Malthusian stagnation to Boserupian expansion and back again. In this simplified representation, w_t is individual well-being, $f(w_t)$ is the distribution (probability density function) of w_t among individuals in the population, θ is the subsistence level of mean well-being (i.e. the level that just supports population replacement), and σ^2 is the variance in well-being. The vertical and horizontal lines within each distribution are intended to convey the location and size of, respectively, the distribution's mean and variance. During Boserupian expansion, both the mean and the variance in well-being increase by an amount proportional to the magnitude of the expansion. When the population returns to Malthusian stagnation, however, the distribution is expected to fall back to exactly the same state it was in before the expansion – but at a higher population size owing to the population growth experienced during the expansion when the mean value of well-being was greater than θ.

make a few feeble stabs at an answer using what few data exist. Consider, for example, the estimates of peasant landholdings in medieval England shown in Table 5.3, all of which come from the century leading up to the first outbreak of the Black Death.[22] If we can assume that landholding size is an indirect or partial

---

[22] I omit the post-Black Death period because the population decline associated with the epidemic initiated dramatic changes in the rural English economy (Dyer, 1989).

Table 5.3 Statistics on the distribution of peasant household land holdings in England during the century leading up to the Black Death of 1349–50. From (1) Dyer (1983: 200); (2) Hassall and Beauroy (1993: 47); (3) Dyer (1989: 141); (4) Hallam (1957: 343, 349); (5) Campbell (1984: 106); (6) Kosminsky (1956: 216, 223); (7) Poos (1991: 16,18); (8) Smith (1984: 140).

Location	Period	Number of households	Mean size of holding (acres)	Variance	CV (%)[a]	Source
Midlands, East Anglia, the south	1248–1349	60	14.8	121.4	74.6	(1)
Holkham (Norfolk)	1250–73	62	6.0	17.1	68.9	(2)
Holywell (Hunts.)	1252	56	11.7	93.2	82.5	(3)
Pinchbeck (Lincs.)	1259–60	319	9.5	112.5	111.6	(4)
Spalding (Lincs.)	1259–60	426	7.7	147.9	157.9	(4)
	1287	587	6.0	86.5	155.0	
Coltishall (Norfolk)	1275–99	34	12.0	196.2	116.7	(5)
	1300–24	58	15.3	486.1	144.1	
	1325–48	52	8.0	74.6	107.9	
All of England	1279					(6)
villein		15 902	13.6	112.0	78.1	
free		6 154	14.8	427.0	139.2	
combined		22 056	13.9	200.2	101.7	
Essex	1288–1340	605	8.2	85.5	112.8	(7)
Redgrave (Suffolk)	1289	101	11.9	61.5	65.4	(8)
Sutton (Lincs.)	1304–5	165	5.6	48.3	124.1	(4)
Stoughton (Leics.)	1341	62	16.4	127.2	68.9	(3)

[a] Coefficient of variation, equal to the ratio of the square root of the variance to the mean, multiplied by 100.

measure of household well-being – a big conceptual leap, I admit – can we use these figures to infer anything about whether these peasant households were well-off or just getting by? We cannot, of course, answer this question on a village-by-village basis, never mind a household-by-household one. But we can provide a provisional generic answer by doing a few simple calculations based loosely on what we think we know about the medieval English agrarian economy (see, for example, Titow, 1972; McCloskey, 1976, 1991; McCloskey and Nash, 1984; McDonald and Snooks, 1986; Dyer, 1989, 2002; Townsend, 1993; McDonald, 1998; Hatcher and Bailey, 2001). (I write "what we *think* we know" advisedly: there is much that is uncertain in this exercise.) Suppose, to begin with, that an average person in the community needs to consume about 1700 kcal day^{-1} to survive and function at the subsistence level (the requirement for hardworking adults would be somewhat higher at over 2000 kcal day^{-1}, but the *average* would also involve small children who needed less; see, for example, Anderson *et al.*, 1946). This adds up to an annual per capita requirement of some 620 500 kcal.[23] If we assume that the average medieval peasant household had 5.5 members (probably not too far from the truth), it would need to consume just over 3.4×10^6 kcal yr^{-1}. Now, we know from manorial records kept by Winchester Cathedral, a major landowner in medieval England, that yields for the staple grains wheat, barley, and oats averaged about 15 bushel per acre during a reasonably good year (Titow, 1972). (Winchester's holdings were all located in the richer areas of SSW England, and its records mostly predate the onset of the Little Ice Age, so this figure may be somewhat high as a general proposition). As it happens, a bushel of threshed and winnowed grain weighs about 26 kg.[24] And 1 kg of grain yields about 3600 kcal. Thus, assuming that a medieval bushel was the equivalent of a modern one, the average acre during the average year in the high Middle Ages yielded roughly 1.4×10^6 kcal. Based on this crude guestimate, it would appear that the average household needed to eat the produce of about 2.4 acres in a normal year.

But now we need to factor in what *wasn't* available to eat. According to the Winchester yield ratios, about 25–30 percent of each year's harvest needed to be set aside as seed for next year's sowing. And perhaps 20–25 percent went to pay rents, dues and fines imposed by the manorial court. Taking numbers from Table 2.6, an extremely conservative estimate of postharvest grain losses (including losses during processing and storage) would be 15 percent (I am ignoring grain fed to livestock). Erring on the low side of all these numbers, it would probably not be too extreme to suggest that something like 60 percent of the annual harvest would normally be unavailable for peasant consumption. Thus, to eat the equivalent of 2.4 acres, the household would need to *cultivate* six acres each year. But the household's *total* landholding would also include fields lying fallow. Under a two-field system of

---

[23] Note that all my figures are based solely on energetic needs and ignore secondary foods such as cheese, meat and vegetables (e.g. cabbage and onions). To allow for such things would only add to the peasants' land hunger.

[24] I am grateful to David Webster for going to a local health food store and actually weighing (but not buying!) a bushel of whole, unground wheat, and to Lena Scholten, the store's owner, for graciously letting him get away with it.

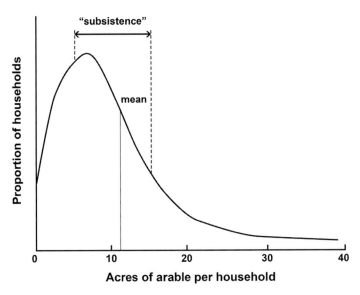

Figure 5.16 Hypothetical distribution of landholding sizes in a "typical" English peasant village during the pre-Black Death medieval period in relation to the approximate amount of land needed to support household food consumption at the subsistence level.

rotation (i.e. half of all arable lying fallow each year), access to 12 acres would be needed to keep six acres under cultivation each year; under a three-field system (one-third of arable lying fallow), nine acres would be needed. The average peasant household would, therefore, have needed access to approximately 10 acres of arable – or, in view of all the uncertainties in our calculations, perhaps we should say a number somewhere in the range of about 6–15 acres – to continue operating at the subsistence level of consumption.

How do these crude guestimates help us interpret Table 5.3? Well, bear in mind everything that we *don't* know about the tabulated villages: Were the rotations two- or three-field systems? (There were probably some of each.) How much were the customary rents, dues and fees? (It varied from one manor to another.) How much did average yields vary by, say, latitude or elevation. (We simply don't know.) Were some of the village economies expanding, others stagnant, and perhaps a few actually shrinking – that is, was Boserup or Malthus in play? (Again we don't know.) But fools rush in... Most of the mean landholdings in Table 5.3 hover near 10 acres or slightly above. In all cases, the variances are considerably larger than the corresponding means. Since no one could have had a *negative* holding – although some households could certainly have been landless – it must be the case that the distributions are markedly right-skew, with long upper tails and means somewhat higher than the corresponding modes. Figure 5.16 is my best guess as to what the "typical" distribution of peasant household landholdings in a medieval English village may have looked like. The figure also shows my range of guesses for the subsistence level of food production (I am assuming, in effect, that household size was not correlated

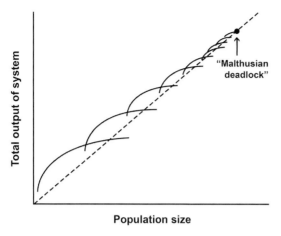

Figure 5.17 Declining marginal productivity of innovation leading to "Malthusian deadlock" where further change is effectively impossible. The only escape from deadlock is for some exogenous force to decrease the size of the population so that the system can enter a different trajectory of intensification.

with landholding size, which it almost certainly was – see Chapter 12). If we take this figure at all seriously – and I cannot make a strong argument that we should – it suggests that a substantial majority of households were operating near the subsistence level, with a not inconsiderable minority below that level, including a subgroup of poor landless peasants. Another minority of households were comfortably above the subsistence level and might even be considered "rich" (although in Chapter 10 I will suggest that their comparatively favorable condition may well have been temporary). More than this we cannot say, except that the results are not obviously inconsistent with the predictions of the MaB ratchet when it is at Malthusian stagnation. Does this mean that, at least in pre-Black Death England, most local populations were close to Malthusian stagnation? I suspect it does, but I'd hate to have to prove the point. Perhaps someday medieval archaeology will tell the tale.

Malthusian Deadlock

Contemplation of the MaB ratchet over the past few years has led me to other ideas not discussed in my original paper on the subject. One that I find intriguing, if far from verified, is the notion that the handle of the ratchet may become harder and harder to turn as ratcheting progresses – that is, there may in the long-run be declining marginal productivity of agricultural innovation itself in preindustrial farming systems (Figure 5.17). Imagine, for example, a system of dry rice farming with long fallows. If population growth leads to a shortening of fallows, simple stone walls may be built along the contours of the fields to check soil loss. If further population pressure occurs, small streams may be diverted to irrigate the fields, turning the stone walls into the lower boundaries of flooded terraces. Eventually, the formerly nonintensive system of shifting cultivation may evolve under population pressure into a highly intensive system of wet rice cultivation – a process that may be going on today in parts of West Kalimantan, Indonesia (Seavoy, 1973; Padoch *et al.*, 1998). Now, the fact that stone walls had already been built to stop erosion may have made it that much easier to switch to irrigated terraces – the earlier round of intensification, in other words, may have guided or even constrained later options for intensification. As innovations accumulate, they may progressively narrow the field of further development and lead eventually to extreme specialization and little capacity for further change – the point marked "Malthusian deadlock" in Figure 5.17. At that point the farming system may be effectively frozen unless some exogenous force comes along to knock it entirely out of its former trajectory.

Which brings us back to pre-Black Death England. Perhaps the single most convincing real-world case of Malthusian deadlock and its subsequent escape was the evolution and later collapse of the open-field grain farming system in the "champion" region of medieval England (Hatcher, 1977; Hatcher and Bailey, 2001). For some 250 years after the Norman Conquest, grain farming in this region intensified and became more specialized and more demanding of labor, in close parallel with the growth of the English population, most of which was still rural and heavily concentrated in the champion region. By about 1300, however, the intensification (and the population growth) had halted and had even begun to retreat, perhaps in part because of the onset of the Little Ice Age. But mostly the system was stagnant, just as suggested by our arithmetic exercise above. Then, after 1349 the system collapsed, an event clearly sparked by the Black Death, which killed off something like 30–50 percent of the English population (Miller, 1991: 2–8). Depopulation meant that farm workers were suddenly enjoying a sellers' market for their labor, and their earnings and standards of living improved greatly for a time (Dyer, 1989: 157–60). Eventually, however, large landowners responded by switching to a pastoral economy based on commercial wool production, which imposed much lower on-farm labor demands than had open-field cultivation; much of the rural population was siphoned off to towns and cities, which grew rapidly during this period (Dyer, 1991). After some 150 years, population growth and economic intensification picked up again, but in a wholly new direction. It has even been argued, with some plausibility, that the Industrial Revolution might never have happened had the Black Death not knocked the British economy out of Malthusian deadlock a few centuries earlier (Levine, 2001: 380*ff.*). A lovely, MaB-ratchety kind of story, and it may even be true.

At any rate, thanks to the MaB ratchet, one can (if one wishes) be a Malthusian *and* a Boserupian without feeling the discomfort of cognitive dissonance or committing the sin of inconsistency. But I have to admit that the MaB ratchet is, like Malthus and Boserup's own models, a macrodemographic tool that provides limited insight into what is likely to be going on at the microlevel where both demographic processes and farming practices are actually determined. In this respect, the MaB ratchet falls squarely into the tradition of the post-Boserup debate on agricultural intensification, which has been conducted almost exclusively at the macrolevel. At the same time, the post-Boserup debate has been (blessedly) less abstract than the theoretical models discussed in this chapter, including the MaB ratchet, thanks in large part to the influence of several authors who have had rich experiences in the field. We will discuss the fieldwork of these authors in the next chapter.

6   The Intensification Debate after Boserup

I have sometimes been impressed . . . by the question of an intelligent [Bemba] chief, 'Why do the government officers ask me about the history of the Bemba and their magic, and never about our gardens and the growing of food?'   – A. I. Richards (1939: 404)

In this chapter I hope to put some real-world flesh on the bare theoretical bones of Malthus and Boserup, especially the latter. Although Malthus and Boserup both drew upon empirical evidence in their writings, neither did the sort of long-term fieldwork on traditional farming that would satisfy a modern-day anthropologist. I have no wish or warrant to disparage their efforts at theoretical modeling – but the comparison of model to reality is also important, not only to test the model for possible rejection but to suggest ways in which it might be improved or extended. It is worth emphasizing, however, that there is nothing to be gained by attempting to make any model perfectly realistic, even if that were possible, for to do so would be to make it too complicated to understand and would destroy its generalizability. Even as we complicate our model, we should still seek simplicity and generality: we still want the model to be a *model.* If complications are to be added, they should be *important* complications – things that significantly increase our understanding, not just things that improve the fit of the model *ex post facto* to a particular set of field observations or that merely satisfy an esthetic preference for holism or complexity.

This chapter reviews the fieldwork, findings and ideas of several authors who have written on agricultural intensification since the time of – and often inspired by – Boserup's 1965 book *The Conditions of Agricultural Growth*. The aim of the review is to identify useful theoretical complications that have emerged from empirical research in the field. Most of the ideas summarized here are still concentrated at the macrodemographic level, but some begin to suggest links to the microlevel. Before adopting a more thematic treatment, however, I want to mention three especially influential fieldworkers, one of whose work pertaining to agricultural intensification actually predated Boserup by a couple of years.

Three Early Fonts of Complication

Clifford Geertz and Agricultural Involution

The anthropologist Clifford Geertz is perhaps best known for his later work in symbolic anthropology and "thick" ethnography, but he wrote an early, influential monograph on the ecology of Indonesian rice farming entitled *Agricultural*

Involution: The Processes of Ecological Change in Indonesia (Geertz, 1963). Although much of the book was based on archival materials, it was inspired by his own fieldwork in Bali starting in the 1950s. Writing two years before Boserup's first book, he addressed many of the same questions she did but framed them in terms of *labor absorption capacity* rather than agricultural intensification *per se* (see Booth and Sundrum, 1985, for an extended exploration of labor absorption in farming, including a chapter on Geertz's ideas). That is, he emphasized the ability of an agricultural system to continue producing increases in marginal productivity sufficient to keep agricultural laborers alive rather than the increases in total production achieved by higher labor inputs. The complex of interrelated economic, demographic and ecological changes that Geertz called *agricultural involution* encompasses the absorption of labor (and hence of population) by an increase in household farm work toward its maximum, an increase in the spatial concentration of production, shrinking household landholdings, declining marginal productivity, up to a stable equilibrium and a progressive impoverishment of individuals and households leading to a state that he describes as "shared poverty" in a "labor-stuffed" economy (Geertz, 1963: 80). Thus, the concept covers much of the same ground as Boserup's agricultural intensification, but from an altogether more pessimistic vantage point. Geertz's involution is not a force for progress but for immiseration.[1]

It is fundamental to Geertz's view that different agricultural systems have different capacities for labor absorption and involution. According to Geertz, wet rice farming as practiced in East and Southeast Asia probably has the highest capacity to absorb labor of any form of traditional agriculture; widespread practices such as irrigation, terracing, frequent weeding, and transplanting of rice seedlings, all of which are labor intensive but also highly productive, allow multiple crops to be harvested each year and support enormous populations, but with individual households controlling a smaller and smaller share of the total productive apparatus. Geertz's 1963 book is organized around a comparison of "Inner" and "Outer" Indonesia (Figure 6.1), the former characterized by intensive wet rice farming (*sawah*) and the latter by shifting cultivation of dry rice (Figure 6.2). Shifting cultivation, Geertz argues, has a very low capacity for labor absorption compared to *sawah*. In consequence, if local population grows in Outer Indonesia it rapidly leads to system breakdown, especially deforestation and other forms of environmental degradation that serve to reduce population growth, whereas in Inner Indonesia population growth can be absorbed up to a very high limit, but at the cost of involution and misery. The net demographic result is an eight-fold difference in population density between the two regions: 60 persons km^{-2} in Outer Indonesia versus 480 persons km^{-2} in Inner Indonesia (Geertz, 1963: 13).

Geertz has been criticized for a selective and uncritical use of historical material from Indonesia (White, 1973, 1983). And his sharp distinction between *sawah* and

---

[1] It should be noted that, in one brief paragraph in her 1965 book, Boserup does acknowledge the potential immiseration that can accompany population growth and intensification (Boserup, 1965: 41), but elsewhere (p. 118) she claims that such misery is merely "an intermediary stage" in the development of better conditions.

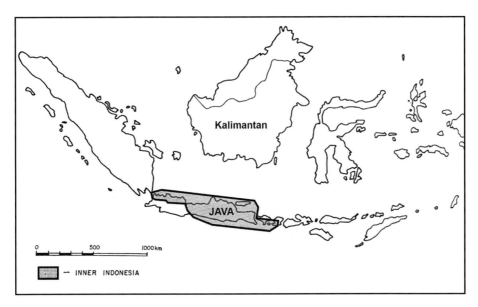

Figure 6.1 Inner versus outer Indonesia. Inner Indonesia, comprising Java, Southern Bali, and Western Lombok, is densely populated and dominated by intensive paddy and terraced rice cultivation (*sawah*). Outer Indonesia, comprising the rest of the nation, including Kalimantan (Borneo), is lightly peopled and (as of the 1950s) was mostly fed by shifting cultivation of dry hill rice. Modified from Geertz (1963: 14), by permission of the University of California Press Berkeley.

shifting cultivation, which seems to imply that shifting cultivators would find it hard to switch to more intensive wet-rice farming, is contradicted by ethnographic evidence of mixed *sawah*/shifting cultivation systems in Inner Indonesia and of recent construction of at least small-scale irrigation systems in Sumatra and West Kalimantan, major parts of Outer Indonesia (Seavoy, 1973; Padoch *et al.*, 1998). Nonetheless, his ideas are valuable in emphasizing the economic and societal *costs* of agricultural intensification, which Boserup treats largely as a beneficent force.

Harold C. Brookfield and the Multiplicity of Causes and Effects

If Geertz's interest in agricultural ecology was short-lived, Harold Brookfield's has been life-long. Brookfield began work as an agricultural geographer in highland New Guinea in the 1950s, including as part of an unusual (for the time) collaboration with a cultural anthropologist, Paula Brown (see Brookfield, 1962, 1968; Brookfield and Brown, 1963). Now well into his eighties, he continues to travel the world exploring the implications of agricultural intensification for human well-being and the loss of biodiversity, as well as other forms of environmental degradation (Blaikie and Brookfield, 1987; Brookfield *et al.*, 1995). He has pursued a spectacularly wide range of fieldwork opportunities, not only in the New Guinea highlands but also in the rest of Melanesia, in Polynesia and the West Indies, in Mauritius and more recently in Southeast Asia. Few researchers can claim as broad a knowledge of traditional and

(a)

(b)

Figure 6.2 Contrasting farming landscapes, Inner and Outer Indonesia: (a) Terraced, irrigated rice fields (*sawah*) in Bali and (b) a newly cleared field in Aceh. Figure credits: (a) Edmund Lowe Photography / Moment / Getty Images and (b) Photography by Mangiwau / Moment Getty Images.

developing-world farming as he possesses (for a summary of much of his life's work, see Brookfield, 2001a).

Early in his career Brookfield appears as a fairly confirmed Boserupian, as best exemplified in the regional geography of Melanesia he wrote with Doreen Hart in 1971. But even then his view of intensification was more nuanced and multidimensional than Boserup's. In *Melanesia: A Geographic Interpretation of an Island World* (Brookfield and Hart, 1971: 105–20), he and his coauthor showed that intensification was indeed correlated with population density, but at a low enough level to implicate other, nondemographic forces. He also emphasized that intensification could take many forms beyond the Boserupian substitution of labor for land (Brookfield, 1972; see the quote from Brookfield near the beginning of Chapter 5 above). He was, for example, one of the first to highlight the importance of landesque capital, even in shifting cultivation: field clearance itself could be considered an investment in landesque capital if it resulted in secondary growth that was easier to clear the next time around, thus representing a simple capital improvement that may actually save human labor.

In other words, Brookfield went far beyond the shortening of fallows as a form of intensification (Brookfield, 1972, 1984). In one of his most recent reflections on the whole intensification issue, he has argued that two broad classes of factors have been insufficiently investigated in "the large post-Boserup literature" – namely, "farmers' use of capital investment of all forms, and the importance of organisational skills, as distinct from the technical skills on which the literature has concentrated" (Brookfield, 2001a: 181). As noted, Brookfield has emphasized landesque capital; I would also emphasize, among other things, crop genetic resources as a form of capital. And, more generally, as I argued in Chapter 2 (and Brookfield has argued at length), the range of possible capital investments made by traditional farmers has been grossly underestimated in the literature (see Figure 2.17). When Brookfield speaks of organizational skills, he has in mind such things as the spatial organization of the farm and the allocation of labor.

In addition to his insight that intensification could take manifold forms unexplored by Boserup, Brookfield believed that it could be *caused* by multiple forms of "pressure" beyond population pressure (see especially Brookfield, 2001b). In particular, he differentiated subsistence production from *economic* or *trade production* (food production for reciprocal exchange or trade, including marketing) and *social production* (food production to meet social obligations or political ends) and argued that the latter two forms were especially sensitive to nondemographic pressures. His favorite example of social production is the ceremonial pig exchange found throughout the New Guinea highlands – described in detail by Strathern (1975), among others – in which the rearing of pigs (and the cultivation of plant foods to feed them) was converted through ceremonial distribution into political status and power.[2] It is entirely possible, as Brookfield acknowledges, that increases in social and trade production may themselves sometimes be a secondary outcome of population pressure, but they need not be (cf. Börjeson, 2004a,b; Loiske, 2004).

Finally, in some of his writings Brookfield emphasized *disintensification* almost as much as intensification (see especially Brookfield, 1984). Consistent with hints provided by Boserup (1965), Brookfield believed that agricultural disintensification could result from depopulation or the colonization of thinly occupied habitats, but

---

[2] Some authors have suggested that Brookfield has placed too much emphasis on the role of highland New Guinea pig exchanges in the traditional economy, since such exchanges were mostly observed after fairly sustained contact with the outside world, which may have resulted in gross inflation of the ceremonial economy (Gardner, 2001).

could also result from political collapse. Thus, he argued that disintensification, like intensification, had multiple causes and could take multiple forms.

Robert McC. Netting and the Question of Scale

Another researcher with a life-long interest in agrarian ecology and agricultural intensification was Robert Netting, who did several rounds of fieldwork among Kofyar farmers of the Jos Plateau in central Nigeria (see Netting, 1965, 1968, 1973) and later worked with smallholder farmers in the Swiss Alps (Netting, 1972, 1974b, 1976, 1979, 1981). His early fieldwork in Nigeria was summarized in the classic monograph *Hill Farmers of Nigeria: Cultural Ecology of the Kofyar of the Jos Plateau* (Netting, 1968). Although parts of this book are now quite dated (and statistically naïve), it was remarkably sophisticated for its time, when the detailed ecology of traditional farmers was just beginning to be explored. I find it humbling to reread the book now, more than 40 years after it was written, and discover how many of the themes highlighted in the present volume were anticipated by Netting. His later work in Switzerland was especially notable for his use of historical demographic sources as well as his own ethnographic material (Netting, 1979, 1981), something of a first in cultural anthropology. In later years he collaborated with his graduate students Priscilla and Glenn Stone, who had done their own fieldwork among the Kofyar, in exploring determinants of household structure, the division of labor by sex, agricultural seasonality and disintensification of farming in the lowlands south of the Jos Plateau (Stone *et al.*, 1990, 1995). He also worked with another former graduate student, Rick Wilk, in highlighting the household as a universal locus for the organization of resources in traditional farming (Netting *et al.*, 1984; Wilk, 1989b). Near the end of his short life, Netting wrote a major synthetic work, his 1993 book *Smallholders, Householders: Farm Families and the Ecology of Intensive, Sustainable Agriculture*, essentially a summary of his life's work. His enduring contribution, in my opinion, is a wealth of fine-grained descriptive detail on day-to-day farming practices and the organization of the family farm in traditional and developing-world economies.

On the theoretical side, Netting was an avowed Boserupian, dedicating *Smallholders, Householders* to her:

FOR ESTER BOSERUP
who broke new ground with her sense of how smallholders intensify their cultivation and with her vision of the economics of agrarian change. (Netting, 1993: v)

He was firmly convinced that population pressure played a significant role in agricultural intensification, but he shared Brookfield's belief that intensification was multidimensional and that pressure operated at multiple scales. He also pros-elytized vigorously for the view that the household is the single most important scale at which to study intensification (Netting, 1965, 1968, 1979, 1981, 1993; Netting *et al.*, 1984) and wrote an influential comparative study of variation in household size and its economic implications (Netting, 1982). Most of the rest of the present book is devoted to traditional farming households, and Netting's work has been a major inspiration for it.

Other Theoretical Lessons from Empirical Fieldwork

Over the years, several other field-based studies have claimed to provide at least partial or provisional support for Boserup's model of agricultural intensification under population pressure (e.g. Gleave and White, 1969; Brown and Podolefsy, 1976; Lagemann, 1977; Turner *et al.*, 1977, 1993; Metzner, 1982; Lele and Stone, 1987; Pingali *et al.*, 1987; Palte, 1989; Eder, 1991; Wiggins, 1995; Stone, 1996; Turner and Ali, 1996; Adams and Mortimer, 1997; Allen, 2001; Bourke, 2001; Sirén, 2007). Criticisms of one of the *best* of these studies (Allen, 2001), discussed in Chapters 1 and 5 above, apply to most of the others as well, *viz.*: crude population density is a poor measure of population "pressure" (which remains poorly defined), analyses are cross-sectional rather than longitudinal, the ecological fallacy is a danger in the kinds of cross-population comparisons that have been done, the shortening of fallows is only one dimension of intensification. Recent fieldwork has also led to suggestions for significant *improvements* to Boserup's original model that stop short of rejecting it outright (for reviews, see Brookfield, 2001b; Stone, 2001).[3] The following paragraphs discuss some of the suggested changes that seem to me to be the strongest candidates for ways in which Boserup ought to be revised.

Does Shifting Cultivation Really Work the Way Boserup Thought it Did?

Boserup's typology of agricultural systems (Table 5.1) took as its baseline what she called "forest-fallow cultivation" and what others variously call shifting cultivation, slash-and-burn cultivation, swiddening, or horticulture.[4] "Minimally defined, shifting cultivation is a system of continuous farming in which impermanent fields are cleared with fire and are cropped for fewer years than they are fallowed"

---

[3] There have also been suggestions for purely theoretical modifications of Boserup's model (see, for example, Datoo, 1978; Robinson and Schutjer, 1984).

[4] The term "swidden" was introduced to anthropology by Izikowitz (1951: 7) to refer to the clearing of fields by fire. It is an obsolete English dialect word that is cognate to the Swedish word *svedja* (a burnt clearing, to burn a clearing, especially in forest). It is arguably inappropriate as a generic label for shifting cultivation (the term I prefer) since historically fire clearance has been used widely throughout the world, including by farmers no one would call shifting cultivators (Steensberg, 1993). Conklin (1963: 3) also questions the use of "slash-and-burn" as a generic term since in some savannah areas *hoe*-and-burn clearance is applied (de Schlippe, 1956: 119) and in one especially drenched area of the Colombian Chocó, where burning is not usually an option, slash-and-*mulch* cultivation is practiced (West, 1957). In my opinion, "horticulture" is an especially inapt term for shifting cultivation, as is the word "gardens" when applied to shifting cultivators' fields. In its most extensive form, shifting cultivation is the very opposite of horticulture or gardening, defined in agricultural science as the most intensive type of crop production (with "crops" that are often ornamentals instead of edibles). Gardeners work the soil with care, weed frequently, apply heavy doses of fertilizer, herbicides, and pesticides, are generous with mulches and generally treat their gardens as permanent fields they have no intention of abandoning. Some of them may be "organic" but none are shifting cultivators.

(Ruddle, 1974: 1) – which is fine as a not-too-detailed description, but perhaps not enough to pin down a worldwide, unitary type (it would, in fact, include Boserup's category of bush-fallow cultivation as well as forest-fallow). Nonetheless shifting cultivation *conceived as a type* played a fundamental role in Boserup's contribution to the debate over population and agriculture: all forms of agricultural intensification in Boserup's scheme acted by modifying the one variable that was deemed to be supremely important under shifting cultivation, the length of fallow periods relative to periods of cultivation. It would not be an exaggeration to claim that almost everything in Boserup (1965) rests on a particular view of how shifting cultivation works. But shifting cultivation is spectacularly heterogeneous and is practiced in a wide variety of agrarian contexts, including alongside farming practices that are extremely intensive (see Figure 2.2, as well as Conklin, 1980, on the Ifugao of the Philippines). As noted in the previous chapter, Boserup's ideas about shifting cultivation crystallized at a time when our thinking about it was still rather new and untested. Has more recent research altered the Boserupian view of how shifting cultivation works?

By the time Boserup wrote *The Conditions of Agricultural Growth*, a conventional portrait of shifting cultivation had already come into being; it is still to be found in almost all introductory anthropology textbooks written today. The most commonly cited elements of this textbook portrait can be summarized as follows:

- Fields are cropped for a few years and then allowed to lie fallow. The fallow period is typically (much) longer than the period of continuous cropping – according to figures frequently mentioned in the secondary literature, perhaps 20–25 years of fallow on average as opposed to 1–2 years of cropping.
- Land is allowed to return to fallow when crop yields start to be compromised by declining soil fertility or increasing problems with weeds and pests.
- Land going into fallow is completely abandoned and allowed to return to natural vegetation – indeed, to something that resembles primary forest if the fallow period is long enough.
- The degree of soil regeneration is completely determined by the length of the fallow period.
- If fallows are sufficiently long, shifting cultivation can survive in an area indefinitely without causing major long-term degradation of soils or vegetation.
- Fields are cleared by slashing and burning. Burning of vegetation releases the nutrients stored in the natural plant biomass to the field's soils, making them immediately available to crop plants.
- No fertilizer or other soil amendment is used other than what is burned when the field is cleared.
- No elaborate soil tillage is done.
- Little if any weeding is done.
- It is normal to grow a large number of crop species in a single field during a particular season, often mixed together in a way that is seemingly random. This practice of mixed cropping reduces risk by (i) lowering the probability that

host-specific plant diseases will spread and (ii) ensuring that the field will yield at least some food when other crops fail.

- At maturity, the crops on the field form a closed, stratified canopy similar to that of mature tropical rainforest. This canopy protects the soil from raindrop erosion and desiccation.

Now, it is perfectly possible to find descriptions of subsistence farming in the literature that conform fairly closely to this stereotype (including among the Gainj, the group we worked with in highland New Guinea). But recent, "post-Boserup" field research has shown that some elements of this portrait are based on weak empirical evidence and others are simply wrong or at least not generally true.

To understand the conventional view accepted by Boserup, turn back to Figure 5.9, which illustrates the purported relationship between soil quality (or crop yield) and the length of the period of continuous cultivation and of fallow. Consistent with this figure, Boserup (1965) held that the length of fallowing and its effect on soils and yields are the primary mechanisms linking population and traditional farming: the main reason fallows are shortened is to feed a growing population, and the resultant, if unanticipated, declines in soil fertility and yield are the main motivators for adopting new farming practices. It comes as something of a shock, then, to learn that there is very little evidence supporting the relationships shown in Figure 5.9 (Sanchez, 1976; Szott et al., 1999; Mertz, 2002; Bruun et al., 2006, 2009). Only a few researchers have studied the impact of fallow lengths on soil quality or crop yields. In India (Swamy and Ramakrishnan, 1988) and Brazil (Silva-Fosberg and Fearnside, 1997), fallow lengths and yield appear to be positively but weakly correlated, whereas in Laos (Roder et al., 1995) and Borneo (Bruun et al., 2009) no clear correlation has been found (Figure 6.3).[5]

The use of the R statistic to classify preindustrial farming systems implies that the length of both continuous cultivation and fallow is more or less fixed and can be summarized by an average number of years as a way to characterize the farming system's practices as a whole. But there is no evidence whatsoever that shifting cultivators use the number of years a plot of land has lain fallow in deciding whether to clear it again. No one thinks, "It's been 20 years, so I can farm this land again." Instead, shifting cultivators examine the vegetation that has sprung up on fallow land (especially so-called *indicator species* that provide reliable information about soil quality) to judge whether it is ready for recultivation (author's field observations). Subsistence farmers themselves do not think in terms of the absolute length of the fallow, so why should we?

Boserup believed that the average length of the fallow period was one of the most important statistics characterizing a farming system. But surely innumerate

---

[5] A shortcoming that makes all these empirical studies difficult to interpret is that they are cross-sectional, whereas the theoretical relationships shown in Figure 5.9 are longitudinal. That is, multiple fields with differing antecedent fallow periods are contrasted, without much statistical or experimental control for differences in slope, drainage or other field characteristics. The studies are also based on small samples, which may account for some of the apparently negative findings.

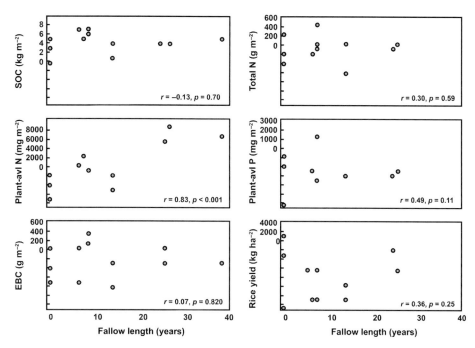

Figure 6.3 The effects of fallow length on soil characteristics and upland dry rice yields under shifting cultivation, Sarawak, Borneo ($n = 12$ fields). Fallow lengths ranged from five to 38 years, except for three fields that were being cultivated for a second year. (Top panels, left to right) Soil organic carbon content (SOC), total nitrogen (N). (Middle panels, left to right) Plant-available N, plant-available phosphorus (P). (Lower panels, left to right) Exchangeable base cations (EBC), rice yields. Only plant-available N is significantly associated with fallow length. Redrawn from Bruun *et al.* (2009), by permission of Springer Publishing.

subsistence farmers are even less inclined to consider average fallows than they are the absolute length of one particular fallow? Paradoxically, it may not even be possible for the numerate outsider to compute a meaningful average fallow length. Working in the Amazonian region of Ecuador, Anders Sirén (2007) estimated the lengths of 31 standing fallows that were about to be cleared and re-cultivated.[6] These were then turned into estimates of fallow survival using life-table methods. As can be seen in Figure 6.4, there is very little sign of any central tendency or "typical" fallow length – some of the distributions look very nearly uniform, with scarcely a hint of a

---

[6] Sirén estimated the ages of fallows using multiple satellite images and extensive informant interviews. Both methods are likely to be error-prone, especially at higher fallow lengths (the satellite images only went back about 20 years). I have often wondered why cross-sectional estimates of fallow age could not be based on coring of trees to count their tree-rings. This approach would require multiple trees to be cored on each fallow plot because (i) not all trees on the plot germinated during the first postcultivation year, and (ii) some older outliers may be present on the plot having survived from an earlier fallow period. Thus, the entire distribution of tree-ring ages would need to be examined carefully. Still, I see no fundamental reason that the method should not work – except for the fact that trees in the humid tropics often have poorly developed rings, especially in the absence of a distinct dry season.

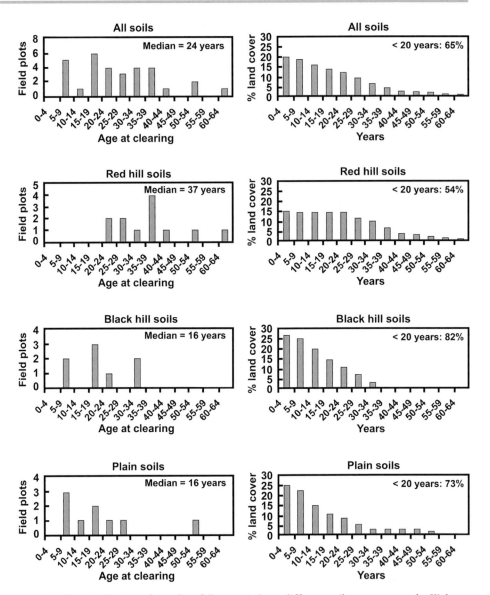

Figure 6.4 The distribution of standing fallow periods on different soil types among the Kichwa, Sarayaku region, Ecuadorian Amazon (*n* = 31 fallow plots). (Left) Age (in years) of fallows at the time of most recent clearing. (Right) Life-table estimates of the survival of fallows (in years) expressed as a percentage of land cover. From Sirén (2007), by permission of Springer Publishing.

mode.[7] From such data, it would be very hard to say anything about the "normal" or average fallow length. Gleave (1996) has made much the same point with respect to shifting cultivation in Sierra Leone, emphasizing that fallow lengths are likely to

---

[7] Technically a uniform distribution does have an arithmetic mean, but it is entirely determined by the range of observed values, not by their detailed distribution or central tendency (which is nonexistent).

vary by microhabitat, making it meaningless to talk about the average for an entire community or region.

Nor is there very much support for the claim that burning of slashed vegetation releases an immediate if transitory "flush" of soil nutrients. In their classic study, Nye and Greenland (1960) found that soil organic content could be improved by burning, but to an extent that depends on the quality of the burn, which is in turn determined by the residual moisture content of the slashed vegetation after it has dried a while. A good burn can release plant-available phosphorus (P) to the soil (Ramakrishnan and Toky, 1981; Andriesse, 1989; Roder *et al.*, 1995; Lawrence and Schlesinger, 2001) because P has a high temperature threshold for volatilization (DeBano *et al.*, 1998). Nitrogen (N), however, is volatized at much lower temperatures, and estimated losses of the N stored in slashed vegetation attributable to burning range from 25 to 67 percent (DeBano *et al.*, 1998). Such losses can be serious since N is often the most limiting of the soil macronutrients. Finally, burning can kill much of the microbial community in the topsoil, partly because of heat and partly as a result of an increase in soil pH (Andriesse and Koopmans, 1984; Andriesse and Schelhaus, 1987; Giardina *et al.*, 2000; Jensen *et al.*, 2001). Microbial die-offs, which affect both bacterial and fungal species, can compromise the decomposition of soil organic matter and thus impede the release of plant-available ions. They can also destroy the mycorrhizae (fungus-rootlet symbioses in many species of vascular plants) that enhance the ability of crops to absorb those ions. The soil microbial community can potentially recover over one or two seasons of cropping, but the rate of recovery is dependent upon the size and geometry of the field, which influence how quickly microbial inocula from the surrounding forest reach all parts of the burnt area. In sum, the effects of burning on soil fertility are mixed and are likely to vary in both strength and direction under different circumstances. The effects cannot always be assumed to be purely beneficial. The only consistent virtues of burning are that it makes field clearance easier and it kills many potential weeds.[8]

Shifting cultivators have all sorts of tricks for prolonging the period of cultivation without extending the subsequent fallow period or resorting to manuring or other labor-intensive practices. For example, what de Schlippe (1956: 204–16) called "pseudorotations" are used widely in sub-Saharan Africa (Richards, 1939; Miracle, 1967: 110; Ruthenberg, 1971: 58–65) and elsewhere (Ruddle, 1974: 123–31; Uhl *et al.*, 1982); that is, different crop mixtures and sequences of mixtures are used from year to year on different types of soils to slow down the rate of soil depletion (Figure 6.5). Earlier phases of the pseudorotation are often devoted to the primary energy crops and later phases to legumes as available soil nitrogen declines (Norman *et al.*, 1995: 7–8). During the final phase of the pseudorotation, just before the field is to be abandoned, it is common to plant crops that are tall, robust, and able to

---

[8] Note, however, that in the East African *citimene* form of shifting cultivation, people clear an area much larger than the field to be planted and stack all the slashed vegetation in the field so that it can be burned (Allan, 1965:66–76; Strømgaard, 1985, 1992). The implication is that the farmers themselves believe that the more ash from the burn, the better it is for the field's soil.

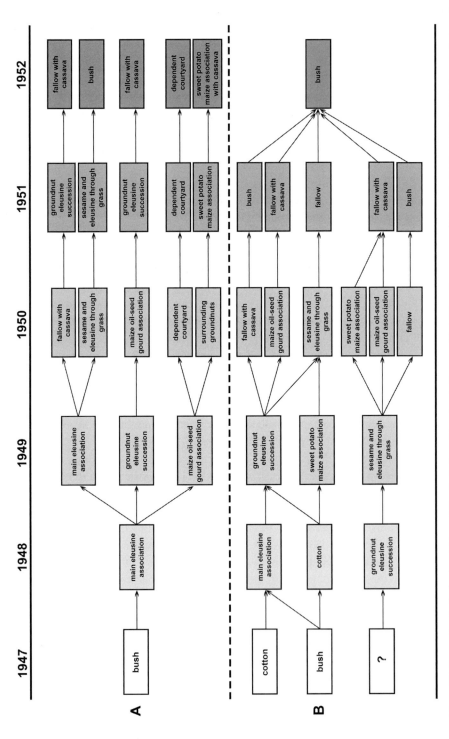

Figure 6.5 Some Zande "pseudorotations," South Sudan. Eleusine is finger millet (*Eleusine coracana*). From de Schlippe (1956: 208), by permission of Routledge and Kegan Paul Publishers.

out-compete weeds, able to grow moderately well on poor soils, and are biennials or perennials that will continue to grow during the fallow period with little or no encouragement from the farmer (Norman *et al.*, 1995: 8). Cassava (*Manihot esculenta*) scores well on all these counts, and in Zaire Miracle (1967) found that cassava was five times more likely to be planted as the last crop rather than earlier in the cultivation sequence under long-fallow shifting cultivation, and eleven times more likely in short-fallow systems. The actual duration of cultivation (and perhaps of subsequent fallow as well) is almost certainly conditioned to some degree on the precise sequence of pseudorotations applied to a particular field in a particular series of agricultural years.

There are other considerations that are relevant to the textbook stereotype of shifting cultivation. Mixed cropping, for example, is not universal among shifting cultivators, even those that otherwise conform closely to the stereotype; the Iban, for example, monocrop (and diligently weed) their dryland rice fields (Freeman, 1955). Moreover, the hypothesized advantages of mixed cropping (to reduce risk and to discourage the spread of plant diseases) are largely unsubstantiated.[9] In fact, mixed cropping can potentially *lower* yields, depending upon how the crops interact with each other (Figure 2.15). The idea that, under shifting cultivation in the humid tropics, mature fields mimic the rainforest in having closed, multistory canopies and a great diversity of plant species – an idea usually attributed to Clifford Geertz (1963: 16–17) – has been comprehensively debunked, at least in Amazonia (Beckerman, 1983a,b; Boster, 1983; Flowers *et al.*, 1983; Stocks, 1983; Vickers, 1983).

A relatively new insight into shifting cultivation is that fallows are rarely "abandoned" as in the textbook view, but are actively managed in a variety of ways, some of which were described in Chapter 2. Recent researchers have pointed out that these fairly labor-intensive forms of fallow management often amount to a form of agroforestry, in which the careful tending of trees is an integral part of the system (Denevan and Padoch, 1987; Cairns *et al.*, 2007). To his credit Conklin (1957: 3) recognized over 50 years ago that shifting cultivation often incorporates an element of agroforestry.

For a variety of reasons, then, the textbook portrait of shifting cultivation now appears to be too problematic to serve as the basis for an entire theory of agricultural intensification, and Boserup's ideas about fallows and soil fertility need to be reconsidered in light of more recent research. At the very least we need to take seriously Harold Brookfield's argument that intensification takes many forms beyond the shortening of fallow periods.

The Environmental Contingency of Intensification

To quote Boserup (1965: 117) again, "it is unrealistic to regard agricultural cultivation systems as adaptations to different natural conditions..."; on the contrary, "cultivation systems can be more plausibly explained as the results of differences in population density." As noted in the previous chapter, this statement is perfectly

---

[9] It is well known that permanent fields with rotations including a "cleaning" crop do quite well in limiting the spread of infection. Under shifting cultivation, the proper pseudorotations should be just as effective.

fine as a model assumption, but completely unconvincing as a statement about reality – and I seriously doubt that any present-day supporter of Boserup accepts this radical claim. Perhaps the first researcher to reject the claim explicitly was the geographer Eric Waddell, based on his work among Raiapu Enga farmers in the central highlands of Papua New Guinea. Noting that local cultivation practices varied significantly across, for example, contrasting soil and vegetation types, Waddell argued that "[t]he greatest weakness in Boserup's thesis, indicated by this study of Raiapu agriculture, is its failure to account for physical and biological variables in the ecosystem" (Waddell, 1972: 219). Interestingly, this criticism did not lead Waddell to reject Boserup's ideas altogether: "while a close relationship between population density and agricultural intensification is indicated, the data that have been presented do not lend themselves to a *simple* Boserupian-type interpretation" (Waddell, 1972: 217; emphasis added). If we regard Boserup's claim about the irrelevance of the environment as a model assumption rather than a would-be factual statement, then Waddell's results appear to offer a fair amount of support for her model. Indeed, had he taken Boserup's advice and ignored environmental differences, he would have missed some important confounding variables that needed to be controlled in order to give her model a fair test. In addition, it seems very probable that avenues of intensification can differ widely by environment – for example, in dry versus wet tropical environments, a difference explored in detail for Polynesia by Kirch (1994). It has even been suggested that there is an important dichotomy in the opportunities for and means of intensification between areas whose staples are grains versus areas that primarily cultivate root crops (Harris, 1972) – and that even different tropical root crops may differ in these regards (Hildebrand, 2007). To ignore local adaptations to specific natural resources, including crop varieties, in traditional farming seems a profound error. To figure out how to include those adaptations formally in Boserup's model is, on the other hand, not a simple task.

Does Intensification Always (or Even Usually) Compromise the Marginal Productivity or Energy Efficiency of Labor?

Boserup challenged earlier views that any innovation that increases crop yield is obviously desirable and thus should be adopted spontaneously by traditional farmers once they become aware of it. Such a view ignores what Boserup considered a fundamental fact – that increases in crop yield are almost always accompanied by decreases in the marginal productivity and energy efficiency of human labor.[10] Innovations, in other words, require more work and may well be resisted by rational farmers. This kind of "Boserupian inertia" is a critical component of her scheme, the very thing that requires population pressure as a force to overcome it. Some early commentators questioned on logical and empirical grounds whether Boserupian

---

[10] This idea should be carefully distinguished from that of the declining marginal productivity of labor *per se*. What Boserup was claiming, controversially as it turns out, was that *everything* that increases yield, no matter what particular input it involves, reduces the productivity of human work.

Table 6.1 A semicontrolled comparison of rice cultivation in Southeast and island Asia. From Hunt (2000: 268, 270); data from Geddes (1954), Freeman (1955), Janlekha (1955), Moerman (1968), Durrenberger (1978, 1979).

I. Shifting cultivation	Dayak	Iban	Lisu	Shan
Country	Sarawak	Sarawak	Thailand	Thailand
Period	1949–51	1949–51	1968–70	1976–7
No. farms observed	1	4	20	25
Mean farm size (ha)	0.7	2.2	1.2	0.8
Labor input (days ha^{-1} yr^{-1})	252	172	135	220
Total rice yield (kg ha^{-1} yr^{-1})	1776	941	1240	1384
Labor productivity (kg day^{-1})	7.0	5.5	9.2	6.3

II. Irrigated paddy	Bang Chan	Ban Ping	Shan
Country	Thailand	Thailand	Thailand
Period	1949–54	1960	1976–7
No. farms observed	1	31	25
Mean farm size (ha)	7.8	1.0	1.0
Labor input (days ha^{-1} yr^{-1})	91	99	111
Total rice yield (kg ha^{-1} yr^{-1})	2946	3099	2571
Labor productivity (kg day^{-1})	32.4	31.3	23.2

inertia was universal or even very common (Bronson, 1972; Barlett, 1976; Grigg, 1979), pointing out that if it were rare then Boserup's model would have little general applicability. Later field-based studies of this question were done by Padoch (1985), Cramb (1989), Eder (1991), Conelly (1992), Hunt (2000) and Nielson *et al.* (2006), all of whom concluded that Boserupian inertia is not inevitable but were unable to say whether it is widespread. Results from one set of "semicontrolled" comparisons (semicontrolled in the sense that all the cases come from one general area, all involve rice production, and all provide the data needed to compute comparable indices) are shown in Table 6.1. This comparison, taken at face value, suggests that the labor efficiency of intensive wet rice farming is some four times *greater* than that of shifting cultivation. The small number of cases does not, admittedly, allow for much generalization. In addition, it may be that comparing shifting cultivation with full-blown irrigated farming may stack the deck in favor of the latter: to be fair, we really ought to discount the *current* productivity of wet rice farming for the labor investments made in constructing the irrigation system by the venerable ancestors of the present-day population. Nonetheless, Boserup's assumption that intensification almost always reduces the efficiency of labor has come to seem less and less plausible over the years.

Defending Boserup from this criticism, Stone (2001: 178) comments that it is true that labor efficiency does not always decline as production is increased, but that *Boserupian* intensification *by definition* involves lowered efficiency and therefore the need for population pressure as an inducement. One wonders how many reported cases of agricultural intensification would be rendered irrelevant for Boserup's model as a result of this definition. In addition, Stone would seem to come perilously close to the circular argument that Boserup's model *by definition* can only be tested against data that already conform to it.

If labor efficiency does not decline with increased yields, are there *non-Boserupian* forms of inertia standing in the way of agricultural intensification? If there are, then Boserup's model need not hinge entirely on a decline in labor efficiency resulting from intensification. Two possible sources of non-Boserupian inertia seem particularly pertinent: *risk aversion* (all genuine innovations are locally untested and thus perceived as at least potentially risky) and *start-up costs* (innovations may require large initial investments – for example, labor for constructing irrigation channels or other kinds of landesque capital – that may take considerable time to pay off). Such types of inertia may still need population pressure – or some *other* type of pressure – to be overcome, thus rescuing Boserup's model in altered form.[11]

Agricultural Change as a Slow and Messy Process

Two important field studies, one in Sonora, Mexico (Doolittle, 1984), and the other in West Kalimantan, Indonesia (Padoch *et al.*, 1998), have provided insights into the actual, on-the-ground *processes* of agricultural intensification. Doolittle begins by pointing out that there are in theory at least two distinct types of agricultural change, which he calls the *systematic* and the *incremental*. Under systematic intensification, a new agro-ecosystem (to use his preferred term) is created in one fell swoop, as it were, before any crops are cultivated on it. Thus, the system of farming takes on its final form over a relatively short period of time, more or less necessitating some kind of coordination of the process at a political level well above the individual farm. Incremental intensification, in contrast, involves small modifications to existing fields, even as they are being cropped, that only become discernible as part of any significant agricultural change after a long, slow process of accumulation. Such intensification, according to Doolittle, is usually done by the farmers themselves on their individual holdings, with only minimal coordination across farms. Indeed, he notes, in any one year it may be difficult to distinguish the changes from routine tillage and field maintenance.

Doolittle provides a detailed (and very interesting) description of run-off (*decrué*) irrigation within periodically flooded arroyos in Eastern Sonora State, locally called the *temporales* system. *Temporal* farming can take various forms, partly as adaptations to particular arroyo topography but also as different phases of a longer-term process of change – a process identifiable only by long-term prospective observation or carefully controlled comparison of different fields (in this study, Doolittle does the latter). Changes between "phases" can be small – for example, piling up some brush to

---

[11] Other forms of pressure may emanate from Brookfield's social or economic production, as suggested by Turner and Ali's model of "induced intensification" arising from a combination of demographic conditions and market forces (Turner and Ali, 1996; see also Eder, 1991; Berry, 1993; Kates *et al.*, 1993). In our study of *subsistence* farming, these other forms of pressure are of dubious relevance.

slow water coming onto the field or scraping tiny, evanescent channels a few inches wide and only one or two inches deep to help direct water onto the field. The digging of larger, more permanent channels, when it is done, may require some coordination and labor-sharing with neighboring households, but it is rare for more than two or three households to be involved. Although he never quite says so, Doolittle clearly thinks that this kind of small-scale, incremental change is the norm for preindustrial farming (I would go even further and argue that systematic change is exceedingly rare in the preindustrial world). What Doolittle does say, however, is that many studies of agricultural intensification, especially in archaeology, seem to assume that it always represents systematic change (see, for example, most of the papers in Marcus and Stanish, 2006; Thurston and Fisher, 2007). This assumption, he points out, may be an almost inevitable result of viewing agricultural change backwards in time. Retrospectively we tend to see the fully formed agro-ecosystem that came to prevail in any one area but not the earlier stages, which are often hidden or obliterated by the final form. "In this case, the resulting [observable] constructional form of the agro-ecosystem alone does not allow assessment of the process of its development" (Doolittle, 1984: 124). Archaeology also tends to telescope time, making the changes appear to be rapid when in fact they may have taken many decades or generations to accumulate. But the study of present-day farming systems is not immune to this distortion either; for example, Geertz's comparison of shifting cultivation in its least intensive form to an old and elaborately developed system of *sawah* almost makes it look as if it is impossible to go from the former to the latter in small intermediate steps.

It is not. This is shown clearly by another field study, carried out in Geertz's Outer Indonesia (the Province of West Kalimantan on the island of Borneo). In this study, Padoch *et al.* (1998) document the early stages of the transition from shifting cultivation to *sawah*. They view the transition among Tara'n Dayak farmers as just the sort of slow, incremental process posited by Doolittle. In addition, they point to what they regard as another significant feature of the transition: "distinct, unstable, suboptimal, and often confusing forms of production [may] figure as transitional stages" (Padoch *et al.*, 1998: 3). Boserup's scheme was unidirectional – resulting in greater and greater intensification – and each step involved a reduction in labor efficiency. Padoch and her colleagues emphasize the reality observed among the Dayak – that change can go in the direction of either greater or lesser intensification, some specific changes may increase labor efficiency, some not, and when labor efficiency *is* lowered, farmers may adopt the changes anyway (even in the absence of population pressure) because they consider them to be necessary but temporary and unstable intermediate stages on the way to what they ultimately have in mind. The views of both Doolittle and Padoch *et al.* suggest that gradualism and path-dependence are important elements of preindustrial agricultural change and should be included in any model of it.[12]

---

[12] The point about path-dependence has also been emphasized by Morrison (1996, 2006).

What Else Changes Under Intensification?

Several researchers have suggested that other aspects of the agrarian economy and society change in predictable ways under intensification. Boserup herself, for example, pointed to increasing security of land tenure (Boserup, 1965; see also Guillet, 1981) and increasing formalization of sex roles in farming (Boserup, 1970; see also Ember, 1983; Stone et al., 1995). Others have cited the degree of land fragmentation (Goland, 1993b), the spatial concentration of farming (Stone, 1996), the efficiency of resource allocation in general (Brookfield, 2001b), the inspiration for technical innovation (Binswanger and Ruttan, 1978), and increasing out-migration and market participation (Netting et al., 1993; Snyder, 1996). Less positive outcomes of intensification may include declining biodiversity and other forms of environmental damage (Zimmerer, 1996; Kaihura and Stocking, 2003), narrowing dietary breadth (Kennett and Winterhalder, 2006), and widening social differentials (Gray 2005). Insofar as such things affect or are correlated with agricultural production and human well-being, they seem worth trying to include in the model – some of them may, in effect, be important dimensions of agricultural intensification itself.

The Role of Environmental Degradation in Agricultural Change

I argued in Chapter 3 that some degree of environmental degradation may be common in subsistence agriculture. It may in fact sometimes result from agricultural intensification itself (Phillips-Howard and Lyon, 1994). As Blaikie and Brookfield (1987: 30) put it, Boserup's model "may be likened to a toothpaste tube – population growth applies pressure on the tube, and somehow, in an undefined way, squeezes out agricultural innovation at the other end. However,…what appears at the other end of the tube is often not innovation but degradation." But this claim raises an important question: can environmental degradation per se, whether associated with increased population or not, act as a positive impetus for change in farming practices? This possibility is explored by Tiffen et al. (1994) and Alexander (1996). The particular example of it I have in mind is the development of agricultural terraces, which may look complicated in mature form but may start out as a simple response to erosion (Figure 6.6). An apparent ethnographic example of this hypothetical scheme is shown in Figure 6.7. Archaeological sedimentation evidence sometimes suggests a similar origin for ancient terracing, although not always (Schjellerup, 1985).

A More Rounded View of Agricultural Change

Based on his long experience of fieldwork (both archaeological and ethnographic) in Oceania, Patrick Kirch has offered an expanded version of Boserup's model in graphical form (Kirch, 1994: 15–20). His scheme builds on a distinction drawn by Harold Brookfield (1984) between *intensification* and *innovation*. I agree that this

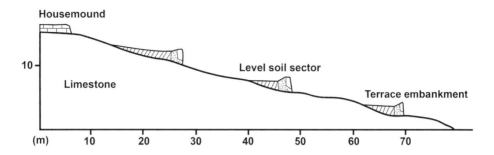

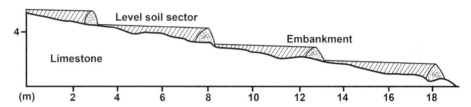

Figure 6.6 Hypothetical development of agricultural terraces from simple embankments built to impede soil erosion. Erosion itself leads to the accumulation of topsoil behind the embankments, which in turn gradually converts the embankments into terraces. From Simmons (1987: 65), by permission of John Wiley & Sons, Inc.

Figure 6.7 Severe gully erosion reclaimed by agricultural terraces, northeastern highlands of Ethiopia. From Holt and Lawrence (1993); photo ©Save the Children UK.

distinction is important, but I would take it one step further: much of the post-Boserup literature on preindustrial agricultural change has not only failed to distinguish intensification and innovation, but has confused both concepts with *involution* in Geertz's sense of the term. Now, intensification and involution (when it occurs) are obviously related, but the latter is one possible *consequence* of the former, not the

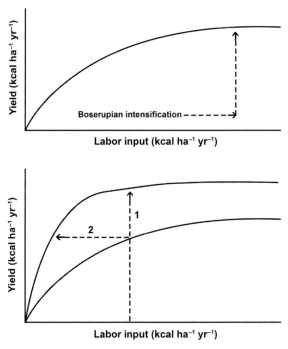

Figure 6.8 Agricultural intensification via an increase in human labor (top) versus one achieved through innovation (e.g. adopting a new crop variety or tool) (bottom). Note that innovation involves moving to a new production function, which is not necessarily the case for other forms of intensification. The innovation trajectory marked 1 involves a substantial increase in output while maintaining a fixed level of labor input; the trajectory marked 2 involves a maintenance of the previous output while realizing a substantial saving in labor input.

same thing as it – increases in yield do not always result in immiseration. Brookfield's distinction between intensification *sensu stricto* (an increase in yield without an increase in land) and innovation (adoption of some new practice, technology, or resource) is equally important, even though innovation often results in intensification (see, for example, the consequences of adopting new genetic resources in Figure 3.10). Shortening of fallows (Boserupian intensification) is not especially innovative: it is a mere quantitative change in an element of the system that is already present. Its effect (if Boserup is right about the need for additional labor) is to push us a wee bit further up the slope of the *current* production function for labor (Figure 6.8, top), perhaps resulting in some small increase in human misery (involution) or perhaps not. Genuine innovation, in contrast, moves us to a different production function altogether (Figure 6.8, bottom). In addition, there are at least two distinct ways to reach that new production function. Arrow 1 in Figure 6.8 results from an attempt to maintain labor inputs at their current level while achieving a significant increase in yield, arrow 2 an attempt to maintain yield while achieving a significant reduction in the labor needed to produce it (arrow 2 thus represents a genuinely labor-saving move). The first form of innovation results in intensification, the second does not – but it may make people happier.

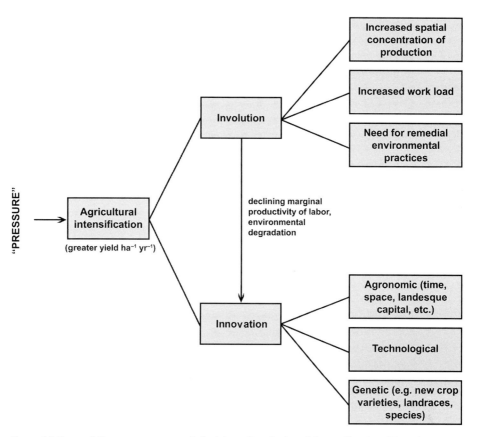

Figure 6.9 Beyond Boserup: an expanded vision of agricultural intensification. Note that innovations may actually be labor-saving, thus increasing the efficiency of human labor inputs. Modified from Kirch, P. V. (1994) *The Wet and the Dry: Irrigation and Agricultural Intensification in Polynesia*. Chicago: University of Chicago Press, p. 19, by permission of The University of Chicago Press.

While I laud (and borrow) Kirch's use of Brookfield's distinction, I'd like to elaborate on it a bit more in light of some of the issues raised in this chapter. In Figure 6.9, the pressure to intensify can take many forms, demographic, economic, social or political. Intensification can involve involution, with its attendant decline in marginal productivity and potential for environmental damage and immiseration, but these very ills may inspire people to concoct genuine innovations that serve to increase the efficiency of human labor and thus boost marginal productivity. These innovations can be agronomic (for example, more efficient organization of the farm in time or space) or technological (the adoption or invention of new agricultural implements). They can also involve genetic resources, i.e. a more efficient allocation of various plant and animal varieties.[13] None of these elaborations puts paid to

---

[13] It should be noted that all these innovations are subject to declining marginal productivity – albeit at higher yields – if their necessary inputs are pushed too far (again see Figure 3.10).

Boserup, or to Malthus for that matter, as long as we regard their conceptual frameworks as *models* rather than complete pictures of reality. Boserup's model is submerged in Figure 6.9, as is Geertz's, and can be lifted up out of it whenever it is useful to do so for analytical purposes. Malthus, on the other hand, provides a model for agricultural stasis, not change, and thus serves to blockade the processes shown in Figure 6.9. Both stasis and change can both occur in the preindustrial world, meaning that we need not choose between Malthus and Boserup.

And that, in a nutshell, is where the debate over traditional farming and population stands at the beginning of the twenty-first century: lots of complications to consider but little effort thus far to incorporate them into formal models – and not many meaningful tests of such models.

Intensive Subsistence Farming: An Extended Example from East Africa

I want to switch gears now and examine one particular example of intensive farming in East Africa studied by several agronomists and described in detail by Hans-Dieter Ludwig, who did his own extended fieldwork there in the 1960s (Ludwig, 1968). This example, involving the Wakara people living and farming on Ukara Island in Lake Victoria, offers what seems to me an especially interesting case study because it involves the development of an extraordinarily intensive set of farming practices (approaching the intensity of wet rice farming in parts of Geertz's Inner Indonesia) while still retaining a dominant focus on subsistence production. As an island, Ukara is spatially circumscribed and partially isolated from other groups, and at the time of study its inhabitants had little involvement in marketing and even less exposure to centralized political authority. Ukara is also one of the most densely populated parts of rural sub-Saharan Africa, a fact that Ludwig certainly does not think is a coincidence. In fact, Ludwig's interpretation of the Ukara situation is in many respects quite Boserupian in flavor. This is remarkable because, although it was written three years after Boserup's *Conditions of Agricultural Growth*, it seems to have been completely uninfluenced by it. At least Ludwig does not cite Boserup's work, nor does any other paper in the volume where his account appears. In effect, Ludwig's study appears to represent an independent invention of Boserupian thought, and it shares many of the strengths and weaknesses of her approach. But, whatever the soundness of Ludwig's interpretation (which we shall discuss below), his *description* of Wakara farming practices is excellent.

Ukara is one of several isolated "islands" of intensive farming, surrounded by a sea of shifting cultivation and nomadic pastoralism, that have recently been recognized in East Africa (Figure 6.10). It is also a literal island, measuring only about 9 km × 9 km in area and located near the southern shore of Lake Victoria in Tanzania. The climate is mesic, with about 1500 mm of rainfall each year and distinct wet and dry seasons (rain falls mainly between December and May, with March and April being the wettest months). The natural vegetation, which can scarcely be said to exist anymore, ranges from dry tropical forest to open savannah. Ukara has a flat, narrow lakeshore, a gently sloping lowland interior dominated by the alluvial plains of

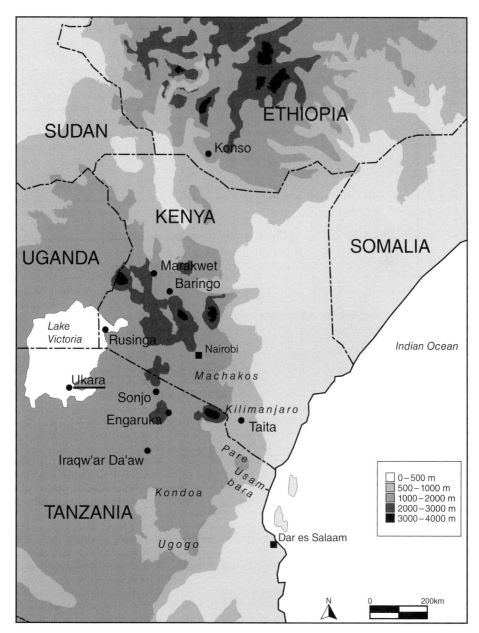

Figure 6.10 "Islands" of intensive grain-based agriculture in East Africa. All examples (dots) are contemporary except Engaruka, which is attested archaeologically. From Widgren (2004: 8). Reprinted by permission of Boydell & Brewer Ltd, *Islands of Intensive Agriculture in Eastern Africa: Past and Present*, ISBN 9780852554272, James Currey, 2004, edited by Mats Widgren and John E. G. Sutton.

several rivers, a slightly higher and hillier inter-riverine zone that Ludwig refers to as "pediment" land, and a rough, more steeply sloping interior rising to an altitude of about 1250 m and characterized by unimproved grassland and scattered outcrops of granitic rock or "inselbergs" (Figure 6.11). *Contra* Boserup, it is clear that local

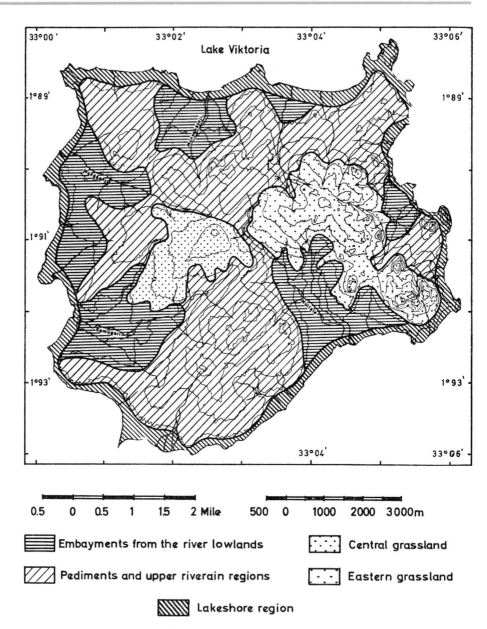

0.5   0   0.5   1   1.5   2 Mile   500   0   1000   2000   3000m

▤ Embayments from the river lowlands   ⬚ Central grassland

▨ Pediments and upper riverain regions   ⬚ Eastern grassland

▧ Lakeshore region

Figure 6.11 The physiography of Ukara Island, Tanzania. From Ludwig (1968: 98).

Wakara farmers carefully adjust their practices to these different environmental zones (Figure 6.12): the lake shore supports water meadows and irrigated grass pits for growing animal fodder; the lower river valleys are the site of irrigated permanent cultivation of rice and other crops, as well as fodder; pediment land is given over to dry rice and other unirrigated food crops; the rugged interior (whose soils are unsuitable for arable farming) is used seasonally for pasturing cattle while fodder crops are maturing. Table 6.2 shows the amount and use of each of these land types, and makes the point that fully 98.6 percent of the land surface of Ukara Island is

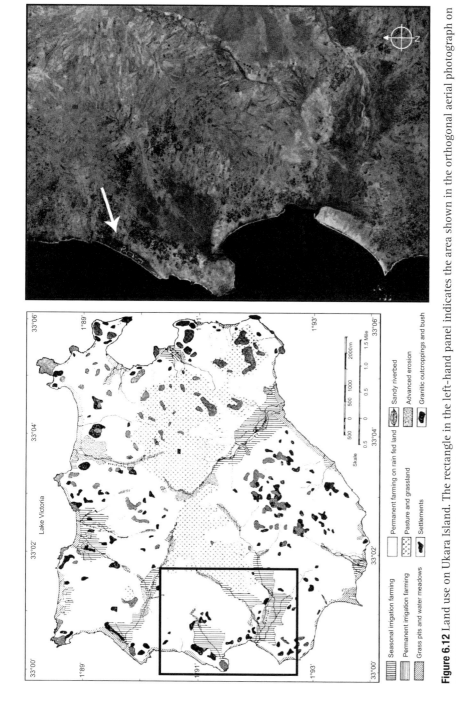

Figure 6.12 Land use on Ukara Island. The rectangle in the left-hand panel indicates the area shown in the orthogonal aerial photograph on the right. (Right) Note the areas of permanent irrigated rice farming, which show up as darkened areas in the lower river courses. The arrow indicates lakeside irrigated water meadows where fodder is grown; the rectilinear structures are grass pits. From Ludwig (1968: 96–7).

Table 6.2 A summary of land use on Ukara Island. From Ludwig (1968: 101).

Land type	Area (ha)	%
Arable	6185	80.3
Farming on rain-fed land	5668	73.6
Seasonal irrigation in lower river valley	511	6.6
Permanent irrigation with water meadows	6	0.1
Grassland	1385	18.3
Grazing areas	1362	18.0
Water meadows and grass pits near shore	23	0.3
Unproductive areas	109	1.4
Rocky outcrops and bush	46	0.6
Settlements	31	0.4
Areas of advanced erosion	18	0.2
Sandy river beds	14	0.2

Table 6.3 Estimated population densities on Ukara Island, 1965. From Ludwig (1968: 91–4).

Total population	> 16 000
Total land area (km^2)	78
Population densities (persons km^{-2}):	
total land	210
arable land	260
intensively cultivated land[a]	470

[a] Irrigated land and permanent dryland arable.

devoted to food production (including for livestock). This, in short, is an area in which the land is used about as completely as possible for the growing of food, and cultivation practices are carefully adjusted to make full use of the available environmental zones. Combined with evidence of high population densities (Table 6.3), this pattern of land use convinces Ludwig that the island is about as populous as it could possibly be under preindustrial agriculture and the prevailing environmental constraints. According to local tradition, the combination of high population density and intensive farming on Ukara dates back to at least the seventeenth century, well before the colonial period.

The Wakara (baKara, Kara) people of Ukara Island all speak a single Bantu language, and they are the island's sole inhabitants. The Wakara as a whole, however, are not confined to Ukara, but have recently colonized parts of the nearby island of Ukerewe and Northern Sukumaland on the mainland of Tanzania. Consistent with what Boserup and Brookfield would have predicted, the Wakara who have migrated to these less densely settled areas have reverted (if that is the right word) to shifting cultivation – plus some wage labor, which is uncommon on Ukara. This movement of people allows a revealing demographic comparison. Table 6.4 presents

Table 6.4 Estimated population size, Wakara-speakers 1928–57. From Ludwig (1968: 94).

Year	Wakara on Ukara	Wakara elsewhere	Total
1928	16 989	6 478	23 467
1931	17 506	8 069	25 575
1948	16 501	15 321	31 822
1957	16 052	18 365	34 417

estimates of the size of the Wakara population on and off Ukara Island between 1928 and 1957. The Wakara population as a whole almost doubled over that 30-year interval, a decidedly high rate of growth, but all the increase was registered off-island. The number of people on Ukara itself remained fairly constant and perhaps even declined slightly. Elsewhere (Laurie and Trant, 1952: 37) we are told that the crude birth and death rates on Ukara as of about 1950 were approximately 0.035 and 0.021 respectively, suggesting that the island population was experiencing a fairly high rate of natural increase. If these figures are correct, then the relative constancy of Ukara's population must have been attributable to out-migration. (One wonders if this demographic safety valve would have been an option before the *pax Britannica*.) Ludwig argues that Ukara is experiencing severe population pressure whereas Ukerewe and Northern Sukumaland, where Wakara farming practices appear to have undergone significant disintensification, are not. If so, then contrary to Boserup but consistent with the MaB ratchet, pressure is associated with demographic equilibrium, not with population growth *per se*.

The main food crops on Ukara are wet and dry rice, millet,[14] cassava (*Manihot esculenta*), bambara groundnuts (*Vigna subterranea*) and other legumes, sweet potatoes (*Ipomoea batatas*), yams (*Dioscorea* spp.), and a variety of vegetables. Some maize is also grown. Fields are organized by altitude and soil type according to the catena shown in Figure 6.13. Except for bambara groundnuts, which are an important part of the diet, legumes are mostly grown as green manure crops and are harvested before their seedpods dehisce. All cultivation is permanent (except for the occasional short fallow on rain-fed land), and all land, including upland grazing, is privately owned by individual households. The Wakara raise a dwarf breed of Zebu cattle plus some sheep and goats, all of which play a central role in the ecology of farming by providing manure. Wakara householders also keep chickens, which are the most common source of animal protein since larger livestock are too valuable to slaughter on a regular basis (except for bullocks, some of which are butchered and eaten when about two years old).

Single farmsteads or small villages (both of which are permanent) are located either on the edges of the river basins or on the slopes extending into the pediment area. Settlements are situated as close as possible to the fields that are cultivated most

---

[14] Ludwig glosses several species as "millet", including finger millet (*Eleusine coracana*), bulrush millet (*Pennisetum typhoideum*), and red sorghum (*Sorghum vulgare*).

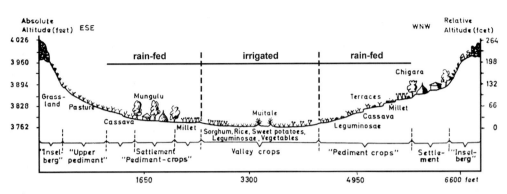

Figure 6.13 A typical farming catena, Ukara Island. Relative altitude is elevation above the valley bottom. Based on a 1965 transect of the lower Muitale River near the village of Chigara. From Ludwig (1968: 100).

intensively, "where farmyard manure and crops must be carried back and forth" frequently (Ludwig, 1968: 99–101). Farmsteads are typically placed nearest the irrigated fields, which must be tended daily; dryland plots are more widely scattered. The greater distances to upland grazing areas is not a serious problem since the grass is only harvested (for roofing material) once a year, few cattle are taken to pasture in any given year and they spend little time there, the beasts transport themselves from farmstead to pasture, and the smaller children of the household are able to tend the grazing animals. (As cattle are driven to and from the upland pastures through the densely sown arable, they are muzzled to prevent them from stealing other households' crops.) It would seem, as predicted by Brookfield, that the Wakara have intensified their food production not only by increasing labor inputs but also by organizing space as efficiently as possible given the range and spatial distribution of microhabitats.

Rain-fed farming is done mainly on the mid-elevation pediment land. A typical set of unirrigated fields is shown in Figure 6.14. Individual plots are narrow and oriented parallel to the slope of the land, which gives each household access to the full soil catena but also encourages erosion; often stone dykes or terraces are constructed at the lower margins of the fields to impede soil loss. In some fields, mounds are constructed for cassava, sweet potatoes, and groundnuts. Adjacent plots are likely to be growing different crops at any one time, reflecting the fact that each plot undergoes a complex rotation sequence and the rotational stages of neighboring plots are not synchronized. Over the course of each three-year rotation cycle (Table 6.5) the Wakara obtain three bulrush millet harvests, one sorghum harvest, one harvest of bambara nuts, and one harvest of green manure. These gains are purchased at the price of careful tillage and weeding, as well as yearly applications of manure: animal manures are worked into the soil every other year, green manures in the intervening year (Figure 6.14, left). Despite the frequent dressings of manure, the yields on rain-fed fields are judged to be "rather low" because of nutrient-poor soils (Ludwig, 1968: 105).

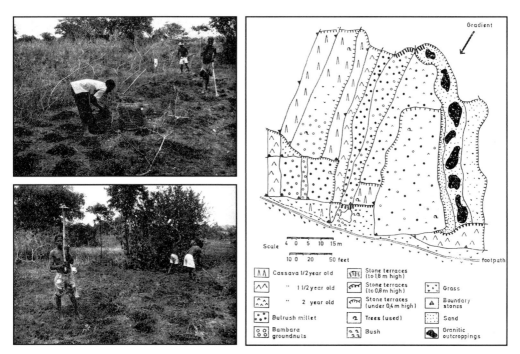

Figure 6.14 Rain-fed farming at Mbule on Ukara Island. (Top left) Part of a rain-fed field with a three-year-old stand of cassava is being manured in preparation for new cultivation. Animal manure brought in by basket is being spread by hand. (Bottom left) Tillage of soil is usually done by small groups of men or women using long-handled hoes with iron blades. Animal manure, green manure, and crop residues are worked in to a depth of 20–50 cm. (Right) Orientation of plots. From Ludwig (1968: 107).

Productivity is much higher on the irrigated fields situated on the alluvial soils of lowland river valleys. Irrigated fields are of two types: (i) permanent, year-round irrigated rice fields lying just above the mouths of the rivers (see Figure 6.12, right), and (ii) seasonally irrigated fields further up the valleys, devoted to dry rice during the summer months and a mix of irrigated crops, including rice, during winter (Figure 6.15). Both types of field are tended with great care, including frequent weeding. Irrigated fields are located near the spring branches or rivers that feed them, requiring only a fairly small-scale (but "closely interwoven") network of embankments, dams, canals, and culverts (Ludwig, 1968: 108). When nonrice crops are cultivated, they are often placed on mounds up to 1 m high to protect their roots from water-logging. The banks of the natural watercourses that line the irrigated fields are often planted in grasses that are later harvested for animal fodder – they are in effect water meadows, and they are separated from the irrigated fields by reed-covered embankments (Figure 6.15). The normal cropping sequence observed on seasonally irrigated fields is listed in Table 6.6; note that each plot receives *two* dressings of animal manure each year. Young rice seedlings are allowed to grow on special nursery beds and then carefully transplanted to the larger fields once the previous crop has been harvested, a practice commonly observed on highly intensive

Table 6.5 Typical cropping sequence on rain-fed land, Ukara. From Ludwig (1968: 105–6).

Year/month of rotation	Activity
First year	
August	Animal manure is applied and worked in to a depth of 20–50 cm
September–October	Millet (bulrush millet and red sorghum) is sown, a green manure crop (e.g. *Crotalaria striata* or legumes) is sown after first hoeing when millet is about 0.3 m high
November–December	Millet and green manure crop grow
January–February	Millet is harvested
March–June	Green manure crop grows to a height of 1–2 m
Second year	
July	Green manure crop is cut and worked into the soil during dry season
September–October	At beginning of rains, self-sown millet germinates and starts to grow
November–January	Bambara groundnuts are inter-planted among the growing millet
February	Millet is harvested
March–May	Bambara groundnuts grow
June	Bambara groundnuts are harvested
Third year	
July–September	Animal manure is worked in
September–October	Self-sown millet germinates
November–January	Millet matures
January–February	Millet is harvested
February–April	Cassava is planted
June	Cassava is harvested, the rotation is restarted *or* a short fallow (1–2 years) may begin

wet rice farms in East, Southeast, and South Asia but only rarely in sub-Saharan Africa. Irrigated land of both types makes up less than 10 percent of all arable (with seasonally irrigated fields representing by far the larger portion), but provides a disproportionately large fraction of the island's total annual yield. In unusually good years, irrigated fields may even produce enough rice to justify farmers crossing over to Ukerewe or Sukumaland in order to market some of it.

The key to the Wakara system of permanent farming, both irrigated and unirrigated, is intensive manuring. Green manure crops are cultivated and are important on dryland fields – especially legumes with their high nitrogen content. Goats and sheep are penned and their droppings carefully collected. But most manure comes

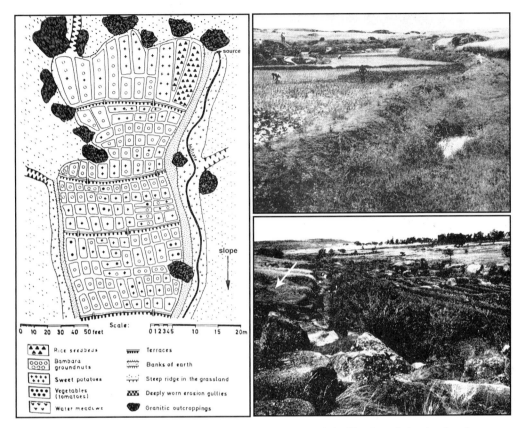

Figure 6.15 Seasonal irrigation farming on Ukara Island. (Left) Winter irrigation farming on an upper river-course (in summer almost all plots would be flooded to grow rice). (Top right) Rice growing: earthen banks regulate water via culverts. Rice seeds are being replanted in flooded fields. Water meadows, where fodder is grown, are to right. (Bottom right) Water meadow (arrow) separated from arable by reed-covered back. Small beds (right) are planted with sweet potato and bambara groundnuts. From Ludwig (1968: 109–10).

from cattle. The traditional Wakara house has a byre (cow shed) built into one side (Figure 6.16), the floor of which is dug to a depth of just under a meter, and the resulting pit lined with stones so that the cow cannot damage it. Fodder is provided twice a day, piled up at the outer edge of the pit where the beast can reach it. The resulting manure, mixed with feed litter, crop residues, and leaves, is mucked out of the byre two or three times a year and piled up in the farmyard (Figure 6.16). Cattle spend most of the year in the byre, although many households drive their heifers and calves up to the high pastures to feed for a short period while fodder crops are growing (bulls leave the byre only to be watered). Fodder for penned cattle and other livestock is carefully cultivated. Grass is sown in water meadows located on the lake foreshore or along river banks (Figure 6.17; see also Figure 6.15, right-hand panels). In addition, special structures, which Ludwig calls grass pits, are dug down about 1.5 m along the foreshore and connected to the lake by irrigation channels (Figure 6.17;

Table 6.6 Crop rotation on seasonally irrigated land, Ukara. From Ludwig (1968: 111).

Month	Activity
December–February	Rice is sown in small seed-beds, covered with leafy branches to protect them from birds and strong sunlight
February–March	Fields are tilled, animal manure worked in to depth of 20–50 cm, rice seedlings transplanted from seed-beds to flooded fields
April–June	Rice grows and begins to ripen
July–August	Rice is harvested by cutting stalks 50–100 cm under panicles with a knife
August–September	Fields are tilled and animal manure worked in for a subsequent planting of sweet potatoes, bambara groundnuts, sorghum, and vegetables
September–January	Nonrice crops grow and are harvested when ripe, new rice seed-beds are prepared
January–February	Harvested fields are tilled and animal manure worked in for the next rice crop

Figure 6.16 The primary source of manure on Ukara Island. (Top left) House with open byre (arrow) built into its side. The heap of manure in the right foreground has been shoveled out of the byre. (Bottom left) Dwarf Zebu cow tethered in byre, the floor of which is approximately 80 cm below ground level. (Right) Hauling manure from byre to field. Each basket weighs c. 15 kg; a mean of 12 baskets are used per rain-fed field each year. From Ludwig (1968: 103, 113).

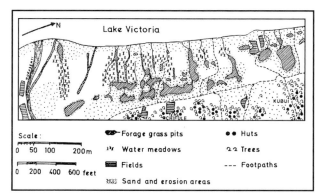

Figure 6.17 Lake-side water meadows and irrigated grass pits where fodder for livestock is grown, Ukara Island. Irrigation is done year-round by groundwater and by flooding with lake water via canals. (Top right) Excavated and irrigated grass pits. Most pits are *c.* 1.5 m deep. (Bottom right) Harvesting fodder by hand or knife in a grass pit. Man is standing hip-deep in water. From Ludwig (1968: 116–17).

see also Figure 6.12 right). The Wakara also cultivate 39 species of trees and shrubs whose leaves are periodically trimmed for fodder. Other sources of fodder include nonpoisonous weeds, one green manure crop (*Crotalia striata*), other crop residues (except for some varieties of cassava that are too high in cyanogenic glucosides), and the occasional catchcrop of rice. Cultivation, collection and carriage of animal fodder makes up a large part of the food production economy, almost exclusively geared to the production of manure.[15]

These cattle-rearing practices require an enormous investment of human labor, averaging about three to four hours out of a typical 12-hour workday. Most of this labor is spent in transporting fodder and manure. Baskets of manure or fodder typically weigh 14–15 kg, and multiple headloads must be hauled every day. The labor for this heavy work is provided by each household's able-bodied members, men, women and older children, who together move some 360 kg of fodder and manure *daily* (Table 6.7). It is probable that the inescapable need for manure and fodder is a major factor – perhaps the principal factor – limiting Ukara's capacity for permanent farming, as well as its prospects for further intensification. At least it is difficult to imagine that much more time and energy could be invested in fodder and manure production and transport without compromising other necessary parts of the

---

[15] The Wakara also use dairy products and, very rarely, eat beef, primarily from animals that have died of natural causes.

Table 6.7 Average quantity of fodder and farmyard manure carried daily by members of a single household, based on 50 sample households, Ukara, 1965. From Ludwig (1968: 120).

			Number of baskets		
	men	women	children	total	Total weight day^{-1} (kg)
Manure	4.4	4.2	2.7	11.1	158
Fodder	5.4	5.5	3.5	14.4	202
Total	9.8	9.7	6.2	25.5	360

Figure 6.18 A farmstead in Nyamanga, Ukara Island: h = house, b = byre (cow shed), g = granaries, ch = open cooking hearth, fw = firewood stacked in bushes, m = manure pile. The byre in the center of the picture is newly constructed, presumably to accommodate a growing herd of cattle. Lines of stones are placed to demarcate different functional areas. *Inset*, schematic of house interior. From Ludwig (1968: 101–2).

farming regime. I would even suggest, as a hypothesis, that Ukara was approaching a state of Malthusian deadlock that could only be broken by the introduction of inorganic fertilizers, which had not happened by the time of Ludwig's fieldwork.

Ludwig does not tell us much about individual households and their farms, but what he does report is interesting. Figure 6.18 shows a typical farmstead on Ukara, with a single house, byres, cooking areas, granaries and so on; average characteristics of households and their holdings are given in Table 6.8. The average number of

Table 6.8 Mean characteristics of households and their holdings, 50 sample households, Ukara, 1965. From Ludwig (1968: 102).

Persons per household	10.9
Total holding area (ha)	2.5
Number of arable fields	7.5
Number of grazing plots	2.2
Arable (ha):	1.7
millet	0.7
rice	0.3
cassava	0.3
bambara groundnuts + other legumes	0.3
sweet potatoes	0.1
other crops + short-term fallow	<0.1
Pasture (ha)	0.8
Livestock per holding:	
cattle	2.6
goats	3.3
sheep	0.7
chickens	7.4
Number of trees grown for fodder	25.0

household members is just under 11, a very high figure for traditional farmers, whose households usually average around five to seven individuals (see Chapter 7). It is difficult to explain this high number since we are not given any detailed information about household composition; but Ludwig ascribes it to land shortage, which prevents married sons from leaving their parents' household to set up new, independent farms. If this explanation is correct, then a large fraction of households on Ukara Island must be what are known as *stem households*, made up of an older couple (or widow/widower) plus one or more married sons, along with their wives and any coresident children. (In this connection it would be very interesting to compare the composition of Wakara households on Ukara to that on Ukerewe and in Northern Sukumaland, where land shortage is apparently not a problem.) The household's total land holding is very small, about 2.5 hectares. Arable is broken up into seven or eight fields, each tiny (<0.25 ha) and all of them widely dispersed (on average about 2 km from the farmstead). The average household has two or three head of cattle, three goats, one sheep, and seven or eight chickens. It also owns 25 trees or shrubs whose leaves are harvested as fodder.

Despite the comparatively large size of households on Ukara, the average labor force on each farm is small (Table 6.9) and subject to unexpected reductions owing to illness, temporary absences and migration to other areas. As a consequence, the members of the household labor force usually work hard. Small children contribute little labor, though they may tend cattle or scare birds away from newly sown fields. Children over 10 years of age, on the other hand, contribute appreciably to household labor. Men and women share more or less equally in farm work. In general, household members work about 12 hours a day (with significant seasonal variation,

Table 6.9 Mean labor capacity per household in "man equivalents" (MEs),[a] based on 50 sample households, Ukara, 1965. From Ludwig (1968: 125).

Age (years)	Males		Females		Total	
	ME	%	ME	%	ME	%
10–18	0.9	35	0.7	36	1.6	35
19–60	1.6	60	1.0	56	2.6	58
>60	0.1	5	0.1	8	0.3	7
Total	2.7	59	1.8	41	4.5	100

[a]Computed using the following ME weights:

Age group (years):	0–9	10–14	15–19	20–50	>50	
Males	0.0	0.25	0.67	1.00	0.67	
Females	0.0	0.25	0.50	0.67	0.50	

of course), some eight hours of which are devoted to arable farming and the rest to tending livestock and occasional fishing and hunting of birds. Ludwig reckons that most households use their available labor supply to its full capacity. In 1965, 58 percent of households had to enlist help from neighbors and relatives to cultivate their fields (this assistance was either reciprocated or paid in produce). As two colonial medical officers put it in the early 1950s, "There is a never-ending struggle on the part of the Wakara, men, women and children, to get food; so far the people are holding their own, but it is difficult to believe that this can continue much longer, in view of the rapid continued increase of the population" (Laurie and Trant, 1952: 37–8).

Which brings us to Ludwig's Boserupian interpretation of the Ukara case. That interpretation comes largely from the comparative material on Ukara, Ukerewe and North Sukumaland laid out in Table 6.10. Now, no correlation based on a sample size of three can be very convincing – and no correlation of any kind can reveal much about the direction of causation or the mechanisms driving the correlation, no matter how large the sample. But let's allow Ludwig his argument, which is that all the differences listed in Table 6.10 are fundamentally a reflection of differences in population density. To begin with, the size of households appears to increase with population density, resulting in an increase in the effective size of the household labor supply as measured in "man equivalents" (MEs). As already noted, Ludwig attributes this phenomenon to land shortage, which forces married sons to remain with their wives and children in their parents' household. (I would suggest that it may also reflect the relative labor absorption capacities of the three sets of farming practices.) Even more striking is the increase in labor supply relative to hectares of cultivated land, which is double on densely settled Ukara which is in the more sparsely populated North Sukumaland. This, of course, reflects the marked decrease in holding size with population density (7.8 ha in Sukumaland, 4.9 in Ukerewe, 2.5 in Ukara). Equally striking is that Ukara is substantially *less* involved in cash cropping than the other areas. In Sukumaland, "semicommercial farms" predominate, and

Table 6.10 Farm data from three neighboring areas of Tanzania with similar environments: North Sukumaland (mainland), Ukerewe Island (Lake Victoria) and Ukara Island (Lake Victoria). All yields are expressed as Tanzanian shilling equivalents. ME, "man equivalents" in labor (see Table 7.9). From Ludwig (1968: 130–1).

Variable	North Sukumaland	Ukerewe	Ukara
Population density	low	medium	high
Persons per holding	6.6	9.0	10.9
ME per holding	3.0	4.2	4.5
ME per ha land	1.3	1.7	2.6
Cattle (head per holding)	11.8	1.9	2.6
Total farm area (ha)	7.8 (100%)	4.9 (100%)	2.5 (100%)
Grazing area (ha)	5.5 (71%)	2.4 (47%)	0.8 (32%)
Cropped land (ha):	2.3 (29%)	2.5 (53%)	1.7 (68%)
subsistence crops	1.3	1.6	1.4
cash crops (rice, sisal, cotton)	1.0	0.9	0.3
Gross yield from all crops	1420 (100%)	828 (100%)	1135 (100%)
Gross yield from subsistence crops	434 (56%)	414 (50%)	838 (74%)
Gross yield from cash crops	632 (44%)	414 (50%)	297 (26%)
Gross yield per ha farm land	189	190	506
Gross yield per ME	492	222	283
Gross yield per hour of work	0.50	0.54	0.16

approximately half of all produce from agriculture and animal husbandry is sold (Ludwig, 1968:132).[16] On Ukara, in contrast, only about 25 percent of agricultural yield is marketed and animal products are apparently never sold, suggesting either that markets are too inaccessible to the island or that cash cropping is not viewed as an effective solution to land shortages there.

Paralleling the differences in cash cropping, far more attention is paid to subsistence food production on Ukara than elsewhere. Farms there may be small, but hectare for hectare they are more than twice as productive as farms on Ukerewe or in North Sukumaland, repaying all that work hauling manure and fodder. In addition, Ludwig judges that the quality of the diet on Ukara is better since it is based on a mixture of crops whereas Ukerewe and North Sukumaland are heavily dependent on cassava, which is productive in terms of calories but light on other nutrients and hard on the soil. And even what little market activity is conducted by Ukara farmers is oriented toward food for the family. "Of the 50 farmers [on Ukara] asked what they would purchase if they had an additional cash surplus, 91% decided on high quality foods, 65% on farm investments, 59% on increasing their stock of cattle, and only 24% wanted to buy consumer goods, such as bicycles and transistor radios"

---

[16] Indeed, Sukumaland's principal cash crop is cotton, which obviously cannot be consumed as food by the producing household. Ukara has no crops that are grown exclusively for cash sale.

(Ludwig, 1968:132). Despite their partial involvement in the cash economy, the people of Ukara clearly remain subsistence farmers at heart.

The last three lines in Table 6.10 are central to Ludwig's Boserupian argument. Ukara farms may be relatively productive, but the island does not compare favorably with respect to gross yields per "man equivalent" of household labor, and it does very poorly in terms of yields per hour of farm work. The returns on labor for North Sukumaland and Ukerewe are more than three times greater than for Ukara. Translating this finding into language that would appeal to Boserup, Ludwig essentially argues that intensification of food production under population pressure leads to a sharp reduction in the marginal productivity of farm labor. Ukara land is productive, Ukara labor is not – which means that the farmers of Ukara feed themselves through sheer hard work. Ludwig's observations suggest that farmers on Ukara work in their fields from dawn to dusk all year round. "Obviously the Wakara must work very long hours indeed to secure their livelihood. This is certainly the main reason they prefer to migrate to Sukumaland and to become cash-cropping, soil-mining, semipermanent [shifting] cultivators with a much higher return per hour of work" (Ludwig, 1968: 133).

To his credit, Ludwig provides a good discussion of various problems of data quality, which led him to conclude that this comparison "should be made with caution" (Ludwig, 1968: 130).[17] For my part, I would also have liked some information about variation *within* each of the three cases; without data on differences among households and their farms, the ecological fallacy is a real danger. And of course I don't care much for gross population density as a measure of "pressure." Still, I find Ludwig's linkage of dense population and intensive farming fairly convincing if not definitive. Ukara has a lot of people squeezed into a small space, and its inhabitants work hard to feed themselves. But there is a deeper question left completely unanswered by Ludwig's (and Boserup's) explanatory scheme: Where did the tightly packed demographic situation on Ukara come from in the first place? Why hasn't it affected neighboring areas? Why is Ukara an island of high population density and intensive agriculture in a region of thin populations, shifting cultivators, and nomadic pastoralists? (The same could be asked of the other East African islands of intensive cultivation shown in Figure 6.10.) Even if we accept population as a driver of intensification on Ukara, why is the population there as large as it is? If it is the result of a history of MaB ratcheting, what set off the ratchet on Ukara but not in other nearby areas, including on the environmentally similar island Ukerewe? These questions are difficult to answer because the trajectory of development of both the farming and the demographic regimes on Ukara is, as Doolittle (1984) would not be surprised to learn, impossible to reconstruct at this late date. And static comparisons cannot settle questions about temporal dynamics.

---

[17] He is most concerned about potential selectivity bias in the original samples from which the statistics in Table 6.10 were computed (Ludwig, 1968: 130–1). He also acknowledges many difficulties in measuring yields.

As good as Ludwig's account of Wakara farming practices is (and it is very good), there is something else missing from it. It is at heart a description of what comes across as a rather homogeneous "system" of farming – homogeneous in the sense that every farmer appears to be doing much the same thing – seemingly running on autopilot and explicable using data on the island and its population as a whole, as in Table 6.10. Although Ludwig acknowledges that Wakara households are largely independent of each other in food production and consumption, we get little sense of the individual farm as a single (if spatially fragmented) functional unit – as an *enterprise*; little sense of its owners and operators as intellectually active agents – managers, decision-makers, risk-takers, risk-avoiders, people who choose to migrate or to stay put. We are given some averages concerning farms and households, but nothing about variation among them or what causes it. We are told that the Wakara seem, as a *population*, to be reasonably well nourished in terms of calories if not protein, but not how nutrition, health, birth and death vary among households or how such variation may result from differences in farming decisions and behaviors. Somehow the basic *motor* of the system – the farming family and its farm – has largely been left out of the account. And what is lacking in Ludwig's description is, to my mind, equally lacking in much of the literature on traditional farming.

Reopening the Debate

The classic debate over agriculture and population has not been wholly misdirected; in fact, I think we have learned a great deal from it. But it seems to have ground to something of a halt without any final resolution of its most fundamental issues. I suspect that most people are simply tired of it and have moved on to other things, as Brookfield (2001b) seems to intimate. These days, explanations that incorporate population processes are viewed as being rather reductionist, and reductionism is currently out of fashion, at least in the social sciences. The premature closing of the agriculture/population debate is, in my opinion, unfortunate, because I think the relationship between demographic processes and traditional farming is even *more* profound than did either Malthus or Boserup.

What are my dissatisfactions with the post-Boserupian debate over intensification and population processes? First, it has focused exclusively on agrarian *change* rather than stability – despite the fact (acknowledged by both Malthus and Boserup) that traditional farming practices undergo long periods with little if any sustained directional change (as opposed to transient, nondirectional fluctuations). A focus on change is perhaps understandable given that most of the surviving remnants of traditional farming studied in recent years by anthropologists, geographers and other scientists are themselves undergoing rapid and often cataclysmic change in response to global influences. But those influences did not exist in the distant past. The focus on intensification and other forms of change assumes in effect that the rapid population growth occurring today in parts of the developing world can be extrapolated uncritically to the past. Boserup, however, remarked that "[u]ntil recently rates of population growth were low or very low in most pre-industrial communities and from time to time the size of the population would be reduced by wars, famines or epidemics" (Boserup, 1965: 56). And Malthus put forward a model of demographic *stagnation*, not growth. As explained in Chapter 4, there are reasons to believe that preindustrial populations may have been subject to forces that would tend toward a stable equilibrium in population size. Change did occur, of course, and an expanded version of Boserup's model can play a part in helping us understand such change. But stasis also occurred and was arguably the norm. It too requires explanation.

Second, despite decades of progress on some issues, the debate is still centered on a disturbingly opaque notion of population "pressure" – which, whatever it is, does not seem to have much to do with any actual, nuts-and-bolts demography. We have little good theory about why, when or where pressure is likely to build up, or how that pressure results from (or feeds back upon) fertility, mortality or migration, the basic forces of demographic change. For most participants in the debate, pressure seems to be synonymous with population density, which I have repeatedly characterized as difficult to interpret and perhaps even meaningless in all but its narrowest usage. Any theory that cannot specify its principal predictor variable in a satisfactory way is a poor foundation for scientific investigation.

Finally, the debate has focused too much on the macrodemographic scale, treating populations, farming communities and (worst of all) farming "systems" as the units that experience and respond to demographic forces. With some exceptions (most notably Robert Netting and his students), the debate has generally ignored individual farmers, farms and farming households. But in subsistence farming, these are the key actors; the larger community (or some segment of it) can certainly play a role, but a distinctly limited and secondary one (see Chapter 12). The focus on the aggregate has resulted in models that conform to the general logic schematized in Figure 6.19, wherein population and agriculture are distinct entities that act upon each other at remove. As I argued in Chapter 1, I think this is a mistake. When viewed from the perspective of the individual farming household, the interplay of demography and farming looks much more intimate (Figure 6.20). The subsistence farming household is, in essence, a demographic enterprise: demography (i.e. creating and rearing a family) is its whole *raison d'être*. Accordingly, there may be two, if not more, distinct levels of population pressure that are at least partly independent of each other: one operating at the macrodemographic or aggregate level (what we have called *Boserupian pressure*) and the other at the microdemographic or household/farmstead level (which I shall call *Chayanovian pressure* for reasons that will become clear in Chapter 10). It is entirely possible for Chayanovian pressure to exist in the total absence of Boserupian pressure – which does not absolve us from the need to clarify what we mean by "pressure" at whatever level it occurs. It is also possible, as I shall

Figure 6.19 How *not* to think about population and traditional farming.

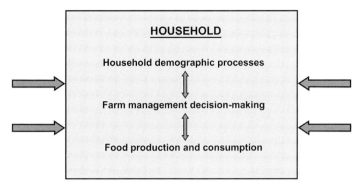

Figure 6.20 A more fruitful way to think about population and traditional farming. Single-headed arrows indicate unspecified inputs.

argue, that demographic and economic processes going on within households can be potent sources of population stasis as well as change.

In sum, our investigation of population and subsistence farming (i) must deal with demographic stasis as well as change, (ii) must pay more attention to the precise mechanisms, both demographic and agrarian, driving the relationship between the two and (iii) must disaggregate the scale of analysis to the household level. These are the goals of the remainder of this book.

Part III

Microdemographic Approaches to Population and Subsistence Farming

7 The Farming Household as a Fundamental Unit of Analysis

In the small tribal societies which are the traditional subject of anthropological research, direct exploitation of natural resources is usually carried out for the most part by families, and the economic processes of distribution, use, and consumption of goods occur largely within the family context. Thus in most African societies a family group of some kind produces food by cultivating its own land or herding its own cattle and consumes most of this food at its own homestead. Natural resources are major points of ecological contact between human communities and their physical environment, and in tribal societies the ecological processes of exploitation occur mainly in a family milieu. The labour and skills necessary for exploiting the natural resources are funneled through the family in actual application, while the goods consumed are distributed through family channels. Individuals obtain their vital sustenance largely through the mediation of the family structure. Thus the family is a principal locus of ecological processes.   – R. F. Gray (1964: 5)

I believe that a convincing case can be made out in favour of the household as the fundamental unit in pre-industrial European society for social, economic, even educational and political purposes... The relationship between parents, children, servants and kin within the English household, and the interplay of its size and structure with economic and demographic development, make up an intricate adaptive mechanism which we are only now beginning to understand.   – P. Laslett (1969)

In many societies the household is the one unit through which almost the whole of the economy can be studied as a connected and functioning whole.   – R. U. Firth (1966: 1)

In preceding chapters, I have urged repeatedly, first, that the population/agriculture debate needs to be disaggregated to some spatial scale lower than the total population and, second, that the household, the most conspicuous functional group in the everyday working life of all preindustrial farming communities, is the best place to start the disaggregation. Note that I say "start": other scales may turn out to be useful – perhaps even more useful for some purposes – but the household level would seem, as many researchers have suggested, to be the smallest scale that *as a general rule* captures the essential processes linking traditional farming and demography (Laslett, 1983; Fricke, 1984; Netting, 1993).

Gene Hammel once remarked that the household "is the next bigger thing on the social map after an individual" (1984: 40–1). Many students of preindustrial households have taken this idea to heart, further disaggregating their material from the level of the household *per se* to that of the individual and treating households, in effect, as changing environments through which individuals pass during their life courses (e.g. Hareven, 1974; Vinovskis, 1977, 1988; Kertzer, 1986; Bongaarts, 1987; Elder, 1987; Willekins, 1988; Kertzer and Hogan, 1991; Ruggles, 1990, 2009). For some research questions, this reorientation has been useful. But there is still considerable merit in treating the farming household as a unit of fundamental demographic and economic importance in its own right. An individual cannot possess demography, which can only belong to a *group* of individuals. The household, in contrast, does have demography – can even be regarded in itself as a tiny population for some analytical purposes, as this chapter will suggest. By the same token, an individual cannot have an age or sex *composition*, a sexual division of labor (see Chapter 9) or a ratio of food consumers to food producers (Chapter 10). The household can. Finally, the *family farm*, the most basic spatial and ecological unit in traditional agriculture, is operated and relied upon by an entire household, even if only one member is viewed as its rightful owner.

Still, it is important not to lose sight of the fact that all households (except, of course, those with only one member) are made up of diverse individuals with overlapping but not identical self-interests, among whom both cooperation and competition are to be expected (Laslett, 1984). The household is not, to borrow an old wheeze from seventeenth-century philosophy, a monad: self-sufficient, noninteracting, indivisible, impenetrable and unchanging. But it is arguably the most important arena for organizing food production and consumption among traditional farmers, the most important level at which behaviors and decisions influencing fertility, mortality and migration take place and thus the single most important place where agriculture and demography interact in traditional rural societies. As recently argued, the household is also the basic level at which to begin understanding the environmental impact of smallholder farming (An *et al.*, 2001; Perz, 2002; Perz *et al.*, 2006; VanWey *et al.*, 2007).

This chapter introduces the subsistence farming household as a fundamental unit of analysis. Although more general topics will be discussed, the primary emphasis will be on household demography. Later chapters will link the demography to food and farming. All these chapters will be motivated by our model of the subsistence-oriented household as a demographic enterprise (Figure 7.1).

What is a Household?

The household is rather like art (or obscenity): we may not know how to define it, but we recognize it when we see it.[1] If, however, we wish to *study* households in multiple cultural settings, we need to be able to define them so that they can be observed and measured in a way that has cross-cultural validity. Households have been defined in terms of (among other things) day-to-day coresidence, familial relationships, control of a physical "estate" such as arable land, livestock or a collection of farm tools, or the range of practical tasks their members routinely perform (Gray, 1964; Bender,

---

[1] To quote Gene Hammel again, the household is a "unit of social structure recognizable by anyone but a caviling social scientist" (1984: 30).

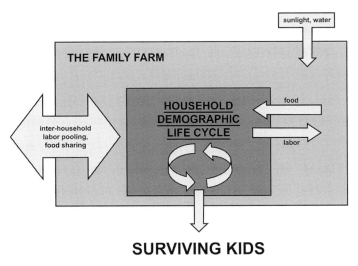

SURVIVING KIDS

Figure 7.1 The subsistence-oriented family farm as a demographic enterprise.

1967; Laslett, 1983, 1988; Carter, 1984: 45). It has even been suggested that households do so many different things, which differ so radically from one society to another, that a single definition can never be concocted (Yanagisako, 1979). In ecological analysis, by way of contrast, an empirical "you'll know 'em when you see 'em" approach is sometimes adopted – attractive as a way to avoid a lot of tedious hairsplitting, but insufficient for ensuring comparability in cross-cultural work. Change over time makes households even harder to separate from each other (Carter, 1984), and some individuals may view themselves as belonging to more than one household at the same time.[2] Identifying households may thus involve an element of arbitrariness on the researcher's part, especially in longitudinal studies – not necessarily an insurmountable problem as long as the researcher is clear on how the identification was made. But, as demonstrated by Keilman (1995), the way in which we define households will probably have at least some effect on the results we obtain from our statistical analyses and from comparative studies.

My own preferred definition, which reflects my interest in food, nutrition and the household demographic enterprise, is the one used by tax assessors in early fifteenth-century Tuscany: a household is "a uno vino e uno pane" (Klapisch and Demonet, 1972) – that is, a group of individuals who *regularly* pool food (and wine!) and eat together.[3] The adverb *regularly* is subject to interpretation but generally means on a daily basis unless a recognized household member is temporarily absent. Note that

---

[2] Most definitions used in modern empirical research are designed to ensure that a person belongs to one and only one household at any given moment so that no one in the sample is enumerated more than once. It is in this connection that the approach based on individual life courses may be most useful since individuals persist as discrete "units" over their lifetimes.

[3] Similar definitions of households as "eating at one table" or "sharing one cook pot" are common in the literature. These definitions do not differ dramatically from the formal one adopted for the National Census of the United Kingdom in 1998 (after field-testing of several alternatives): a household is one person living

this definition, based strictly on common food consumption, does not necessarily imply the coresidence or biological relatedness of household members, even if these turn out to be common features of households so defined. And in fact they turn out to be *very* common features in all traditional rural societies – although close relatedness does not mean that exactly the same set of relatives is always present (or that nonrelatives are never present), and coresidence does not mean that everyone in the household always lives in one physical structure. Sometimes members of a single household can reside in a cluster of spatially contiguous buildings, once a common arrangement in parts of rural Mesoamerica (Redfield and Villa Rojas, 1934: 33–5). In other cases, such as quasi-urbanized farming communities in medieval northern Italy, a single "house" constitutes in effect an apartment building with several to many farming households residing in it (Klapisch, 1972; Kertzer, 1991).

Some researchers carefully distinguish *de jure* from *de facto* members and treat the former as "real" household members as opposed to the latter, who may be temporary visitors or hangers-on (Siegel and Swanson, 2004: 205–8, 524). However, in traditional societies without formal laws, the operative meaning of *de jure* may be unclear or the entire concept inappropriate. Moreover, someone present in the household may be a jural member to some "proper" members of the household but not to others. My inclination is to stick with *de facto* membership as long as it is consistent with the idea of regularly eating together over a more or less prolonged period of time (weeks? months? years?), although this approach can be problematic since we often do not *observe* households over prolonged periods of time. Sometimes we just have to punt on our definitions.

This may be a good place to address the claim sometimes put forward, that in some traditional farming communities larger, nonhousehold-based residential groups exist that "communally" take on many of the roles ascribed in this book to individual households. I have in mind specifically the traditional matrilineal longhouses of the Iroquois living in what is now the northeastern United States and southeastern Canada, the even larger longhouses or *rumah*s of the Iban of Sarawak, and the circular *shabono* houses of the Yanomama of interior Venezuela and Brazil.

The Iroquois are the most difficult to evaluate on this score since no systematic ethnographic observations were ever made back when longhouses were still intact, functioning institutions. By the early to mid-nineteenth century, when Louis Henry Morgan attempted to reconstruct traditional Iroquois society based on oral histories, the longhouse was at best a relic and no longer a dwelling place (Morgan, 1851). The modern longhouse, where it exists, is essentially a self-conscious recreation by Iroquois "traditionalists" and almost certainly bears little similarity to traditional longhouses (Myers, 2006). It is known from ethnohistory and archaeology that longhouses were subdivided into separate hearths where smaller kin groups, apparently equivalent to households, regularly cooked and ate (Eric Jones, personal communication). On the other hand, there is a one-sentence remark from an

on his/her own with their own kitchen or cooking facilities *OR* a group of people (not necessarily related) sharing a kitchen or cooking facilities (www.statistics.gov.uk/census/pdf/ag9812.pdf).

Figure 7.2 A traditional Iban longhouse, Sarawak. Photograph © Dennis Lau (1999).

eighteenth-century Jesuit observer, Fr. Joseph François Lafitau, to the effect that "All the women of the village [which may contain several longhouses] join together for the heavy [farming] work" (Lafitau, 1724). This statement probably refers to special-purpose work groups that came together seasonally around labor-intensive tasks such as land clearance or harvest, which would make them more or less identical to seasonal, multihousehold work groups observed in most preindustrial farming communities (see Chapter 12). But we just do not know.

The situation is clearer for the Iban, who were studied in detail by Derek Freeman (1955, 1970) during the 1940s and 1950s when traditional *rumah*s were still common (Figure 7.2). Among many other things, Freeman was interested in testing the then-popular belief that Iban longhouses were truly corporate landholding and farming operations that completely submerged their constituent households. As his careful observations show, they were not. *Rumah*s were not single domiciles but, in effect, apartment houses (as Freeman himself called them) made up of multiple independent, physically distinct household apartments called *bilek*s (Figure 7.3). The *bilek* was occupied by a small group of close kin with its own living space walled off from other *bilek*s, its own material possessions, and its own farm holding, albeit fragmented and scattered among the holdings of other *bilek*s. *Bilek* apartments were built on to an existing longhouse one at a time, and over the long run *bilek* families had a tendency to hive off the longhouse as single units or as small collections of closely related *bilek*s (Freeman, 1955: 21–6). When the distribution of *bilek* size (i.e. number of occupants) is compared to that of separate households in other preindustrial farming communities, they turn out to be remarkably similar to each other (Table 7.1; Table 7.6 shows additional comparative data).

The Yanomama *shabono* appears to be similar to the Iban *rumah* in many respects (Chagnon, 2009: 56–9). Unlike the *rumah*, however, the ring-shaped wood and thatch *shabono* often comprises a single continuous space opening onto a shared central courtyard. But discrete household subunits are delimited by piles of

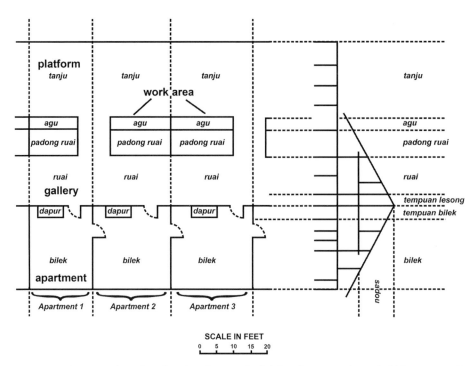

Figure 7.3 Schematic plan of an Iban longhouse. The *bilek* is the private household "apartment". *Padong ruai* and *dapur* are storage units. From Freeman (1955: 2), by permission of Her Majesty's Stationery Office.

household possessions, and each subunit has its own sleeping hammocks and cook fires (Smole, 1976: 59–67). Landholding and farming are organized at the level of the single household rather than that of the *shabono* as a whole (Smole, 1976: 111–13). Like the *rumah*, the *shabono* is in effect a sort of apartment house.

Five Ways of Looking at Households

Social units closely matching our definition of "households" were thus well-nigh universal in traditional farming communities – or at least no clear counter-examples have been discovered to date. Unsurprisingly in light of this fact, households are accepted as important units of analysis in several distinct fields of research, even though they are viewed from rather different perspectives as we move from one field to another. The disciplines most relevant to this book are listed in Table 7.2, along with some of the household characteristics or within- and between-household processes deemed most important to each field.

From the vantage point of this book, *all these fields and perspectives are equally important*. Household demography is a well-established part of mainstream demography. In trying to think about the family-based, subsistence-oriented farming

Table 7.1 Numerical composition of *bilek* families in three Iban longhouses, May 1950. For comparison, the percent distribution of household sizes for Norwegian peasants in 1801 (who did not reside in longhouses or similar multihousehold structures) is shown. Iban data from Freeman (1970: 10); Norwegian data from Drake (1969: Table 18).

Longhouse	Size of *bilek* family ($N = 107$)[a]												
	2	3	4	5	6	7	8	9	10	11	12	13	14
Rumah Nyala	0	7	3	4	3	2	2	1	3	0	0	0	0
Ruman Sibat	3	2	7	4	9	4	0	0	3	0	0	0	0
Ruman Tungku	2	4	9	9	6	7	7	1	3	0	1	0	1
Total	5	13	19	17	18	13	9	2	9	0	1	0	1
%	17		51			22			10				
Norway 1801[b] %	21		46			24			9				

[a] Mean = 5.75, inter-quartile range = 4–6.
[b] Mean = 5.70, inter-quartile range = 4–6.

household as a demographic enterprise, we start with the assumption that the goal of the operation is inherently demographic – to create and raise a family. And the household characteristics and processes studied by household demographers are a direct reflection of, are indeed driving forces within, the demographic enterprise. Moreover, if the household demographic enterprise is to succeed, then agricultural yields must meet the household's joint nutritional requirements. To achieve that goal the household must organize its farm and manage its limited resources carefully. Thus, the household demographic enterprise is both demographic *and* economic in its essential nature – although, in my view, the economic is subservient to the demographic. Social and cultural factors inevitably exert their own influences on the household enterprise, and some of these factors, including the ones identified in Table 7.2, have such direct influences on household demography and economy as to be integral to the demographic enterprise. Finally, if the household's yield of food is to meet its joint nutritional requirements each year, it must be responsive to the fact that these requirements vary by age and sex, as well as by workload and health status (which also vary by age and sex). It follows, then, that the food needs of the household as a whole are determined in large part by the changing age and sex composition of its members, as well as its absolute size – in other words, by household demography. Insofar as household members constitute the usual labor force for farming, the physiological work capacity of the household members is a major determinant of how much labor can be invested in food production. As detailed in Chapter 9, physiological work capacity also varies by age and sex as well as by nutritional status. Thus, among the various factors that drive the household subsistence enterprise, demographic, economic, sociocultural and nutritional variables would seem to be of special and universal importance.

Table 7.2 Household characteristics or processes identified as paramount by selected scientific disciplines.

The household as a unit of demographic analysis

o size (i.e. number of members)
o age and sex composition
o dynamics (formation, expansion, extension, contraction, dissolution)
o flow of members into and out of the household (migration)
o effects of household-level characteristics on fertility, mortality and migration

The household as a unit of economic analysis

o production goals
o organization and management of production
o allocation of household labor
o allocation of other scarce resources
o ratio of producers to consumers
o relationship to land and other resources (tenure)
o within- and between-household cooperation and competition

The household as a unit of social analysis

o age patterns of marriage
o patterns of postmarital residence
o kinship composition
o degree of extension
o effects of plural marriage on household composition
o social ties to other households

The household as a unit of cultural analysis

o transmission of cultural capital (enculturation)
o rules or expectations regarding an individual's eligibility for marriage
o rules or expectations regarding postmarital residence
o rules or expectations regarding household formation, extension and dissolution
o rules or expectations regarding inheritance of land, livestock, farming capital and other resources

The household as a unit of nutritional analysis

o nutritional status of household members
o gross and net consumption needs (i.e. net of energy put into food production)
o physiological work capacity
o intra- and inter-household distribution of food
o effects of household characteristics on nutritional status and on nutrition-related morbidity and mortality

General Features of Subsistence-Oriented Farming Households

At the cost of repeating material from Chapter 1, I want to assert (admittedly without much supporting evidence at this point) a series of propositions about subsistence-level farming households that I believe to have wide if not strictly universal empirical validity. Since we are concerned in this chapter with the household as a separate unit on its own, this particular set of assertions ignores relations among households, which will be discussed in Chapter 12.

- The farming household is the primary unit of food production and consumption: most food grown by a household is eaten by that same household, most food eaten by a household is grown by that same household.
- The domicile of the farming household is a discrete spatial cluster, but not necessarily a single house.
- Farming households are farming families, typically made up of a core of close consanguineal kin – usually within one or two degrees of relatedness – plus their spouses. In some circumstances more distant relatives and even nonrelatives may also be present, but these are almost always additions to a core membership of close kin.
- Exclusive access to arable land and disposition of its produce is vested in the household (at least temporarily as under usufruct, wherein exclusive access to land lasts only as long as the household is actively cultivating it).
- Most farm management decisions originate in the household. Most are made by the male head of household (if he is living) under the influence of other members.
- Subsistence farms are small operations: small in membership (usually falling between one and twelve members, with a mean of about five to seven) and small in the area of arable land allotted to each (often much less than ten hectares).[4]
- Farming households change over time – they can even be said to have a built-in demographic life cycle.

In Chapter 1 I presented these assertions as working assumptions underlying a model of the subsistence farming household, but I think they are also valid empirical generalizations, even if they admit of exceptions. (A small number of exceptions does not a model or generalization murder.) I will start documenting these assertions in this chapter and continue in the following chapters.

The Demography of Households

Basic Demographic Models

Household characteristics are undeniably influenced by demographic variables – for example, the rate at which new children are produced within the household, or the probability that a child will survive to the age of marriage or establishment of a new household, if the two are distinct events. We can start to identify and assess such

---

[4] Dramatic exceptions to the generalization that households are small in membership can be found scattered through the literature. One example, the Wakara of Ukara Island, was discussed in Chapter 6. An even more extreme case from Mali is described by Toulmin (1992). In both instances, there are special circumstances that appear to encourage large households.

demographic influences by building deliberately over-simplified models in which interesting household characteristics are determined *solely* by demographic variables (or rather demographic variables plus a handful of cultural rules concerning such things as where a newly married couple is expected to reside). These models assume that demographic variables are exogenous to the household – i.e. there are no household-level feedbacks influencing the demography itself. In these simple models, then, demography is treated as a completely autonomous determinant of household characteristics – not a claim anyone would ever want to make about real households, but a useful simplification for isolating the effects of the relevant demographic variables.

Most such modeling efforts have focused on total household size and build upon early work by Ansley Coale (1965). As Coale himself acknowledged, his models were so over-simplified and schematic as to be of dubious usefulness. But Burch (1970) elaborated on them, adding considerably more demographic detail and increasing the models' range of application. During the 1970s and 1980s, computer-based micro-simulation models became popular as a way to mimic household demography (Dyke and MacCluer, 1974; Wachter *et al.*, 1978, especially chapters 1–4; Wachter, 1987b). These computer models permitted the study of more complex and realistic demographic regimes, and allowed the investigation of household composition as well as overall size – but sometimes at the expense of clarity and generalizability. More recently, agent-based computer models have been used to explore household dynamics (see Billari *et al.*, 2003; Todd *et al.*, 2005), but these efforts are so few and so new that it would be premature to try to summarize them.

The sensitivity analyses calculated by Thomas Burch (1970) would seem to strike a reasonable balance between realism and simplicity. The results of Burch's analyses are summarized in Table 7.3.[5] In these analyses, average household size is determined by age-specific mortality rates taken from a model life table specified by a given life expectancy at birth (e_0), the mean ages of women at marriage and childbirth, the overall level of fertility as indicated by the total fertility rate (*TFR*), and the rules governing where a newly married couple should live during the earliest phase of their marriage (postmarital residence rules). The latter rules, when combined with a woman's probability of surviving long enough to marry and her mother's probability of surviving to the ages at which her daughter marries and then reproduces, determine how common larger stem families are under each scenario (in the scenario labeled stem family type 2, the level of fertility – more specifically, the total number of daughters produced – is also important). The selected values of age at marriage, mortality, and fertility included in Table 7.3 are intended to bracket the range of

---

[5] Burch published only the results for wife's age at marriage = 20 years, commenting that other analyses suggested that age at marriage had little effect on household size. I have recalculated his models for age at marriage = 15 and 25 years. These additional calculations would seem to suggest that age at marriage should not be altogether ignored as a determinant of household size, but Burch was probably right to consider its effects modest.

Table 7.3 Model-predicted average household size by woman's age at marriage (in years), mortality ($e_0 =$ life expectancy at birth), fertility level (*TFR* = total fertility rate), and family type.[a] *Simple family* (nuclear family): every woman who survives to the given age at marriage marries at that age and immediately establishes a new household. *Stem family type 1*: every woman who survives to the given age at marriage marries at that age; if her mother is dead, she establishes her own household immediately, otherwise she does so at the time of her mother's death. *Stem family type 2*: every woman who survives to the given age at marriage marries at that age; if her mother is dead she establishes her own household immediately; if the mother is alive, one surviving sister in each family remains in the mother's household until the mother's death. Modified and extended from Burch (1970); see also Coale (1965: 65–6).

Mortality/ fertility level	Age at marriage = 15 Family type			Age at marriage = 20 Family type			Age at marriage = 25 Family type		
	Simple	Stem 1	Stem 2	Simple	Stem 1	Stem 2	Simple	Stem 1	Stem 2
e_0 = 20 years									
TFR = 4	2.7	2.8	3.7	3.0	3.3	3.8	3.4	3.5	4.2
6	3.1	3.2	4.6	3.6	4.1	4.7	4.3	4.4	5.4
8	3.4	3.5	5.4	4.2	4.8	5.6	5.2	5.3	6.7
e_0 = 40 years									
TFR = 4	2.9	3.7	5.6	3.4	4.3	5.4	3.9	4.7	6.0
6	3.4	4.0	7.2	4.2	5.2	7.2	5.1	5.9	8.4
8	3.9	4.3	9.0	5.0	6.0	9.2	6.4	7.1	11.0
e_0 = 60 years									
TFR = 4	3.1	4.9	7.7	3.6	5.1	7.5	4.2	6.0	8.2
6	3.7	5.0	11.9	4.5	5.8	10.9	5.6	7.3	12.4
8	4.2	5.2	14.8	5.4	6.6	14.4	7.1	8.6	17.1

[a] Based on the Coale–Demeny model "West" female life tables and stable populations for mortality levels 1, 9 and 17 (Coale and Demeny, 1983). The mean age of women at childbearing is assumed to be 30 years in all cases, regardless of age at marriage.

variation observed in preindustrial societies. In view of the many simplifying assumptions made by Burch, the precise household sizes listed in the table ought not to be taken too seriously. But the analyses are convincing in showing that fertility, mortality and postmarital residence exert important influences on household size (with age at marriage rather less important). At the same time, however, it is striking what a narrow range of household sizes arises from remarkably wide differentials in fertility and mortality. Expected household sizes in excess of ten are found only in extreme circumstances, mostly under a level of mortality (e_0 = 60) that is so low as to be rare in rural preindustrial populations. Most predicted household sizes fall between about 3.0 and 7.0. Thus, a quite wide range of demographic regimes gives rise to a fairly narrow range of expected household sizes, a finding also supported by microsimulation studies (Dyke, 1981).

Burch's models have several deficiencies, all of which he is careful to discuss in detail. Most are too technical to describe here, but one is too important to ignore.

Burch assumes that the level of fertility, as captured by the *TFR*, can be varied independently of the age at marriage. But age at marriage is a fundamentally important determinant of fertility levels. Two women who marry at 15 and 25, respectively, must reproduce at dramatically different rates within marriage if they are to end up with the same completed family size by the termination of their reproductive lives (which is what the *TFR* is intended to measure): the marital fertility rates of the woman who marries late must generally be higher than those of the early-marrying woman if the former is to catch up with the latter in total number of children produced. The *TFR* is not a "factor" that can be held constant in a sensitivity analysis, but rather a statistic that summarizes the joint effects of a congeries of factors, of which age at marriage is indubitably one. Moreover, if age at marriage changes, then the average age at childbearing almost necessarily changes as a result, despite the fact that Burch holds it constant at 30 years. If Burch's models were complicated enough to take these interactions into account, household size would turn out to *decline* with later marriage, as microsimulation studies have suggested. As it is, households are larger with later marriage under Burch's models precisely because late marriage does not reduce childbearing and unmarried daughters remain in their natal homes longer than they otherwise would. This is important for understanding the expected range of variation in household sizes because it suggests that the larger households shown in Table 7.3 are unlikely to occur in reality.

These sorts of exercises are enlightening because they show that fertility and mortality on their own can be important determinants of household characteristics. In particular, they consistently show that the comparatively high mortality rates experienced by preindustrial populations limit the size and complexity of kin-based households. Because of high mortality, large households containing three generations of close kin are always likely to be rare, whatever the rules governing postmarital residence, and four-generation households will almost never occur. In all these models, however, household size (as well as composition) is determined by *aggregate-level* fertility and mortality as summarized by life tables and stable population models (a criticism originally leveled by Kunstadter, 1974). Up to a point this makes sense, in that households in populations with high fertility and mortality tend themselves to have high fertility and mortality. But surely there are also *household-specific* variables influencing household demography – for example, an unusually large household with limited land may suffer higher-than-average child mortality owing to intra-household competition. In other words, processes occurring within a household can shape the household's demography: the relationships between demography and household characteristics are reciprocal, in reality if not in our simpler models (see Chapter 8). Such household-level feedbacks might be expected to limit variation in household size and composition even further.[6] And such feedbacks, I would point out, are fundamental to the rest of this book.

---

[6] On the other hand, microsimulation models, which are inherently stochastic, demonstrate that a lot of variation in the size and composition of households can be generated by purely random variation among households in births and deaths (see especially Wachter *et al.*, 1978).

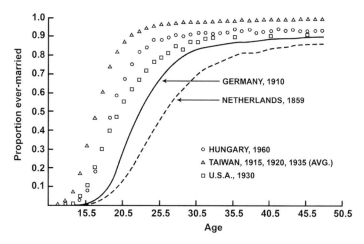

Figure 7.4 Age patterns of marriage: proportion of women ever-married by age (years), selected populations. From Coale (1971: 196), by permission of the Taylor Francis Group.

Interrelations of Demographic and Sociocultural Determinants

The models discussed in the previous section simplify reality by stripping away many of the social and cultural factors influencing household size and composition, thereby unmasking the influence of raw demographic forces. Some of these social and cultural factors vary too idiosyncratically from one community to another to allow easy generalization, but a subset of them turn out to be of universal importance, including age patterns of marriage, postmarital residence rules, rules for household extension (including the cultural permissibility of plural marriages), the age of accession to household headship and migration patterns operating at several spatial scales. All these factors are tightly interwoven in traditional societies and often appear to have important reciprocal effects on each other.

The distribution of women's ages when they first marry has been shown to vary widely across human societies, as has the fraction of women who never marry before the end of their potential reproductive lives at around age 50 (Figure 7.4). The two variables seem to be related – the later the age at first marriage, the larger the fraction who never marry – and Coale and McNeil (1972) showed that the fraction of women not marrying by 50 can be regarded as nothing more than the cumulative outcome of the rates of first marriage at younger ages (mathematically, of course, that has to be true). But it's an *important* outcome because it determines the fraction of adult females who are (presumably) never exposed to the risk of childbearing. And the actual rates of first marriage determine how much of a woman's potential reproductive life is given over to celibacy (again, presumably), even if she does marry before age 50.[7] Alongside an age-specific schedule of survival probabilities, the distribution

---

[7] These two sentences should be modified, of course, to reflect the incidence of bastardy (as historical demographers like to call it), which is itself known to vary widely across human populations (Laslett *et al.*, 1980).

Table 7.4 Traditional postmarital residence rules (redefined for use in household demography).

Virilocal residence – newly married couple expected to move into *existing* household of husband's close relatives (e.g. his parents)

Uxorilocal residence – newly married couple expected to move into *existing* household of *wife's* close relatives (e.g. her parents)

Neolocal residence – newly married couple expected to establish a new autonomous household, which may or may not be near any of their parents' existing households

Ambilocal residence – newly married couple can choose to live in *existing* household of *either* husband's or wife's close relatives

Bilocal residence – newly married couple periodically switches, living virilocally, then uxorilocally, then virilocally, etc.

of ages at marriage has at least some effect on the expected size of households, as our discussion of Burch's sensitivity analyses suggests (Table 7.3). Remarkably little is known about what factors determine the distribution of ages at marriage – but see Hajnal (1965, 1982) for an important set of empirical hypotheses and Todd *et al.* (2005) for some interesting model-based musings.[8] But two things seem clear: (i) very late ages at marriage in traditional societies are mostly confined to post-medieval northwestern Europe (see below), and (ii) the age at marriage in traditional societies tends to covary with local postmarital residence rules.

Postmarital residence rules – norms or exceptions about where a couple should reside immediately after marriage – have long been studied by anthropologists, although rarely from a demographic perspective. Conventional anthropological terms for postmarital residence, modified slightly for use in household demography, are given in Table 7.4. With the exception of neolocality, all these rules allow for some degree of household extension (see below). Burch's analyses (Table 7.3) suggest how important the rules can be in explaining household size. Postmarital residence rules have become an important subject within the field of household and family demography, and we return to them below.

Academic interest in the demographic concomitants of household extension has spawned an enormous literature, far too complex (and resistant to consensus) to summarize here. But a few general points ought to be made. Defining types of household extension has been a major subindustry in its own right within this larger field of research. Hammel and Laslett (1974) undertook one of the first attempts at a comprehensive classification; precisely insofar as they *were* comprehensive, their typology was horrifyingly complicated. More recent efforts have led to little agreement on basic terminology, and one begins to wonder if there are platonic "types" of household extension to begin with. Table 7.5 presents some highly simplified terminology for describing the most common forms of extension. My intention in providing these definitions is merely to fix some terms for use in the following

---

[8] In many cultural settings outside of Europe, some degree of pubertal development seems to be an important determinant of a female's *eligibility* for marriage – although eligibility is only a prelude to marriage itself, which may lag several years behind (Udry and Cliquet, 1982).

Table 7.5 Terms for types of household extension used in this book. Note that these terms are neither well established nor used consistently in the literature, and polygamy is not usually considered a form of household extension.

Simple household – a household consisting of a single married couple or its relict[a] plus any coresident unmarried children of the marriage. If both members of the married couple are living in the household, it can be called a *nuclear-family household.*

Extended-family household – a simple household with at least one additional kin member (e.g. a married couple, their children, and the wife's sister). Can be shortened to *extended household.*

Stem-family household – an extended-family household containing at least two currently or ever-married members spanning at least two generations and linked by a parent-offspring relationship (e.g. a widowed mother and her adult married offspring with his/her spouse and children). Can be shortened to *stem household.*

Joint-family household – an extended-family household containing at least two nuclear families of the same generation linked by a sibling relationship (e.g. two married brothers plus their wives and children). Can be shortened to *joint household.*

Other kin-based household – a household consisting of second-degree or higher-order consanguineal kin in the absence of the first-degree linking relatives (e.g. a widowed woman living with her niece, who may be married with children).

Nonkin-based household – a household consisting exclusively of nonrelatives or distant relatives, or a household consisting of only one individual living on his/her own.

Polygamous (polygynous, polyandrous) household – a household centered on a married individual and his/her multiple spouses and their coresident children, if any. Polygynous households involve a husband with multiple wives, polyandrous households a wife with multiple husbands. Polyandrous households are rare.

[a] Unfortunate technical term for the widowed former partner to a marriage, male or female.

discussion, not to invent a framework for future analysis. Incidentally, when we speak of "types" of – or "rules" for – household extension, we should not assume that the corresponding forms of extension are prescribed or even statistically normative; they may be allowable and even desirable, but they are not mandated.

One major issue in the demography of household extension has to do with how much effect extension has on the size of households. Intuitively, we would expect households in societies that encourage extension to be larger on average than in those that do not. But that does not seem to be the case: on the contrary, the overall distribution of household sizes in extended and nonextended systems seems to be eerily invariant (Table 7.6). Hajnal (1982) came up with a clever explanation for why this should be so, having to do with the age of accession to household headship (usually, but not always, on the part of a married male). The average size of a household, he notes, is just the total population size divided by the number of households in the population. Assuming that every household has one and only one head, then it follows that the average size of a household is inversely proportional to the number of household *heads* in the population – the fewer the heads, the fewer the households and hence the larger their average size. Now, under any particular age pattern of mortality, late accession to headship should result in fewer heads than early accession, simply because fewer individuals will survive to the age

Table 7.6 Percentage distribution of households by size, selected preindustrial populations (*italics*, simple nuclear-family household systems; boldface, extended-family household systems). From Hajnal (1982: 463); data from Barclay (1954), Drake (1969), Laslett (1972), Wall (1972), Johansen (1975).

| Population | Period | Number of persons | | | | Total | Mean number of persons per household |
		1–3	4–6	7–9	10+		
100 rural English communities	*1574–1821*	*36*	*42*	*17*	*5*	*100*	*4.8*
Rural India	1951	34	43	17	6	100	4.9
Rural Denmark (26 parishes)	*1787*	*30*	*43*	*21*	*6*	*100*	*5.2*
Taiwan	1915	30	42	18	10	100	5.3
Norway (3 areas)	*1801*	*21*	*46*	*24*	*9*	*100*	*5.7*

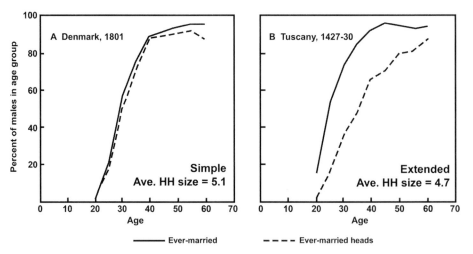

Figure 7.5 The relationship between men's entry into marriage and accession to household headship, (A) Denmark, 1801, a simple household system, (B) Tuscany, 1427–30, an extended household system. Note the similar average household sizes, although the Tuscan value is slightly lower. From Hajnal (1982: 465); data from Johansen (1975), Herlihy and Klapisch-Zuber (1978), by permission of John Wiley & Sons, Inc.

of accession if it is late. In stem and joint household systems (by far the most common forms of household extension where it exists) couples often marry early but spend some time in a parent or sibling's household before going on to establish their own independent household. Thus, extended household systems often have early marriage but late accession to headship. Simple, nuclear-family household systems, in contrast, often have comparatively late marriage but accession to headship that follows more or less immediately upon marriage (neolocal residence). Thus, in both the extended and nonextended cases, the age of accession to household headship is similar. In the two examples shown in Figure 7.5, Danish men

Table 7.7 Mean number of individuals per household by relationship to household head. "Other heads" would include widowed or divorced heads. From Hajnal (1982: 456, 460); data from Census of India (1951: Table C.I[ii]), Johansen (1975).

I. Extended household pattern: rural India, 1951

Sex	Married heads and wives	Other heads	Children	Other relatives	Unrelated	Total
Males	0.71	0.19	1.10	0.48	0.03	2.51
Females	0.71	0.10	0.81	0.74	0.03	2.39
Both sexes	1.42	0.29	1.91	1.22	0.06	**4.90**

II. Simple household pattern: rural Denmark, 1781–1801

Sex	Married heads and wives	Other heads	Children	Other relatives	Servants	Others	Total
Males	0.88	0.05	0.99	0.08	0.50	0.05	2.55
Females	0.88	0.07	0.96	0.15	0.40	0.09	2.55
Both sexes	1.76	0.12	1.95	0.23	0.90	0.14	**5.10**

experienced late marriage followed by rapid accession to headship, whereas Tuscan men underwent earlier marriage but delayed accession to headship owing to social pressures to reside for a few years after marriage in an already existing household, usually that of the groom's parents (virilocal residence). Because the two accession curves are similar, the two cases had similar average household sizes (5.1 vs. 4.7). In fact, because headship accession in Tuscany was slightly later than in Denmark, its average household size was slightly lower, despite – or rather because of – the presence of extended households.

As I say, this explanation is clever, but it is not necessarily correct as the *general* solution to the problem. We simply do not know the age-of-accession curves for enough preindustrial societies to decide the point. Other factors may be equally important (and to Hajnal's credit he considered them all in his 1982 paper). For example, nuclear-family households are sometimes unexpectedly large because they include temporary nonkin members who rarely show up in extended-family households. In early modern Europe, to cite the classic example, household members unrelated (or not obviously related) to the other members and referred to in the records as "servants" were not uncommon (Kussmaul, 1981; Laslett, 1987).[9] As hinted by the comparison in Table 7.7, these nonrelatives in simple households

[9] Male servants were sometimes referred to as "farm laborers." Occasionally nonkin members of preindustrial households were listed as "lodgers" or "boarders". While they ate and slept in the household, the latter two were not involved with the life and work of the household the way servants and farm laborers were, and it might be better not to include them among the household's members. Thankfully lodgers and boarders were found mainly in urban settings, so we can duck this conundrum here.

Table 7.8 Percentages of households with different numbers of married couples in varying relationships, three extended-family household systems in South Asia and Southern Europe. From Hajnal (1982: 461, 466); data from Dandekar and Pethe (1960), Herlihy and Klapisch-Zuber (1978), Kabir (1980).

Married couples	Maharashtra (India) 1947–51	Nepal 1976	Tuscany 1427–30
No intact couple	19	17	23
One couple	58	63	58
Two couples			
Father and son	10 ⎤		
Two brothers	5 ⎬ 16	15	15
Other relations	1 ⎦		
Three or more couples	5	3	4
Total	100	99	100
Number of households	12 030	5 537	59 770

may, in effect, have assumed the functional roles in the household economy played by relatives attached to the core nuclear family in extended households. We return below to the question of who these apparently unrelated European servants (now known as "life-cycle servants") were and what they were up to (see Kussmaul, 1981; Smith, 1999).

In comparing the demography of extended and simple household systems, it is critical to bear in mind that extended forms are not static "structural" types but rather transient phases of a dynamic process, a point strongly emphasized by Lutz Berkner (1972, 1975). In a cross-sectional study, few households may actually be extended even in the most unambiguously extended-family "system" (Table 7.8). This fact is partly attributable to the high mortality found throughout the preindustrial world, which limits the number of surviving close kin with whom to live. Longitudinally, however, many or even most households may undergo at least a brief *phase* of extension. In other words, few households in extended-family societies are likely to be extended at any one time, but almost *all* such households may experience extension at some point during their life cycles. And while they are extended, these households may indeed be larger on average than simple households from the same community (though not necessarily so). At any one time, however, extended households may be too infrequent to have much impact on the cross-sectional distribution of household sizes in the community as a whole. A similar point could be made about coresident polygamous households. Even where polygamy is highly valued, a minority of households are likely to be polygamous at any one time, owing both to the restricted availability of potential spouses and the costs of marrying again (e.g. bride wealth or the expense of constructing additional living space). Moreover, no household starts out polygamous; additional spouses are typically acquired one at a time sometime after the original establishment of the household by a single nuclear family. Empirically, polygamous marriages rarely involve more than three spouses – i.e. one spouse of one sex and two of the other – at one time.

Table 7.9 Normal life-cycle service in rural northern Europe: servants as a percent of total population by sex and age. Note that servants were not found exclusively in the wealthiest households, but in households of almost all ranks. Most servants were unmarried at the time of service. From Hajnal (1982: 471); data from Drake (1969), Hansen (1975), Laslett (1977), Wall (1982).

Age interval (years)	Iceland, 1729 (3 counties)		Norway, 1801 (3 areas)	Flanders, 1814 (9 villages)		England, 1599–1796 (6 communities)	
	Males	Females	Both sexes	Males	Females	Male	Females
10–14	21	20	10	14	5	5	4
15–19	33	34	32	38	31	35	27
20–24	39	44	33	48	36	30	40
25–29	34	32	19	35	25	15	15
30–39	12	24	8	23	6	6	7
40–49	9	17	3	8	2	2	2

In the preindustrial world, especially where movement of people from the countryside to towns or cities was rare, marriage or the formation of a new household was often the principal cause of inter-household migration (Fix, 1999: *passim*). In Chapter 1, we have already discussed how short most marriage distances were under preindustrial conditions of transport; these highly localized movements were not at all like the rural–urban or transnational migration we observe in the modern world. But marriage always involves movement from one household to another for at least one of the partners. In areas where neolocality does not prevail, both partners to the marriage might later move again, perhaps with already-born children, when they establish their own household. These kinds of movements can be viewed as part of a larger strategy of household formation.

In northwest Europe during the early modern or postmedieval period, another kind of inter-household migration, generally occurring *before* marriage, was common (Table 7.9). This pattern of movement by so-called *life-cycle servants* has already been mentioned, and it has been described in more detail by Hajnal (1982: 473):

(1) Servants were numerous, apparently always constituting at least 6 per cent, and usually over 10 per cent, of the total population [at any one time]. (2) Almost all servants were unmarried and most of them were young (usually between 10 and 30 years of age). (3) A substantial proportion of young people of both sexes were servants at some stage in their lives. (4) Most servants were not primarily engaged in domestic tasks, but were part of the work force of their master's farm or craft enterprise. (5) Servants lived as members of their master's household. (6) Most servants were members of their master's household by contract for a limited period. (7) There was no assumption that a servant, as a result of being in service, would necessarily be socially inferior to his or her master. The great majority of servants eventually married and ceased being servants. Their social class before service (i.e., usually the class of their parents) and their social class after service could be the same as their master's (and in some Northwest European populations at some periods this was not infrequently the case).

In contemporary legal texts this pattern of service was often described as *intra moenia* ("within the walls"), alluding to the fact that these servants slept within the master's domicile (Blackstone, 1979 [orig. 1765]: 413–15). Sometimes servants moved fairly long distances from their birthplaces to live with their masters, but typically the distance between the servant's natal household and his or her master's household was small – indeed, both households usually resided in the same local community (Laslett, 1987; Jennings, 2010). As Hajnal suggests, servants were not found exclusively, or even most commonly, in rich households (while rich families often had more servants than poor ones, rich households made up a tiny fraction of the community as a whole). The age-specific rates of service were usually fairly similar for male and female servants (see Table 7.9), although little is known about how tasks were split between the serving sexes. In the richer households, female servants were likely to fill "luxury" domestic roles such as maids or cooks, but in poorer households both male and female servants appear to have been more or less exclusively involved in farm work, although presumably given rather different tasks. In parts of preindustrial Scotland, for example, at harvest time male farm laborers were allowed to wield both sickles and scythes, whereas it was considered inappropriate for females to use the scythe, which requires much greater upper body strength than the sickle (Howatson, 1984).

In two enduringly influential papers, Hajnal (1965, 1982) pulled together many of the strands running through the preceding paragraphs into a model that has come to be called "the Hajnal hypothesis" (Engelen and Wolf, 2005). Hajnal posited an imaginary line (Figure 7.6), running approximately from St. Petersburg, Russia, to Trieste, Italy, that separated early-modern, rural Eurasian populations into two distinct regimes of marriage and household formation, as summarized in Table 7.10. To the West of the line was found a pattern of household formation he called the northwest European simple household system, combining late marriage, neolocal residence and frequent life-cycle service before marriage. To the East, stretching from eastern Europe to the Pacific, lay a pattern of household formation (the stem household system) character-ized by earlier marriage than in western Europe, residence for several years after marriage in the already-existing household of one or both parents of either the bride or, more commonly, the groom (creating a stem-family household), little or no life-cycle service and a tendency for stem households to split eventually into their constitu-ent simple-family components.[10] He went on to speculate that the European regime operated to adjust households to resources by delaying childbearing and the establish-ment of a new domestic enterprise until a couple had secured at least the minimal resources (especially arable land) needed to support a family – much as Malthus thought *ought* to happen if population growth is to be restrained for the advancement of human happiness and well-being (see Chapter 5).

As Engelen and Wolf (2005: 18–20) have pointed out, the Hajnal hypothesis is really a cluster of three related hypotheses, which they call the "ethnographic" hypothesis, the "niche" hypothesis and the "equilibrium" hypothesis. The ethnographic hypothesis has to

---

[10] What I am here calling the "stem" household system to conform to Table 7.5 above, Hajnal originally called the "joint" household system.

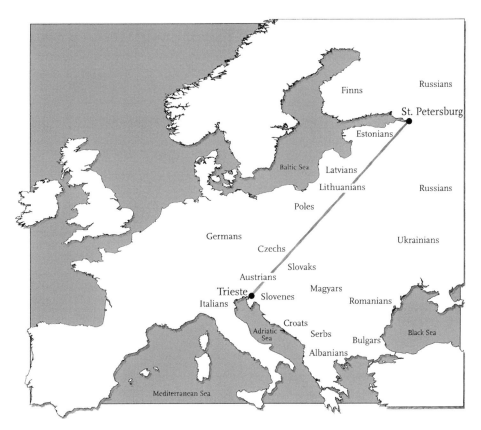

Figure 7.6 The Hajnal line, literally interpreted. Names are ethnic groups straddling or close to the line *c.* 1850. From Plakans and Wetherell (2005: 108), by permission of Aksant Academic Publishers.

do with the empirical validity of Hajnal's description of the Hajnal line and the two household-formation regimes purportedly lying on either side of it. Does the whole edifice hold up against our expanding historical knowledge about marriage, households and life-cycle service across Eurasia? The niche hypothesis is about the different ways in which the two household-formation systems tried to guarantee an economic "niche" (e.g. a farm) for each new household – with the northwest European system clearly coming out ahead in the comparison. And the equilibrium hypothesis is that the northwest European system operated at the *household* level to regulate fertility and hence population growth at the *aggregate* level – unlike in the rest of the preindustrial world, which as a result was more vulnerable to Malthusian positive checks. In other words, the equilibrium hypothesis claims that preindustrial European populations had, by postmedieval times, developed mechanisms for population regulation based primarily on resource-conditioned adjustments of fertility (couples could not initiate childbearing until they had access to the necessary resources), not mortality, the critical regulator in other regions and periods. Both the niche and equilibrium hypotheses fall if the ethnographic hypothesis is rejected, but neither one is proven by acceptance of the ethnographic hypothesis – both need to be tested on their own. If they both survive the test, however, it would be a major advance in

Table 7.10 John Hajnal's summary of household formation rules West and East of the Hajnal line (see Figure 7.6). West of the line is the so-called northwest European simple (nuclear) family system. To the East is the stem family system that, according to Hajnal, characterizes much of the rest of Eurasia (Hajnal, 1982: 452). Reproduced with permission of John Wiley & Sons, Inc, from J. Hajnal (1982) Two kinds of preindustrial household formation system. *Population and Development Review*, 8, 449–94.

Household formation rules common to northwest European simple household systems

- Late marriage for both sexes (e.g. mean ages at first marriage over 26 for men and over 23 for women
- Immediately after marriage a couple establish their own household, the husband becoming household head (neolocal postmarital residence)
- Before marriage young people often circulate between households as servants (life-cycle service)

Household formation rules common to stem household systems

- Earlier marriage for men and quite early marriage for women (mean ages at first marriage under about 26 for men and under 21 for women)
- A young married couple often start life together either in a household of which an older couple is and remains in charge or in a household of which an unmarried older person (such as a widower or widow) continues to be head. Usually the young wife joins her husband in the household of which he is a member (virilocal postmarital residence).
- Households with several married couples may eventually split to form two or more households, each containing one or more couples.

our understanding of the relationship between farming households and resources, especially land, in one part of the preindustrial world (Wrigley, 1981).

Recent research suggests that the ethnographic portion of the Hajnal hypothesis passes the test, albeit with slightly drooping colors. The empirical evidence suggests that the Hajnal line is both fuzzy and porous – complex in its geography (a squiggle not a line) and with many outliers falling on the wrong side of the line. To give one example, it is starting to look as if early modern Japan may have shared many features with the "European" pattern (Cornell, 1987; Saito, 1998, 2000; Nagata, 2005). In addition Hajnal's ethnographic hypothesis tends to underestimate the extent of variation within Europe west of the Hajnal line (Laslett, 1983). The strength and coherence of the European pattern tend to lessen as we move south and east within Europe – which Hajnal presumably knew since he consistently spoke of the *northwest* European system of household formation. Particular exceptions to the European pattern have been studied in some detail in central France (Berkner and Shaffer, 1978), among Italian sharecroppers (Kertzer and Hogan, 1991) and southern Europeans in general (Viazzo, 2005), in eastern Europe (Plakans and Wetherell, 2005), and among peasants in Russia west of the Urals (Czap, 1982; Avdeev *et al.*, 2004/6).[11] Yet despite the evidence uncovered by all this research, Hajnal's ethnographic hypothesis has held up

---

[11] Hajnal himself (1982: 467–9) was the first to identify European Russian peasant households as likely exceptions to his European pattern.

Table 7.11 Life cycle of the neolocal, nuclear-family household (idealized – events may not occur in the exact order specified). Modified from Höhn (1987: 66). Reproduced by permission of Oxford University Press from C. Höhn (1987) The family life cycle: Needed extensions of the concept. In *Family Demography: Methods and their Applications*, ed. J. Bongaarts, T. K. Burch, and K. W. Wachter. Oxford: Oxford University Press, pp. 65–80. Reproduced with permission of the Licensor through PLSclear.

Phase of the household life cycle	Beginning	End
Formation	marriage	birth of first child
Expansion	birth of first child	birth of last child
Completed expansion	birth of last child	exit of first child[a]
Contraction	exit of first child[a]	exit of last child[a]
Dissolution	death of first spouse	death of survivor (extinction)

[a] "Exiting" includes death, out-marriage and other forms of out-migration operating at the household level, including, for example, life-cycle service.

reasonably well. As Engelen and Wolf (2005: 33) summarize the ethnographic issue, "There is a clear, readily identifiable difference between European household systems and those found in the rest of the world. It is a finding that we must not allow critics to bury prematurely because it is our best hope for writing books that add up rather than just stack up." It is now time, they suggest, to think about how best to test the niche and equilibrium hypotheses, which will be much more difficult than testing the ethnographic one.[12] We also have no idea why rural northwestern Europe was so different from the rest of Eurasia, if indeed it was, and what precise mechanism was operating in that subregion to discourage the establishment of new households before sufficient resources had been secured. It is still too early to pass final judgment on the various things that make up the Hajnal hypothesis.

The Household Demographic Life Cycle

If you refer back to Figure 7.1, you can see that it highlights something called the "household demographic life cycle" as one of the central processes driving the household demographic enterprise. This phenomenon and its linkages to food production will be the principal focus of Chapter 10. I introduce the concept here in order to emphasize that households are dynamic, not static, and that the inevitable changes in household size and composition arising from all the demographic and sociocultural factors reviewed in this chapter may have fundamentally important consequences for the household's joint nutritional needs and the availability of household labor to meet them. What I mean by the household demographic life cycle is illustrated for the simplest possible case, the nonpolygamous nuclear-family household with neolocal residence, in Table 7.11. More elaborate schemes will need to be

---

[12] Preliminary assaults on the niche hypothesis have been made by Fertig (2003, 2005) and Engelen (2005). Both authors end up undecided but skeptical. If the niche hypothesis fails, then the equilibrium hypothesis must also be rejected, since it is predicated on the validity of the niche concept.

formulated for other household systems (see Goody, 1958). But all households, whether simple or complex, undergo a definite life cycle, although the fine details of its history, phases, and velocity will differ from one household to another even within a single community (Otterbein, 1970; Fjellman, 1977; Otterbein and Otterbein, 1977; Mitteraurer and Sider, 1979). As later chapters will endeavor to show, the household demographic life cycle is potentially an important unifying concept in the study of subsistence farming.

Households and Access to Basic Farming Resources

To succeed in their demographic enterprise, farming households need secure and predictable access to essential farming resources, especially arable land. Rules of land tenure and inheritance are fundamentally important for tying households to those resources. In the older literature on population and agriculture, with its ingrained love of the aggregate, the terms "over-population" and "population pressure" usually denoted situations in which the *average* farming household (or indeed *every* farming household) lacks the land needed to meet its nutritional needs. But any *one* household may lack adequate land, not because of an absolute shortage of land affecting the entire community, but because that particular household does not have secure title to sufficient land under the prevailing system of land tenure and inheritance (Sen, 1981). Land is never divided equally among households in traditional farming communities, even in the most ardently egalitarian ones (Netting, 1982). But even if it were, variation in household size and age composition generated by each household's particular life-cycle trajectory (including those resulting from purely stochastic fluctuations in births and deaths) would after a few years generate differential *needs* for land among households – an insight that goes back to Malthus. Thus, when Cuffaro (2001: 3) writes that "[p]roperty rights on land are the most important population-related institution in agriculture," she is implicitly referring to processes that originate within households. Demographic pressure, whatever actual mechanisms and responses it may entail, can act at the household level even when it is not affecting the population as a whole (see Chapter 10).

Traditional rules for the transfer of land, including inheritance, are summarized in Table 7.12. Usufruct is often found in areas where land is abundant relative to human needs (Wilk and Netting, 1984: 12). Presumably there is little danger in allowing a family's current holding to revert to a common pool if there is ample land for everyone. But as the land available per household declines – perhaps because of population growth – land tenure and inheritance rules tend to become more formalized. In fact, Boserup (1965: 77–87) has argued that changes in land tenure and inheritance are an almost-inevitable consequence of population growth and agricultural intensification.

Most ideas about the relationship between land tenure/inheritance rules and other aspects of the household demographic enterprise have been rather speculative, but they at least provide some interesting hypotheses to test. For example, it has been suggested that impartible inheritance may be associated (in a chicken-and-egg sort

Table 7.12 Traditional non-market forms of land acquisition, inheritance and transfer.

Usufruct

- Land reverts to common community pool for reallotment when it goes out of active cultivation

Inheritance (usually male to male only)[a]

- *Impartible inheritance* (mono-, unigeniture)
  o *Primogeniture* – land passes intact to *oldest* surviving heir
  o *Ultimogeniture* – land passes intact to *youngest* surviving heir (uncommon)
- *Partible inheritance* – land is divided (not necessarily equally) among all surviving (male) heirs

Provision for female heirs

- *Dower* – widow retains c. ¼–½ of late husband's land for life or until remarriage
- *Dowry* – daughter is given plot(s) of land as part of her marriage settlement; the land usually reverts to her husband or his kin

Excambion (Scottish law, late Middle English)

- Direct exchange of land parcels by common agreement between owners or tenants

Assarting (Anglo-Norman, from Latin *sarriere* to hoe)

- Authorized use of land formerly held in common, esp. forest or open grazing

[a] May include mother's brother to sister's son in matrilineal societies.

of way) with stem household systems, although this claim has not gone unchallenged (see Verdon, 1979; Kertzer, 1991). If it is true, it may reflect the ability of a household head to "blackmail" one married son into staying on the farm and helping with the work.[13] Whatever the reason for impartible inheritance, the relative advantages of primogeniture versus ultimogeniture are unclear, except that the youngest son may be too young at the death of the household head to run the farming operation. On the other hand, under conditions of high mortality and a wide distribution of the ages of women at the birth of their children – both characteristic of preindustrial populations – younger heirs are more likely to be alive at the time of the head's death than are older heirs. In addition, older heirs are more likely already to have left the home farm and established themselves elsewhere at the time of the head's death. Partible

---

[13] In medieval England, formal premortem inheritance contracts were common, whereby a still-living household head would agree to turn the farm over to his designated heir on the condition that the latter stay on the farm and support the prior head and his wife in their old age (Homans, 1942: 144–59). Manorial court rolls suggest that these contracts were often honored in the breach: they are full of complaints from elderly parents that their heir was not providing the provisions to which they felt entitled under the contract, not even so much as a threadbare blanket (Homans, 1942: 158).

inheritance is often associated with simple household systems of Hajnal's northwest European type (Wilk and Netting, 1984: 12). Perhaps partible inheritance and its attendant need to put together a large enough holding was a major motivator of life-cycle service: the amount of inherited land provided by partible inheritance may not have been sufficient to support a new household, but perhaps more could have been purchased with the wages earned in service.[14] Finally, excambion (and sometimes even outright sale) were important for countering land fragmentation, often assumed to be a consequence of partible inheritance (but see Chapter 2). Even in tenant-farming or sharecropping communities, permanent land transfers were often arranged by the tenants or sharecroppers themselves – the landlord apparently did not care much who was working his parcels of land so long as rents and other dues were paid.

It is important to remember that rules for ownership and inheritance apply not only to land *per se* but to other farming resources such as animals, tools, stored food, cooking implements, water sources and landesque capital. Writing of a Spanish peasant community with partible inheritance, Behar (1986: 81) has described how even manure piles are subdivided at the death of the household head – with many attendant ructions among the inheriting offspring. This case also reminds us that ownership and inheritance are frequently contested in traditional communities. Vital resources often spark violent passions.

Household, House, Farmstead and Farm Possessions

As a final point in this introductory essay on the preindustrial agrarian household, I want to remind the reader, at least in passing, that farming households reside in a concentric series of physical settings, encompassing the house and farmstead (house plus outbuildings), the entire farm (including fields, meadows, pastures, and water sources), and the larger physical and social environments. In Chapters 1 and 2, I have already discussed the spatial organization of the farm relative to the location of the farmhouse itself, as well as placement of the farmhouse with respect to other basic physical resources. But there is much more to say about the farmhouse and farmstead as practical, physical entities. Owing to limitations of space, this subject cannot be discussed in detail here, but it has been remarked upon (rather pointedly) by Smith (1982):

Most contemporary anthropological accounts of housing and house styles in exotic pre-industrial cultures illustrate the predominantly semiotic interests and goals of their authors. Under these influences, social and cultural anthropologists seem to regard dwellings and other types of construction as primarily of interest because of their symbolic character and signifi-cance. From such perspectives, a house is readily perceived as a code to be cracked by a semiotic analysis which will no doubt display a deep structure that integrates and coordinates the redundant symbolic contrast sets which together order and constitute the house. Now

---

[14] Which raises another chicken-and-egg question: did late marriage allow for service, or did premarital service cause late marriage?

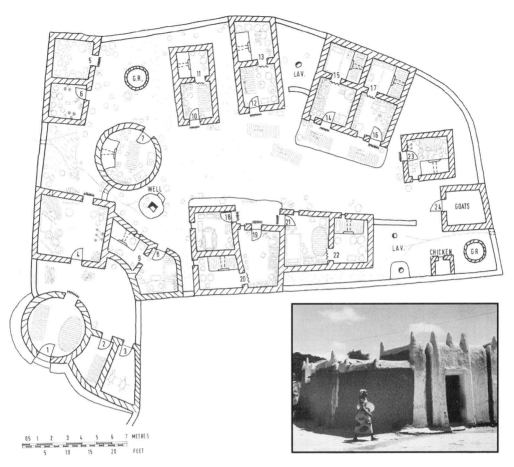

Figure 7.7 Plan of polygynous household compound in the predominantly Hausa town of Zaria, northern Nigerian, c. 1968. *LAV.*, lavatory (pit latrine); *GR.*, granary; *striated rectangles or ovals*, sleeping mats; 1, entranceway fronting on street. Other numbers are keyed to Figure 7.8. *Insert*, typical house façade in Zaria. From Schwerdtfeger (1982: 2, 344), by permission of John Wiley & Sons, Inc.

clearly, all human dwellings must embody and reflect the symbolism that pervades the culture of those who constructed and occupy them; but such expression occurs within limits set by the materials and techniques of construction, the affluence, number, and rank of the occupants, the location, layout, and size of the building and similar mundane but relevant factors. These material constraints are normally sufficient to ensure that dwellings, though laden with symbolic purposes and meanings, must first fulfil certain practical requirements as suitable homes, before serving as vehicles for symbolism. These limiting conditions and functions should therefore be particularly important objects of ethnographic documentation and analysis in order properly to contextualize and illuminate the symbolic motivations and patterns that inform and overlay the house itself. Unfortunately it is precisely in this respect that anthropological studies of housing in pre-industrial societies have been most systematically incomplete...(Smith, 1982: xii–xiii).

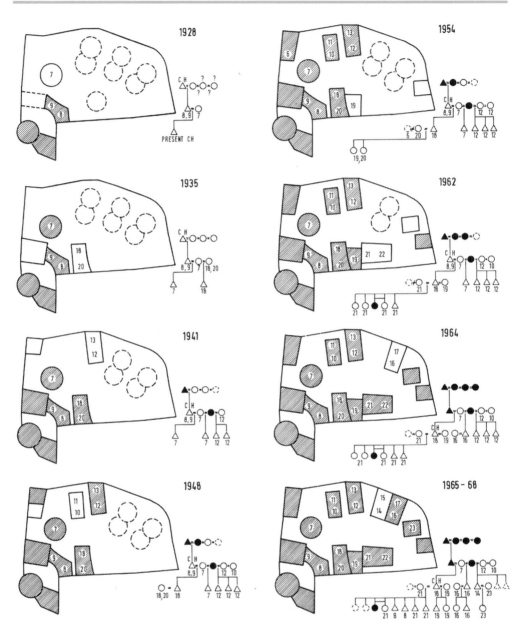

Figure 7.8 The demographic and architectural history (1928–68) of the house compound shown in Figure 7.7. Structures indicated by broken lines are older huts that have been pulled down (round huts are more traditional than rectilinear ones). Hatched structures are those already present in the immediately preceding period. Each genealogy shows residents in the year indicated (*triangles*, males; *circles*, females; =, marriage). Individuals with filled-in symbols are deceased; those with broken symbols reside elsewhere. From Schwerdtfeger (1982: 49), by permission of John Wiley & Sons, Inc.

Table 7.13 The findings of a postmortem household inventory for Andro Peatrie, a "middling" farmer who died July 27, 1685, in Foubister, Orkney, northern Scotland (Fenton, 1978: 140). Reproduced with permission of John Donald from A. Fenton (1978) *The Northern Isles: Orkney and Shetland*, Edinburgh: John Donald. Reproduced with permission of the Licensor through PLSclear.

Value	Item £ s d
One dun horse 6 years old	14.00.00
One black horse 16 years old	04.00.00
One red sheltie [pony] 21 years old	02.00.00
Two old kye [cows]	10.00.00
Two young oxen	04.00.00
One quoyack in halveris [heifer with calf]	02.10.00
One young wether sheep [uncastrated male]	01.06.00
In the barn 1 meil oats [1 meil equals about 54 kg]	02.00.00
In the stackyard, 2 meils of unthreshed bere [a landrace of barley]	06.00.00
In the house, 1 meil of meal [flour]	05.00.00
Two geese and a gander	01.00.00
Inside and furnishings of house[a]	12.00.00
Subtotal	63.16.00
Owed to the deceased	+03.09.00
Owed by the deceased (inc. funeral @ £10)	−49.09.00
Net Assets	15.16.12

[a] According to other inventories, typical plenishings of the house of such a farmer might include two to three wooden box beds with mattresses filled with bere or oat husks, some quilts, a couple of storage chests and a girnel (meal storage chest), a musket, a few pewter plates, bowls and cups, several wooden trenchers; a quern (hand mill); a pair of bellows, at least one chamber pot, an iron kettle, vessels for brewing ale, stools, a table, a cupboard, pots, an iron griddle and a chain from which to hang it over the fire, a few spoons, and one or two cruizie lamps (open iron vessels that burned seal or whale oil using wicks made of grass stems). The household would also own a collection of simple, handmade farm tools – spades, rakes, hoes, scythes, sickles, and perhaps a plow for the two oxen to pull. A seventeenth-century Orcadian household with such a range of belongings would be considered fairly prosperous. Most householders did not have enough possessions to warrant a postmortem inventory.

Whatever the symbolic significance of the house – and no doubt it exists – the physical, functional, economic, even physiological and demographic aspects of domestic architecture (including not only domiciles but outbuildings, cook houses, storage facilities, etc.) are surely worthy of study in their own right.[15] The "physiology" of the house and outbuildings would include such things as their worthiness as shelters for people and livestock, their thermal properties, ventilation, hygiene,

---

[15] Arguably the single best example of such a study undertaken in the preindustrial world can be found in the book from which Smith's quote was taken (Schwerdtfeger, 1982). Alas (from my point of view) it was conducted in urban areas, not in the agrarian countryside. Other good examples include Andersen (1978), Larsson and Larsson (1984), and Oliver (2003). A wonderful book that manages to combine the symbolic, the practical, and the *affective* dimensions of a preindustrial house is Berliner (2003).

separation of functional areas (e.g. cooking areas, sleeping areas, work areas), differential usage by household members (e.g. men and women), the management of human and animal waste and so forth. "Economic" factors might cover building costs in labor, material and time, as well as who bears those costs. What I mean by "demographic" aspects of domestic architecture is illustrated in Figures 7.7 and 7.8. As these figures show, housing can change in tandem with the size and life-cycle stage of the household "population" that dwells within it. Abandonment of the house or farmstead, perhaps coinciding with the dissolution of the household, is also a "demographic" event of some note. Further discussion of such topics is beyond the scope of this book. But all these aspects of houses, farmsteads and farms as physical and functional units are, in my opinion, of great importance for understanding the traditional farming household as a practical enterprise. They deserve much more study than they have received to date.

Another important fact about the physical equipage of the preindustrial farming household is that, by our ethnocentric standards, such households were almost unfathomably poor in material possessions. This poverty is hinted at by archaeological investigations of domestic sites (Yentsch, 1990) and made more explicit in

Figure 7.9 A household and its possessions in Kouakourou village, Mali, West Africa. The household consists of a 39-year-old male head, his two wives, and their eight children (one daughter was absent on the day the photograph was taken). Household possessions include mortars and pestles to pound sorghum, millet and other grains (left), sieves for sifting cracked grain (leaning against mortars), an ancient, broken musket, sleeping platforms and mosquito nets (left rear), a bicycle, various cooking pots and implements, storage pots and baskets, a battery-powered radio/cassette player, a few chairs and stools, and locally made farm implements (center right). Except for another mortar and pestle, two more wooden sleeping platforms, some old radio batteries that the children use as toys, and whatever land and crops the household currently holds claim to, this is the sum total of the household's worldly possessions. The woman in the lower left courtyard and her children and possessions belong to a neighboring household. From Menzel and Mann (1994: 14–15), by permission of the Sierra Club Foundation. Photo © *Material World* (1994).

historical inventories of household possessions (Rutman, 1967; Bedell, 2000). House-hold inventories, usually recorded for tax purposes following the death of the household head, are far from representative since they almost always ignore the poorer households that make up the bulk of the community – but the case of a "middling" farming household in northern Scotland is presented in Table 7.13. Other, more vivid if non-quantitative accounts of household possessions from the modern developing world are provided by the book *Material World* (Menzel and Mann, 1994), which should be on the shelf of everyone interested in the everyday practicalities of domestic life. One farming household from Mali is shown with its possessions in Figure 7.9. Archaeological finds, formal inventories, and ethnographic case studies, including the examples shown in Table 7.13 and Figure 7.9, point to one important feature of the material property belonging to most preindustrial farming households: it mostly has something to do with food and its production, storage, processing, cooking and eating. Subsistence-oriented households in particular are unlikely to have many possessions that are not immediately relevant to their demographic enterprise in some very practical way.

8 Under-Nutrition and the Household Demographic Enterprise

The move from poverty to wealth [during the transition from the preindustrial to the modern world] is, in a social sense, an advance in material well-being... Death has always been the ultimate threat, and the move from poverty to wealth is first of all a move away from death. Its first indicators are statistics on life expectancy, death rates, and infant mortality. Famine and hunger are next on the list; again, the move from poverty to wealth is a move from famine and hunger, as indicated statistically by a declining incidence of malnutrition and its related diseases. Plague is the next of the ancient afflictions, and it may be taken as symbolic of all fatal or disabling diseases; the move away from them is another move from poverty to wealth. – N. Rosenberg and L. E. Birdzell (1986: 4)

Fears are sometimes expressed that the nutritive value of foods will be lowered by the means that are proving so successful in giving increased yields – fertilizers, insecticides, herbicides and intensive methods of animal husbandry. Certainly the most intensive checks and research will be needed to guard against this, but we should keep a sense of perspective and remember that the highest death-rates and incidence of crippling disablements, particularly amongst young children, are found where low-yield, natural foods are eaten. – K. J. Carpenter (1969: 74)

Progress [is] an episode in the history of hunger. – E. P. Prentice, 1947 (quoted by Fussell, 1952: 35)

In the previous chapter we examined models of the influence of fertility and mortality on the size of households. Two major (and quite deliberate) simplifying assumptions underlying all these models are (i) that fertility and mortality are exogenous to the household and (ii) that all households in a community are exposed to exactly the same demographic conditions. This assumption is patently false, even if it is convenient for some analytical purposes. Starting in the present chapter, we reverse the causality, asking whether mortality, fertility and migration differ among households owing to material conditions (especially those influencing food availability) that are peculiar to each individual household. Do all households in a community have the same level of, for example, early childhood mortality – and, if not, why not? I will argue that an important part of the answer is that feedbacks operate within the household involving food production and the household's demographic life-cycle, and these feedbacks are powerful enough on their own to differentiate households even in the absence of clear social and political differences dividing the community as a whole. The critical linkage in this feedback, I believe, involves the relationship between dietary adequacy and various aspects of human physiology. If I am right about the importance of this relationship, it would point to a basic (and perhaps ever-present) form of population regulation operating at the level of the subsistence farming household. But before we can examine this claim, we need to review what is currently known about the relationship between dietary adequacy and the basic forces of demography – fertility, mortality and migration. And before we do *that*, we need to think more carefully about what we mean by "dietary adequacy" and how to measure it. This chapter does both. Because little of the evidence I marshal in this chapter is explicitly organized at the household level, households will play a somewhat covert role in this treatment. But, while contemplating the relationship between under-nutrition and, say, fertility or mortality, the reader should really be thinking about the role that under-nutrition plays as a potential impediment to the household demographic enterprise. Subsequent chapters return the household to center stage.

Are Subsistence Farmers and their Families Under-Nourished?

The question posed in the heading of this section is fundamental for evaluating the Malthusian model of preindustrial population dynamics and more recent extensions of it, including the MaB ratchet (Chapters 5 and 6). It is also fundamental for understanding the relationship between food production and household demography in the premodern agrarian world. If preindustrial farming communities spend most of their time near the stable demographic equilibrium I have characterized as Malthusian stagnation, then the *average* household ought to be close to the "subsistence" level of dietary adequacy – the level that just supports replacement-level fertility and survival.[1] This prediction implies in turn that a substantial fraction of households ought to be under-nourished (according to some appropriate standard) at any given time. A variety of studies, ethnographic, epidemiological and even osteological (skeletal), have attempted to test this prediction, without necessarily framing the problem in the same theoretical terms I use here. We will review some of those studies later in this chapter. But first we need to understand that nutritional adequacy may be difficult to measure or even define in a biologically meaningful way.

Conceptual and Measurement Issues in Nutritional Assessment

Imagine that our job is to examine one particular person – say, a woman from a remote farming village in the mountainous interior of Whateverland who is 35 years old, married, has four living children (one of whom is nursing) and belongs to a household with access to 3 ha of arable land – and determine whether she has an adequate diet. Before we even start to measure anything, we are confronted with a difficult but profoundly important question: adequate for *what*? For avoiding death? Hoeing a field? Nursing a baby? Sitting in front of a computer eight hours a day?

---

[1] It is important to point out that this level of dietary adequacy may not come anywhere close to what we in the West would consider healthy or normal. It is a purely demographic benchmark, not a clinical or psychological one.

Running a marathon? The correct answer for our Whateverlandish woman will, one suspects, differ rather sharply from the answer we would arrive at for a 35-year-old woman working as a day-trader in modern-day Manhattan.

What diet would meet the specific nutritional needs of our Whateverlandish farm woman? It is, of course, impossible to say in any detail without a careful examination of her day-to-day life. In a very general way, however, Figure 4.20 summarized the range of essential physiological "tasks" that *must*, depending on age and sex, be subsidized by the dietary intake of people living in a subsistence farming community.[2] These five tasks generally do not all come into play at each stage of an individual's life. Evolution has done us the favor of separating (albeit imperfectly) the phases of rapid somatic growth and reproduction, and traditional culture often does a nice job of separating periods of rapid growth or pregnancy from those of hard physical work, thereby reducing the competing demands of these various jobs for their share of an individual's energy intake. Nonetheless, multiple tasks need to be accommodated at every age. It is reasonably well established, for example, that women who are pregnant or nursing (especially under the prolonged and intensive modes of breastfeeding practiced in many traditional societies) require additional food if the women are to continue performing energetically costly farm work, and if they do not receive it they lose physical condition with every successive round of pregnancy and lactation (Bongaarts and Delgado, 1979; Miller and Huss-Ashmore, 1989). Similarly, individuals doing hard physical labor or battling heavy loads of micro- and macroparasites will lose condition on a diet that is perfectly adequate to sustain others of similar age and sex. If food intake is not sufficient to fuel all the essential tasks that occur at a specific age or under a specific set of circumstances, something has to give – and there are likely to be adverse functional consequences, ranging from ill-health and compromised work capacity to death.

Returning to our Whateverlandish woman, then, we first need to estimate how much food she would require in order to lead the kind of life she leads at an adequate level of functionality. Thus, we need to estimate her normal levels of energy expenditure. As it happens, portable, backpack-style respirometers, heart-rate monitors, body-motion sensors, and stable isotopes give us a way to do that (if a bit imprecisely) in remote field locations (see Chapter 9). Since activity levels change by season, we need to do repeat studies of energy expenditure over *at least* a year – and multiple years would be better since farm work can vary with year-to-year fluctuations in weather. We would have to estimate (somehow) any additional energetic burdens associated with disease load, pregnancy or nursing, all of which can also vary seasonally and from one year to the next. But none of that is too daunting (!) since we have only one subject to keep up with.

---

[2] Note that this figure omitted any reference to "leisure," "entertainment," "sports," or the like, including such things as ritual, dancing, play, even warfare. It is a common observation during food shortages that these kinds of "inessential" expenditures of energy are severely curtailed. Indeed *resting quietly* may become the dominant daytime behavior observed in a severely under-nourished individual.

In addition to the precise dietary requirements imposed by the woman's way of life, we need to determine her actual dietary intake, carefully recording both the quantity and types of food she consumes. Small samples of all the foods she eats ought to be set aside for later chemical analysis, not only to determine kilocalories of energy but also to evaluate the quality of her food in terms of its supply of proteins and other nutrients. And, since diet almost always varies widely season-to-season and year-to-year, we again need to monitor her dietary intake over a prolonged period. It would also be good to take the occasional blood sample from her to assess her circulating levels of important micro-nutrients, metabolic products, indicators of protein adequacy and even hormones that may tell us something about her reproductive state.[3] The costs of doing the associated lab work will be high, but then we only have one woman to evaluate. We could even run a weak electrical current through her body and measure the resistance of her tissues to it (bioelectric impedance) as an indirect way to estimate her total body fat. Finally, we could record any clinical symptoms known from previous studies to be associated (sometimes) with poor nutrition, e.g. enamel hypoplasias in her teeth, hyperplasia of her parotid salivary glands, retinitis pigmentosa, erythematous rashes, dispigmentation of skin or hair, easy pluckability of hair, alopecia, muscle wasting, general weakness, pallor caused (perhaps) by anemia, etc.[4] With all this information in hand, we have a fair chance of evaluating the woman's dietary adequacy in a way that is meaningful for the particular life she lives.

In a scientific survey of nutritional adequacy under conditions approximating preindustrial farming, however, we want samples representing some larger community or population, not just a single individual. Unfortunately, the evaluation protocol described above is, quite simply, impossible to apply to a sample of even modest size. The simplest of dietary intake studies are difficult to do reliably in the field, and are generally considered not worth the effort. Poorly funded nutritional surveys in developing countries cannot afford elaborate lab assays on large numbers of subjects. Estimation of energy expenditure using respirometers or other methods is time-consuming and hard to do on more than a very few individuals during any one field season (Uliaszeck, 1995). Given the infeasibility of doing "proper" nutritional studies on sufficiently large samples from remote developing-world communities, what is the alternative? The usual answer is, we do anthropometrics.[5] That is, we measure

---

[3] Standardized laboratory methods are now available to assay a wide variety of nutritional indicators in serum (or even saliva, urine or breastmilk), including iron, albumin and transferrin (measures of total protein intake), folate, thiamin, riboflavin, niacin and other vitamins, calcium, phosphorus, creatine (presumed to be a proxy measure of muscle mass or protein turnover), zinc, iodine, selenium and a host of other signs of a subject's state of nutritional adequacy at the time of the blood draw (Gibson, 2005: v373*ff*).

[4] Such clinical signs must always be taken with a grain of salt because (i) they are not very *sensitive* (they are readily observable only in advanced cases of under-nutrition), and (ii) they are not very *specific* (they can occur for several distinct reasons, not all of them associated with under-nutrition).

[5] Some fieldworkers also attempt to collect nonanthropometric data, including, for example, crude estimates of food intake based on 24-hr dietary recalls or semi-qualitative reports of physical activity. But anthropometrics are the tool of necessity for most nutritionists working in the rural developing world.

various aspects of a person's gross morphology that we believe to be indicative of his or her nutritional condition – including such things as height, weight, skinfold thickness, mid-upper-arm circumference, head circumference – and either analyze the raw data or construct multimeasure indices such as height-for-age and weight-for-height (in children), body mass index (in adults), or the ratio of upper-arm circumference to head circumference, indices thought to capture nutritional effects better than the raw data. Highly standardized protocols and reliable, durable instruments (anthropometers, baby boards, skinfold calipers, flexible metal tapes, sling or standing scales) have been developed for measuring these anthropometric variables. A standard suite of such measures can easily be taken from one individual in a matter of minutes, permitting coverage of large samples.

But what do anthropometrics actually measure? That is, what is the precise relationship between a given anthropometric measure and the individual's true level of dietary adequacy, past or present? This can be a difficult question to answer, because the relationship is often indirect and subject to many confounding influences, and there may be a long lag between an episode of dietary inadequacy and the appearance of measurable effects on the phenotype. Most anthropometric variables purport to measure either the cumulative effect of past disturbances in somatic growth (e.g. height-for-age) or something about current fat reserves (e.g. weight-for-height or skinfold thickness). Nutritionists look for anthropometric signs of *stunting* (small body size) or *wasting* (low fat reserves) on the assumption that the former reflects past nutritional stress during somatic growth, whereas the latter is more sensitive to recent, perhaps acute under-nutrition. But stunting can also reflect severe psychological stress in the past, and wasting can be caused by a recent bout of diarrhea. Neither necessarily represents nutritional adequacy alone.

How, then, do we try to make functional sense of anthropometric measures? For simplicity, let us confine our attention to variables that attempt to measure something about fat stores. We know that morbidly obese people are prone to excess risks of cardiovascular disease, diabetes, certain cancers and other unquestionably bad functional outcomes, which can shorten lifespan. Of course, if we're interested in subsistence farming, obesity is rarely a concern. More relevantly, morbidly thin people, such as victims of anorexia or famine, are at elevated risk of severe electrolyte imbalances, heart failure, kidney failure, all manner of tissue deterioration, restricted work capacity, near-total suppression of the immune system and a resulting inability to fight off deadly infectious diseases and a variety of other unambiguously pathological conditions that can also shorten lifespan. Thus, we know something about the outer extremes of nutritional adequacy as reflected, for example, by weight-for-height, skinfold thickness, mid-upper arm circumference or other anthropometric measures of body fat. But when surveying traditional farming communities during normal (nonfamine) years, we almost always observe a range of anthropometric values that fits within the space between morbid thinness and morbid obesity with plenty of room left over on either side – though as a general rule falling much closer to the thin end than the fat. The question we have to decide is this: where along this observed range of phenotypes is it reasonable to say that some degree of under-nutrition is present? Again, this is less a question of absolute thinness and more one of functional capacity. Will an individual's current fat reserves sustain whatever activities need to be done without causing deterioration in the individual's physical condition? Unfortunately, most anthropometric surveys in the rural developing world either do not stay around long enough to observe the relevant functional consequences or do not bother to try to measure them. (Later we shall examine studies that do both.) But if in such an anthropometric survey we observe someone who is thin (according to some yardstick), how can we decide that he or she is *too* thin if we do not stick around to see if, for example, the person becomes immunocompromised or unable to perform necessary farm work? The only possible answer is that we need a *standard* – objective and well-validated, of course – that tells us if this person is too thin. Where in the world does such a standard come from? Should all human communities be held to the same standard? Is too thin too thin the world round?

There is a longstanding debate in the field of practical nutritional assessment about whether anthropometric standards should be *local* or *international*. It is by no means clear that there is a single, simple answer to the question. I would guess that, over the long history of nutritional assessment in the developing world, most studies have used international standards. Thus, the growth performance (and its supposed nutritional implications) of countless children in the rural developing world – from Gambia to Guyana to New Guinea and beyond – has been assessed against the age-specific heights observed back in the 1960s by nutritionists from Harvard studying "normal" children in the Boston area (Jelliffe, 1966).[6] Nutritionists who advocate this approach often justify it by claiming that all human populations have roughly the same distribution of individual-level *genetic growth potentials* (except perhaps for some extreme cases such as African pygmies), and that attaining the individual's potential is an indicator of adequate nutrition and good health (Schroeder, 2008:345–6). Since the distribution of growth potentials is everywhere more or less the same, it is argued, only samples from poorly nourished groups will deviate sharply from the growth curves observed in (presumably) well-fed communities like the Boston Greater Metropolitan Area. In light of all the new-found complexities of developmental genetics, however, it is unclear that the concept of "genetic growth potential" has much biological validity. But even if it has, there is no obvious reason to believe that all human populations should possess similar distributions of it, or that the successful attainment of the average growth potential is a sign of optimal health or nutrition.[7] Furthermore, arguments based on the

---

[6] More recent international standards, including for anthropometric measures other than height, have been developed by the WHO, NCHS, NHANES I-III, the National Diet and Nutrition Survey (UK), and many other agencies and projects (for a comprehensive if uncritical review, see Gibson, 2005: 20–3, 240–3). All these standards are subject to the doubts raised here.

[7] If we have a genetic growth potential for height, why not one for body mass? According to an absolutely unimpeachable scientific reference work (*The Guinness Book of World Records*, best studied over a pint of Guinness), the heaviest known human being alive today weighs more than 1230 pounds (558 kg) and

distribution of growth potentials provide no grounds for assessing the nutritional status of an *individual* – unless, that is, we adopt arbitrary cut-off points along the distribution of some physical measurement to indicate the dividing line between the well- and poorly nourished. For example, we may decide that any child falling below the fifth percentile of the corresponding height-for-age distribution observed among Boston children is likely to be under-nourished. But the fifth percentile has no inherent biological meaning,[8] and the use of *any* cut-off point may erroneously assume that sharp threshold effects exist in the relationship between anthropometric variables and functionality (e.g. that falling at the fourth percentile places a child in danger, but falling at the sixth does not).

From the vantage point of the historian of human material conditions, it also seems rather strange that the promulgators of international standards take it for granted that "modern" populations, i.e. those that have undergone industrialization and the demographic/epidemiological transition, and that have the lowest fertility and mortality rates, the lightest physical workloads and the most secure and abundant food supplies that have ever been attained in human history – in short, the *strangest* populations that have ever existed – should provide the norms against which all other human communities are to be evaluated. This choice of comparison population introduces a definite bias into nutritional assessment. A modern child is unlikely to be fighting off malaria or cholera, to be helping herd cattle or hauling loads of manure or to be at risk of facing a dramatically reduced food supply next year. Thus, a child in a subsistence economy who falls below the fifth percentile of, say, Boston's height-for-age may be *less* well-nourished than its Boston counterpart at the same percentile simply because it faces greater physiological challenges that must be met if the child is to survive and thrive. Once again, nutritional adequacy can only be gauged against functional requirements.

If international standards are unsatisfactory, are local ones better? Unfortunately, there are problems with this alternative too. How, for example, do we know that everyone in the local population is not under-nourished in the absence of an external standard? Perhaps everyone in the local community looks short to us, but we cannot really judge them to be pathologically short (and thus under-nourished?) without an external standard to compare them to. Well, then, let's compare members of the population strictly to each other – whereupon we discover some individuals are shorter than others even after we adjust for age and sex. Can we at least consider relatively short members to be *more* poorly nourished than taller ones from the same community? That depends. Sukhatme and Margen (1978, 1982) have argued that somatic stunting may actually be an adaptation to a restricted food supply: the

---

is completely bed-ridden. I am perfectly willing to accept that this weight may be approaching the maximal genetic growth potential for body mass in the human species as a whole. But can anyone suggest any sense in which this weight is "optimal" for anything other than getting into *The Guinness Book of World Records*?

[8] Except insofar as it reflects the biological fact that most of us have five fingers on each hand. Were we to have seven, would we prefer the seventh percentile? Or would we be thinking in terms of perseptaniles instead of percentiles?

smaller you are in height or weight the less you need to eat to maintain your current condition.[9] Should that turn out to be true (which would surprise me), are taller people with their heavier food requirements effectively *less* well-nourished than their shorter neighbors on a similar diet? Or, contrariwise, perhaps anything near or above the local average height (which may still be quite short by international standards) represents the well-adapted norm. In the latter situation, how far below the local average does someone have to fall in order to be classified as under-nourished? The conventional answer is at least two (local) standard deviations. In a normally distributed variable, the mean − 2 s.d. is approximately equivalent to the fifth percentile − and we're back to the problems of arbitrary cut-offs, unrealistically sharp thresholds and the untoward influence of having five fingers. Worse, this criterion will always make it look as if exactly 5 percent of the population is under-nourished even if *all* the locals are well-nourished − or indeed starving, as the case may be. Local standards are not a panacea and may even introduce additional problems of their own.

There is a final, deeper concern regarding the concept of "nutritional status" itself, the very thing we would like to assess. Is it really a fairly static, unitary *state*, or is it a multidimensional dynamic *process*? Everyone agrees that it is, of course, the latter, but until recently it has not usually been assessed that way. For example, experimental studies suggest that, for some physiological functions, longitudinal energy *balance* may be more important than cross-sectional energy *stores* (Cameron, 1996), but in the field few researchers take the repeated measures needed to track energy balance (this is changing). In addition, different aspects of what we lump together under the term "nutritional status" may have different functional consequences. Energy balance may influence reproductive capacity, protein intake may influence immunocompetence and vitamin deficiencies may have specific influences on growth. All this is further complicated by the dynamic, lagged relationship between the onset of dietary inadequacy and the appearance of detectable changes in functionality or phenotype. There remain many unanswered questions about what we actually mean by nutritional status (Osmani, 1992).

So, Are Subsistence Farmers and their Families Under-Nourished?

In view of all the conceptual and practical problems associated with the assessment of nutritional status, what if anything can we say about the prevalence of under-nutrition among traditional farmers? Not surprisingly, less than we would like. If we take their results at face value, nutritional surveys of living agricultural populations in the developing world, based primarily on anthropometrics, suggest that many

---

[9] Over the years, this "small but healthy" hypothesis has enjoyed some popularity in nutritional circles. In general, however, follow-up studies conducted in the rural developing world that use initial nutritional status as a predictor of prospective risk of death indicate that shorter and lighter individuals consistently experience higher subsequent mortality than their less-stunted compatriots (see Sommer and Lowenstein, 1975; Chen *et al.*, 1980; Heywood, 1982; Beaton, 1989; Schroeder and Brown, 1994).

contain sizeable fractions of moderately-to-severely under-nourished individuals, perhaps something like 15–40 percent or more, especially at younger ages (Whyte, 1974; Robson and Wadsworth, 1977; Lawrence *et al.*, 1989; Payne, 1989; Waterlow, 1992; de Onis *et al.*, 1993; de Onis and Blössner, 1997; United Nations, 1998; Ferro-Luzzi *et al.*, 2001; Popkin, 2008). Of course, living developing-world populations may not be especially good models for genuinely preindustrial farming communities, even if they are often the best living analogs we have. In addition, it is likely that the choice of study population for this kind of survey injects an unhealthy dose of selectivity bias into our conclusions. Nutritional surveys under difficult field conditions are usually mounted in areas already suspected of having high prevalences of under-nutrition. The surveys, after all, are usually conducted as a basis for medical interventions or policy decisions, not for purely scientific purposes. Our sample of samples may thus be biased toward groups with comparatively poor nutrition.

Recently, several scholars, most of them economists, have become interested in what they call *anthropometric history* (Floud and Wachter, 1982; Fogel *et al.*, 1983; Floud *et al.*, 1990, 2011; Mokyr and Ó Gráda, 1996; Steckel and Rose, 2002; Fogel, 2004). Studies in this field draw upon historical collections of anthropometric data to make inferences about past standards of living. It is in the nature of things that such collections are rare and often involve peculiar subgroups (e.g. slaves, military recruits, Union Army veterans) that may not be representative of the general population from which they were drawn. In addition, it is usually the case that only a single anthropometric measure, stature, is recorded, although sometimes weight is as well. But one result of these studies seems reasonably robust. Over the long run (and despite some short-term reversals and periods of stagnation), industrialization has generally resulted in increases in mean stature, suggesting that preindustrial people may have been nutritionally stunted relative to their industrialized descendants.[10] Braver (or less finicky) anthropometric historians have gone so far as to conclude that these increases in mean stature point to improvements in nutrition that contributed significantly to declining mortality during the epidemiological transition. But that may be too great a burden of explanation to place on a single anthropometric measure like stature – or even two when we toss in weight.

Ethnographic studies of traditional farmers may provide additional evidence. For example, Dinks (1993) has presented some empirical generalizations about hunger in preindustrial societies based on the Standard Cross-Cultural Sample of 186 preindustrial societies drawn from the ethnographic literature and selected to represent all parts of the world proportionately. His results are difficult to interpret because different methods and standards were almost certainly used in the various studies that contributed to the database, and the comparability of the data cannot be gauged short of re-examining all the original ethnographic accounts (which I certainly have not done). Nonetheless, Dinks's examination of the ethnographic material included in

---

[10] The same studies also suggest that the *variance* in stature often increased during industrialization, perhaps owing to widening economic differentials. As noted in Chapter 5, this finding may be consistent with expectations based on the MaB ratchet.

the Standard Cross-Cultural Sample found that (i) chronic under-nutrition (in all seasons and in nonfamine years) was mentioned in 31 percent of studies, (ii) regular seasonal under-nutrition in 38 percent of studies, and (iii) recurrent famine in 75 percent of studies. (We are told only whether these conditions were present or absent, not how widespread or severe they were within each society.) Setting aside the problem of comparability, these figures might be expected to be *under-estimates* since they assume that the ethnographer actually paid attention to the adequacy and variability of the food supply. In addition, many ethnographers spend a rather short time at their field sites (typically a year at any one time, perhaps with an equally short return visit or two some years later); as a consequence they may miss intermittent and short-lived episodes of food shortage and hunger. By the way, while Dinks's generalizations cover a wide variety of subsistence types, he found no consistent difference in the evidence of food shortages among traditional farmers as opposed to hunter-gatherers or pastoralists (see also Benyshek and Watson, 2006).

One important and convincing finding in ethnographic studies concerns the uneven distribution of under-nutrition within many traditional farming households, reflecting inequitable allocation of either food resources or physiological burdens among household members (Chen *et al.*, 1981; McMillan, 1986; Wheeler and Abdullah, 1988; Thomas, 1990; Dercon and Krishnan, 2000; Bolt and Bird, 2003; Dubois and Ligon, 2010). To summarize a complicated situation in a few words, female household members are often at a distinct disadvantage (Figure 8.1). We should not assume, therefore, just because a household commands enough food in the aggregate, that its members all get sufficient food to meet their individual needs.

Finally, the question of the nutritional condition of preindustrial (and usually prehistoric) farming communities has been of keen interest to so-called bioarchaeologists (paleodemographers, paleopathologists, paleoepidemiologists), scholars interested in reconstructing past morbidity and mortality patterns based on skeletons excavated at archaeological sites. I think it is fair to say that most bioarchaeologists believe that preindustrial farmers were under-nourished not only by modern standards, but also in comparison to most hunter-gatherers past and present (see Cohen and Armelagos, 1984; Cohen, 1989; Larsen, 1999; Cohen and Crane-Kramer, 2007).[11] For a variety of reasons, I have long been skeptical of this claim (see Wood *et al.*, 1992b; Wood, 1998), but I have to admit that I am in a small professional minority on this point (but see Kaplan, 2000; Bogin, 2011, among others). But setting aside the controversial comparison between prehistoric farmers and hunter-gatherers, bioarchaeology shows unambiguously that boney lesions believed to be indicative of under-nutrition – especially lesions such as enamel hypoplasias, Harris lines, and short height-for-age that reflect growth disruption and stunting – are common among the skeletons of ancient farmers (see Cohen and Crane-Kramer, 2007).

---

[11] The empirical evidence taken to support this claim comes mainly from studies of the skeletons themselves. *Ex-post* explanations include a purported narrowing of dietary breadth following domestication, an increase in infectious disease prevalence resulting from increased sedentism and population density, and widening economic inequality among early farmers (Cohen, 1989).

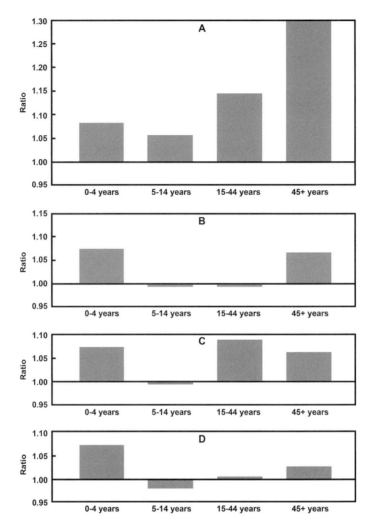

Figure 8.1 Ratio of male/female caloric intake in relation to requirements by age in rural Bangladesh (N = 1927 males, 1599 females). (A) unadjusted; (B) adjusted for body weight; (C) adjusted for body weight, pregnancy and lactation; (D) adjusted for body weight, pregnancy, lactation and physical activity. Comparison of (C) and (D) suggests that women's activities may be substantially curtailed during pregnancy and/or lactation. From Chen *et al.* (1981: 62), by permission of John Wiley & Sons, Inc.

Whether those farmers were in better or worse shape than the hunter-gatherers who preceded them is a separate question and quite irrelevant to the discussion here.

In sum, several lines of evidence, each admittedly problematic, converge to suggest that under-nutrition was far from rare in traditional farming communities, even during nonfamine years. More than that we really cannot say – especially when it comes to making precise quantitative statements about the distribution of under-nutrition both within and across preindustrial populations. Moreover, it is difficult to assess how the apparent levels of under-nutrition reported in historical, archaeological or developing-world studies relate to replacement-level fertility, mortality or migration – the core issue with respect to the Malthusian model and its descendants – unless we examine some of the studies that try to relate under-nutrition to demographic outcomes. We do just that in the next section.

What is the Most Important Nutrition-Related Impediment to the Household Demographic Enterprise?

From a purely demographic perspective, the household enterprise "fails" if it produces fewer offspring who survive to adulthood than are needed to replace the household founders numerically in the next generation. (This deliberately narrow definition of failure ignores the possibility that the founders have no desire to replace themselves.) The demographic performance of the enterprise is thus the net result of fertility (the number of offspring produced) and preadult mortality.[12] In this section we examine the effects of under-nutrition on mortality and fertility separately; we also try to assess whether the demographic effects of under-nutrition are channeled primarily via its effects on fertility or on mortality, or whether the two demographic forces are more or less equally important. Since inter-household migration is also a vital part of the household demographic enterprise, we briefly discuss decisions to migrate as possible responses to local shortfalls in the food supply.

Mortality, Especially Childhood Mortality

Preindustrial and modern communities differ dramatically in general death rates, but most especially in the death rates observed among young children (Figure 8.2). This difference is graphically illustrated by mortality rates estimated before, during and after the nineteenth- and twentieth-century epidemiological transition in England and Wales, a trend that eventuated in an almost quantum disjunction between modern and premodern levels of early childhood mortality (Figure 8.3). Mortality during the first year of life, for example, declined by about 90 percent during the transition from the preindustrial to the modern. Today infant mortality is almost nonexistent in industrialized nations, whereas in the past it was one of the largest components of age-specific mortality across the lifespan (Gage, 1993; Bideau *et al.*, 1997).

What, if anything, was the contribution of dietary inadequacy to the high child mortality characteristic of the preindustrial past, as well as of present-day farmers in the Third World? Well, whatever else it means and however it is measured, under-

---

[12] Since death during the reproductive span of one or the other partner to a marriage can obviously lower household fertility, adult mortality is also important to the demographic enterprise (and, of course, death of an economically productive adult in the household can also endanger children's survival). However, since the mortality rates of reproductive-age adults are much lower than those of young children, and adult mortality appears to be comparatively insensitive to under-nutrition, adult mortality will not be considered in this chapter. A more important effect of under-nutrition in adults is an impairment of physiological work capacity, which is examined in Chapter 9.

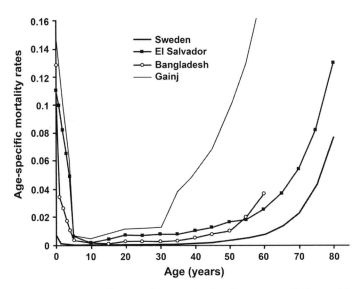

Figure 8.2 Age-specific mortality rates in four human populations with widely differing levels of mortality: Sweden, 1985 (females); El Salvador, 1950 (males); Bangladesh, 1978 (both sexes); the Gainj of highland Papua New Guinea, 1970–7 (males). Note that the Gainj, a small group of shifting cultivators, was the only one of the four without regular access to modern medical care at the time of data collection. The Gainj curve is based on a small sample (<150 deaths) and therefore appears somewhat more "jagged" than the other examples. In addition, in light of biases known from other anthropological demographic studies, it is likely that the ages of older Gainj adults have been underestimated systematically and their mortality rates therefore overestimated to some extent. Thus, inter-population variation in rates among children less than five years old (which are well-estimated for all four groups) is almost certainly greater than at any other age. Data from Keyfitz and Flieger (1968, 1990), Chowdhury *et al.* (1981), Wood (1987).

nutrition is predictive of the death of young children in much of the contemporary rural developing world. In Table 8.1, for example, children under the age of 10 in rural Bangladesh who were moderately-to-severely under-nourished (according to the local distribution of one particular anthropometric index) were also at substantially elevated relative risk of death (R) over an 18-month follow-up period compared to their mildly under-nourished counterparts.[13] Figure 8.4 shows similar results from highland New Guinea, where 18-month prospective mortality rates in children under two-and-a-half years of age increased sharply with lower nutritional status (as evaluated at the beginning of follow-up against the Harvard standards). And Figure 8.5 shows the same basic pattern using age-specific weight-for-age as a predictor of early childhood death in various populations from the rural preindustrial or developing world. Shockingly, the juvenile mortality rates observed in most of

---

[13] The especially sharp rise in R among moderately and severely under-nourished children at age 3 years *may* reflect the fact that this is the normal age at weaning in the study population (Sommer and Lowenstein, 1975), although this is not known with certainty.

Table 8.1 Children at risk (C), percent mortality (M) and relative risk of death (R) by degree of under-nutrition, as assessed by the ratio of arm circumference to height, 18-month follow-up study of 8292 children from rural Bangladesh. Relative risks of death under moderate and severe under-nutrition are assessed against the risks associated with mild under-nutrition (R = 1.0) (Sommer and Loewenstein, 1975). Reproduced from A. Sommer and M. S. Loewenstein, Nutritional status and mortality, *American Journal of Clinical Nutrition* (1975) 28, 287–92, by permission of Oxford University Press.

| | Degree of under-nutrition[a] | | | | | | | | |
| | Mild | | | Moderate | | | Severe | | |
Age at initial assessment (years)	C	M	R	C	M	R	C	M	R
1	492	3.0	1.0	408	4.4	1.5	59	11.9	3.9
2	507	3.7	1.0	435	6.0	1.6	66	13.6	3.6
3	515	2.5	1.0	406	4.9	2.0	62	17.7	7.0
4	420	1.4	1.0	321	1.9	1.3	66	6.1	4.2
5–9	2032	0.5	1.0	1791	0.6	1.2	389	1.0	2.0

[a] Degree of under-nutrition according to the local distribution of ratios of arm circumference to height: mild, >50th percentile; moderate, 10th–50th percentile; severe, <10th percentile.

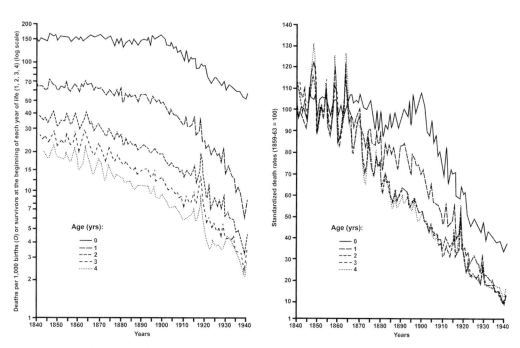

Figure 8.3 Decline in early childhood mortality rates (ages 0–4 years), England and Wales 1840–1940. (Left) Absolute rates on a log scale. (Right) Standardized rates (1859–63 = 100) on a linear scale. The transient spike in mortality just before 1920 reflects the 1917 global pandemic of "Spanish" influenza. From Woods *et al.* (1988), by permission of the Taylor Francis Group.

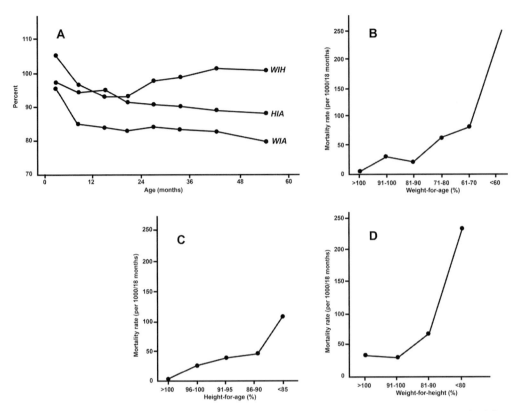

Figure 8.4 The association between nutritional status, as measured by weight-for-age (W/A), height-for-age (H/A) and weight-for-height (W/H) at the beginning of the study, and prospective rate of death over an 18-month follow-up period, in 1147 children of ages 6–30 months at initial recruitment, Tari Basin, Southern Highland Province, Papua New Guinea. All anthropometric indices are expressed as percentages of the Harvard growth standards. (A) Distribution of mean nutritional indices (as percentage of mean age-specific Harvard standards) at the beginning of the study. Prospective 18-month mortality rate as a function of weight-for-age (B), height-for-age (C) and weight-for-height (D). The two major conclusions of the study were (i) that weight-for-height is the most sensitive of the tested indicators of reduced functionality, resulting in substantial increases of mortality at levels as high as 81–90 percent of the Harvard standards, and (ii) there is no evidence to support the Sukhatme hypothesis that small body size is an adaptation to dietary inadequacy. From Heywood (1982: 16–18), by permission of Jscholar, Inc.

these populations were actually greater than *neonatal* mortality in the USA (universally neonatal mortality is the highest component of childhood mortality within a population). Many more examples could have been adduced (for a recent summary of the literature, see Christian, 2008), but the general pattern is clear enough. In many (probably most, perhaps nearly all) farming communities in the Third World, the normal, nonfamine range of nutritional conditions observed in young children is, at least at its lower tail, associated with substantially elevated risks of death. Childhood mortality is without doubt an important nutrition-related impediment to the

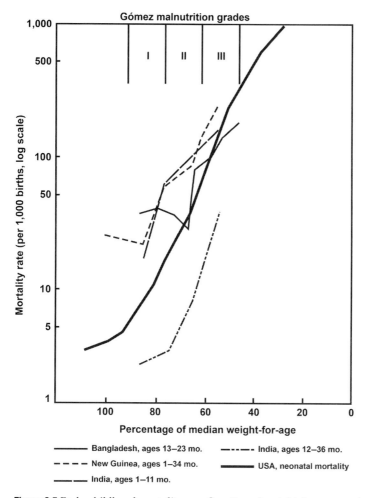

Figure 8.5 Early childhood mortality as a function of weight-for-age, various populations. From Mosley and Chen (1984: 31), by permission of Cambridge University Press.

household demographic enterprise in a variety of developing-world farming communities. From all available evidence, the same is almost certain to have been true in the preindustrial past (Aykroyd, 1971; Bengtsson, 1999; Bengtsson *et al.*, 2004; Fogel, 2004; Floud *et al.*, 2011).

But to understand the significance of inadequate diets for child mortality in the preindustrial world, we need to examine the mechanisms linking the two in more detail. The first step is to ascertain what preindustrial people actually die of, a question that has been investigated in the field by several anthropologists and other researchers. Now, before going any further, it is necessary to point out that retrospective diagnosis of the primary cause of any particular death that occurs during field research, based as it is on "verbal autopsy" (a postmortem interview with witnesses), is problematic (Snow and Marsh, 1992). This is so principally because the symptoms elicited in interviews are often rather vague and nonspecific

Table 8.2 Causes of death (as percentage of recorded deaths at all ages) in selected preindustrial and developing-world societies, for three broad categories of causes. The !Kung (Kalahari Desert) and Aka (Congo Basin) were predominantly hunter-gatherers at the time of study. The Yanomama (Orinoco Basin) and Gainj (highland New Guinea) were shifting cultivators. From Preston *et al.* (1972), Howell (1979: 69), Wood (1980: 122), Melancon (1982: Table 3.1), Hewlett *et al.* (1986: 54).

	!Kung		Aka		Yanomama		Gainj	Developing countries[a]	
Causes	M	F	M	F	M	F	M + F	M	F
Infectious	77	82	91	95	76	72	79	80	80
Degenerative	8	10	0	0	5	8	7	14	17
Violent and accidental	15	8	9	5	19	20	14	6	3
Total	100	100	100	100	100	100	100	100	100
No. of deaths	342		669		111		44	10 000+	

[a] Based on data from eight national populations with life expectancy at birth <40 years, similar to the life-table estimates for the other four populations.

(Kalter *et al.*, 1990; Marsh *et al.*, 2003). But if we are content to settle for an extremely crude classification of causes, a strong and consistent pattern emerges: preindustrial and rural Third World people mostly die of infectious diseases, which collectively lead other categories of causes by a large margin (Table 8.2). Even in developing-world communities with some access to modern health care and with rapidly falling mortality rates, infectious diseases remain the most important class of serious clinical problems in young children – serious enough, that is, to warrant admission to hospital (Table 8.3). Historically, the dropping away of deaths by infectious disease accounted for almost all the decline in childhood mortality during the modern epidemiological transition in the West (Figure 8.6).[14]

But if most deaths of children in the preindustrial past were the direct result of infection, does that mean that under-nutrition was unimportant as a cause of death? Not at all, though it may indicate that under-nutrition was mostly a *contributing* cause of death rather than an immediate one. But it was a profoundly important contributing cause. One of the most thoroughly investigated functional effects of under-nutrition, in both humans and lab animals, is reduced *immunocompetence* or the ability of the immune system to defend its owner from contracting or succumbing to infectious disease (for reviews, see Keusch, 1998; Woodward, 1998; Gershwin *et al.*, 2004). Table 8.4 summarizes elements of the immune system known to be

---

[14] Compare Figures 8.3 and 8.6, but be careful to note the difference in both the scale of rates (deaths per 1000 versus per 100 000) and the time span along the *x*-axis. Figure 8.6 begins in 1900, by which time infectious diseases as a percentage of all causes of death had already fallen substantially in comparison to 1840.

Table 8.3 Frequency of pediatric hospital admissions by cause in a birth cohort of 452 infants (<1 yr old at admission), Vellore, south India, 2002 (Gladstone *et al.*, 2008). Reproduced from *Archives of Disease in Childhood*, B. P. Gladstone, J. P. Muliyil, S. Jaffar, J. G. Wheeler, A. Le Fevre, M. Itturiza-Gomara, J. J. Gray, A. Bose, M. K. Estes, D. W. Brown and A. Kang, 93, 479–84, 2008, with permission from BMJ Publishing Group Ltd.

Cause of admission	Frequency of admission (%)	
Respiratory infection	51	
Diarrhea	21	All infections 80%
Other infections	8	
Neonatal conditions	12	
Genetic anomalies	3	
Malnutrition	2	
Others	3	
Total	100	
Number of admissions	106	

compromised by protein-energy malnutrition.[15] Anyone with even an elementary knowledge of the immune system will recognize that Table 8.4 includes things that are important to every arm of the immune response, from innate immunity to acquired or adaptive immunity, from the complement system to cell-mediated immunity to the passive immunity conveyed to babies in mothers' milk. While the different components of the immune system are variably sensitive to the influence of under-nutrition, some are very sensitive indeed. And the lower range of variation in nutritional status found in traditional populations during years of *normal* food availability is enough to cause substantial impairments in immunocompetence, including at the extreme complete *anergy* or lack of any measurable immune response (Shell-Duncan and Wood, 1997). Little surprise, then, that nutritional status is predictive of both the frequency and severity of such important, potentially fatal infections as diarrheal disease in Third-World children (Table 8.5). In addition, the clear linkages among nutrition, immunocompetence, infectious disease and death explain a not uncommon finding – that deaths during famines are mostly attributable to infection rather than overt starvation, even in famines caused by such a profound dearth of foodstuffs as was the Great Irish Potato Famine of the mid-nineteenth century (Table 8.6).[16]

Some years ago, the epidemiologists Henry Mosley and Lincoln Chen put together a useful analytical framework for studying the determinants of childhood mortality in developing countries (Mosley and Chen, 1984). Quite reasonably, their scheme focuses on deaths from infectious diseases, since this is the leading class of causes of death in such settings. Figure 8.7 shows a slightly simplified and updated version of the Mosley–Chen framework, modified (among other ways) so that the effects of

---

[15] Shortages of specific micronutrients can also have immunosuppressive effects (for recent reviews, see Keen *et al.*, 2004; Ramakrishnan *et al.*, 2004).
[16] See also Mokyr and Ó Gráda (2002) and Ó Gráda (2009: 109–21).

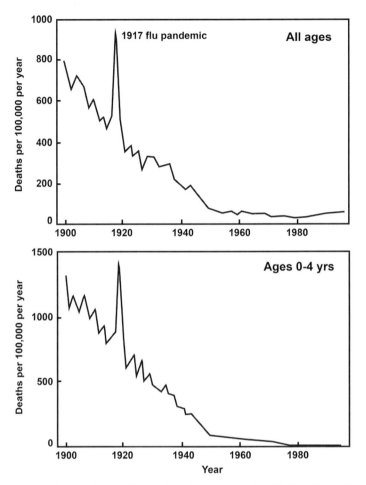

Figure 8.6 Annual rates of infectious disease mortality, United States 1900–96. (Top) Deaths at all ages. (Bottom) Deaths among children less than five years old. From Armstrong *et al.* (1999: 63–4), by permission of the American Medical Association.

nutritional status on mortality are channeled through their impact on immunocompetence. Almost any aspect of the physical or socioeconomic environment can exert an influence on early childhood mortality, but only if it has some effect on at least one of a small number of more proximate factors intimately related to the risk of death in young children and acting mainly at the level of the household. Among the latter, exposure to pathogens in the child's immediate home environment is obviously important to the child's likelihood of moving from the healthy to the sick state.[17] By "maternal factors" Mosley and Chen mostly mean the mother's ability to produce sufficient high-quality breastmilk (see Brown *et al.*, 1986), critical to the child's health for both nutritional and immunological reasons. Physical trauma can

---

[17] In the Mosley–Chen framework, "sick" and "healthy" refer to the presence or absence, respectively, of an active, symptomatic infection by a single, specific pathogen.

Table 8.4 Components of the immune system known to be impaired by protein-energy under-nutrition. Cytokines (inter- and paracellular messengers): IL, interleukin; IFN, interferon; TNF, tumor necrosis factor. Ig, immunoglobulin (antibody). Modified from Jackson and Calder (2004: 79).

Mucus production
Integrity of the intestinal mucosa
Weight of thymus, spleen, tonsils and lymph nodes (e.g. nutritional thymectomy)
Number of T-lymphocytes in the bloodstream
Number of CD4+ and CD8+ cells in the bloodstream
Proliferation of T-lymphocytes
Production of Th1-type cytokines (IL-2, IFN-γ)
Delayed-type hypersensitivity
Concentration of secretory IgA in breastmilk, the intestinal mucosa, tears, saliva, etc.
Concentration of C3 (from complement system) in the bloodstream
Natural killer cell activity
Respiratory bursts in neutrophils
Bacterial killing by neutrophils
Production of the cytokines TNF, IL-1 and IL-6 by monocytes/macrophages
Concentration of acute-phase proteins in the bloodstream

Table 8.5 The relationship between nutritional status and the incidence and duration of diarrheal disease in 343 children of ages 6–32 months in rural Nigeria (Tompkins, 1981). Reprinted from *The Lancet*, 317(8225), A. Tomkins, Nutritional status and severity of diarrhoea among pre-school children in rural Nigeria, 18 April, 860–2, copyright 1981, with permission from Elsevier.

Nutritional status	Number of children	Diarrhea attack rate[a]	Percent of time ill with diarrhea
Weight-for-age			
≥75 percent	220	1.25	8.5
<75 percent	123	1.52	11.3
Height-for-age			
≥90 percent	245	1.37	7.9
<90 percent	98	1.45	10.8
Weight-for-height			
≥80 percent	302	1.29	7.6
<80 percent	41	1.90	13.6

[a] Cases per child in three months.

provide multiple routes of infection by damaging the child's integument – for example, untreated burns and their attendant damage to skin and other tissues often result in serious local or systemic infections. And central to the whole scheme is the child's nutritional status as it affects its immunocompetence. But under-nutrition sneaks in again through the backdoor during illness itself. If a sick child does not recover, it may die immediately or may first pass through a state known as *growth faltering*. If the child does experience growth faltering, its risk of dying rather than recovering is substantially increased (Pelletier *et al.*, 1993). Growth faltering thus

Table 8.6 Recorded causes of death (by percentage) during the Irish famine of 1846–9 (Ó Gráda, 1999: 93). Reprinted with permission of John Wiley & Sons, Inc, from C. Ó Gráda (1999) *Black '47 and Beyond: The Great Irish Famine in History, Economy, and Memory,* Princeton, NJ: Princeton University Press.

	County Mayo	Counties Tipperary/Clare
Dysentery/diarrhea	28.2	21.2
Unspecified fever	27.5	29.7
Starvation	9.1	3.6
Consumption (tuberculosis)	4.6	6.9
Cholera	2.2	5.3
Dropsy (nutritional edema)	2.0	1.4
Marasmus (severe protein-energy malnutrition)	1.6	2.7
Other (inc. unknown)	24.8	29.2
Total	100.0	100.0

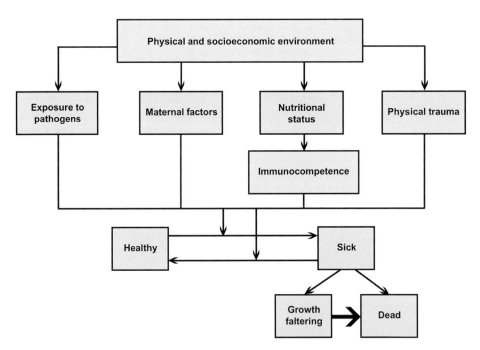

Figure 8.7 A framework for studying the major determinants of early childhood mortality in the preindustrial world, where most juvenile deaths are caused by infectious disease. Conceptually, the framework refers to the risk of death in a single child. Modified from Mosley and Chen (1984: 29), by permission of Cambridge University Press.

plays a critical role in early childhood death in the developing world, and it needs to be examined in more detail.

The phenomenon of growth faltering is illustrated in Figure 8.8. This classic figure, which has been reproduced countless times, shows the longitudinal growth performance of one young English girl who was born in the mid-1950s

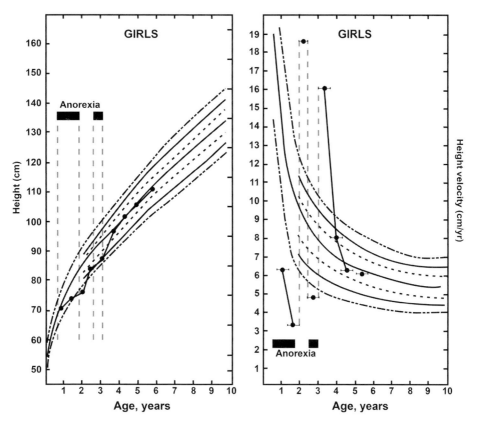

Figure 8.8 Growth faltering in one young girl who experienced two episodes of anorexia of unreported etiology (not necessarily anorexia nervosa), Great Britain *c.* 1960. Smooth curves are percentiles of values in normal British girls (solid curve is the median); points represent prospective observations on the one girl. From Tanner (1963), by permission of John Wiley & Son, Inc.

(Tanner, 1963). Both her height-for-age and her age-specific height velocity (annual increment in height) are shown against the distributions observed in presumably healthy and well-nourished British girls. Earlier in her life, the girl had experienced two rounds of anorexia.[18] Although when first measured she was near the median height-for-age in the general British population, her growth velocity declined ("faltered") during both periods of anorexia, dropping well below the first percentile observed in well-fed girls. Astonishingly, though, once her normal appetite had returned, her height velocity skyrocketed, reaching values well over the *99th* percentile – so-called "catch-up growth," a common sequel to growth faltering in populations with good health care and an ample food supply (Boersma and Wit,

---

[18] "Anorexia" just means a pathological loss of appetite, whatever its cause. It does not necessarily imply anorexia nervosa. We are not told why the girl in Figure 8.8 failed to eat enough, although it was the reason she was first taken to a clinic and had her height measured, and why her growth was repeatedly monitored for several years thereafter.

1997). Despite the cumulative effects of growth faltering, catch-up growth pushed the girl back up near the population median height-for-age by about age four or five.

It has been argued that the *function* of growth faltering is to lessen the intense competition between somatic growth and maintenance resulting from food shortages that coincide with ages when normal growth rates are at their highest (Shrimpton *et al.*, 2001; McDade, 2003; McDade *et al.*, 2008) – and that the *function* of catch-up growth is to mitigate the potentially adverse future effects of growth faltering (Tanner, 1986). Perhaps. But in physiology it is often difficult to differentiate a function (an evolved adaptive response) from a simple occurrence (something that just happens) or even a pathology. The logic of the adaptationist argument is simple enough. If food consumption is too low to support both rapid growth and mainten-ance, it makes evolutionary sense to suspend growth in order to increase the likelihood that the child will survive the immediate crisis. But, it is further argued, growth is still important for future survival and reproduction, so once the crisis has passed it makes just as much evolutionary sense to invest the now-plentiful food being consumed disproportionately into growth. There are, I think, two problems with this argument, aside from the fact that "making evolutionary sense" does not constitute evidence.[19] First, it is difficult to decide whether growth faltering is an adaptation or a simple pathology. It certainly signals that not enough food is being taken in to support normal functionality. But the key to the adaptationist argument is that maintenance is always given *priority* over growth – that growth will always fail at levels of under-nutrition less severe than those needed to compromise mainten-ance – and that is simply not established. Epidemiological evidence indicates that some degree of nutrition-related immunosuppression can occur even in the absence of measurable growth faltering – i.e. that immune function, a critical component of maintenance, may be *more* sensitive to under-nutrition than is growth (Shell-Duncan and Wood, 1997). The concept of catch-up growth as adaptation is equally problem-atic. Being short *per se* doesn't kill you (otherwise *Homo floresiensis* could never have evolved). Growth faltering is a sign of elevated risk of death not because it makes the child shorter than it "ought" to be, but because it is telling us that functionally significant under-nutrition is occurring. Resumption of normal growth rates is doubtless a good sign from this perspective, but there does not seem to be any clear advantage to attaining *super-normal* rates, the key feature of catch-up growth. The idea that catch-up growth is an adaptation would seem to hark back to the notion that each individual has a genetic growth potential and that fulfilling that potential is essential for optimal health – a strange concept that has never, to my knowledge, been critically evaluated.

Catch-up growth occurs only if plentiful food is actually made available to the child during and after the period of growth faltering. All too often, the reality in much of the developing world (and probably the preindustrial past) is that catch-up growth never gets a chance to happen. Figure 8.9 shows the experience of one rural

---

[19] I thank Anne Buchanan for helping me think through these problems.

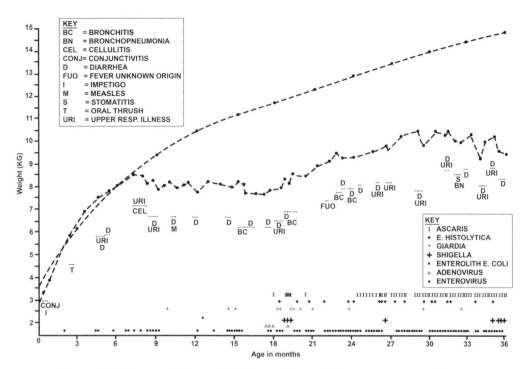

Figure 8.9 A three-year history of infection and growth faltering in a young child in rural Guatemala. *Smooth broken line*, mean weight (kg) for age in healthy Guatemalan children. *Jagged broken line*, prospective observations on one child. From Mata (1992), by permission of the American Society of Tropical Medicine.

Guatemalan child whose growth first faltered at about age seven months and had not caught up by the age of 36 months. And Figure 8.9 makes another important point – namely, that growth faltering (or rather the under-nutrition that causes it) often promotes the onset and virulence of infectious disease, which in turn worsen the growth faltering (Martorell *et al.*, 1975; Scrimshaw, 1981; de Onis and Blössner, 1997). Malnutrition impairs the child's ability to fight infectious diseases, but just as importantly infectious diseases (especially diarrheal disease, a pernicious killer of children in the Third World) can contribute to malnutrition (Caulfield *et al.*, 2003). Prolonged growth faltering represents a vicious cycle involving under-nutrition and infection. It is very likely that the poor child in Figure 8.9 would never have survived to its third birthday had there not been a well-run maternal-child-health clinic nearby to treat its infections (nor would we have had such detailed prospective information on the child).

It may be that growth faltering occurs *in order* to reduce competition between growth and maintenance in young children during periods of dearth. Even so, the statistical finding from many nutritional and epidemiological studies of children in the rural developing world – that in the absence of effective medical intervention growth faltering is predictive at the level of the individual child of a substantially elevated prospective risk of death from infectious disease (Pelletier *et al.*, 1993, 1995;

de Onis and Blössner, 1997) – suggests that the reduced competition often does not work. Whatever the evolutionary meaning of growth faltering and catch-up growth, I suggest that the ugly synergy among under-nutrition, growth disruption, compromised immune function, life-threatening infectious diseases and early childhood death is a central feature of virtually all preindustrial and developing-world demographic regimes, just as argued by Moseley and Chen and many others (e.g. Scrimshaw, 1983a,b, 2000; Watkins and van de Walle, 1983; Martorell and Ho, 1984; Lunn, 1991; Wrigley 1991b; Pelletier *et al.*, 1993, 1995; Fogel, 1994, 2004; Bideau *et al.*, 1997; Scott and Duncan, 2002: 275–302; Bengtsson *et al.*, 2004; Allen *et al.*, 2005; Popkin, 2008). The synergy is, in short, one of the most formidable challenges facing the household demographic enterprise in traditional farming communities.

Fertility

The relationship between under-nutrition and childhood mortality appears to be undeniable. But what about fertility? Does under-nutrition hamper the household's demographic enterprise by reducing the number of infants born? Most scientific attention has thus far been focused on maternal under-nutrition and its reproductive and demographic consequences. Within this area of research, there have long been two quite distinct approaches, and, generally speaking, they have reached diametrically opposed conclusions (see Wood, 1994b, for a review). The *demographic* approach examines the relationship between a woman's nutritional status and her *fertility* in the strict technical sense (the actual number of live-born children she produces), while the *physiological* approach examines the relationship between a woman's nutritional status and various measurable physiological variables thought to be related to her *fecundity* (her biological capacity for reproduction). According to the physiologists, "The reproductive [hypothalamo-pituitary-gonadal] axis is closely linked to nutritional status, especially undernutrition in the female..." (ESHRE Capri Workshop Group, 2006). The majority view among demographers, in contrast, is that the range of nutritional conditions normally observed in rural developing-world communities has almost no measurable effect on fertility (Bongaarts, 1980; Hobcraft, 1985; Pebley *et al.*, 1985; John *et al.*, 1987; Ford and Huffman, 1993; John, 1993; Wood, 1994b).[20] But fertility and fecundity are not the same thing, and they may not even be strongly correlated (if, for example, a woman is celibate for her entire postpubertal life, she may be perfectly fecund, but she will remain completely

---

[20] To mention one area of agreement, both physiologists and demographers accept that fertility is suppressed during extreme famine conditions, although there is little consensus about the precise causes of the suppression. For example, Bongaarts and Cain (1982) have argued that the decline in fertility sometimes observed during and immediately following a famine is not primarily physiological in origin but rather reflects marital disruption (owing to the death of one or both spouses) or postponement of marriage while famine conditions prevail. Many demographers, however, do accept that the severe malnutrition associated with famine can affect reproductive physiology in demographically important ways (Stein and Susser, 1975; Bongaarts, 1980; Hugo, 1984; Watkins and Menken, 1985; Duncan and Scott, 2002; Ó Gráda, 2009).

Table 8.7 Reproductive status of 65 postmenarcheal and premenopausal Gainj women who were married and living with their husbands, highland Papua New Guinea, 1982–3. Tabulated figures are the age-specific percentages (with standard errors in parentheses) of women in each reproductive category based on serum hormone concentrations and self-reports of lactation. Test of difference between age groups: log likelihood ratio = 8.6, df = 3, $p = 0.034$. From Wood (1994a: 112). Copyright © 1994 From *Dynamics of Human Reproduction: Biology, Biometry, Demography* by J. W. Wood. Hawthorne, NY: Aldine de Gruyter. Reproduced by permission of Taylor and Francis Group, LLC, a division of Informa plc.

Age of woman (years)	N	Pregnant	Lactating, not pregnant Acyclic	Cyclic	Not pregnant, not lactating	Total
20–39	45	33 (7)	33 (7)	20 (6)	13 (5)	100
40–49	20	10 (7)	20 (9)	30 (10)	40 (7)	100

infertile). In addition, unlike fertility, fecundity is unobservable, a "capacity" not a measurable variable; we can only observe things we believe on *a priori* grounds to be related to it (not unlike the example of anthropometrics and nutritional status). As I have emphasized elsewhere, it is perfectly possible that both the physiologists and the demographers are correct within their respective scientific domains (Wood, 1994b). But, in the present context, it is fertility and demography that count.

The fundamental source of uncertainty in reconciling the two approaches is the difficulty of linking fecundity "factors" (i.e. observables thought to be related to fecundity) and fertility, especially in developing-world settings. Table 8.7, which shows data on the Gainj women we studied in highland New Guinea, illustrates the problem. Ovarian physiology and its possible impairment by under-nutrition are best studied in women who are neither pregnant nor lactating since both pregnancy and breastfeeding powerfully interfere with ovarian function even in well-nourished women. But, as the reproductive physiologist Roger Short (1976) has argued, in a preindustrial population without access to modern contraceptives or widespread tubal sterility, most reproductive-age women are likely to be pregnant or lactating at any given time.[21] In the case of the Gainj in Table 8.7, the exclusion of pregnant or lactating women from our study would eliminate almost 90 percent of women at peak reproductive ages (20–39 years), almost all of whom are married. Some of the women at those ages who are *not* pregnant or lactating might be experiencing some form of impaired ovarian function – perhaps that is *why* they are not pregnant or lactating when most other women are – and the impairment may have nothing to do with nutrition. Virtually all Gainj women are under-nourished to some degree by

[21] As Short points out, this is just as true of traditional societies with comparatively low fertility as it is of high-fertility communities. Given the absence of effective methods of birth control, low-fertility preindustrial communities usually have low fertility because of the contraceptive effects of prolonged breastfeeding. High-fertility communities, in contrast, tend to be characterized by shorter and less intensive breastfeeding. Under low fertility a woman spends less time pregnant but more time breastfeeding, while the reverse is true of high-fertility women.

Western standards, so the discovery of under-nutrition among women with impaired ovarian function would tell us nothing about the *causal* relationship between fertility and nutrition. The excluded fraction falls to 60 percent among women over age 40 (Table 8.7), but many women over age 40 are likely to be experiencing various forms of irregular ovarian function associated with normal aging (e.g. long cycles and cycles of variable length, anovulatory cycles, cycles with low levels of luteal-phase progesterone).

In statistical jargon, then, there is likely to be severe selectivity bias in almost any sample of preindustrial women who are not currently pregnant or lactating, especially since almost all women in preindustrial communities are married by about age 20 (see Chapter 7). However, a series of studies among Lese farmers and Efe hunter-gatherers in what is now the Democratic Republic of Congo (Ellison,1990, 2003) was able to examine ovarian function in something approximating a representative (nonselective) sample of adult females and found some evidence of a link between under-nutrition and low progesterone secretion during the postovulatory phase of women's cycles (low, that is, in comparison to Western women). But the very reason they were able to look at a more or less representative sample of Lese and Efe women even while excluding pregnant or lactating subjects was that tubal sterility (apparently caused by gonorrhea or chlamydia infections) was extremely widespread in these groups – the primary sterility rate in Lese and Efe women is about 40 percent (the secondary sterility rate is not reported) and the total fertility rate is 2.4, well below replacement level given local mortality rates. Because of the widespread pathological sterility, the studies were unable to link under-nutrition and disrupted ovarian function with fertility *per se*. To this day, we still do not know if comparatively low luteal progesterone has any measurable effect on actual fertility.[22]

There are further complications. Some of the best studies of the relationship between ovarian physiology and nutrition, done on laboratory monkeys to avoid the problems associated with work on humans, suggest that the linkage may have less to do with current nutritional status and more to do with energy *balance* (for reviews, see Cameron, 1996; ESHRE Capri Workgroup, 2006). Even so slight a change in energy balance as missing a meal can cause detectable changes in the hypothalamo-pituitary-gonadal axis, but these can be rapidly reversed by eating a small quantity of carbohydrate-rich food. I once asked a physiologist centrally involved in this research if nutrition-induced amenorrhea could be "cured" by eating a single Big

[22] Many studies of these issues have been conducted among Western women, but most have focused on women who are unusually lean, such as ballet dancers, marathon runners, competitive rowers and anorectics. It is now well-established that such women do tend to experience various forms of ovarian dysfunction, including complete amenorrhea in many cases (see Cumming *et al.*, 1994, for a review). But it is difficult to attribute the dysfunction entirely to leanness or dietary inadequacy since these women differ from the general population in multiple ways, particularly with respect to activity levels and psychological stress. More to the point, both the leanness and activity levels observed in, say, ballet dancers or marathon runners are so extreme that they are unlikely to be typical of the everyday conditions experienced by women in preindustrial farming communities. At least with respect to leanness and psychological stress, however, they may yet turn out to be useful models for reproductive physiology during famines.

Mac; she replied, "Heck, it can be cured by just eating the bun!" (Judy L. Cameron, personal communication). Preindustrial farming women may not eat much, but in my experience they rarely miss a meal, even if it is just a fire-baked tuber or a small bowl of rice. More recent research on monkeys suggests that these effects may have less to do with energy balance itself and more to do with the stress response associated with sudden, negative changes in energy balance, whether associated with food limitation or an increase in physical activity (Bethea *et al.*, 2013). These findings suggest that we need to rethink the link between ovarian function and under-nutrition.

That such a link exists is, in my estimation, very probable but its quantitative effects on fertility are largely unknown. But even if we cannot yet arrive at a conclusion about the absolute effect of hunger on fertility, we can make a tentative judgment about its *relative* effects on fertility in comparison to mortality by examining the demographic response to known famine conditions. Two cases will suffice. Figure 8.10 shows changes in mortality and fertility that occurred during the Finnish famine of 1865–9, which has been studied in great detail by the historical demographer Kari Pitkänen (1993, 2002). The crop failure of 1869 was particularly dire and came on top of two lesser food shortages in 1866–7 (earlier shortages often intensify later ones, primarily by reducing the carry-over of stored grain for eating and sowing). The famine of 1869 was severe enough to induce a fertility response, which lagged peak mortality by about nine months, consistent with either a direct biological effect on the rate of conception *or* postponement of marriages during the crisis. The apparent rebound in births following the 1869 famine may have been caused by an upswing in previously postponed marriages, or it could have been attributable to the many infant and early childhood deaths during the famine that terminated breastfeeding and its contraceptive effects and thus left an unusually high proportion of women in a fecund state once the famine was resolved – a mortality effect and not really a fertility effect at all. But, whatever its cause, the decline in fertility was small compared to the increase in mortality.[23] Moreover, the mortality response to the famine was, I suspect, almost entirely a result of the direct physiological effects of hunger, whereas the fertility response almost certainly combined both biological and behavioral factors. But even ignoring this issue, it is clear at least in this case that profound, famine-level under-nutrition has a much larger effect on mortality than on fertility.

A second case is shown in Figure 8.11, which clarifies certain questions but obscures others. From 1895 to 1898 there was a series of severe food shortages culminating in outright famine in the state of Punjab, then part of the British Raj. Trends in the monthly average price of the staple grain crop jowar (*Sorghum vulgare*)

---

[23] This comparison is further confused by a difference in the number of people at risk of experiencing each of the two events: deaths occur at all ages, whereas births occur only to a much narrower age group of adult females. But in fact most excess deaths during famine also occur in a very narrow age range, i.e. among youngsters and the elderly (Watkins and Menken, 1985; Ó Grada, 2009). Thus, this complicating factor is unlikely to have a very marked effect on the comparison.

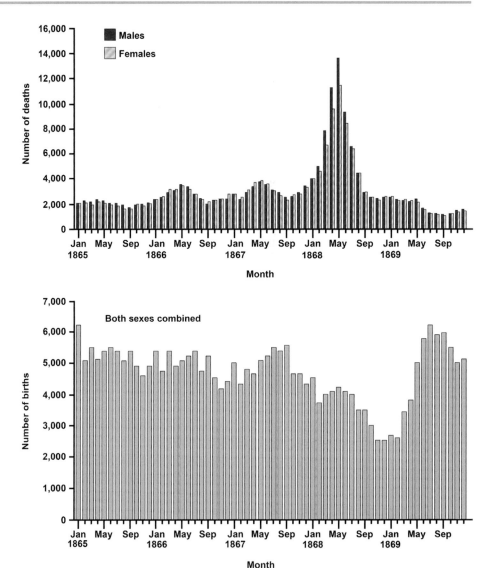

Figure 8.10 The monthly number of deaths (by sex) and births (sexes combined) in regions of Finland affected by the famine of 1865–9. The total monthly number of deaths (both male and female) is roughly double the number for either sex alone. It is that total number that should be compared to the total number of births. Note too the large difference in the scale of the y-axes in the two panels: all the changes in fertility fit well within the bottom half of the mortality panel. From Pitkänen (2002: 71), by permission of Oxford University Press, USA.

track the course of the crisis. At the peak of the famine in 1897, the demographic effects of hunger were blunted by the widespread provision of food relief by the state and colonial governments. But the periods of severe food shortage on either side of the peak tell the story. The top portion of Figure 8.11 shows two indices of fertility and mortality across the famine period. The mortality index (MI) shows the percent

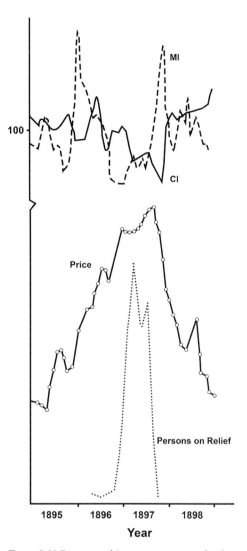

100

Figure 8.11 Demographic consequences of a famine in the Punjab lasting from 1895 to 1898. Shown are monthly trends in the price of the staple grain jowar, the number of people on poor relief, and the mortality index (MI) and "conception" index (CI). MI is computed against the average baseline mortality during a period of five years before the famine (baseline MI = 100). CI, which refers to legitimate births only (i.e. marital fertility), is computed from live births in a similar way, but back-dated by nine months to reflect fertile conceptions rather than births *per se*. This back-dating conflates the total number of conceptions with the number of pregnancies lost through intrauterine mortality. Redrawn from Maharatna (1996: 99), by permission of Oxford University Press, USA.

change in number of deaths relative to average baseline mortality (MI = 100) calculated for the five years leading up to the famine. The so-called conception index (CI) is computed in similar fashion from legitimate live births, but then back-dated by nine months to reflect the time of conception. But it is important to note that the CI does not really refer to all conceptions but only *fertile* ones (those that ultimately result in live births), thus confounding actual conceptions and intrauterine mortality. The *y*-axis provides no scale for the percent changes in vital rates (or anything else), but then we are only interested in the relative responses in fertility and mortality anyway. Usefully, the data on fertility in Figure 8.11 all pertain to fertility within intact marriages, thus removing the effects of marital disruption and postponement of marriage. And there does seem to be a distinct trough in the CI just after the absolute peak in jowar prices, at a time when food relief was declining rapidly (plus a possible postfamine rebound in fertility). But the overall message of Figure 8.11 is similar to what we took away from the Great Finnish Famine: there may well have been an impact of famine on fertility, but at its greatest it was small relative to the impact on mortality.

These aggregative comparisons cannot possibly answer all our questions, especially about households. But both patterns, which accord with other studies of the demographic effects of famine (Ó Gráda, 2009), suggest that death is much more sensitive to extreme hunger than birth. Under-nutrition may not be the sole factor responsible for these effects, but it is almost certain to be a major one, especially in the case of mortality.

Hunger and Migration

The final force of population change is, of course, migration. Alas, this section must be brief because the effects of nonfamine levels of under-nutrition on individual decisions to move are almost completely unstudied. Mass movements during famines are common in the modern developing world (Findley, 1994; Findley *et al.*, 1995), and we know quite a lot about them (see Ó Gráda, 2009:81–9, for a review). Because these modern movements require trains, trucks and reasonably good roads, as well as refugee centers, the occurrence of famine-induced mass migration in the preindustrial world is more doubtful. But the real question concerns smaller-scale movements in response to normal day-to-day hunger, about which we know next to nothing for either the modern or the preindustrial world. In the modern developing world, *poverty* often motivates migration, especially rural–urban and transnational migration (Findley and Salif, 1998), but is poverty sufficiently well correlated with under-nutrition that we can call this movement a response to food supply *per se*? And do the much more restricted opportunities for long-distance migration observed in preindustrial communities (see Chapter 1) allow for migration to be an effective response to food shortages? We don't really know but it would be worth trying to find out.

Population Regulation at the Household Level?

In Chapter 4, I suggested that most subsistence farming populations are limited by food and that the resulting density-dependent population regulation mostly involves early childhood mortality, which, in its turn, is caused mainly by infectious diseases taking advantage of young immune systems that have been impaired by under-nutrition. Density-dependent fertility and migration may also be important, but early childhood mortality, I believe, is the strongest and most general mechanism regulating the size of traditional farming communities. The present chapter has outlined the major reasons I take this view. But it has done little to place the mechanism in the context of the subsistence farming household. In the following chapters I argue that density-dependent changes in early childhood mortality arise in part from the internal dynamics of the household demographic enterprise itself, suggesting in turn that the constellation of variables linking food supply and childhood death operate partly, perhaps predominantly, at the level of households. If true, this all means that the tendency toward demographic stasis that appears to be characteristic of many preindustrial farming communities arises in good part from what is going on inside households. Forces acting at more aggregated levels are almost certainly involved too, but I would guess they pale in comparison with household-level processes. In addition, since separate households are often out of sync with each other in their internal dynamics, those dynamics and their interactions with both food production and dietary adequacy can lead to the demographic and economic differentiation of households even in the absence of institutionalized social or political differences. The following chapters explore these ideas.

9   The Nature of Traditional Farm Work and the Household Labor Force

Because contemporary writers on manpower in prehistory have little direct experience of manual labour they often grossly overestimate average human strength.   – B. Cotterell and J. Kamminga (1990: 24)

> Hoe, rice plant, midday heat,
> Sweat falls on black earth.
> Who knows how a bowl is filled?
> Each grain from hard work comes.
>   – Li Shen (AD 772–845)[1]

To feed a family of five, a farmer must work like an ox. But to feed six people, even a whipped ox would refuse to work.   – Old saying from Shansi, Northern China (modified from Gourou, 1975:116)

In every preindustrial farming operation, some of the most important and insurmountable limits to a household's food supply are imposed by the size and demographic makeup of the work force it can muster to produce it. Apart from the energy for photosynthesis provided by the Sun, the energy for food production in subsistence farming is almost entirely biological in nature – mostly human and secondarily animal (in some places), with wind or water power very occasionally playing a minor role. Almost universally, the labor needed for household food production is organized by the household itself and is indeed made up overwhelmingly of its own members. Granted, as will be discussed in more detail in Chapter 12, voluntary work groups that draw in members of several neighboring households may be mobilized at certain times of year for particularly heavy tasks that need to be done quickly, often in return for some kind of payment in kind (perhaps a part of the harvest, a feast, or a beer-drinking party) or a promise of reciprocation; in addition, individual labor contributions by close relatives living in nearby households may be requested on a day-to-day basis. In this chapter and the next, however, I shall make the model assumption – one of those tactical "lies" discussed in Chapter 1 – that labor on the household farm is provided *exclusively* by the household itself. I do this to show some of the built-in limitations to household-based food production,

---

[1] Based on the translation by Renee Liang (www.thebigidea.co.nz/news/blogs/talkwrite/2009/nov/63250-cultural-storytellers-tusiate-avia), who also corrects a common misattribution of the poem to Chang Chen-Pao.

Figure 9.1 A husband and wife hoeing a field for planting sorghum, Sukumaland, Tanganyika, c. 1950. Note baby in sling. As Malcolm (1953: 38) notes, "the vast bulk of the regular agricultural work is done without assistance by each family on its own holding." From Malcolm (1953: plate opposite p. 33), by permission of Oxford University Press, USA.

limitations that require special social arrangements – the expenditure of "social capital" – if they are to be overcome. The idea that households are wholly on their own when it comes to farm labor may be a tactical lie, but the truth is that most labor in traditional farming *is* provided by the household that runs the farm (Figure 9.1). The subsistence-oriented household provides by far the largest contribution of non-solar energy for its own food production.

The preindustrial household labor force is characterized by several features that are germane to this chapter and the next.

- The labor force is small, often no more than two adults and perhaps one or two older children. Because it is small, the labor force is subject to proportionately large random fluctuations in size and composition; illness, death, or out-migration of just one person can have a major impact on available labor.[2] In addition, the small labor force may make it difficult to organize an efficient division of labor – by sex, age or anything else. And, of course, the small household labor force can provide only a very limited total productive capacity. The hiring of unrelated farm laborers may speed the process, but this is rare in subsistence farming – with the

[2] The unanticipated death of an adult producer, for example, can be analogous to wiping out as much as 50 percent of a nation's productive capacity in an instant, a feat that saturation bombing was unable to achieve in World War II.

notable exception of the northwest European pattern of life-course servitude described in Chapter 7.

- The supply of household labor changes according to the stage of the household's demographic life cycle, simply because the size and composition of the household change over its life cycle. As will be discussed in Chapter 10, the *demand* for farm labor in food production also changes in broadly predictable ways over the household life cycle.
- Within the limits set by the household's size and life cycle, farm labor is allocated according to the customary division of labor by age and sex, as well as the need to invest labor as efficiently as possible.
- The energy expended in household labor (whether human or animal) is provided almost entirely by the food grown on the household's own land. The net energy content of the food produced by the household must be discounted for this unavoidable expenditure.

From Seed to Stomach – What Constitutes Farm Work?

When thinking about traditional farm work, it is important to recall one fundamental fact: When the household is the principal unit of both food production and food consumption, the *growing, processing, cooking, distribution* and *eating* of food are but phases of a single integrated process of getting nutrients into the bellies of close kin and dependents. The "agricultural" sphere, the purely productive part of the enterprise, should not be thought of as separate from the "domestic" sphere – the domain of economic activity most oriented toward family food consumption and child care, which are of course the whole point of the endeavor. Our view of farm labor as a part of the household demographic enterprise should therefore cover everything from food production to food consumption and beyond – including field clearing, tillage, sowing, weeding, manuring, harvesting and transport, but also food processing, storage, and distribution, haulage of fuel and water, cooking, eating, carry-over of seed and, perhaps most importantly, child care. In subsistence farming, there is no gap between the agricultural and the domestic – both are essential parts of the household demographic enterprise.

The single most important implication of this perspective is that the work of female household members is accorded more importance than is often the case in studies of traditional agriculture. Female labor, compared to male labor, is disproportionately "domestic" and thus (to some authors) not of any particular *economic* significance. But, as part of the household demographic enterprise, domestic work is as essential as any other farm work – and is often equally arduous (Figure 9.2). Giving women due credit for their work means that, as a general rule, men and women make roughly equal contributions to traditional farm work, at least in terms of hours of work if not sheer brute strength (Haswell, 1985). Similarly, the labor of older children (Figure 9.3) and the elderly (Figure 9.4), while often less physically demanding than the work of younger adults, should not be ignored when estimating the household's total energy budget.

Figure 9.2 (Left) Sisters pounding cassava into flour, Ushi, Northern Rhodesia 1959. (Right) Yanoama woman returning home after a visit to a neighboring village, Parima Highlands, Venezuela *c.* 1970. She carries food, building material (leaves for roofing), cooking pots, baskets and other personal belongings. A third child (partly obscured) follows her on foot. From Kay (1964: plate 6), Smole (1976: 171), the latter by permission of the University of Texas Press.

The Physiology of Preindustrial Farm Work

How Hard do Traditional Farmers Work?

It is sometimes claimed that traditional farmers, especially shifting cultivators, work less than we do – an assertion that is made with even greater conviction about hunter-gatherers. With respect to *hours* of work across the course of a year, the claim may have some merit (although I doubt we have enough comparative data to support it with any confidence). But before we jump to the conclusion that hunter-gatherers or shifting cultivators led enviable lives of leisure – that they lived in "the original affluent society" or were blessed with a Zen-like disdain for the accumulation of material wealth that so obsesses us foolish Westerners (Sahlins, 1972) – we need to take three things into consideration. First, as argued in Chapter 3, traditional farming (I set hunting-gathering aside as irrelevant to this book, although I suspect the same was true of it) seems to have been characterized by sharp declines in the marginal productivity of labor (see Figure 3.12). If so, there was nothing to be gained by working beyond the point at which absolute yields reached their peak. Thus, if our ancestors worked short hours, it was not because they could achieve affluence, or at least satisfy their limited desires, by doing so, but because they could not wrest more from a recalcitrant environment by working longer hours. As Kaplan (2000) comments, there is a difference between leisure and enforced inactivity. Second, the input of labor needed for traditional farming varied widely by time of the year (see Chapter 11). The farming household had to have been capable (perhaps with some

Figure 9.3 Children's labor in traditional farming. (Top) Mayan boys transporting maize from milpa to village with their father and uncle, northern Yucatan, Mexico. (Bottom) Children helping to single neeps (thin out turnips), Orkney, Scotland *c.* 1900. Informants tell us that singling neeps was especially hard work. From Kramer (2005: 99), by permission of Harvard University press; Tom Kent (1910).

help) of meeting seasonal peaks in the demand for labor – but that almost necessarily means that its members did not need to work long hours to satisfy the much lower demand during the rest of the year (Bleiberg *et al.*, 1981; Brun *et al.*, 1981; Stone *et al.*, 1990). Indeed, development economists used to fret over "seasonal under-employment" as a near-universal structural problem plaguing farmers in the developing world (Leibenstein, 1957; Fisk, 1971; Cleave, 1974; Booth and Sundrum, 1985). Third, if it really is true that traditional farmers worked comparatively short

Figure 9.4 "After seventy years, toil may not cease" (King, 1911: 430). An elderly woman and man doing household craft production (spinning and ginning of cotton), rural Japan *c.* 1900. From King (1911: 431).

hours, they may still have worked so hard when they *did* work that they might have found the idea of sitting behind a desk staring at a computer screen all day long pretty attractive. Perhaps we should not be too quick to abandon our day jobs in order to become fulltime subsistence farmers.

So how hard was traditional farm work when it did in fact take place? How much energy had to be expended per unit time (say, per minute or hour or day) in performing necessary farming tasks? This is a difficult question to answer, both because only a few field investigations have been done under conditions that approximate traditional farming and because the methods available for measuring energy expenditure in remote field sites are not terribly reliable (see Dufour and Piperata, 2008). In the laboratory, energy expenditure can be measured by multiple instruments with exquisite reliability and accuracy on subjects using a treadmill or stationary bicycle, the speed and resistance of which can be controlled by the investigator. But in the field things are more difficult. The usual method is to measure oxygen consumption and/or heart rate as proxies for energy costs – and indeed those variables have fairly simple and repeatable relationships to energy expenditure (for technical details, see Ulijaszek, 1995: 62–74). For many years, measurement of oxygen consumption using a backpack-style respirometer (Figure 9.5) appears to have been the method of choice among fieldworkers studying the energetics of traditional farm work, and most of the results reviewed here were obtained by that method. Unfortunately, although there was a surge in such studies during the 1960s and 1970s, when more compact and lightweight respirometers became available, they seemed to have tailed off in more recent years, perhaps as machines have

Max Planck Respirometer

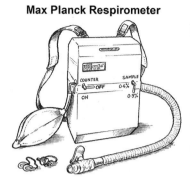
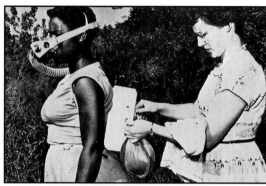

Figure 9.5 The field measurement of energy expenditure using a backpack-style respirometer to monitor oxygen uptake, tropical Africa c. 1965. The technology has changed little except for further miniaturization, a digital display, and computerized data logging. It should be noted that even the most compact modern respirometers are still somewhat bulky and heavy and may interfere to some degree with normal work behavior. From Durnin and Passmore (1967: 21, plate IIIa), by permission of Heinemann Publishing.

replaced more and more human effort in agriculture throughout the world. Most studies of the energetics of "work" are now done on athletes.[3]

Based on the small number of detailed bioenergetic studies that have been done over the years on human work in traditional or developing-world farming, specific farm tasks seem to have ranged from the light to the onerous (Table 9.1). Depending on the mode of farming in question, tasks involved in clearing and preparing fields (tree felling, clearing brush, hoeing, ridging) and in harvesting (binding and stacking sheaves of grain, hay mowing) tend to be especially heavy, although more day-to-day chores such as weeding can also involve heavy work. On the other hand, weeding, unlike clearing or harvesting, need not be done on a tight schedule and may therefore allow for more periods of rest in the field or even whole days of leisure.

To provide a clearer idea of the limits to human labor, it is perhaps more telling to scale energy expended in work to the individual's basal metabolism rate (BMR). Figure 9.6, which is very approximate when it comes to absolute numbers (which would vary among subjects anyway), highlights the inevitable inefficiency of the net energy made available for metabolic processes (including work but excluding digestion) compared to food energy ingested. It also shows that the energy available for work itself plateaus as other limiting factors such as body mass, cross-sectional muscle area, heat build-up, water loss and lack of training come into play. At its upper limit, sustained aerobic work requires about the same amount of metabolically

---

[3] This unfortunate state of affairs is beginning to change (for reviews of recent research see Dufour and Piperata, 2008; Snodgrass, 2012). In addition, field studies of farm work are likely to be reinvigorated in the near future by new technical developments, such as validation studies currently being done on combing heart-rate monitors and body-motion sensors and on the doubly-labelled water method as comparatively simple ways to monitor energy expenditure (Cole and Coward, 1992; Crouter et al., 2004; Brage et al., 2005; Assah et al., 2011).

Table 9.1 Estimated energy expenditure in traditional farming tasks. The categorization of activities by work intensity follows the guidelines developed by Durnin and Passmore (1967: 47). From Fox (1953), Phillips (1954), van Loon (1963), Durnin and Passmore (1967: 66–7).

Region	Farm activity	kcal min^{-1}	Intensity of work
Europe	hay mowing with a scythe	5.6–10.2	moderate–heavy
	binding sheaves (men)	6.2–8.6	heavy
	binding sheaves (women)	3.0–4.9	light–moderate
	stacking sheaves	5.1–8.4	moderate–heavy
	loading sheaves	5.0–6.5	moderate
	threshing (men)	4.2–6.0	light–moderate
	threshing (women)	3.8–5.5	moderate
	plowing	5.2–7.8	moderate
Africa	clearing bush and scrub	5.8–8.4	moderate–heavy
	hoeing (women)	4.8–6.8	moderate–heavy
	weeding	3.8–7.8	light–heavy
	planting groundnuts	3.1–4.5	light–moderate
	ridging, deep digging	5.5–15.2	moderate–unduly heavy
	tree felling	8.4	heavy
	head carrying (20–35 kg loads)	3.2–5.6	light–moderate
India	hay mowing with machete	5.1–7.9	moderate–heavy
	watering	4.1–7.5	light–moderate
	weeding, digging, transplanting	2.3–9.1	light–heavy

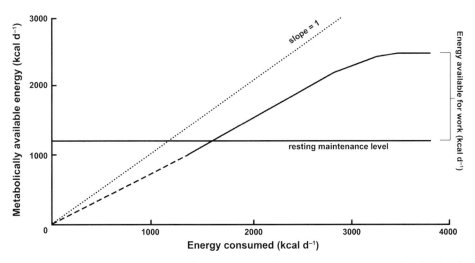

Figure 9.6 Schematic representation of the relationship between energy consumed as food and energy available for sustained aerobic work in a hypothetical adult male (i.e. no cost of growth, pregnancy or lactation). *Dotted line*, theoretical maximum if the conversion of food energy to metabolically available energy were perfectly efficient, which it is not. *Broken line*, metabolically available energy too low to sustain life. Note that brief bursts of work, especially those involving anaerobic metabolism, can reach levels of energy expenditure substantially higher than shown here, but only for short periods before a spell of rest is needed.

Table 9.2 Energy costs of various physical activities, including those involved with traditional farming. From James and Schofield (1990), Pasquet and Koppert (1993), Ulijaszek (1995: 35–40).

Activity	Physical activity ratio[a]
Sitting at rest	1.2
Walking on level at 1–2 km hr^{-1}	2.3
Carrying 20–30 kg load	3.1
Climbing stairs with 11–16 kg load	6.8
Chopping wood with machete	3.5
Clearing bush	4.4
Field ridging	8.3
Hoeing	6.5
Planting groundnuts	3.1
Planting manioc	1.9
Harvesting manioc	3.5
Peeling manioc	1.9
Pounding manioc	2.6
Sieving manioc	2.6
Pounding rice	5.6
Weeding, moderate crop of weeds	5.0
Timber cutting with steel axe	5.1
Pulling a rickshaw with 180 kg load	10.4

[a] Energy expenditure as a multiple of basal metabolism rate.

available energy as the BMR itself. In other words, the *gross* energy cost of labor, which necessarily includes basal metabolism if the worker is to stay alive, can be sustained without frequent rest and snacking only if it is less than about twice the cost of basal (resting) metabolism by itself.

Table 9.2 lists the so-called physical activity ratio (energy expended as a multiple of the basal metabolism rate) for several activities either involved in traditional farming or likely to be familiar to the reader. Even walking at a moderate pace on a flat surface falls near the upper limit of sustained aerobic work. More arduous tasks such as hoeing, ridging and pounding grain can be done only in short bursts that exhaust anaerobic energy (the ATP-PC and lactic acid systems) and require very frequent rest breaks; in the course of such tasks, individual bursts of work may last only about 90 seconds before muscles need to be reoxygenated and lactic acid cleared from their tissues. If we average the physical activity ratio over an entire work day, including periods of rest and eating, we get the results shown in Table 9.3. Most of these activity ratios fall between about 1.5 to 2.0, which suggests that, over the day as a whole, traditional farmers are often working near the upper limit of sustained energy expenditure (see Dufour and Piperata, 2008).

For any task that involves a high energetic rate during an active burst of work, time in the field spent resting must be considered a necessary component since frequents rests are essential to maintain the overall rate of work. In rural Gambia,

Table 9.3 Mean daily physical activity (as multiple of basal metabolism rate) for adults involved in traditional farming. From Viteri *et al.* (1971), de Guzman *et al.* (1974), Norgan *et al.* (1974), Montgomery and Johnson (1977), Brun *et al.* (1979, 1981), Bleiberg *et al.* (1980, 1981), Schutz *et al.* (1980), Ferro-Luzzi (1985).

Location	Sex	Sample size	Mean or range of age (yrs)	Type of work	Physical activity ratio
Upper Volta, Africa	F	12	31	Farming, rainy season	1.7
	F	12	31	Farming, dry season	2.1
	F	14	31	Harvesting	1.5
	M	16	36	Farming, rainy season	2.2
	M	23	36	Farming, dry season	1.6
New Guinea (Kaul)	F[a]	23	23	Shifting cultivation	1.6
	F[a]	17	40	Shifting cultivation	1.4
	F[b]	7	27	Shifting cultivation	1.5
	M	19	18–29	Shifting cultivation	1.7
	M	32	30+	Shifting cultivation	1.4
New Guinea (Lufa)	F[a]	31	23	Shifting cultivation	1.8
	F[a]	7	36	Shifting cultivation	1.7
	F	7	25	Shifting cultivation	1.8
	M	28	18–25	Shifting cultivation	1.6
	M	15	30+	Shifting cultivation	1.7
Peru (Machiguenga)	F	20	25	Shifting cultivation, rainy season	1.7
	F	8	27	Shifting cultivation, dry season	1.7
	M	15	30	Shifting cultivation	1.9
	M	8	25	Shifting cultivation	2.3
Guatemala	F	6	23	Peasant farming	1.6
	F[c]	18	28	Peasant farming	1.6
	M	18	30	Hired agricultural labor	2.3
Philippines (Laguna)	M	9	28	Rice farming	2.2
Iran (Varanin)	M	10	39	Hired agricultural labor, spring	2.2
	M	14	38	Hired agricultural labor, summer	2.3
	M	10	35	Hired agricultural labor, autumn	2.3
	M	12	38	Hired agricultural labor, winter	1.7

[a] Nonpregnant, nonlactating.
[b] Pregnant.
[c] Lactating.

for example, the energy expended during active work appears to be roughly correlated with the percentage of time in the field spent resting (Table 9.4), although the relationship is no doubt complicated by the worker's body size, need for water, and posture during work, as well as other factors such as ambient temperature and humidity. With reference to female rice cultivators in Gambia, Margaret Haswell (1985: 27–8) argues that

the different rates of energy cost for each [agri]cultural operation are compensated for by the time spent resting in the field. The net effect of this is to hold more or less constant the energy cost per unit of time [i.e. time spent actively working plus rest and meal time] of all agricultural tasks involved in the production of rice. Clearly this solution prolongs the time taken to undertake the more energetically expensive tasks such as hoeing heavy clay soils prior to transplanting rice seedlings for which activity the time spent resting was 41 percent, compared with only 9 percent when performing the relatively light task of harvesting. This method of resolving energy needs adds a further dimension to the problem however, that of the time constraint imposed by scarcity of season during which a particular task can be undertaken. Traditionally it is the combination of these two factors which has strongly motivated societies to organize their resources in human labour by allocating clear cut functions specifically to men or women and also to divide many of the tasks according to age-sex groups.

Net Gain in Food Energy for Each Unit of Energy Expended in Farm Work

If traditional farmers put a lot of energy into the production of food for their families, how much energy do they produce in return? Very few figures are available, largely because of the difficulties of estimating both the energy expended and the quantity and caloric value of the food produced in the field. For Lamotrek Atoll in the Pacific, Lawton (1973) estimated the ratio of net food energy yield to energy expended in producing that food to be approximately 18–19, which would appear to be a very high figure (it is in fact the highest estimated rate of return I could find in the literature on traditional farming).[4] But this community's staple starches are provided largely by permanent tree crops (breadfruit and coconut), which require little labor once they are established and are located next to house plots so that transport costs are minimized. In Table 1.1 we saw that the Iban, who grow dry rice by shifting cultivation, had a ratio of about 11, but this figure excludes energy expended on transport. Estimates typical of a traditional farm system containing a mixture of cultivation types of differing intensities are shown in Table 9.5, which suggests an overall mean return ratio of eight or nine, with transport accounting for about one-eighth of the net energy expended. Note, however, that these figures ignore the energy costs on the "domestic" side of the operation (food processing, haulage of fuel and water, etc.), as well as the fact that something like a quarter to a third of the

---

[4] In modern mechanized farming, the return on human labor by itself is on the order of 2000–3000, although if we include machines and fossil fuels (as we should) the ratio drops to four or five. Modern farming is powered by petroleum, not by food.

Table 9.4 Energy expenditure and time in the field spent working versus resting, various staple crops, Genieri Village, Gambia, West Africa. Time spent chasing away birds and monkeys is not tabulated, since work rate is set by the animals, not the workers. From Haswell (1985: 100–3). Reproduced from M. R. Haswell (1985) *Energy for Subsistence*, 2nd edn, London: Macmillan, by permission of Palgrave Macmillan Scholarly. Reproduced with permission of the Licensor through PLSclear.

Crop and activity	kcal min^{-1} of work	Percent of time in field spent:	
		working	resting
Adult males (mean wt. 58.8 kg)			
Groundnuts (*Arachis hypogaea*)			
Clearing land before planting	5.3	82	18
Ridging and planting	6.2	84	16
Planting on flat	3.4	83	17
Weeding	4.3	79	21
Lifting	4.8	70	30
Windrowing	3.8	61	39
Stacking	3.7	96	4
Beating	4.6	67	33
Winnowing	2.9	67	33
Late millet (*Pennisetum typhoides* var.)			
Clearing	5.4	82	18
Planting	3.4	83	17
Weeding	4.3	83	17
Harvesting:			
flattening stems	3.1	90	10
cutting heads	3.3	91	9
bundling	3.3	91	9
Early millet (*Pennisetum typhoides* var.)			
Clearing	5.0	82	18
Planting	3.4	83	17
Weeding	4.3	83	17
Harvesting:			
flattening stems	3.1	90	10
cutting heads	3.3	91	9
bundling	3.3	91	9
Sorghum (*Sorghum* spp.)			
Clearing	5.3	82	18
Ridging and planting	6.2	84	16
Weeding	4.3	83	17
Harvesting	3.2	90	10
Maize (*Zea mays*)			
Clearing	5.3	82	18
Ridging and planting	6.2	84	16
Weeding	4.3	83	17
Harvesting	3.2	90	10

Table 9.4 (cont.)

Crop and activity	kcal min^{-1} of work	Percent of time in field spent:	
		working	resting
Adult females (mean wt. 51.6 kg)			
Findi (*Digitaria exilis*)			
Broadcasting and covering	3.7	89	11
Harvesting	2.9	90	10
Swamp rice (*Oryza sativa*)			
Hoeing	5.1	59	41
Pulling grass	3.9	73	27
Transplanting	4.2	75	25
Harvesting	3.0	91	9
Upland rice (*Oryza sativa*)			
Manuring	3.0	82	18
Hoeing and broadcasting	5.3	58	42
Weeding	3.6	71	29
Thinning	3.4	71	29
Lifting	3.4	77	23
Harvesting	2.8	91	9

energy yield must be reserved as seed for next year. They also ignore losses of stored food to insect and rodent pests and to rot. If the energetic returns on work in Table 9.5 average around eight to nine, that does *not* mean that each worker can feed eight or nine people in a normal year. In addition, these figures are aggregate estimates and therefore do not reflect variation attributable to household-level factors such as the amount and quality of available land, the household's life-cycle stage, or its ratio of consumers to producers. Nor do they reflect the fact that crops are grown and valued not just for their energy content but also as sources of other nutrients and for their palatability.

Are Traditional Farmers Efficient Workers?

Classical economists assumed that people, being entirely rational, omniscient and in perfect control of their behavior and environment, would organize things to minimize production costs, including energy inputs – an assumption sometimes called the *principle of least effort* (after Zipf, 1949). A similar assumption has been made specifically about traditional farmers (Schultz, 1964; Makhijani and Poole, 1975; Barlett, 1980a). For a variety of reasons – including antipathy toward classical economics – this idea has come under heavy criticism in recent years. But I would argue that an assumption of optimal efficiency can be justified in the case of traditional farm work – *if* we exercise due caution. And caution is definitely needed because people waste all kinds of energy in nonproductive activities such as playing, dancing, singing, drumming and fighting when food is abundant and work

Table 9.5 Summary of the ratios of food energy produced to energy expended in subsistence farming by microenvironment and crop, Genieri Village, Gambia, West Africa 1949–50. Ratios are shown both with and without transport costs (including walking to and from farm plots) included. Transport reduces the net energy gain by about one-eighth on average. From Haswell (1985: 28).

Microhabitat and crop	Percent of total area cultivated	Ratio of energy gained to energy expended:		Percent of total human labor energy costs
		including transport	omitting transport	
Guinea savanna grey soils (above scarp)[a]				
Late millet	12.0	8.1	10.9	7.2
Grey soils and ochre-brown sandy loams (below scarp)[b]				
Early millet	1.8	12.4	12.4	0.9
Sorghum	1.7	13.9	15.1	0.4
Digitaria exilis	11.3	16.8	18.2	1.3
Maize	0.8	13.4	13.4	0.8
Groundnuts	35.5	14.7	15.6	28.1
River flats, upland and swamp[c]				
Wet rice	36.9	5.3	6.1	61.3
Net energy gain ratio (weighted mean)		**8.4**	**9.6**	
Σ	100.0	100.0		100.0

[a] Highest elevation and greatest distance from domicile. Generally low quality soils poor in organic matter, deficient in phosphorus and calcium and tending to acidity. Cropped for three to four years and then left to long fallow. Least intensive form of cultivation.

[b] Intermediate elevation and closest to domicile. Good quality, well-drained soils, periodically manured. Cropped annually for several years and then subject to short fallow.

[c] Lowest elevation and moderately distant from domicile. Annually flooded or permanently waterlogged grassland just inside mangrove swamp forest lining the bank of the Gambia River. Rich but salt-contaminated soils (the Gambia is tidal and brackish at this point despite being 190 km inland from the ocean) farmed annually for periods between 15–50 years, followed by brief fallows. The local strain of wet rice (*Oryza sativa* var.) is moderately salt-tolerant. Wet rice is the most intensively cultivated crop, requiring careful soil preparation, frequent weeding and transplanting from nursery beds.

is light – this despite the fact that they could store some of that energy as body fat to draw upon in leaner seasons (Johnson and Behrens, 1982). Moreover, even if farmers were to strive for *perfect* efficiency, the unpredictability of the environment would make it impossible to achieve anyway. Fortunately a certain amount of wastage is tolerable except under unusually stringent conditions (during food shortages, for example, traditional farmers often curtail most nonproductive activities and spend a considerable amount of nonwork time resting in the shade). But when it comes to hard, necessary, but unentertaining physical work – what the great Russian agronomist Aleksandr Chayanov (1925) called "drudgery" (*tyagostnost*) – traditional farmers do seem to strive for something like optimal efficiency, even if they are rarely able to achieve it. Energy is finite and only a limited amount of it can be invested in productive work *per se*. If you want to stay alive under subsistence conditions, you might want to try to allocate your productive energies as prudently as possible within the constraints imposed by the physical environment (see E. A. Smith, 1979, for a general evolutionary argument).

There is, in fact, ample empirical evidence (admittedly not often from traditional farmers) that people do try, consciously or unconsciously, to minimize drudgery. For example, a series of experiments performed by the Hungarian ergonomist Gavriel Salvendy back in the early 1970s found that people doing unrewarding, repetitive work tend to settle spontaneously into the optimal rate of energy expenditure when allowed to do so (Figure 9.7). More recent work has confirmed this finding (Almås-bakk *et al.*, 2000; Sparrow *et al.*, 2000). Another line of evidence concerns what is known as *least-cost pathfinding*: when free to form their own paths between fixed destinations (i.e. when not channeled by such things as sidewalks, walls or "keep off the grass" signs), people on foot routinely find, after a period of exploration to gauge the unevenness of the landscape, pathways that minimize total energy expenditure (see e.g. Rees, 2004). Least-cost pathfinding models have been applied retrospectively to historical trackways, adjusting appropriately for the difference in slopes negotiable by humans on foot or on horseback as opposed to humans in motor vehicles (people and ponies can climb hills that are too steep even for a four-wheel drive vehicle). The fit of the least-cost predictions to old, often abandoned farm trails and trackways is usually very close (de Smith, 2003). Even wild mammals in mountainous landscapes and livestock on hilly pasture have been found to travel along energetically efficient pathways they create for themselves (Reichman and Atchison, 1981; Ganskoop *et al.*, 2000). Hill walkers in Great Britain are often advised to follow sheep tracks.

Some fascinating studies have been done on the energetics and biomechanics of headloading (carrying loads on top of the head or suspended from it) among men and women in traditional farming communities. Women of the Luo and Kikuyu tribes in Kenya, for example, are much more efficient at headloading than are untrained Western subjects (Figure 9.8). They even seem to be able to carry loads up to 20 percent of their own body mass without any measurable increase in energy consumption over unloaded walking (Maloiy *et al.*, 1986). The secret to their efficiency appears to lie in the posture they assume and the gait they use – the special way they walk – during headloading (Heglund *et al.*, 1995). Semiprofessional Nepali porters are even more efficient (Figure 9.9), although they need to take frequent rest stops (Bastien *et al.*, 2005).

Finally, many of the simple agricultural implements and techniques developed by preindustrial farmers can be viewed as genuinely labor-saving devices – devices that reduce energy costs or allow human power to be applied more efficiently – which is

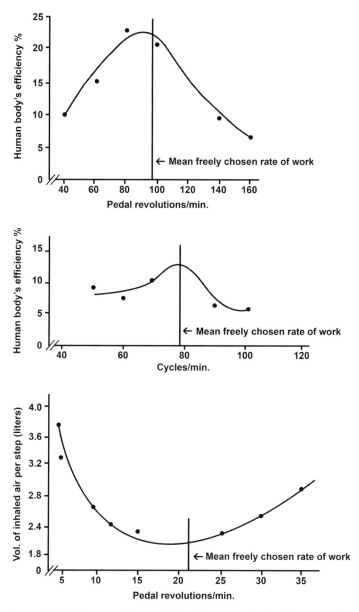

Figure 9.7 Effect of paced (forced, ●) and unpaced (freely chosen) work rate on the efficiency of the human body. (Top) bicycle ergometer; (middle) pump ergometer; (bottom) Harvard step test. Curves are theoretical models fit to the paced results. From Salvendy (1972: 271), by permission from Magyar Tudományos Akadémia.

presumably why they were adopted in the first place. For example, shifting cultivators who need to clear fields out of mature rainforest often spend a few easy minutes making a simple scaffold to raise them above the thick buttress roots of older trees, thereby avoiding several hard hours of chopping (Figure 9.10). Water is surprisingly heavy in the quantities needed for daily household use, and water-lifting devices are

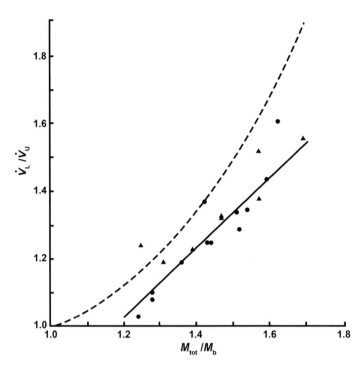

Figure 9.8 The energetics of headloading in African women. Ratio of individual woman's rate of oxygen consumption ($\dot{V}$) during loaded walking (L) to that during unloaded walking (U) plotted against the ratio of total loaded mass ($M_{tot} = M_b$ + load) to unloaded body mass (M_b) for Luo (▲) and Kikuyu (●) women walking at the optimal speed of 3.25 km hr^{-1}. (Broken line) Estimated relationship for untrained US army recruits. Note that African women appear to be able to carry loads up to 20 percent of their own body mass without any measurable increases in oxygen consumption. From Maloiy *et al.* (1986), by permission of Springer Publishing.

common, especially in irrigated farming where mass transfers of water are necessary (Figure 9.11). Hoes not only have blades to bite into soil, but also handles to provide leverage (Figure 9.1). Plows are often adopted because they reduce human labor (Weil, 1970; Pryor, 1985), although the draft animals that pull them seem to be no more efficient at converting food energy into work than are people (see below). In general, it seems that traditional farmers are more than willing to work hard when they have to, but are unashamed to lighten their work load whenever possible. In view of the severely limited supplies of energy available to preindustrial farming, such a "work-shy" attitude seems quite sensible.

Are Traditional Farmers like Well-Trained Athletes?

The efficient use of traditional farm practices and implements often requires a considerable amount of prior training. In Chapter 2, we saw that an older, experienced Iban woman appeared to be more efficient at sowing rice than her younger counterparts (see Table 2.8). As I can attest, use of an old-fashioned scythe or plow by

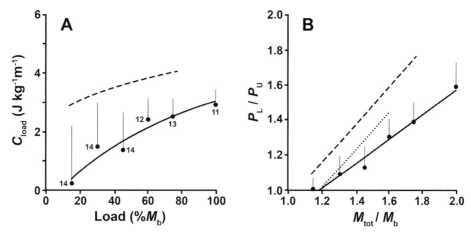

Figure 9.9 The energetics of headloading in male Nepalese porters. (A) Metabolic cost of carrying a 1 kg load over a distance of 1 m (C_{load}) plotted against the total weight of the load relative to individual body mass (M_b). (Circles) Nepalese porters (numbers are sample sizes, vertical lines are error bars, heavy line is a fitted polynomial equation). (B) Gross metabolic increase in power (power loaded, P_L, divided by power unloaded, P_U) plotted against M_{tot}/M_b as defined in Figure 9.8. (Broken lines) untrained US control subjects. (Dotted line) the Luo and Kikuyu women shown in Figure 9.8. From Bastien, G. J., Schepens, B., Willems, P. A. and Heglund, N. C. (2005) Energetics of load carrying in Nepalese porters. *Science*, 308, 1755, reprinted with permission from the American Association for the Advancement of Science.

Figure 9.10 Iban man clearing primary rainforest, Sarawak 1949. Note scaffolding to raise the axe-man above the thick buttress roots. (Inset) A traditional Iban hafted iron adze (*bilong*). From Freeman (1955: 42, plate 7), by permission of Her Majesty's Stationery Office.

Figure 9.11 Traditional water lifter for rice irrigation, China, *c.* 1900. (Insert) Men working the foot treadles on a small water lifter. From King (1911: 79, 300).

Figure 9.12 Using the traditional African short-handled hoe, an implement that requires considerable experience to wield efficiently, especially because of the extreme posture that needs to be assumed. (Left) Kofyar household members ridging a sloping garden, Jos Plateau, Nigeria *c.* 1961. (Right) Zande brothers clearing a garden in second-growth grassland, Southern Sudan *c.* 1950. From Netting (1968: plate IIA), by permission of the University of Washington Press; de Schlippe (1956: plate 24), by permission of Routledge and Kegan Paul Publishers.

a rank amateur is a laughably clumsy and wasteful business.[5] Certain tools, no matter how simple they may seem, can be wielded effectively only by well-trained users (Figure 9.12), and much of the employment of children in traditional farming no doubt has an element of training attached to it. The apparent primitiveness (to our

---

[5] I am indebted to a plowman (whose name, alas, I do not know) at Den Fynske Landsby in Odense, Denmark, for giving me an opportunity to make a laughing stock of myself.

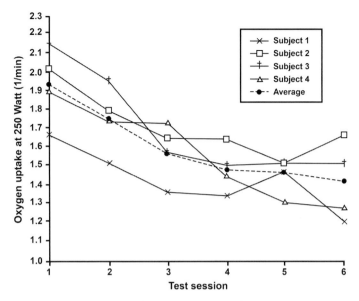

Figure 9.13 Progressive decline in energy expenditure over six training sessions, four subjects working at a constant output of 250 W min^{-1}. From Almåsbakk *et al.* (2000: 247), by permission of Human Kinetics Publishing.

eyes) of preindustrial farming implements masks the real sophistication of their application:

> The technical equipment of agriculture [among the Sonjo of northern Tanzania] is extremely simple, but appears to be adequate for exploiting the arable land. The exploitative technology of the Sonjo requires little comment, though its simplicity is perhaps deceptive. Rather than elaborate equipment, the most important elements are knowledge and sound judgement as to water control, seeds, crops, seasons, and the various operations of cultivation. (Gray, 1963: 156.)

Bioenergetic studies have shown that even simple tasks can be done more efficiently after training (Figure 9.13). But it is important to bear in mind that training, no matter how rigorous and prolonged, cannot increase human work capacity or efficiency without limit (Figure 9.14). Even the well-trained human body remains a frail vessel.

Variation by Age and Sex in Maximum Physiological Work Capacity

It will surprise no one to learn that the total work capacity of humans, as measured by their maximum attainable rate of energy expenditure or oxygen consumption, varies widely according to age and sex (Figure 9.15).[6] But even if unsurprising, this simple biological fact is of fundamental importance for understanding the allocation of subsistence household labor, where age and sex are factors of universal

---

[6] Since measurement of maximum physiological work capacity requires a treadmill, stationary bicycle, or other adjustable ergometric device plus continuous monitoring by electrocardiogram, it is rarely done outside of the laboratory – which is why most results come from Western subjects.

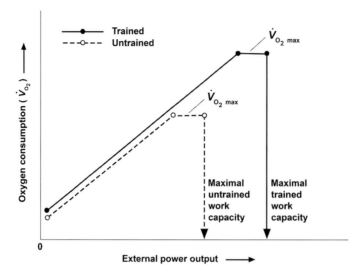

Figure 9.14 Work experience ("training") increases work capacity and maximal power output, but only by a fairly small amount and still subject to declining marginal output. From Brooks *et al.* (1996: 6), by permission of the McGraw-Hill Companies.

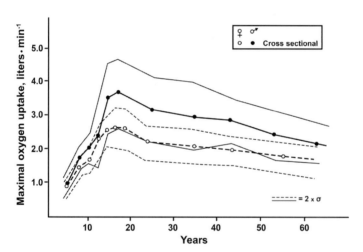

Figure 9.15 Physiological work capacity by age and sex, measured on a treadmill at controlled speeds. Mean values ($\pm 2\sigma$) for healthy, well-nourished Scandinavians of ages 4 to 65 years. From Rodahl (1989: 20), by permission of the Taylor Francis Group.

significance. In both sexes, physiological work capacity (PWC) peaks in early adulthood and declines gradually as age increases, falling by about a third to a half by age 60. In early childhood, both sexes have roughly the same PWC, but they diverge markedly during puberty, as male adolescents lay down greater muscle mass than females. Throughout adulthood, female PWC is about 25 percent lower than male PWC on average.

Although it has never been tested rigorously, the idea that traditional age–sex patterns of labor allocation roughly parallel these changes in PWC would seem to make a great deal of economic sense – although in the course of actual behavior these patterns are likely to be obscured to a greater or lesser degree by individual-level factors. In general, however, we might expect that a farm task that would place a 30-year-old woman (for example) near the upper limit of her PWC and thus performing it inefficiently, slowly, and with a need for frequent rest stops would be done more comfortably, more rapidly, and with lower overall cost by a 35-year-old man – at least on average. But, as shown by the approximate 5th and 95th percentiles in Figure 9.15 (mean $\pm 2\sigma$), there is plenty of overlap in PWC between the sexes, as there is for many phenotypic traits. Hence traditional *norms* about the division of labor by sex (or age) may appear to be absolute, but actual practice may not be (see below). In addition, there is likely to be some degree of variation among populations in the age–sex patterns of PWC for either environmental or genetic reasons (e.g. factors affecting the age at puberty), so we should not take it for granted that the standards illustrated in Figure 9.15 will be appropriate for all human communities. Healthy, well-nourished Scandinavians are not a random sample of the entire human species.

The Effect of Under-Nutrition on Physiological Work Capacity

One factor that is known to have a (potentially) large effect on an individual's work capacity is his or her nutritional status, however defined or measured (see Chapter 8). Perhaps the starkest demonstration of this effect – at least from published, ethically acceptable research – was provided by a study done at the University of Minnesota during World War II (see Keys *et al.*, 1950). In this study, 12 otherwise healthy adult male volunteers were put on semistarvation rations (daily energy intake 1570 kcal, with 50 grams of protein and 30 grams of fat) for 12 weeks while under medical supervision; during that time they lost an average of 24 percent of their body mass and 28 percent of their PWC (Keys *et al.*, 1950: 716). Their actual unpaced work performance, as measured by a standard fitness test, declined by about 82 percent (Figure 9.16), probably reflecting a loss of motivation as well as a decline in PWC *per se*. All these changes were completely reversed over the course of 20 weeks of dietary rehabilitation.

The Minnesota experiment involved a fairly extreme form of under-feeding, and its results may not reflect the "normal" under-nutrition observed in many rural preindustrial communities. What is perhaps a more pertinent study (albeit of urban dwellers) was conducted in Cali, Colombia, on chronically under-nourished local men (Spurr, 1984, 1988). The study classified 47 subjects according to their weight for height, serum albumin level, and daily creatinine excretion (scaled to height) into three groups – mildly, intermediately, and severely malnourished – as shown in Table 9.6.[7] The groups were then compared to each other and to a control group of

---

[7] Serum albumin and urinary creatinine serve as proxy measures for dietary protein intake.

Table 9.6 A study of aerobic work capacity and nutritional status in Cali, Colombia: selection criterion and observed mean ± standard deviation of physical variables in adult male subjects who are mildly (M), intermediately (I) and severely malnourished (S). From Spurr (1988).

Subject group	Sample size	Weight/height (kg m^{-1})	Serum albumin (g dl^{-1})	Daily creatinine/height (mg dy^{-1} m^{-1})
M	11	>32	>3.5	>600
		33.3 ± 2.1	3.8 ± 0.5	660 ± 67
I	18	29–32	2.5–3.5	450–600
		30.8 ± 2.0	3.0 ± 0.7	559 ± 75
S	18	<29	<2.5	<450
		27.4 ± 2.1	2.1 ± 0.5	391 ± 76

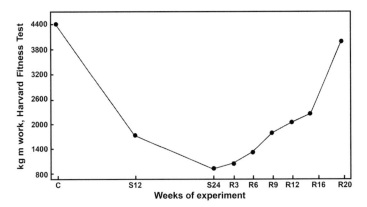

Figure 9.16 The effect of semistarvation on physical work. Mean performance (in kg m) on the Harvard Fitness Test during 24 weeks of semistarvation (S) and 20 weeks of subsequent dietary rehabilitation (R) in 12 otherwise healthy adult male volunteers. The energy intake during the period of semistarvation was limited to 1570 kcal, with 50 g of protein and 30 g of fat. On this diet, subjects lost an average of 24 percent of their body weight and 28 percent of their aerobic work capacity. Keys *et al.* (1950, vol. 1: 728), by permission of the University of Minnesota Press.

well-nourished men (Figures 9.17 and 9.18). Severe malnutrition reduced total PWC by more than 60 percent compared to well-nourished controls and 52 percent compared to mildly malnourished men. Most of the latter loss of PWC was restored over four months of *ad libitum* dietary supplementation (repletion). These results suggest – and the results of dietary repletion drive home the conclusion – that the degree of under-nutrition affects PWC in a roughly dose-dependent manner.

The Energy Trap

In sum, the physiological work capacity of the human body, as measured by maximum oxygen consumption per minute of work, is strictly limited even in well-nourished individuals. In under-nourished individuals, the limits are even tighter.

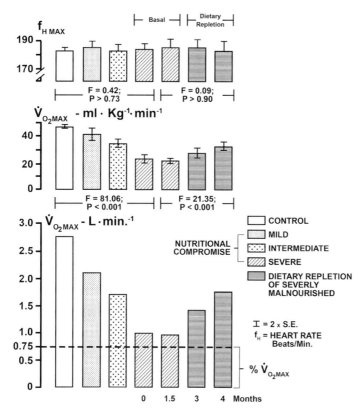

Figure 9.17 Aerobic work capacity and nutritional status in three groups of chronically malnourished men and a well-nourished control group, Cali, Colombia. Maximum heart rate ($f_{H\ MAX}$), maximum aerobic power ($\dot{V}_{O_2 MAX}$ per kg of body mass) and maximum work capacity ($\dot{V}_{O_2 MAX}$ total) in mildly, intermediately and severely malnourished adult males, during dietary repletion of severely malnourished subjects and in well-nourished controls, Cali, Colombia. The bold numbers in the lowest panel show a fixed submaximal work load ($\dot{V}_{O_2}$ of 0.75 l min^{-1}) as a percentage of each group's maximum work capacity. From Spurr (1988), by permission of Cambridge University Press.

Thus, in an actual preindustrial farming community, where nutritional status inevitably varies among individuals, the PWC is likely to vary as well, even after adjusting for differences in age, sex and other obvious characteristics. While conducting nutritional research in northern Nigeria during the 1970s, Richard Longhurst came to the realization that this linkage could have important inter-generational implications for household health and demography – implications he summarized by the catchphrase "the energy trap" (Longhurst, 1984). Figure 9.19 schematizes Longhurst's logic. For simplicity, imagine three households whose food is provided entirely by the physical exertions of their 35-year-old male heads. In one case (the "rich man" in Figure 9.19) food intake is well above the subsistence level, and once the man has satisfied his basal maintenance requirements, he can effectively invest effort into sharp increases in energy production for his household. A "poor man" struggles

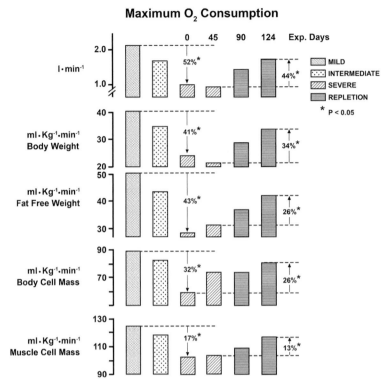

Figure 9.18 The effect of nutritional status on the maximum oxygen consumption (aerobic work capacity) of various body compartments in mildly, intermediately and severely malnourished adult males and during dietary repletion of severely malnourished subjects, Cali, Colombia. From Spurr (1988), by permission of Cambridge University Press.

closer to the edge of subsistence but – again, once he has supplied his basal metabolic requirements – he may still be capable of lifting his family further above the subsistence level by additional effort, even if he cannot duplicate the productive gains of the rich man. Given a few more generations, the poor man's descendants may be able to pull themselves upward into comparative wealth. The "trapped man", however, is so under-nourished that he loses nutritional condition even while trying to meet his basal needs; as a result, he can never surpass the subsistence level no matter how close to his PWC he works, thus miring his household in poverty and under-nutrition. If the trapped man is never able to feed his family adequately, his offspring will pay the price: they will either die of malnutrition or grow up to be so under-nourished that they become trapped as household heads themselves – and so on down the generations. In other words, variation in nutritional status among productive household members, argues Longhurst, can lead to semipermanent differences in the physical and economic well-being of families that persist across generations – quasi-class differences, if you will.

This is an interesting – and quite Malthusian – idea, but one that is inherently difficult to test empirically. Longhurst's own data from Nigeria were not up to the

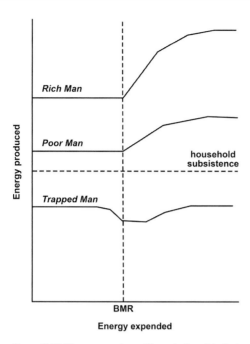

Figure 9.19 The energy trap. The relationship between work-related energy expenditure and the amount of food energy produced for the household by three men. The men's dietary energy levels before they reach their basal metabolic rates (BMR) condition their ability to convert work energy into further energy production. Modified from Longhurst (1984: 11), by permission of the Cornell Program in International Nutrition.

task. One possible case has been offered by Stanley Ulijaszek from his work in Papua New Guinea (Table 9.7). The reporting of this case is frustrating because the samples are small and no indicators of variability (standard errors, variances, confidence intervals) are provided, making it impossible to assess the statistical credibility of the results. But taking the figures in Table 9.7 at face value, it appears that men who are stunted and wasted have lower PWCs, need to spend more time clearing fields (presumably because of more frequent rest stops), and can sustain work for fewer hours each day; apparently their households also contain a larger fraction of children with low BMIs and a higher early childhood mortality rate than those of other male household heads.[8] Whether this is a genuine inter-generational effect or just a reflection of the "trapped" households' general conditions of poverty (for example, an unhygienic environment) is uncertain. Nor can we tell if the observed level of under-nutrition will be transmitted to yet another generation of offspring, or if the children will recover at least to the "short but not thin" level by adulthood. But insofar as these data are credible, they may point to a *possible* example of Longhurst's energy trap. If they do, they may signal a major demographic effect of the

---

[8] Presumably a child's risk of death was partly dependent on its nutritional status; had the children who died survived, then the *average* nutritional status of the household's offspring would probably have been even worse.

Table 9.7 The energy trap in New Guinea? Adult male body size, work capacity (head of household only) and household demography for three groups of men classified by height and weight, Wopkaimin, Papua New Guinea ($n = 36$ households). From Ulijaszek (1995: 161).

	Tall, not thin	Short, not thin	Short and thin
Sample size (households)	10	21	5
BMI (kg m^{-2})	>18.5	>18.5	<18.5
Height (cm)	>164.0	<164.0	<164.0
Physiological work capacity ($\dot{V}_{O_2\,MAX}$, 1 min^{-1})	2.4	2.0	1.8
Percentage PWC spent in most costly activity (field clearing)	37.0	43.0	49.0
Energy intake (MJ dy^{-1})	8.8	8.6	7.5
Duration of daily activity sustainable at existing level of daily energy intake (hr)	6.4	8.4	3.1
Number of offspring in household	2.7	2.6	3.0
Percentage of children in family with BMI < US median – 2 s.d.	11	6	40
Death rate in children <5 yr old (per 1000 live births)	207	214	286

Table 9.8 Farm labor and grain yields in dryland rice cultivation, four selected households (HH) among the Iban of Sarawak 1949. From Norman (1979: 132); data from Freeman (1955).

	HH1	HH2	HH3	HH4
Persons per HH	8	6	5	5
Labor force (over age 15)	4	4	4	3
Area of rice planted (ha)	2.6	2.2	1.9	2.0
Total rice yield (kg)	1950	1760	1710	2640
Yield ha^{-1} (kg)	741	800	891	1360
Yield as percentage of family requirements	78	93	109	168

bioenergetics of human work, channeled through the differential nutrition and survival of young children and operating across birth cohorts. Certainly there is, worldwide, variation in householders' abilities to meet their families' nutritional needs, as Freeman (1955) found among the Iban of Sarawak (Table 9.8). During a bad (but not disastrous) year, when rains came too early to allow for a thorough burning of slashed vegetation on new fields, almost 70 percent of Iban households could not feed their families adequately by their own labor (Table 9.9).

Animal versus Human Energy

If humans are such frail vessels, then surely they can do better by exploiting the power of large draft animals (Figure 9.20). Well, yes and no. Table 9.10 suggests that oxen and water buffalo are about three to four times stronger when it comes to farm

Table 9.9 Rice yields of 25 Iban households (HHs) in relation to their total energy requirements, Sarawak 1949–50. From Freeman (1955: 104).

Yield as %-age of HH requirements	No. of HHs	%-age of all HHs	
≥100	8	32	
75-99	6	24	⎫
50-74	6	24	⎬ 68%
25-49	4	16	⎭
<25	1	4	

Figure 9.20 Plowing with a water buffalo, Vietnam. Image credit: Visoot Uthairam/Moment/Getty Images.

work than are humans; but, like humans, the beasts need to be fed from local produce, most of it provided by the farm that owns them. In both humans and animals, the energy expended in work (relative to food energy consumed) is about the same multiple (3) of basal energy expenditure (Table 9.11). Apparently, traditional farmers do not use draft animals for their energy *efficiency*, but to lighten their own workload or perhaps to speed up work whenever possible. Moreover, draft animals need a lot of food, which competes, in effect, with food for humans: both require investments of limited time, energy and land.

Wherever land reached the limit of absolute scarcity, feeding the animals became one of the most agonizing problems of the village community. 'The horse eats people' is an adage in which the Rumanian peasant has crystallized a substantial dose of economic 'analysis'. (Georgescu-Roegen, 1970: 90)

Table 9.10 The amplification of human energy by draft animals used in plowing and harrowing (mainly cattle and water buffalo), India (Norman, 1979: 160). Reproduced, with permission, from M. J. T. Norman (1979) *Annual Cropping Systems in the Tropics.* Gainesville, FL: University Presses of Florida.

State	Crop	A Net human energy input for land preparation (MJ ha^{-1})	B Net human energy input for all tasks (MJ ha^{-1})	C Net animal energy input for land preparation (MJ ha^{-1})	D Total net energy input [B + C] (MJ ha^{-1})	D ÷ B
Bombay	wheat	78	234	585	819	3.5
Madhya Pradesh	wheat	126	282	945	1227	4.4
Punjab	wheat	66	198	495	693	3.5
Bombay	sorghum	42	150	315	465	3.1
Madras	sorghum	36	234	270	504	2.2
Bombay	gram	42	198	315	513	2.6
Mean	–	65	216	488	704	3.2

Table 9.11 Estimated rates of energy expenditure (MJ hr^{-1}) during farm work, humans and draft animals (oxen and water buffalo), India. One draft animal provides six times the work as one human, but also requires six times as much energy intake for basal maintenance, resulting in no net gain in energy efficiency (Norman, 1979: 49, 150). Reproduced, with permission, from M. J. T. Norman (1979) *Annual Cropping Systems in the Tropics.* Gainesville, FL: University Presses of Florida.

	Humans	Draft animals
Basal energy expenditure	0.25	1.5
Gross work energy expenditure	1.00	6.0
Net work energy expenditure	0.75	4.5

In preindustrial farming, whether we are talking about human labor or animal labor, work is powered by food *and* it is limited by food. The food energy available for labor is a primary determinant of the food energy produced, a substantial part of which is reinvested in further labor. The rest, such as it is, goes to support other aspects of the household demographic enterprise. Whenever energy for food production is provided predominantly by biological sources (other than fossil fuels), there is a firm cap on the achievable success rate of the demographic enterprise.

The Logic of Labor Allocation and the Division of Labor by Sex

Applying the cautious principle of least effort adumbrated above to farm-related drudgery provides a basis for thinking about the way work is normally parceled out on subsistence farms. The household workforce is, as has been emphasized, small and thus limited in its aggregate work capacity. In addition, its members vary among themselves in their *individual* capacities, reflecting their age and sex as well as other physical attributes (nutritional status, absence of crippling deformity, overall health, reproductive state, etc.). Subsistence farmers are certainly aware of this variation and allocate household labor to make the most of whatever work capacity is available to them. Their general logic of labor allocation is perhaps best explained with a specific example – the division of labor by sex, probably the best-studied dimension of traditional labor investment.

It is worth repeating that *all* work that contributes to the household demographic enterprise of subsistence farmers is important, most certainly including "domestic" tasks such as food processing, transport of fuel and water, cooking, child care, etc. Under this broad definition of farm work, men and women appear to contribute more or less equally (in terms of hours of work) to the household demographic enterprise across a wide range of traditional farming communities (Haswell, 1985). This does not, of course, mean there are no differences in the type of work they do or that work is allocated to females and males at random. Contrary to the claim of some observers that the sexual division of labor is purely a "cultural construct," there is in fact a strong degree of cross-cultural regularity to the tasks normally handled by each sex (Table 9.12). It is difficult to believe that this regularity does not arise, at least in part, from basic biological differences between the sexes. But to understand how those differences operate – and to understand labor allocation in general – we need to invoke the economic concept of *comparative advantage*. The question is not whether one sex absolutely can or cannot do a particular job (Figure 9.21), but which sex can do it more *efficiently* or at lower *opportunity costs*. Efficient, low-cost allocation of tasks across the household labor force acts to the net benefit of the household as a whole. Many nondomestic farm tasks (e.g. clearing fields or plowing) are not only energetically costly but often last from dawn to dusk and therefore entail high opportunity costs. In contrast, domestic work (e.g. cooking, fetching water, cleaning) tends to involve a series of largely independent tasks of comparatively short duration, thus allowing for greater flexibility in time use over the course of the day (Figure 9.22).[9] Domestic work also tends to be aseasonal, making the demand for it relatively constant over the year (Figure 9.23); thus, individual domestic chores are not usually subject to severe seasonal bottlenecks requiring heavy and rapid work. Therefore, domestic work generally involves lower opportunity costs and allows those who perform it to "multitask" more easily. Domestic work is, so to speak, more *interruptible* than many other forms of farm work – but no less essential.

In terms of their comparative advantages in farm work, men and women differ biologically in two important respects, the first quantitative, the second qualitative: (i) On *average* men are larger and heavier, have greater muscle mass and upper body strength, have higher physiological work capacities and are better at lifting heavy

---

[9] Figure 9.22 is interesting because it shows the activity patterns of an unmarried man living on his own, with only limited access to female labor (in the person of his sister-in-law). Of necessity, his days are dominated by *domestic* chores, which must be done if he is to eat and keep his home reasonably hygienic. Fortunately he is paid to do some teaching, so he can afford to buy some of the plant food he has no time to grow for himself.

Table 9.12 The division of labor by sex in 185 preindustrial societies including in the standard cross-cultural sample. Tasks are ranked by proportion exclusively male among societies in which the task was observed. F = 0, females not involved in task. M > F, task more commonly done by males. M = F, task more or less equally shared between the sexes. F > M, task more commonly done by females. M = 0, males not involved in task. Adapted from Murdock and Provost (1973: Table 1); Factors in the division of labor by sex: A cross-cultural analysis by George P. Murdock and Caterina Provost 12(2): 203–225; 1973, with permission.

	F = 0	M > F	M = F	F > M	M = 0
Metalworking	85	1	0	0	0
Hunting of large animals	139	5	0	0	0
Trapping of small animals	136	12	1	1	0
Butchering	122	9	4	4	4
Land clearance	95	34	6	3	1
Fishing	83	45	8	5	2
Tending large animals	54	24	14	3	3
House building	105	30	14	9	20
Soil preparation	66	27	14	17	10
Fire making	40	6	16	4	20
Gathering small animals	27	3	9	13	15
Crop planting	27	35	33	26	20
Harvesting	10	37	34	34	26
Crop tending	22	23	24	30	32
Milking	15	2	8	2	21
Burden carrying	18	12	46	34	36
Care of small animals	19	8	14	12	44
Weaving	24	0	6	8	50
Fuel gathering	25	12	12	23	94
Gathering wild plant food	6	4	18	42	65
Dairy production	4	0	0	0	24
Spinning	7	3	4	5	72
Laundering	5	0	4	8	49
Water fetching	4	4	8	13	131
Grain grinding	2	4	5	13	114
Cooking	0	2	2	63	117

objects than women. (ii) On the other hand, only women can produce breastmilk. Breastfeeding is one task that cannot be shared by the sexes. Traditional breastfeeding patterns tend to be "intensive" by modern-day standards – suckling is typically frequent through the day, with intervals between episodes of suckling often less than 15–30 minutes on average, and the age of each child at weaning is comparatively late, often two to four years or more (Wood, 1994a: 362–70). Breastfeeding thus requires lactating women to spend a great deal of time near their nursing children (Nerlove, 1974).[10]

---

[10] Prolonged breastfeeding is also hard "work" in that it is energetically costly, even if the energy expenditures involve tissues other than muscle (Schutz et al., 1980). (Ideally, these energy costs should

Figure 9.21 Working with oxen in Orkney, Scotland, c. 1900. (Top) A harrowing team being driven by a man, who is standing on the harrow to provide weight. (Bottom) A plow team driven by a woman whose husband is off island. Working with draft animals was traditionally male work in Orkney and is often described as being exclusively so. But there are few if any farm tasks that either sex absolutely cannot perform if necessary. Photographs by Tom Kent, c. 1900.

be included in the household's total energy budget.) For example, Widdowson (1976) estimates that the 36 000 kcal stored by the average, well-nourished Western woman during pregnancy is sufficient to support only four to five months of lactation, even under what is by non-Western standards a comparatively nonintensive regime of nursing. The National Academy of Sciences recommends that lactating women consume 500 kcal day^{-1} over their normal requirements (Worthington-Roberts *et al.*, 1985). This recommendation is based on the assumption that the average woman gains about 3.5 kg of fat during pregnancy that can be mobilized to provide the 300 kg day^{-1} needed to produce 850 ml of milk every day for approximately three months. But the typical woman in a preindustrial or rural developing-world community is unlikely to conform to this picture of a well-nourished, modern

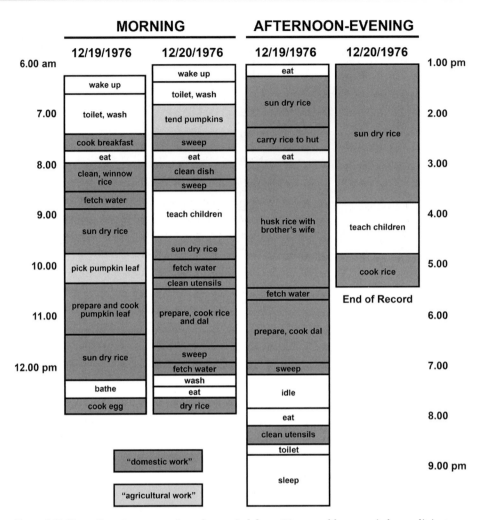

Figure 9.22 Time allocation over a two-day period for a 50-year-old unmarried man living on his own, rural Bangladesh. Notice that he earned some cash working part-time as a village teacher. From Cain (1977: 205), by permission of John Wiley & Sons, Inc.

Studies in rural Bangladesh (Huffman *et al.*, 1980) have shown that seasonal involvement in nondomestic farm work can interfere significantly with women's ability to invest time in breastfeeding. By comparison, domestic work is, as we have seen, more interruptible.

Western woman. She often begins pregnancy with lower nutritional reserves; she gains little if any body fat during pregnancy; she may lactate for more than three years, not three months; she often does not supplement her own diet significantly during lactation; and her milk provides virtually all the nutriment required by her child for at least the first six months of its life. The net effect of these differences is that the nutritional status of women in traditional societies often declines sharply over the course of lactation (Bongaarts and Delgado, 1979; Miller and Huss-Ashmore, 1989).

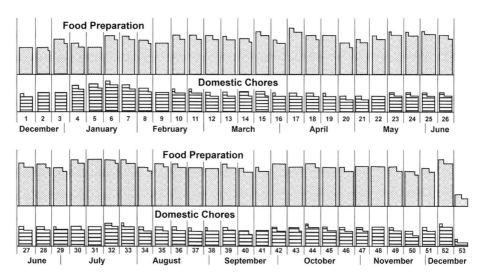

Figure 9.23 Domestic work tends to be aseasonal. Hours per week devoted to "female" work among the Ushi, Northern Rhodesia, 1959–60. From Kay (1964: 63), by permission of Manchester University Press.

Other generalizations about the sexual division of labor taken from the literature (Murdock, 1937; Brown, 1963; Burton and White, 1984; Stone *et al.*, 1995) include the following:

- Women tend to work close to home, men at greater distances.
- Women's work in agriculture (in the narrow sense) tends to decline when large domestic animals are used for traction – but their work in *tending* animals often increases (Burton and Reitz, 1981).
- Women's work in agriculture (in the narrow sense) may increase with agricultural involution (e.g. paddy farming in East Asia) but decrease with other forms of intensification (Ember, 1983). It depends in part on whether intensification results in greater *spatial concentration* of food production near the domicile (see Chapter 1).
- House gardens tend to be planted, tended and harvested primarily by women, often with the help of children and the elderly.
- When grains are the staple crop, women tend to spend less time in agriculture (in the narrow sense) but more time in food processing (e.g. threshing, winnowing, grinding).
- Child care, food preparation and cooking are universally dominated by women.
- Men tend to dominate tasks that are energetically intensive and under severe time constraints (e.g. clearing forest).

There are, of course, exceptions to every rule. Nonetheless, most of these patterns can be explained by a simple, parsimonious model based on four plausible assumptions (Burton *et al.*, 1977; White *et al.*, 1981):

- Production tasks are not independent. They can be organized into sequences, such that the products of one step are used in the next step. Whichever sex is involved in the earlier steps in the sequence will have a higher probability of being involved in later steps as well, especially if the steps are close together in time and space.

- Breastfeeding requires women to stay close to their nursing children, which often puts them near their other dependent children as well. Women therefore dominate childcare responsibilities in general, as well as other tasks that do not take them far from home, at least as long as any of the children in question need to be carried.
- Breastfeeding often competes with other tasks for a woman's time and attention. Women's jobs therefore tend to be interruptible or of fairly short duration.
- Men tend to dominate arduous and physically risky tasks, as well as tasks done far from the domicile (this assumption may partly be a corollary of the previous two).

Data on 50 tasks from the standard cross-cultural sample (n = 185 preindustrial societies) provide very strong support for the model (Burton *et al.*, 1977; White *et al.*, 1981), suggesting, first, that brute strength and breastfeeding may be the two primary factors underlying traditional patterns of labor allocation by sex and, second, that machines and baby bottles may have surprising knock-on effects on gender roles. But remember that, except for breastfeeding, the biological differences between the sexes provide only comparative, not absolute, differences in the ability to do traditional farm work. There seem to be plenty of jobs on the farm that can be done more or less equally well by women and men (see Table 9.12, M = F).

Labor Needs and the Economic "Demand" for Children

When interviewed about their family size goals, people in rural developing countries sometimes say they want children "to help us on the farm" or "to support us in our old age" (Nag *et al.*, 1978). Based on such observations, Caldwell (1976) has suggested that parents in preindustrial rural societies were motivated to produce large families because the net flow of material wealth over the long term in such societies ran from the offspring generation to the parental generation – hence the production of more children maximized the parents' economic "utility". In other words, there was an economic demand for children's labor in farming that could only be met by producing large families. Consistent with this suggestion, Cain (1977) once estimated that the average son in rural Bangladesh became a net food producer by the age of 12, paid off his own cumulative consumption by age 15, and compensated for his own and one sister's cumulative consumption by age 22. (These estimates imply that the son survived without disability and continued living and working on his parents' farm until early adulthood.) These results have been cited in support of Caldwell's belief that a reversal in net inter-generational wealth flows, associated with the monetary costs of childrearing and education in modern capitalist societies, has been a major factor in the recent decline in fertility worldwide (Caldwell, 1982).

More recent research on traditional farming communities has, however, questioned the generalizability of Cain's findings from Bangladesh, indicating that the cumulative productive contributions of children, male or female, usually do not equal their parents' investment of energy in them before the children have left their natal

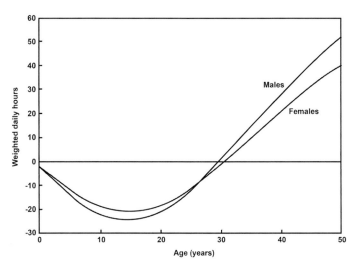

Figure 9.24 Estimated cumulative net production of offspring (by sex) from birth to age 50, Mayan Indians, Xculoc village, Yucatan, Mexico. Based on semilongitudinal time-allocation data collected by Kramer (1998) over the course of an entire year, including over 17 000 time-scan sample observations of 112 individuals of all ages. From Lee and Kramer (2002: 486), by permission of John Wiley & Sons, Inc.

homesteads and started working to support their own households (Kaplan, 1994, 1996; Lee, 1994; Kramer, 1998, 2005; Stecklov, 1999; Lee and Kramer, 2002). Figure 9.24, for example, suggests that, in a subsistence-oriented Maya village in the Yucatan, offspring do not attain a cumulative net productivity of zero until about age 30, by which time they are producing primarily for their own households, not their parents'.[11] Moreover, adult children may or may not be readily available to help their parents in their dotage. Depending in part on rules dictating post-marital residence and the inheritance of land, for example, half or more *surviving* children may leave the farm well before their parents retire from farm work, and redirect their energies into raising their own offspring. And, of course, the parents themselves may not live to retirement age. Counting on newborns for their possible *future* economic value seems a perilous undertaking.

Several authors (Kaplan, 1994, 1996; Kramer, 2005; Kramer and Boone, 2002) have suggested that the desire for children may be more deeply rooted in biology than in superficial economics – or, to put it differently, that the utility parents *really* want to maximize is their genetic fitness, not their economic security in old age. Both positions have their defenders and detractors, and both are nearly impossible to test critically against empirical evidence. One particular version of the argument from genetic fitness – the so-called "grandmother hypothesis" for the evolution of menopause – posits that women in traditional societies continue to make net positive

---

[11] Neither Cain's nor Lee and Kramer's estimates are adjusted to take account of the high risk of death during childhood in these populations, which would increase the average age at which a cumulative net production contribution of zero would be attained, perhaps by a substantial amount.

contributions to their children's and even grandchildren's welfare well into old age (Hawkes *et al.*, 1998); this hypothesis has now undergone some 20 years' worth of testing against field data, with results that can only be called inconclusive. Nonetheless, it has to be said that the old idea that preindustrial farming couples have comparatively high fertility levels because of a high economic "demand" for children's labor in farm work appears to be much more problematic than we used to believe.

Last Thoughts

The household demographic enterprise in traditional farming communities, if it is to succeed, requires the production of offspring who survive to adulthood. Young children make extravagant demands on their parents' capacity to produce food (including breastmilk). If their food needs are not met, those children are placed at a high risk of dying during preadult life, thus endangering the whole business. But the energy required to make food in the preindustrial world is biological and itself requires food for its support. Indeed, an inadequate food supply can be one of the principal factors limiting the physiological capacity of the household to produce more food. Added to that is the problem that the household labor force, for all its changes in size over the household life cycle, is always extremely small and thus has a strictly limited capacity to produce food even when it is well-nourished. As discussed in the next chapter, almost every subsistence-farming household passes through one or more phases during which the supply of labor for food production has to struggle to keep up with demand. All this adds up to a potentially important negative feedback loop reining in the household demographic enterprise and thus limiting the potential of the farming community as a whole for population increase. These limiting factors can also contribute to what might be thought of as a kind of "population pressure" for agrarian change working at the household level – a spatial scale Boserup never seriously contemplated – and potentially working just as relentlessly at low population densities as at high ones. I have called such pressure "Chayanovian pressure." The next chapter explains why.

10 The Economics of the Household Demographic Life Cycle

No man knows, I think, who is worthy to have;
but the most needy are our neighbors, if we note it well.
Like prisoners in pits are poor folk in crofts,
charged with children and chief-lord's rent.
What they can spare from their spinning they spend on house-hire,
and on milk and on meal to make into gruel
to quiet their children who cry after food.
And they themselves also suffer much hunger,
and woe in winter-time, and waking at night
to rise by the bedside for rocking the cradle,
to card and comb wool, to clean and to mend,
and to rub and to reel, rushes to peel,
that hard it is to write or in rhyme to show
the woe of these women who work in the crofts.
And of many other men that much woe suffer,
both hunger and thirst, to turn a fair face outward,
and are abashed to beg and would not have it known
what they need of their neighbors at noon and at eve.
   And well I know, as the wide world teaches,
what else befalls those who have many children
and have no cattle but their craft to clothe and to feed them,
and many to grasp at the few pence they own.
       – William Langland (*c.* 1390) *Piers Ploughman* (the C-text).
           Passus IX, lines 70–91 (free translation)

In discussing Richard Longhurst's model of the energy trap in the previous chapter, we speculated that differences among households in nutritional status could be amplified, via their effects on work capacity, into semipermanent, inter-generational differences in a family's material well-being. But the energy trap, if it is to operate at all, must act on *preexisting* differences in household well-being. Thus far, we have said nothing about where those initial differences come from. A large part of the answer, of course, is that traditional farmers, like all people, vary among themselves in such things as industriousness, cleverness, prudence, fecklessness, even sheer dumb luck – not to mention the political nous to turn a temporary advantage into something more enduring. In addition, environmental unpredictability can be a potent source of differential household success, even in communities that appear to us to be egalitarian. In this chapter, however, we focus on one possible source of economic differentiation that is inherent in the household demographic enterprise – the household's built-in demographic life cycle, the ebb and flow of household size and age–sex composition resulting from births, deaths, marriages and other forms of inter-household migration (see Chapter 7). More specifically, inter-household differentiation arises from two facts: (i) that the life cycles of all the households in a community are never in perfect synchrony, and (ii) that an element of randomness always plays a part in every household's life cycle. No two life cycles are ever quite the same in their intensity and timing – and these dissimilarities can have important economic consequences.

Formal study of the economics of the demographic life cycle of traditional farming households can be traced back to the great (and doomed) Russian agricultural economist A. V. Chayanov.[1] Chayanov thrived professionally, as both a theoretician and a fieldworker, from about 1912 to 1930. His work was largely unknown to Western scholars until the mid-1960s, when an English translation of one of his major works first appeared (Chayanov, 1966).[2] This publication sparked great interest, especially among economic anthropologists and students of peasant economies (see Millar, 1970; Sahlins, 1971, 1972; Minge-Kalman, 1977; Hunt, 1978, 1979; A. E. Smith, 1979; Durrenberger, 1980, 1984; Lewis, 1981; Chibnik, 1984, 1987). It also inspired numerous attacks from Marxist critics (e.g. Harrison, 1975, 1977; Littlejohn, 1977; Patnaik, 1979). By the late 1980s, the flurry of interest in Chayanov's work had largely subsided, although it played a prominent role in Robert Netting's influential book of 1993, *Smallholders, Householders*.[3] Currently his ideas are undergoing a bit of a renaissance, albeit in greatly modified form (see below). For my part, Chayanov has long been and remains, along with Malthus and Boserup, part of the intellectual triumvirate that has most influenced my thinking about the demography of subsistence farming.

Shanin (1986: 2–4) has suggested that Chayanov made two major contributions to agricultural economics, one profound and the other less so. The lesser contribution takes the form of specific models of the economics of the household life cycle and of the balance between production and what he called "drudgery." The more profound contribution, according to Shanin, was an entirely novel approach to peasant economics:

---

[1] Being Russian, Chayanov's surname was not of course *Chayanov* but rather Уаяюв, which can be transliterated into English in a variety of ways. Before the mid-twentieth century the rare references to Chayanov's writings in the non-Russian literature mostly drew upon German translations, which generally used the transliteration *Tschaianoff* or *Tschajanoff*. Starting in the mid-1960s, however, English editions became available that were translated directly from the Russian. Since then, *Chayanov*, which is somewhat closer to the Russian original, has become the preferred English transliteration.

[2] It is sometimes claimed that this translation was the first of his writings to appear in English. But see Tschaianoff (1931 [orig. 1918]). This short excerpt, however, was hardly a major work, although it is an interesting one.

[3] That role, however, was predominantly negative since Netting did not believe that the ethnographic evidence supported Chayanov's ideas (Netting, 1993: 312–19). I discuss that evidence below.

The analytical approach suggested [by Chayanov] was to begin the consideration of peasant agriculture "from below," that is, from *the operational logic of the family farms* rather than from the national and international flows of resources, goods, and demands... [He] defined a particular peasant economy by the characteristics of family labor and the relative autonomy of its usage at the roots of peasant survival strategies which are systematically different from those of capitalist enterprises. (Shanin, 1986: 3; emphasis added)

I pay homage to both contributions (although I would change "peasant" to "traditional farmer"). Some of Chayanov's specific models are reviewed below, as are statistical results intended to test them. I also appreciate his use, very von Thünian in flavor, of deliberately over-simplified models to isolate particular components of complex real-world situations. But it is the "profound" contribution, Chayanov's "bottom-up" approach, that makes the current book most deeply Chayanovian in spirit.

In what follows, I do not attempt to review all of Chayanov's theoretical and empirical contributions, many of which are tangential to the concerns of this book. In addition, I shamelessly translate some of his ideas into my own terms (I promise to confess the crime whenever I commit it). Finally, I apply elements of his theory of peasant economy to nonpeasant subsistence or near-subsistence farmers, for whom I consider it even more appropriate than it was for the peasants studied by Chayanov, who were involved to some degree in marketing and the cash economy. Chayanov himself thought his theory inapplicable to nonmonetized economies because cash value was for him the only currency in which economic production and consumption could be measured, a task essential to his modeling approach. One of *our* tasks will be to consider other, noncash currencies.

A.V. Chayanov and the Economics of the Household Life Cycle

Chayanov's Life, Death and Resurrection

Aleksandr Vasil'evich Chayanov (Figure 10.1) was born in Moscow in 1888, the grandson of a peasant farmer whose son had migrated to the city and prospered.[4] Chayanov graduated from the Moscow Agricultural Academy and established his national reputation in 1912 with an analysis of the demographic determinants of peasant flax production in Russia. In 1913 he was appointed to the faculty at the Agricultural Institute of Petrovskoe Razumovskoe (later renamed the Institute of Agricultural Economy) near Moscow. There he joined a brilliant group of agronomists and economists charged with helping to modernize what was at the time still a very backward peasant economy – barely 50 years after the abolition of serfdom. This group, with Chayanov's central involvement, produced an impressive body of field data and economic analysis, primarily concerning the "black earth" region of

---

[4] There is no definitive biography of Chayanov in English. Partial details are provided by Kerblay (1966), Jasny (1972), Danilov (1991), Bourgholtzer (1999) and Shanin (2009), from all of whom the current account has been pieced together.

Figure 10.1 Aleksandr Vasil'evich Chayanov (1888–1937). From Chayanov (1986: frontispiece), by permission of the University of Wisconsin Press.

southwestern Russia and Ukraine. Within a short time, Chayanov became director of the Institute, which he headed until 1930.

By that time, Chayanov had survived the Bolshevik revolution of 1917, the period of "war communism," Lenin's New Economic Policy and the early phases of Stalin's collectivization of Soviet agriculture (see Jasny, 1972, for an account of the political and economic context of Chayanov's career). He never joined the Communist Party, but was for years considered a useful "non-party expert" by the government (Shanin, 2009: 85). In 1930, however, he was fired from his position at the Institute and arrested for "wrecking" Soviet agriculture. The main complaint against him seems to have been that he opposed the top-down imposition of collective farming, advocating instead the organization of farm cooperatives controlled locally by the peasants themselves; it cannot have helped that he also suggested that collectives or cooperatives from different agricultural regions should be allowed to find their own optimum sizes, contrary to Stalin's belief that all collectives should be as large as possible. He was duly convicted, sentenced to five years' hard labor in a camp in Kazakhstan and, after his release, exiled from Moscow. In 1937 he was arrested again and charged with the more serious crime of treason, because he had allegedly joined a *neo-Narodnik* (neopopulist) plot to topple the dictatorship of the industrial proletariat and replace it with a peasant utopia (no one now seems to believe he was guilty of the charge). He was quickly tried and convicted, and, on Stalin's orders, was immediately taken to the back of the courthouse and shot.

Teodor Shanin has provided an eloquent eulogy and a more rounded portrait of Chayanov:

[He] was much more than an agrarian master-economist of a country in which 80 percent of the population made their living in agriculture. A man of extremely rich mind, trained within the best humanist traditions of Europe, by the age of 40 he combined important analytical work, field research and methodological studies concerning peasantry with five novels, a 'utopia', a play, a book of poetry, and a half-finished guide to Western painting and a history of the city of Moscow. He spoke a number of languages, travelled extensively in Europe – before and after 1917 – and was closely knit into the cultural encounters of the educated Muscovites. He was a Moscow intellectual of the day at their best, deeply committed to the cause of improvement of the livelihood of the mass of common people, of human liberties and of his country's educational standards. Chayanov's rural focus of attention was rooted accordingly in a basic moral stand. As to his scholarly endeavour, Chayanov's thought breached disciplinary frontiers between economics, sociology, history, arts, agriculture and epistemology. His particular personal strength lay in a remarkable power of disciplined imagination and ability to put it in words, an outstanding and original models-creating ability, a capacity which bridged between his scholarly and artistic achievements and made him a theorist and leader among his peers. (Shanin, 2009: 85)

In 1987, Chayanov was officially rehabilitated by the Gorbachev government. His work was republished in Russian for the first time in almost 60 years and was greeted with rapturous applause from the then still-Soviet academy. For Chayanov himself, it was 50 years too late.

Chayanov's Model of the Farming Household's Life Cycle

Chayanov succinctly summarized his essential views in a short paper delivered at the Third Russian Congress of the League of Agrarian Reforms, held just before the Bolshevik revolution of November 1917:

The farm economy of the peasant differs essentially from farm economy organized on those capitalistic principles that customarily serve as a basis for the solution of economic problems.

1. The first fundamental characteristic of the farm economy of the peasant is that it is a family economy. Its whole organization is determined by the size and composition of the peasant family and by the coordination of its consumptive demands with the number of its working hands...
2. The second fundamental characteristic of peasant economy is that its character depends to a great extent on the size and composition of the family, because its organization is familistic. A change in the size and composition of the family calls forth a corresponding change in the size of the family landholding and hence makes the size of the peasant farm unstable and changeable...
3. A third characteristic is that, aside from organic changes in the amount of the labor power of a family caused by its natural development, there are temporary fluctuations in the amount of labor power, caused by the departure of some members from the family or by long visits paid to the family by some of its members. These numerous fluctuations in the composition of the family are reflected immediately in variations in the amount of land

cultivated by the family. Hence we see that in peasant economy the amount of land is as flexible as clay; it is adapted to, and accordingly responds to all the changes in, the labor apparatus of the family. (Tschaianoff, 1931 [orig. 1918]: 144–6)

Now Chayanov did not speak of this set of characteristics as a "model," a term that was not then current, at least not in the sense meant here. But that he had something like our notion of a model in mind is confirmed by a later statement: "we must, of course, recognize that our constructs reduce life to a scheme and, like any abstract theory, have as their subject an imaginary farm much purer in type than those we must encounter in reality" (Chayanov, 1986 [orig. 1925]: 48). Accordingly, we can take the characteristics listed above as model assumptions rather than infallible statements about reality, namely: (i) the farm is operated entirely by the family members making up the farming household, with no hired labor or contributions from other households, (ii) farm land is freely available and workable (i.e. arable land is plentiful and there is no declining marginal productivity of land), and (iii) the size and composition of the farming household fluctuate owing both to semipredictable changes resulting from its internal demographic dynamics ("its natural develop-ment") and from less predictable movements of individuals between households. To translate assumption (iii) into modern terms, household size and composition are subject to both systematic and stochastic (random) demographic changes. Assump-tion (i) may occasionally be correct (if only approximately) in the real world, assumption (ii) is rarely if ever so, and assumption (iii) always and inescapably so. But it's Chayanov's model and he is free to make whatever assumptions he wishes so long as they take us in interesting directions.

In his *Theory of Peasant Economy*, Chayanov illustrated his view of the household demographic life cycle with a simple numerical example, which he characterized as "*a rough scheme*" (Chayanov, 1986: 57, emphasis as in original) and which I, predictably, would call a model. Assuming that men marry at age 25 and women at 20, that strictly neolocal postmarital residence is practiced, that a first child is born in the second year of marriage, that subsequent children arrive at exactly three-year intervals, that no one in the household dies, and that no one leaves until the first child marries at 25, then the size and age composition of the household's membership change over its existence as shown in Table 10.1.[5] In terms of household economic activity, of course, these members are far from equivalent. Infants and toddlers need to eat but contribute nothing of substance to food production; older children may well help farm, but their productive contributions are unlikely to match those of their

---

[5] This example made no pretense to demographic realism. As Chayanov noted, "Undoubtedly, due to the death rate of grown children or a somewhat higher birth rate than we have taken, family development in reality will differ from our figures. We will always meet families that consist of only three or four persons, despite having lasted fifteen years. Families will frequently break down prematurely, taking the full cycle as 25 years, as we have done, more or less. However, the type of normal family development which occurs without catastrophe will always resemble these figures, and the scheme is adequate for a *theoretical* description of family development" (Chayavnov, 1986: 57; emphasis added).

Table 10.1 Chayanov's model for the growth of a household by year of its existence. For simplicity a neolocal nuclear-family household (HH) is shown, with no entry of additional members (beyond the original conjugal pair) except by birth, no mortality, and no exit from the household for any reason; intervals between births are all three years long (Chayanov, 1986: 57). From Chayanov, A. V., *The Theory of Peasant Economy* © 1986 by the Board of Regents of the University of Wisconsin System. Reprinted by permission of the University of Wisconsin Press.

Year of HH's existence	Husband	Wife	Age of children (years)										Total no. of members
			1st	2nd	3rd	4th	5th	6th	7th	8th	9th	
1	25	20										2
2	26	21	0									3
3	27	22	1									3
4	28	23	2									3
5	29	24	3	0								4
6	30	25	4	1								4
7	31	26	5	2								4
8	32	27	6	3	0							5
9	33	28	7	4	1							5
10	34	29	8	5	2							5
11	35	30	9	6	3	0						6
12	36	31	10	7	4	1						6
13	37	32	11	8	5	2						6
14	38	33	12	9	6	3	0					7
15	39	34	13	10	7	4	1					7
16	40	35	14	11	8	5	2					7
17	41	36	15	12	9	6	3	0				8
18	42	37	16	13	10	7	4	1				8
19	43	38	17	14	11	8	5	2				8
20	44	39	18	15	12	9	6	3	0			9
21	45	40	19	16	13	10	7	4	1			9
22	46	41	20	17	14	11	8	5	2			9
23	47	42	21	18	15	12	9	6	3	0		10
24	48	43	22	19	16	13	10	7	4	1		10
25	49	44	23	20	17	14	11	8	5	2		10
26	50	45	24	21	18	15	12	9	6	3	0	11

parents and may not even meet their own consumption requirements.[6] To understand changes in both consumer demand and productive capacity over the household life cycle, we need to weight the individual members by their evolving needs and

---

[6] An important point needs to be made here. Chayanov was concerned with all economic activity within the household, including, for example, craft production for sale at market. My intention, in contrast, is to model subsistence farming households in nonmonetized economies; accordingly I restrict attention to food production and consumption. The difference should not, however, be exaggerated. In many "peasant" societies, market participation is limited and most of the money earned from the market is spent on food for the household.

Table 10.2 Chayanov's age- and sex-specific weights for household production and consumption. Note there is no change in production or consumption weights after age 25 years.

Age (years)	Production		Consumption	
	Males	Females	Males	Females
0	0	0	0.1	0.1
1–13	0	0	0.3	0.3
14–18	0.7	0.7	0.5	0.5
19–24	0.9	0.7	0.9	0.7
25+	1.0	0.8	1.0	0.8

abilities. Based loosely on rates estimated from field data collected in Vologda Oblast, Chayanov proposed the age- and sex-specific weights for consumption and production shown in Table 10.2, expressed as scale-free "adult-male equivalents". (As discussed below, estimation of appropriate weights turns out to be one of the thorniest problems in the empirical application of Chayanov's model.)

Applying these weights to the numbers in Table 10.1 and assuming a sex ratio at birth of 100 or 1:1, we get the figures listed in Table 10.3 and illustrated in Figure 10.2. Note that the ratio of weighted consumers to weighted producers (the C/P ratio) itself undergoes cyclical change over the course of the household life cycle, initially increasing as young, nonproductive children are added and then falling again as children become increasingly involved in food production. At its peak, the C/P ratio is almost double what its initial value was back when the household consisted solely of the newly wed couple. Compared to how much they needed to do to support themselves on their own, the husband and wife would need to produce twice as much food to meet the household's nutritional needs at the peak of its C/P curve.

To Chayanov, this was an enormous change in household consumer demand and might be expected to have significant knock-on effects on the household economy in general:

Thus, *every family*, depending on its age, is in its different phases of development a completely distinct labor machine as regards labor force, intensity of demand, consumer-worker ratio, and the possibility of applying the principles of complex cooperation [i.e. a division of labor].

In accordance with this, we can pose the first problem of our inquiry: *Does the state of this continually changing machine affect the economic activity of a family running its labor farm, and if it does, how and to what extent?*

Since the labor family's basic stimulus to economic activity is the necessity to satisfy the demands of its consumers, and its work hands are the chief means of this, we ought first of all to expect the family's *volume of economic activity* to quantitatively correspond more or less to these basic elements in family composition. (Chayanov, 1986: 60; emphasis as in original)

In other words, insofar as the household works primarily to meet its own needs, its changing demography should be an ever-present factor affecting the intensity of household food production ("the family's *volume of economic activity*"). With respect to the peasant communities in the black earth region of Russia and Ukraine studied by Chayanov and his colleagues, for which (as they thought) high-quality land was freely

Table 10.3 Household members as in Table 10.1 but weighted by the production and consumption values in Table 10.2. For each child, the given weight is the average of the male and female weights. Individuals making a contribution to food production in a given year are shown in boldface (Chayanov, 1986: 57). From Chayanov, A. V., *The Theory of Peasant Economy* © 1986 by the Board of Regents of the University of Wisconsin System. Reprinted by permission of the University of Wisconsin Press.

Year of HH's existence	Married couple	Children									Weighted number of:		C/P
		1	2	3	4	5	6	7	8	9	Consumers (C)	Producers (P)	
1	1.8										1.8	1.8	1.00
2	1.8	0.1									1.9	1.8	1.06
3	1.8	0.3									2.1	1.8	1.17
4	1.8	0.3									2.1	1.8	1.17
5	1.8	0.3	0.1								2.2	1.8	1.22
6	1.8	0.3	0.3								2.4	1.8	1.33
7	1.8	0.3	0.3								2.4	1.8	1.33
8	1.8	0.3	0.3	0.1							2.5	1.8	1.39
9	1.8	0.5	0.3	0.3							2.9	1.8	1.61
10	1.8	0.5	0.3	0.3							2.9	1.8	1.61
11	1.8	0.5	0.3	0.3	0.1						3.0	1.8	1.66
12	1.8	0.5	0.5	0.3	0.3						3.4	1.8	1.88
13	1.8	0.5	0.5	0.3	0.3						3.4	1.8	1.88
14	1.8	0.5	0.5	0.3	0.3	0.1					3.5	1.8	1.94
15	1.8	**0.7**	0.5	0.5	0.3	0.3					4.1	2.5	1.64
16	1.8	**0.7**	0.5	0.5	0.3	0.3					4.1	2.5	1.64
17	1.8	**0.7**	0.5	0.5	0.3	0.3	0.1				4.2	2.5	1.68
18	1.8	**0.7**	**0.7**	0.5	0.5	0.3	0.3				4.8	3.2	1.50
19	1.8	**0.7**	**0.7**	0.5	0.5	0.3	0.3				4.8	3.2	1.50
20	1.8	**0.9**	**0.7**	0.5	0.5	0.3	0.3	0.1			5.1	3.4	1.50
21	1.8	**0.9**	**0.7**	**0.7**	0.5	0.5	0.3	0.3			5.7	4.1	1.39
22	1.8	**0.9**	**0.7**	**0.7**	0.5	0.5	0.3	0.3			5.7	4.1	1.39
23	1.8	**0.9**	**0.9**	**0.7**	0.5	0.5	0.3	0.3	0.1		6.0	4.3	1.39
24	1.8	**0.9**	**0.9**	**0.7**	**0.7**	0.5	0.5	0.3	0.3		6.6	5.0	1.32
25	1.8	**0.9**	**0.9**	**0.7**	**0.7**	0.5	0.5	0.3	0.3		6.6	5.0	1.32
26	1.8	**0.9**	**0.9**	**0.9**	**0.7**	0.5	0.5	0.3	0.3	0.1	6.9	5.2	1.32

accessible, it was natural to assume that rising C/P ratios could effectively be countered by increases in the area of the household's arable land, thus explaining the positive correlation they had observed between family size and farm size (Table 10.4). But larger farms require more work, and consequently a relationship between C/P ratio and both amount and productivity of work was also expected and duly observed (Table 10.5). Neither finding, it should be said, provides unimpeachable support for Chayanov's model. Perhaps the causation reflected in these correlations runs in a direction opposite to that assumed by Chayanov. Perhaps, as his Marxist critics have asserted, in categorizing farms by size he is really exposing underlying class

Table 10.4 The relationship between area sown per farm (in desyatinas) and the number of individuals of both sexes in the farming household (HH), several regions of European Russia. One desyatina is approximately equal to a hectare (Chayanov, 1986: 62). From Chayanov, A. V., *The Theory of Peasant Economy* © 1986 by the Board of Regents of the University of Wisconsin System. Reprinted by permission of the University of Wisconsin Press.

Vyatka (Kirov Oblast)		Tula Oblast		Samara Oblast	
Area sown	Mean HH size	Area sown	Mean HH size	Area sown	Mean HH size
0.0	2.8	0.0	1.0	0.0	3.5
0.1–0.9	3.5	0.1–0.9	3.4	0.1–2.9	4.4
1.0–2.4	4.4	1.0–1.9	4.4	3.0–5.9	5.2
2.5–4.9	5.3	2.0–4.9	6.2	6.0–8.9	6.1
5.0–7.4	6.2	5.0–9.9	8.4	9.0–11.9	6.9
7.5–9.9	7.2	10.0–14.9	11.0	12.0–14.9	7.5
10.0–14.9	8.6	15.0–24.9	17.7	15.0–19.9	8.2

Table 10.5 C/P ratio, income and working days, Volokolansk Oblast, Russia 1910 (Chayanov, 1986: 78). From Chayanov, A. V., *The Theory of Peasant Economy* © 1986 by the Board of Regents of the University of Wisconsin System. Reprinted by permission of the University of Wisconsin Press.

C/P ratio	Working days per worker	Income per worker (rubles)
1.01–1.20	98.8	131.9
1.21–1.40	102.3	151.5
1.41–1.60	157.2	218.8
>1.60	161.3	283.4

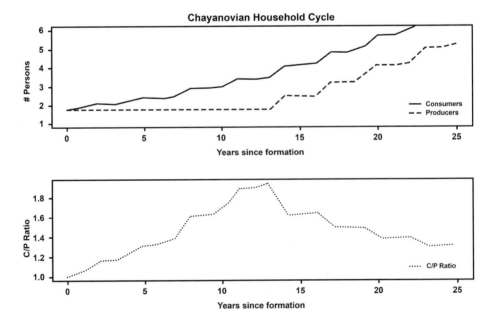

Figure 10.2 Curves showing the weighted number of food consumers (C) and food producers (P), and weighted consumer/producer ratio (C/P), by years since marriage for the example shown in Tables 10.1 and 10.3. The curves are jagged because births and age-related changes in weights are discontinuous.

differences: wealthier farmers can afford more land, and they can also, presumably, support larger families – and perhaps the labor of wealthier farmers is more productive simply because they can combine it with more capital (wealth is indeed an important potential confounding factor in testing Chayanov's model). Chayanov's evidence carries exactly the same conclusiveness (or lack thereof) as any correlational study.

Has Chayanov's Model already been Falsified?

It is appropriate to pause here to consider if we may be beating a dead or seriously disabled horse. During the 20 years or so following publication of Chayanov's *Theory of Peasant Economy* in English, several attempts were made to test his model against real-world data collected among peasants or other preindustrial farmers. Some authors have interpreted the results of these various efforts as providing, at best, only weak or mixed support and, at worst, no support or outright falsification of Chayanov's predictions (Tannenbaum, 1984; Shanin, 1986; Ellis, 1993: 116–18; Netting, 1993: 312–19). More positive results were reported by Minge-Kalman (1977), Durrenberger (1979), Hunt (1979), Dove (1984, 1985) and Chibnik (1984, 1987). Results deemed to falsify Chayanov were presented by Due and Anadajayasekeram (1984), Herring (1984), McGough (1984), Tannenbaum (1984) and Wiber (1985).

Frankly, I find none of these earlier studies, pro or con, terribly convincing, for all of them suffer from serious deficiencies of study design and statistical reasoning. For one thing, almost all are based on extremely small samples, usually in the range of 10–50 cases, too few to provide the statistical power needed to reject the hypothesis that C/P ratios have no effect on household production. In addition, all the analyses use very defective measures of C and P. (Indeed, many of them use preexisting data collected for entirely different purposes and not really suited to the purpose at hand.) So, for example, almost none of the estimates of P include domestic work, which I regard as essential to the household enterprise and likely to be sensitive to the C/P ratio (the only exception is Minge-Kalman, 1977, who rightly criticizes other measures of P for being gross under-estimates). Some of the studies draw upon production statistics concerning only a single dominant crop, even though secondary crops often require considerable labor. And no one attempts to estimate age- and sex-specific weights for computing values of C and P that are appropriate for the particular population being studied – often using Chayanov's own weights, which were estimated for a specific region of Russia, or falling back on the old-fashioned, imprecise and usually culturally inappropriate dependency ratio taken from demography (i.e. the ratio of the number of household members younger than 15 and older than 65 to the number between 15 and 65 – a measure that under-values the work of children and the elderly in many preindustrial societies). An even more serious criticism is that – again, with one exception (the historical data from Iowa examined by Chibnik, 1984, 1987) – all the empirical analyses were cross-sectional and cross-household, whereas Chayanov's model is about longitudinal changes *within* households.[7]

---

[7] Chayanov's own supporting evidence suffered from this same shortcoming.

But there is an even deeper problem with all these analyses: they examine simple bivariate relationships, with no controls for potential confounding variables. This is more than a minor statistical impropriety – it reflects a fundamental lack of understanding of the whole logic of scientific modeling. To cite an author whose work I admire but who I think was wrongheaded in the present connection, Netting (1993: 315) lodged the following complaint against Chayanov:

Chayanov's analysis does incorporate other factors besides the consumer/worker ratios in determining the utility curves..., but the model's radical simplifications, by glossing over the complexities of differing household productive strategies and ignoring cash-producing activities, encourage an emphasis on the easily computed consumer/worker ratios as correlated with product per worker. The attractive shortcut to household labor input misses the complexities introduced by shortages of land and market participation that consistently enter into smallholder household decision making. Using 12 data sets covering societies as distant as the Tsembaga swiddeners [of highland New Guinea] and Iowa farmers in 1880, Michael Chibnick found a positive correlation between consumer/worker and production/worker ratios [as predicted by the model] in 11 of 12 cases, but only in 4 cases was the correlation greater than 0.3. This suggests that nondemographic variables, such as access to land and capital, value of farm implements, and location of farm in relation to transportation and market centers, are more important factors in affecting household production (Chibnik, 1987:96).

This statement contains a considerable amount of truth and one glaring falsehood – that C/P ratios are "easily computed" (see below) – but it is basically irrelevant.[8] Of course Chayanov's model radically oversimplifies household production strategies – it's a *model*. At the risk of nagging the reader, I repeat that the whole purpose of a model is to simplify reality in order to isolate important effects that might otherwise be swamped by other variables. To provide any kind of fair test of such a model, those other confounding variables need to be controlled statistically in some form of multivariate analysis. Earlier studies simply did not attempt to do this – and their small sample sizes would have precluded it anyway.

There are two other issues. First, in trying to construct *general* models, we are wise to emphasize *general* variables and relationships – and special attention ought to be paid to ones that are *inevitably* present in some form or another. The household demographic life cycle is an inevitable part of all household economies, whereas several of the other factors mentioned by Netting (cash-producing activities, location of market centers, land shortages) may or may not be relevant. When they *are* present, as Netting rightly notes, those other factors may well obscure the effects of the C/P ratio – which is precisely why they need to be controlled statistically if we are to test Chayanov's model properly. It may even turn out that changes in C/P ratios are correlated with

---

[8] And, anyway, Chayanov himself made essentially the same point: "[I]n order to avoid incorrect treatment of our conclusions we ought to stress that at any particular moment the family *is not the sole determinant of the size of a particular farm*, and determines its size only in a general way. The comparatively high correlation coefficients established between these figures are, nevertheless, far from 1.00. This alone indicates the existence of parallel factors which in their turn exert a pressure on the figure being studied" (Chayanov, 1986: 69; emphasis as in original).

CHAYANOV ACTING ON THE SUPPLY SIDE:

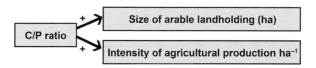

CHAYANOV ACTING ON THE DEMAND SIDE:

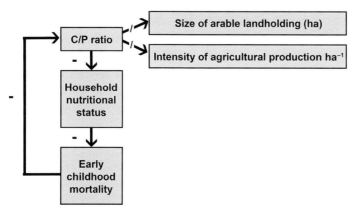

Figure 10.3 The conventional model that has C/P ratio acting purely on the supply side of the household economy (top) and an extended model that allows for possible effects on the demand side when supply-side responses are blocked or impeded (bottom). Pluses and minuses indicate the direction of the *bivariate* relationship between boxes. Thus, the closed loop in the bottom panel represents a negative feedback that should keep C/P within bounds.

those other factors – e.g. a high C/P ratio may be one thing motivating household market participation – introducing simultaneity problems that make it even harder to isolate the effects of C/P ratios statistically. A well-specified multivariate model and high-quality longitudinal data are needed to overcome such problems.

Finally, all the tests reviewed above considered the possible effects of C/P ratios strictly on the supply side of the household economy – on food production – whereas the demographically important effects might well fall on the demand side. An unfavorable C/P ratio may have negligible effects on food production if other limiting factors prevent an effective agricultural response. In that very case, we might expect a high C/P ratio to feed back on C via mortality, especially early childhood mortality associated with under-nutrition (Figure 10.3). We turn now to some recent analyses that have examined that possibility.

Do C/P Ratios Matter?

After a hiatus of some years, several researchers have recently turned again to Chayanovian principles in an attempt to understand preindustrial farming households. None of these studies is entirely free of the kinds of statistical shortcomings and deficiencies of study design discussed above – but they all have multiple advantages over earlier analyses.

The Shuar of Ecuador are a large group of Jivaroan-speaking shifting cultivators living along the western margins of Amazonia and the eastern foothills of the Andes. Hagen *et al.* (2006) have reported findings on the effects of household C/P ratio on dependent children's nutritional status (as reflected in their anthropometrics) in one Shuar village. This study was cross-sectional, and it used a poor measure of the C/P ratio (basically a slight modification of the dependency ratio), but it was otherwise statistically sophisticated. Typical findings from one of several analyses are shown in Table 10.6. In all the analyses, including those not shown here, high C/P ratios appear to depress children's nutritional status, even when adjusted for several confounding variables (see notes to Table 10.6). While the R^2 values in this analysis are small, supporting the suggestion by Netting and indeed Chayanov himself that other, nondemographic factors may also have important and sometimes dominating effects, that does not mean that the effect of C/P ratio is not real, but only that other effects may swamp it. Whatever additional variables might be involved, it would seem that Shuar parents struggle to feed their children adequately when C/P ratios are unfavorable. This suggests, in turn, that Shuar householders are not fully able to compensate for changing C/P ratios. (Paradoxically, with perfect compensation the C/P ratio would have no discernible statistical influence at all, even if it were the most powerful force driving the household's economic behavior.) For similar results from Ethiopia, see Hadley *et al.* (2011).

Taking the implications for child health one step further, Campbell and Lee (1996) found a large effect of the C/P ratio on infant mortality among peasant farmers in

Table 10.6 Robust regression of dependents' age-adjusted anthropometric variables on household C/P ratio in 85 children (<20 years of age) in 27 Shuar households, eastern Andean foothills of Ecuador.[a] Observations were clustered by household to correct for within-household correlations (Hagen *et al.*, 2006). Reprinted, with permission of John Wiley & Sons, Inc, from E. H. Hagen, H. C. Barrett and M. E. Price (2006) Do human parents face a quantity-quality tradeoff? Evidence from a Shuar community. *American Journal of Physical Anthropology*, 130, 405–18.

Response variable	Estimated coefficient (s.e.)	t	p	R^2
Height (residual)	– 0.44 (0.09)	– 4.95	<0.001	0.19
Weight (residual)	– 0.41 (0.06)	– 6.51	<0.001	0.03
Body mass index (residual)	– 0.40 (0.08)	– 2.72	0.011	0.05
Body fat (residual)	– 0.46 (0.08)	– 5.03	<0.001	0.03
Arm circumference (residual)	– 0.23 (0.08)	– 5.90	<0.001	0.21
Height (z-score)	– 0.40 (0.09)	– 4.44	<0.001	0.03
Weight (z-score)	– 0.49 (0.09)	– 5.52	<0.001	0.24
Body mass index (z-score)	– 0.41 (0.10)	– 4.21	<0.001	0.03

[a] *Notes*: (1) C/P ratio remains significant when adjusted for father's social status and household landholding size/soil quality. (2) C/P ratio remains significant when anthropometric residuals were combined into two independent variables by principal components analysis. (3) C/P ratio remains significant when multiple-test corrections are made.

Table 10.7 Results of Cox proportional hazards analysis of infant mortality on four northern islands of Orkney, Scotland, 1855–2001 (*n* = 1275 live births, excluding twins). All results are adjusted for period (birth cohort) and island of occurrence. Effect sizes are expressed as relative risks of infant death, either in comparison to the reference category or attributable to a unit increase in the corresponding predictor variable. Household (HH)-level frailty variance adjusts for unmeasured heterogeneity among households (Sparks *et al.*, 2013). Reprinted, with permission of John Wiley & Sons, Inc, from C. S. Sparks, J. W. Wood and P. L. Johnson (2013) Infant mortality and intra-household competition in the northern islands of Orkney, Scotland, 1855–2001. *American Journal of Physical Anthropology*, 151, 191–201.

Predictor variable	Relative risk of infant death	95 percent confidence interval
Household C/P ratio	1.49	1.15–1.93
Mother's age at child's birth	0.99	0.94–1.00
Child's sex (male = 1)	1.20	0.93–1.55
Length of previous birth interval	0.64	0.38–1.09
Birth order:		
first (reference)	1.00	–
second to fifth	1.02	0.66–1.57
greater than fifth	0.44	0.18–1.09
Previous child died? (yes = 1)	1.32	0.76–2.29
Father's occupation:		
farmer (reference)	1.00	–
farm laborer	1.20	0.90–1.62
merchant, minister, etc.	1.81	1.26–2.61

HH-level frailty variance = 0.18.

Liaoning, China, where long-term prospective data were available (see also Lee and Campbell, 2005). Sparks *et al.* (2013) also examined the influence of the C/P ratio on infant mortality in the northern islands of Orkney, Scotland, from the mid-nineteenth century to the present (Table 10.7). This historical demographic study was prospective, covering about a century and a half of household experience, the sample size was large (1275 live births recorded in the vital registers of five islands) and the statistical controls were well thought-out. In this analysis, it appears that a unit increase in C/P ratio raises the risk of infant death by almost 50 percent.

We also examined the situation over recent decades in an irrigated rice-farming village in northern Laos (Tomita *et al.*, 2015). This village is far enough off the beaten track that it was, until very recently, largely noncommercialized in its agricultural production. Table 10.8 shows the results of our analyses of prospective data for the period from 1971, when written records on the village become reliable, to 2006, when the effects of economic modernization were taking hold. What the results show is that, once several possible confounding effects of additional household demographic variables and other chronological changes are controlled for, there is a substantial and significant effect of C/P ratio on the probability of early childhood mortality within the household. All the other predictor variables have effects that are in the

Table 10.8 Mixed-effect logit hazard model with random household-level intercept, early childhood mortality (ages <5 years), Na Savang Village, northern Laos 1971–2006. $N = 148$ early childhood deaths among 3075 children at risk. Parameters of the random household intercept are presented as estimate ± one standard error. The parity of the birth in question was not entered as a control variable because of its high correlation with mother's age (Tomita et al., 2015). Reprinted from S. Tomita, D. M. Parker, J. A. Jennings and J. W. Wood (2015) Household demography and early childhood mortality in a rice-farming village in northern Laos. *PLOS ONE* 10, e0119191. Doi:10.1371/journal. pone.0119191. Copyright © 2015 Tomita et al.

Predictor variable	Estimated β coefficient	Standard error	Effect size[a]	z-value	Corrected[b] p
Demographic and household (HH) variables:					
Child's age	– 1.182	0.222	0.307	– 5.335	0.001
Child's age^2	0.172	0.062	1.187	2.766	0.018
Child's sex (female = 1)	0.116	0.179	1.123	0.645	0.999
Mother's age	– 0.027	0.012	0.973	– 2.206	0.081
HH landholding (ha)	– 0.000	<0.001	1.000	– 2.125	0.102
HH size	0.047	0.024	1.048	1.945	0.156
C/P ratio	2.199	0.865	9.020	2.541	0.032
Chronological control variables:					
Collectivization? (yes = 1)	0.059	0.252	1.060	0.233	0.999
Disaster? (yes = 1)	0.050	0.256	1.051	0.194	0.999
Period 1 (1971–1980)	1.244	0.507	3.470	2.455	0.126
Period 2 (1981–1990)	1.048	0.520	2.851	2.014	0.132
Period 3 (1991–2000)	0.594	0.515	1.812	1.154	0.747
Period 4 (2001–2006)	———————— reference category ————————				

Random household intercept:
Estimated mean = – 5.317 ± 1.274
Estimated variance = 0.107 ± 0.029

[a] Effect size = exp(estimated β coefficient). No effect = 1.0.
[b] Bonferroni correction for multiple tests against alternative pretested models.

anticipated direction, but that are much smaller than that of the C/P ratio, as indicated by the column labeled "Effect size." In other words, increasing C/P ratios within the household appear to be associated with a large increase in early childhood mortality.

Finally, there are other ways to look at the agricultural effects of household composition. For example, several recent studies concerned with the interaction of population and deforestation in the Amazon Basin (Lutzenheiser and Hackett, 1993; Pichón, 1996; Godoy et al., 1997; McCraken et al., 1999; Perz, 2001, 2002; Perz et al., 2006) have suggested that household-level demographic variables, including the C/P ratio or dependency ratio, may be just as important as population-level ones in predicting land-use patterns and environmental degradation. To cite one study, Perz (2002) has investigated land use among recent migrants to Uruará, in Brazil's Pará

District, who have established small farms along the Transamazonian Highway. In particular he examined decisions about whether 314 plots of land owned by 261 households would be left as primary forest, cultivated as active cropland, converted into more or less permanent pasture, or allowed to lie fallow as secondary growth. His data were cross-sectional and his analyses in effect used the dependency ratio (or rather its components), but his attempts at statistical control were impressive. His analyses suggest that the age structure of the household has significant and comparatively large effects on land use, especially decisions to crop a plot or allow it to lie fallow. No clear effects were found on the use of pasture, which is devoted primarily to commercial beef production rather than household subsistence.

How should Age- and Sex-Specific Consumption and Production Weights be Estimated?

Despite their more sophisticated statistical models, one way in which the studies just discussed were as deficient as earlier analyses of the C/P ratio was in their use of arbitrary, nonlocal age- and sex-specific weights for computing C and P. The failure of so many studies to compute appropriate age- and sex-specific weights raises a discomfiting question: Is it actually *possible* to estimate C and P in any credible, population-specific way? Chayanov himself defined both variables semisubjectively, in terms of the marginal utility of food output and the marginal disutility of labor – consumer satisfaction (judged against local consumption standards) versus perceived drudgery. In my reformulation, I prefer to operationalize them in terms of more objective metrics, even if these are not necessarily easier to measure. In the previous chapter, I used bioenergetic units (or proxies for them such as investment of time) as my currency for evaluating work in subsistence. Numerous studies suggest that both the biological energy available for aerobic work and the dietary energy required for active life vary by age and sex in ways that would not, I think, have surprised Chayanov (Figure 10.4). Based on such studies, at least one attempt has been made to reformulate Chayanov's model in bioenergetic terms (Ulijaszek and Strickland, 1993; see also Ulijaszek, 1995: 158–64). But both quantities – work energy available and dietary energy required – are also affected by local or individual factors such as disease burden, available tools, ambient temperature and perhaps even genetics. More importantly, both quantities are inextricably related – the more you work, the more you need to eat – rendering any attempt to estimate them separately in the same population problematic. Thus, while the general *shapes* of the age and sex patterns in Figure 10.4 may be more or less universal in humans, the precise values almost certainly are not. Logically, the curves in Figure 10.4 represent the kinds of things we are trying to get at, but we cannot take it for granted that the curves estimated for healthy, well-nourished, moderately active Westerners are at all appropriate for any group of traditional farmers.

The most successful attempt, by far, to estimate age- and sex-specific consumption and production weights for a particular local community of near-subsistence farmers

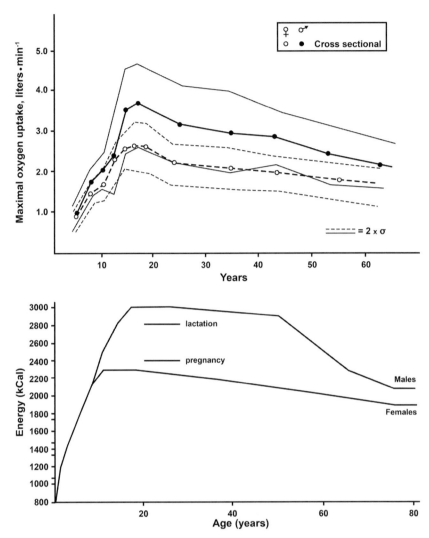

Figure 10.4 (Top) Aerobic work capacity ("production") by age and sex, measured on a treadmill at controlled speeds. Mean values (± 2 s.d.) for healthy, well-nourished Scandinavians of ages 4 to 65 years. (Bottom) Recommended daily energy consumption for healthy, moderately active individuals from the United Kingdom, c. 1970. From *Reports on Public Health and Medical Subjects, Great Britain*, 1970, London, pp. 1–14, by permission of Her Majesty's Stationery Office; Rodahl (1989: 20), by permission of the Taylor Francis Group.

was carried out by the demographer Ron Lee and anthropologist Karen Kramer (2002). In the 1990s, Kramer (1998, 2005) did an extraordinary piece of fieldwork among Maya shifting cultivators living in a village called Xculoc in the northern Yucatan of Mexico. At the time of study, Xculoc had almost no involvement in the cash economy. Travel to the nearest markets involved a five-hour hike to a paved road where villagers might be able to catch a ride to several market towns 40–60 km away. It sounds as if their diet was virtually unchanged from the precolonial past:

The majority of calories consumed comes from maize, but the Maya also cultivate beans, squash, sweet potatoes, and peanuts. Many families maintain a kitchen garden where they grow a variety of citrus, avocado, banana, and papaya trees, and numerous other fruits and vegetables. Domesticated turkeys, ducks, chickens, and pigs [the latter two postcontact introductions from the Old World] are raised for occasional consumption, and deer, peccaries, coatis, armadillos, and various birds are hunted to supplement the diet. Honey is collected for sale from hives they maintain in the forest, and small quantities of maize may be exchanged in the village store for a limited range of commodities such as vegetable oil, eggs, and candles. Otherwise no cash crops are grown. (Lee and Kramer, 2002: 477)

Data on the farmers of Xculoc come from a time-allocation survey based on scan sample techniques: an individual's spot activity (i.e. what he or she was doing at the moment of observation) was recorded at 15-minute intervals over a period of three to four hours during a single day, and these observations were repeated once every few weeks over the course of an entire agricultural year. Through the combined efforts of multiple recorders fluent in Mayan, over 17 000 observations were made on 112 individuals of ages 0–65 years from 19 households, with an average of 155 observations per individual (Kramer, 2005: 93). Kramer collaborated with Lee to estimate production and consumption patterns from these data (Lee and Kramer, 2002), using an admirably expansive definition of productive work:

Productive activities include any agricultural task (ground preparation, planting, weeding, harvesting, transporting field goods), domestic task (washing, cleaning, food processing, food preparation, cooking, serving, running errands, hauling water, chopping firewood, tending animals), and wage labor [which was rare]. (Lee and Kramer, 2002: 496)[9]

Initially, *production* (P) was measured as the mean number of hours per day (averaged over the whole year) invested by an individual in these activities. (Scan sampling is, in comparison to more continuous observation of time allocation, a poor way to estimate the mean number of hours spent in any given activity.) But, since productivity per hour of work was unlikely to be the same for all ages and both sexes, task-specific weights intended to reflect each individual's labor efficiency (productivity hr^{-1} ÷ energy expenditure hr^{-1}) relative to young adults were estimated using data from a small pilot study (see Kramer, 2005: 125–7, 194). In addition, each task

---

[9] While this study is to be commended for including so much domestic labor, it does suffer one important omission: child care. "While direct child care (activities such as washing, feeding, bathing, and nursing) can be clearly observed and recorded, many indirect forms of child care (carrying a child, talking to a child) may or may not be recorded depending on observer discretion and what suites of activities he or she classifies as child care. In some households, for example, babies and young children are put in a hammock (the Maya equivalent of a playpen) much more often than is the case in other households, where young children are constantly held or carried. We do not include child care as work because personal parenting preferences would lead to marked individual differences in overall work effort. Nonetheless, child care is an important activity especially in young girls' lives. Maya girls allocate 7 percent of their time to child care compared to the 1 percent boys spend on that activity. If child care were included as work, it would considerably boost the time girls spend working while having little effect on boys' work effort" (Lee and Kramer, 2002: 496).

was weighted by its presumed caloric cost, using values taken from the literature (Lee and Kramer, 2002: 495).

Consumption (C) needs to be measured in the same time-based currency as production if the C/P ratio is to be scale-free. This poses a number of problems, forcing Lee and Kramer to make several assumptions that may or may not have been warranted. Since inter-household exchanges of food appeared to be uncommon, it was assumed that the household is a genuinely autonomous unit of food production and consumption, and that on average the amounts of food produced and eaten by the household as a whole are equal to each other (it is unclear how seed stock and losses during storage were handled in this calculus). Under this assumption, total household food consumption is simply equal to total household food production expressed as the weighted time required to produce that quantity of food. The next assumption is a big one. Each household member's share of the food produced was assumed to be proportional to his or her nutritional requirements, as extrapolated from "standard tables" (i.e. nonlocal estimates of dietary requirements) adjusted for the member's age, sex, body mass and activity level (Lee and Kramer, 2002: 481). Setting aside the question of whether the nonlocal standards are really appropriate, there is a worrying question as to whether food is normally divided within the household according to each member's needs (recall from Chapter 8 that females are often at a disadvantage when it comes to food allocation). Nevertheless, *if these assumptions are correct*, then C as calculated by Lee and Kramer can be interpreted as the mean hours of weighted household time required to produce the food consumed by an individual each day, averaged over the whole year.

Figure 10.5 plots the individual age- and sex-specific estimates of C and P computed for Xculoc by these methods, as well as the smoothed patterns revealed by fitting spline functions to these estimates. Perhaps unsurprisingly, the individual values vary a great deal, with the sexes and age groups overlapping to a considerable extent. The smoothed patterns, however, correspond in a rough way to expectations based on the bioenergetic curves in Figure 10.4 – and perhaps that should give us some confidence that Lee and Kramer are headed in the right direction. Based on the smoothed curves in Figure 10.5, Figure 10.6 shows the changes in the C/P ratio across the average household life cycle in Xculoc (as reconstructed from cross-sectional data).[10]

---

[10] There is a subtle but important technical detail in how Lee and Kramer (2002: 488–9, 496) go from the smoothed curves in Figure 10.5 to the average C/P ratio among all households by year of marriage. The values of P and C in Figure 10.5 already include any additional production investments or cuts in consumption made in response to high C/P ratios. "For example, the average production effort of a 30-year-old woman already reflects the fact that 30-year-old women typically live in households with many young children and therefore experience economic pressure in response to which they have already adjusted their production or consumption. The smoothed profiles already assume a response to the very household pressures that we now wish to measure, hence their use would lead us to underestimate the extent of these pressures" (Lee and Kramer, 2002: 488). This is one aspect of the problem of estimating C and P separately when they are necessarily interrelated. To circumvent this problem, Lee and Kramer model the C and P values estimated for each individual as the product of a standard age–sex profile (which they wish to retrieve) and a household-specific fixed effect (which they wish to eliminate). By removing the household-specific effect, they correct for the problem that

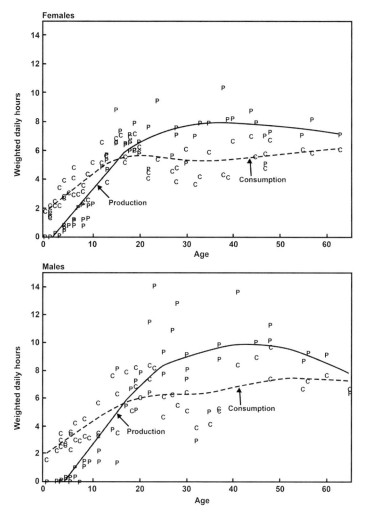

Figure 10.5 Food production (solid lines) and consumption (dashed lines) across the life course of Maya females and males, shifting cultivators, Xculoc village, Northern Yucatan (*n* = 112 individuals of ages 0–65 years). Letters are individual estimates; smoothed curves are fit to the estimates by spline functions. Note that C does not equal the average time an individual spends consuming each day, but rather the average time (weighted by the workers' productivity) that it takes the individual's household to *produce* the food he or she consumes each day. From Lee and Kramer (2002: 483), by permission of John Wiley & Sons, Inc.

C/P ratios appear to peak some 10 years after the marriage that established the household, and the peak is almost 250 percent higher than the initial value, quite a bit more than originally reckoned by Chayanov. Moreover, there is a secondary increase in C/P after the thirtieth year of marriage as working-age children leave home

individuals at particular stages of their own lives are likely to live in households experiencing particular levels of economic stress. And Netting (1993: 315) thought C/P ratios were easy to compute!

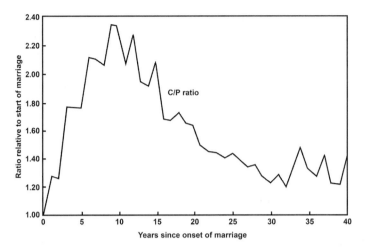

Figure 10.6 Ratio of consumers (C) to producers (P), each calculated as the weighted average of family members by age and sex, across the life cycle of the average Maya family. Age- and sex-specific C and P weights are taken from Figure 10.5. The jaggedness of the curves reflects the fact that births and deaths in the household are discontinuous. From Lee and Kramer (2002: 491), by permission of John Wiley & Sons, Inc.

and the original married couple, whose productivity is declining with age, is forced to rely more and more on its own labor. Alas, Lee and Kramer provide no evidence for how household production or consumption may have changed in response to these changes in C/P.

These estimates from Xculoc seem plausible if difficult to verify, and they almost have to be better than the dependency ratio or the arbitrary numbers used in other studies. But they are still to some extent indirect and based on assumptions that go well beyond the empirical evidence at hand. We have not yet reached the Promised Land where C/P ratios are estimated by perfect and simple methods – or even convinced ourselves that such an earthly paradise exists. But it may not matter a great deal. Julia Jennings (2010: 218–35) has recently performed a series of sensitivity analyses using several different sets of age- and sex-specific production and consumption weights – including Lee and Kramer's (Figure 10.5) and those based on bioenergetic data (Figure 10.4), as well as Chayanov's original weights (Table 10.2) and a new set suggested by Hammel (2005 – see below). She also threw in the crude dependency ratio for comparison. Using historical demographic data from north Orkney, Scotland, and applying the resulting C/P ratios or dependency ratios as predictor variables in regression analyses of several important demographic and economic outcomes (household birth rate, early childhood deaths, deaths among the elderly, household size and form, presence of servants in the household and value of the household's landholding), it turns out that all sets of weights – with the notable exception of the dependency ratio – yield similar regression coefficients for the effect of C/P ratio. The Lee–Kramer's weights and the bioenergetic weights were highly correlated ($r = 0.88$) and gave consistently similar parameter estimates, but the performance of Chayanov and Hammel's weights was not far off the mark. Thus, if the various weights among which we have to choose are more or less similar and biologically plausible, they may all provide equally valid statistical results. If so, future investigations of the C/P ratio will be considerably easier than they otherwise would have been. Of course, it is also possible that all the weights examined by Jennings were equally *bad* for the Orkney case. Much more research needs to be done before we can settle the issue.[11] In the meantime, Lee and Kramer's efforts, as imperfect as they may be, set the standard: they are unlikely to be bettered any time soon.

Possible Household Strategies for Coping with a High C/P Ratio

As argued by Chayanov, an increase in the household's C/P ratio must be countered by an increase in its intensity of food production if the health and survival of its members are not to be compromised. For the moment, let's stop worrying about empirical estimation and consider from a purely theoretical point of view how a household might try to cope with a high C/P ratio. There are several possibilities for offsetting an increase in C/P, but all are likely to be of limited value in the face of the many factors constraining traditional food production (see Chapter 3). Starting with the coping strategy that Chayanov himself considered most important among the land-rich Russian and Ukrainian peasants he worked with, the household might be able to *obtain more arable land*. But in other situations land may be scarce and households may compete for any additional land, as Chayanov's critics have pointed out (e.g. Millar, 1970; Netting, 1993). More fundamentally, declining marginal productivity of land may be common in traditional household-based farming systems (see Figure 3.14) – meaning that, past some point, additional land cannot be farmed productively by a small household labor force no matter how hard it works (Binswanger and McIntire, 1987).

Which brings us to the next coping strategy: those household members who do work can *work harder*, as does seem to happen in some cases (Minge-Kalman, 1977; Chibnick, 1987).[12] But, as emphasized in Chapter 9, the household's total physiological work capacity is sharply limited by its small labor force, even if draft animals are used. In addition, steeply declining marginal productivity of labor appears to be widespread in subsistence farming (see Figure 3.12). That Chayanov himself recognized this problem is illustrated by his famous graph of the balance between consumer satisfaction and drudgery (Chayanov, 1986: 82), reinterpreted in bioenergetic terms in Figure 10.7. But if you cannot work harder, perhaps you can *work more efficiently* – allocate your labor more judiciously, perhaps even adopt new tools that do a better job of minimizing wastage of human energy. By the same token, you can

[11] For a different, equally encouraging, sensitivity-analysis approach to C/P ratios, see Tomita *et al.* (2015).

[12] Indeed, if the household obtains more land, it *must* work harder if it is to exploit it. But intensification of work can also be done on a landholding of fixed size.

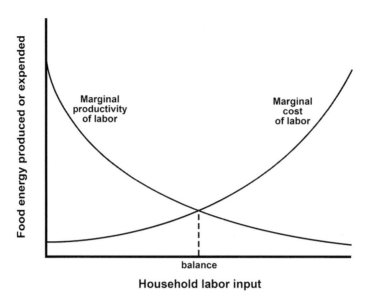

Figure 10.7 A bioenergetic reinterpretation of Chayanov's balance between consumer satisfaction (marginal productivity of labor) and drudgery (marginal cost of labor). There is absolutely no practical reason for a subsistence farming household to invest labor beyond the balance point, for the net return on labor would then be negative.

organize your farm more efficiently, perhaps by arranging it in space along von Thünian lines. (This, of course, is also a matter of using human energy more efficiently – in this case, energy expended in transport.) In other words, a high C/P ratio may induce improvements in farming techniques and organization, which may even endure after the C/P ratio starts to decline again. But these improvements can only go so far. Once you have arranged your farm as close to the von Thünian ideal as possible on an anisotropic landscape, for example, you've exhausted that option.

Perhaps you can *invest more capital* – if, that is, more capital exists. Formation of landesque capital – terraces, irrigation canals, dikes, raised fields, etc. – is one possibility (see Chapter 2); but such capital, being expensive and semipermanent, may not be warranted in view of the transitoriness of high C/P values: the ratio may already be dropping well before landesque capital has recouped its initial costs. This idea introduces an important time element into our discussion, in that strategies for offsetting high C/P ratios, which normally last only a few years, must yield results fairly quickly if they are to be of much use.

Confining ourselves to strategies that can be implemented to good effect in the short term, you might be able to counter a high C/P ratio by *changing this year's decisions about land use or cropping regimes*, as suggested by Perz's (2002) research in Transamazonia. Or perhaps you can *move somewhere better*, if somewhere better exists and the costs of the move are low enough. If you are unable to increase the work performed per hour or per kilocalorie by each worker in the household, then perhaps you can *bring in more workers* – i.e. lower the C/P ratio by increasing

P. Although it violates one of Chayanov's basic assumptions (which is, after all, the ultimate fate of all model assumptions), the household may be able to hire labor from the outside if it can afford to do so. Consistent with this idea, Jennings *et al.* (2011) have found that the number and characteristics of hired farm workers in nineteenth-century Orkney changed as expected with the hiring household's C/P ratio. Alternatively, it may be possible to *form extended households* in a way that improves the overall C/P ratio for at least one of the constituent nuclear families – what Reyna (1976) once called "the extending strategy." This is an interesting possibility, and I consider it in more detail below.

When some marketing of food is done, it may be prudent (depending on market conditions) for you to *sell less food*. Peasant farmers often do this in times of regional food shortages (Vanhaute, 2011), so why not when household C/P ratios are unfavorable? This strategy does not literally increase P, but it may increase the *effective* amount of food available to the household. Alternatively, when agricultural produce is a drug on the market, it might be a good idea to *buy more food*. One might even contemplate going into nonagricultural production (e.g. craft production) for sale at market if prices are such that it is profitable to trade your own nonagricultural labor for someone else's labor in growing food. Finally, you may be able to *go into debt* to some more successful household – a classic "solution" in peasant communities but one with unpleasant potential long-term consequences of a political nature (i.e. the formation of enduringly asymmetrical patron–client relationships).

Aside from these last three options, most of the responses listed thus far would be considered forms of *household* agricultural intensification, affecting the household but not necessarily the whole population. They suggest (but do not exhaust) the range of household responses that scientists trying to test Chayanov ought to examine. While none of these strategies is perfect, risk-free or ultimately unconstrained, each represents a deliberate attempt to reduce the C/P ratio by increasing P – an attempt, in other words, to respond to "Chayanovian" demographic pressure by intensifying household food production. (Note the similarity to Boserup's logic but now operating at the level of the individual household.) But it is also possible, if inherently dangerous, to try to lower C. For example, the entire household can try to *make do with less food* – although Malthus and the MaB ratchet suggest that it may already be close to the margins of under-nutrition (see Chapter 5). And if the household's total food intake cannot be increased substantially, it may still be possible to *change the intra-household allocation of food* to some advantage, perhaps by diverting more to dependent, nonproductive children who are especially vulnerable (Abdullah and Wheeler, 1985; Wheeler and Abdullah, 1988). Steering food away from productive adults, however, may affect their physiological work capacity in a way that ultimately works to the disadvantage of the entire household, as once suggested by Schofield (1974).

If none of these options, separately or together, is adequate to solve the problems of a high C/P ratio, then the ultimate response comes into play – *have fewer children or let some of the ones you've already had die* – i.e. Malthus's preventive or positive check. Although it is contrary to the whole aim of the household demographic

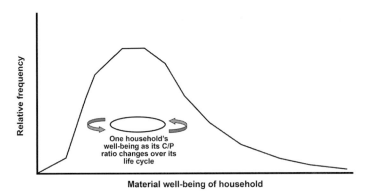

Figure 10.8 Cycling C/P ratios as a possible source of inter- and intra-household variation in material well-being.

enterprise, this "option" is arguably, on a worldwide basis, the most common response to unfavorable C/P ratios – which does not make it the most *preferred* one.

This discussion suggests some hypotheses concerning cycling C/P ratios as a possible factor in the success or failure of the household demographic enterprise.

- The material well-being of a subsistence farming household is liable to change as its C/P ratio changes. Since the life cycles of different households are out of sync, cycling C/P ratios are likely to explain some non-trivial fraction of inter-household variation in well-being. Precisely because of the dynamic nature of the C/P ratio, however, a household's relative position on the distribution of material well-being across the community is unlikely to be constant (Figure 10.8).
- The C/P ratio is a major factor determining the intensity of food production by the subsistence farming household. An unfavorable C/P ratio can constitute a kind of "Chayanovian" population pressure for agricultural intensification operating purely at the household level, in distinction to "Boserupian" pressure acting at the population level. A population not subject to Boserupian pressure can still contain households experiencing Chayanovian pressure.[13] When *both* are present, however, the two forms of pressure are likely to operate on different time scales: in general we expect Chayanovian pressure to be more transitory (but perhaps more acute) than Boserupian.

[13] There is an important technical point here, and I beg forgiveness for this footnote from readers not familiar with mathematical demography. For those who are, imagine a perfectly stationary population with constant age- and sex-specific fertility and mortality, no external migration, age- and sex-distributions at stable equilibrium, and a zero growth rate. Viewed in the aggregate, nothing about the population is changing: it is at an absolute equilibrium. But when we examine the individual households it contains, we find that *nothing* is at equilibrium: each household's total size and age/sex composition are changing (age composition continuously so). Households continue to cycle even when they are part of a strictly stationary population. Moreover, households, being in effect tiny populations, are always subject to random demographic fluctuations, even when the larger population, for all practical purposes, is not. Finally, inter-household migration will still be going on (e.g. because of marriage) even if no one enters or leaves the larger population. Household-level disequilibrium prevails even in the face of absolute population-level equilibrium.

- Limits on the household's ability to intensify food production in response to an increasing C/P ratio are major factors determining the nutritional status and work capacity of its members – *and* a major factor determining changes in C/P itself, principally via the impact of under-nutrition on early childhood mortality.
- The feedbacks (at the household level) among C/P ratio, work capacity, intensity of food production, under-nutrition and childhood mortality are among the most fundamental linkages between economy and demography in subsistence agriculture. These feedbacks constitute forms of "population" regulation and "population" pressure operating at the scale of the farming household.

The Extending Strategy

Reviving ideas first put forward by Reyna (1976) and Pasternack *et al.* (1976), Gene Hammel (2005) has recently suggested that household extension may sometimes originate as a mechanism for ameliorating the adverse effects of high C/P ratios. As Hammel notes, Chayanov's thinking about the domestic life cycle applies only to nuclear-family households over a single cycle, as in Table 10.1. What would happen, Hammel asks, if we were to follow households over multiple generations and enforce strict virilocal residence, thereby producing, after some period of time, both stem- and joint-family households? And how much difference would it make if we were to compare two contrasting assumptions about how the members of extended households cooperate with each other? On the one hand, we can assume that all household members selflessly pool the food they produce into a single common pot, from which the members draw strictly according to their individual consumption needs (no competition within the household). Alternatively, we can allow parents to cheat – that is, to deflect some of their own produce away from the common pot by a factor proportional to the number of their own surviving offspring, in effect depriving less closely related household members, who naturally enough are also likely to be cheating (intra-household competition). Hammel allows the level of cheating to vary: the greater the cheating (i.e. the more food deflected from the common pot), the more the extended household is acting, in terms of production and consumption, like a collection of independent nuclear-family households rather than a single cooperating unit.

Hammel also modifies Chayanov's model of the household life cycle by introducing more realistic demographic processes (the possibility of deaths within the household, fertility and mortality rates that vary with age, variable rates of marriage by age among adult offspring) and by using what he considers to be more realistic age- and sex-specific consumption and production weights. His suggested weights do seem more plausible than Chayanov's for many preindustrial societies insofar as they allow for a greater productive contribution by children and for declining productive capacity among the elderly. But Hammel's weights, unlike Chayanov's, are not based even loosely on empirical data.

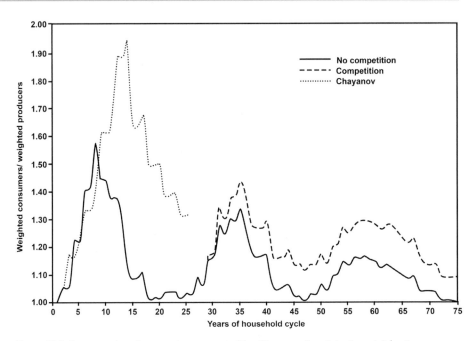

Figure 10.9 Consumer/producer ratios generated by Chayanov's original model (as in Figure 10.2) and by Hammel's model with and without intra-household competition. From Hammel (2005: 7045), by permission of the Proceedings of the National Academy of Sciences.

Hammel conducted simulation studies to explore the implications of all these assumptions, and his general results are illustrated in Figure 10.9. Three scenarios are shown: Chayanov's original results using his own age- and sex-specific weights, Hammel's results for households who are pooling resources (*no competition*), and Hammel's results for households with an intermediate level of cheating (*competition*), both the latter based on Hammel's weights. Chayanov's model is shown over a single household life cycle of 26 years, true to his original presentation, whereas Hammel's chugs along for 75 years and three successive life cycles, each about a generation in length. In both of Hammel's models, the household becomes more and more extended as male offspring marry and remain in the household with their families. During the first cycle all three models produce similar results over the first decade of the household's life span. But both of Hammel's models produce lower peaks than Chayanov's and drop more rapidly on the downward slope of the cycle, owing to the earlier involvement of children in household food production and the lower fertility rates and shorter reproductive span assumed by Hammel. At about the time that Chayanov's household is dissolving, Hammel's no-competition household is entering a second cycle. (We'll come back to the competing household in a moment.) But note that this second cycle reaches a markedly lower peak and is slightly more spread out than the first one. Both phenomena are the direct result of household extension and cooperation. By the second cycle we have a joint household linked by two or more brothers residing virilocally. Because of variation in the age at which the

Table 10.9 The people living at the croft complex of South Hammer according to two decennial censuses separated by 50 years.

Name	Relation to head	Sex	Age (years)	Marital status[a]	"Occupation"
South Hammer 1851					
Charles Paterson	head	♂	41	m	farmer of 4 acres, farm laborer on Tirlot estate
Ann Peterson	wife	♀	40	m	
Stewart Peterson	son	♂	14	s	
Mary Peterson	dau	♀	10	s	
Ann Peterson	dau	♀	6	s	
George Peterson	son	♂	4	s	
William Peterson	son	♂	2	s	
Janet Peterson	dau	♀	1	s	
South Hammer 1901					
1. Stewart Paterson	head	♂	64	m	farmer
1. Mary Paterson	wife	♀	58	m	
1. Robert Paterson	son	♂	24	s	assisting on father's farm
2. William Paterson	head	♂	63[b]	m	fisherman, blacksmith
2. Isabella Paterson	wife	♀	56	m	
2. Robert Paterson	son	♂	29	s	fisherman
3. Janet Rendall	head	♀	51	w	housekeeper
3. William Rendall	son	♂	27	s	plowman on Tirlot estate
3. John Rendall	son	♂	17	s	plowman on Tirlot estate
3. Charles Rendall	son	♂	13	s	scholar[c]
3. Jessie Rendall	dau	♀	11	s	scholar[c]

[a] m = married, w = widowed, s = single.
[b] Probable age misstatement or mistranscription if same William as in 1851.
[c] Attending local grammar school.

South Hammer type a *compound household* to distinguish it from the more usual form of extended household sharing a single domicile.

And what about cycles in South Hammer's C/P ratio? Assuming that the residents of South Hammer were fully cooperating, its C/P trajectory was as shown in the top panel of Figure 10.13. This trajectory is remarkably similar to Hammel's damped cycles. (Figure 10.13 also shows that another of Hammel's predictions is more or less correct – the size of the South Hammer compound household tended to increase over time, at least until it apparently hit a plateau and then declined in later years as the overall fertility in Westray dropped.) For comparison, the bottom panel of Figure 10.13 shows what the C/P ratios would have looked like if the various nuclear families occupying South Hammer over the years had indeed been separate,

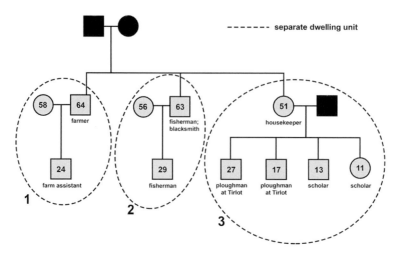

Figure 10.11 Kinship composition of South Hammer complex, 1901 census. Squares are male, circles female. Blacked-in squares and circles represent dead individuals. Numbers inside other squares and circles are ages (in years) in 1901. Numbers of dwellings are keyed to the structures in Figure 10.12. Tirlot is the large estate that then owned the land of South Hammer.

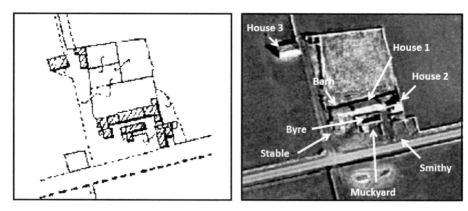

Figure 10.12 South Hammer croft complex. (Left) From 1901 OSGB map (1:2500 scale). (Right) From modern aerial photograph, with archaeological interpretation.

autonomous households. Just as Hammel expected, the total compound C/P ratios are substantially and progressively damped compared to the nuclear-family curves.

By combining documentary and archaeological evidence in this way, we have found that over half the households in our study area were either compound or otherwise extended in the late nineteenth century (Table 10.10). Contrary to Hajnal and Laslett – and much to our own surprise – nuclear-family households were actually in the minority in all six census years. In terms of numbers of members, moreover, compound households were considerably larger on average than other kinds of extended households, which in turn were somewhat larger than simple households (Table 10.11). Consistent with this finding, the size of

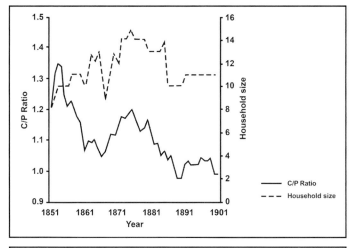

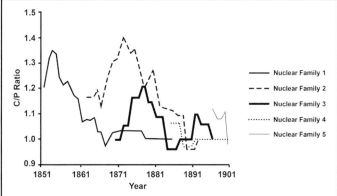

Figure 10.13 Demographic change at South Hammer, 1851–1901. (Top) Total size of the complex's membership (broken line) and C/P ratio of the complex as a whole (solid line). (Bottom) C/P ratios of the individual nuclear families residing at the complex. The age–sex weights for computing C/P ratios were taken from Hammel (2005). (Figure provided by Dr. Julia A. Jennings.)

compound-household *farms* (arable land plus pasture) as reflected in rents was larger than extended-household farms, which were larger than simple-household farms (Table 10.12). Since farm size (i.e. acreage) was virtually fixed over the period of interest, the larger holding size of compound- and extended-household farms was presumably an enabler of extension rather than a result of it: extended-family farms did not grow larger in area because they had to support more members, *à la* Chayanov, but rather larger farms could support greater extension. Finally, Table 10.13 provides the key piece of evidence – how C/P ratios varied by household type. The *mean* C/P ratio varies not at all among simple, extended and compound households. Nor would we expect it to since the average ratio of complex households is just the average of the average ratios of their constituent nuclear families. Hammel did not claim that complex households would *always* have lower C/P ratios than

Table 10.10 Frequency of simple extended and compound households in Northern Orkney (Westray, Papa Westray, Faray, Eday, Sanday and North Ronaldsay) in six decennial censuses, 1851–1901. From Jennings (2010).

Census year	Number of households	Frequency (%) of each household type		
		Simple	Extended	Compound
1851	428	43.0	18.0	39.0
1861	461	39.5	19.3	41.2
1871	475	41.7	21.9	36.4
1881	495	39.4	24.2	36.2
1891	468	47.0	22.2	30.8
1901	463	49.0	25.1	25.9

Table 10.11 Mean household size by household type, same sample as in Table 10.10. From Jennings (2010).

Census year	Number of households	Mean number of household members by type		
		Simple	Extended	Compound
1851	428	5.3	6.6	11.9
1861	461	5.2	6.8	11.0
1871	475	4.8	6.5	12.4
1881	495	4.8	6.6	11.2
1891	468	4.6	6.1	11.4
1901	463	4.3	5.8	11.1

Table 10.12 Mean rent by household type, same sample as in Tables 10.10 and 10.11. Rents are taken from farm valuation rolls and have been shown to be well-predicted ($R^2 = 0.97$) by the regression equation: rent $= \beta_0 + \beta_1$(area of arable) $+ \beta_2$(area of pasture) $+ \beta_{12}$(arable $\times$ pasture). In other words, the rent levied for each tenant farm is basically a measure of the size of its landholding. From Jennings (2010).

Census year	Number of households	Mean annual rent (££) by household type		
		Simple	Extended	Compound
1851	428	13.4	16.5	23.0
1861	461	11.7	13.4	22.5
1871	475	10.2	14.5	29.0
1881	495	15.2	18.2	31.7
1891	468	12.8	9.5	34.0
1901	463	11.2	10.8	30.8

simple ones over the entire life cycle, but that the peak should be lower and the variation in C/P over the whole cycle should be reduced. As the standard deviations in Table 10.13 show, this prediction is supported by the evidence. The reduction in C/P variation by household extension is admittedly small, but it is remarkably consistent.

Table 10.13 Mean and standard deviation in C/P ratios by household type, same sample as in Tables 10.10–10.12. C/P ratios are estimated from the census listings using age- and sex-specific consumption and production weights based on the bioenergetic curves in Figure 10.4. From Jennings (2010).

| | | C/P ratios by household type | | | | | |
| | | Simple | | Extended | | Compound | |
Census year	Number of households	mean	stan. dev.	mean	stan. dev.	mean	stan. dev.
1851	428	1.12	0.118	1.09	0.077	1.11	0.083
1861	461	1.11	0.132	1.11	0.082	1.11	0.087
1871	475	1.09	0.125	1.10	0.096	1.11	0.080
1881	495	1.09	0.122	1.10	0.095	1.10	0.082
1891	468	1.08	0.120	1.10	0.093	1.10	0.092
1901	463	1.07	0.112	1.08	0.087	1.09	0.095
Total	2790	1.09	0.122	1.10	0.090	1.10	0.086

So far, so Hammelish. But if the economic advantages of complex household structure are so patent, why did almost half the households in north Orkney consist of single nuclear families? What countervailing forces acted *against* household extension? As suggested by the curve of household size in Figure 10.13 (top panel) and the numbers in Table 10.11, households tend to grow larger as they become more extended, just as Hammel predicted. This would be fine in a land-rich country such as Chayanov's black earth region, but landholdings in Orkney were more or less constant in acreage over the period in question, and a growing household would eventually strain its farm resources and perhaps increase early childhood mortality. In addition, Hammel alludes to "the micropolitics of internal competition" as a possible constraint on extension. As the household grows in size relative to its landholding, internal competition is likely to worsen, exacerbating tensions between coresident nuclear families and increasing the probability that the household will split into its component parts. And there is another fact that Hammel does not consider. At any moment in the life cycle, household extension moderates the C/P ratio by averaging it across at least two nuclear families, one with a higher ratio and the other with a lower one. The latter family, in effect, "pays" for the moderate C/P ratio of the whole. What's in it for them? Are they likely to be the first to bail out of the enterprise?[15]

Micropolitics are impossible to examine in any straightforward way based on the kinds of historical and archaeological evidence available to us in the Orkney project. But one member of the project, Julia Jennings, has hit on an indirect way to get at some of these issues. What factors, she asks, are predictive of the dissolution or fissioning of extended households? The answers are illuminating (Table 10.14). First, note that the dynamics of dissolution are slightly different for compound households

---

[15] Later in the life cycle, the C/P ratios of the two families may be reversed, but that may not be soon enough to satisfy the family whose composition is more favorable right now.

Table 10.14 The effect of C/P ratio, household size, size of landholding and other control variables on the dissolution of complex households (extended and compound) in the northern islands of Orkney, Scotland, 1851–1901 ($n = 999$ household dissolution events). Coefficients were estimated by interval-censored hazards analysis. From Jennings (2010).

Predictor variable	Rate of household dissolution	
	Regression coefficient	p
Extended households		
C/P ratio[a]	3.4347	0.001
Number of coresident household members[a]	−0.0978	0.214
Farm size (arable and pasture)	0.0473	0.347
Land access (1 = owner, 0 = tenant)	1.0691	0.132
Number of births in intercensal interval[a]	−0.0966	0.181
Number of deaths in intercensal interval[a]	0.3690	0.002
(Farm size × no. coresident HH members)[a]	−0.0019	0.737
Year of census (1851–1901)[a]	−0.0973	0.268
Compound households		
C/P ratio[a]	3.0482	0.001
Number of coresident household members[a]	−0.0433	0.234
Farm size (arable and pasture)	0.0485	0.062
Land access (1 = owner, 0 = tenant)	1.0345	0.112
Number of births in intercensal interval[a]	−0.1807	<0.001
Number of deaths in intercensal interval[a]	−0.0294	0.703
(Farm size × no. coresident HH members)[a]	−0.0051	0.024
Year of census (1851–1901)[a]	0.0557	0.377
Log-likelihood	−630.025	
Bayesian information content	1377.465	
R^2	0.078	

[a] Time-varying covariate.

in comparison to other types of extended household, as indicated by the differential effects of the numbers of births versus deaths during each time interval between censuses. This finding suggests that the two household forms operate in somewhat different ways – although I confess that we do not (yet?) understand this difference. Most of the results, however, are very similar across the two forms. In both cases, high C/P ratios substantially and significantly increase the rate of dissolution. Now, for an extended household to have a high C/P ratio, one of the constituent nuclear families must have a *very* high value of C/P. Thus, a high overall ratio may indicate an unusually large disparity in the demographic fortunes of the families making up the household – which may signal that the family with the most favorable C/P ratio is motivated to leave or to force the other family or families out. In addition, there is a small but significant negative effect of the interaction between household size and landholding on the rate of dissolution, which when combined with the main effects of the two variables (which are not significant) suggest a nonlinear impact of household size relative to household landholding. We are currently doing simulation studies to help us interpret this result.

Broadly speaking, our Orkney findings are for the most part consistent with Hammel's model, but they scarcely add up to a critical test of it. In all likelihood, however, we would never have looked at extended and compound Orcadian households in quite this way had it not been for Hammel's theoretical exercise. Hammel's model is successful in that it suggests an agenda for future studies. That does not, however, mean that the model is necessarily correct. More research, as the saying goes, is needed.

Conclusions

Although the jury may still be out on Chayanov's contributions, and many analytical problems persist concerning how best to evaluate them, I think it is fair to say that Chayanov's emphasis on the linkage between household demography and subsistence production can still make a claim for theoretical significance. In particular, the distinction between Chayanovian and Boserupian "pressure" is, in my opinion, a useful way to think about the multiple scales at which population and preindustrial farming can interact. Across a farming community as a whole, household life cycles are unlikely to be in sync with each other; in fact, they cannot be since the details of their trajectories will always differ because of demographic stochasticity, if for no other reason. At any given time, therefore, some households will be in a comparatively favorable position on their life-cycle trajectories and others not – although within a few years of household development their relative positions may be reversed. Thus, what Chayanov (1966: 68) called *demographic differentiation* (and contrasted sharply with Marxist class differentiation) is always present, no matter how economically egalitarian the community may appear. We can disagree about how *important* fluctuating C/P ratios are in economic and demographic terms, but we can scarcely deny that they exist. From the perspective of a single household, economic fortunes will change as demographic composition changes, which it must (even if a couple is childless, it will still age). Over the course of its career the household is likely to experience *demographic bottlenecks* in food production as C increasingly exceeds P. The household may respond by intensifying its farming efforts, by obtaining more land or by joining its fortunes with other, related households – or it may be forced to compromise the survival of its members (and perhaps its fertility). Again, the magnitude of these effects can – and should – be debated, but the fact that they occur cannot be doubted.

11 Seasonality and the Household Demographic Enterprise

The year bears the crops, not the earth.   – Theophrastus of Eresus (*c.* BC 370–285)

I say to the father of my child, "Father of Podi Sinho," I say, "There is no *kurakkan* [Sinhala: finger millet] in the house, there is no [pearl] millet and no pumpkin, not even a pinch of salt. Three days now and I have eaten nothing but jungle leaves. There is no milk in my breasts for the child." Then I get foul words and blows. "Does the rain come in August?" he says. "Can I make the *kurakkan* flower in July? Hold your tongue, you fool. August is the month in which the children die. What can I do?"   – L. Woolf (1913: 21)[1]

Household C/P ratios, as Chayanov argued, may induce bottlenecks in food availability relative to consumers once every generation or so. Environmental and agricultural seasonality, on the other hand, often induces once-a-year (or more frequent) bottlenecks in *absolute* food availability, to which the household must adapt every year or suffer the consequences. The causes and magnitude of seasonal swings in the food supply differ from place to place, but there is no farming environment in the world that is absolutely aseasonal. In many places, moreover, the seasonal swings can be large enough to threaten the household demographic enterprise. It seems appropriate, therefore, to include seasonality as a critical dimension of household demographic adjustment, as I do in this chapter. But before we examine the agronomic and demographic impact of seasonal changes, I want to take a brief detour to review global patterns of environmental seasonality and their causes, as well as to note a couple of stubborn problems inherent in the analysis of seasonality's effects.

The Physical and Biological Bases of Seasonality

This is not the place for a detailed technical discussion of the causes of environmental seasonality, but the major variables deserve to be mentioned in passing. One overarching generalization that can be made about global patterns of seasonality is that agricultural seasonality in the tropics is primarily the result of cyclical changes in rainfall, while that in the temperate zones is mainly attributable to changes in photoperiod (hours of sunlight in a 24-hr day) and temperature: the tropics have

---

[1] Before marrying his wife Virginia and settling down in bohemian domesticity with the Bloomsbury group, Leonard Woolf spent seven years as a district officer in Ceylon (as it was then called). His novel *The Village in the Jungle*, from which this passage is taken, was based on that experience and is considered scrupulously accurate – including in his use of the teknonymic form of address ("Father of...") customarily used by Sinhalese women when speaking to their husbands.

rainy seasons and dry seasons, the temperate zones summers and winters. This generalization will need to be modified as the discussion proceeds, but for now it can stand as a rule of thumb.

Solar Radiation, Photoperiod and Temperature

Solar radiation is, of course, necessary for photosynthesis in all plants, including crops. The wash of sunlight across the Earth's surface may sometimes seem a veritable flood, but, as noted in Chapter 3, solar radiation is actually a limited resource, and plants compete for it. In particular, nonequatorial regions experience regular yearly cycles in photoperiod and thus in the amount of solar energy available for crops. This fundamental phenomenon is the result of a cosmic accident: a tilt of approximately 23.5° (at present – it varies over geological time) in the Earth's axis of rotation relative to the Sun. The resulting cycles in photoperiod differ sharply by distance from the equator and are most pronounced at higher latitudes (Figure 11.1). The tilt of the Earth's axis also causes seasonal changes in the angle at which solar radiation strikes the Earth's surface. Because of its oblique angle of incidence, the low noontime Sun characteristic of winter at higher latitudes provides less solar energy to a given area of the Earth's surface than does the more orthogonal noontime Sun of the summer, exacerbating the effects of short wintertime photoperiod on crop

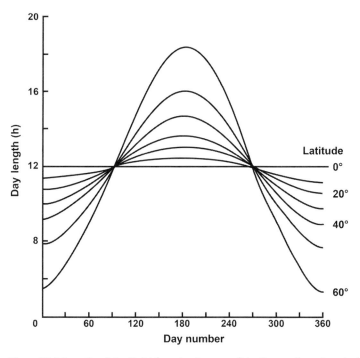

Figure 11.1 Length of daylight (sunrise to sunset) in the northern hemisphere as a function of latitude and day of the year. The pattern is shifted by 182.5 days in the southern hemisphere. From Connor *et al.* (2011: 100), by permission of Cambridge University Press.

production (and confirming our impression that the winter Sun is "weak"). This seasonal difference also becomes greater as latitude increases.

Generally speaking, air temperature follows the cyclic changes in solar radiation, but is also significantly affected by local topography and regional weather systems. Soil temperature is correlated with air temperature and solar radiation; but, because of the insulating properties of the soil itself, changes in the temperature of soil tend to lag behind those in the temperature of the air, and the correlation between the two weakens with soil depth and ground cover (thus accounting for the efficacy of winter mulches). Soil temperature has a rather different effect on crop growth than does air temperature or indeed solar radiation, mainly acting on the capacity of the root system to grow and absorb water and nutrients.

Rainfall and Potential Evapotranspiration

Throughout most of the humid tropics, there are large swings in the monthly amount of rainfall over the course of the year, in sharp contrast to both the temperate zones and the arid tropics (Figure 11.2). If complicating factors such as large land masses and high mountains were swept away, the seasonality of rainfall in the tropics would follow latitudinal patterns almost as simple and elegant as those for photoperiod, with some regions predictably experiencing no dry season and others with one or even two dry seasons. Figure 11.3 provides a simplified picture of what actually happens.

Rainfall by itself, however, does not explain everything about seasonal variation in the water supply available to farmers – potential evapotranspiration must also be taken into consideration. Evapotranspiration combines the water lost to the atmosphere from the soil by evaporation with that lost from plants as a result of transpiration. *Potential* evapotranspiration (PET) is a theoretical quantity defined as the amount of evapotranspiration expected on a field subject to local conditions, but assumed to be (i) covered with a crop of short grass or alfalfa of uniform height, completely shading the ground, and (ii) provided with adequate soil moisture to prevent crop wilting. PET is a function primarily of air temperature – i.e. the heat energy available to evaporate water – plus the effect of wind in moving water vapor away from ground level to the lower atmosphere. In general, temperature contributes about 80 percent to PET, wind about 15 percent, and other factors such as slope and the color of the soil, which affects its absorption of solar radiation, the remainder. If ample water is present, actual evapotranspiration will approximately equal PET (but not exactly because the local reality will deviate from such ideal conditions as a uniform plant cover). If the water present in the soil is insufficient to meet the demands of potential evapotranspiration, then a *water deficit* is said to occur and, if it lasts too long, crops cannot be grown without some form of irrigation.

It is the level of precipitation *relative* to PET that determines the effective amount of water available for growing crops at any particular time of the year. In the two West African examples shown in Figure 11.4, for instance, it might appear that Sokodé in Togo has much more rainwater available for crops than Ibadan, in that the

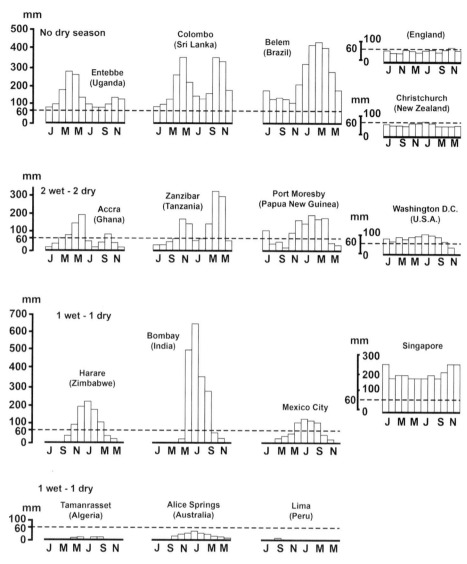

Figure 11.2 Seasonal distribution of rainfall in the tropics, subtropics, and temperate zones (England, Christchurch, Washington). The horizontal broken line at 60 mm rainfall per month is the (somewhat arbitrary) threshold for distinguishing wet and dry months. From Gill (1991: 30), by permission of Cambridge University Press.

area underneath the curve of median rainfall is larger in the former than in the latter. But, after a short period of soil water recharge from April to June, most of the rainfall falling above the PET line in both locales is lost to runoff or subsoil percolation. What is critical is the area *between* the part of the median rainfall curve that falls below PET and the PET line itself, an area that reveals how long and severe a water deficit is experienced over the year. In Sokodé and Ibadan, those areas are similar (indeed in Sokodé it is somewhat larger). The fact that Ibadan experiences a short,

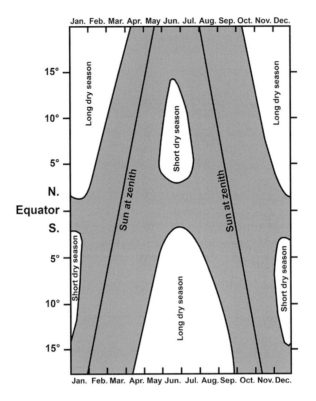

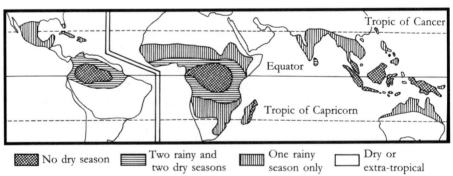

Figure 11.3 Generalized distribution of wet and dry seasons in the topics and subtropics. From Richards (1952: 139), Gill (1991: 36), by permission of Cambridge University Press.

secondary dry spell in July–August does not place it at a very serious disadvantage for it can coast through much of that period by drawing upon residual soil moisture built up during the previous rainy season; the heavy rains that normally fall on Sokodé during July and August, in contrast, are mostly lost.[2]

---

[2] Some traditional farming systems, especially in South Asia, "bank" excess water that falls during the rainy season in tanks or reservoirs, later releasing it for irrigation after the rains have receded and soils have dried out (Agarwal and Naain, 1997).

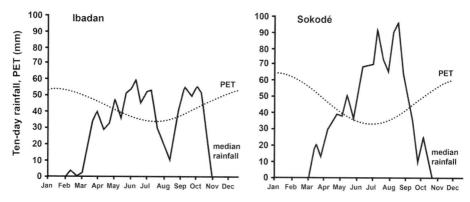

Figure 11.4 Median rainfall and potential evapotranspiration (PET) in Ibadan, Nigeria, and Sokodé, Togo, West Africa. Despite its lower total rainfall, Ibadan sits at the edge of moist, semideciduous forest, whereas rainier Sokodé is well into the dry savannah zone. From Mutsaers (2007: 101–2), by permission of Springer Publishing.

The tropical soil moisture regimes shown in Figure 11.5, which combine rainfall and PET, show just how much more complicated seasonal changes in the effective water supply for farming are than suggested by rainfall alone (compare Figure 11.2). Here for example we see that Singapore, despite a marked drop in rainfall between February and September, has no real dry season (its precipitation is always above PET), while Dodoma in Tanzania, despite a similarly marked *elevation* in rainfall between August and January, has no effective wet season. In other areas, ideas about wet and dry seasons based solely on rainfall data need to be modified to take periods of net soil-moisture recharge and draw-down into consideration.

As a final note, changes in PET can induce "dry" seasons even in temperate zones with ample year-round rainfall (Figure 11.6). This is the main complication to the simple generalization mentioned above, that temperate regions have summers and winters, not wet and dry seasons.

Crop Phenology and the Length of the Growing Season

The agricultural impact of seasonality does not depend exclusively on the physical environment; it is also influenced in important ways by the *phenology* of the crops being grown. In botany, "phenology" refers to the study of the timing of life-cycle events in plants (dormancy, germination, vegetative growth, flowering, seed set, seed dispersal, death) as influenced by their genotype, by seasonal changes in the environment and, most importantly, by the interactions between the two. Different crop species, indeed different varieties of the same species, time their phenological stages differently and, partly as a result, are differentially affected by the physical environment.[3] In Figure 11.7, for example, two widely grown varieties of wheat, generically called "winter" and "spring" wheat, display markedly different phenological patterns in the

---

[3] Weed phenology is also important because it is a major determinant of a weed's ability to out-compete crop plants (see Booth *et al.*, 2003: 81–115).

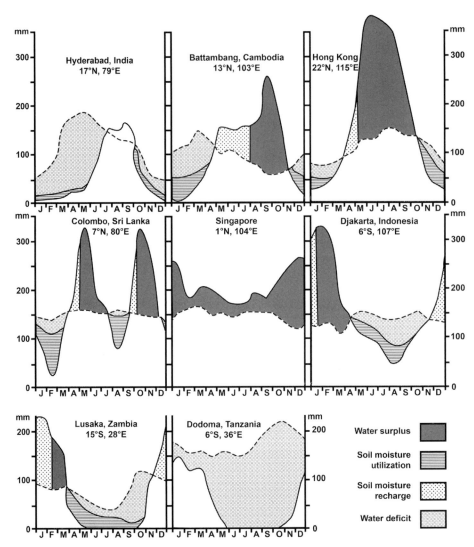

Figure 11.5 Tropical soil water regimes: ——— mean monthly rainfall, - - - - - mean monthly potential evapotranspiration (both in mm). Once soil moisture recharge has been achieved, any rainfall surplus to PET is effectively lost to crop use owing to surface runoff and subsoil drainage. Once precipitation drops below PET, there is a variable period during which plants can draw upon the dwindling soil moisture reserve to support transpiration. Once that reserve is depleted, however, plants will wilt, stop photosynthesizing and eventually die unless more water is provided by rain, irrigation or flooding. From Tivy (1990: 167), by permission of Pearson PLC.

northern plains of North America; winter wheat accommodates its prolonged seedling phase by undergoing a period of dormancy (lowered metabolism, no vegetative growth) during the worst of winter. Since the two environments shown in Figure 11.7 are similar, we can infer (correctly, as it happens) that the large inter-strain differences in phenology are primarily genetic in origin and are likely to be the result of artificial selection by

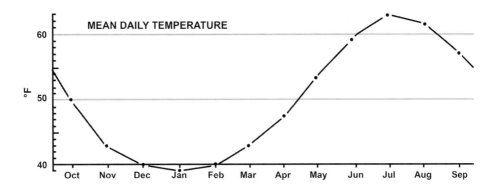

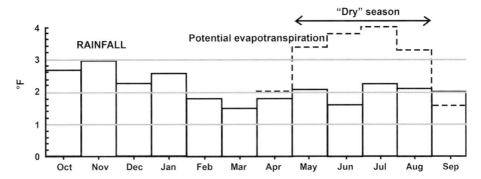

Figure 11.6 How an increase in potential evapotranspiration during the warmth of summer can induce an effective dry season even in Great Britain with its abundant and comparatively equable rainfall. From Duckham (1963: 22), by permission of Chatto and Windus Ltd.

farmers and breeders. But strictly environmental factors can also affect crop phenology, as suggested by Figure 11.8 in which a single nonhybrid strain of barley is grown at different altitudes in Hawaii: the time to maturation at high altitude is some 50 percent longer than that observed near sea level.

Phenological timing and its causes represent an important set of variables determining whether a given crop variety "fits" into a particular pattern of environmental seasonality – a fit summarized by the deceptively simple concept of the *length of the growing season* (LGS). The LGS is not fixed for any one location (although it is often described that way): it is, rather, crop-specific, i.e. determined by the complex interactions between the phenology of the particular crop variety being grown and specific environmental factors, primarily rainfall relative to PET in the tropics and photoperiod/temperature in the temperate regions (elevation is important in both parts of the world). Sometimes those interactions can yield unfortunate results. In Europe, for example, grain crops require longer growing seasons at higher latitudes and elevations (Tivy, 1990: 32); but, alas, higher latitudes and elevations are precisely the parts of Europe that have *shorter* growing seasons for grains (Duckham, 1963: 163–4). To accommodate this regrettable fact about the LGS, species and varieties of staple grains must change as we go further north or into the uplands.

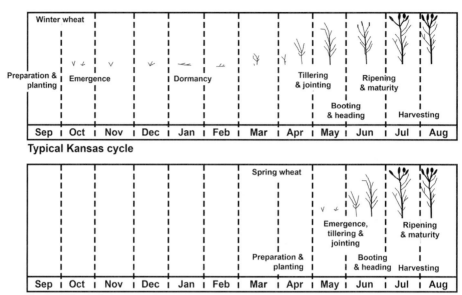

Figure 11.7 Typical phenology (sequence and timing of developmental stages) of winter wheat in Kansas and spring wheat in North Dakota. The two crops have nearly identical harvest periods but very different sowing seasons and rates of growth and maturation. "Tillering" and "jointing" refer respectively to multiple stem formation and the development of clear nodes (joints) and internodes along the stem. "Booting" refers to the period when the developing head becomes visible beneath the sheath of the stalk, but before it has started to emerge; "heading" refers to head emergence, whereas "emergence" refers to visible germination. From MacDonald, R. B. and Hall, F. G. (1980) Global crop forecasting. *Science*, **208**, 670–8, reprinted by permission of the American Association for the Advancement of Science.

Over-simplifying slightly, southern England traditionally grew wheat and rye whereas northern England and Scotland grew oats and barley; similarly, southern Italy quickly adopted the subtropical crop maize after its post-Columbian introduction to Europe, northern Europe did not and indeed could not (in Italy you eat polenta, in Scotland you eat porridge made of oats).

The Unpredictability of Environment Seasonality

Over the *long run*, the average agricultural effects of seasonality (averaged, that is, over many years) tend to be regular and predictable, and local cultural capital often provides a wealth of suggestions for coping with long-term expectations about seasonal variation. Seasonality in this strict sense differs from less predictable environmental fluctuations, which are everywhere imposed to a greater or lesser extent on top of the seasonal pattern. But unpredictability often exerts its dire effects on traditional farmers precisely by obscuring the expected seasonal pattern. Therefore, the interaction of predictable elements of seasonality and inherent environmental unpredictability is important in every traditional farming community. Figure 11.9 shows a particularly striking case: in

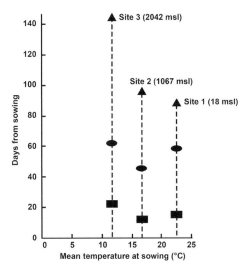

Figure 11.8 Phenology of a single variety of barley (early Bankuti) at different elevations in Hawaii: (rectangles) flower initiation; (ovals) head formation; (triangles) seeds ripening; *msl*, elevation in m above sea level. Redrawn from Aitken (1974: 97). This figure is reproduced from Y. Aitken, *Flowering Time, Climate and Genotype: The Adaptation of Agricultural Species to Climate through Flowering Responses*. Melbourne University Press, Carlton (1974), with permission.

this East African environment, traditional wisdom about clearing and sowing is likely to be frustrated in any given year by inherent variability in the onset of each of the two rainy seasons. Any one year may be anomalous in the details of its seasonal cycle – indeed, in the case shown in Figure 11.9 it is difficult to identify a year that is *not* anomalous! Thus, we should never assume that a given farming year will conform to the long-term pattern.[4] Cultural lore must perforce involve proven ways to cope with the risks imposed by environmental unpredictability, e.g. by planting a variety of crops with different growing seasons or differing degrees of drought resistance. As discussed below, these coping mechanisms do not always work, and the household demographic enterprise may suffer as a result.

Nonsense Correlations in the Study of Agricultural and Demographic Seasonality

In sum, the physical and biological bases of environmental seasonality are well understood – but it is sometimes more difficult to relate such seasonality to agricultural, demographic or behavioral outcomes with any confidence, especially in non-experimental field studies. There is a potential conceptual problem that haunts, not

---

[4] Conversely, neither should we postulate a long-term pattern of seasonality from observations made over a single year. Indeed, the number of years that need to be averaged in order to discern a genuine seasonal pattern is a direct function of just how unpredictable the environment is. Despite this rather obvious fact, it is remarkable how often data for a single year are reported in the literature in order to characterize long-term seasonality.

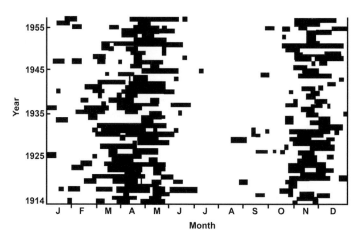

Figure 11.9 Annual variation in rainfall (by pentades) in an East African region characterized by two rainy seasons: Nairobi, Kenya, 1914–57. A pentade is a five-day window, which is blacked in if measurable precipitation falls on at least one of its days. Note the presence of a fairly regular pattern of *average* seasonality along with wide year-to-year fluctuations in the distribution of rainfall. After Griffiths (1959), redrawn by Jackson (1989: 83), by permission of the World Meteorological Organization.

merely studies of seasonality, but all forms of time-series analysis (and the study of seasonality is just a particular kind of time-series analysis). That problem was first highlighted by the pioneering statistician G. Udny Yule in an important paper on the appearance of what he called *nonsense correlations* in data on temporal trends (Yule, 1926). Yule observed (quite correctly) that crude death rates in England during the late nineteenth and early twentieth century were highly correlated ($r > 0.95$) with annual rates of marriage within the Church of England (Figure 11.10). Clearly, as any fool can see, marrying within the established church put people at a higher risk of death, no doubt because a heavier and more lethal variety of rice was thrown at the couple at the end of the Church of England ceremony than in other settings. Yule (rather less absurdly) considered the correlation spurious, "nonsensical" in his terminology. From one point of view, this was simply an example of the ecological fallacy, as well as the general dictum that correlation does not prove causation. But Yule's point was that the ecological fallacy is a special danger in the study of *temporal* trends. Historical periods exist during which many variables are changing at roughly the same time without any direct causal connection among them. It is, I suppose, imaginable that weak and remote connections did exist during the period 1865–1921 between certain social and economic factors, such that the epidemiological transition occurred more or less simultaneously as an increase in secularism that led to (among other things) a reduction in the frequency of weddings in churches of all denominations. But, in and of itself, the correlation between mortality and marriages in the Church of England, though impressively high, is poor evidence for any direct causal connection between the two.

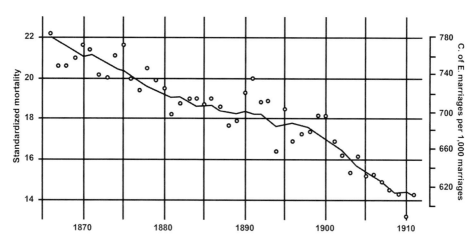

Figure 11.10 The nonsense correlation discovered by G. Udny Yule between the crude annual death rate (solid line) and the annual number of marriages within the Church of England per 1000 total marriages (circles) in England, 1865–1921. The correlation between the two is +0.9512. From Yule (1926: 3), by permission of John Wiley & Sons, Inc.

If spurious correlation is a special risk in all time-series analyses, it is particularly so in the study of seasonality. Virtually *everything* varies seasonally, from the price of pork bellies to the frequency of vacations to sightings of robins, and cross-correlations of any seasonally varying variables are often quite high, especially if time lags are included in the analysis (indeed, seasonal correlations across time-lagged variables often approach one). Many, perhaps most, of these correlations are likely to be spurious. And yet, in the literature on agricultural and demographic seasonality, such lagged cross-correlations are commonly interpreted in causal terms, along with a contrived *ex post* "explanation" of what mechanisms might be linking them (think of my brilliant hypothesis about the lethality of rice thrown at Church of England weddings). As an anthropologist, I regret to say that many field-based studies of seasonality in traditional farming – and of its demographic implications – draw conclusions of exactly this sort. The empirical studies reviewed in this chapter are not entirely innocent of this intellectual sin (or of the equally deplorable sin of trying to infer long-term seasonal patterns from data on a single year), but I have tried to focus on more cautious studies or at least to exercise my own caution in interpreting the results. One key to avoiding nonsense correlations in the study of seasonality is to identify and measure actual *mechanisms* linking the variables being correlated (and not just posit such mechanisms after the fact). If we observe a negative correlation between rainfall and the use of irrigation, for example, the linkage is obvious and can be studied in its own right. If we observe a correlation between rainfall and, say, fertility, the mechanisms involved may be much more difficult to puzzle out – and until they have been identified and shown to explain the observations, we are entitled to regard this as a possible case of nonsense correlation. *Caveat lector.*

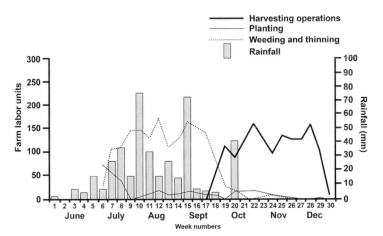

Figure 11.11 Farm labor relative to rainfall in Dagaceri village, northern Nigeria, 1994. Labor is expressed in weighted units (each equivalent to one man-day) per week and rainfall in mm per week. From Mortimore and Adams (1999: 64), by permission of Routledge and Kegan Paul Publishers.

The Shape of the Farming Year

Owing to seasonal changes in such factors as photoperiod, temperature, rainfall and PET – and equally to the way that the phenology of local crops can be shoehorned into those seasonal changes – every part of the arable world, preindustrial and industrial, displays a characteristic annual farming cycle. Figure 11.11, for example, summarizes observations from the Sahel in West Africa. In this region of highly marked wet and dry seasons, planting must be done after the end of the dry season but early enough so that tender new seedlings are not washed out by the heaviest rains. Harvesting, on the other hand, is almost completely confined to the dry season when the ground is not muddy. We can be confident that these obvious correlations between rainfall and work are not spurious since the local farmers themselves point to the relationship as causative.[5]

We might think of such patterns of seasonal work as passive reflections of environmental seasonality and crop phenology – but I suggest they can be more fruitfully viewed as deliberate, calculated responses by farmers to expected seasonal changes in the marginal returns to labor and other inputs. Figure 11.12 shows the hypothetical marginal productivity (MP) of three factors of production, land, labor and irrigation water, applied to a farm in a region with a single clear-cut wet season (this example and my discussion of it are adapted from Gill, 1991: 18–20). Just before the start of the rains the MP of irrigation water is very high; but because (in the absence of irrigation) there is neither sufficient rainfall nor sufficient soil moisture to support a crop, the other two factors have MPs of zero. With the onset of rains, however, the MP of irrigation water falls rapidly, while that of labor increases just as quickly as sowing

---

[5] On the other hand, since these observations were recorded over a single year, Figure 11.11 does not allow us to evaluate year-to-year fluctuations in the onset, adequacy, or duration of the rains, although such fluctuations are likely to be considerable in this notoriously drought-prone region.

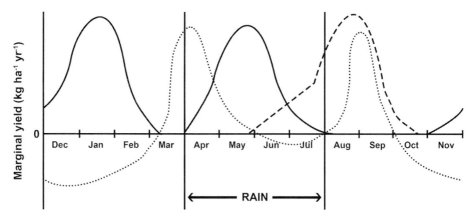

Figure 11.12 A model of seasonal variation in the marginal productivity (MP) of three factors of production: ——— labor, ·········· irrigation water, — — — arable land. From Gill (1991: 18), by permission of Cambridge University Press.

gets under way. The MP of land remains at zero because all available labor is of necessity fully committed to sowing. As the rains continue, the MP of water dips below zero because of the risk of waterlogging or of washing out seeds and seedlings. Once the bulk of the available land is planted and beginning to germinate, the MP of labor falls (unless intensive weeding is done, which is apparently not the case in this fictitious example) and that of land increases. The MP of land remains high for a short time after the rains end because, were additional land available, at least a short-duration catch crop of food could be grown drawing upon residual soil moisture. However, as the dry season advances, this option fades and the MP of land falls as that of water increases – additional moisture in the growing phase would boost crop yield substantially. As the harvest approaches, however, the MP of water drops once again, now falling well below zero since more water at this stage could impede the harvest or cause the crop to rot. With the onset of the harvest, the MP of labor again increases sharply, although as soon as the harvest is in, it falls rapidly, reflecting the fact that the land is once again fallow and labor once again idle awaiting the onset of next year's rains. Plainly, it would be foolish of farmers to invest heavy inputs, including their own labor, at times of the year when their marginal returns would be low or negative. Therefore, subsistence farmers must understand and be reasonably able to predict these changes in marginal productivity (as well as those of other factors of production), must invest resources accordingly and must hedge their bets every year to try to cope with unforeseeable, nonseasonal fluctuations in productivity.

Seasonal variation in the MP of labor on the farm can be rephrased in terms of the *demand* for labor. This demand is never constant over the farming year but shows distinct peaks and troughs (Figure 11.13). Thus, there are typically seasonal *bottle-necks* when demand draws very heavily on the time and energy that a household can provide, perhaps so heavily that certain critical tasks cannot be performed adequately without help from outside the household (see Chapter 12). But there are also periods of what economists have termed seasonal *underemployment*, which might more

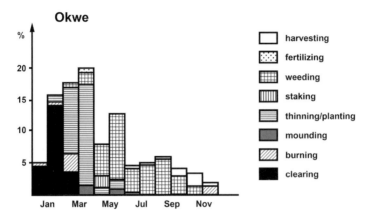

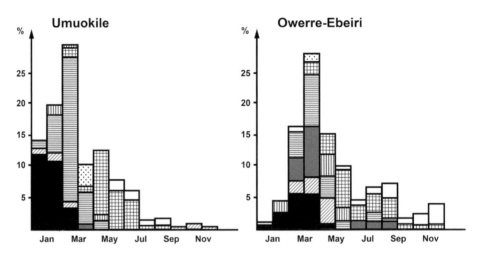

Figure 11.13 Seasonal distribution of farm work in three villages in eastern Nigeria, 1974–5. From Lagemann (1977: 86).

reasonably be called spells of well-earned rest, when the low MP of labor makes working longer or harder pointless. Figure 11.14, from a *chitimene* system of shifting cultivation in East Africa (see Allan, 1965; Strømgaard, 1985, 1988), illustrates the swings in a village's demand for adult male labor as a proportion of the total availability of such labor, which changes over time because of temporary migration, illness and so forth. At certain times of the year, e.g. January, May, late November, the demand comes close to exhausting the local supply of labor; during other months (e.g. February) the supply greatly exceeds the demand. Now, the data in Figure 11.14 pertain to the village community as a whole; but almost all the tasks illustrated by the figure are *organized* by individual households. As emphasized in Chapter 10, the

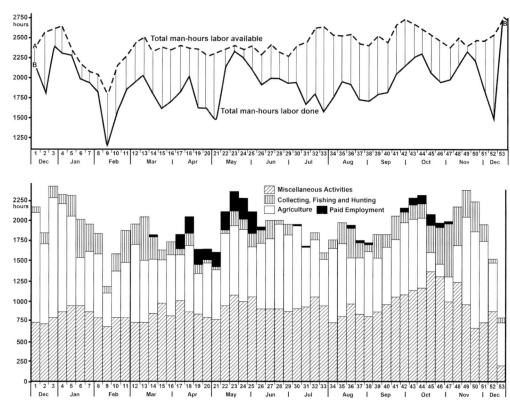

Figure 11.14 Seasonal labour bottlenecks and underemployment among adult males from East Africa practicing the *chitimene* form of shifting cultivation: data from an Ushi-speaking village in Northern Rhodesia (now Zambia). (Top) The supply and demand for labor. (Bottom) The actual distribution of labor. From Kay (1964: 72), by permission of Manchester University Press.

household work force is inherently small and subject to both random and nonrandom perturbations, much more so than the village as a whole (a single adult person-day of illness during a bottleneck may cut the household's ability to accomplish that day's tasks adequately by something like a half). The minimal requirement of the household labor force is that it be able to meet seasonal bottlenecks – either on its own or with help from other households lured by the expenditure of social capital. Unsurprisingly, seasonal bottlenecks, which are often associated with clearing and planting of fields and with harvesting, are periods when households with inadequate labor forces (perhaps because of unfavorable C/P ratios) must try to recruit workers from nearby, related households that are in better shape (see Chapter 12). Incidentally, there is nothing to guarantee that periods of peak labor demand coincide with periods of peak food availability so that household workers can reliably get more and better food to eat when they need it most (Figure 11.15). Following Richard Longhurst's ideas about the energy trap, it is imaginable that the resulting shifts in the nutritional condition of workers (as suggested in the bottom panel of Figure 11.15) may sometimes lower the *effective* household labor force during the worst seasonal

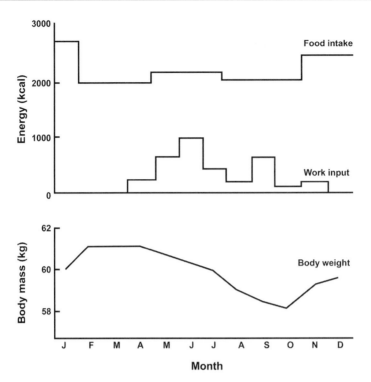

Figure 11.15 Monthly energy intake, work output, and body weight of adult male farmers in the Gambia, West Africa. Reproduced, with permission, from R. H. Fox (1953) *A Study of Energy Expenditure of Africans Engaged in Various Activities, with Special Reference to Some Environmental and Physiological Factors which May Influence the Efficiency of their Work*. PhD dissertation, Department of Nutritional Science, University of London, London.

bottlenecks (compare Dufour, 1983, 1984; Kumar, 1988; Panter-Brick, 1992, 1996a, b; Wandel *et al.*, 1992).

Seasonal changes in the food available to each subsistence farming household reflect the timing and adequacy of the harvest, of course, but also (and just as importantly) the ability of the household to preserve and store the harvested crop until the *next* harvest. Seasonal changes in food stores are a universal feature of preindustrial farming, whether in temperate or tropical zones. Local terms for an annual preharvest "hungry season" are widely encountered in rural developing-world societies (Devereux *et al.*, 2012), and numerous nutritional studies indicate that the locally recognized seasons of relative (and often absolute) dearth are real (Chen *et al.*, 1979; Chambers *et al.*, 1981; Simondon *et al.*, 1993; Devereux *et al.*, 2008).[6] Table 11.1 shows

---

[6] Since many tropical root crops can be "stored" in the ground live and harvested as needed on a day-to-day basis, one might expect that seasonal hunger might be less common in the tropics than in the temperate regions. I know of no evidence to suggest that this is true. We worked in equatorial New Guinea with people almost totally dependent on root crops, and we still witnessed a distinct season of limited food availability and lowered nutritional status.

Table 11.1 Seasonal variation in caloric intake compared with estimated requirements, northern Nigeria, 1956–7. Period I, just after harvest; Period II, midway between harvests; Period III, just before harvest. From FAO (1958: 123).

Region of Nigeria	Estimated energy requirement (kcal person^{-1} day^{-1})	Energy intake (kcal person^{-1} day^{-1})				Energy intake as percentage of requirements			
		Annual average	Period			Annual average	Period		
			I	II	III		I	II	III
Tanganza	2570	2250	2920	1840	2000	88	114	72	78
Langai	2500	2550	2850	2400	2300	102	114	96	92
Southwest Borgu	2550	2060	2570	2000	1620	81	101	78	63

some examples. The problem, as noted, is not just how much food is produced by the household, but how much can be preserved across seasons when no new crops are being harvested. As detailed in Chapter 2, stored food is vulnerable to spoilage and the depredations of mold, insects, rodents and even bears and raccoons in some parts of the world. It is also subject to theft or deliberate destruction by human enemies (Wilson, 1917: 94–7).

In subsistence farming, the possible responses to seasonal hunger may be limited (Flowers, 1983; Panter-Brick and Eggerman, 1997). Intensification of food production (one way, as discussed in Chapter 10, in which a household can try to offset a high C/P ratio) is normally not much of an option, partly because of declining marginal productivity but also because of the very environmental and phenological factors that cause seasonal changes in the marginal productivity of labor and other inputs in the first place. The only real options for poor households may be rationing an already limited food supply, begging for help from neighbors and leaving the area for (one hopes) greener pastures; the rich, in contrast, can survive by borrowing money, selling off assets and drawing on savings. Among the poor Ethiopian farming families surveyed by Devereux and his colleagues in 2006, cutting back on household food consumption was by far the most common response to seasonal hunger (Devereux *et al.*, 2008) – and almost certainly the one that put the household demographic enterprise at the highest risk.

Demographic Seasonality

Seasonal variation in demographically important events (deaths, births, changes in residence, even marriage and sex acts) are as common as seasonal variation in environmental factors and farm practices. Here we concentrate on the seasonality of mortality and fertility, as do most studies of preindustrial demographic seasonality. Over the years, many scientists have tried to determine how seasonal changes in environmental factors, farming behavior or food availability drive seasonal changes in birth and death rates. But here the potential pitfall of nonsense correlation yawns like a chasm. Mortality can be fairly easy to study because cause of death, the physical condition of the victim just before death, and the economic status of the household in question can sometimes be ascertained, making it possible to analyze the underlying mechanisms. Fertility, however, with its complicated biological and behavioral mechanisms, its mixture of deliberate and accidental causes, and its built-in time lags (reflecting, for example, prolonged breastfeeding or pregnancy itself) between any postulated environmental/agronomic effect and the ultimate demographic outcome of interest (a live birth), has proven to be much more resistant to analysis (Wood, 1994a: 529–36).

Seasonality of Death

Under rural preindustrial conditions, mortality appears to be sensitive to seasonal shifts in food availability and exposure to infectious diseases, especially among the most vulnerable members of the household, the very young. In rural Senegal, for example, regular September–October peaks in childhood mortality are observed year after year (Figure 11.16); if anything the peaks appear to be sharper among children of ages 1–4 years than among infants, perhaps because the latter are more likely to be nursing frequently and thus receiving the full nutritional and immunological benefits of breastfeeding. Nutritional status, as indicated by weight-for-height relative to the Harvard standards (see Chapter 8), usually reaches a low point just before the harvest season, closely corresponding to the peak in mortality – and again the amplitude of the seasonal shifts appears to be higher and more regular among somewhat older children. The incidence of diarrheal disease sometimes peaks at about the same time of year, but is so variable that any genuinely seasonal pattern is difficult to detect. However, fevers of *unspecified* origin (but almost certainly including malaria, among other things) do show pronounced and predictable peaks during the preharvest period. Evidence for the causal linkages implied by Figure 11.16 is still correlational in nature, but is nonetheless strongly suggestive of mechanisms that could be studied in more detail.

The causal case has been taken one step further in a study conducted in Senegal's close neighbor, Gambia (Figure 11.17). We saw in Chapter 8 that growth faltering during early childhood was a strong and consistent predictor of elevated childhood mortality in rural developing-world settings. Here we see that growth faltering may worsen during the rainy season (these two cases by themselves do not, of course, prove anything, but the larger data set from which they were taken is reasonably convincing; see McGregor *et al.*, 1970). We are used to thinking of rainfall as an unmitigated blessing for food production, but it can also cause problems if too much of it falls during too short a period. Heavy rains often have two adverse health consequences. First, flooding can physically link sources of drinking water and places where human wastes are deposited – e.g. wells and latrines – and thus increase the incidence of water-borne diseases or diseases spread by the fecal–oral route. (Floods in many parts of the developing world are often followed by outbreaks of cholera.) Second, puddles and pools left by excess rain can provide breeding places for a variety of disease-carrying mosquitoes, including the anopheline species that

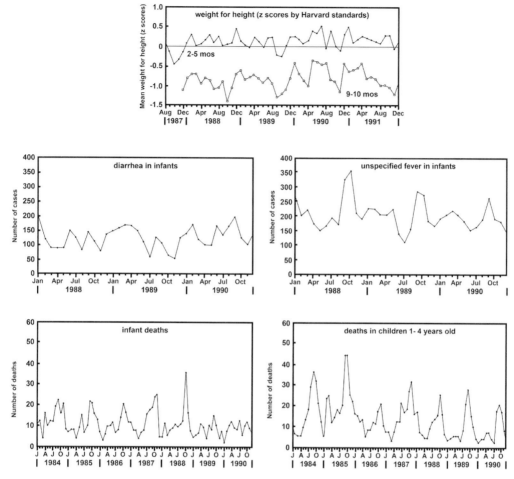

Figure 11.16 Seasonal changes in weight-for-height in young children, the prevalence of diarrhea and unspecified fever in infants, the infant mortality rate and the early childhood mortality rate, rural Senegal. From Simondon *et al.* (1993: 178), by permission of Cambridge University Press.

transmit malaria. The disease occurrences plotted near the bottom of each panel in Figure 11.17 suggest that both adverse effects may have contributed to growth faltering in these two subjects, although the death of the second child may have been more or less immediately precipitated by diarrhea and vomiting and by the rapid somatic wasting that accompanied them.

Seasonality of Birth

Seasonal changes in fertility are more of a puzzle – which is not to say that they are not widespread in rural preindustrial communities as well as other human populations. In an important study, David Lam and Jeffrey Miron (1991, 1994) surveyed global patterns of birth seasonality from 203 different countries, states, provinces and periods, using large datasets, a uniform statistical approach and multiple years of

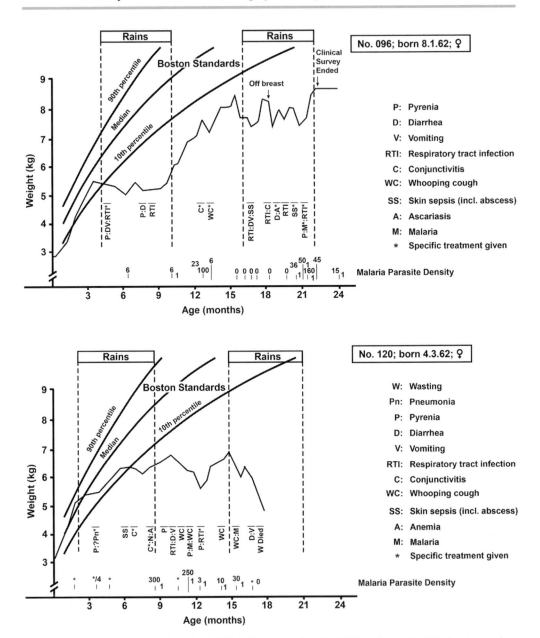

Figure 11.17 Seasonality of rainfall, infection and early childhood growth faltering in rural Gambia, West Africa. Standard growth curves (continuous lines) are from the Harvard Study of children in Boston. Note that the girl shown in the bottom panel died before the survey ended. From McGregor *et al.* (1970), by permission of Oxford University Press, USA.

observation. Their analyses reveal some interesting patterns – or perhaps *nonpatterns* would be more apt in some instances. First, all the populations examined displayed significant birth seasonality, but that seasonality did not vary in any simple way by latitude or photoperiod, nor were the patterns in the northern hemisphere mirror-images of those in the southern hemisphere. Simple climatic variables such as temperature and rainfall did not seem to explain much if any of the variation.[7] Each major region seemed to have its own idiosyncratic pattern, which often persisted right across the Industrial Revolution, the demographic transition and the movement from a rural to an increasingly urban economy. The degree of seasonality within any one country or region did not consistently increase or decrease over time. Other studies have shown that the pattern of birth seasonality (at least in terms of the location of peaks and troughs) has persisted through the introduction of oral contraceptives and other reliable forms of birth control (Seiver, 1985). And there is no obvious ecological reason that the pattern of birth seasonality should shift dramatically as we drive across the border between the United States and Canada (Werschler and Halli, 1992) or fly over the ocean between the United States and Europe (Lam and Miron, 1991). (For what it's worth, Canada looks more "European" than does the USA.)

Over the years, many authors have tried to explain seasonal patterns of birth in terms of observed variation in a myriad of predictor variables, including food availability and maternal nutritional status (Bailey *et al.*, 1992), the timing of marriage (Wood, 1994a: 535), variation in sperm motility and pregnancy loss (Levine *et al.*, 1988; Kallan and Enneking, 1992) – even the frequency of sexual intercourse as influenced (purportedly) by the spread of air conditioning (Seiver, 1989). Most of these studies have been purely correlational and thus prone to nonsense correlations, except in a few cases in which mechanisms have been posited (though not necessarily validated). Thus far, no general patterns of birth seasonality or of predictors have emerged. There certainly does not seem to be a small number of patterns that are widely distributed across traditional farming societies (and *not* observed in most modern urban societies), nor does there appear to be a limited range of plausible explanatory variables, as is the case with mortality. Human birth seasonality, while apparently a near-universal phenomenon, remains a poorly understood one.

Some of the conundrums of birth seasonality are illustrated by the examples shown in Figure 11.18, extracted from official Austrian data sources by Doblhammer-Reiter *et al.* (1999). Most but not all the distributions are bimodal, with a primary peak in February–March and a much smaller secondary peak in August or September – a pattern that is observed in much of Europe, including in areas that are not especially similar to any part of Austria. The primary mode has tended to persist (sometimes increasing, sometimes decreasing) across periods of rapid social and economic change, whereas the secondary mode has usually (but not always) intensified and shifted its position. Although the Tyrol and neighboring Vorarlberg, both in the Austrian alps, are ecologically similar to each other, the weight on the modes reversed itself in the Tyrol but not in Vorarlberg, where seasonal departures from the overall mean number of births increased over time – for completely unknown reasons. The samples on which

---

[7] Later work by the same authors has suggested at least weak effects of both weather and latitude, which are of course partially colinear and therefore difficult to disentangle in observational studies, as indeed are latitude and photoperiod (Lam *et al.*, 1994; Lam and Miron, 1996).

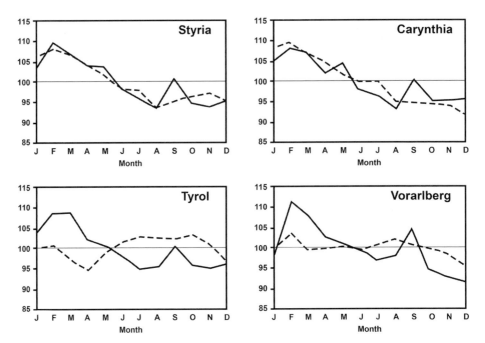

Figure 11.18 Seasonality of births in four of the less urbanized regions of Austria during two periods: - - - - - 1881–1912, ———— 1947–59. The average monthly number of births over each period is expressed as the percentage deviation from the overall average for that period (= 100). From Doblhammer-Reiter *et al.* (1999: 35–6), by permission of Melbourne University Press.

this figure is based are large enough to convince us that both the overall patterns of birth seasonality and their changes over time are real. But, as in almost every other case in the literature, we have no idea why they occur.

Seasonality in Rural Bangladesh

To round out this chapter, I want to examine patterns of seasonality in the rural thana (administrative subdistrict) of Matlab in south-central Bangladesh (Figure 11.19). Matlab thana, though heavily dependent on a form of agriculture that remains largely unmechanized, is very far from being a subsistence economy. On the other hand, more high-quality research on demographic seasonality has been done there than in any other part of the rural developing world, a direct result of the large-scale, prospective Demographic and Health Surveillance System that has been operating continuously there for over 35 years (Holman, 1996).[8] Simply put, more is known about the seasons of birth and death (and their likely causes) in Matlab than anywhere else – which is not to say that all the mysteries of seasonality have been solved there.

---

[8] Because of this surveillance system, all patterns of seasonality in Matlab are well-established based on many years of observation.

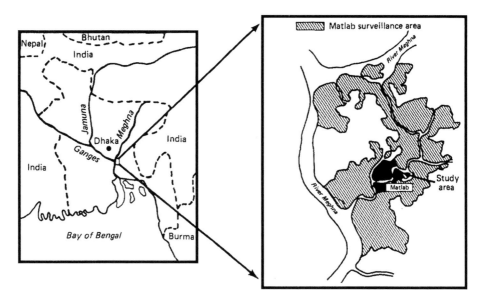

Figure 11.19 Matlab thana, rural Bangladesh, site of the ongoing Demographic and Health Surveillance System operated by the International Centre for Diarrheal Disease Research, 1966 to present. From Becker *et al.* (1986), by permission of the Taylor Francis Group.

The general patterns of environmental and agricultural seasonality in Matlab are summarized in Table 11.2 and Figure 11.20. Bangladesh as a whole lies within the tropical monsoon belt of South Asia with its dramatically contrasting wet and dry seasons. Monsoonal rains cause heavy flooding almost every year in the low-lying portions of the country – and most of Bangladesh, including Matlab, is *very* low-lying. In a normal year, there are three harvests of rice, the principal dietary staple: the main harvest of irrigated rice (*aman*), a secondary harvest of dry rice (*aus*), and a second major, but comparatively small, harvest of an irrigated crop (*boro*). The sowing, growing and harvesting of these three crops dominate the farming year, and the health of both farm women and their children vary in parallel with them (Table 11.2). Among young children, the rains increase the risk of diarrhea caused by pathogenic *E. coli* and rotaviruses (Table 11.2, Figure 11.21). (A second peak in rotavirus infections occurs during the coldest part of winter.) The nutritional status of women, as reflected in their weight, declines during the hot-dry season – which happens to be one of the busiest parts of their work year, when the sowing and transplanting of the *aus* rice crop overlap with the harvest of the *boro* crop. There is a distinct hungry season from August to October, just before the major *aus* harvest, when rice prices in local shops are at their highest (Figure 11.20) and household food stores become seriously depleted, especially among the poor (Figure 11.22). During the hungry season, household energy consumption declines, weight loss occurs in women, and growth faltering is often observed in young children, especially girls (Abdullah and Wheeler, 1985).

Table 11.2 Environmental and agricultural seasonality in Matlab thana, Bangladesh. Season labels are keyed to Figure 11.20 (Becker *et al.*, 1986). From S. Becker, A. Chowdhury and H. Leridon (1986) Seasonal patterns of reproduction in Matlab, Bangladesh. *Population Studies*, 40, 457–72. Copyright © Population Investigation Committee, reprinted by permission of Taylor & Francis Ltd, http://www.tandfonline.com on behalf of Population Investigation Committee.

Season	Events
Monsoon (Jun–Oct)	Time of sowing the main *aman* (irrigated) rice crop (Jun–Aug); time of harvesting the *aus* (dryland) rice crop; peak prevalence of enterotoxigenic *E. coli* diarrhea in children under age 2 yrs (Apr–Sep).
Hungry season (Aug–Oct)	Low demand for agricultural labor; depletion of household food stocks; increase in food prices; retarded growth in children's weight (Sep–Oct); low children's mean percentage of reference weight for age (also Nov–Dec) and for height (also Jul); decreased body mass in women (Sep).
Peak rice harvest (Nov–Dec)	Peak time of harvesting the *aman* rice crop; reduction in breastfeeding (Nov–Dec, also Jan–Feb); peak of births (also Oct).
Time of transplanting rice (Jan–Feb)	Time of transplanting seedlings of the *boro* (secondary irrigated) rice crop.
Hot-dry season (Mar–May)	Time of sowing and transplanting *aus* rice crop (Mar–Apr); time of harvesting *boro* rice crop; decreased body mass in women.

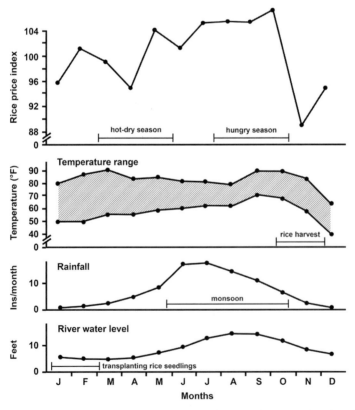

Figure 11.20 Environmental and agricultural seasonality in Matlab, Bangladesh. Modified from Becker *et al.* (1986), by permission of the Taylor Francis Group.

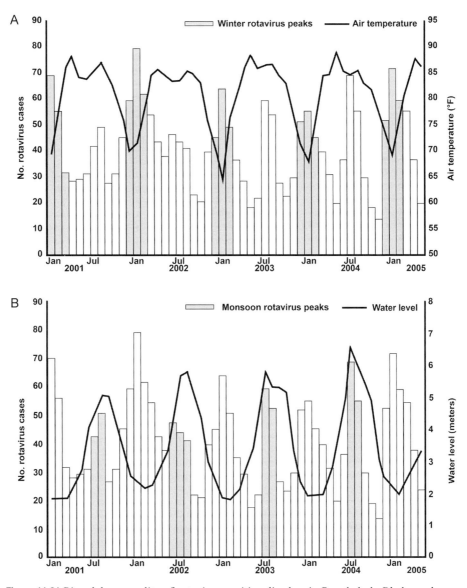

Figure 11.21 Bimodal seasonality of rotavirus-positive diarrhea in Bangladesh, Dhaka and Matlab combined. Correlation between cases of rotavirus-positive diarrhea and air temperature (A) and water level (B) in Dhaka, Jan 2001–May 2005. From Rahman *et al.* (2007), by permission of the Center for Disease Control and Prevention.

The seasonal swings in total mortality (i.e. at all ages) appear to correspond closely to overall food availability, with mortality increasing during the preharvest hungry season and starting to fall as the main *aman* harvest gets under way (Figure 11.23, top). Most of these excess deaths are caused by various infectious diseases, as might be expected if poor nutritional status were compromising immunocompetence (see Chapter 8). Seasonal changes in *neonatal* mortality (deaths during the first week of

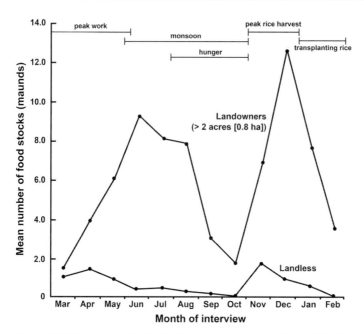

Figure 11.22 Seasonal variation in the average amount of stored food per household, by landholding status, Matlab, Bangladesh (1 maund = 37 kg). Modified from Chen *et al.* (1979), by permission of the Taylor Francis Group.

life) seem to follow a rather different pattern, coinciding more closely with the annual rise and fall of monsoonal rains and local rivers (Figure 11.23, bottom). This finding is consistent with the fact that a large fraction of neonatal deaths in Matlab are attributable to severe diarrhea and neonatal tetanus (Faveau *et al.*, 1990), both of which can be spread by contaminated water used either for hydration or bathing.[9] The deaths of older infants and other young children, in contrast, tend to vary in parallel with the changes in total mortality shown in the top of Figure 11.23 (Muhuri, 1996).

Regular patterns of birth seasonality spanning many years have also been observed in Matlab (Figure 11.24) and have been the subject of extensive study (for a review, see Becker, 1994). Live births peak in October–December and reach a trough in April–June. In contrast, pregnancy losses (spontaneous abortions, miscarriages, stillbirths) usually occur earlier in pregnancy than do full-term births and are therefore spread somewhat more evenly across the year (Figure 11.25, top panel).[10] But combining live births and pregnancy losses (when the latter are known to the

---

[9] Tetanus is caused by contamination of dead tissue by the spores of *Clostridium tetani*, a bacterium commonly found in the soil; the neonatal form is often spread by poor care of the cut umbilical cord, although unhygienic conditions during childbirth are also important (see www.who.int/immunization_monitoring/diseases/neonatal_tetanus/en/). As far as neonatal exposure to contaminated drinking water is concerned, Bangladeshi mothers, especially older ones, sometimes give newborn children sips of water to drink while withholding their colostrum (Huffman *et al.*, 1980; Holman and Grimes, 2001).

[10] The great majority of pregnancy losses in Matlab, as elsewhere, occur very early in pregnancy and are therefore missed in most field surveys (Holman, 1996), including the one summarized in Figure 11.25.

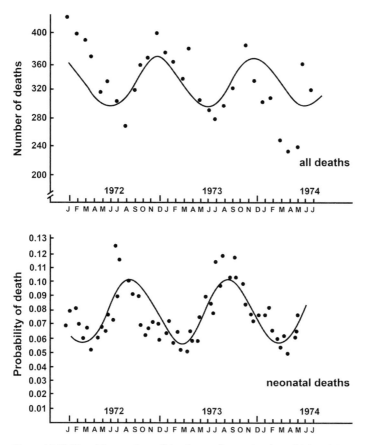

Figure 11.23 Monthly number of deaths at all ages (top), and life-table estimates of the monthly probability of neonatal deaths (bottom), Matlab, Bangladesh 1972–4. Neonatal deaths are deaths occurring during the first week of life. Smooth curves are sine functions fit to the data. From Becker and Sardar (1981: 151).

couple involved) and attempting after the fact to estimate their associated time of conception (insofar as the couple can reconstruct it) suggests a large peak in conceptions falling between January and April (Figure 11.25, middle). Stated differently, the seasonality of live births seems to be caused by seasonal variation in conception rates, not in the incidence of pregnancy loss (for a more detailed examination of this issue, see Holman, 1996). Now this finding, if it is correct, is intriguing, because independent research has shown that the postpartum resumption of menstrual bleeding in nursing women – an indirect, slightly error-prone indicator of the return of full fecundity following a live birth – increases in frequency during October or November, reaches a peak in December–January, and then drops continuously until March or so (Figure 11.25, bottom). Apparent conceptions lag behind the resumption of menses by two to three months on average, about as long as we would expect given the so-called fecund waiting time to conception – the time-lag that results from the fact that the probability of conception from any single act of

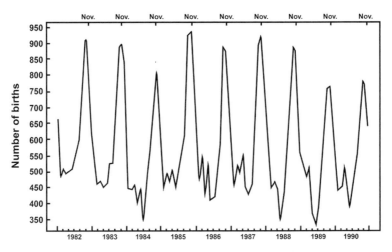

Figure 11.24 Seasonality of live births in Matlab, Bangladesh 1982–90. From Becker (1994), by permission of John Wiley & Sons, Inc.

intercourse never reaches one even in the absence of contraception, so that couples often have to wait some time before a pregnancy occurs (Wood, 1994a: 279–85).

We can, if we're brave, make one more inferential leap by drawing on another study from Matlab, this one examining seasonal variation in breastfeeding behavior (Figure 11.26). In a large prospective study, Huffman *et al.* (1980) found that suckling intensity displayed two characteristic seasonal swings (as well as an overall decline with the nursing child's age): first, a decline in suckling intensity from November to February, corresponding to the period when women are most involved in the *aman* harvest and postharvest processing of the *aman* crop and in the sowing and transplanting of the *boro* crop; and, second, an increase in suckling intensity in May–July just before the preharvest hungry season. Huffman *et al.* (1980) attribute the first of these changes directly to women's heavy involvement in the *aman* harvest-postharvest season and the *boro* sowing/transplanting season, when agricultural work competes with breastfeeding for a new mother's time, attention and energies. Now, Huffman and her coauthors have many years of involvement with the Matlab project, both individually and collectively, and I am inclined to trust their scientific instincts. But it is striking that another period of heavy farm work occurs with the sowing/transplanting of the *aus* crop and the harvesting of the *boro* crop during March–May *without* a clear reduction in suckling intensity – in fact, May overlaps the seasonal *increase* in suckling observed by Huffman *et al.* (1980). But if their original argument proves to be correct, it would be one of very few cases in which an explanatory variable associated with the farming year was tied convincingly to the seasonality of fertility.[11]

---

[11] For one particular subgroup of the Matlab community, comprising households whose male heads are involved in semicommercial fishing along the Meghna River and the estuary of the Ganges and Brahmaputra, another likely source of seasonal fertility has been identified: physical separation of wives

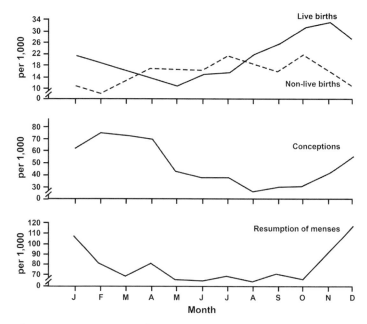

Figure 11.25 Monthly rates (per 1000 women) of live births, pregnancy losses, reported conceptions and resumption of menses during the postpartum period, Matlab, Bangladesh 1976–9. From Becker *et al.* (1986), by permission of the Taylor Francis Group.

Conclusions

For all preindustrial farming households, but especially those with young children, seasonal changes in environment, work, storage and food availability can pose a variety of challenges. Specific patterns of agricultural seasonality vary widely throughout the world, as do the environmental and phenological factors responsible for them, but seasonality is almost everywhere of considerable importance to the household demographic enterprise. In the tropics, childhood mortality rates seem to be correlated with seasonal changes in exposure to infectious diseases and in food availability. In rural *temperate* regions during preindustrial times, seasonality in disease exposure may have been less important, although not necessarily so given the close proximity of people living in the same house throughout winter (in which case the diseases involved would presumably be transmitted by direct person-to-person contact, not by contaminated water or arthropods). But seasonal changes in food availability were almost certainly of great importance in temperate, grain-based rural economies that were heavily dependent on storage (see the papers in Pals and Wijngaarden-Baker, 1998, for extended discussions of agricultural seasonality in preindustrial Europe). Seasonal changes in fertility rates are more of a puzzle. In Matlab, a plausible *prima facie* case has been made that seasonal changes in

from their husbands who are away on extended fishing trips during the apparent period of fewest conceptions (Chen *et al.*, 1974).

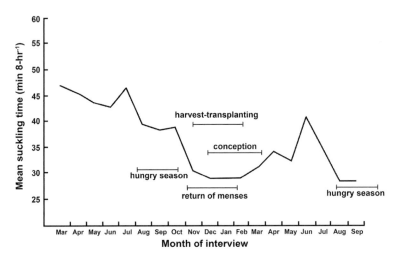

Figure 11.26 Seasonal farm work and breastfeeding may compete for a mother's time in Matlab, Bangladesh. Suckling time (total time spent suckling over a continuous observation period of 8 hours during a single day) in 216 mother–offspring pairs in which the offspring were 17–25 months old at the initiation of observation. Each pair was observed once a month over the entire 18-month study period unless the child was completely weaned first. Modified from Huffman *et al.* (1980), by permission of the American Society for Nutrition.

women's farming activities and their influence on breastfeeding patterns may be important drivers of seasonal fertility. As important as the Matlab study is, however, it still represents a single location and provides limited grounds for generalization. I submit, therefore, that continued analysis of demographic seasonality, including birth seasonality, should be near the top of the agenda in future research on the success or failure of subsistence farming households.

12 Beyond the Household

God save me from what they call *households*. – Emily Dickinson, letter to Abiah Root, 1850

A major goal of this book has been to reframe the scientific debate over the relationship between population and preindustrial farming. One way to see how successful I have been in meeting that goal is to turn back to the section on "Rethinking the relationship between human population and traditional agriculture" in Chapter 1, which posed a series of questions that needed to be answered before further progress could be made. It is now time to revisit those questions in order to judge how far, if at all, we have advanced toward answering them.

Is the Relationship between Population and Preindustrial Agriculture Simple or Complicated?

I think we can safely conclude that the relationship is more complicated than earlier authors, including Malthus and Boserup, have supposed. It operates at many spatial scales (even though, throughout the second half of the book, I've emphasized only one of them) and via multiple mechanisms. It can also involve different effects on different temporal and spatial scales, as hinted at by my mention of second-order (lagged) feedback relationships in Chapter 4 and my discussion of the differences between Boserupian and Chayanovian pressure in Chapter 10. Even if we accept, on purely tactical grounds, my proposed focus on households as a provisional way to simplify our analytical task, the relationship between population and traditional farming *still* appears to be more complex than it did in the earlier literature. Adding additional scales will, of course, only make the subject more complicated – which is no reason not to do it once we have exhausted the analytical utility of our narrower focus on the household.

Is the Relationship Unidirectional or Reciprocal?

If the answer to this question turns out to be "unidirectional" we will need to ask another question: *Who, then, won the debate between Malthus and Boserup?* My own answer to the main question is, unequivocally, "reciprocal," which immediately implies my answer to the second question: "no one." Indeed I have argued that there never really was a legitimate debate between Malthus and Boserup. It turns out that Malthus was right (the growth of all preindustrial populations was limited, and food availability was an inevitable and important part of that limitation) *and* that Boserup was right (preindustrial farming households could respond to limited food availability associated with adverse demographic conditions by intensifying their production of food, although – and here comes Malthus again – their ability to do so was itself limited). The MaB ratchet (Chapter 5) is my most explicit statement of the reciprocal interactions of population and farming behavior at the population level, but, as this book has argued, reciprocal relationships also abound at the level of the household. To pick just two examples: Human and animal labor is a major determinant of household food availability, limited food availability can be a major determinant of the physiological work capacity of the people in the household and of their beasts. High C/P ratios can raise the risk of infant mortality, infant mortality lowers the C/P ratio. Such interactions mean that demographic processes can be both a brake *and* an accelerator of agricultural change – and *vice versa*, that agricultural processes can be both a brake and an accelerator of demographic change. I would suggest that we have only just begun to understand the complicated dynamics that result from these reciprocal interactions.

What are the Precise Mechanisms Underlying the Relationship?

One of the strangest things about the past debate over population and traditional farming is the very great extent to which the actual mechanisms linking the two, both demographic and agronomic, have been ignored. On the demographic side, one must study mortality, fertility and migration in some detail – and I hasten to add that mortality, fertility and migration are themselves all multidimensional and require considerable analytical dissection before we can begin to understand them. On the agronomic side, there is much more to farming behavior (*contra* Boserup) than the average length of fallow periods relative to cropping. Farming practices need to be specified in much more detail before we can understand them as either causes or consequences of demographic change.

I have suggested that important mechanisms channeling the effects of preindustrial farming on population include, at a minimum, such things as the intensity of household food production (reflected only partly by the value of R, the conventional measure of Boserupian intensity), household demographic composition (especially its size and C/P ratio), household physiological work capacity, nutrition, immunocompetence, infectious diseases and childhood mortality. Other mechanisms operating via fertility and migration are also likely but not yet well-established, as is also true of other aspects of mortality. Population feeds back on farming practices by influencing everything a household might do, for example, to offset an unfavorable C/P ratio, such as expanding their access to arable, working longer hours, manuring, carefully allocating their genetic resources and so forth – but the declining marginal productivity of agricultural production always limits the capacity of changes in farming behavior to compensate fully for adverse demographic conditions. Hence, precisely the same feedbacks may ultimately affect childhood mortality as well as (or instead of) farming behavior.

At what Scale or Scales do the Mechanisms Operate?

There will never be a single correct answer to this question – it depends entirely on the questions being asked. Nonetheless, I hope I have succeeded in convincing my readers that the farming household is an enduringly and uniquely important scale at which to address almost all the fundamental questions about population and agriculture in rural, preindustrial societies. Scales both higher (the larger settlement or regional farming system) and lower (the individual) can, of course, also be important. But the farming household and its farm seem to me to be of singular significance as the "cell" that makes up the larger settlement "tissue" and houses, feeds and mobilizes its individual members. Constructing and testing formal models of the farming household and its links to *individuals* in one direction and *the larger settlement system* in the other will be challenging, but the intellectual rewards will, I believe, be great.

The essential first step in this endeavor, I have argued, is to construct a stylized model of the farming household and its farm. This book has attempted to sketch such a model, the elements of which are summarized in Table 12.1. This model, like all models, is a deliberate over-simplification of a complex reality. What to include and what to leave out were conscious and careful decisions on my part. Some readers might choose to make different decisions – putting in more about political ecology or evolutionary biology, for example – but that would result in *their* model, not mine. I believe my choices are defensible, just as different ones would be for different purposes. I believe, in short, that my model identifies basic and universal features of, and relationships within, traditional farming households – features and relationships that may sometimes (perhaps often) be obscured by other variables or linkages omitted from the model, but that must still be present in some form and with some

Table 12.1 Key elements of a model of the family-based subsistence farming household (HH)

The HH as a demographic enterprise

The HH as a quasi-autonomous unit of food production and consumption

The HH and its farm as the basic locus of decision-making regarding the allocation of resources, including HH labor

The inseparability of the "productive" and "domestic" domains of the HH enterprise

The declining marginal productivity of inputs into farming (especially labor inputs)

Density-dependent population regulation acting at the HH level

The synergy of under-nutrition, reduced immunocompetence, infection and childhood mortality within the HH as a central part of density-dependent population regulation

HH age–sex composition as a determinant of HH food requirements

HH age–sex composition (acting via physiological work capacity) as a determinant of the HH's ability to produce sufficient food for itself

The adverse effects of under-nutrition on the HH's physiological work capacity

HH consumer/producer ratio as a determinant of the intensity of HH food production *and* of childhood morbidity and mortality

Exposure of the HH to seasonal changes in food availability and to environmental unpredictability

force. I also believe that my model sets out an important agenda for future research on traditional farming. All the entries in Table 12.1 – and all the relationships among them – need to be specified formally and precisely, tested against field data and rejected or reformulated. My research agenda should not, of course, be the only agenda for studying farming in the preindustrial world, but I think it can be a productive and enlightening one – an agenda that has the potential to inform and supplement *other* agendas. And I would reiterate what I hope this book has made abundantly clear: that most of the elements that make up my model are not in themselves especially new, although I would like to think the particular way I've brought them together is.

The conceptual framework adopted in this book has been based on three model assumptions: (i) the households under investigation are devoted entirely to subsistence farming rather than production for the market, (ii) individual subsistence farms are autonomous when it comes to food production and consumption, and (iii) the subsistence farming household is in essence a demographic enterprise. As I have tried to emphasize throughout the book, none of these three assumptions provides an absolutely true or complete picture of reality. But the three assumptions are otherwise of rather different order: the first is true in some situations (although perhaps only rarely, if ever, nowadays), the second is never more than partially true and the third is always true but only if things are viewed from a certain perspective (my own, of course). All three assumptions should be critically evaluated in future research and modified or abandoned as needed. In the following section of this chapter, I want to take one step in that direction by relaxing the assumption of household autonomy so that we can begin to understand the larger social context of the farming household's demographic enterprise. Earlier chapters were written as if it were every household for itself. This is never true, and it is time to acknowledge that fact.

The Household in its Larger Demographic, Social and Spatial Context

I begin with a simple, uncontestable generalization. Throughout the preindustrial world, farming households are usually found in discrete spatial "clumps" along with other such households – in compounds, hamlets, villages and occasionally even larger, semiurban settlements. Although isolated farmsteads are observed in some areas, mostly what we see are small clusters similar to the examples shown in Figures 12.1 and 12.2. There are several reasons for households to cluster together beyond sheer primate sociality: defense, ties of kinship and affection, the need to share food and the need to work together at least occasionally. In this section, I discuss the importance of kinship ties and the ecology and economics of food-sharing and of cooperative supra-household work parties. Two underlying messages are (i) that the household demographic enterprise is the fundamental unit that generates the population, the network of kinship relations *and* the settlement system at higher, more aggregated levels (*microdemographic processes generate macrodemographic patterns*), and (ii) that inter-household differentials in material well-being within any one settlement are always present, even in supposedly egalitarian farming

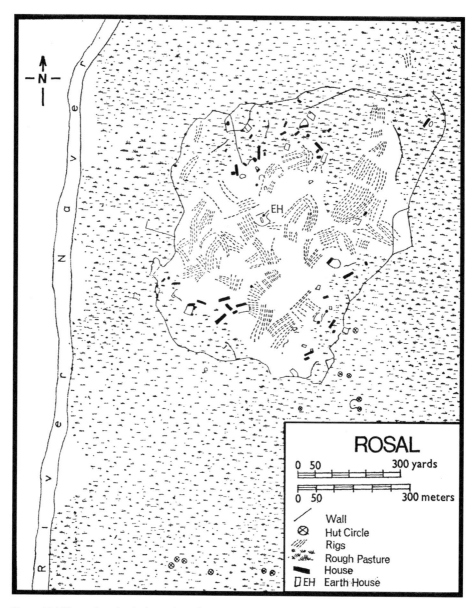

Figure 12.1 The archaeological remains of Rosal township, Strathnaver, in the county of Sutherland, northern Scotland. Rigs were plowed fields planted in oats and barley. The entire settlement was enclosed by a turf wall, portions of which are still visible. Rough pasture was used for cattle and sheep. The township was "cleared" (evicted) by its laird in 1814–18. From Fairhurst (1971: 233), by permission of Macmillan Publishing.

communities, and derive partly from variation in the household demographic enterprise itself (*microdemographic processes generate macrodemographic differentials*).[1] It is these

---

[1] I am not claiming that all macrodemographic features can be reduced to microdemographic processes (what some authors would call "emergent properties" do exist), but only that some of them can, and those that can are important in their own right. In other words, I am still dealing in what are in effect

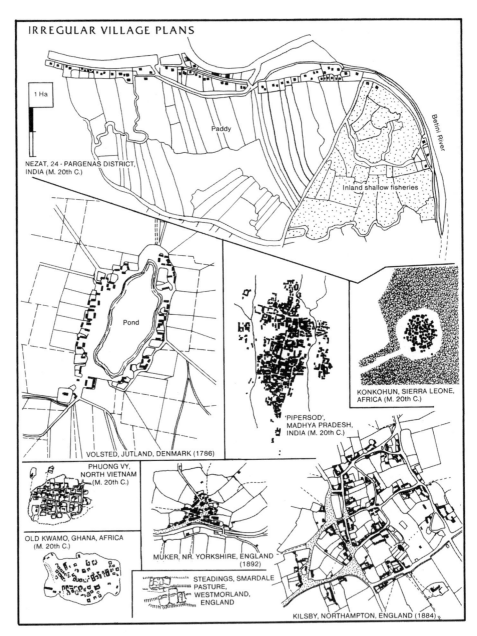

Figure 12.2 Village and hamlet plans from Africa, Europe and Asia. From Roberts (1996: 96), by permission of Routledge and Kegan Paul Publishers.

differentials, I suggest, that combine with close kinship to drive both food-sharing and multihousehold labor groups.

model-based partial-equilibrium analyses that hold constant everything *except* microdemographic processes while examining effects at slightly higher levels of aggregation – which is very far from saying that *only* microdemographic processes are important in the real world.

Population as a Spatially Constrained "Pedigree Process"

Just as the farming household in the preindustrial world is usually made up of a group of close relatives, so the larger spatial cluster of households, whether hamlet, village or something larger, usually comprises a collection of slightly less closely related kinfolk. Indeed, as the example of the Ifugao hamlet in Figure 12.3 suggests, the detailed spatial patterning of houses *within* the settlement often mirrors the kinship relations among them (see Verdery *et al.*, 2012, for an example from rural Thailand, as well as a useful discussion of how to analyze the relationship between kinship and locale using modern spatial methods). The correlation between kinship and spatial propinquity in traditional societies is positive, not so much because relatives opt to move into the same neighborhood from more scattered locations (although that sometimes happens), but because the demographic processes that generate the larger settlement simultaneously create a web of kinship – a pedigree[2] – and in the world of preindustrial farmers those demographic processes are tightly circumscribed spatially (see Chapter 1). Close kin inhabit the same locale mostly because they were born there. For example, the very data (on marriages, births and deaths) that are used by historical demographers in the reconstruction of larger population aggregates can also be used to reconstruct pedigree relationships among individuals. The population-generating process, so to speak, is simultaneously a pedigree-generating process. Given enough time, the pedigree process (to coin a shorter term) can generate as large a population as anyone could wish for (Figure 12.4). Furthermore, under the energetically costly transport conditions of the rural preindustrial world there is always, at any given time, a more or less tight correlation between kinship and location of residence (Wijsman and Cavalli-Sforza, 1984). Most people are, I think we can all agree, born in close physical proximity to their biological mothers. And their mothers frequently live close to the biological fathers involved, often but not always on the same farmstead. Their siblings are apt to be born in more or less the same place as they were (sometimes in the same bed). When they and their siblings grow up and move out to create their own households, they do scatter spatially, but only within a very small radius; what's more, they usually find spouses from the same or

---

[2] By *pedigree* I mean a family tree that reflects the actual biological relationships among individuals. Most traditional societies reckon kinship according to some culturally-sanctioned scheme (e.g. "classificatory" kinship) such that their own kin categories do not correspond exactly or even very closely to the biological relationships. (I would call a local informant's conceptualized network of relatedness a *genealogy* rather than a pedigree.) In other words, social kinship and biological kinship are not the same thing. From the current perspective we are mainly interested in biological kinship – and in fact rural hamlets and villages in the preindustrial past were almost invariably made up, not only of close social kin, but of close biological kin as well. Based on a variety of local population studies, geneticists have estimated that two individuals picked at random from a single small, rural settlement located anywhere in the preindustrial world would have been, on average, at least as closely related biologically as second cousins, an estimate that reflects not just immediate kin ties but more remote inbreeding as well (Cavalli-Sforza and Bodmer, 1971: 352–3; Jacquard, 1974: 495–524).

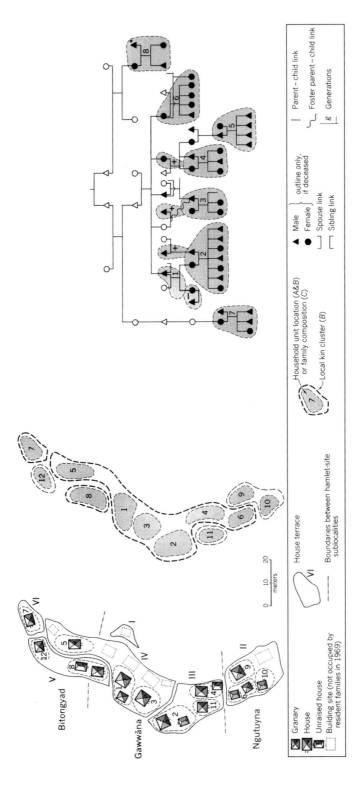

Figure 12.3 Kinship and spatial organization of an Ifugao farming hamlet, north Luzon, the Philippines. (Left) Settlement maps. (Right) Kinship relations among settlement members. The hamlet is surrounded by intensively farmed, terraced wet rice fields. From Conklin (1980: 7), by permission of Yale University Press.

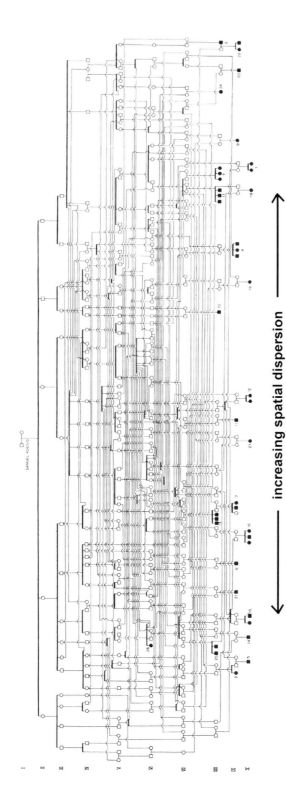

Figure 12.4 The pedigree process as a population-generating process: the biological descendants of Samuel Koenig and his unnamed wife, Old Order Amish, Lancaster County, Pennsylvania. The original couple migrated to North America in 1744. Over the generations, the extended kindred has become somewhat more dispersed spatially, but still resides primarily in Lancaster County. Modified from McKusick (1978: 118), by permission of Johns Hopkins University Press.

increasing spatial dispersion

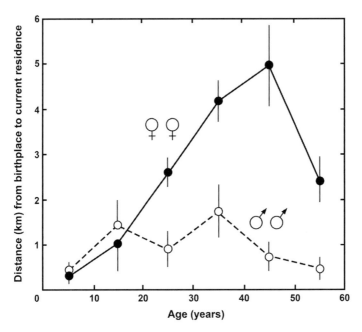

Figure 12.5 Age- and sex-specific average distances (km) between an individual's birthplace and current residence among the Gainj of Papua New Guinea 1978. Error bars are ± 1 s.e. of the age- and sex-specific mean distance. The Gainj practice virilocal postmarital residence. From Wood *et al.* (1985a), by permission of Oxford University Press, USA.

nearby villages (Wijsman and Cavalli-Sforza, 1984:283–4). Any arable to which they have claim is almost certain to be located near their natal homes, often in the same settlement. Similarly, access to the local landesque farming capital built by their parents and more distant ancestors is not blithely foresaken. And so on through the generations. All these forces create a kind of *spatial inertia* acting as a brake on any centrifugal demographic pressures that may be at play. The net effect is that people in traditional farming societies rarely move far from their birthplaces over the course of their lives – although as Figure 12.5 suggests, males and females may move slightly differing distances owing, for example, to asymmetrical postmarital residence rules. But no matter their sex, they almost never end up very far from their close kin. As a consequence, the space around each individual or household itself becomes structured by kinship, as illustrated by a classic study of the population genetics of traditional farming communities in the Upper Parma Valley of Italy (Figure 12.6). Rural settlements in preindustrial farming societies, in short, are typically small islands of close biological kin floating on a wider sea of somewhat less close kin. And insofar as close kinship encourages and channels cooperation, relatedness must be taken into account as we try to understand inter-household food sharing and the pooling of labor within local communities.

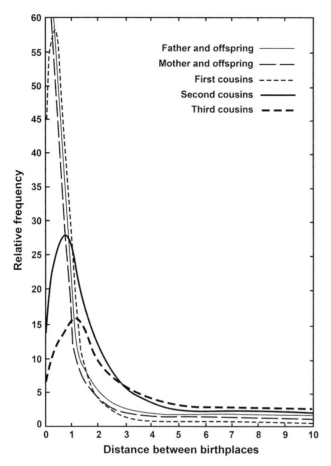

Figure 12.6 Predicted distributions of distances (km) between the birthplaces of relatives of various degrees, based on data from the Upper Parma Valley, Italy (1957–66). Smoothed distributions are approximated by modeling the migration distances as the sum of two exponential random variables. From Cavalli-Sforza and Bodmer (1971: 469), by permission of W. H. Freeman Press.

The Inequality of "Egalitarian" Households

Another salient feature of traditional rural settlements is that their constituent households are never perfectly equal when it comes to material resources, even when they are all closely related. This is true even in prestate societies that most anthropologists would classify as egalitarian (Netting, 1982). Table 12.2, for example, shows several ethnographic examples from sub-Saharan Africa spanning a wide range of environments, agricultural practices, degrees of polygyny and levels of political differentiation. The individual cases summarized in this table have been dichotomized into "wealthy" and "poor" farms according to local informants' subjective judgments about the households in question – or, in the Hausa example, by whether the household owned one piece of essential farming capital, a plow.

Table 12.2 Mean arable landholding size (in hectares) and household size in four groups of traditional African farmers. "Wealthier" and "poorer" farmers were so identifed by local informants; hence the terms have little if any cross-cultural validity (in the Nigerian case, "wealthier" households were simply those that owned at least one entire plow). Sample sizes were 120 households for the Gusii and 60 for all the other groups; in every case, "wealthier" farms made up a minority of the sample. From Goody (1972: 123), reproduced with permission of Cambridge University Press.

Language group	"Wealthier" farms		"Poorer" farms	
	Mean holding size (ha)	Mean no. household members	Mean holding size (ha)	Mean no. household members
Gusii (Kenya)	4.8	10.0	2.8	9.1
Teso (Uganda)	13.9	10.8	5.1	8.3
Tonga (Zambia)	22.7	16.3	8.5	8.0
Hausa (Nigeria)	8.2	11.9	2.7	6.4

Wealthier households or households with plows consistently have larger holdings of arable land and more members than do their neighbors, and we might be tempted to describe them as "rich" even though the absolute differences are mainly small. It should be noted that causation is difficult to untangle in this table. Do wealthy farms or farms with plows have larger holdings because they are better off in other ways (e.g. they can buy more land *and* more food), or does ownership of a plow or other forms of farming capital (including perhaps draft animals) enable the cultivation of a larger holding? Do farms without the necessary capital have fewer members because their holdings (and thus food sources) are smaller, or are their holdings smaller because they need to feed fewer members? Still, though the data can do no more than suggest possible causal explanations, they are sufficient to show that some degree of economic differentiation exists within these rural communities.

Table 12.3 shows the distributions of household landholdings under pre-dominantly rain-fed versus predominantly irrigated farming in Andra Pradesh and Karnataka, neighboring states with similar environments in southern India. In general, the irrigated systems tend to have much smaller holdings, with a majority or near-majority of households having less than one hectare of land in most cases (compared to roughly 10–25 percent in most of the rain-fed examples). Norman (1979: 75) suggests that there is population "pressure" on land in all these cases, but that production can become much more spatially concentrated under irrigation (i.e. more people can be squeezed onto less land). Thus, the smaller average holdings of households practicing irrigation compared to those that are not may not reflect any real disadvantage in the amount of food available to them. But the important point in the current context is that, *within* all cases, whether rain-fed or irrigated, there exists substantial variation in landholding size, no matter what the dominant mode of farming.

Another example, this one from Tokugawa-era Japan, is shown in Table 12.4. Drawing on official population registers, T. C. Smith (1977) has done a demographic

Table 12.3 Farm size distribution (percent) in two Indian states. From Kampen (1974).

State and category	District	Farm size (ha)					
		<1	1–2	2–3	3–4	4–5	>5
Andra Pradesh	Adilabad	26	17	19	9	7	21
Rain-fed	Mehbubnagar	21	20	16	10	8	18
	Medak	43	22	11	6	4	13
Andra Pradesh	East Godovari	70	16	3	3	2	4
Irrigated	Krishna	65	19	7	4	2	4
	West Godovari	62	19	8	4	2	5
Karnataka	Bellary	16	21	17	11	9	26
Rain-fed	Bijapur	10	16	14	11	8	41
	Gulbarga	11	15	13	11	9	41
Karnataka	Mandya	55	24	10	5	2	4
Irrigated	Shimoga	33	30	15	7	5	9
	South Kanara	47	28	12	5	3	4

and economic reconstruction of Nakahara village on Honshu's Nobi Plain during the eighteenth and early nineteenth century.[3] The Tokugawa shogunate was not exactly a "pre-state" situation, although historians argue about just how centralized it was, but the farming village itself seems to have been fairly egalitarian and homogeneous in the formal, sociopolitical sense. Although village headmen tended to *own* more land than other residents, provisions for tenancy "tended to equalize *access* to land" (T. C. Smith, 1977: 44; emphasis added). The size of holdings, including tenants' holdings, was measured at the time in terms of an interesting unit called the *koku*. Originally the *koku* was a measure of volume, notionally the amount of rice needed to support one person for one year. By extension, it was sometimes used to denote the area of land needed to produce one *koku* of rice. (It is impossible to translate this area into an absolute and invariant number of hectares as it varied from place to place; even in any one place, it may have varied over time.) While Table 12.4 shows that mean household size generally varied as might be expected with the number of *koku* farmed by the household – the more *koku*, the more people – the number of household members did not "keep up" with the number of *koku*, presumably reflecting the declining marginal productivity of either land or labor.[4] But the relationship between farm holding and household size seems real enough. For Nakahara the correlations between landholding and household size at the ten observation dates were as follows:

---

[3] "Nakahara" is a pseudonym.
[4] Note too that average household size tended to increase over time. It is difficult to interpret this pattern because it may partly reflect the instability of the *koku* as a measure of land. T. C. Smith (1977), however, considers it real and likely to be part of a pattern of general growth in the village population, reflecting the fact that Nakahara was founded by a small number of settlers not long before the period covered by Smith's study.

Date	Correlation	Date	Correlation
1717	0.71	1780	0.57
1727	0.49	1792	0.38
1738	0.49	1802	0.44
1746	0.50	1812	0.19
1764	0.69	1823	0.13

Table 12.4 Agricultural landholdings and household size in the rice-growing village of Nakahara, Japan 1716–1823. One *koku* nominally equals the amount of rice needed to support one person for a year and, by extension, the land needed to grow one *koku* of rice. From T. C. Smith (1977: 123), reproduced with permission of Cambridge University Press.

	Mean household members by farm holding size		
Year	Small (0–4 *koku*)	Medium (4.1–18.0 *koku*)	Large (>18 *koku*)
1716	1.6	2.5	4.1
1727	2.5	2.9	3.8
1738	2.7	3.8	5.1
1746	2.5	4.5	5.9
1764	2.8	4.5	6.2
1780	3.0	4.3	5.6
1792	3.8	4.8	5.4
1802	4.0	4.5	5.8
1812	5.1	5.0	5.7
1823	4.9	5.1	5.4
Total	3.7	4.2	5.3

These correlations are reasonably substantial at all dates but the last two (T. C. Smith, 1977: 122). Once again, it is difficult to infer causation from these figures: did larger families demand large holdings, or did large holdings enable larger families? Note too that none of the reported correlations comes close to 1.0, suggesting that other factors were in play – including perhaps random variation in demographic events such as births and deaths that influenced household size. Nonetheless, the data do suggest that a certain amount of variation in access to land and in household demography existed within this rather homogeneous farming village.

It is possible that the patterns of household differentiation within rural communities illustrated by Tables 12.2–12.4 signify more or less "latent" class differences – that is, that they are permanent, heritable and institutionalized (whatever that means), and that groups of households consciously share class interests and actively join together to compete with other such groups. Chayanov, however, argued that at least some fraction of the differences within all farming communities was likely to be transitory and to reflect what he called "demographic differentiation" (Chayanov, 1986: 68), especially cycling C/P ratios, rather than class differences *per se* (this claim was part of what got him killed). Other potential causes of inter-household variation in physical well-being that usually stop short of creating class differences include, first, stochastic variation in the number and timing of births and deaths within the household, resulting in fluctuations in household size relative to amount of available land (precisely the source of variation modeled under the MaB ratchet in Figure 5.15); and, second, the prior history of land acquisition, including the vagaries of inheritance, among the household's ancestors from whom the current holding ultimately derives. Such things, including changing C/P ratios, are inevitable no matter how socially and politically homogeneous the community is. The energy trap, discussed in Chapter 9, is another possible mechanism for differentiation in physical well-being – one that may lead to somewhat more permanent, inter-generational differences – but the model of the energy trap has yet to be adequately tested. The fundamental point of importance here is that households within the same local farming community, despite being closely related and socially similar, are very unlikely to be identical in their material conditions as reflected in landholding size and perhaps other variables. I further suggest that the combination of close relatedness, spatial propinquity and material heterogeneity may often act as an important facilitator of the sharing of food and farming tasks among households. Households whose resources exceed their immediate needs may be more inclined to share with their less fortunate next-door kin – and the latter may be more inclined to demand it.

The Ecology of Inter-Household Food Distribution Networks

The sharing of resources within traditional rural villages is occasionally described as "communal". It is not – or at least not in the extreme sense that everyone in the village has equal access to everyone else's resources. Sharing, like the village layout itself, is channeled and constrained by kinship.

During his fieldwork among the Wola of highland New Guinea, Paul Sillitoe (1983) carried out a study of the food grown and consumed by a total of 12 households monitored over a single farming year. One contribution of this study was to show just how small a portion of a household's potential food supply originates or ends up on other farms (Table 12.5). Around 97 percent by weight of the major food crops grown by the average household [in kg, $7551 \div (7551 + 265)$] is eaten by the same household, while about 86 percent of the major crops eaten by the average household [$7551 \div (7551 + 1077)$] is grown by that same household – suggesting that our assumption of household autonomy may not be too far off the mark, at least in this one ethnographic example. The flow of food between households may, of course, still be critical to the recipient family's nutritional well-being even if its volume is relatively small – a point that Sillitoe's survey did not address. Table 12.6 uses data from the same survey to tally the sources of inter-household food gifts broken down by kin relationship and spatial propinquity (whether in the same "village" or

Table 12.5 Sources of plant food (by weight) eaten during a consumption survey of 12 households, Wola, highland New Guiea. Only foods with average consumption per household greater than 50 kg are shown. Weights are all rounded to the nearest kg. Row percentages sum to 100. Modified from Sillitoe (1983: 231), reproduced with permission of Paul Sillitoe.

Plant	Harvested and eaten by household		Received from other households		Given to other households	
	kg	%	kg	%	kg	%
Sweet potato	6211	85.2	846	11.6	236	3.2
Pumpkin	802	84.8	132	14.0	12	1.3
Highland pitpit[a]	218	94.8	9	3.9	3	1.3
Sugar cane	79	68.7	32	27.8	4	3.5
Maize	72	72.0	20	20.0	8	8.0
Taro	60	67.4	27	30.3	2	2.3
Acanthus[b]	63	96.9	2	3.1	0	0.0
Beans	46	83.6	9	16.4	0	0.0
Total	7551	84.9	1077	12.1	265	3.0

[a] *Setaria palmifolia.*
[b] Mostly *Rungia klosii*, both cultivated and collected wild.

not).[5] Most food sharing occurs within the same village, as might be expected if sharing is usually adventitious or haulage costs are high. The most obvious exceptions involve gifts from "close but unrelated associates"; these are often political in nature (note that they go primarily to male recipients) and represent one way in which a so-called big man (*ol howma*) can augment his multivillage client base (Sillitoe, 1979: 113). There is nothing adventitious about gifts of food from big men: they are political tools. Another feature is that gifts of food from kin are somewhat more likely to be given to male recipients, especially if they come from affines (gifts from extremely close consanguines tend to go to females). But whether the recipient is male or female, the gift is almost always shared with the other members of his or her household (Sillitoe, 1983).

The Wola trace social kinship bilaterally; as a consequence, their conceptualized scheme of kin relations hews fairly closely to the patterns of biological kinship. What happens when the divergence between the two is greater? The Bemba of East Africa, who are matrilineal, provide an interesting comparison. Figure 12.7 reproduces Audrey Richards's 1934 sketch map of Kasaka, a Bemba village in Northern Rhodesia where she did much of her fieldwork (Richards, 1939: 167). The map is hard to read (as it was in the original), but it contains a wealth of information about the

[5] As in much of highland New Guinea, the Wola do not reside in compact settlements of the sort we would normally call villages. What I have labeled the "village" in the present context is what the Wola would call the *semoda*, a named, exogamous, discrete territorial unit that claims shared usufructory access to a recognized area of land and a common genealogy, the latter often not known in any detail (Sillitoe, 1983: 24).

Table 12.6 Number of times food was received from various categories of relatives living in different households during consumption survey of 12 households, Wola, highland New Guinea. Modified from Sillitoe (1983: 258), reproduced with permission of Paul Sillitoe.

| Relationship (ego = recipient) | Mean no. of relatives in each category[a] | | Mean no. of times food received from each relative, by category | | | |
| | | | Male recipients | | Female recipients | |
	M	F	From same village	From other village	From same village	From other village
Consanguines						
Children	1	2	4.0	5.0	10.5	2.5
Siblings	4	3	8.0	1.8	11.0	2.0
Siblings' children	4	1	3.2	0.5	4.0	0
Father	0	1	0	0	1.0	0
Mother	1	1	0	3.0	10.0	15.0
Father's relatives	12	2	12.2	2.0	1.5	0
More distant paternal relatives	51	19	5.2	0.2	2.2	0.1
Mother's relatives	4	1	2.0	0.2	0	0
More distant maternal relatives	36	1	9.6	0.6	1.0	0
Affines						
Spouse's siblings	2	2	9.5	8.0	0.5	0.5
Spouse's siblings children	2	0	1.5	0.5	0	0
Spouse's parents	2	1	7.5	5.0	0	0
Spouses' father's relatives	3	7	0.3	1.7	0.3	0.1
Spouses' mother's relatives	0	1	0	0	0	0
Spouses' more distant paternal relatives	13	23	1.0	0.2	1.4	0.1
Spouses' more distant maternal relatives	2	1	0	1.0	0	0
Children's affines	2	4	1.5	0.5	1.2	1.0
Sibling's affines	3	3	6.7	0.3	0	0.7
Sibling's children's affines	6	0	0.8	0.5	0	0
Father's relatives' affines	44	38	2.8	0.7	0.8	0.2
Mother's relatives' affines	15	1	3.4	0.9	1.0	1.0
Spouse's siblings' affines	4	2	0.8	2.0	0	0
Spouse's father's relatives' affines	0	3	0	0	0	1.0
Spouse's mother's relatives' affines	0	1	0	0	0	0
Spouse's more distant relatives' affines	3	19	1.3	0.7	1.4	0.4
Close but unrelated associates	3	2	0	29.0	0	6.5

[a] As recognized by recipients in survey, broken down by sex of recipient.

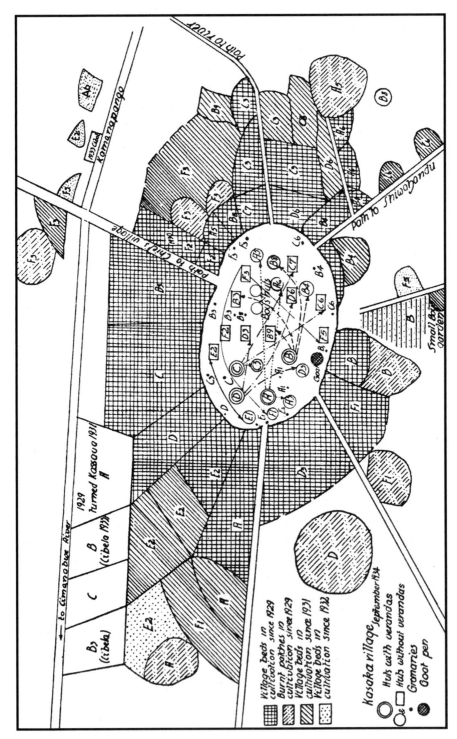

Figure 12.7 Sketch map of the Bemba farming village of Kasaka (1934), Northern Rhodesia (now Zambia), south central Africa. From Richards (1939: 167), by permission of Oxford University Press, USA.

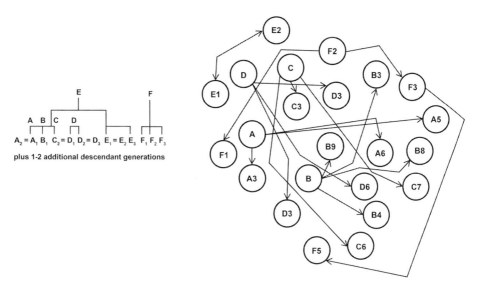

Figure 12.8 An expanded plan of the 23 huts in the center of the village shown in Figure 12.7, plus the matrilineal and affinal relationships linking them (households not explicitly shown in the genealogy are in the youngest one or two descending generations). Every household belongs to one of six local matrilines (A–F). Arrows indicate observed pathways of food-sharing among households in 1934. All the food shared among households was restricted to a single local matriline, and almost all of it originated in the household of the oldest surviving kinswoman in that particular matriline. Adapted from Richards (1939: 177).

interrelatedness of households, the size of holdings and other village features. The center of the map, which is almost completely unreadable, shows the patterns of inter-household food flows recorded by Richards during a survey lasting from September 1 to October 7, 1933.[6] Figure 12.8 provides an enlarged and simplified version of the central part of Richards' sketch map, and also shows the matrilineal relationships among households (house numbers not shown in the genealogy are all in the two youngest descending generations). The village comprised four major matrilines (A, B, C, D) and two minor ones (E, F). All inter-household transfers of food were confined to a single local matriline, and almost all originated in the household of the oldest surviving female member of that particular matriline. Since every household within the matriline regularly helped the senior-most woman with her farm work, these transfers might be viewed as representing, in effect, *redistributions* of food to the cooperating families rather than gifts. Richards suggests that food-giving households usually had more grain in their granaries than recipients; givers also had, on average, slightly more fields. (Richards also suggests that the availability of female labor was an important determinant of household yields.) It appears that gifts to direct matrilineal descendants are not markedly more frequent

---

[6] Had the survey lasted longer, the number of inter-household food gifts would undoubtedly have been greater, perhaps substantially so, as would the number of households linked by food-sharing.

than those to in-marrying affines, which suggests that consanguinity *per se* may not be the sole guiding principle involved here. Moreover, purely patrilateral food transfers were entirely absent, even in the case of contiguous households. Thus, at least in this case, social kinship would seem to trump biological kinship. It is important to remember, however, that close social kin are also close biological kin in such small farming communities.

Such detailed empirical information on food-sharing is rare in the literature on traditional farming societies. The few studies that exist, however, are consistent in suggesting that food transfers among households tend to be confined to close neighbors and close kin, either biological or social or, most likely, both. Even less information, unfortunately, is available on the role of these transfers in maintaining the health of household members and the success of the demographic enterprise. Is the major role of these transfers nutritional or purely social and political – or is it some mixture of the two? Does the likelihood or the size of the transfer reflect the relative needs or demographic conditions of the two households involved? For example, are households with favorable C/P ratios more likely to give to households with poor ones than the reverse? We simply do not know.

The Ecology of Supra-Household Labor

Households in rural preindustrial settlements share not only the food they grow, but also their respective stocks of farm labor. They have to, because there are certain farming operations that require more labor than the individual household can supply by itself. In the Taiwanese wet rice example shown in Table 12.7, the size of the

Table 12.7 Average work team size and contributions for various field operations in lowland irrigated rice farming, Taiwan 1963, before mechanization of labor. From Connor *et al.* (2011: 414); data from Chang (1963).

Operation	No. in team	Days worked	Time worked (hr ha^{-1})
First plowing	1	4.4	44
Application of manure	2	2.2	44
Harrowing and puddling	1	14.0	140
Transplanting	7	1.7	119
First additional fertilizer	1	1.3	13
and cultivation	5	1.7	85
Second additional fertilizer	1	1.3	13
and cultivation	4	2.0	80
First disease control	1	1.2	12
Third additional fertilizer	1	1.3	13
and cultivation	4	2.1	84
Weeding barn grass	2	1.5	30
Second disease control	1	1.3	13
Harvesting	8	2.9	232
Cleaning, drying, transport	2	5.0	100

necessary work team varies markedly from task to task. Certain jobs in particular, such as the transplanting of rice seedlings, cultivation (hoeing) following the application of fertilizer and harvesting, require a daily labor force that is likely to be beyond what the household can supply by itself. It is important to add that these data concern work on permanent paddy fields, so that field clearance is not involved; if it were, it would have required a work team of a size similar to that of, say, transplanting or harvesting.

Obviously, helping other households meet their labor needs, no matter what the specific task is, has a built-in cost: you are required to expend time and energy, which are always limited, in activities not directly related to your own demographic enterprise. Is it reasonable to suppose that the cost is more than offset by tangible benefits of some kind? In exploring this question, we can draw on two fairly typical cases from the savannah regions of West Africa. The first case is the Tiv of the Benue Plains of Central Nigeria, studied by ethnologist Paul Bohannon in the 1940s and 1950s. Figure 12.9 shows a party of about 25 Tiv men and boys working together to clear a field from well-established grassland using short-handled hoes and digging sticks (the figure also illustrates a basic principle adumbrated in Chapter 9, that arduous work requires frequent rest breaks). This particular farming task entails two difficulties: (i) fields must be cleared quickly if one is to take maximum advantage of the coming rains, and (ii) established grasslands, with their densely interwoven mats of rhizomes lying just beneath the soil surface, are especially hard to clear. If nothing else, the work party is speeding up the task by allowing some members to work while others rest, a division of "labor" that might be difficult to achieve in a smaller group. Among traditional farmers in general, field clearing is one of the jobs that most frequently involve supra-household labor contributions (harvest is the other). A Tiv settlement is shown in Figure 12.10, along with the pedigree linking households and the composition of the work parties observed by Bohannon (work parties are

Figure 12.9 Men and boys of a Tiv hoeing party taking a break, central Nigeria 1949. From Bohannan (1954: plate XIII), by permission of Her Majesty's Stationery Office.

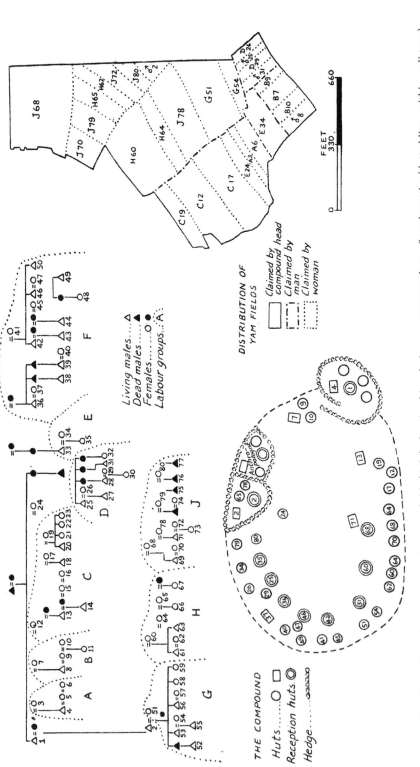

Figure 12.10 A Tiv residential compound and its yam fields (right), showing kin relations among members of work parties (dotted lines within pedigrees). From Bohannan (1954: 18), by permission of Her Majesty's Stationery Office.

indicated in the pedigree by dotted lines). As with food-sharing among households, it would seem that kinship and spatial propinquity are important principles in the mobilization of supra-household farm work among the Tiv.

The second West African example involves the Tiv's immediate neighbors to the west, the Kofyar – or, rather, that segment of the Koyfar population that has colonized the Namu Plains of Central Nigeria in recent decades (Netting, 1968; Stone, 1996). In 1984–5, Stone *et al.* (1990) conducted a year-long survey of 15 Kofyar households and found that three labor mobilization strategies accounted for more than 98 percent of all farm work (Stone, 1996: 108): (i) Simple household labor, in which household members work their own fields (including fields to which they have only temporary usufruct rights), is responsible for the great bulk of agricultural work; household work teams, controlled by the household head, rarely have more than five members. (ii) *Wuk* labor parties are somewhat larger multihousehold groups made up of 5–20 individuals whose members voluntarily take turns working on each other's fields (i.e. for direct reciprocation – and the balance of reciprocation is carefully tallied). (iii) *Mar muos* labor teams are much larger groups of 30–60 voluntary workers attracted and paid off by a festive party devoted to drinking millet beer made by the women of the household whose fields are being worked. Over the entire year, 75 percent of labor was provided by individual households, 11 per cent by *wuk* groups, and 14 percent by *mar muos* parties (Figure 12.11). The allocation of labor from each set of groups to specific tasks having to do with the main staple food crops, millet, sorghum and yams, is illustrated in Figures 12.12 and 12.13, to which I return presently. Secondary crops such as cowpeas and groundnuts (peanuts) are grown almost exclusively using household labor.

Stone *et al.* (1995) have questioned whether Kofyar inter-household labor exchanges make economic sense at all. What, they ask, is the advantage of putting in *x* days on your neighbors' farms so that *x* neighbors will each put in one day on your own? Viewed in this way, reciprocation of work by itself would not seem to be enough to justify the labor exchange. The Kofyar arrangements seem especially uneconomical in view of the fact that the women of your household have to devote extra time, labor and potential food to brewing beer for the *mar muos* festivities – and that the merry folk making up the *mar muos* group are universally acknowledged by the Kofyar as doing less careful work than you would do on your own fields (Stone, 1996: 110–11). In addition, extra time and energy will be wasted in travelling to neighbors' fields that could have been conserved by concentrating exclusively on your own. Stone (1996: 111) does note that individuals in *mar muos* teams compete with each other ("at a frantic pace") to show who can work the hardest. In addition, *mar muos* labor is said to be "well adapted to agricultural tasks in which several activities such as ridging and weeding are conducted concurrently...;" it "also allow[s] 'banking' of labor, since the means of under-writing the group labor (beer) is produced by work distributed across the previous farming season (millet cultivation) and across the five days preceding the labor party (brewing)" (Stone *et al.*, 1990: 12). It is not clear, however, whether these virtues are enough to compensate fully for the costs of holding *mar muos* parties.

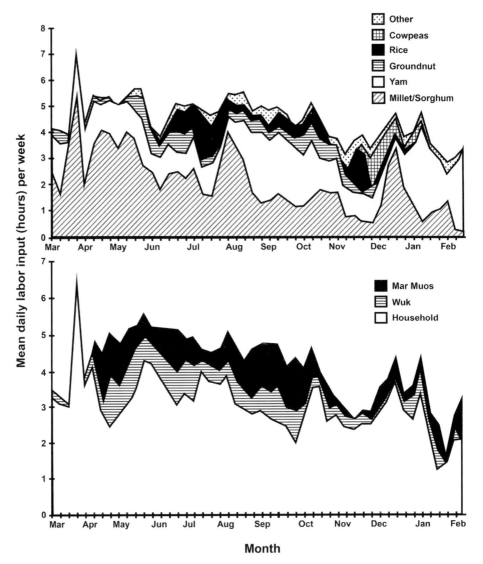

Figure 12.11 Mean daily labor inputs (in hours) per individual, all crops, 15 households among the Kofyar living on the Namu Plains of central Nigeria 1984–5. Data were not collected for two weeks in the dry season (February 18 to March 3). (Top) Agricultural labor inputs by crop. Note the dominance of the annual work cycle by millet, sorghum and yams (*Dioscora* spp.). (Bottom) Apportionment of work hours to different work groups (*wuk*, small work groups repaid by direct reciprocation of labor; *mar muos*, larger work groups organized around a millet beer-drinking party). Redrawn from Stone *et al.* (1990: 11), by permission of John Wiley & Sons, Inc. (top panel); and from *Settlement Ecology: The Social and Spatial Organization of Kofyar Agriculture* by Glenn Davis Stone, p. 108, © The Arizona Board of Regents, by permission of the University of Arizona Press (bottom panel).

Several factors presumably encourage households to work together. Payment and reciprocation help, of course, as no doubt do close kinship and spatial proximity, the latter of which minimizes travel costs. But these factors serve to reduce the costs of cooperation without necessarily providing clear-cut benefits. In general, I suggest

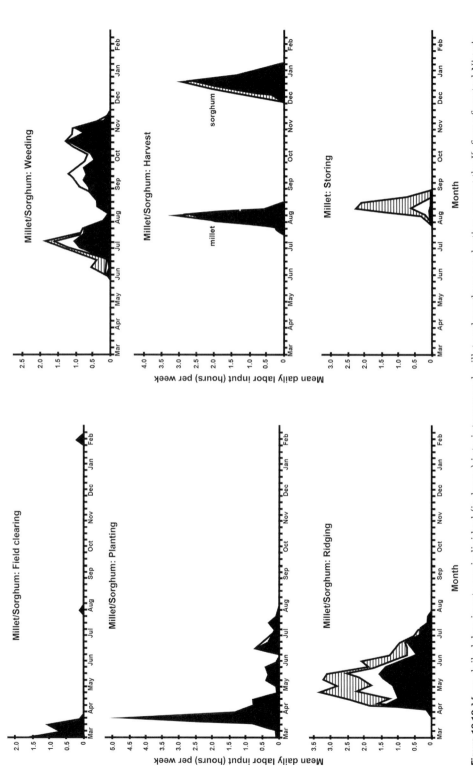

Figure 12.12 Mean daily labor inputs per individual (in hours) into intercropped millet and sorghum production among the Kofyar of central Nigeria 1984–5. Black areas represent household labor; white areas represent *wuk*, small work groups repaid by direct reciprocation of labor; hatched areas represent *mar muos*, larger work groups organized around a millet beer-drinking party. From Stone *et al.* (1990: 13–14), by permission of John Wiley & Sons, Inc.

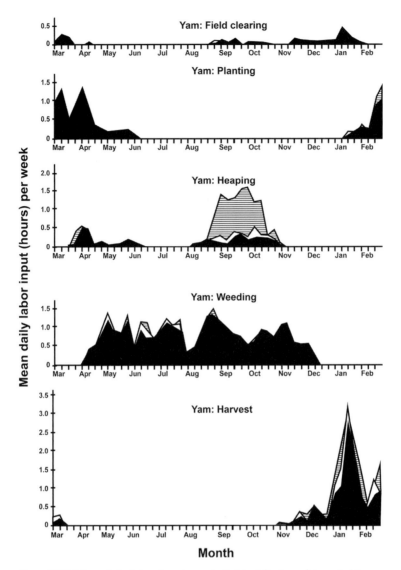

Figure 12.13 Mean daily labor inputs per individual (in hours) invested in yam production among the Kofyar of central Nigeria, 1984–5. Shading as in Figure 12.12. From Stone *et al.* (1990: 18), by permission of John Wiley & Sons, Inc.

that inter-household pooling of labor tends to occur when some or all of the following three conditions are met:

- *Tasks involve bulk transfers of heavy material (e.g. soil, timber, stones) that workers from a single household cannot do by themselves.* This consideration may explain the use of supra-household labor by the Kofyar in such tasks as the ridging of millet and sorghum fields (Figure 12.12) and the mounding (heaping) of yam plants (Figure 12.13), both of which involve fairly large-scale movements of

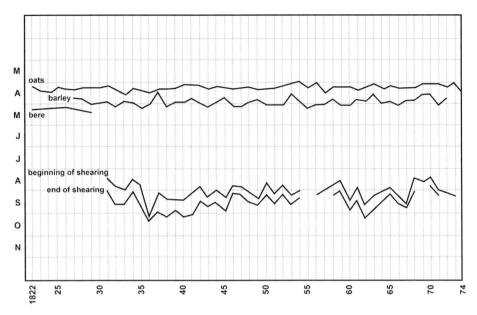

Figure 12.14 Sowing and harvesting (shearing) dates for oats, bere and barley, 1822–74. Calculated from Andrew MacGregor's account book of Camserney Farm, Perthshire, Scotland. From Fenton (1976: 62), by permission of John Donald Publishers Ltd.

soil. Tasks such as planting and weeding, which do not involve bulk transfers of soil, can be handled mostly with household labor.

• *Tasks need to be accomplished in a very short time, and an effective division of labor can speed things up.* In the Kofyar case, getting millet into storage may represent an example of such a temporal bottleneck (Figure 12.12). Again, tasks such as weeding can be extended over a longer period and thus do not draw as heavily on the household's labor force at any one time. Another example, from a quite different part of the world, is provided by Figure 12.14, which shows the narrow time constraints involved in sowing and harvesting grain in preindustrial Scotland. Figure 12.15 indicates the divisions of labor in these two tasks that could be achieved by traditional Scottish farmers – but only if enough hands were available. No single household could provide sufficient personnel to support such task specialization.

• *Tasks require working capital beyond the means of a single household.* Turning again to historic Scotland (Figure 12.16), the capital needed for sowing (including both plowing and harrowing) included a heavy plow, a spike harrow, sufficient draft animals (in this case, four horses and four oxen) and the tackle needed to harness the animals. Very few farming households possessed all the necessary equipment and livestock to get the staple crops in the ground and thus were forced to cooperate with other households to complete the tasks.

In essence, what I am suggesting is that supra-household work parties are a means of overcoming the limitations built into the individual household's small-scale farming operation, especially the tight limits on household labor and capital. In other words,

Figure 12.15 Division of labor for broadcasting (sowing) seed and harrowing (top) and for cutting, binding and stacking sheaths during harvesting of grain (bottom), Scotland 1855. Note assignment of workers to different tasks, presumably speeding up the work. From Fenton (1976: 48, 55), by permission of John Donald Publishers Ltd.

supra-household work groups may entail significant *economies of scale*. With regard to limits on household labor, it would be very interesting to know if cooperating households tend to differ sharply in their C/P ratios, such that the household with a high ratio needed extra help to feed its dependents. As in the case of food-sharing, the household with the favorable C/P ratio would be subsidizing the benefits going to the one with the unfavorable ratio, perhaps in hopes of future reciprocation when their respective positions switch, as sooner or later they almost inevitably will. Alas, as in the case of food-sharing, we do not know the answer to this question.

* * *

Despite their particular interest in their own narrow demographic destiny, then, subsistence farming households do not act alone. They are embedded in spatial clusters made up of close kin and nearby neighbors (who are generally the same people), and over the generations dense networks of cooperation, sharing and informal reciprocation almost inevitably develop. It seems likely that these interactions among households, including the sharing of food and farm work, are important from a nutritional and demographic perspective – although surprisingly little work has

Figure 12.16 The capital needed for harrowing (top) and plowing (bottom), including four horses and four oxen, in Scotland 1753. Note that the harrow is following a sower, who is broadcasting seed, in order to break up clods and lightly spread the soil to cover the seed. From a gravestone in Liberton kirkyard, Edinburgh. From Fenton (1976: 33), by permission of John Donald Publishers Ltd.

been done on the subject from that perspective. Some ethnographers might argue that the import of these interactions is primarily social and political, but we ought not to ignore the potential physiological and demographic benefits. Nor should we lose sight of the fact that neighboring households can be sharp competitors as well as cooperators; after all, you are more likely to compete for local resources with nearby households, whose interests may overlap but will never coincide perfectly with your own. A final lesson is that, no matter how complex the web of social relations, both cooperative and competitive, in the rural preindustrial world, the universe of such relations was small, both numerically and spatially. As the anthropological demographer Nancy Howell (1979: 307–30) has emphasized, the high mortality levels characteristic of preindustrial populations guaranteed that local kin networks contained remarkably few living members. Similarly, the high energetic and opportunity costs of movement and haulage meant that the sharing of food and work was confined to a small geographical area. During even fairly localized food shortages or hungry seasons, therefore, households that might otherwise have been willing and able to help you and your family when you need it are unlikely to be in a position to do so. Shared kin relations can imply shared suffering as well as shared success. While the subsistence farming household is not in fact completely autonomous for food production and consumption, the larger pool of social resources on which it can draw on a daily basis is itself severely limited by both demographic and environmental constraints. The larger community can certainly help the household in its demographic enterprise, but it cannot solve all the household's problems.

Envoi

I admit that the picture this book has sketched of the subsistence farming community and its constituent households is not especially rosy. We are not talking about a primitive arcadia where everyone was free, happy and equal *à la* Jean-Jacques Rousseau. Work was hard, the seasons could be bitter, and life was often short, even in the presence of helpful kin and the absence of powerful oppressors. But neither do I subscribe to the increasingly popular view that the development of agriculture was – to quote Jared Diamond (1987) – "the worst mistake in the history of the human race." For one thing, I am by no means convinced that the lives of earlier hunter-gatherers were easier or less precarious (for my reasons, see Wood, 1998; for a broader perspective, see Kaplan, 2000). In addition, the hard existences of our farming ancestors had manifold compensations – the warmth of hearth and family, traditional music and dance, the celebrations marking the farming year, the intimate familiarity of people and place. For better or worse, these things have had no place in this book. To redress that omission, I want to end with a quote that I think shows a fine sense of balance. It comes from the great Orcadian poet George Mackay Brown, who wrote in his autobiography *For the Islands I Sing* (1997: 166–7):

It seems too that the people of my generation, though much better off materially than their grandfathers, have lost a richness and strength of character. . .[through] the slow seepings and rottings of the new [industrial] age. But here we must be careful. The new age, though it carries in one hand the cup of poison, brings in the other the benefits of science. Without the 'miracle drugs', streptomycin and PAS and INAH,[7] I might have died sometime in the 1950s. I don't think, either, that I would have written much beside a fish-oil lamp in one of those old crofts that still exist as museum pieces here and there, with pigs grunting and hens fluttering behind the peat-fire in the center; and a dame-school a mile or so away where I might have gone to learn reading and writing. Yet that was a time, 150 years ago, when life was dangerous and the language rich, and the community was invested with a kind of ceremony. The people lived close to the springs of poetry and drama, and were not aware of it. I draw any art I have from great-grandparents, and further back; I acknowledge the gift and the debt, but I would not have wished to live their hard lives.

---

[7] Antibiotics used to treat Brown's tuberculosis.

Appendix: A Bibliographic Essay on Subsistence Farming

There exists an enormous literature on subsistence and near-subsistence farming, written mainly by anthropologists, geographers, agronomists, ethnobotanists, ecologists and agricultural economists. This literature tends to be scattered and is sometimes difficult to track down. Much of it is out of print – indeed, much of the best of it is decades old since styles of research and the questions that seem worth pursuing have changed dramatically in the past few decades, and not always for the better. Sadly, there is no up-to-date, sophisticated, comprehensive book-length treatment of the ethnology and ecology of traditional farming, a real gap in the literature. So here I offer some pointers to the larger literature. The only criteria guiding my choice of citations are that (i) the work is historically important, (ii) the work is useful or (iii) I like it. Criterion (iii) tends to dominate.

Two ambitious attempts to write comprehensive histories of farming, both interesting but neither entirely satisfying, are Vasey (1992) and Mazoyer and Roudart (2006). Oddly, neither book has much to say about living subsistence farmers. Other interesting historical overviews are Harlan (1992, 1995) and Evans (1998). A comparative survey of surviving forms of traditional agriculture can be found in Turner and Brush (1987), although the authors try to shoehorn everything into an analytical framework that seems too constricting. Two outdated but still excellent treatments of tropical agriculture as a practical endeavor are Norman (1979) and Ruthenberg (1971). New editions of both are badly needed. A book that covers some of the same ground as the present one, with less demography but more ethnography, is Netting (1993).

Anyone who wants to study traditional farming has to learn about crop species, many of which may initially be unfamiliar. An encyclopedic compilation is van Wyk (2005), which has excellent photographs and capsule descriptions of more than 350 crop species. This book is indispensable. Another good compilation, less comprehensive but with more botany, is Vaughan and Geissler (1997), worth the price if only for the gorgeous artwork. Elzebroek and Wind (2008) is another useful compendium, if organized a bit oddly. It also helps to have some general botany and plant physiology, at least at the introductory level; I recommend Norman *et al.* (1995), Raven *et al.* (1999) and Larcher (2003).[1] Hay and Porter (2006) and Connor *et al.* (2011) are excellent on crop physiology, but pitched at fairly high technical levels. Less technical are Langer and Hill (1991), Forbes and Watson (1992) and Evans (1993), the last of which is also very thought-provoking.

Anyone who wants to study traditional farming also has to know something about the relevant environmental factors. First and foremost, some knowledge of soils is a

---

[1] Avoid the most recent edition of Raven *et al.*, which omits much of the material on plant ecology and farming. It's all on the web – but if you're like me, you prefer your books nonvirtual.

must. Soil science is, unfortunately, inherently complicated, and most textbooks fail to convey its intellectual excitement. (Soil science intellectually exciting? Well, yes, actually.) An excellent introduction is Ashman and Puri (2002). Once you have that slim volume under your belt you can turn fearlessly to one of the giants such as Brady and Weil (2007). Brady and Weill is probably the most widely used textbook on soil science in the USA, but it is weak on soil microbiology, a critical subject if you want to understand, say, agricultural nitrogen cycling. I recommend Coleman *et al.* (2004) and Bardgett (2005) to fill the hole. On ethnopedology, see Wilshusen and Stone (1990). Preindustrial methods of soil tillage were described long ago by Malden (1891). Kramer (1966) compiled an interesting, if incomplete, worldwide catalog of traditional tillage tools, while Raghavan (1960) presents, in an absorbing volume, the results of a pan-India survey of indigenous agricultural implements of all types. (Both may be hard to find.) Another useful source is the journal *Tools & Tillage*, published by the National Museum of Denmark.

To love traditional farming is perforce to love muck. Preindustrial fertilizer – manures green and not so green, marl, slaked lime and so forth – is a rich and redolent subject in its own right. Alas, such fertilizers are also largely obsolete except in organic gardening. But there is an extensive older literature on muck. The work at the Rothamsted Experimental Station was (and still is) of fundamental importance; the best books to come out of Rothamsted concerning the preindustrial era (or at least the era before the invention of industrial nitrogen fixation) are Hall (1905, 1909). Older texts on muck that are available in recent facsimile editions are Morfit (1848), Browne (1858) and Sempers (1899). Interesting modern discussions of preindustrial fertilizers are provided by Shiel (1991), Catt (1994) and Smil (2001: 1–38).

Meteorology is another essential but inherently complicated subject. As a complete novice, I found Bonan (2002) stimulating, especially for the way it relates global climate and local weather to ecosystems and plant communities. A classic volume – badly outdated but still indispensable for anyone interested in agriculture – is Geiger (1965). For hydrology and water–soil relations, one standard American text is Ward and Trimble (2003). Jackson (1989) is a useful synthesis of climate, hydrology and tropical farming.

Some other topics of special relevance to traditional farming include: mixed cropping (planting more than one crop species in the same field) and multi-cropping (harvesting more than one crop of the same species from the same field in a single year) (Stelly, 1976; Beets, 1982; Vandermeer, 1989; Innis, 1997), irrigation (Cressey, 1950; Leach, 1968; Kawaguchi and Kyuma, 1977; Coward, 1980; Bray, 1984, 1986; Beaumont *et al.*, 1989; Mitchell and Guillet, 1994; Barnes, 1990, Marby, 1996), house gardens (Abdoellah and Marten,1986; Niñez, 1987; Landauer and Brazil, 1990; Lamont *et al.*, 1999; Eyzaguirre and Linares, 2004), nitrogen fixation by symbiotic microbes (Postgate, 1998), weeds (Holm *et al.*, 1991; Booth *et al.*, 2003) and water, potable or otherwise (White *et al.*, 1972; Pereira, 1973; Wilkinson, 1977).

And finally to accounts of local or regional patterns of subsistence and near-subsistence farming. To begin with, I want to mention four of my favorite books, each of which easily meets all three of my criteria for inclusion in this note. The first is Audrey Richards's classic monograph on the Bemba of what is now Zambia (Richards, 1939). What is the best way to pack threshed millet into a granary? She tells you. How do traditional farmers decide where to put new gardens? She tells you. Best of all, she erases the line between the "agricultural" and the "domestic," just as I advocated in Chapters 1 and 10. (True, her book is thin on quantitative data and statistical analysis, but what a cornucopia of descriptive detail!) Another favorite is John Hatch's 1974 book on the Motupe Indians of lowland western Peru. Hatch was originally trained as an agricultural economist and began his fieldwork in Peru about the way you'd expect – by conducting a formal economic survey. By the end of the survey, however, he had come to believe that he was missing something important. So he advertised himself as a farm laborer and agreed to work for free for any farmer who would train him and explain why the farming practices he was being taught made sense. (Talk about *field*work!) Yes, it really does turn out that traditional farmers do what they do for good, practical reasons. The same message is also conveyed in considerable technical detail in Gene Wilken's 1987 book *Good Farmers: Traditional Agricultural Resource Management in Mexico and Central America*, the third of my four favorites. By the end of the book, you should know how to do pot irrigation and how to build a drywall terrace, along with many other useful skills (you'll also learn how to *think* about preindustrial resource management problems). Finally, a book that I consider one of anthropology's finest accomplishments: the late Hal Conklin's interpretive atlas of the astonishing wet-rice terraces of the Ifugao in the northern Philippines (Conklin, 1980). I doubt that many books on traditional farming have required as much work, either in the field or in book production, as this one. There is nothing else remotely like it in the ethnographic literature. (Now, if only someone would devote several decades to digitizing the maps. . .) Putting these four books together would arguably provide a wonderful introductory course on traditional farming.

The rest of the citations are organized by geographical area. I have concentrated on book-length monographs and edited volumes and have not cited many individual journal papers, references to which appear throughout this book. I have emphasized accounts that are heavy on practical detail – how farming is actually done. As noted before, many of my sources are old, but that bothers me not at all. Good descriptions of traditional farming systems are, as noted by Mathewson (1984: xix), obsolescence proof. Of necessity, I have included cases in which more or less rapid economic change was occurring at the time of study, but only if enough information about the prechange situation shines through. Finally, I note a distinct tropical and subtropical bias in my choices, owing to the fact that most temperate farming systems had already changed beyond recognition (unless reconstructed historically) by the time anthropologists and other scholars became interested in the ecology of traditional farming. This bias, in general, is perhaps the most important way in which recent traditional farming systems are unrepresentative of those in the genuinely preindustrial past.

Sub-Saharan Africa: Richards (1939), Trapnell (1943), Allan *et al.* (1948), Haswell (1953, 1963, 1985), Bohannan (1954), de Schlippe (1956), Johnston (1958), Huffnagel

(1961), Scudder (1962), Gray (1963), Kay (1964), Allan (1965), Shack (1966), Miracle (1967), Bohannan and Bohannan (1968), Ludwig (1968), Netting (1968), McLoughlin (1970), Stauder (1971), Bernard (1972), Hill (1972, 1977), Cleave (1974), FAO (1974), Westphal (1975), Lagemann (1977), Kowal and Kassam (1978), Grove and Klein (1979), Burnham (1980), Richards (1985, 1986), Strømgaard (1985, 1988), McCann (1987), Thom and Wells (1987), Skjønsberg (1989), Carney (1991), McIntire *et al.* (1992), Toulmin (1992), Reij *et al.* (1996), Stone (1996), Lockwood (1998), Mortimore (1998), Mortimore and Adams (1999), Smith (2002), Börjeson (2004a,b), Widgren and Sutton (2004).

North Africa and the Near East: Johnson (1903), Erinç and Tunçdilek (1952), Wilkinson (1977), Watson (1979), Abdulfattah (1981), Eger (1987), Beaumont *et al.* (1989), Craig *et al.* (1993), Bowman and Rogan (1999).

Europe and early Anglo-America: Thirsk (1957), Slicher van Bath (1963a,b), Rutman (1967), Le Roy Ladurie (1976), Russell (1976), R. E. F. Smith (1977), Netting (1981), Behar (1986), Bell and Watson (1986), McDonald and Snooks (1986), Campbell and Overton (1991), Bentley (1992), Foster and Smout (1994), Pospisil (1995), Astill and Davies (1997), Sereni (1997), McDonald (1998), Almås (2004), Donahue (2004), Campbell and Bartley (2006), Mathieu (2009), Halstead (2014).

South Asia: Kanitkar (1944), Randhawa and Nath (1959), Raghavan (1960), Randhawa *et al.* (1961, 1964, 1968), Haswell (1967), Leach (1968), Wyon and Gordon (1971), Macfarlane (1976), Biswanger *et al.* (1980), Watabe (1981), Hill (1982), Maclachlan (1983), Engelhardt (1984), Ramakrishnan (1992), Stevens (1993), Agarwal and Narain (1997), Adhikari (2000), Baker (2005), Chakravarty *et al.* (2006).

China (especially prerevolutionary) and Japan: King (1911), Buck (1930, 1937), Hommel (1937), Fei (1939), Fei and Chang (1945), Yang (1945), Beardsley *et al.* (1959), T. C. Smith (1959, 1977), Zhong (1982), Bray (1984), Ruddle and Zhong (1988), Xu and Peel (1991), Yin (2001), von Verschuer (2016).

Mainland and Island Southeast Asia: Izikowitz (1951), Sharp *et al.* (1953), Geddes (1954, 1976), Judd (1961), Freeman (1955, 1970), Conklin (1957, 1980), Geertz (1963), Hendry (1964), Hickey (1964), Ho (1967), Moerman (1968), Takahashi (1969), Wallace (1970), Lewis (1971), Purcal (1971), Hanks (1972), Claus and Lintner (1975), Hayami (1978), Kunstadter *et al.* (1978), Ping (1978), Sharp and Hanks (1978), Kuchiba *et al.* (1979), Schlegel (1979), Binswanger *et al.* (1980), Watabe (1981), Metzner (1982), Lopez-Gonzaga (1983), Dove (1985), Lambert (1985), Marten (1986), Hardjono (1987), Palte (1989), Fukui (1993), Schneider (1995), Tsubouchi (1996), Gönner (2002), Cramb (2007), Viên *et al.* (2009).

Highland New Guinea: Brookfield and Brown (1963), Pospisil (1963), Rappaport (1967), Clarke (1971), Waddell (1972), Steensberg (1980), Sillitoe (1983, 1996, 2010), Dwyer (1990), Healey (1990), Sillitoe *et al.* (2002).

Lowland New Guinea and the rest of Oceania: Best (1925), Firth (1939), Handy (1940), Bascom (1949), Barrau (1958, 1961), Fox and Cumberland (1962), Sahlins (1962), Serpenti (1965), Waddell and Krinks (1968), Christiansen (1975), Harding (1985), Ohtsuka and Suzuki (1990), Yen and Mummery (1990), Kirch (1994), Manner (2008).

Native America: Wilson (1917), Cook (1920), Castetter and Bell (1942, 1951), Hack (1942), Tax (1953), Pennington (1963, 1980), Denevan (1971), Harris (1971), Watters (1971), Cancian (1972), de Ortiz (1973), Nietschmann (1973), Hatch (1974), Ruddle (1974), Collier (1975), Gade (1975), Smole (1976), Brush (1977), Donkin (1979), Brush *et al.* (1981), Soldi (1982), Johnson (1983, 2003), Hames and Vickers (1983), Mathewson (1984), Denevan and Padoch (1987), Hunt (1987), Rhoades and Bidegaray (1987), Wilken (1987), Posey and Balée (1989), Salick (1989), Mitchell and Guillet (1994), Zimmerer (1996), Doolittle (2000), Denevan (2001), Whitmore and Turner (2001), Posey (2002), Schjellerup *et al.* (2003, 2005), Schreiber and Rojas (2003), Kramer (2005), Ingram and Hunt (2015).

References

Abdoellah, O. S. and Marten, G. G. (1986) The complementary roles of homegardens, upland fields, and rice fields for meeting nutritional needs in west Java. In *Traditional Agriculture in Southeast Asia: A Human Ecology Perspective*, ed. G. G. Marten. Boulder, CO: Westview, pp. 293–325.

Abdulfattah, K. (1981) *Mountain Farmer and Fellah in 'Asir, Southwest Saudi Arabia: The Conditions of Agriculture in a Traditional Society*. Erlangen, GDR: Erlanger Geographische Arbeiten.

Abdullah, M. and Wheeler, E. F. (1985) Seasonal variations, and the intra-household distribution of food in a Bangladeshi village. *American Journal of Clinical Nutrition*, 41, 1305–13.

Abernethy, V. D. (1979) *Population Pressure and Cultural Adjustment*. New York: Human Sciences Press.

Adams, W. M. (1986) Traditional agriculture and water use in the Sokoto Valley, Nigeria. *The Geographical Journal*, 152, 30–43.

Adams, W. M. and Mortimer, M. J. (1997) Agricultural intensification and flexibility in the Nigerian Sahel. *The Geographical Journal*, 163, 150–60.

Adams, W. M., Potkanski, T. and Sutton, J. E. G. (1994) Indigenous farmer-managed irrigation in Sonjo, Tanzania. *The Geographical Journal*, 160, 17–32.

Adhikari, J. (2000) *Decisions for Survival: Farm Management Strategies in the Middle Hills of Nepal*. Delhi: Adroit Publishers.

Agarwal, A. and Narain, S., eds. (1997) *Dying Wisdom: Rise, Fall and Potential of India's Traditional Water Harvesting Systems*. New Delhi: Centre for Science and Environment.

Aitken, Y. (1974) *Flowering Time, Climate and Genotype: The Adaptation of Agricultural Species to Climate through Flowering Responses*. Melbourne: Melbourne University Press.

Albert, W. (1972) *The Turnpike Road System in England 1663–1840*. Cambridge: Cambridge University Press.

Alexander, M. J. (1996) The effectiveness of small-scale irrigated agriculture in the reclamation of mine land soils on the Jos Plateau of Nigeria. *Land Degradation and Development*, 7, 77–84.

Alexander, R. M. (1999) *Energy for Animal Life*. Oxford/New York: Oxford University Press.

Ali, A. M. S. (2005) Homegardens in smallholder farming systems: Examples from Bangladesh. *Human Ecology*, 33, 245–70.

Allan, W. (1949) How much land does a man require? In *Studies in African Land Usage in Northern Rhodesia*. Rhodes-Livingstone Paper 15. Cape Town: Oxford University Press, pp. 1–23.

Allan, W. (1965) *The African Husbandman*. Edinburgh: Oliver and Boyd.

Allan, W., Gluckman, M., Peters, D. U., *et al.* (1948) *Land Holding and Land Usage among the Plateau Tonga of Mazabuka District: A Reconnaissance Survey, 1945*. Oxford: Oxford University Press.

Allen, B. J. (2001) Boserup and Brookfield and the association between population density and agricultural intensity in Papua New Guinea. *Asia Pacific Viewpoint*, 42, 237–54.

Allen, B. J. and Crittenden, R. (1987) Degradation and a pre-capitalist political economy. In *Land Degradation and Society*, ed. P. Blaikie and H. C. Brookfield. London: Routledge, pp. 145–56.

Allen, R. C., Bengtsson, T. and Dribe M, eds. (2005) *Living Standards in the Past: New Perspectives on Well-Being in Asia and Europe*. Oxford: Oxford University Press.

Almås, R., ed. (2004) *Norwegian Agricultural History*. Trondheim: Tapir Academic Press.

Almåsbakk, B., Whiting, H. T. A. and van den Tillaar, R. (2000) Optimisation in the learning of cyclical actions. In *Energetics of Human Activity*, ed. W. A. Sparrow. Champaign, Ill.: Human Kinetics, pp. 228–54.

Altieri, M. A. (1990) Why study traditional agriculture? In *Agroecology*, ed. C. R. Carroll and J. H. Vandermeer. New York: McGraw-Hill, pp. 331–64.

Alvarez, N., Garine, E., Khasah, C., *et al.* (2005) Farmers' practices, metapopulation dynamics, and conservation of agricultural diversity on-farm: A case study of sorghum among the Duupa in sub-Sahelian Cameroon. *Biological Conservation*, 121, 533–43.

Amanor, K. S. (1991) Managing the fallow: Weeding technology and environmental knowledge in the Krobo District of Ghana. *Agriculture and Human Values*, 8, 5–13.

An, L., Lin, J., Ouyang, Z., *et al.* (2001) Simulating demographic and socioeconomic processes on the household level and implications for giant panda habitats. *Ecological Modelling*, 140, 31–49.

Andersen, K. B. (1978) *African Traditional Architecture: A Study of Housing and Settlement Patterns of Rural Kenya*. Nairobi: Oxford University Press.

Anderson, R. K., Calvo, J., Serrano, G. and Payne, G. C. (1946) A study of the nutritional status and food habits of Otomi Indians in the Mezquital Valley of Mexico. *American Journal of Public Health*, 36, 883–903.

Andriesse, J. P. (1989) Nutrient management through shifting cultivation. In *Nutrient Management for Food Crop Production in Tropical Farming Systems*, ed. J. van der Heide. Haren, the Netherlands: Institute for Soil Fertility, pp. 29–62.

Andriesse, J. P. and Koopmans, T. T. (1984) A monitoring study of nutrient cycles in soils used for shifting cultivation under various climatic conditions in tropical Asia. I. The influence of simulated burning on forms and availability of plant nutrients. *Agriculture, Ecosystems and Environment*, 12, 1–16.

Andriesse, J. P. and Schelhaas, R. M. (1987) A monitoring study of nutrient cycles in soils used for shifting cultivation under various climatic conditions in Asia. III. The effects of land clearing through burning on fertility level. *Agriculture, Ecosystems and Environment*, 19, 311–32.

Anonymous (1960) Working models in medicine. *Journal of the American Medical Association*, 174, 407–8.

Armstrong, G. L., Conn, L. A. and Pinner, R. W. (1999) Trends in infectious disease mortality in the United States during the 20th century. *Journal of the American Medical Association*, 281, 61–8.

Ashman, M. R. and Puri, G. (2002) *Essential Soil Science*. Oxford: Blackwell.

Assah, F. K., Ekelund, U., Brage, S., *et al.* (2011) Accuracy and validity of combined heart rate and motion sensor for the measurement of free-living physical activity energy expenditure in adults in Cameroon. *International Journal of Epidemiology*, 40, 112–20.

Astill, G. (1988) Fields. In *The Countryside of Medieval England*, ed. G. Astill and A. Grant. Oxford: Blackwell, pp. 62–85.

Astill, G. and Davies, W. (1997) *A Breton Landscape*. London: University College London Press.

Avdeev, A., Blum, A. and Troitskala, I. (2004/6) Peasant marriage in nineteenth-century Russia. *Population*, 59, 721–64.

Ayala, F. J. (1966) Dynamics of populations, I: Factors affecting population growth and population size in *Drosophila serrata*. *The American Naturalist*, 100, 333–4.

Aykroyd, W. R. (1971) Nutrition and mortality in infancy and early childhood: Past and present relationships. *American Journal of Clinical Nutrition*, 24, 480–7.

Bailey, R. C., Jenike, M. R., Ellison, P. T., *et al.* (1992) The ecology of birth seasonality among agriculturalists in central Africa. *Journal of Biosocial Sciences*, 24, 393–412.

Bailyn, B. (1986) *Voyagers to the West: A Passage in the Peopling of America on the Eve of the Revolution*. New York: Random House.

Baker, J. M. (2005) *The Kuhls of Kangra: Community-Managed Irrigation in the Western Himalayas*. Seattle: University of Washington Press.

Baker, P. T. and Sanders, W. T. (1972) Demographic studies in anthropology. *Annual Review of Anthropology*, 1, 151–78.

Ballard, C. (2001) Wetland drainage and agricultural transformations in the Southern Highlands of Papua New Guinea. *Asia Pacific Viewpoint*, 42, 287–304.

Barclay, G.W. (1954) *Colonial Development and Population in Taiwan*. Princeton, NJ: Princeton University Press.

Bardgett, R. D. (2005) *The Biology of Soil: A Community and Ecosystem Approach*. Oxford: Oxford University Press.

Barker, D. J. P (2002) *Mothers, Babies and Disease in Later Life*. New York: B. M. J. Books.

Barker, G. (1985) *Prehistoric Farming in Europe.* Cambridge: Cambridge University Press.

Barker, G. (2006) *The Agricultural Revolution in Prehistory: Why Did Foragers Become Farmers?* Oxford: Oxford University Press.

Barlett, P. F. (1976) Labor efficiency and the mechanism of agricultural evolution. *Journal of Anthropological Research*, 32, 124–40.

Barlett, P. F. (1980a) Adaptive strategies in peasant agricultural production. *Annual Review of Anthropology*, 9, 545–73.

Barlett, P. F., ed. (1980b) *Agricultural Decision Making: Anthropological Contributions to Rural Development.* New York: Academic Press.

Barlett, P. F. (1980c) Introduction: Dimensions and dilemmas of householding. In *The Household Economy: Reconsidering the Domestic Mode of Production*, ed. R. R. Wilk. Boulder, CO: Westview, pp. 3–10.

Barlett, P. F. (1982) *Agricultural Choice and Change: Decision Making in a Cost Rica Community.* New Brunswick, NJ: Rutgers University Press.

Barnes, G. (1990) Paddy soils now and then. *World Archaeology*, 22, 1–17.

Barrau, J. (1958) *Subsistence Agriculture in Melanesia.* Honolulu: Bernice P. Bishop Museum.

Barrau, J. (1961) *Subsistence Agriculture in Polynesia and Micronesia.* Honolulu: Bernice P. Bishop Museum.

Bartlett, M. S. (1960) *Stochastic Population Models in Ecology and Epidemiology.* London: Methuen.

Bascom, W. (1949) Subsistence farming on Ponape. *The New Zealand Geographer*, 5, 115–29.

Bastien, G. J., Schepens, B., Willems, P. A. and Heglund, N. C. (2005) Energetics of load carrying in Nepalese porters. *Science*, 308, 1755.

Bates, R. P. (1986) Postharvest considerations in the food chain. In *Food in Sub-Saharan Africa*, ed. A. Hansen and D. E. McMillan. Boulder, CO: Lynne Rienner, pp. 230–59.

Bayliss, P. and Choquenot, D. (2003) The numerical response: Rate of increase and food limitation in herbivores and predators. In *Wildlife Population Growth Rates*, ed. R. M. Sibly, J. Hone and T. H. Clutton-Brock. Cambridge: Cambridge University Press, pp. 148–79.

Beach, T., Dunning, N., Luzzadder-Beach, S., Cook, D.E. and Lohse, J. (2006) Impacts of the ancient Maya on soils and soil erosion in the central Maya lowlands. *Catena*, 65, 166–78.

Beardsley, R. K., Hall, J. W. and Ward, R. E. (1959) *Village Japan.* Chicago: University of Chicago Press.

Beaton, G. H. (1989) Small but healthy: Are we asking the right question? *European Journal of Clinical Nutrition*, 43, 863–75.

Beaumont, P., Bonine, M. and McLachlan, K., eds. (1989) *Qanat, Kariz and Khattara: Traditional Water Systems in the Middle East and North Africa.* Wisbech: MENAS Press.

Becker, S. (1994) Understanding seasonality in Bangladesh. *Annals of the New York Academy of Sciences*, 709, 370–8.

Becker, S., Chowdhury, A. and Leridon, H. (1986) Seasonal patterns of reproduction in Matlab, Bangladesh. *Population Studies*, 40, 457–72.

Becker, S. and Sardar, M. A. (1981) Seasonal patterns of vital events in Matlab thana, Bangladesh. In *Seasonal Dimensions to Rural Poverty*, ed. R. Chambers, R. Longhurst and A. Pacey. London: Frances Pinter, pp. 149–54.

Beckerman, S. (1983a) Does the swidden ape the jungle? *Human Ecology*, 11, 1–12.

Beckerman, S. (1983b) Barí swidden gardens: Crop segregation patterns. *Human Ecology*, 11, 85–101.

Bedell, J. (2000) Archaeology and probate inventories in the study of eighteenth-century life. *Journal of Interdisciplinary History*, 31, 223–45.

Beets, W. C. (1982) *Multiple Cropping and Tropical Farming Systems.* Boulder, CO: Westview.

Behar, R. (1986) *Santa María del Monte: The Presence of the Past in a Spanish Village.* Princeton, NJ: Princeton University Press.

Bell, J. and Watson, M. (1986) *Irish Farming: Implements and Techniques 1750–1900.* Edinburgh: John Donald.

Bellon, M. R. (1991) The ethnoecology of maize variety management: A case study from Mexico. *Human Ecology*, 19, 389–418.

Bellon, M. R., Pham, J.-L., Sebastian, L. S., *et al.* (1998) Farmers' perceptions of varietal diversity: Implications for on-farm conservation of rice. In *Farmers, Gene Banks and Crop Breeding: Economic Analyses of Diversity in Wheat, Maize, and Rice*, ed.

M. Smale. Dordrecht: Kluwer Academic Publishing, pp. 95–108.

Bellon, M. R. and Taylor, J. E. (1993) "Folk" soil taxonomy and the partial adoption of new seed varieties. *Economic Development and Cultural Change*, **41**, 763–86.

Bellwood, P. (2005) *First Farmers: The Origins of Agricultural Societies.* Oxford: Blackwell.

Bender, D. R. (1967) A refinement of the concept of household: Families, coresidence and domestic functions. *American Anthropologist*, **69**, 493–503.

Bengtsson, T. (1999) The vulnerable child: Economic insecurity and child mortality in pre-industrial Sweden – a case study of Västanfors, 1757–1850. *European Journal of Population*, **15**, 117–51.

Bengtsson, T., Campbell, C. and Lee, J. Z., eds. (2004) *Life under Pressure: Mortality and Living Standards in Europe and Asia, 1700–1900.* Cambridge, MA: MIT Press.

Benneh, G. (1973) Small-scale farming systems in Ghana. *Africa*, **43**, 134–46.

Bennett, B. C., Baker, M. A. and Andrade, P. G. (2001) *The Ethnobotany of the Shuar of Eastern Ecuador.* New York: New York Botanical Garden Press.

Bentley, J. W. (1987) Economic and ecological approaches to land fragmentation. *Annual Review of Anthropology*, **16**, 37–67.

Bentley, J. W. (1992) *Today There is no Misery: The Ethnography of Farming in Northwest Portugal.* Tucson, AZ: University of Arizona Press.

Benyshek, D. C. and Watson, J. T. (2006) Exploring the thrifty genotype's food-shortage assumptions: A cross-cultural comparison of ethnographic accounts of food security among foraging and agricultural societies. *American Journal of Physical Anthropology*, **131**, 120–6.

Berkner, L. K. (1972) The stem family and the developmental cycle of the peasant household: An eighteenth-century Austrian example. *American Historical Review*, **77**, 398–418.

Berkner, L. K. (1975) The use and misuse of census data for the historical analysis of family structure. *Journal of Interdisciplinary History*, **7**, 721–38.

Berkner, L. K. and Shaffer, J. W. (1978) The joint family in the Nivernais. *Journal of Family History*, **3**, 150–62.

Berliner, N. (2003) *Yin Yu Tang: The Architecture and Daily Life of a Chinese House.* Boston: Tuttle Publishing.

Bernard, F. E. (1972) *East of Mount Kenya: Meru Agriculture in Transition.* Munich: Weltforum Verlag.

Berry, S. (1993) *No Condition is Permanent: The Social Dynamics of Agrarian Change in Sub-Saharan Africa.* Madison, WI: University of Wisconsin Press.

Berryman, A. A. (1994) Population dynamics: Forecasting and diagnosis from time series. In *Individuals, Populations and Patterns in Ecology*, ed. K. E. F. Watt, S. A. Leather and D. M. Hunter. Andover, UK: Intercept Press, pp. 119–28.

Berryman, A. A. (2004) Limiting factors and population regulation. *Oikos*, **105**, 667–70.

Best, E. (1925) *Maori Agriculture: The Cultivated Food Plants of the Natives of New Zealand, with Some Account of Native Methods of Agriculture, its Ritual and Origin Myth.* Wellington: Dominion Museum.

Bethea, C. L., Phu, K., Reddy, A. P. and Cameron, J. L. (2013) The effect of short moderate stress on the midbrain corticotrophin-releasing factor system in a macaque model of functional hypothalamic amenorrhea. *Fertility and Sterility*, **100**, 1111–21.

Bhandari, M. M. (1974) Famine foods in the Rajasthan desert. *Economic Botany*, **28**, 73–81.

Bideau, A., Desjardins, B. and Brignoli, H. P., eds. (1997) *Infant and Child Mortality in the Past.* Oxford: Oxford University Press.

Bil, A. (1990) *The Shieling 1600–1840: The Case of the Central Scottish Highlands.* Edinburgh: John Donald.

Billari, F. C., Preskawetz, A. and Fürnfranz, J. (2003) On the cultural evolution of age-at-marriage norms. In *Agent-Based Computational Demography: Using Simulation to Improve our Understanding of Demographic Behaviour*, ed. F. C. Billari and A. Preskawetz. Heidelberg: Physica-Verlag, pp. 139–57.

Bingham, H. (1948) *Lost City of the Incas: The Story of Machu Picchu and its Builders.* New York: Duell, Sloan and Pierce.

Binswanger, H. P., Evenson, R. E., Florencio, C. A. and White, B. N. F., eds. (1980) *Rural Households in Asia.* Singapore: Singapore University Press.

Binswanger, H. P. and McIntire, J. (1987) Behavioral and material determinants of production relationships in land-abundant tropical agriculture. *Economic Development and Cultural Change*, **36**, 73–99.

Binswanger, H. P. and Ruttan, V. (1978) *Induced Innovation: Technology, Institutions, and Development*. Baltimore: Johns Hopkins University Press.

Blackstone, W. (1979) *Commentaries on the Laws of England: A Facsimile of the First Edition of 1765–1769*. Chicago: University of Chicago Press.

Blaikie, P. M. (1971) Spatial organization of agriculture in some north Indian villages: Parts I and II. *Transactions of the Institute of British Geographers*, **52**, 1–40; **53**, 15–30.

Blaikie, P. M. and Brookfield, H. C. (1987) Approaches to the study of land degradation. In *Land Degradation and Society*, ed. P. M. Blaikie and H. C. Brookfield. London: Routledge, pp. 27–48.

Bleiberg, F. M., Brun, T. A. and Goihman, S. (1980) Duration of activities and energy expenditure of female farmers in dry and rainy seasons in Upper Volta. *British Journal of Nutrition*, **43**, 71–82.

Bleiberg, F. M., Brun, T. A., Goihman, S. and Lippman, D. (1981) Food intake and energy expenditure of male and female farmers from Upper Volta. *British Journal of Nutrition*, **45**, 505–15.

Boersma, B. and Wit, J. M. (1997) Catch-up growth. *Endocrine Reviews*, **18**, 646–61.

Bogaard, M., Fraser, R., Heaton, T. H. E., *et al.* (2013) Crop manuring and intensive land management by Europe's first farmers. *Proceedings of the National Academy of Sciences*, early edition www.pnas.org/cgi/doi/10.1073/pnas.1305918110.

Bogin, B. (2011) !Kung nutritional status and the original "affluent society" – a new analysis. *Anthropologischer Anzeiger: Journal of Biological and Clinical Anthropology*, **68**, 349–66.

Bohannan, P. (1954) *Tiv Farm and Settlement*. London: HMSO.

Bohannan, P. and Bohannan, L. (1968) *Tiv Economy*. Evanston, IL: Northwestern University Press.

Bolt, V. J. and Bird, K. (2003) *The Intrahousehold Disadvantages Framework: A Framework for the Analysis of Intra-household Difference and Inequality*. CPRC Working Paper No. 32. Manchester: Chronic Poverty Research Centre, University of Manchester.

Bonan, G. (2002) *Ecological Climatology: Concepts and Applications*. Cambridge: Cambridge University Press.

Bonar, J. (1885) *Malthus and His Work*. London: Macmillan.

Bongaarts, J. (1980) Does malnutrition affect fecundity? A summary of evidence. *Science*, **208**, 564–9.

Bongaarts, J. (1987) The projection of family composition over the life course with family status life tables. In *Family Demography: Methods and their Applications*, ed. J. Bongaarts, T. K. Burch and K. Wachter. Oxford: Oxford University Press, pp. 189–212.

Bongaarts, J. and Cain, M. (1982) Demographic responses to famine. In *Famine*, ed. K. M. Cahill. Maryknoll, NY: Orbis Books, pp. 44–59.

Bongaarts, J. and Delgado, H. (1979) Effects of nutritional status on fertility in rural Guatemala. In *Natural Fertility*, ed. H. Leridon and J. A. Menken. Liège: Ordina Editions, pp. 107–33.

Booth, A. and Sundrum, R. M. (1985) *Labour Absorption in Agriculture: Theoretical Analyses and Empirical Investigations*. Oxford: Oxford University Press.

Booth, B. D., Murphy, S. D. and Swanton, C. J. (2003) *Weed Ecology in Natural and Agricultural Systems*. Cambridge, MA: CABI Publishing.

Borges, J. L. (1970) *A Universal History of Infamy*, trans. N. T. di Giovanni. New York: E. P. Dutton.

Börjeson, L. (2004a) *A History under Siege: Intensive Agriculture in the Mbulu Highlands, Tanzania, 19th Century to the Present*. Stockholm: Department of Human Geography, Stockholm University.

Börjeson, L. (2004b) The history of Iraqw intensive agriculture, Tanzania. In *Islands of Intensive Agriculture in Eastern Africa*, ed. M. Widgren and J. E. G. Sutton. Oxford: James Currey, pp. 68–104.

Borrie, W. D. (1970) *The Growth and Control of World Population*. London: Weidenfeld and Nicolson.

Boserup, E. (1965) *The Conditions of Agricultural Growth: The Economics of Agrarian Change under Population Pressure.* Chicago: Aldine.

Boserup, E. (1970) *Women's Role in Economic Development.* London: George Allen and Unwin.

Boserup, E. (1976) Environment, population, and technology in primitive societies. *Population and Development Review*, 2, 21–36.

Boserup, E. (1981) *Population and Technological Change: A Study of Long-Term Trends.* Chicago: University of Chicago Press.

Boserup, E. (1990) *Economic and Demographic Relationships in Development*, ed. T. P. Schultz. Baltimore: Johns Hopkins University Press.

Boserup, E. (1999) *My Professional Life and Publications 1929–1998.* Copenhagen: Museum Tusculanum Press, University of Copenhagen.

Boster, J. S. (1983) A comparison of the diversity of Jivaroan gardens with that of the tropical forest. *Human Ecology*, 11, 47–68.

Boster, J. S. (1985) Selection for perceptual distinctiveness: Evidence for Aguaruna cultivars of *Manihot esculenta. Economic Botany*, 39, 310–25.

Bourgholtzer, F. (1999) *Aleksandr Chayanov and Russian Berlin.* London: Frank Cass.

Bourke, R. M. (2001) Intensification of agricultural systems in Papua New Guinea. *Asia Pacific Viewpoint*, 42, 219–35.

Bourke, R. M. (2007) Managing the species composition of fallows in Papua New Guinea by planting trees. In *Voices from the Forest: Integrating Indigenous Knowledge into Sustainable Upland Farming*, ed. M. Cairns. Washington: Resources for the Future, pp. 379–88.

Bourke, R. M., Allen, B. J., Hobsbawn, P. and Conway, J. (1998) *Papua New Guinea: Text Summaries (two volumes).* Agricultural Systems of Papua New Guinea Working Paper No. 1. Canberra: Department of Human Geography, The Australian National University.

Bowman, A. K. and Rogan, E., eds. (1999) *Agriculture in Egypt: From Pharaonic to Modern Times.* Proceedings of the British Academy 96. Oxford: Oxford University Press.

Boyce, A. J., Küchemann, C. F. and Harrison, G. A. (1967) Neighborhood knowledge and the distribution of marriage distances. *Annals of Human Genetics*, 30, 335–8.

Boyd, R. and Richerson, P. J. (1985) *Culture and the Evolutionary Process.* Chicago: University of Chicago Press.

Boyd, R. and Richerson, P. J. (2002) Group beneficial norms spread rapidly in a structured population. *Journal of Theoretical Biology*, 215, 287–96.

Boyd, R. and Richerson, P. J. (2009) Culture and the evolution of human cooperation. *Philosophical Transactions of the Royal Society B (Biological Sciences)*, 364, 3281–8.

Boyd, R., Richerson, P. J. and Henrich, J. (2011) The cultural niche: Why social learning is essential for human adaptation. *Proceedings of the National Academy of Sciences*, 108 (10), 918–25.

Bradfield, M. (1971) *The Changing Pattern of Hopi Agriculture.* London: Royal Anthropological Institute.

Brady, N.C. and Weil, R. R. (2007) *The Nature and Properties of Soils*, 14th edn. Upper Saddle River, NJ: Prentice Hall.

Brage, S., Brage, N., Franks, P., Ekelund, U. and Wareham, N. (2005) Reliability and validity of the combined heart rate and movement sensor Actiheart. *European Journal of Clinical Nutrition*, 59, 561–70.

Brasier, C. M. (2001) Rapid evolution of introduced plant pathogens via interspecific hybridization. *BioScience*, 51, 1213–33.

Bray, F. (1984) *Science and Civilisation in China, Volume 6 (Biology and Biological Technology), Part II (Agriculture)*, ed. J. Needham. Cambridge: Cambridge University Press.

Bray, F. (1986) *The Rice Economies: Technology and Development in Asian Societies.* Berkeley, CA: University of California Press.

Brenton, B. P. (1989) The seasonality of storage. In *Coping with Seasonal Constraints*, ed. R. Huss-Ashmore, J. J. Curry and R. K. Hithcock. Philadelphia: The University Museum, University of Pennsylvania, pp. 45–54.

Bronson, B. (1972) Farm labor and the evolution of food production. In *Population Growth: Anthropological Perspectives*, ed. B. Spooner. Cambridge, MA: MIT Press, pp. 190–218.

Brookfield, H. C. (1962) Local study and comparative method: An example from central New Guinea.

Annals of the Association of American Geographers, **52**, 242–54.

Brookfield, H. C. (1968) New directions in the study of agricultural systems in tropical areas. In *Environment and Evolution*, ed. E. T. Drake. New Haven, CT: Yale University Press, pp. 413–39.

Brookfield, H. C. (1972) Intensification and disintensification in Pacific agriculture: A theoretical approach. *Pacific Viewpoint*, **13**, 30–48.

Brookfield, H. C. (1984) Intensification revisited. *Pacific Viewpoint*, **25**, 15–44.

Brookfield, H. C. (2001a) *Exploring Agrodiversity*. New York: Columbia University Press.

Brookfield, H. C. (2001b) Intensification, and alternative approaches to agricultural change. *Asia Pacific Viewpoint*, **42**, 181–92.

Brookfield, H. C. and Brown, P. (1963) *Struggle for Land: Agriculture and Group Territories among the Chimbu of the New Guinea Highlands*. Melbourne: Oxford University Press.

Brookfield, H. C. and Hart, D. (1971) *Melanesia: A Geographical Interpretation of an Island World*. London: Methuen.

Brookfield, H. C., Potter, L. and Byron, Y. (1995) *In Place of the Forest: Environment and Socio-economic Transformation in Borneo and the Eastern Malay Peninsula*. Tokyo: United Nations University Press.

Brooks, G. A., Fahey, T. D. and White, T. P. (1996) *Exercise Physiology: Human Bioenergetics and Its Applications*. Mountain View, CA: McGraw-Hill.

Browman, D. L. (1987) Agro-pastoral risk management in the Central Andes. *Research in Economic Anthropology*, **8**, 171–200.

Brown, A. G. and Barber, K. E. (1985) Late Holocene paleoecology and sedimentary history of a small lowland catchment in central England. *Quaternary Research*, **24**, 87–102.

Brown, G. M. (1997) *For the Islands I Sing*. London: John Murray.

Brown, J. K. (1963) A note on the division of labor by sex. *American Anthropologist*, **72**, 1073–8.

Brown, K. H., Roberston, A. D., Akhtar, N. A. and Ahmed, M. G. (1986) Lactational capacity of marginally nourished mothers: Relationships between maternal nutritional status and quantity and proximate composition of milk. *Pediatrics*, **78**, 909–19.

Brown, L., ed. (1993) *The New Shorter Oxford English Dictionary (Volume 1, A–M)*. Oxford: Clarendon Press.

Brown, P. and Padolefsky, A. (1976) Population density, agricultural intensity, land tenure and group size in the New Guinea highlands. *Ethnology*, **15**, 211–38.

Browne, D. J. (1858) *The Field Book of Manures, or the American Muck Book*. New York: A. A. Moore Agricultural Book Publisher.

Brun, T. A., Bleiberg, F. and Goihman, S. (1981) Energy expenditure of male farmers in dry and rainy seasons in Upper-Volta. *British Journal of Nutrition*, **45**, 67–75.

Brun, T. A., Geissler, C. A., Mirbagheri, I., *et al.* (1979) The energy expenditures of Iranian agricultural workers. *American Journal of Clinical Nutrition*, **32**, 2154–61.

Brush, S. B. (1975) The concept of carrying capacity for systems of shifting cultivators. *American Anthropologist*, **77**, 799–811.

Brush, S. B. (1977) *Mountain, Field, and Family: The Economy and Human Ecology of an Andean Valley*. Philadelphia: University of Pennsylvania Press.

Brush, S. B. (1986) Genetic diversity and conservation in traditional farming systems. *Journal of Ethnobiology*, **6**, 151–67.

Brush, S. B. (2004) *Farmers' Bounty: Locating Crop Diversity in the Contemporary World*. New Haven, CT: Yale University Press.

Brush, S. B., Carney, H. and Huaman, Z. (1981) The dynamics of Andean potato agriculture. *Economic Botany*, **35**, 70–88.

Brush, S. B. and Meng, E. (1998) Farmers' evaluation and conservation of crop genetic resources. *Genetic Resources and Crop Evolution*, **45**, 139–50.

Bruun, T. B., de Neergaard, A., Lawrence, D. and Ziegler, A. (2009) Environmental consequences of the demise in swidden agriculture in Southeast Asia: Carbon storage and soil quality. *Human Ecology*, **37**, 375–88.

Bruun, T. B., Mertz, O. and Elberling, B. (2006) Linking yields of upland rice in shifting cultivation to fallow length and soil properties. *Agriculture, Ecosystems and Environment*, **113**, 139–49.

Buck, J. L. (1930) *Chinese Farm Economy: A Study of 2866 Farms in Seventeen Localities and*

Seven Provinces in China. Chicago: University of Chicago Press.

Buck, J. L. (1937) *Land Utilization in China: A Study of 16,786 Farms in 168 Localities, and 38,256 Families in Twenty-two Provinces in China, 1929-1933.* Nanking: University of Nanking Press.

Burch, T. K. (1970) Some demographic determinants of average household size: An analytical approach. *Demography,* **7**, 61–9.

Burnham, P. (1980) *Opportunity and Constraint in a Savanna Society: The Gbaya of Meiganga, Cameroon.* London: Academic Press.

Burton, M. L., Brudner, L. A. and White, D. R. (1977) A model of the sexual division of labor. *American Ethnologist,* **4**, 227–51.

Burton, M. L. and Reitz, K. (1981) The plow, female contribution to agricultural subsistence and polygyny: A log linear analysis. *Behavior Science Research,* **16**, 272–305.

Burton, M. L. and White, D. R. (1984) Sexual division of labor in agriculture. *American Anthropologist,* **86**, 568–82.

Cain, M. T. (1977) The economic activities of children in a village in Bangladesh. *Population and Development Review,* **3**, 201–27.

Cairns, M., ed. (2007) *Voices from the Forest: Integrating Indigenous Knowledge into Sustainable Upland Farming.* Washington: Resources for the Future.

Cairns, M., Keitzar, S. and Yaden, T. A. (2007) Shifting forests in northeast India: Management of *Alnus nepalensis* as an improved fallow in Nagaland. In *Voices from the Forest: Integrating Indigenous Knowledge into Sustainable Upland Farming,* ed. M. Cairns. Washington: Resources for the Future, pp. 341–78.

Caldwell, J. C. (1976) Toward a restatement of demographic transition theory. *Population and Development Review,* **2**, 321–66.

Caldwell, J. C. (1982) *Theory of Fertility Decline.* London: Academic Press.

Cameron, J. L. (1996) Regulation of reproductive hormone secretion in primates by short-term changes in nutrition. *Reviews of Reproduction,* **1**, 117–26.

Campbell, B. M. S. (1984) Population pressure, inheritance and the land market in a fourteenth-century peasant community. In

Land, Kinship and Life Cycle, ed. R. M. Smith. Cambridge: Cambridge University Press.

Campbell, B. M. S. and Bartley, K. (2006) *England on the Eve of the Black Death: An Atlas of Lay Lordship, Land and Wealth, 1300-49.* Manchester: Manchester University Press.

Campbell, B. M. S., Galloway, J. A. and Murphy, M. (1992) Rural land-use in the metropolitan hinterland, 1270–1330: The evidence of *inquisitiones post mortem. Agricultural History Review,* **40**, 1–22.

Campbell, B. M. S. and Overton, M., eds. (1991) *Land, Labour and Livestock: Historical Studies in European Agricultural Productivity.* Manchester: Manchester University Press.

Campbell, C. D. and Lee, J. Z. (1996) A death in the family: Household structure and mortality in rural Liaoning – life-event and time-series analysis, 1792–1867. *History of the Family,* **1**, 297–328.

Cancian, F. (1972) *Change and Uncertainty in a Peasant Economy: The Maya Corn Farmers of Zinacantan.* Berkeley, CA: University of California Press.

Carlson, T. (1913) Über geschwindigkeit und grösse der Hefevermehrung in Würze. *Biochemische Zeitschrift,* **57**, 313–34.

Carney, J. (1991) Indigenous soil and water management in Senegambian rice farming systems. *Agriculture and Human Values,* **8**, 37–48.

Carpenter, K. J. (1969) Man's dietary needs. In *Population and Food Supply: Essays on Human Needs and Agricultural Prospects* ed. J. Hutchinson. Cambridge: Cambridge University Press, pp. 61–74.

Carrier, E. H. (1932) *Water and Grass: A Study in the Pastoral Economy of Southern Europe.* London: Christophers.

Carter, A. T. (1984) Household histories. In *Households: Comparative and Historical Studies of the Domestic Group,* ed. R. M. Netting, R. R. Wilk and E. J. Arnould. Berkeley, CA: University of California Press, pp. 44–83.

Castetter, E. F. and Bell, W. H. (1942) *Pima and Papago Indian Agriculture.* Albuquerque, NM: University of New Mexico Press.

Castetter, E. F. and Bell, W. H. (1951) *Yuman Indian Agriculture.* Albuquerque, NM: University of New Mexico Press.

Caswell, H. (2006) *Matrix Population Models*, 2nd edn. Sunderland, CT: Sinauer Associates.

Catt, J. A. (1994) Long-term consequences of using artificial and organic fertilisers: The Rothamsted experiments. In *The History of Soils and Field Systems*, ed. S. Foster and T. C. Smout. Aberdeen: Scottish Cultural Press, pp. 119–34.

Caulfield, L. E., de Onis, M., Blossner, M. and Black, R. E. (2003) Undernutrition as an underlying cause of child deaths associated with diarrhea, pneumonia, malaria, and measles. *American Journal of Clinical Nutrition*, 80, 193–8.

Cavalli-Sforza, L. L. and Bodmer, W. F. (1971) *The Genetics of Human Populations*. San Francisco: W. H. Freeman.

Ceccarelli, S., Acevedo, E. and Grando, S. (1991) Breeding for yield stability in unpredictable environments: Single traits, interaction between traits, and architecture of genotypes. *Euphytica*, 56, 169–85.

Census of India (1951) *Census of India, Volume 1, India: Part IA, Demographic Tables*. New Delhi: Office of the Registrar General and Census Commissioner, Government of India.

Chagnon, N. A. (2009) *Yąnomamö*, 5th edn. Belmont, CA: Wadsworth.

Chakravarty, K. K., Badam, G. L. and Parnjpye, V. (2006) *Traditional Water Management Systems of India*. Bhopal: Indira Gandhi Rashtriya Manav Sangrahalaya.

Chaloner, W. H. and Ratcliffe, B. M., eds. (1977) *Trade and Transport: Essays in Economic History in Honour of T. S. Willam*. Manchester: Manchester University Press.

Chamberlain, A. T. (2006) *Demography in Archaeology*. Cambridge: Cambridge University Press.

Chambers, J. D. and Mingray, G. E. (1966) *The Agricultural Revolution 1750–1880*. London: Batsford.

Chambers, R., Longhurst, R. and Pacey, A. (1981) Seasonal patterns in births and deaths. In *Seasonal Dimensions to Rural Poverty*, ed. R. Chambers, R. Longhurst and A. Pacey. London: Frances Pinter, pp. 135–62.

Chambers, R., Pacey, A. and Thrupp, L. A., eds. (1989) *Farmer First: Innovation and Agricultural Research*. London: Intermediate Technology.

Chang, C. C. (1963) *An Agricultural Engineering Analysis of Rice Farming Methods in Taiwan*. Los Baños, Philippines: International Rice Research Institute.

Charbonneau, H. (1970) *Tourouvre-au-Perche aux XVIIe et XVIIIe Siècles: Étude de Démographie Historique*. Paris: PUF.

Charlesworth, B. (1980) *Evolution of Age-Structured Populations*. Cambridge: Cambridge University Press.

Chayanov, A. V. (1925) *Organizatsiia Krest'ianskogo Khoziaĭstva*. Moscow: The Co-operative Publishing House.

Chayanov, A. V. (1966 [orig. 1925]) *The Theory of Peasant Economy*, trans. R. E. F. Smith, ed. D. Thorner, B. Kerblay and R. E. F. Smith. Homewood, IL: Richard D. Irwin, Inc.

Chayanov, A. V. (1986 [orig. 1925]) *The Theory of Peasant Economy*, new edition, trans. R. E. F. Smith, ed. D. Thorner, B. Kerblay and R. E. F. Smith. Madison, WI: University of Wisconsin Press.

Chen, L. C., Ahmed, S., Gesche, M. and Mosley, W. H. (1974) A prospective study of birth interval dynamics in rural Bangladesh. *Population Studies*, 28, 277–97.

Chen, L. C., Chowdhury, A. K. M. A. and Huffman, S. L. (1979) Seasonal dimensions of energy protein malnutrition in rural Bangladesh: The role of agriculture, dietary practices and infection. *Ecology of Food and Nutrition*, 8, 175–8.

Chen, L. C., Chowdhury, A. K. M. A. and Huffman, S. L. (1980) Anthropometric assessment of energy-protein malnutrition and subsequent risk of mortality among preschool-aged children. *American Journal of Clinical Nutrition*, 33, 1836–43.

Chen, L. C., Huq, E. and D'Souza, S. (1981) Sex bias in the family allocation of food and health care in rural Bangladesh. *Population and Development Review*, 7, 55–70.

Chibnik, M. (1984) A cross-cultural examination of Chayanov's theory. *Current Anthropology*, 25, 335–40.

Chibnik, M. (1987) The economic effects of household demography: A cross-cultural assessment of Chayanov's theory. In *Household Economies and Their Transformations*, ed. M. D. Maclachlan. Lanham, MD: University Press of America, pp. 74–106.

Chisholm, M. (1962) *Rural Settlement and Land Use: An Essay in Location.* London: Hutchinson University Library.

Chowdhury, M. K., Becker, S., Razzaque, A., *et al.* (1981) *Demographic Surveillance System, Matlab: Vital Events and Migration 1978.* Scientific Report No. 47. Dhaka: International Centre for Diarrheal Disease Research.

Christanty, L., Abdoellah, O. S., Marten, G. C. and Iskander, J. (1986) Traditional agroforestry in West Java: The *pekarangan* (housegarden) and *kebun-talun* (annual-perennial rotation) cropping systems. In *Traditional Agriculture in Southeast Asia: A Human Ecology Perspective*, ed. G. C. Marten. Boulder, CO: Westview Press, pp. 132–58.

Christian, P. (2008) Infant mortality. In *Nutrition and Health in Developing Countries*, 2nd edn, ed. R. D. Semba and M. W. Bloem. Totowa, NJ: Humana Press, pp. 87–111.

Christiansen, S. (1975) *Subsistence on Bellona Island (Mungiki): A Study of the Cultural Ecology of a Polynesian Outlier in the British Solomon Islands Protectorate.* Copenhagen: Reitzels Forlag.

Cipolla, C. M. (1993) *Before the Industrial Revolution: European Society and Economy 1000–1700.* New York: W. W. Norton.

Claidière, N. and André, J.-B. (2012) The transmission of genes and culture: A questionable analogy. *Evolutionary Biology*, 39, 12–24.

Clark, C. and Haswell, M. (1967) *The Economics of Subsistence Agriculture*, 3rd edn. London: Macmillan.

Clarke, W. C. (1971) *Place and People: An Ecology of a New Guinean Community.* Berkeley, CA: University of California Press.

Claus, P. J. and Lintner, S. (1975) The cultural ecology of a paddy tract. *Tools and Tillage*, 2, 211–27.

Clawson, D. L. (1985) Harvest security and intraspecific diversity in traditional tropical agriculture. *Economic Botany*, 39, 56–67.

Cleave, J. H. (1974) *African Farmers: Labor Use in the Development of Smallholder Agriculture.* New York: Praeger.

Cleveland, D. A. and Soleri, D. (2007) Extending Darwin's analogy: Bridging differences in concepts of selection between farmers, biologists, and plant breeders. *Economic Botany*, 61, 121–36.

Coale, A. J. (1965) Appendix: Estimates of average size of household. In *Aspects of the Analysis of Family Structure*, ed. A. J. Coale, L. A. Fallers, M. J. Levy, D. M. Schneider and S. S. Tomkins. Princeton, NJ: Princeton University Press, pp. 64–9.

Coale, A. J. (1971) Age patterns of marriage. *Population Studies*, 25, 193–214.

Coale, A. J. and Demeny, P. (1983) *Regional Model Life Tables and Stable Populations*, 2nd edn. London: Academic Press.

Coale, A. J. and McNeil, D. R. (1972) Distribution by age of the frequency of first marriage in a female cohort. *Journal of the American Statistical Association*, 67, 743–9.

Cohen, J. E. (1995) *How Many People can the Earth Support?* New York: W. W. Norton.

Cohen, M. N. (1989) *Health and the Rise of Civilization.* New Haven, CT: Yale University Press.

Cohen, M. N. and Armelagos, G., eds. (1984) *Paleopathology at the Origins of Agriculture.* Orlando, FL: Academic Press.

Cohen, M. N. and Crane-Kramer, G. M. M., eds. (2007) *Ancient Health: Skeletal Indicators of Agricultural and Economic Intensification.* Gainesville, FL: University Press of Florida.

Cole, T. J. and Coward, W. A. (1992) Precision and accuracy of doubly labeled water energy expenditure by multipoint and two-point methods. *American Journal of Physiology – Endocrinology and Metabolism*, 263, 965–73.

Coleman, D. C., Crossley, D. A. and Hendrix, P. F. (2004) *Fundamentals of Soil Ecology*, 2nd edn. London: Elsevier Academic.

Collier, G. A. (1975) *Fields of the Tzotzil: The Ecological Basis of Tradition in Highland Chiapas.* Austin, TX: University of Texas Press.

Collinson, M. P., ed. (2000) *A History of Farming Systems Research.* Wallingford: CABI Publishing.

Conelly, W. T. (1992) Agricultural intensification in a Philippine frontier community: Impact on labor efficiency and farm diversity. *Human Ecology*, 20, 203–23.

Conklin, H. C. (1957) *Hanunóo Agriculture: A Report on an Integral System of Shifting Cultivation in the Philippines.* Rome: Food and Agriculture Organization of the United Nations.

Conklin, H. C. (1961) The study of shifting cultivation. *Current Anthropology*, **2**, 27–61.

Conklin, H. C. (1963) *El Estudio del Cultivo de Roza: The Study of Shifting Cultivation.* Washington, DC: Union Panamericana.

Conklin, H. C. (1980) *Ethnographic Atlas of Ifugao: A Study of Environment, Culture, and Society in Northern Luzon.* New Haven, CT: Yale University Press.

Connell, J. H. (1961) Effects of competition, predation by *Thais lapillus*, and other factors on natural populations of the barnacle *Balanus balanoides*. *Ecological Monographs*, **31**, 61–104.

Connor, D. J., Loomis, R. S. and Cassman, K. G. (2011) *Crop Ecology: Productivity and Management in Agricultural Systems*, 2nd edn. Cambridge: Cambridge University Press.

Cook, H. and Williamson, T., eds. (1999) *Water Management in the English Landscape: Field, Marsh and Meadow.* Edinburgh: Edinburgh University Press.

Cook, O. F. (1920) Foot-plow agriculture in Peru. In *Annual Report of the Smithsonian Institution 1918.* Washington: Smithsonian Institution, pp. 487–91.

Cook, O. F. (1921) Milpa agriculture: A primitive tropical system. In *Annual Report of the Smithsonian Institution 1919.* Washington: Smithsonian Institution, pp. 207–26.

Cornell, L. L. (1987) Hajnal and the household in Asia: A comparativist history of the family in preindustrial Japan, 1600–1870. *Journal of Family History*, **12**, 143–62.

Cotterell, B. and Kamminga, J. (1990) *Mechanics of Pre-industrial Technology.* Cambridge: Cambridge University Press.

Cotton, C. M. (1996) *Ethnobotany: Principles and Applications.* New York: Wiley and Sons.

Coward, E. W., ed. (1980) *Irrigation and Agricultural Development in Asia: Perspectives from the Social Sciences.* Ithaca, NY: Cornell University Press.

Cowgill, G. (1975) On causes and consequences of ancient and modern population changes. *American Anthropologist*, **77**, 505–25.

Cowles, A. and Chapman, E. N. (1935) Statistical study of climate in relation to pulmonary tuberculosis. *Journal of the American Statistical Association*, **30**, 517–36.

Craig, D., Meechan, J. G. and Skelly, M., eds. (1993) *The Agriculture of Egypt.* Oxford: Oxford University Press.

Cramb, R. A. (1989) Labor efficiency and intensity of land use in rice production: An East Malaysian case. *Agricultural Systems*, **29**, 97–115.

Cramb, R. A. (2007) *Land and Longhouse: Agrarian Transformation in the Uplands of Sarawak.* Copenhagen: NIAS Press.

Cramer, H. H. (1967) *Plant Protection and World Crop Production.* Leverkusen, GDR: Bayer.

Cressey, G. B. (1950) Qanats, karez, and foggaras. *Geographical Review*, **48**, 27–44.

Crouter, S. E., Albright, C. and Bassett, D. R. (2004) Accuracy of Polar S410 heart rate monitor to estimate energy cost of exercise. *Medicine and Science in Sports and Exercise*, **36**, 1433–9.

Cuffaro, N. (2001) *Population, Economic Growth and Agriculture in Less Developed Countries.* London: Routledge.

Cumming, D. C., Wheeler, G. D. and Harber, V. J. (1994) Physical activity, nutrition, and reproduction. *Annals of the New York Academy of Sciences*, **709**, 55–76.

Curwin, E. C. and Hatt, G. (1953) *Plough and Pasture: The Early History of Farming.* New York: Henry Schuman.

Czap, P. (1982) The perennial multiple family household. *Journal of Family History*, **1**, 5–26.

de Guzman, P. E., Dominguez, D. R., Kalaw, J. M., Basconcillo, R. O. and Santos V. F. (1974) A study of the energy expenditure, dietary intake, and pattern of daily activity among various occupational groups. I. Languna rice farmers. *Philippine Journal of Science*, **103**, 53–65.

de Onis, M. and Blössner, M. (1997) *WHO Database on Child Growth and Malnutrition.* Geneva: World Health Organization.

de Onis, M., Monteiro, C., Akr, J. and Clugston, G. (1993) The worldwide magnitude of protein-energy malnutrition: An overview from the WHO database on child growth. *Bulletin of the World Health Organization*, **71**, 703–12.

de Ortiz, R. R. (1973) *Uncertainties in Peasant Farming: A Colombian Case.* London: The Athlone Press.

de Schlippe, P. (1956) *Shifting Cultivation in Africa: The Zande System of Agriculture.* London: Routledge and Kegan Paul.

de Smith, M. J. (2003) GIS, distance, paths and anisotropy. In *Advanced Spatial Analysis*, ed. P. A. Longley and M. Batty. Redlands, CA: ESRI Press, pp. 309–26.

Dandekar, V. M. and Pethe, V. (1960) Size and composition of rural families. *Artha Vijñana*, **2**, 189–99.

Danilov, V. (1991) Introduction: Alexander Chayanov as a theoretician of the co-operative movement. In A. V. Chayanov, *The Theory of Peasant Co-operatives*. Columbus, OH: Ohio State University Press, pp. xi–xxxv.

Darwin, C. (1859) *On the Origin of Species by Means of Natural Selection, or the Preservation of Favoured Races in the Struggle for Life*. London: John Murray.

Datoo, B. A. (1978) Toward a reformulation of Boserup's theory of agricultural change. *Economic Geography*, **54**, 134–44.

Davidson, J. (1938) On the ecology of the growth of the sheep population in South Australia. *Transactions of the Royal Society of South Australia*, **62**, 141–8.

Dearing, J. A., Håkansson, H., Liedberg-Jönsson, B., *et al.* (1987) Lake sediments used to quantify the erosional response to land use change in southern Sweden. *Oikos*, **50**, 60–78.

DeBano, L. F., Neary, D. G. and Folliott, P. F. (1998) *Fire's Effects on Ecosystems*. New York: Wiley and Sons.

Dejene, A., Shishira, E. K., Yanda, P. Z. and Johnsen, F. H. (1997) *Land Degradation in Tanzania*. Washington: The World Bank.

Delang, C. (2006) Not just minor forest products: The economic rationale for the consumption of wild plant foods by subsistence farmers. *Ecological Economics*, **59**, 64–73.

Denevan, W. M. (1971) Campa subsistence in the Gran Pajonal, Eastern Peru. *Geographical Review*, **61**, 496–518.

Denevan, W. M. (2001) *Cultivated Landscapes of Native Amazonia and the Andes*. Oxford: Oxford University Press.

Denevan, W. M. and Padoch, C., eds. (1987) *Swidden-Fallow Agroforestry in the Peruvian Amazon*. New York: New York Botanical Garden Press.

Dercon, S. and Krishnan, P. (2000) In sickness and health: Risk sharing within households in rural Ethiopia. *Journal of Political Economy*, **108**, 688–727.

Devereux, F., Sabates-Wheeler, R. and Longhurst, R., eds. (2012) *Seasonality, Rural Livelihoods and Development*. London: EarthScan.

Devereux, S., Vaitla, B. and Swan, S. H. (2008) *Seasons of Hunger: Fighting Cycles of Quiet Starvation among the World's Rural Poor*. London: Pluto Press.

Dewalt, B. R. (1985) Farming systems research. *Human Organization*, **44**, 106–14.

Dewar, R. E. (1984) Environmental productivity, population regulation, and carrying capacity. *American Anthropologist*, **86**, 601–14.

Diamond, J. (1987) The worst mistake in the history of the human race. *Discover Magazine*, May, 64–6.

Dijkman, J. (1999) Carrying capacity: Outdated concept or useful livestock management tool? In Crop and Grassland Service (AGPC), *Livestock: Coping with Drought* (www.odi.org.uk/work/projects/pdn/drought/dijkman.html). London: Pastoral Development Network, Overseas Development Institute, unpaginated.

Dinks, R. (1993) Starvation and famine. *Cross-Cultural Research*, **27**, 28–69.

Doblhammer-Reiter, G., Rodgers, J. L. and Rau, R. (1999) *Seasonality of Birth in Nineteenth and Twentieth Century Austria: Steps toward a Unified Theory of Human Reproductive Seasonality*. MPIDR Working 1999-013. Rostock: Max Planck Institute for Demographic Research.

Donahue, B. (2004) *The Great Meadow: Farmers and the Land in Colonial Concord*. New Haven, CT: Yale University Press.

Donkin, R. A. (1979) *Agricultural Terracing in the Aboriginal New World*. Tucson, AZ: The University of Arizona Press.

Doolittle, W. E. (1984) Agricultural change as an incremental process. *Annals of the Association of American Geographers*, **74**, 124–37.

Doolittle, W. E. (2000) *Cultivated Landscapes of Native North America*. Oxford: Oxford University Press.

Dove, M. R. (1984) The Chayanovian slope in a swidden society: Household demography and extensive agriculture in West Kalimantan. In *Chayanov, Peasants, and Economic Anthropology*, ed. E. P. Durrenberger. New York: Academic Press, pp. 97–132.

Dove, M. R. (1985) *Swidden Agriculture in Indonesia: The Subsistence Strategies of the Kalimantan Kantu'*. Berlin: Mouton Publishers.

Drake, M. (1969) *Population and Society in Norway 1735–1865*. Cambridge: Cambridge University Press.

Drechsel, P. and Penning de Vries, F. W. T. (2001) Land pressure and soil nutrient depletion in sub-Saharan Africa. In *Response to Land Degradation*, ed. E. M. Bridges, I. D. Hannam, L. R. Oldeman, *et al.* Plymouth: Scientific Publishers, pp. 55–64.

Dubois, P. and Ligon, E. (2010) *Nutrition and Risk Sharing within the Household*. CUDARE Working Paper 1096. Department of Agricultural and Resource Economics, University of California, Berkeley, CA.

Duckham, A. N. (1963) *Agricultural Synthesis: The Farming Year*. London: Chatto and Windus.

Duckham, A. N. and Masefield, G. B. (1969) *Farming Systems of the World*. New York: Praeger.

Due, J. M. and Anandajayasekeram, P. (1984) Contrasting farming systems in Morogoro Region, Tanzania. *Canadian Journal of African Studies*, 18, 583–91.

Dufour, D. L. (1983) Nutrition in the northwest Amazon: Household dietary intake and time-energy expenditure. In *Adaptive Responses of Native Amazonians*, ed. R. B. Hames and W. T. Vickers. New York: Academic Press, pp. 328–55.

Dufour, D. L. (1984) The time and energy expenditure of indigenous women horticulturalists in the northwest Amazon. *American Journal of Physical Anthropology*, 65, 37–46.

Dufour, D. L. and Piperata, B. A. (2008) Energy expenditure among farmers in developing countries: What do we know? *American Journal of Human Biology*, 20, 249–58.

Dumont, R. (1957) *Types of Rural Economy: Studies in World Agriculture*. London: Methuen.

Dupâquier, J., ed. (1983) *Malthus Past and Present*. New York: Academic Press.

Durnin, J. V. G. A. and Passmore, R. (1967) *Energy, Work and Leisure*. London: Heinemann.

Durrenberger, E. P. (1978) *Agricultural Production and Household Budgets in a Shan Peasant Village in Northwestern Thailand: A Quantitative Description*. Athens, OH: Ohio University Press.

Durrenberger, E. P. (1979) Rice production in a Lisu village. *Journal of Southeast Asian Studies*, 10, 139–45.

Durrenberger, E. P. (1980) Chayanov's economic analysis in anthropology. *Journal of Anthropological Research*, 36, 133–48.

Durrenberger, E. P., ed. (1984) *Chayanov, Peasants, and Economic Anthropology*. New York: Academic Press.

Dwyer, P. D. (1990) *The Pigs that Ate the Garden: A Human Ecology from Papua New Guinea*. Ann Arbor, MI: University of Michigan Press.

Dyer, C. (1983) English diet in the later middles ages. In *Social Relations and Ideas*, ed. T. H. Aston, P. R. Cross, C. Dyer and J. Thirsk. Cambridge: Cambridge University Press, pp. 191–216.

Dyer, C. (1989) *Standards of Living in the Later Middle Ages: Social Change in England c. 1200–1520*. Cambridge: Cambridge University Press.

Dyer, C. (1991) *Decline and Growth in English Towns 1400–1640*. Cambridge: Cambridge University Press.

Dyer, C. (2002) *Making a Living in the Middle Ages: The People of Britain 850–1520*. New Haven, CT: Yale University Press.

Dyke, B. (1981) Computer simulation in anthropology. *Annual Review of Anthropology*, 10, 193–207.

Dyke, B. and MacCluer, J. W., eds. (1974) *Computer Simulation in Human Population Studies*. New York: Academic Press.

Dyke, G. V. (1993) *John Lawes of Rothamsted: Pioneer of Science, Farming and Industry*. Harpenden: Hoos Press.

Eder, J. F. (1991) Agricultural intensification and labor productivity in a Philippine vegetable gardening community: A longitudinal study. *Human Organization*, 50, 245–55.

Eger, H. (1987) *Run-off Agriculture: A Case Study of the Yemeni Highlands*. Wiesbaden: Ludwig Reichert.

Ehrlich, P. R. (1968) *The Population Bomb*. New York: Ballantine Books.

Elder, G. H. (1987) Families and lives: Some developments in life-course studies. *Journal of Family History*, 12, 179–99.

Ellis, F. (1993) *Peasant Economics: Farm Households and Agrarian Development*, 2nd edn. Cambridge: Cambridge University Press.

Ellison, P. T. (1990) Human ovarian function and reproductive ecology: New hypotheses. *American Anthropologist*, **92**, 933–52.

Ellison, P. T. (2003) *On Fertile Ground: A Natural History of Human Reproduction*. Cambridge, MA: Harvard University Press.

El Titi, A., ed. (2003) *Soil Tillage in Agroecosystems*. Boca Rotan, FL: CRC Press.

Elzebroek, T. and Wind, K. (2008) *Guide to Cultivated Plants*. Wallingford: CABI International.

Ember, C. R. (1983) The relative decline in women's contribution to agriculture with intensification. *American Anthropologist*, **85**, 285–304.

Engelen, T. (2005) The Hajnal hypothesis and transition theory. In *Marriage and the Family in Eurasia: Perspectives on the Hajnal Hypothesis*, ed. T. Engelen and A. P. Wolf. Amsterdam: Aksant Academic Publishers, pp. 51–71.

Engelen, T. and Wolf, A. P. (2005) Introduction: Marriage and family in Eurasia – Perspectives on the Hajnal hypothesis. In *Marriage and the Family in Eurasia: Perspectives on the Hajnal Hypothesis*, ed. T. Engelen and A. P. Wolf. Amsterdam: Aksant Academic Publishers, pp. 15–34.

Engelhardt, T. (1984) *Economics of Traditional Smallholder Irrigation Systems in the Semi-Arid Tropics of South Asia*. Stuttgardt-Hohenheim, GDR: Institut für Agrar- und Sozialökonomie in den Tropen und Sutropen Fachgebiet Ökonomik der landwirtschaftlichen Produktion.

Engels, F. (1954 [orig. 1844]) Outlines of a critique of political economy. In *Marx and Engels on Malthus: Selections from the writings of Marx and Engels dealing with the theories of Thomas Robert Malthus*, ed. R. L. Meek. New York: International Publishers, pp. 57–63.

Erinç, S. and Tunçdelik, N. (1952) The agricultural regions of Turkey. *The Geographical Review*, **42**, 179–203.

ESHRE Capri Workshop Group (2006) Nutrition and reproduction in women. *Human Reproduction Update*, **12**, 193–207.

Evans, L. T. (1993) *Crop Evolution, Adaptation and Yield*. Cambridge: Cambridge University Press.

Evans, L. T. (1998) *Feeding the Ten Billion: Plants and Population Growth*. Cambridge: Cambridge University Press.

Eyzaguirre, P. B. and Linares, O. F., eds. (2004) *Home Gardens and Agrobiodiversity*. Washington: Smithsonian Books.

FAO (1958) *The State of Food and Agriculture 1958*. Rome: Food and Agriculture Organization of the United Nations.

FAO (1974) *Shifting Cultivation and Soil Conservation in Africa*. Rome: Food and Agriculture Organization of the United Nations.

FAO (1997) Estimated post-harvest losses of rice in Southeast Asia (www.fao.org/FACTFILE/FF9712-e.htm). Rome: Food and Agriculture Organization of the United Nations.

Fairhurst, H. (1971) The study of deserted medieval settlements in Scotland (to 1968), Part I: Rural settlement. In *Deserted Medieval Village*, ed. M. Beresford and J. G. Hurst. London: Macmillan, pp. 229–35.

Farmer, B. H. (1960) On not controlling subdivision in paddy-lands. *Transactions and Papers of the Institute of British Geographers*, **28**, 225–35.

Faveau, V., Wojtyniak, B., Mostafa, G., Sarder, A. M. and Chakraborty, J. (1990) Perinatal mortality in Matlab, Bangladesh: A community-based study. *International Journal of Epidemiology*, **19**, 606–12.

Fei, H.-T. (1939) *Peasant Life in China: A Field Study of Country Life in the Yangtze Valley*. London: Routledge and Kegan Paul.

Fei, H.-T. and Chang, C.-I. (1945) *Earthbound China: A Study of Rural Economy in Yunnan*. Chicago: University of Chicago Press.

Fenton, A. (1974) The cas-chrom: A review of the Scottish evidence. *Tools and Tillage*, **2**, 131–48.

Fenton, A. (1976) *Scottish Country Life*. Edinburgh: John Donald.

Fenton, A. (1978) *The Northern Isles: Orkney and Shetland*. Edinburgh: John Donald.

Fenton, A. (1984) Wheelless transport in northern Scotland. In *Loads and Roads in Scotland and Beyond: Road Transport over 6000 Years*, ed. A. Fenton and G. Stell. Edinburgh: John Donald, pp. 105–23.

Fenton, A. and Stell, G., eds. (1984) *Loads and Roads in Scotland and Beyond: Road Transport over 6000 Years*. Edinburgh: John Donald.

Fernea, R. A. (1970) *Shaykh and Effendi: Changing Patterns of Authority among the El Shabana of Southern Iraq.* Cambridge, MA: Harvard University Press.

Ferro-Luzzi, A. (1985) Work capacity and productivity in long-term adaptation to low energy intakes. In *Nutritional Adaptation in Man*, ed. K. Blaxter and J. C. Waterlow. London: John Libbey, pp. 61–9.

Ferro-Luzzi, A., Morris, S. S., Taffesse, S., Demissie, T. and D'Amato, M. (2001) *Seasonal Undernutrition in Rural Ethiopia: Magnitude, Correlates, and Functional Significance.* Research Report 118. Washington: International Food Policy Research Institute.

Fertig, G. (2003) The invisible chain: Niche inheritance and unequal social reproduction in pre-industrial Continental Europe. *History of the Family*, 8, 7–19.

Fertig, G. (2005) The Hajnal hypothesis before Hajnal. In *Marriage and the Family in Eurasia: Perspectives on the Hajnal Hypothesis*, ed. T. Engelen and A. P. Wolf. Amsterdam: Aksant Academic Publishers, pp. 37–48.

Findley, S. E. (1994) Does drought increase migration? A study of migration from rural Mali during the 1983–85 droughts. *International Migration Review*, 28, 539–53.

Findley, S. E. and Salif, S. (1998) From season to season: Agriculture, poverty and migration in the Senegal River Valley, Mali. In *Emigration Dynamics in Developing Countries, Volume 1: Sub-Saharan Africa*, ed. R. Appleyard. Aldershot: Ashgate, pp. 69–143.

Findley, S. E., Traore, S., Ouedraogo, D. and Diarra, S. (1995) Emigration from the Sahel. *International Migration*, 33, 469–520.

Firth, R. U. (1966) *Housekeeping among Malay Peasants*, 2nd edn. London: The Athlone Press.

Firth, R. W. (1939) *Primitive Polynesian Economy.* London: Routledge and Kegan Paul.

Firth, R. W. (1969) Social structure and peasant economy: The influence of social structure upon peasant economies. In *Subsistence Agriculture and Economic Development*, ed. C. R. Wharton. Chicago: Aldine, pp. 23–37.

Fisher, C. T. (2007) Agricultural intensification in the Lake Pátzcuaro Basin: Landesque capital as statecraft. In *Seeking a Richer Harvest: The Archaeology of Subsistence Intensification, Innovation, and Change*, ed. T. T. Thurston and C. T. Fisher. New York: Springer Science, pp. 91–106.

Fisk, E. K. (1971) Labour absorption capacity of subsistence agriculture. *The Economic Record*, September, 366–78.

Fix, A. G. (1999) *Migration and Colonization in Human Microevolution.* Cambridge: Cambridge University Press.

Fjellman, S. M. (1977) The Akamba domestic cycle as Markovian process. *American Ethnologist*, 4, 699–713.

Flew, A., ed. (1970) *Thomas Malthus's An Essay on the Principle of Population and A Summary View of the Principle of Population.* Harmondsworth: Penguin Books.

Floud, R., Fogel, R. W., Harris, B. and Hong, S. C. (2011) *The Changing Body: Health, Nutrition, and Human Development in the Western World since 1700.* Cambridge: Cambridge University Press.

Floud, R. and Wachter, K. (1982) Poverty and physical stature: Evidence on the standard of living of London boys 1770–1980. *Social Science History*, 6, 422–52.

Floud, R., Wachter, K. and Gregory, A. (1990) *Height, Health and History: Nutritional Status in the United Kingdom 1750–1980.* Cambridge: Cambridge University Press.

Flowers, N. M. (1983) Seasonal factors in subsistence, nutrition, and child growth in a central Brazilian Indian community. In *Adaptive Responses of Native Amazonians*, ed. R. B. Hames and W. T. Vickers. New York: Academic Press, pp. 357–90.

Flowers, N. M., Gross, D. R., Ritter, M. L. and Werner, D. W. (1983) Variation in swidden practices in four central Brazilian Indian societies. *Human Ecology*, 10, 203–17.

Fogel, R. W. (1994) The relevance of Malthus for the study of mortality today: Long-run influences on health, mortality, labour force participation, and population growth. In *Population, Economic Development and the Environment: The Making of our Common Future*, ed. K. L. Kiessling and H. Landberg. Oxford: Oxford University Press, pp. 231–84.

Fogel, R. W. (2004) *The Escape from Hunger and Premature Death, 1700–2100: Europe, America, and the Third World.* Cambridge: Cambridge University Press.

Fogel, R. W., Engerman, S. L., Floud, R., *et al.* (1983) Secular changes in American and British stature and nutrition. *Journal of Interdisciplinary History*, **14**, 445–81.

Forbes, J. C. and Watson, R. D. (1992) *Plants in Agriculture*. Cambridge: Cambridge University Press.

Forbes, S. (2005) *A Natural History of Families*. Princeton, NJ: Princeton University Press.

Ford, K. and Huffman, S. (1993) Maternal nutrition, infant feeding, and post-partum amenorrhea: Recent evidence from Bangladesh. In *Biomedical and Demographic Determinants of Reproduction*, ed. R. Gray, H. Leridon and A. Spira. Oxford: Clarendon Press.

Foster, S. and Smout, T. C., eds. (1994) *A History of Soils and Field Systems*. Erskine: Scottish Historical Press.

Fourastié, J. (1959) De la vie traditionelle à la vie 'tertiaire': Recherches sur le calendrier demographique de l'homme moyen. *Population*, **14**, 417–32.

Fox, J. W. and Cumberland, K. B., eds. (1962) *Western Samoa: Land, Life and Agriculture in Tropical Polynesia*. Christchurch: Whitcombe and Tombs.

Fox, R. H. (1953) *A Study of Energy Expenditure of Africans Engaged in Various Activities, with Special Reference to Some Environmental and Physiological Factors which May Influence the Efficiency of their Work*. PhD dissertation, Department of Nutritional Science, University of London, London.

Franklin, S. H. (1969) *The European Peasantry: The Final Phase*. London: Methuen.

Freeman, J. D. (1955) *Iban Agriculture: A Report on the Shifting Cultivation of Hill Rice by the Iban of Sarawak*. London: HMSO.

Freeman, J. D. (1970) *Report on the Iban*. London: The Athlone Press.

Fricke, T. E. (1984) *Himalayan Households: Tamang Demography and Domestic Processes*. Ann Arbor, MI: UMI Research Press.

Friedrich, K.-H. (1968) Coffee-banana holdings at Bukoba: The reasons for stagnation at a higher level. In *Smallholder Farming and Smallholder Development in Tanzania*, ed. H. Ruthenberg. Munich: Weltforum-Verlag, pp. 175–212.

Fuchs, M., Lang, A. and Wagner, G. A. (2004) The history of Holocene soil erosion in the Philous Basin, NE Peloponnese, Greece, based on optical dating. *Holocene*, **14**, 334–45.

Fukui, H. (1993) *Food and Population in a Northeast Thai Village*. Honolulu: University of Hawaii Press.

Fussell, G. I. (1952) *The Farmer's Tools: The History of British Farm Implements and Machinery AD 1500–1900*. London: Orbis Books.

Gade, D. W. (1975) *Plants, Man and the Land in the Vilcota Valley of Peru*. The Hague: Dr. W. Junk B. V.

Gade, D. W. and Rios, R. (1974) Chaquitaclla: The native footplough and its persistence in central Andean agriculture. *Tools and Tillage*, **2**, 3–15.

Gage, T. B. (1993) The decline of mortality in England and Wales 1861 to 1964: Decomposition by cause of death and component of mortality. *Population Studies*, **47**, 47–66.

Galloway, J. A. and Murphy, M. (1991) Feeding the city: Medieval London and its agrarian hinterland. *The London Journal*, **16**, 3–14.

Ganskoop, D., Cruz, R. and Johnson, D. E. (2000) Least-effort pathways? A GIS analysis of livestock trails in rugged terrain. *Applied Animal Behaviour Science*, **68**, 179–90.

Gardner, D. (2001) Intensification, social production, and the inscrutable ways of culture. *Asia Pacific Viewpoint*, **42**, 193–207.

Gavin, W. (1951) The way to higher crop yields. *Journal of the Ministry of Agriculture*, **58**, 176–7.

Geddes, W. R. (1954) *The Land Dayaks of Sarawak*. London: HMSO.

Geddes, W. R. (1976) *Migrants of the Mountains: The Cultural Ecology of the Blue Miao (Hmong Njua) of Thailand*. Oxford: Clarendon Press.

Geertz, C. (1963) *Agricultural Involution: The Processes of Ecological Change in Indonesia*. Berkeley, CA: University of California Press.

Geiger, R. (1965) *The Climate near the Ground (revised edition)*. Cambridge, MA: Harvard University Press.

Georgescu-Roegen, N. (1970) The institutional aspects of peasant communities: An analytical view. In *Subsistence Agriculture and Economic Development*, ed. C. R. Wharton. Chicago: Aldine, pp. 61–93.

Gepts, P. (2004) Crop domestication as a long-term selection experiment. *Plant Breeding Reviews*, **24**, 1–44.

Gershwin, M. E., Nestel, P. and Keen, C. L., eds. (2004) *Handbook of Nutrition and Immunity*. Totowa, NJ: Humana Press.

Giardina, C. P., Sanford, R. L., Dockersmith, I. C. and Jaramillo, V. J. (2000) The effects of slash burning on ecosystem nutrients during the land preparation phase of shifting cultivation. *Plant Soil*, 220, 247–60.

Gibson, R. D. (2005) *Principles of Nutritional Assessment*, 2nd edn. Oxford: Oxford University Press.

Gilbert, G., ed. (2008) *Thomas Malthus's An Essay on the Principle of Population*. Oxford: Oxford University Press.

Gilg, J. P. (1970) Culture commercial et discipline agraire Dobadéné (Tchad). *Etudes Rurales*, 37–39, 173–97.

Gill, G. J. (1991) *Seasonality and Agriculture in the Developing World: A Problem of the Poor and Powerless*. Cambridge: Cambridge University Press.

Gladstone, B. P., Muliyil, J. P., Jaffar, S., *et al.* (2008) Infant morbidity in an Indian slum birth cohort. *Archives of Disease in Childhood*, 93, 479–84.

Gleave, M. B. (1996) The length of the fallow period in tropical fallow farming systems: A discussion with evidence from Sierra Leone. *The Geographical Journal*, 162, 14–24.

Gleave, M. B. and White, H. P. (1969) Population density and agricultural systems in West Africa. In *Environment and Land Use in Africa*, ed. M. F. Thomas and G. W. Whittington. London: Methuen, pp. 273–300.

Gliessman, S. R. (2007) *Agroecology: The Ecology of Sustainable Food Systems*, 2nd edn. Boca Raton, FL: CRC Press.

Godoy, R., O'Neill, K., Groff, S., *et al.* (1997) Household determinants of deforestation by Amerindians in Honduras. *World Development*, 25, 977–87.

Goland, C. (1993a) *Cultivating Diversity: Field Scattering as Agricultural Risk Management in Cuyo Cuyo, Department of Puno, Peru*. Production, Storage, and Exchange Research Project, Working Paper No. 4. Chapel Hill, NC: University of North Carolina.

Goland, C. (1993b) Field scattering as agricultural risk management: A case study from Cuyo Cuyo, Department of Puno, Peru. *Mountain Research and Development*, 13, 317–38.

Golson, J. (2007) Unraveling the story of early plant exploitation in highland Papua New Guinea. In *Rethinking Agriculture:*

Archaeological and Ethnoarchaeological Perspectives, ed. T. Denham, J. Iriarte and L. Vrydaghs. Walnut Creek, CA: Left Coast Press, pp. 109–25.

Gönner, C. (2002) *A Forest Tribe of Borneo: Resource Use among the Dayak Benuaq*. Nagar, Bali: D.K. Printworld.

Goodnight, C. J. and Stevens, L. (1997) Experimental studies of group selection: What do they tell us about group selection in nature? *The American Naturalist*, 150, S59–S79.

Goody, J., ed. (1958) *The Developmental Cycle in Domestic Groups*. Cambridge: Cambridge University Press.

Goody, J. (1972) The evolution of the family. In *Household and Family in Past Time*, ed. P. Laslett and R. Wall. Cambridge: Cambridge University Press, pp. 103–24.

Goody, J. (1976) *Production and Reproduction: A Comparative Study of the Domestic Domain*. Cambridge: Cambridge University Press.

Gourou, P. (1975) *Man and Land in the Far East*. London: Longman.

Gray, L. C. (2005) What kind of intensification? Agricultural practice, soil fertility and socioeconomic differentiation in rural Burkina Faso. *The Geographical Journal*, 171, 70–82.

Gray, R. F. (1963) *The Sonjo of Tanganyika: An Anthropological Study of an Irrigation-Based Society*. Oxford: Oxford University Press.

Gray, R. F. (1964) Introduction. In *The Family Estate in Africa*, ed. R. F. Gray and P. H. Gulliver. London: Routledge and Kegan Paul, pp. 1–33.

Grégoire, E. (1980) *Etude Socio-économique du Village de Gourjae (Départment de Maradi, Niger)*. Programme de Recherches sur la Région de Maradi. Bourdeaux: Université de Bourdeaux.

Griffiths, J. F. (1959) Bioclimatology and the meteorological services. In *Proceedings of the Symposium on Tropical Meteorology in Africa*. Nairobi: World Meteorological Organization, pp. 282–300.

Grigg, D. B. (1974) *The Agricultural Systems of the World: An Evolutionary Approach*. Cambridge: Cambridge University Press.

Grigg, D. B. (1979) Ester Boserup's theory of agrarian change: A critical review. *Progress in Human Geography*, 3, 64–84.

Grove, A. (1993) Water use by the Chagga on Kilimanjaro. *African Affairs*, **92**, 431–48.

Grove, A. T. and Klein, F. M. G. (1979) *Rural Africa*. Cambridge: Cambridge University Press.

Guillemin, R. (1956) Evolution de l'agriculture autochtone dans les savannes de l'Oubangui. *Agronomie Tropicale*, **11**, 143–76.

Guillet, D. (1981) Land tenure, ecological zone, and agricultural regime in the Central Andes. *American Ethnologist*, **8**, 139–58.

Gunasena, H. P. M., ed. (2001) *Food Security and Small Tank Systems in Sri Lanka*. Colombo: National Science Foundation of Sri Lanka.

Hack, J. T. (1942) *The Changing Physical Environment of the Hopi Indians of Arizona*. Cambridge, MA: Peabody Museum.

Hadley, C., Belachew, T., Lindstrom, D. and Tessema, F. (2011) The shape of things to come? Household dependency ratio and adolescent nutritional status in rural and urban Ethiopia. *American Journal of Physical Anthropology*, **144**, 643–52.

Hagen, E. H., Barrett, H. C. and Price, M. E. (2006) Do human parents face a quantity–quality tradeoff? Evidence from a Shuar community. *American Journal of Physical Anthropology*, **130**, 405–18.

Hajnal, J. (1965) European marriage patterns in perspective. In *Population in History: Essays in Historical Demography*, ed. D. V. Glass and D. E. C. Eversley. Chicago: Aldine, pp. 101–43.

Hajnal, J. (1982) Two kinds of preindustrial household formation system. *Population and Development Review*, **8**, 449–94.

Hall, A. D. (1905) *The Book of the Rothamsted Experiments*. London: John Murray.

Hall, A. D. (1909) *Fertilisers and Manures*. London: John Murray.

Hallam, H. E. (1957) *The Lincolnshire Fenland in the Early Middle Ages: A Social and Economic History*. PhD dissertation, Department of History, University of Nottingham, Nottingham, UK.

Halstead, P. (2014) *Two Oxen Ahead: Pre-Mechanized Farming in the Mediterranean*. Chichester, UK: Wiley-Blackwell.

Halstead, P. and O'Shea, J., eds. (1989) *Bad Year Economics: Cultural Responses to Risk and Uncertainty*. Cambridge: Cambridge University Press.

Hames, R. B. and Vickers, W. T., eds. (1983) *Adaptive Responses of Native Amazonians*. New York: Academic Press.

Hammel, E. A. (1984) On the *** of studying household form and function. In *Households: Comparative and Historical Studies of the Domestic Group*, ed. R. M. Netting, R. R. Wilk and E. J. Arnould. Berkeley, CA: University of California Press, pp. 29–43.

Hammel, E. A. (2005) Chayanov revisited: A model for the economics of complex kin units. *Proceedings of the National Academy of Sciences*, **102**, 7043–6.

Hammel, E. A. and Laslett, P. (1974) Comparing household structure over time and between cultures. *Comparative Studies in Society and History*, **16**, 73–109.

Handy, E. S. C. (1940) *The Hawaiian Planter, Volume I: His Plants, Methods and Areas of Cultivation*. Honolulu: Bernice P. Bishop Museum.

Hanks, L. M. (1972) *Rice and Man: Agricultural Ecology in Southeast Asia*. Chicago: Aldine-Atherton.

Hansen, H. O. (1975) *Population Census of 1729 in Three Counties*. Statistics of Iceland II, 59. Reykjavik: Iceland Statistical Bureau.

Hanson, R. (2000) *Long-term growth as a sequence of exponential models*. (http://hanson.gmu.edu/longgrow.html).

Hanus, H. and Schoop, P. (1989) Influence of nitrogen and fungicide on yield and yield variability in wheat and barley. In *Variability in Grain Yields*, ed. J. R. Anderson and P. B. R. Hazell. Baltimore: Johns Hopkins University Press, pp. 265–9.

Haraldsson, H. V. and Olafsdottir, R. (2006) A novel modeling approach for evaluating the preindustrial natural carrying capacity of human population in Iceland. *Science of the Total Environment*, **372**, 109–19.

Hardin, G. (1968) The tragedy of the commons. *Science*, **162**, 1243–8.

Hardin, G. (1998) The feast of Malthus: Living within limits. *The Social Contract*, Spring, 181–7.

Harding, T. G. (1985) *Kunai Men: Horticultural Systems of a Papua New Guinea Society*. Berkeley, CA: University of California Press.

Hardjono, J. (1987) *Land, Labour and Livelihood in a West Java Village*. Yogyakarta, Indonesia: Gadjah Mada University Press.

Hareven, T. K. (1974) The family process: The historical study of the family cycle. *Journal of Social History*, **7**, 322–9.

Harlan, J. R. (1992) *Crops and Man*, 2nd edn. Madison, WI: American Society of Agronomy, Crop Science Society of America.

Harlan, J. R. (1995) *The Living Fields: Our Agricultural Heritage.* Cambridge: Cambridge University Press.

Harlan, J. R. and Pasquereau, J. (1969) Décrue agriculture in Mali. *Economic Botany*, **23**, 70–4.

Harris, D. R. (1971) The ecology of swidden cultivation in the Upper Orinoco rain forest, Venezuela. *Geographical Review*, **61**, 475–95.

Harris, D. R. (1972) The origin of agriculture in the tropics. *The American Scientist*, **60**, 180–93.

Harris, F. (1999) Nutrient management strategies of small-holder farmers in a short-fallow farming system in north-east Nigerian. *The Geographical Journal*, **165**, 275–85.

Harrison, M. (1975) Chayanov and the economics of the Russian peasantry. *Journal of Peasant Studies*, **2**, 389–417.

Harrison, M. (1977) The peasant mode of production in the work of A. V. Chayanov. *Journal of Peasant Studies*, **4**, 323–36.

Hassall, M. and Beauroy, J., eds. (1993) *Land and Landscape in Norfolk 1250-1350.* Oxford: Oxford University Press.

Haswell, M. R. (1953) *Economics of Agriculture in a Savannah Village.* London: HMSO.

Haswell, M. R. (1963) *The Changing Pattern of Economic Activity in a Gambia Village.* London: HMSO.

Haswell, M. R. (1967) *Economics of Development in Village India.* London: Routledge and Kegan Paul.

Haswell, M. R. (1973) *Tropical Farming Economics.* London: Longman.

Haswell, M. R. (1985) *Energy for Subsistence*, 2nd edn. London: Macmillan.

Haswell, M. R. and Hunt, D., eds. (1991) *Rural Households in Emerging Economies: Technology and Change in Sub-Saharan Africa.* Providence, RI: Berg.

Hatch, J. K. (1974) *The Corn Farmers of Motupe: A Study of Traditional Farming Practices in Northern Coastal Peru.* Madison, WI: Land Tenure Center, University of Wisconsin.

Hatcher, J. (1977) *Plague, Population and the English Economy 1348-1530.* Basingstoke: Macmillan.

Hatcher, J. and Bailey, M. (2001) *Modelling the Middle Ages: The History and Theory of England's Economic Development.* Oxford: Oxford University Press.

Hawkes, K., O'Connell, J. F., Blurton-Jones, N. G., Alvarez, H. P. and Charnov, E. L. (1998) Grandmothering, menopause, and the evolution of human life histories. *Proceedings of the National Academy of Sciences*, **95**, 1336–9.

Hay, R. K. M. and Porter, J. R. (2006) *The Physiology of Crop Yield*, 2nd edn. Oxford: Blackwell.

Hayami, Y. (1978) *Anatomy of a Peasant Economy: A Rice Village in the Philippines.* Manila: International Rice Research Institute.

Hazlett, W. (1807) *A Reply to the Essay on Population by the Rev. T. R. Malthus.* London: Longman, Hurst, Rees and Orme.

Heady, E. O. and Dillon, J. L. (1961) *Agricultural Production Functions.* Ames, IA: Iowa State University Press.

Healey, C. (1990) *Maring Hunters and Traders: Production and Exchange in the Papua New Guinea Highlands.* Berkeley, CA: University of California Press.

Heglund, N. C., Willems, P. A., Penta, M. and Cavagna, G. A. (1995) Energy-saving gait mechanics with head-supported loads. *Nature*, **375**, 52–4.

Hegmon, M. (1989) Risk reduction and variation in agricultural economies: A computer simulation of Hopi agriculture. *Research in Economic Anthropology*, **11**, 89–121.

Heine, K. (2003) Paleopedological evidence of human-induced environmental change in the Puebla-Tlaxcala area (Mexico) during the last 3,500 years. *Revista Mexicana de Ciencias Geológicas*, **20**, 235–44.

Hendry, J. B. (1964) *The Small World of Khanh Hau.* Chicago: Aldine.

Herlihy, D. and Klapisch-Zuber, C. (1978) *Les Toscans et leurs Familles: Une Étude du Castato Florentin de 1427.* Paris: Presses de la Fondation national des Sciences Politiques.

Heron, R. (1794) *General View of the Natural Circumstances of the Isles adjacent to the North West Coast of Scotland which are distinguished by the Common Name of Hebudae or Hebrides.* Great Britain Board of Agriculture. Edinburgh: John Paterson.

Herring, R. J. (1984) Chayanovian versus neoclassical perspectives on land tenure and productivity interactions. In Durrenberger, E. P. (ed.), *Chayanov, Peasants, and Economic Anthropology.* Academic Press, New York, pp. 133–49.

Heston, A. and Kumar, D. (1983) The persistence of land fragmentation in peasant agriculture: An analysis of South Asian cases. *Explorations in Economic History,* **20**, 199–220.

Hewlett, B., van de Koppel, J. and van de Koppel, M. (1986) Causes of death among Aka pygmies of the Central African Republic. In *African Pygmies,* ed. L. L. Cavalli-Sforza. New York: Academic Press, pp. 45–63.

Heywood, P. (1982) The functional significance of malnutrition – growth and prospective risk of death in the highlands of Papua New Guinea. *Journal of Food and Nutrition,* **39**, 13–19.

Hickey, G. C. (1964) *Village in Vietnam.* New Haven, CT: Yale University Press.

Hildebrand, E. A. (2007) A tale of two tuber crops: How attributes of ensete and yams may have shaped prehistoric human–plant interactions in southwest Ethiopia. In *Rethinking Agriculture: Archaeological and Ethnoarchaeological Perspectives,* ed. T. Denham, J. Iriarte and L. Vrydaghs. Walnut Creek, CA: Left Coast Press, pp. 273–98.

Hill, D. J. (1977) The role of *Anabaena* in the *Azolla-Anabaena* symbiosis. *New Phytologist,* **78**, 611–16.

Hill, P. (1972) *Rural Hausa: A Village and a Setting.* Cambridge: Cambridge University Press.

Hill, P. (1977) *Population, Prosperity and Poverty: Rural Kano 1900 and 1970.* Cambridge: Cambridge University Press.

Hill, P. (1982) *Dry Grain Farming Families: Hausaland (Nigeria) and Karnataka (India) Compared.* Cambridge: Cambridge University Press.

Hill, R. W., Wyse, G. A. and Anderson, M. (2008) *Animal Physiology,* 2nd edn. Sunderland, MA: Sinauer Associates.

Hinde, P. R. A. (1998) *Demographic Methods.* London: Hodder and Arnold.

Hindle, P. (2002) *Medieval Roads and Tracks.* Princes Risborough: Shire Archaeology.

Ho, R. (1967) *Farmers of Central Malaya.* Canberra: Australian National University Press.

Hobcraft, J. (1985) Comments from a demographer. In *Maternal Nutrition and Lactational Infertility,* ed. J. Dobbing. New York: Raven Press, pp. 129–37.

Hoffpauir, R. (1978) Subsistence strategy and its ecological consequences in the Nepal Himalaya. *Anthropos,* **73**, 215–52.

Höhn, C. (1987) The family life cycle: Needed extensions of the concept. In *Family Demography: Methods and their Applications,* ed. J. Bongaarts, T. K. Burch, and K. W. Wachter. Oxford: Oxford University Press, pp. 65–80.

Holm, L. G., Plucknett, D. L., Pancho, J. V. and Herberger, J. P. (1991) *The World's Worst Weeds: Distribution and Biology.* Malabar, FL: Krieger Publishing.

Holman, D. J. (1996) *Total Fecundability and Pregnancy Loss in Rural Bangladesh.* PhD dissertation, Department of Anthropology and Population Research Institute, Pennsylvania State University, University Park, PA.

Holman, D. J. and Grimes, M. A. (2001) Colostrum feeding behaviour and initiation of breast-feeding in rural Bangladesh. *Journal of Biosocial Science,* **33**, 139–54.

Holt, J. and Lawrence, M. (1993) *Making Ends Meet: A Survey of the Food Economy of the Ethiopian North-East Highlands.* London: Save the Children UK.

Homans, G. C. (1942) *English Villagers of the Thirteenth Century.* Cambridge, MA: Harvard University Press.

Hommel, R. P. (1937) *China at Work: An Illustrated Record of the Primitive Industries of China's Masses, whose Life is Toil, and thus an Account of Chinese Civilization.* New York: The John Day Company.

Hone, J. and Sibly, R. M. (2003) Demographic, mechanistic and density-dependent determinants of population growth rate: A case study in an avian predator. In *Wildlife Population Growth Rates,* ed. R. M. Sibly, J. Hone and T. H. Clutton-Brock. Cambridge: Cambridge University Press, pp. 41-54.

Howatson, W. (1984) Grain harvesting and harvesters. In *Farm Servants and Labour in*

Lowland Scotland, 1770–1910, ed. T. M. Devine. Edinburgh: John Donald, pp. 124–42.

Howell, N. (1979) *Demography of the Dobe !Kung*. New York: Academic Press.

Hudson, N. (1992) *Land Husbandry*. Ithaca, NY: Cornell University Press.

Huffman, S. L., Chowdhury, A. K. M. A, Chakraborty, J. and Simpson, N. K. (1980) Breastfeeding patterns in rural Bangladesh. *American Journal of Clinical Nutrition*, 33, 144–54.

Huffnagel, H. P. (1961) *Agriculture in Ethiopia*. Rome: Food and Agriculture Organization of the United Nations.

Hughes, P. J., Sullivan, M. E. and Yok, D. (1991) Human induced erosion in a highlands catchment in Papua New Guinea: The prehistoric and contemporary records. *Zeitschrift für Geomorphologie*, 83, 227–39.

Hugo, G. J. (1984) The demographic impact of famine: A review. In *Famine as a Geographical Phenomenon*, ed. B. Currey and G. J. Hugo. Dordrecht: Reidel, pp. 7–31.

Hunt, D. (1978) Chayanov's model of peasant household resource allocation and its relevance to Mbere division, Eastern Kenya. *Journal of Development Studies*, 15, 59–86.

Hunt, D. (1979) Chayanov's model of peasant household resource allocation. *Journal of Peasant Studies*, 6, 247–85.

Hunt, R. C. (1988) Size and the structure of authority in canal irrigation systems. *Journal of Anthropological Archaeology*, 44, 335–55.

Hunt, R. C. (2000) Labor productivity and agricultural development: Boserup revisited. *Human Ecology*, 28, 251–77.

Hunt, R. D. (1987) *Indian Agriculture in America: Prehistory to Present*. Lawrence, KA: University Press of Kansas.

Hunter, P. (1997) *Waterborne Disease: Epidemiology and Ecology*. New York: Wiley-Blackwell.

Hutchinson, G. E. (1978) *An Introduction to Population Ecology*. New Haven, CT: Yale University Press.

Igbozurike, M. U. (1970) Fragmentation in tropical agriculture: An overrated phenomenon. *The Professional Geographer*, 22, 321–5.

Ingram, S. E. and Hunt, R. C., eds. (2015) *Traditional Arid Lands Agriculture:*

Understanding the Past for the Future. Tucson: University of Arizona Press.

Imminck, M. D. C. (1990) Measuring food production and consumption, and the nutritional effects of tropical home gardens. In *Tropical Home Gardens*, ed. K. Landauer and M. Brazil. Tokyo: United Nations University Press, pp. 126–37.

Innis, D. Q. (1997) *Intercropping and the Scientific Basis of Traditional Agriculture*. London: Intermediate Technology Publications.

Izikowitz, K. G. (1951) *Lamet: Hill Peasants in French Indochina*. Gothenberg: Ethnographic Museum.

Jackson, A. A. and Calder, P. C. (2004) Severe undernutrition and immunity. In *Handbook of Nutrition and Immunity*, ed. M. E. Gershwin, P. Nestel and C. L. Keen. Totowa, NJ: Humana Press, pp. 71–92.

Jackson, I. J. (1989) *Climate, Water and Agriculture in the Tropics*, 2nd edn. London: Longman.

Jacquard, A. (1974) *The Genetic Structure of Populations*. Berlin: Springer-Verlag.

James, P., ed. (1989) T.R. Malthus's *An Essay on the Principle of Population; or A View to its Past and Present Effects on Human Happiness; With an Inquiry into our Prospects Respecting the future Removal or Mitigation of the Evils which it Occasions (edition of 1803 with the variora of 1806, 1807, 1817 and 1826; two volumes)*. Cambridge: Cambridge University Press.

James, W. P. T. and Schofield, E. C. (1990) *Human Energy Requirements: A Manual for Planners and Nutritionists*. Oxford: Oxford University Press.

Janlekha, K. (1955) *A Study of the Economy of a Rice Growing Village in Central Thailand*. Bangkok: Ministry of Agriculture, Division of Agricultural Economics.

Jasny, N. (1972) *Soviet Economists of the Twenties: Names to be Remembered*. Cambridge: Cambridge University Press.

Jelliffe, D. B. (1966) *The Assessment of the Nutritional Status of the Community (with Special Reference to Field Surveys in Developing Regions of the World)*. Geneva: World Health Organization.

Jennings, J. A. (2010) *Household Structure, Dynamics, and Economy in a Preindustrial*

Farming Population: The North Orkney Islands, 1851–1901. PhD dissertation, Department of Anthropology and Population Research Institute, Pennsylvania State University, University Park, PA.

Jennings, J. A., Wood, J. W. and Johnson, P. L. (2011) Household-level predictors of the presence of servants in Northern Orkney, Scotland, 1851–1901. *History of the Family*, 16, 278–91.

Jensen, M., Michelsen, A. and Menassie, G. (2001) Responses in plant, soil inorganic and microbial nutrient pools to experimental fire, ash and biomass addition in a woodland savanna. *Oecologia*, 128, 85–93.

Johansen, H. C. (1975) *Befolkningsudvikling og Familiestruktur i det 18 Arhundrede*. Odense, Denmark: Odense University Press.

John, A. M. (1993) Statistical evidence of links between maternal nutrition and post-partum infertility. In *Biomedical and Demographic Determinants of Reproduction*, ed. R. Gray, H. Leridon and A. Spira. Oxford: Oxford University Press, pp. 372–82.

John, A. M., Menken, J. A. and Chowdhury, M. A. (1987) The effects of breastfeeding and nutrition on fecundability in rural Bangladesh: A hazards-model analysis. *Population Studies*, 41, 433–46.

Johnson, A. W. (1972) Individuality and experimentation in traditional agriculture. *Human Ecology*, 1, 149–59.

Johnson, A. W. (1974a) "Carrying capacity" in Machiguenga ecology: Theory and practice. Paper presented at the 73rd annual meeting of the American Anthropological Association.

Johnson, A. W. (1974b) Ethnoecology and planting practices in a swidden agricultural system. *American Ethnologist*, 1, 87–101.

Johnson, A. W. (1983) Machiguenga gardens. In *Adaptive Responses of Native Amazonians*, ed. R. B. Hames and W. T. Vickers. New York: Academic Press, pp. 29–63.

Johnson, A. W. (1989) How the Machiguenga manage resources: Conservation or exploitation of nature? In *Resource Management in Amazonia: Indigenous and Folk Strategies*, ed. D. A. Posey and W. Balée. New York: New York Botanical Garden, pp. 213–22.

Johnson, A. W. (2003) *Families of the Forest: The Matsigenka Indians of the Peruvian Amazon*. Berkeley, CA: University of California Press.

Johnson, A. W. and Behrens, C. A. (1982) Nutritional criteria in Machiguenga food production decisions: A linear-programming approach. *Human Ecology*, 10, 167–89.

Johnson, C. T. (1903) *Egyptian Irrigation: A Study of Irrigation Methods and Administration in Egypt*. US Department of Agriculture, Office of Experimental Stations, Bulletin No. 130. Washington: Government Printing Office.

Johnston, B. F. (1958) *The Staple Food Economies of Western Tropical Africa*. Stanford, CA: Stanford University Press.

Judd, L. C. (1961) *Chao Rai Thai: Dry Rice Farmers in Northern Thailand*. Bangkok: Suriyaban Publishers.

Kabir, M. (1980) *The Demographic Characteristics of Household Populations*. World Fertility Survey Comparative Studies, no. 6. The Hague: International Statistical Institute.

Kahneman, D. (2003) Maps of bounded rationality: Psychology for behavioral economics. *American Economic Review*, 93, 1449–75.

Kaihura, F. and Stocking, M., eds. (2003) *Agricultural Biodiversity in Smallholder Farms of East Africa*. Tokyo: United Nations University Press.

Kallan, J. E. and Enneking, E. A. (1992) Seasonal patterns of spontaneous abortion. *Journal of Biosocial Sciences*, 24, 71–5.

Kalter, H. D., Gray, R. H., Black, R. E. and Gultiano, S. A. (1990) Validation of postmortem interviews to ascertain selected causes of death in children. *International Journal of Epidemiology*, 19, 380–6.

Kampen, J. (1974) *Soil and Water Conservation and Management in Farming Systems Research for the Semi-Arid Tropics*. Hyderabad: ICRISAT.

Kanitkar, N. V. (1944) *Dry Farming in India*. New Delhi: Indian Council of Agricultural Research.

Kaplan, D. (2000) The darker side of the "original affluent society". *Journal of Anthropological Research*, 56, 301–24.

Kaplan, H. (1994) Evolutionary and wealth flow theories in fertility: Empirical tests and new models. *Population and Development Review*, 20, 753–91.

Kaplan, H. (1996) A theory of fertility and parental investment in traditional and modern human societies. *Yearbook of Physical Anthropology*, 39, 91–135.

Karasov, W. H. and Martínez del Rio, C. (2007) *Physiological Ecology: How Animals Process Energy, Nutrients, and Toxins*. Princeton, NJ: Princeton University Press.

Kates, R. W., Hyden, G. and Turner, B. L. (1993) Theory, evidence, study design. In *Population Growth and Agricultural Change in Africa*, ed. B. L. Turner, G. Hyden and R. W. Kates. Gainesville, FL: University Press of Florida, pp. 1–40.

Kawaguchi, K. and Kyuma, K. (1977) *Paddy Soils in Tropical Asia: Their Material Nature and Fertility*. Honolulu: University Press of Hawaii.

Kay, G. (1964) *Chief Kalaba's Village: A Preliminary Survey of Economic Life in an Ushi Village, Northern Rhodesia*. Manchester: Manchester University Press.

Keeley, L. H. (1996) *War before Civilization*. New York: Oxford University Press.

Keen, C. L., Uriu-Adams, J. Y., Emsimsa, K. and Gershwin, M. E. (2004) Trace elements/minerals and immunity. In *Handbook of Nutrition and Immunity*, ed. M. E. Gershwin, P. Nestel and C. L. Keen. Totowa, NJ: Humana Press, pp. 117–40.

Keilman, N. (1995) Household concepts and household definitions in western Europe: Different levels but similar trends in household developments. In *Household Demography and Household Modeling*, ed. E. van Imhoff, A. Kuijsten, P. Hooimeijer and L. van Wissen. New York: Plenum Press, pp, 111–35.

Kendal, J. R., Tehrani, J. J. and Odling-Smee, J., eds. (2011) *Human Niche Construction*. Special issue of *Philosophical Transactions of the Royal Society, Series B (Biological Sciences)*, 366, 784–934.

Kende, H., van der Knaap, E. and Cho, H.-T. (1998) Deepwater rice: A model plant to study stem elongation. *Plant Physiology*, 118, 1105–10.

Kennett, D. J. and Winterhalder, B. (2006) *Behavioral Ecology and the Transition to Agriculture*. Berkeley, CA: University of California Press.

Kerblay, B. (1966) A. V. Chayanov: Life, career, works. In *A. V. Chayanov on the Theory of Peasant Economy*, ed. D. Thorner, B. Kerblay and R. E. F. Smith. Madison, WI: University of Wisconsin Press, pp. xxv–lxxv.

Kertzer, D. I. (1986) A life course approach to coresidence. In *Family Relations in Life Course Perspective*, ed. D. I. Kertzer. Greenwich, CT: JAI, pp. 1–22.

Kertzer, D. I. (1991) Household history and sociological theory. *Annual Review of Sociology*, 17, 155–79.

Kertzer, D. I. and Hogan, D. P. (1991) Reflections on the European marriage pattern: Sharecropping and proletarianization in Casalecchio, Italy, 1861–1921. *Journal of Family History*, 16, 31–45.

Kessler, J. J. (1994) Usefulness of the human carrying capacity concept in assessing environmental sustainability of land-use in semi-arid regions. *Agriculture, Ecosystems and Environment*, 48, 273–84.

Keusch, G. T. (1998) Nutrition and immunity: From A to Z. *Nutrition Reviews*, 56, S3–S4.

Keyfitz, N. (1975) How do we know the facts of demography? *Population and Development Review*, 1, 267–88.

Keyfitz, N. and Flieger, W (1968) *World Population: An Analysis of Vital Data*. Chicago: University of Chicago Press.

Keyfitz, N. and Flieger, W. (1990) *World Population Growth and Aging: Demographic Trends in the Late Twentieth Century*. Chicago: University of Chicago Press.

Keys, A., Brožek, J., Henschel, A., Mickelsen, O. and Taylor, H. L. (1950) *The Biology of Human Starvation (two volumes)*. Minneapolis: University of Minnesota Press.

King, F. H. (1911) *Farmers of Forty Centuries, or Permanent Agriculture in China, Korea and Japan*. Madison, WI: Democrat Press.

King, G. (1869) Famine foods of Marwar. *Proceedings of the Asia Society of Bengal*, 38, 116–22.

King, R. and Burton, S. (1982) Land fragmentation: Notes on a fundamental rural spatial problem. *Progress in Human Geography*, 6, 475–94.

Kirch, P. V. (1994) *The Wet and the Dry: Irrigation and Agricultural Intensification in Polynesia*. Chicago: University of Chicago Press.

Klapisch, C. (1972) Household and family in Tuscany in 1427. In *Household and Family in Past Time*, ed. P. Laslett. Cambridge: Cambridge University Press, pp. 267–82.

Klapisch, C. and Demonet, M. (1972) 'A une vino e uno pane': La famille rurale toscane au début du XVe siècle. *Annales Economies, Sociétés, Civilisations*, **27**, 873–901.

Komatsu, Y., Tsunekawa, A. and Ju, H. (2005) Evaluation of sustainability based on human carrying capacity in drylands: A case study in rural villages in Inner Mongolia, China. *Agriculture, Ecosystems and the Environment*, **108**, 29–43.

Kosminsky, E. A. (1956) *Studies in the Agrarian History of England in the Thirteenth Century*, trans. R. Kisch, ed. R. H. Hilton. Oxford: Oxford University Press.

Kowal, J. M. and Kassam, A. H. (1978) *Agricultural Ecology of Savanna: A Study of East Africa*. Oxford: Clarendon Press.

Kramer, F. L. (1966) *Breaking Ground: Notes on the Distributions of Some Simple Tillage Tools*. Sacramento, CA: Sacramento State College.

Kramer, K. L. (1998) *Variation in Children's Work among Modern Maya Subsistence Agriculturalists*. PhD dissertation, Department of Anthropology, University of New Mexico, Albuquerque, NM.

Kramer, K. L. (2005) *Maya Children: Helpers at the Farm*. Cambridge, MA: Harvard University Press.

Kramer, K. L. and Boone, J. L. (2002) Why intensive agriculturalists have higher fertility: A household energy budget approach. *Current Anthropology*, **43**, 511–17.

Krausmann, F. (2004) Milk, manure, and muscle power: Livestock and the transformation of preindustrial agriculture in central Europe. *Human Ecology*, **32**, 735–72.

Krishna, R. (1969) Models of the family farm. In *Subsistence Agriculture and Economic Development*, ed. C. R. Wharton. Chicago: Aldine, pp. 185–90.

Kuchiba, M., Tsubouchi, Y. and Maeda, N., eds. (1979) *Three Malay Villages: A Sociology of Paddy Growers in West Malaysia*. Honolulu: University Press of Hawaii.

Kumar, S. K. (1988) Effect of seasonal food shortage on agricultural production in Zambia. *World Development*, **16**, 1051–63.

Kunstadter, P. (1974) Footnotes on implications of aggregated data used in population simulation. In *Computer Simulation in Human Population Studies*, ed. B. Dyke and J. W. MacCluer. New York: Academic Press, pp. 435–46.

Kunstadter, P., Chapman, E. C. and Sabhasri, S., eds. (1978) *Farmers in the Forest: Economic Development and Marginal Agriculture in Northern Thailand*. Honolulu: University Press of Hawaii.

Kussmaul, A. (1981) *Servants in Husbandry in Early Modern Europe*. Cambridge: Cambridge University Press.

Lafitau, S. F. (1724) *Moeurs des Sauvages Ameriquains, Comparées aux Moeurs des Premiers Temps*. Paris: Saugrain et Hochereau.

Lagemann, J. (1977) *Traditional African Farming Systems in Eastern Nigeria: An Analysis of Reaction to Increasing Population Pressure*. Munich: Weltforum Verlag.

Lam, D. A. and Miron, J. A. (1991) Seasonality of births in human populations. *Social Biology*, **38**, 51–78.

Lam, D. A. and Miron, J. A. (1994) Global patterns of seasonal variation in human fertility. *Annals of the New York Academy of Sciences*, **709**, 9–28.

Lam, D. A. and Miron, J. A. (1996) The effect of temperature on human fertility. *Demography*, **33**, 291–306.

Lam, D. A., Miron, J. A. and Riley, A. (1994) Modeling seasonality in fecundability, conceptions, and births. *Demography*, **31**, 321–46.

Lambert, D. H. (1985) *Swamp Rice Farming: The Indigenous Pahang Malay Agricultural System*. Boulder, CO: Westview.

Lamont, S. R., Eshbaugh, W. H. and Greenberg, A. M. (1999) Species composition, diversity, and use of home gardens among three Amazonian villages. *Economic Botany*, **53**, 312–26.

Landauer, K. and Brazil, M., eds. (1990) *Tropical Home Gardens*. Tokyo: United Nations University Press.

Lande, R., Engen, S., Sæther, B.-E., *et al.* (2002) Estimating density dependence from population time series using demographic theory and life history data. *The American Naturalist*, **159**, 321–37.

Lang, A. (2003) Phases of soil erosion-derived colluviation in the loess hills of southern Germany. *Catena*, **51**, 29–31.

Langdon, J. (1986) *Horses, Oxen and Technological Innovation: The Use of Draught Animals in English Farming from 1066–1500*. Cambridge: Cambridge University Press.

Langer, R. H. M. and Hill, G. D. (1991) *Agricultural Plants*, 2nd edn. Cambridge: Cambridge University Press.

Larcher, W. (2003) *Physiological Plant Ecology*, 4th edn. Berlin: Springer-Verlag.

Larsen, C. S. (1999) *Bioarchaeology: Interpreting Behavior from the Human Skeleton.* Cambridge: Cambridge University Press.

Larsson, A. and Larsson, V. (1984) *Traditional Tswana Housing: A Study of Four Villages in Eastern Botswana.* Stockholm: Swedish Council for Building Research.

Laslett, P. (1969) Size and structure of the household in England over three centuries. *Population Studies*, **23**, 199–223.

Laslett, P. (1972) Introduction: The history of the family. In *Household and Family in Past Time*, ed. P. Laslett and R. Wall. Cambridge: Cambridge University Press, pp. 1–89.

Laslett, P. (1977) *Family Life and Illicit Love in Earlier Generations.* Cambridge: Cambridge University Press.

Laslett, P. (1983) Family and household as work group and kin group: Areas of traditional Europe compared. In *Family Forms in Historic Europe*, ed. R. Wall, J. Robin and P. Laslett. Cambridge: Cambridge University Press, pp. 513–63.

Laslett, P. (1984) The family as a knot of individual interests. In *Households: Comparative and Historical Studies of the Domestic Group*, ed. R. M. Netting, R. R. Wilk and E. J. Arnould. Berkeley, CA: University of California Press, pp. 353–79.

Laslett, P. (1987) The institution of service. *Local Population Studies*, **40**, 55–60.

Laslett, P. (1988) Family, kinship and collectivity as systems of support in pre-industrial Europe: A consideration of the 'nuclear-hardship hypothesis'. *Continuity and Change*, **3**, 153–75.

Laslett, P. (2004) *The World We Have Lost: Further Explored*, 4th edn. London: Routledge.

Laslett, P., Oosterveen, K. and Smith, R. M., eds. (1980) *Bastardy and Its Comparative History: Studies in the History of Illegitimacy and Marital Non-conformism in Britain, France, Germany, Sweden, North America, Jamaica and Japan.* Cambridge, MA: Harvard University Press.

Laurie, W. and Trant, H. (1952) Dietary survey Ukara. *East African Medical Survey Annual Report, 1951.* Nairobi: Colonial Office of Health.

Lawrence, D. and Schlesinger, W. H. (2001) Changes in soil phosphorus during 200 years of shifting cultivation in Indonesia. *Ecology*, **82**, 2769–80.

Lawrence, M., Lawrence, F., Cole, T. J., *et al.* (1989) Seasonal pattern of activity and its nutritional consequence in Gambia. In *Seasonal Variability in Third World Agriculture: The Consequences for Food Security*, ed. D. E. Sahn. Baltimore: Johns Hopkins University Press, pp. 47–56.

Lawton, J. H. (1973) The energy cost of "food-gathering". In *Resources and Population*, ed. B. Benjamin, P. R. Cox and J. Peel. London: Academic Press, pp. 59–76.

Le Roy Ladurie, E. (1976) *The Peasants of Languedoc.* Urbana, IL: University of Illinois Press.

Leach, E. R. (1968) *Pul Eliya, A Village in Ceylon: A Study of Land Tenure and Kinship.* Cambridge: Cambridge University Press.

Lee, C. T., Tuljapurkar, S. and Vitousek, P. M. (2006) Risky business: Temporal and spatial variation in preindustrial dryland agriculture. *Human Ecology*, **34**, 739–63.

Lee, J. Z. and Campbell, C. D. (2005) Living standards in Liaoning, 1749–1909: Evidence from demographic outcomes. In *Living Standards in the Past: New Perspectives on Well-Being in Asia and Europe*, ed. R. C. Allen, T. Bengtsson and M. Dribe. Oxford: Oxford University Press, pp. 403–25.

Lee, R. D. (1974) The formal dynamics of controlled populations and the echo, the boom, and the bust. *Demography*, **11**, 563–85.

Lee, R. D. (1986) Malthus and Boserup: A dynamic synthesis. In *The State of Population Theory: Forward from Malthus*, ed. D. Coleman and R. S. Schofield. Oxford: Blackwell, pp. 96–130.

Lee, R. D. (1987) Population dynamics of humans and other animals. *Demography*, **24**, 443–65.

Lee, R. D. (1988) Induced population growth and induced population progress: Their interaction in the accelerating stage. *Mathematical Population Studies*, **1**, 265–88.

Lee, R. D. (1994) Fertility, mortality and intergenerational transfers: Comparisons across steady states. In *The Family, the Market and the State in Ageing Societies*, ed. J. Ermisch and N. Ogawa. Oxford: Oxford University Press, pp. 135–57.

Lee, R. D. and Kramer, K. L. (2002) Children's economic roles in the Maya family life cycle: Cain, Caldwell, and Chayanov revisited. *Population and Development Review*, 28, 475–99.

Lehmann, J., Kern, D. C., Glaser, B. and Woods, W. I. (2004) *Amazonian Dark Earths: Origins, Properties, Management*. Berlin: Springer.

Leibenstein, H. (1957) The theory of underemployment in backward economies. *Journal of Political Economy*, 65, 91–103.

Lele, U. and Stone, S. W. (1987) *Population Pressure, the Environment, and Agricultural Intensification: Variations on the Boserup Hypothesis – Managing Agricultural Development in Africa*. Washington: The World Bank.

Lerche, G. (1994) *Plowing Implements and Tillage Practices in Denmark from the Viking Period to about 1800 – Experimentally Substantiated*. Herning, Denmark: Poul Kristensen.

Levine, D. (2001) *At the Dawn of Modernity: Biology, Culture, and Material Life in Europe after the Year 1000*. Berkeley, CA: University of California Press.

Levine, R. J., Bordson, B. L., Mathew, R. M., *et al.* (1988) Deterioration of semen quality during summer in New Orleans. *Fertility and Sterility*, 49, 900–7.

Lewis, H. T. (1971) *Ilocano Rice Farmers: A Comparative Study of Two Philippine Barrios*. Honolulu: University Press of Hawaii.

Lewis, J. V. D. (1981) Domestic labor intensity and the incorporation of Malian peasant farms into localized descent groups. *American Ethnologist*, 8, 53–73.

Littlejohn, G. (1977) Peasant economy and society. In *Sociological Theories of the Economy*, ed. B. Hindess. London: Macmillan, pp. 118–56.

Lockett, C. T., Calvert, C. C. and Grivetti, L. E. (2000) Energy and micronutrient composition of dietary and medicinal wild plants consumed during drought: Study of rural Fulani, Northeastern Nigeria. *International Journal of Food Sciences and Nutrition*, 51, 195–208.

Lockwood, M. (1998) *Fertility and Household Labour in Tanzania: Demography, Economy, and Society in Rufiji District, c. 1870–1986*. Oxford: Oxford University Press.

Loiske, V.-M. (2004) Institutionalized exchange as a driving force in intensive agriculture: An Iraqw case study. In *Islands of Intensive Agriculture in Eastern Africa*, ed. M. Widgren and J. E. G. Sutton. Oxford: James Currey, pp. 105–13.

Longhurst, R. (1984) *The Energy Trap: Work, Nutrition and Child Malnutrition in Northern Nigeria*. Ithaca, NY: Program in International Nutrition, Cornell University.

Lopez-Gonzaga, V. (1983) *Peasants in the Hills: A Study of the Dynamics of Social Change among the Buhid Swidden Cultivators in the Philippines*. Quezon: University of the Philippines Press.

Lozada, M., Lado, A. and Weigandt, M. (2006) Cultural transmission of ethnobotanical knowledge in a rural community of northwestern Patagonia, Argentina. *Economic Botany*, 60, 374–85.

Ludwig, H.-D. (1968) Permanent farming on Ukara: The impact of land shortage on husbandry practices. In *Smallholder Farming and Smallholder Development in Tanzania: Ten Case Studies*, ed. H. Ruthenberg. Munich: Weltforum Verlag, pp. 87–135.

Lumpkin, T. A. and Plucknett, D. L. (1980) *Azolla*: Botany, physiology, and use as a green manure. *Economic Botany*, 34, 111–53.

Lunn, P. G. (1991) Nutrition, immunity and infection. In *The Decline of Mortality in Europe*, ed. R. S. Schofield, D. Reher and A. Bideau. Oxford: Oxford University Press, pp. 131–45.

Lutzenheiser, L. and Hackett, B. (1993) Social stratification and environmental destruction: Understanding household CO_2 production. *Social Problems*, 40, 50–73.

Lyimo, M. H., Nyagwegwe, S. and Mnkeni, A. P. (1991) Investigations on the effect of traditional food processing, preservation and storage methods on vegetable nutrients: A case study in Tanzania. *Plant Foods for Human Nutrition*, 41, 53–7.

MacDonald, R. B. and Hall, F. G. (1980) Global crop forecasting. *Science*, 208, 670–8.

Macfarlane, A. (1976) *Population and Resources: A Study of the Gurungs of Nepal*. Cambridge: Cambridge University Press.

Macintyre, M. and Allen, J. (1990) Trading for subsistence: The case from the southern Massim. In *Pacific Production Systems: Approaches to Economic Prehistory*, ed. D. E. Yen and J. M. J. Mummery. Canberra: Research School of Pacific

Studies, Australian National University, pp. 120–36.

Maclachlan, M. D. (1983) *Why They did not Starve: Biocultural Adaptation in a South Indian Village*. Philadelphia: Institute for the Study of Human Issues.

McAuliffe, J. R., Sundt, P. C., Valiente-Banuet, A., Casas, A. and Viveros, J. L. (2001) Pre-columbian soil erosion, persistent ecological changes, and collapse of a subsistence agricultural economy in the semi-arid Techuacán Valley, Mexico's 'cradle of maize'. *Journal of Arid Environments*, 47, 47–75.

McCann, J. (1987) *From Poverty to Famine in Northeast Ethiopia: A Rural History 1900-1935*. Philadelphia: University of Pennsylvania Press.

McCloskey, D. N. (1976) English open fields as behavior towards risks. *Research in Economic History*, 1, 124–70.

McCloskey, D. N. (1991) The prudent peasant: New findings on open fields. *Journal of Economic History*, 51, 343–55.

McCloskey, D. N. and Nash, J. (1984) Corn at interest: The extent and cost of grain storage in medieval England. *American Economic Review*, 74, 174–87.

McCracken, S. D., Brondizio, E. S., Nelson, D., *et al.* (1999) Remote sensing and GIS at farm property level: Demography and deforestation in the Brazilian Amazon. *Photogrammetric Engineering and Remote Sensing*, 65, 1311–20.

McDade, T. W. (2003) Life history theory and the immune system: Steps toward a human ecological immunology. *Yearbook of Physical Anthropology*, 46, 100–25.

McDade, T. W., Reyes-Garcia, V., Blackinton, P., *et al.* (2007) Ethnobotanical knowledge is associated with indices of child health in the Bolivian Amazon. *Proceedings of the National Academy of Sciences*, 104, 6134–9.

McDade, T. W., Reyes-Garcia, V., Tanner, S., Huanca, T. and Leonard, W. R. (2008) Maintenance versus growth: Investigating the costs of immune activation among children in lowland Bolivia. *American Journal of Physical Anthropology*, 136, 478–84.

McDonald, J. (1998) *Production Efficiency in Domesday England, 1086*. London: Routledge.

McDonald, J. and Snooks, G. D. (1986) *Domesday Economy: A New Approach to Anglo-Norman History*. Oxford: Oxford University Press.

McGough, J. P. (1984) The domestic mode of production and peasant social organization: The Chinese case. In *Chayanov, Peasants, and Economic Anthropology*, ed. E. P. Durrenberger. New York: Academic Press, pp. 183–201.

McGregor, I. A., Rahman, A. K., Thomson, A. M. and Billewicz, W. Z. (1970) The health of young children in a West African (Gambian) village. *Transactions of the Royal Society of Tropical Medicine and Hygiene*, 64, 48–77.

McIntire, J., Bourzat, D. and Pingali, P. (1992) *Crop-Livestock Interaction in Sub-Saharan Africa*. Washington: The World Bank.

McKusick, V. A., ed. (1978) *Medical Genetic Studies of the Amish*. Baltimore: Johns Hopkins University Press.

McLoughlin, P. R. M., ed. (1970) *African Food Production Systems: Cases and Theory*. Baltimore: Johns Hopkins University Press.

McMillan, D. E. (1986) Distribution of resources and products in Mossi households. In *Food in Sub-Saharan Africa*, ed. A. Hansen and D. E. McMillan. Boulder, CO: Lynne Rienner, pp. 26–73.

McNab, B. K. (2002) *The Physiological Ecology of Vertebrates: A View from Energetics*. Ithaca, NY: Cornell University Press.

McNab, B. K. (2012) *Extreme Measures: The Ecological Energetics of Birds and Mammals*. Chicago: University of Chicago Press.

McNeil, J. R. (1992) *The Mountains of the Mediterranean World: An Environmental History*. Cambridge: Cambridge University Press.

Mäckel, R., Schneider, R. and Sidel, J. (2003) Anthropogenic impact on the landscape of Southern Badenia (Germany) during the Holocene – documented by colluvial and alluvial sediments. *Archaeometry*, 45, 487–501.

Maharatna, A. (1996) *The Demography of Famines: An Indian Historical Perspective*. Bombay: Oxford University Press.

Makhijani, A. and Poole, A. (1975) *Energy and Agriculture in the Third World*. Cambridge, MA: Ballinger.

Malcolm, D. W. (1953) *Sukumaland: An African People and Their Country – A Study of Land Use in Tanganyika*. Oxford: Oxford University Press.

Malden, W. J. (1891) *Tillage*. London: George Bell and Sons.

Maloiy, C. M. O., Heglund, N. C., Prager, L. M., Cavagna, G. A. and Taylor, C. R. (1986) Energetic costs of carrying loads: Have African women discovered an economic way? *Nature*, 319, 668–9.

Malthus, T. R. (1798) *An Essay on the Principle of Population, as it affects the Future Improvement of Society with remarks on the Speculations of Mr. Godwin, M. Concordet, and Other Writers.* London: J. Johnson.

Malthus, T. R. (1803) *An Essay on the Principle of Population; or, a View of its Past and Present Effects on Human Happiness; with an enquiry into our Prospects respecting the Future Removal or Mitigation of the Evils which it occasions*, 2nd edn. London: J. Johnson.

Malthus, T. R. (1807) *An Essay on the Principle of Population; or, a View of its Past and Present Effects on Human Happiness; with an enquiry into our Prospects respecting the Future Removal or Mitigation of the Evils which it occasions*, 4th edn. London: John Murray.

Malthus, T. R. (1826) *An Essay on the Principle of Population, or A View of its Past and Present Effects on Human Happiness*, 6th edn. London: John Murray.

Malthus, T. R. (1830) *A Summary View of the Principle of Population.* London: John Murray.

Malthus, T. R. (1986 [orig. 1872]) *An Essay on the Principle of Population, or a View of its Past and Present Effects on Human Happiness*, 7th posthumous edn. Fairfield, NJ: Augustus M. Kelley Publishers.

Manner, H. I. (2008) Directions for long-term research in traditional agricultural systems of Micronesia and the Pacific Islands. *Micronesica*, 40, 63–86.

Marby, J. B., ed. (1996) *Canals and Communities: Small-Scale Irrigation Systems.* Tucson, AZ: University of Arizona Press.

Marcus, J. and Stanish, C., eds. (2006) *Agricultural Strategies.* Los Angeles: University of California at Los Angeles Press.

Marsh, D. R., Sadruddin, S., Fikree, F. F., Krishnan, C. and Darmstadt, G. L. (2003) Validation of verbal autopsy to determine the cause of 137 neonatal deaths in Karachi, Pakistan. *Paediatric and Perinatal Epidemiology*, 17, 132–42.

Marten, G. G., ed. (1986) *Traditional Agriculture in Southeast Asia: A Human Ecology Perspective.* Boulder, CO: Westview.

Marten, G. G. and Vityakon, P. (1986) Soil management in traditional agriculture. In *Traditional Agriculture in Southeast Asia: A Human Ecology Perspective*, ed. G. G. Marten. Boulder, CO: Westview, pp. 199–225.

Martorell, R., Habicht, J.-P., Yarbrough, C., *et al.* (1975) Acute morbidity and physical growth in rural Guatemalan children. *American Journal of the Diseases of Childhood*, 129, 1296–301.

Martorell, R. and Ho, T. J. (1984) Malnutrition, morbidity, and mortality. In *Child Survival: Strategies for Research*, ed. W. H. Mosley and L. C. Chen. Cambridge: Cambridge University Press, pp. 49–68.

Marx, K. (1954 [orig. 1862]) Malthus as an apologist [from *Theories of Surplus Value, Volume II*]. In *Marx and Engels on Malthus: Selections from the writings of Marx and Engels dealing with the theories of Thomas Robert Malthus*, ed. R. L. Meek. New York: International Publishers, pp. 115–25.

Mata, L. (1992) Diarrheal disease as a cause of malnutrition. *American Journal of Tropical Medicine and Hygiene*, 47, 16–27.

Mathewson, K. (1984) *Irrigation Horticulture in Highland Guatemala: The Tablón System of Panajachel.* Boulder, CO: Westview.

Mathieu, J. (2009) *History of the Alps 1500–1900: Environment, Development, and Society.* Morgantown, WV: West Virginia University Press.

Matley, I. M. (1968) Transhumance in Bosnia and Herzegovina. *Geographical Review*, 58, 231–61.

Matsuo, T. (1959) *Rice Culture in Japan.* Tokyo: Japanese Ministry of Agriculture.

Maynard Smith, J. (1964) Group selection and kin selection. *Nature*, 201, 1145–7.

Mazoyer, M. and Roudart, L. (2006) *A History of World Agriculture: From the Neolithic Age to the Current Crisis.* New York: Monthly Review Press.

Mead, W. R. (1953) *Farming in Finland.* London: The Athlone Press.

Meertens, H. C. C., Ndege, L. J. and Enserink, H. J. (1995) *Dynamics in Farming Systems: Changes in Time and Space in Sukumaland, Tanzania.* Amsterdam: Royal Tropical Institute.

Melancon, T. (1982) *Marriage and Reproduction among the Yanomamo Indians of Venezuela.* PhD dissertation, Department of Anthropology, Pennsylvania State University, University Park, PA.

Menzel, P. and Mann, C. C. (1994) *Material World: A Global Family Portrait.* San Francisco: Sierra Club.

Mertz, H. C., ed. (1994) *Madagascar: A Country Study.* Washington: The Library of Congress (available at http://countrystudies.us/madagascar/10.html).

Mertz, O. (2002) The relationship between length of fallow and crop yields in shifting cultivation: A rethinking. *Agroforestry Systems*, **55**, 149–59.

Metzner, J. K. (1982) *Agriculture and Population Pressure in Sikka, Isle of Flores: A Contribution to the Study of the Stability of Agricultural Systems in the Wet and Dry Tropics.* Canberra: Australian National University.

Millar, J. R. (1970) A reformulation of A. V. Chayanov's theory of the peasant economy. *Economic Development and Cultural Change*, **18**, 219–29.

Millat-e Mustafa, M., Hall, J. B. and Teklehaimanot, Z. (1996) Structure and floristics of Bangladesh homegardens. *Agroforestry Systems*, **33**, 263–80.

Miller, E. (1991) Introduction: Land and people. In *The Agrarian History of England and Wales, Volume III: 1348–1500*, ed. E. Miller. Cambridge: Cambridge University Press, pp. 1–33.

Miller, J. E. and Huss-Ashmore, R. (1989) Do reproductive patterns affect maternal nutritional status? An analysis of maternal depletion in Lesotho. *American Journal of Human Biology*, **1**, 409–19.

Millington, A. and Jepson, W., eds. (2008) *Land-Change Science in the Tropics: Changing Agricultural Landscapes.* New York: Springer Scientific.

Minge-Kalman, W. (1977) On the theory and measurement of domestic labor intensity. *American Ethnologist*, **4**, 273–84.

Miracle, M. P. (1967) *Agriculture in the Congo Basin: Tradition and Change in African Rural Economies.* Madison, WI: University of Wisconsin Press.

Mitchell, W. P. and Guillet, D., eds. (1994) *Irrigation at High Altitudes: The Social Organization of Water Control Systems in the Andes.* Washington: American Anthropological Association.

Mitteraurer, M. and Sider, R. (1979) The developmental process of domestic groups: Problems of reconstruction and possibilities of interpretation. *Journal of Family History*, **4**, 257–84.

Miyagawa, S. (2002) Utilization of plant resources as famine foods in northeast Thailand. *Japanese Journal of Tropical Agriculture*, **46**, 136–42.

Mock, D. W. (2004) *More than Kin and Less than Kind.* Cambridge, MA: Harvard University Press.

Moerman, M. (1968) *Agricultural Change and Peasant Choice in a Thai Village.* Berkeley, CA: University of California Press.

Mokyr, J. and Ó Gráda, C. (1996) Height and health in the United Kingdom 1815–1860: Evidence from the East India Company Army. *Explorations in Economic History*, **33**, 141–68.

Mokyr, J. and Ó Gráda, C. (2002) What do people die of during famines? The Great Irish Famine in comparative perspective. *European Review of Economic History*, **6**, 339–64.

Montgomery, D. R. (2007) *Dirt: The Erosion of Civilizations.* Berkeley, CA: University of California Press.

Montgomery, E. and Johnson, A. W. (1977) Machiguenga energy expenditure. *Ecology of Food and Nutrition*, **6**, 97–105.

Moore, A. M. T., Hillman, G. C. and Legge, A. J. (2000) *Village on the Euphrates: From Foraging to Farming at Abu Hureyra.* Oxford: Oxford University Press.

Morfit, C. (1848) *Manures, Their Composition, Preparation, and Action upon Soils.* Philadelphia: Lindsay and Blakiston.

Morgan, L. H. (1851) *League of the Ho-de-no-sau-nee or Iroquois.* Rochester, NY: Sage and Brothers.

Morgenstern, H. (1982) Uses of ecologic analysis in epidemiologic research. *American Journal of Public Health*, **72**, 1336–44.

Morrison, K. (1996) Typological schemes and agricultural change: Beyond Boserup in south India. *Current Anthropology*, **37**, 583–608.

Morrison, K. (2006) Intensification as situated process: Landscape history and collapse. In *Agricultural Strategies*, ed. J. Marcus and C. Stanish. Los Angeles: University of California at Los Angeles Press, pp. 71–91.

Mortimore, M. (1998) *Roots in the African Dust: Sustaining the Drylands*. Cambridge: Cambridge University Press.

Mortimore, M. and Adams, W. M. (1999) *Working the Sahel: Environment and Society in Northern Nigeria*. London: Routledge.

Mosley, W. H. and Chen, L. C. (1984) An analytical framework for the study of child survival in developing countries. In *Child Survival: Strategies for Research*, ed. W. H. Mosley and L. C. Chen. Cambridge: Cambridge University Press, pp. 25–45.

Mueller, L. D. (1997) Theoretical and empirical examination of density-dependent selection. *Annual Review of Ecology and Systematics*, 28, 269–88.

Muhuri, P. K. (1996) Estimating seasonality effects on child mortality in Matlab, Bangladesh. *Demography*, 33, 98–110.

Muller, J. and Almedom, A. M. (2008) What is "famine food"? Distinguishing between traditional vegetables and special foods for times of hunger/scarcity (Boumba, Niger). *Human Ecology*, 36, 599–607.

Murdoch, W. W. (1994) Population regulation in theory and practice. *Ecology*, 75, 271–85.

Murdock, G. P. (1937) Comparative data on the division of labor by sex. *Social Forces*, 15, 551–3.

Murdock, G. P. and Provost, C. (1973) Factors in the division of labor by sex: A cross-cultural analysis. *Ethnology*, 12, 203–25.

Murphy, D. J. (2007) *People, Plants and Genes*. Oxford: Oxford University Press.

Murtha, T. M. (2009) *Land and Labor – Classic Maya Terraced Agriculture: An Investigation of the Settlement Ecology and Intensive Agricultural Landscape of Caracol, Belize*. Berlin: V. D. M. Verlag.

Mutsaers, H. J. W. (2007) *Peasants, Farmers and Scientists: A Chronicle of Tropical Agricultural Science in the Twentieth Century*. Dordrecht: Springer.

Myers, M. G. (2006) *Households and Families of the Longhouse Iroquois at Six Nations Reserve*. Lincoln, NE: University of Nebraska Press.

Nag, M., White, B. F. and Peet, R. C. (1978) An anthropological approach to the study of the economic value of children in Java and Nepal. *Current Anthropology*, 19, 293–306.

Nagata, M. L. (2005) One of the family: Domestic service in early modern Japan. *History of the Family*, 10, 355–65.

Naylor, P. E. (1961) Farming organization in central Iraq. *Journal of Experimental Agriculture*, 29, 19–34.

Nazarea-Sandoval, V. D. (1995) *Local Knowledge and Agricultural Decision Making in the Philippines*. Ithaca, NY: Cornell University Press.

Neel, J. V. (1972) The genetic structure of a tribal population, I: Introduction. *Annals of Human Genetics*, 35, 255–9.

Neel, J. V. and Chagnon, N. A. (1968) The demography of two primitive, relatively unacculturated American Indian tribes. *Proceedings of the National Academy of Sciences*, 59, 680–9.

Neel, J. V. and Weiss, K. M. (1975) The genetic structure of a tribal population, XII: Biodemographic studies. *American Journal of Physical Anthropology*, 42, 25–51.

Nerlove, S. B. (1974) Women's workload and infant feeding practices: A relationship with demographic implications. *Ethnology*, 13, 207–14.

Netting, R. M. (1965) Household organization and intensive agriculture: The Kofyar case. *Africa*, 35, 422–9.

Netting, R. M. (1968) *Hill Farmers of Nigeria: Cultural Ecology of the Kofyar of the Jos Plateau*. Seattle: University of Washington Press.

Netting, R. M. (1972) Of men and meadows: Strategies of Alpine land use. *Anthropology Quarterly*, 45, 132–44.

Netting, R. M. (1973) Fighting, forest, and the fly: Some demographic regulators among the Kofyar. *Journal of Anthropological Research*, 29, 164–79.

Netting, R. M. (1974a) Agrarian ecology. *Annual Review of Anthropology*, 3, 21–56.

Netting, R. M. (1974b) The system nobody knows: Village irrigation in the Swiss Alps. In *The Impact of Irrigation on Society*, ed. M. Gibson and T. E. Downing. Tucson, AZ: University of Arizona Press, pp. 67–75.

Netting, R. M. (1976) What Alpine peasants have in common: Observations in communal land tenure in a Swiss village. *Human Ecology*, 4, 135–46.

Netting, R. M. (1979) Household dynamics in a nineteenth-century Swiss village. *Journal of Family History*, **4**, 39–58.

Netting, R. M. (1981) *Balancing on an Alp: Ecological Change and Continuity in a Swiss Mountain Community*. Cambridge: Cambridge University Press.

Netting, R. M. (1982) Some home truths on household size and wealth. *American Behavioral Scientist*, **25**, 641–62.

Netting, R. M. (1993) *Smallholders, Householders: Farm Families and the Ecology of Intensive, Sustainable Agriculture*. Stanford, CA: Stanford University Press.

Netting, R. M., Wilk, R. R. and Arnould, E. J., eds. (1984) *Households: Comparative and Historical Studies of the Domestic Group*. Berkeley, CA: University of California Press.

Newton, J. W. and Cavins, J. F. (1976) Altered nitrogenous pools induced by the *Azolla-Anabaena* symbiosis. *Plant Physiology*, **58**, 798–9.

Nielsen, U., Mertz, O. and Noweg, G. T. (2006) The rationality of shifting cultivation systems: Labor productivity revisited. *Human Ecology*, **34**, 201–18.

Nietschmann, B. (1973) *Between Land and Water: The Subsistence Ecology of the Miskito Indians, Eastern Nicaragua*. New York: Seminar Press.

Niñez, V. C. (1987) Household gardens: Theoretical and policy considerations. *Agricultural Systems*, **23**, 167–86.

Norgan, N. G., Ferro-Luzzi, A. and Durnin, J. V. G. A. (1974) The energy and nutrient intake and the energy expenditure of 204 New Guinea adults. *Philosophical Transactions of the Royal Society, London (Series B)*, **268**, 309–48.

Norman, D. W. (1977) Economic rationality of tradition Hausa dryland farmers in the north of Nigeria. In *Tradition and Dynamics in Small-Farm Agriculture: Economic Studies in Asia, Africa, and Latin America*, ed. R. D. Stevens. Ames, IA: Iowa State University Press, pp. 63–91.

Norman, D. W. and Baker, C. D. (1986) Components of farming systems research, FSR credibility, and experiences in Botswana. In *Understanding Africa's Rural Households and Farming Systems*, ed. J. L. Moock. Boulder, CO: Westview, pp. 36–57.

Norman, M. J. T. (1979) *Annual Cropping Systems in the Tropics*. Gainesville, FL: University Presses of Florida.

Norman, M. J. T., Pearson, C. J. and Searle, P. G. E. (1995) *The Ecology of Tropical Food Crops*, 2nd edn. Cambridge: Cambridge University Press.

Nye, P. H. and Greenland, D. J. (1960) *The Soil under Shifting Cultivation*. Farnham Royal: Commonwealth Agricultural Bureaux.

Nyerges, A. E. (1989) Coppice swidden fallows in tropical deciduous forest: Biological, technological, and sociocultural determinants of secondary forest successions. *Human Ecology*, **17**, 379–400.

Nyerges, A. E., ed. (1997) *The Ecology of Practice: Studies of Food Crop Production in Sub-Saharan West Africa*. Amsterdam: Overseas Publishers Association.

O'Gorman, R., Wilson, D. S. and Sheldon, K. M. (2008) For the good of the group? Exploring group-level evolutionary adaptations using multilevel selection theory. *Group Dynamics – Theory, Research, and Practice*, **12**, 17–26.

Ó Gráda, C. (1999) *Black '47 and Beyond: The Great Irish Famine in History, Economy, and Memory*. Princeton, NJ: Princeton University Press.

Ó Gráda, C. (2009) *Famine: A Short History*. Princeton, NJ: Princeton University Press.

O'Hara, S. L., Street-Perrott, F. A. and Burt, T. P. (1993) Accelerated soil erosion around a Mexican highland lake caused by prehispanic agriculture. *Nature*, **362**, 48–51.

Odend'hal, S. (1972) Energetics of Indian cattle in their environment. *Human Ecology*, **1**, 3–22.

Ohtsuka, R. and Suzuki, T. (1990) *Population Ecology of Human Survival: Bioecological Studies of the Gidra in Papua New Guinea*. Tokyo: University of Tokyo Press.

Oliver, P. (2003) *Dwellings: The Vernacular House World Wide*. London: Phaidon Press.

Orlove, B. S. and Godoy, R. (1986) Sectoral fallowing systems in the central Andes. *Journal of Ethnobiology*, **6**, 169–204.

Osmani, S. R. (1992) On some controversies in the measurement of undernutrition. In *Nutrition and Poverty*, ed. S. R. Osmani. Oxford: Oxford University Press, pp. 121–64.

Östberg, W. (2004) The expansion of Marakwet hill-furrow irrigation in the Kerio Valley of Kenya. In *Islands of Intensive Agriculture in*

Eastern Africa: Past and Present, ed. M. Widgren and J. E. G. Sutton. Oxford: James Currey, pp. 19–48.

Otterbein, K. F. (1970) The developmental cycle of the Andros household: A diachronic analysis. *American Anthropologist*, **72**, 1412–19.

Otterbein, K. F. and Otterbein, C. S. (1977) A stochastic process analysis of the developmental cycle of the Andros household. *Ethnology*, **16**, 415–26.

Overton, M. (1996) *Agricultural Revolution in England: The Transformation of the Agrarian Economy 1500–1850*. Cambridge: Cambridge University Press.

Padoch, C. (1985) Labor efficiency and intensity of land use in rice production: An example from Kalimantan. *Human Ecology*, **13**, 271–89.

Padoch, C. and de Jong, W. (1991) The house gardens of Santa Rosa: Diversity and variability in an Amazonian agricultural system. *Economic Botany*, **45**, 166–75.

Padoch, C., Harwell, E. and Susanto, A. (1998) Swidden, sawah, and in-between: Agricultural transformation in Borneo. *Human Ecology*, **26**, 3–20.

Pals, J. P. and Wijngaarden-Bakker, L. V., eds. (1998) Special issue on seasonality. *Environmental Archaeology*, **3**, 1–128.

Palte, J. G. L. (1989) *Upland Farming on Java, Indonesia: A Socio-Economic Study of Upland Agriculture and Subsistence under Population Pressure*. Utrecht: Faculty of Geographical Sciences, University of Utrecht.

Panter-Brick, C. (1992) The energy costs of common tasks in rural Nepal: Levels of energy expenditure compatible with sustained physical activity. *European Journal of Applied Physiology*, **64**, 447–84.

Panter-Brick, C. (1996a) Physical activity, energy stores, and seasonal energy balance among men and women in Nepali households. *American Journal of Human Biology*, **8**, 263–74.

Panter-Brick, C. (1996b) Season and sex variation in physical activity levels among agro-pastoralists in Nepal. *American Journal of Physical Anthropology*, **100**, 7–21.

Panter-Brick, C. and Eggerman, M. (1997) Household responses to food shortages in Western Nepal. *Human Organization*, **56**, 190–8.

Pasquet, P. and Koppert, G. J. A. (1993) Activity patterns and energy expenditure in Cameroonian tropical forest populations. In *Tropical Forests, People and Food: Biocultural Interactions and Applications to Development*, ed. C. M. Hladik, A. Hladik, O. F. Linares, *et al.* Paris: UNESCO Press, pp. 311–20.

Pasternack, B., Ember, C. R. and Ember, M. (1976) On the conditions favoring extended family households. *Journal of Anthropological Research*, **35**, 109–24.

Patnaik, U. (1979) Neo-populism and Marxism: The Chayanovian view of the agrarian question and its fundamental fallacy. *Journal of Peasant Studies*, **6**, 375–420.

Payne, P. (1989) Public health and functional consequences of seasonal hunger and malnutrition. In *Seasonal Variability in Third World Agriculture: The Consequences for Food Security*, ed. D. E. Sahn. Baltimore: Johns Hopkins University Press, pp. 19–46.

Payton, F. V., Rhue, R. D. and Hensel, D. R. (1989) Mitserlich–Bray equation used to correlate soil phosphorus and potato yields. *Agronomic Journal*, **81**, 571–6.

Pearl, R. (1925) *The Biology of Population Growth*. New York: Knopf.

Pearl, R. (1927) The growth of populations. *Quarterly Review of Biology*, **2**, 532–48.

Pearl, R. and Reed, L. J. (1920) On the rate of growth of the population of the U.S.A. since 1790, and its mathematical representation. *Proceedings of the National Academy of Sciences*, **6**, 275–88.

Pearl, R., Reed, L. J. and Kish, J. F. (1940) The logistic curve and the census count of 1940. *Science*, **92**, 486–8.

Pebley, A. R., Huffman, S. L., Chowdhury, A. K. M. A. and Stupp, P. W. (1985) Intra-uterine mortality and maternal nutritional status in rural Bangladesh. *Population Studies*, **39**, 425–40.

Pelletier, D. L., Frongillo, E. A. and Habicht, J.-P. (1993) Epidemiologic evidence for a potentiating effect of malnutrition on child mortality. *American Journal of Public Health*, **83**, 1130–3.

Pelletier, D. L., Frongillo, E. A., Schroeder, D. G. and Habicht, J.-P. (1995) The effects of malnutrition on child mortality in developing countries. *Bulletin of the World Health Organization*, **73**, 443–8.

Pelzer, K. J. (1945) *Pioneer Settlement in the Asiatic Tropics: Studies in Land Utilization and Agricultural Colonization in Southeastern Asia.* New York: American Geographical Society.

Pennington, C. W. (1963) *The Tarahumar of Mexico: Their Environment and Material Culture.* Salt Lake City, UT: University of Utah Press.

Pennington, C. W. (1980) *The Material Culture of the Pima Bajo of Central Sonora, Mexico, Volume 1.* Salt Lake City, UT: University of Utah Press.

Perales, H. R., Brush, S. B. and Qualset, C. O. (2003a) Landraces of maize in Central Mexico: An altitudinal transect. *Economic Botany,* 57, 7–20.

Perales, H. R., Brush, S. B. and Qualset, C. O. (2003b) Dynamic management of maize landraces in Central Mexico. *Economic Botany,* 57, 21–34.

Pereira, H. C. (1973) *Land Use and Water Resources in Temperate and Tropical Climates.* Cambridge: Cambridge University Press.

Perz, S. G. (2001) Household demographic factors as life cycle determinants of land use in the Amazon. *Population Research and Policy Review,* 20, 159–86.

Perz, S. G. (2002) Household demography and land use allocation among small farms in the Brazilian Amazon. *Human Ecology Review,* 9, 1–16.

Perz, S. G., Walker, R. T. and Caldas, M. M. (2006) Beyond population and environment: Household demographic life cycles and land use allocation among small farms in the Amazon. *Human Ecology,* 34, 829–49.

Pestalozzi, H. (2000) Sectoral fallow systems and the management of soil fertility: The rationality of indigenous knowledge in the high Andes of Bolivia. *Mountain Research and Development,* 20, 64–71.

Petersen, W., ed. (1972) *Readings in Population.* New York: Macmillan.

Petersen, W. (1979) *Malthus.* Cambridge, MA: Harvard University Press.

Phillips, P. G. (1954) The metabolic cost of common West African agricultural activities. *Journal of Tropical Medicine,* 57, 12–20.

Phillips-Howard, K. D. and Lyon, F. (1994) Agricultural intensification and the threat to soil fertility in Africa: Evidence from the Jos

Plateau. *The Geographical Journal,* 160, 252–65.

Pichón, F. J. (1996) Land-use strategies in the Amazon Frontier: Farm-level evidence from Ecuador. *Human Organization,* 55, 416–24.

Pielou, E. C. (1977) *An Introduction to Mathematical Ecology,* 2nd edn. New York: Wiley-Interscience.

Pierce, J. E. (1964) *Life in a Turkish Village.* New York: Holt, Rinehart.

Ping, A. K. (1978) *A Geographical and Socio-Economic Study of the Paddy Cultivation in Sekinchang, Selangor, Peninsular Malaysia.* Singapore: Department of Geography, Nanyang University.

Pingali, P., Bigot, Y. and Binswanger, H. P. (1987) *Agricultural Mechanization and the Evolution of Farming Systems in Sub-Saharan Africa.* Baltimore: Johns Hopkins University Press.

Pitkänen, K. J. (1993) *Deprivation and Disease: Mortality during the Great Finnish Famine of the 1860s.* Helsinki: The Finnish Demographic Society.

Pitkänen, K. J. (2002) Famine mortality in nineteenth-century Finland: Is there a sex bias? In *Famine Demography: Perspectives from the Past and Present,* ed. T. Dyson and C. Ó Gráda. Oxford: Oxford University Press, pp. 64–92.

Plakans, A. and Wetherell, C. (2005) The Hajnal line and eastern Europe. In *Marriage and the Family in Eurasia: Perspectives on the Hajnal Hypothesis,* ed. T. Engelen and A. P. Wolf. Amsterdam: Aksant Publishers, pp. 105–26.

Plaster, E. J. (2003) *Soil Science and Management,* 4th edn. Clifton Park, NJ: Thomson.

Poos, L. R. (1991) *A Rural Society after the Black Death: Essex 1350–1525.* Cambridge: Cambridge University Press.

Popkin, B. A. (2008) The nutrition transition and its relationship to demographic change. In *Nutrition and Health in Developing Countries,* 2nd edn, ed. R. D. Semba and M. W. Bloem. Totowa, N.J.: Humana Press, pp. 601–16.

Posey, D. A. (2002) *Kayapó Ethnoecology and Culture.* London: Routledge.

Posey, D. A. and Balée, W., eds. (1989) *Resource Management in Amazonia: Indigenous and Folk Strategies.* New York: New York Botanical Garden.

Pospisil, L. (1963) *Kapauku Papuan Economy.* New Haven, CT: Yale University Press.

Pospisil, L. (1995) *Obernberg: A Quantitative Analysis of a Tirolean Peasant Economy*. New Haven, CT: Connecticut Academy of Arts and Sciences.

Postgate, J. (1998) *Nitrogen Fixation*. Cambridge: Cambridge University Press.

Preston, S. H., Heuveline, P. and Guillot, M. (2000) *Demography: Measuring and Modeling Population Processes*. New York: Wiley-Blackwell.

Preston, S. H., Keyfitz, N. and Schoen, R. (1972) *Causes of Death: Life Tables for National Populations*. New York: Academic Press.

Proctor, D. L., ed. (1994) *Grain Storage Techniques: Evolution and Trends in Developing Countries*. Rome: Food and Agriculture Organization of the United Nations.

Pryor, F. L. (1982) An international perspective on land scattering. *Explorations in Economic History*, **19**, 296–320.

Pryor, F. L. (1985) The invention of the plow. *Comparative Studies in Society and History*, **27**, 727–43.

Pryor, F. L. and Maurer, S. T. (1982) On induced economic change in precapitalist economies. *Journal of Development Economics*, **10**, 325–53.

Purcal, J. T. (1971) *Rice Economy: A Case Study of Four Villages in West Malaysia*. Kuala Lumpur: University of Malaya Press.

Raghavan, D., ed. (1960) *Indigenous Agricultural Implements of India: An All-India Survey*. New Delhi: Indian Council of Agricultural Research.

Rahman, M., Sultana, R., Ahmed, G., *et al.* (2007) Prevalence of G2P[4] and G12P[6] rotavirus, Bangladesh. *Emerging Infectious Diseases*, **13**, 18–24.

Ramakrishnan, P. S. (1992) *Shifting Agriculture and Sustainable Development: An Interdisciplinary Study from North-Eastern India*. Paris: UNESCO.

Ramakrishnan, P. S. and Toky, O. P. (1981) Soil nutrient status of hill agro-ecosystems and recovery pattern after slash and burn agriculture (*jhum*) in north-eastern India. *Plant Soil*, **60**, 341–61.

Ramakrishnan, U., Webb, A. L. and Ologoudou, K. (2004) Infection, immunity, and vitamins. In *Handbook of Nutrition and Immunity*, ed. M. E. Gershwin, P. Nestel and C. L. Keen. Totowa, NJ: Humana Press, pp. 93–115.

Randhawa, M. S., Mitra, A. and Hehta, G. (1964) *Farmers of India, Volume III: Assam, Orissa, West Bengal, Andamans and Nicobars, Manipur, Nefa, Tripura*. New Delhi: Indian Council of Agricultural Research.

Randhawa, M. S. and Nath, P. (1959) *Farmers of India, Volume I: Punjab, Himachal Pradesh, Jammu and Kashmir*. New Delhi: Indian Council of Agricultural Research.

Randhawa, M. S., Nath, V., Vaidya, S., *et al.* (1968) *Farmers of India, Volume IV: Madhya Pradesh, Rajasthan, Gujarat, Maharashtra*. New Delhi: Indian Council of Agricultural Research.

Randhawa, M. S., Sivaraman, M. S., Naidu, I. J. and Vaidya, S. (1961) *Farmers of India, Volume II: Madras, Andhra Pradesh, Mysore and Kerala*. New Delhi: Indian Council of Agricultural Research.

Rappaport, R. A. (1967) *Pigs for the Ancestors: Ritual in the Ecology of a New Guinea People*. New Haven, CT: Yale University Press.

Raven, P. H., Evert, R. F. and Eichorn, S. E. (1999) *Biology of Plants*, 6th edn. New York: W. H. Freeman.

Redfield, R. and Villa Rojas, A. (1934) *Chan Kom: A Maya Village*. Washington: Carnegie Institution.

Redman, C. (1999) *Human Impact on Ancient Environments*. Tucson, AZ: University of Arizona Press.

Rees, W. G. (2004) Least-cost paths in mountainous terrain. *Computers and Geosciences*, **30**, 203–9.

Reichel-Dolmatoff, G. and Reichel-Dolmatoff, A. (1961) *The People of Aritama: The Cultural Personality of a Colombian Mestizo Village*. Chicago: University of Chicago Press.

Reichman, O. J. and Atchison, S. (1981) Mammal trails on mountain slopes: Optimal paths in relation to slope angle and body weight. *The American Naturalist*, **117**, 416–20.

Reij, C., Scoones, I. and Toulmin, C., eds. (1996) *Sustaining the Soil: Indigenous Soil and Water Conservation in Africa*. London: EarthScan.

Reyes, R. D. (1973) Analysis of some factors affecting rice yield response. In *Water Management in Philippine Irrigation Systems*. Los Bano, Philippines: International Rice Research Institute, pp. 37–52.

Reyna, S. P. (1976) The extending strategy: Regulation of household dependency ratio.

Journal of Anthropological Research, 32, 182–98.

Rhoades, R. E. and Bedegaray, P. (1987) *The Farmers of Yurimaguas: Land Use and Coping Strategies in the Peruvian Jungle*. Lima: The International Potato Center.

Rice, E., Smale, M. and Blanco, L.-L. (1998) Farmer's use of improved seed selection practices in Mexican maize: Evidence and issues from the Sierra de Santa Marta. *World Development*, 26, 1625–40.

Richards, A. I. (1939) *Land, Labour and Diet in Northern Rhodesia: An Economic Study of the Bemba Tribe*. Oxford: Oxford University Press.

Richards, P. (1985) *Indigenous Agricultural Revolution: Ecology and Food Production in West Africa*. London: Hutchinson.

Richards, P. (1986) *Coping with Hunger: Hazard and Experiment in an African Rice-Farming System*. London: Allen and Unwin.

Richards, P. (1995) The versatility of the poor: Wetland rice farming systems in Sierra Leone. *Geoforum*, 35, 197–203.

Richards, P. W. (1952) *The Tropical Rain Forest*. Cambridge: Cambridge University Press.

Richerson, P. J. and Boyd, R. (1998) Homage to Malthus, Ricardo, and Boserup: Toward a general theory of population, economic growth, environmental degradation, wealth, and poverty. *Human Ecology Review*, 4, 83–8.

Roberts, B. K. (1996) *Landscapes of Settlement*. London: Routledge.

Robinson, W. and Schutjer, W. (1984) Agricultural development and demographic change: A generalization of the Boserup model. *Economic Development and Cultural Change*, 32, 355–66.

Robson, J. R. K. and Wadsworth, G. R. (1977) The health and nutritional status of primitive populations. *Ecology of Food and Nutrition*, 6, 187–202.

Rodahl, K. (1989) *The Physiology of Work*. London: Taylor and Francis.

Roder, W., Phengchanh, S. and Keoboulapha, B. (1995) Relationships between soil, fallow period, weeds and rice yield in slash-and-burn systems of Laos. *Plant Soil*, 176, 27–36.

Rosenberg, N. and Birdzell, L. E. (1986) *How the West Grew Rich: The Economic Transformation of the Industrial World*. New York: Basic Books.

Rowley-Conwy, P. (1981) Shifting cultivation in the temperate European Neolithic. In *Farming Practice in British Prehistory*, ed. R. Mercer. Edinburgh: Edinburgh University Press, pp. 85–96.

Ruddle, K. (1974) *The Yukpa Cultivation System: A Study of Shifting Cultivation in Colombia and Venezuela*. Berkeley, CA: University of California Press.

Ruddle, K. and Zhong, G. (1988) *Integrated Agriculture-Aquaculture in South China: The Dike-Pond System of the Zhujiang Delta*. Cambridge: Cambridge University Press.

Ruggles, S. (1990) Family demography and family history: Problems and prospects. *Historical Methods*, 23, 22–30.

Ruggles, S. (2009) Reconsidering the northwest European family system: Living arrangements of the aged in comparative historical perspective. *Population and Development Review*, 35, 249–73.

Russell, H. S. (1976) *A Long, Deep Furrow: Three Centuries of Farming in New England*. Hanover, NH: University Press of New England.

Ruthenberg, H. (1971) *Farming Systems in the Tropics*, 2nd edn. Oxford: Clarendon Press.

Rutman, D. B. (1967) *Husbandmen of Plymouth: Farms and Villages in the Old Colony, 1620–1692*. Boston: Beacon Press.

Saccheri, I. and Hanski, I. (2006) Natural selection and population dynamics. *Trends in Ecology and Evolution*, 21, 341–7.

Sahlins, M. D. (1962) *Moala: Culture and Nature on a Fijian Island*. Ann Arbor, MI: University of Michigan Press.

Sahlins, M. D. (1971) The intensity of domestic production in primitive societies: Social inflections of the Chayanov slope. In *Studies in Economic Anthropology No. 7*, ed. G. Dalton. Washington: American Anthropological Association, pp. 30–51.

Sahlins, M. D. (1972) *Stone Age Economics*. Chicago: Aldine.

Saito, O. (1998) Two kinds of stem-family system? Traditional Japan and Europe compared. *Continuity and Change*, 13, 167–86.

Saito, O. (2000) Marriage, family labor and the stem-family household: Traditional Japan in a comparative perspective. *Continuity and Change*, 15, 17–45.

Salick, J. (1989) Ecological basis of Amuesha agriculture, Peruvian upper Amazon. *Advances in Economic Botany*, **7**, 189–212.

Salick, J., Cellinese, N. and Knapp, S. (1997) Indigenous diversity of cassava: Generation, maintenance, use and loss among the Amuesha, Peruvian Upper Amazon. *Economic Botany*, **51**, 6–19.

Salvendy, G. (1972) Physiological and psychological aspects of paced and unpaced performance. *Acta Physiologica Academiae Scientiarum Hungaricae*, **42**, 267–75.

Sambatti, J. B. M., Martins, P. S. and Ando, A. (2001) Folk taxonomy and evolutionary dynamics of cassava: A case study in Ubatuba, Brazil. *Economic Botany*, **55**, 93–105.

Samuelson, P. A. (1972) *The Collected Scientific Papers of Paul Samuelson, vol. 3*. Cambridge, MA: MIT Press.

Sanchez, P. A. (1976) *Properties and Management of Soils in the Tropics*. New York: Wiley and Sons.

Sarmela, M. (1987) Swidden cultivation in Finland as a cultural system. *Suomen Antropologi*, **4**, 1–36.

Sasaki, Y. and Box, P. (2003) Agent-based verification of von Thünen's location theory. *Journal of Artificial Societies and Social Simulation*, **6** (http://jasss.soc.surrey.ac.uk/6/2/9.html).

Scheer, S. J. and McNeely, A. J., eds. (2007) *Farming with Nature: The Science and Practice of Ecoagriculture*. Washington: Island Press.

Schjellerup, I. (1985) Observations on ridged fields and terracing systems in the northern highlands of Peru. *Tools and Tillage*, **5**, 100–21.

Schjellerup, I., Quipuscoa, V., Espinoza, C., Peña, V. and Sørensen, M. K. (2005) *The Chilcos Valley Revisited: Life Conditions in the Ceja de Selva, Peru*. Copenhagen: National Museum of Denmark.

Schjellerup, I., Sørensen, M. K., Espinoza, C., Quipuscoa, V. and Peña, V. (2003) *The Forgotten Valleys: Past and Present in the Utilization of Resources in the Ceja de Selva, Peru*. Copenhagen: National Museum of Denmark.

Schlegel, S. A. (1979) *Tiruray Subsistence: From Shifting Cultivation to Plow Agriculture*. Quezon City, Philippines: Ateneo de Manila University Press.

Schneider, J. (1995) *From Upland to Irrigated Rice: The Development of Wet-Rice Agriculture in Rejang Musi, Southwest-Sumatra*. Berlin: D. Reimer Verlag.

Schofield, S. (1974) Seasonal factors affecting nutrition in different age groups and especially preschool children. *Journal of Development Studies*, **2**, 22–40.

Schreiber, K. and Rojas, J. L. (2003) *Irrigation and Society in the Peruvian Desert: The Puquios of Nasca*. Lanham, MD: Lexington Books.

Schroeder, D. G. (2008) Malnutrition. In *Nutrition and Health in Developing Countries*, 2nd edn, ed. R. D. Semba and M. W. Bloem. Totowa, N.J.: Humana Press, pp. 341–76.

Schroeder, D. G. and Brown, K. H. (1994) Nutritional status as a predictor of child survival: Summarizing the association and quantifying it global impact. *Bulletin of the World Health Organization*, **72**, 569–79.

Schultz, T. (1964) *Transforming Traditional Agriculture*. New Haven, CT: Yale University Press.

Schutz, Y., Lechtig, A. and Bradfield, R. B. (1980) Energy expenditure and food intakes of lactating women in Guatemala. *American Journal of Nutrition*, **33**, 892–902.

Schwerdtfeger, F. W. (1982) *Traditional Housing in African Cities: A Comparative Study of Houses in Zaria, Ibadan, and Marrakech*. Chichester: Wiley and Sons.

Scott, S. and Duncan, C. J. (1999) Characteristics of population cycles in preindustrial England. *Local Population History*, **62**, 70–6.

Scott, S. and Duncan, C. J. (2002) *Demography and Nutrition: Evidence from Historical and Contemporary Populations*. Oxford: Blackwell Science.

Scrimshaw, N. S. (1981) Significance of the interaction of nutrition and infection in children. In *Textbook of Pediatric Nutrition*, ed. R. M. Suskind. New York: Raven Press, pp. 229–40.

Scrimshaw, N. S. (1983a) Functional consequences of malnutrition for human populations: A comment. In *Hunger and History: The Impact of Changing Food Production and Consumption Patterns on Society*, ed. R. I. Rotberg and T. K. Rabb. Cambridge: Cambridge University Press, pp. 211–13.

Scrimshaw, N. S. (1983b) The value of contemporary food and nutrition studies for historians. In *Hunger and History: The Impact of Changing Food Production and Consumption Patterns on Society*, ed. R. I. Rotberg and T. K. Rabb. Cambridge: Cambridge University Press, pp. 331–6.

Scrimshaw, N. S. (2000) Infection and nutrition: Synergistic interactions. In *The Cambridge World History of Food*, ed. K. F. Kiple and K. C. Ornelas. Cambridge: Cambridge University Press, pp. 1397–411.

Scudder, T. (1962) *The Ecology of the Gwembe Tonga*. Manchester: Manchester University Press.

Seavoy, R. E. (1973) The transition to continuous rice cultivation in Kalimantan. *Annals of the Association of American Geographers*, **63**, 218–25.

Seiver, D. A. (1985) Trends and variation in the seasonality of U.S. fertility. *Demography*, **22**, 89–100.

Seiver, D. A. (1989) Seasonality of fertility: New evidence. *Population and Environment*, **10**, 245–57.

Seligman, C. (1910) *The Melanesians of British New Guinea*. Cambridge: Cambridge University Press.

Sempers, F. W. (1899) *Manures: How to Make and Use Them*. Philadelphia: W. Atlee Burpee and Co.

Sen, A. (1981) *Poverty and Famines: An Essay on Entitlement and Deprivation*. Oxford: Oxford University Press.

Sena, L. P., Vanderjagt, D. J., Rivera, C., *et al.* (1998) Analysis of nutritional components of eight famine foods of the Republic of Niger. *Plant Foods for Human Nutrition*, **52**, 17–30.

Sereni, E. (1997) *History of the Italian Agricultural Landscape*. Princeton, NJ: Princeton University Press.

Serpenti, L. M. (1965) *Cultivators in the Swamps: Social Structure and Horticulture in a New Guinea Society (Frederik-Hendrik Island West New Guinea)*. Assens, the Netherlands: Van Gorcum.

Shack, W. A. (1966) *The Gurage: A People of the Ensete Culture*. Oxford: Oxford University Press.

Shanin, T. (1986) Chayanov's message: Illuminations, miscomprehensions, and the contemporary "development" theory. In *A. V. Chayanov on the Theory of Peasant Economy*

(new edition), ed. D. Thorner, B. Kerblay and R. E. F. Smith. Madison, WI: University of Wisconsin Press, pp. 1–24.

Shanin, T. (2009) Chayanov's treble death and tenuous resurrection: An essay about understanding, about roots of plausibility and about rural Russia. *The Journal of Peasant Studies*, **36**, 83–101.

Sharp, L. and Hanks, L. M. (1978) *Bang Chan: Social History of a Rural Community in Thailand*. Ithaca, NY: Cornell University Press.

Sharp, L., Hauck, H. Z., Janlekha, K. and Textor, R. B. (1953) *Siamese Rice Village: A Preliminary Study of Bang Chan 1948–1949*. Bangkok: Cornell Research Center.

Shell-Duncan, B. and Wood, J. W. (1997) The evaluation of delayed-type hypersensitivity responsiveness and nutritional status as predictors of gastro-intestinal and acute respiratory infection: A prospective field study among traditional nomadic Kenyan children. *Journal of Tropical Pediatrics*, **43**, 5–32.

Shiel, R. S. (1991) Improving soil productivity in the pre-fertiliser era. In *Land, Labour and Livestock: Historical Studies in European Agricultural Productivity*, ed. B. M. S. Campbell and M. Overton. Manchester: Manchester University Press, pp. 51–77.

Shigeta, M. (1990) Folk *in-situ* conservation of ensete (*Ensete ventricosum* (Welw.) E.E. Cheesman): Towards the interpretation of indigenous agricultural science of the Ari, southwestern Ethiopia. *African Study Monographs*, **10**, 93–107.

Short, R. V. (1976) The evolution of human reproduction. *Proceedings of the Royal Society of London (series B)*, **196**, 3–24.

Shrimpton, R., Victora, C. G., de Onis, M., *et al.* (2001) Worldwide timing of growth faltering: Implications for nutritional intervention. *Pediatrics*, **107**, 1–7.

Sibly, R. M. and Calow, P. (1986) *Physiological Ecology of Animals: An Evolutionary Approach*. Oxford: Blackwell Scientific.

Sibly, R. M. and Hone, J. (2003) Population growth rate and its determinants: An overview. In *Wildlife Population Growth Rates*, ed. R. M. Sibly, J. Hone and T. H. Clutton-Brock. Cambridge: Cambridge University Press, pp. 11–40.

Siegel, J. S. and Swanson, D. A., eds. (2004) *The Methods and Materials of Demography*, 2nd edn. New York: Academic Press.

Siemens, A. H. (1983) Wetland agriculture in pre-Hispanic Mesoamerica. *Geographical Review*, **73**, 166–81.

Sigaut, F. (1988) A method for identifying grain storage techniques and its application for European agricultural history. *Tools and Tillage*, **6**, 3–32.

Sigaut, F. (1989) Storage and threshing in pre-industrial Europe: Additional notes. *Tools and Tillage*, **6**, 119–24.

Sillitoe, P. (1979) *Give and Take: Exchange in Wola Society*. Canberra: Australian National University Press.

Sillitoe, P. (1983) *Roots of the Earth: Crops in the Highlands of Papua New Guinea*. Kensington, Australia: New South Wales University Press.

Sillitoe, P. (1996) *A Place Against Time: Land and Environment in the Papua New Guinea Highlands*. Amsterdam: Harwood.

Sillitoe, P. (1998) It's all in the mound: Fertility management under stationary shifting cultivation in the Papua New Guinea highlands. *Mountain Research and Development*, **18**, 123–34.

Sillitoe, P. (2010) *From Land to Mouth: The Agricultural "Economy" of the Wola of the New Guinea Highlands*. New Haven, CT: Yale University Press.

Sillitoe, P., Stewart, P. J. and Strathern, A. (2002) *Horticulture in Papua New Guinea: Case Studies from the Southern and Western Highlands*. Ethnology Monographs, No. 18. Pittsburgh: Department of Anthropology, University of Pittsburgh.

Silva-Fosberg, M. C. and Fearnside, P. M. (1997) Brazilian Amazonian *caboclo* agriculture: Effect of fallow period on maize yield. *Forest Ecology and Management*, **97**, 3–24.

Simmons, I. G. (1987) Transformation of the land in pre-industrial time. In *Land Transformation in Agriculture*, ed. M. G. Wolman and F. G. A. Fournier. New York: Wiley and Sons, pp. 45–77.

Simon, H. (1957) *Models of Man*. New York: Wiley and Sons.

Simondon, K. B., Bénéfice, E., Simondon, F., Delaunay, V. and Chahzazarian, A. (1993) Seasonal variation in nutritional status of adults and children in rural Senegal. In *Seasonality and Human Ecology*, ed. S. Ulijaszek and S. S. Strickland. Cambridge: Cambridge University Press, pp. 166–83.

Sinclair, T. R. and Gardner, F. P. (1998) Environmental limits to plant production. In *Principles of Ecology in Plant Production*, ed. T. R. Sinclair and F. P. Gardner. New York: CAB International, pp. 63–78.

Sirén, A. H. (2007) Population growth and land use intensification in a subsistence-based community in the Amazon. *Human Ecology*, **35**, 669–80.

Skjønsberg, E. (1989) *Change in an African Village*. Hartford, CT: Kumarian Press.

Slicher van Bath, B. H. (1963a) *Yield Ratios, 810–1820*. Wageningen: Afdeling Agrarische Geschiedenis, Landbouwhogeschool.

Slicher van Bath, B. H. (1963b) *The Agrarian History of Western Europe A.D. 500–1850*. London: Edward Arnold.

Slobodkin, L. B. (1954) Population dynamics in *Daphnia obtusa* Kurz. *Ecological Monographs*, **24**, 69–88.

Smil, V. (2001) *Enriching the Earth: Fritz Haber, Carl Bosch, and the Transformation of World Food Production*. Cambridge, MA: MIT Press.

Smith, A. E. (1979) Chayanov, Sahlins, and the labor-consumer balance. *Journal of Anthropological Research*, **35**, 477–80.

Smith, E. A. (1979) Human adaptation and energy efficiency. *Human Ecology*, **7**, 53–74.

Smith, J. M. B. (1977) Man's impact upon some New Guinea mountain ecosystems. In *Subsistence and Survival: Rural Ecology in the Pacific*, ed. T. P. Bayliss-Smith and R. G. Feachem. London: Academic Press, pp. 185–214.

Smith, M. G. (1982) Foreword. In F. W. Schwerdtfeger, *Traditional Housing in African Cities: A Comparative Study of Houses in Zaria, Ibadan, and Marrakech*. Chichester: Wiley and Sons, pp. xi–xvii.

Smith, R., ed. (2002) *Ecological Survey of Zambia: The Traverse Records of C.G. Trapnell 1932–43*. Kew: Royal Botanic Gardens.

Smith, R. E. F. (1977) *Peasant Farming in Muscovy*. Cambridge: Cambridge University Press.

Smith, R. M. (1984) Families and their land in an area of partible inheritance: Redgrave, Suffolk

1260-1320. In *Land, Kinship and Life-Cycle*, ed. R. M. Smith. Cambridge: Cambridge University Press, pp. 135–96.

Smith, R. M. (1999) Relative prices, forms of agrarian labour and female marriage pattern in England, 1350–1800. In *Marriage and Rural Economy: Western Europe since 1400*, ed. I. Devos and L. Kennedy. Turnhout, Belgium: Brepols Publishers, pp. 19–48.

Smith, T. C. (1959) *The Agrarian Origins of Modern Japan*. Stanford, CA: Stanford University Press.

Smith, T. C. (1977) *Nakahara: Family Farming and Population in a Japanese Village, 1717–1863*. Stanford, CA: Stanford University Press.

Smith, T. L. (1959) Fragmentation in agricultural holdings in Spain. *Rural Sociology*, **24**, 140–9.

Smole, W. J. (1976) *The Yanoama Indians: A Cultural Geography*. Austin, TX: University of Texas Press.

Snodgrass, J. J. (2012) Human energetics. In *Human Biology: An Evolutionary and Biocultural Perspective*, ed. S. Stinson, B. Bogin and D. O'Rourke. Hoboken, NJ: Wiley-Blackwell, pp. 325–84.

Snow, B. and Marsh, K. (1992) How useful are verbal autopsies to estimate childhood causes of death? *Health Policy Planning*, **7**, 22–9.

Snyder, K. A. (1996) Agrarian change and land-use strategies among Iraqw farmers in northern Tanzania. *Human Ecology*, **24**, 315–40.

Sober, E. (1994) Reintroducing group selection to the human behavioral sciences. *Behavioral and Brain Sciences*, **17**, 585–654.

Soldi, A. M. (1982) *La Agricultura Tradicional en Hoyas*. Lima: Pontificia Universidad Catolica del Peru.

Soleri, D. and Cleveland, D. A. (2001) Farmers' genetic perceptions regarding their crop populations: An example with maize in the central valleys of Oaxaca, Mexico. *Economic Botany*, **55**, 106–28.

Soltow, L. (1990) The distribution of private wealth in land in Scotland and Scandinavia in the seventeenth and eighteenth centuries. In *Scotland and Scandinavia 800–1800*, ed. G. G. Simpson. Edinburgh: John Donald, pp. 130–47.

Sommer, A. and Loewenstein, M. S. (1975) Nutritional status and mortality. *American Journal of Clinical Nutrition*, **28**, 287–92.

Sparks, C. S., Wood, J. W. and Johnson, P. L. (2013) Infant mortality and intra-household competition in the northern islands of Orkney, Scotland, 1855–2001. *American Journal of Physical Anthropology*, **151**, 191–201.

Sparrow, W. A., Hughes, K. M., Russell, A. P. and Le Rossignol, P. F. (2000) Movement economy, preferred modes, and pacing. In *Energetics of Human Activity*, ed. W. A. Sparrow. Champaign, IL: Human Kinetics, pp. 96–123.

Spurr, G. B. (1984) Physical activity, nutritional status, and physical work capacity in relation to agricultural activity. In *Energy Intake and Activity*, ed. E. Pollitt and P. Amante. New York: Alan R. Liss, pp. 207–61.

Spurr, G. B. (1988) Marginal malnutrition in childhood: Implications for adult work capacity and productivity. In *Capacity for Work in the Tropics*, ed. K. J. Collin and D. F. Roberts. Cambridge: Cambridge University Press, pp. 107–40.

Stanhill, G. (1976) Trends and deviations in the yield of the English wheat crop during the last 750 years. *Agroecosystems*, **3**, 1–10.

Stauder, J. (1971) *The Majangir: Ecology and Society of a Southwest Ethiopian People*. Cambridge: Cambridge University Press.

Steckel, R. H. and Rose, J. C. (2002) *The Backbone of History: Health and Nutrition in the Western Hemisphere*. Cambridge: Cambridge University Press.

Stecklov, G. (1999) Estimating the economic returns to childbearing in Côte d'Ivoire. *Population Studies*, **53**, 1–17.

Steensberg, A. (1980) *New Guinea Gardens: A Study of Husbandry with Parallels in Prehistoric Europe*. London: Academic Press.

Steensberg, A. (1993) *Fire-Clearance Husbandry: Traditional Techniques throughout the World*. Herning, Denmark: Poul Kristensen.

Stein, Z. and Susser, M. (1975) Fertility, fecundity, famine: Food rations in the Dutch famine 1944/5 have a causal relation to fertility, and probably to fecundity. *Human Biology*, **47**, 131–54.

Stelly, M., ed. (1976) *Multiple Cropping*. Madison, WI: American Society of Agronomy, Crop Science Society of America, Soil Science Society of America.

Stevens, S. F. (1993) *Claiming the High Ground: Sherpas, Subsistence, and Environmental Change in the Highest Himalayas*. Berkeley, CA: University of California Press.

Stocks, A. (1983) Candoshi and Cocamilla swiddens in eastern Peru. *Human Ecology*, **11**, 69–84.

Stone, G. D. (1996) *Settlement Ecology: The Social and Spatial Organization of Kofyar Agriculture*. Tucson, AZ: University of Arizona Press.

Stone, G. D. (2001) Theory of the square chicken: Advances in agricultural intensification theory. *Asia Pacific Viewpoint*, **42**, 163–80.

Stone, G. D., Netting, R.M. and Stone, M. P. (1990) Seasonality, labor scheduling and agricultural intensification in the Nigerian savanna. *American Anthropologist*, **92**, 7–23.

Stone, M. P., Stone, G. D. and Netting, R. M. (1995) The sexual division of labor in Kofyar agriculture. *American Ethnologist*, **22**, 165–86.

Stout, B. A., Myers, C. A., Hurrand, A. and Faidley, L. W. (1979) *Energy for World Agriculture*. Rome: Food and Agriculture Organization of the United Nations.

Strathern, A. J. (1975) *The Rope of Moka: Big-men and Ceremonial Exchange in Mount Hagen, New Guinea*. Cambridge: Cambridge University Press.

Street, J. M. (1969) An evaluation of the concept of carrying capacity. *The Professional Geographer*, **21**, 104–7.

Strømgaard, P. (1985) The infield outfield system of shifting cultivation among the Bemba of South Central Africa. *Tools and Tillage*, **5**, 67–84.

Strømgaard, P. (1988) The grassland mound-system of the Aisa-Mambwe of Zambia. *Tools and Tillage*, **6**, 33–46.

Strømgaard, P. (1992) Immediate and long-term effects of fire and ash fertilization on a Zambian miombo woodland soil. *Agriculture, Ecosystems and Environment*, **41**, 19–37.

Sugiyama, Y. and Ohsawa, H. (1982) Population dynamics of Japanese monkeys with special reference to the effect of artificial feeding. *Folia Primatologica*, **39**, 238–63.

Sukhatme, R. V. and Margen, S. (1978) Models for protein deficiency. *American Journal of Clinical Nutrition*, **31**, 1237–56.

Sukhatme, R. V. and Margen, S. (1982) Autoregulatory homeostatic nature of energy balance. *American Journal of Clinical Nutrition*, **35**, 355–65.

Swamy, P. S. and Ramakrishnan, P. S. (1988) Nutrient budget under slash and burn agriculture (*jhum*) with different weeding regimes in north-eastern India. *Acta Oecologica*, **9**, 85–102.

Szott, L. T., Pal, C. A. and Buresh, R. J. (1999) Ecosystem fertility and fallow function in the humid and subhumid tropics. *Agroforestry Systems*, **47**, 163–96.

Takahashi, A. (1969) *Land and Peasants in Central Luzon: Socio-Economic Structure of a Bulacan Village*. Tokyo: Institute of Developing Economies.

Tannenbaum, N. (1984) The misuse of Chayanov: Chayanov's rule and empiricist bias in anthropology. *American Anthropologist*, **86**, 924–42.

Tanner, J. M. (1963) The regulation of human growth. *Child Development*, **34**, 817–47.

Tanner, J. M. (1986) Growth as a target-seeking function: Catch up and catch down growth in man. In *Human Growth: A Comprehensive Treatise (Volume II)*, ed. F. T. Falkner and J. M. Tanner. New York: Plenum Press, pp. 167–79.

Tax, S. (1953) *Penny Capitalism: A Guatemalan Indian Economy*. Washington: US Government Printing Office.

Taylor, D. C. (1981) *The Economics of Malaysian Paddy Production and Irrigation*. Bangkok: The Agricultural Development Council.

Terao, A. and Tanaka, T. (1928) Influence of temperature upon the rate of reproduction in the water-flea *Moina macropa* Strauss. *Proceedings of the Imperial Academy (Japan)*, **4**, 553–5.

Tesfaye, T., Getachew, B. and Worede, M. (1991) Morphological diversity in tetraploid wheat landrace populations from the central highlands of Ethiopia. *Hereditas*, **114**, 171–6.

Teshome, A., Fahrig, L., Torrance, J. K., *et al.* (1999a) Maintenance of sorghum (*Sorghum bicolor*, Poaceae) landrace diversity by farmers' selection in Ethiopia. *Economic Botany*, **53**, 79–88.

Teshome, A., Torrance, J. K., Baum, B., *et al.* (1999b) Traditional farmers' knowledge of sorghum (*Sorghum bicolor* [Poaceae]) landrace storability in Ethiopia. *Economic Botany*, **53**, 69–78.

Thirsk, J. (1957) *English Peasant Farming: The Agrarian History of Lincolnshire from Tudor to Recent Times*. London: Methuen.

Thom, D. J. and Wells, J. C. (1987) Farming systems in the Niger inland delta, Mali. *Geographical Review*, **77**, 328–42.

Thomas, D. (1990) Intra-household resources allocation: An inferential approach. *Journal of Human Resources*, **25**, 635–64.

Thurston, T. L. and Fisher, C. T., eds. (2007) *Seeking a Richer Harvest: The Archaeology of Subsistence Intensification, Innovation, and Change.* New York: Springer.

Tiffen, M., Mortimore, M. and Gichuki, F. (1994) *More People, Less Erosion: Environmental Recovery in Kenya.* New York: Wiley.

Titow, J. Z. (1972) *Winchester Yields: A Study in Medieval Agricultural Productivity.* Cambridge: Cambridge University Press.

Tivy, J. (1990) *Agricultural Ecology.* London: Longman.

Todd, P. M., Billari, F. C. and Simao, J. (2005) Aggregate age-at-marriage patterns from individual mate-search heuristics. *Demography*, **42**, 559–74.

Tomita, S., Parker, D. M., Jennings, J. A. and Wood, J. W. (2015) Household demography and early childhood mortality in a rice-farming village in northern Laos. *PLOS ONE*, **10**, e0119191. Doi:10.1371/journal.pone.0119191.

Tomkins, A. (1981) Nutritional status and severity of diarrhoea among pre-school children in rural Nigeria. *The Lancet*, **317**(8225), 18 April, 860–2.

Toulmin, C. (1992) *Cattle, Women, and Wells: Managing Household Survival in the Sahel.* Oxford: Oxford University Press.

Townsend, R. M. (1993) *The Medieval Village Economy: A Study of the Pareto Mapping in General Equilibrium Models.* Princeton, NJ: Princeton University Press.

Trapnell, C. G. (1943) *The Soils, Vegetation and Agriculture of North-Eastern Rhodesia.* Oxford: Oxford University Press.

Trenbath, B. R. (1976) Plant interactions in mixed crop communities. In *Multiple Cropping*, ed. M. Stelly. Madison, WI: American Society of Agronomy, Crop Science Society of America, Soil Science Society of America, pp. 129–69.

Tschaianoff [Chayanov], A. V. (1931) The socio-economic nature of peasant farm economy. In *A Systematic Source Book in Rural Sociology (Volume II)*, ed. P. A. Sorokin, C. C. Zimmerman and C. J. Galpin. Minneapolis, MN: University of Minnesota Press, pp. 144–7.

Tsubouchi, U. (1996) *One Malay Village: A Thirty-Year Community Study.* Kyoto: Kyoto University Press.

Tucker, B. (2006) A future discounting explanation for the presence of a mixed foraging-horticulture strategy among the Mikea of Madagascar. In *Behavioral Ecology and the Transition to Agriculture*, ed. D. J. Kennett and B. Winterhalder. Berkeley, CA: University of California Press, pp. 22–40.

Tung, D. X. and Rasmussen, S. (2005) Production function analysis for smallholder semi-subsistence and semi-commercial poultry production systems in three agro-ecological regions in northern provinces of Vietnam. *Livestock Research for Rural Development*, **17** (http://www/lrrd.org/lrrd17/tung17096.htm).

Turchin, P. (1995) Population regulation: Old arguments and a new synthesis. In *Population Dynamics: New Applications and Synthesis*, ed. N. Cappuccino and P. W. Price. New York: Academic Press, pp. 19–40.

Turchin, P. (2003) *Complex Population Dynamics: A Theoretical/Empirical Synthesis.* Princeton, NJ: Princeton University Press.

Turchin, P. (2009) Long-term population cycles in human societies. *Annals of the New York Academy of Sciences*, **1162**, 1–17.

Turner, B. L. and Ali, A. M. S. (1996) Induced intensification: Agricultural change in Bangladesh with implications for Malthus and Boserup. *Proceedings of the National Academy of Sciences*, **93**, 14,984–91.

Turner, B. L. and Brush, S. B. (1987) *Comparative Farming Systems.* London: Guilford Press.

Turner, B. L., Hanham, R. Q. and Portararo, A. V. (1977) Population pressure and agricultural intensity. *Annals of the Association of American Geographers*, **67**, 384–96.

Turner, B. L., Hyden, G. and Kates, R. W., eds. (1993) *Population Growth and Agricultural Change in Africa.* Gainesville, FL: University Press of Florida.

Udry, J. R. and Cliquet, R. L. (1982) A cross-cultural examination of the relationship between ages at menarche, marriage, and first birth. *Demography*, **19**, 53–63.

Uhl, C., Clar, H. and Clark, H. (1982) Successional patterns associated with slash-and-burn agriculture in the Upper Río Negro region of the Amazon Basin. *Biotropica*, **14**, 249–54.

Ulijaszek, S. J. (1995) *Human Energetics in Biological Anthropology.* Cambridge: Cambridge University Press.

Ulijaszek, S. J. and Strickland, S. S. (1993) *Nutritional Anthropology: Prospects and Perspectives.* London: Smith-Gordon.

Unami, K., Kawachi, T. and Yangyuoru, M. (2005) Optimal water management in small-scale tank irrigation systems. *Energy,* **30,** 1419–28.

United Nations (1998) *The State of the World's Children.* U.N. International Children's Emergency Fund. Oxford: Oxford University Press.

van Beukering, J. A. (1947) *Het ladangvraagstuk, enn bedrijfs- en sociaal economisch probleem.* Mededeelingen van het Departement van Economisch Zaken in Nederlandsch-Indië, No. 9.

Vanden Driesen, I. H. (1971) Patterns of land holding and land distribution in the Ife Division of Western Nigeria. *Africa,* **41,** 42–53.

Vandermeer, C. (1971) Water thievery in a rice irrigation system in Taiwan. *Annals of the Association of American Geographers,* **61,** 156–79.

Vandermeer, J. (1989) *The Ecology of Intercropping.* Cambridge: Cambridge University Press.

Vanhaute, E. (2011) From famine to food crisis: What history can teach us about local and global subsistence crises. *Journal of Peasant Studies,* **38,** 47–65.

van Loon, J. H. (1963) Energy expenditure in lifting sheaves. *Proceedings of the XIVth International Congress of Occupational Health,* **62,** 1752–3.

VanWey, L. K., D'Antona, A. O. and Brondizio, E. S. (2007) Household demographic change and land use/land cover change in the Brazilian Amazon. *Population and Environment,* **28,** 165–85.

van Wyck, B.-E. (2005) *Food Plants of the World: An Illustrated Guide.* Portland, OR: Timber Press.

Vasey, D. E. (1992) *An Ecological History of Agriculture, 10,000 B.C.-A.D. 10,000.* Ames, IA: Iowa State University Press.

Vaughan, J. G. and Geissler, C. A. (1997) *The New Oxford Book of Food Plants: A Guide to the Fruit, Vegetables, Herbs and Spices of the World.* Oxford: Oxford University Press.

Verdery, A. M., Entwisle, B., Faust, K. and Rindfuss, R. R. (2012) Social and spatial kinship: Kinship distance and dwelling unit proximity in rural Thailand. *Social Networks* **34,** 112–27.

Verdon, M. (1979) The stem family: Toward a general theory. *Journal of Interdisciplinary History,* **10,** 87–105.

Viazzo, P. P. (1989) *Upland Communities: Environment, Population and Social Structure in the Alps Since the Sixteenth Century.* Cambridge: Cambridge University Press.

Viazzo, P. P. (2005) South of the Hajnal line: Italy and southern Europe. In *Marriage and the Family in Eurasia: Perspectives on the Hajnal Hypothesis,* ed. T. Engelen and A. P. Wolf. Amsterdam: Aksant Publishers, pp. 129–63.

Vickers, W. T. (1983) Tropical forest mimicry in swiddens: A reassessment of Geertz's model with Amazonian data. *Human Ecology,* **11,** 35–45.

Viên, T. D., Rambo, A. T. and Lâm, N. T. (2009) *Farming with Fire and Water: The Human Ecology of a Composite Swiddening Community in Vietnam's Northern Mountains.* Kyoto: Kyoto University Press.

Vinovskis, M. (1977) From household size to the life course: Some observations on recent trends in family history. *American Behavioral Sciences,* **21,** 263–87.

Vinovskis, M. (1988) The historian and the life course: Reflections on recent approaches to the study of American family life in the past. In *Life-Span Development and Behavior,* ed. P. B. Baltes, D. L. Featherman and R. M. Lerner. Hillsdale, NJ: Erlbaum, pp. 33–59.

Viteri, F. E., Torun, B., Garcia, J. C. and Herrera, E. (1971) Determining energy costs of agricultural activities by respirometer and energy balance techniques. *American Journal of Clinical Nutrition,* **24,** 1418–30.

von Rotenham, D. (1968) Cotton farming in Sukumaland: Cash cropping and its implications. In *Smallholder Farming and Smallholder Development in Tanzania,* ed. H. Ruthenberg. Munich: Weltforum Verlag, pp. 51–86.

von Thünen, J. H. (1966 [orig. 1826]) *von Thünen's Isolated State,* ed. P. Hall. Oxford: Pergamon Press.

von Tunzelmann, G. N. (1986) Malthus's 'total population system': A dynamic reinterpretation. In *The State of Population Theory: Forward from Malthus,* ed. D. Coleman and R. S. Schofield. Oxford: Blackwell, pp. 65–95.

von Verschuer, C. (2016) *Rice, Agriculture, and the Food Supply in Premodern Japan*. London: Routledge.

Wachter, K. W. (1987a) Mathematical requirements for homeostasis in prehistory. *Sloan-Berkeley Working Papers in Population Studies, no. 11*. Berkeley: Graduate Group in Demography, University of California.

Wachter, K. W. (1987b) Microsimulation of household cycles. In *Family Demography: Methods and their Applications*, ed. J. Bongaarts, T. K. Burch and K. W. Wachter. Oxford: Oxford University Press, pp. 215–27.

Wachter, K. W., Hammel, E. A. and Laslett, P., eds. (1978) *Statistical Studies of Historical Social Structure*. New York: Academic Press.

Waddell, E. W. (1972) *The Mound Builders: Agricultural Practices, Environment, and Society in the Central Highlands of New Guinea*. Seattle: University of Washington Press.

Waddell, E. W. and Krinks, P. A. (1968) *The Organization of Production and Distribution among the Orokaiva*. Canberra: New Guinea Research Bureau, Australian National University.

Wade, M. J. (1977) An experimental study of group selection. *Evolution*, 31,134–53.

Wall, R. (1972) Mean household size in England from printed sources. In *Household and Family in Past Time*, ed. P. Laslett and R. Wall. Cambridge: Cambridge University Press, pp. 159–203.

Wall, R. (1982) The household: Demographic and economic change in England, 1650-1970. In *Family Forms in Historic Europe*, ed. R. Wall, J. Robin and P. Laslett. Cambridge: Cambridge University Press, pp. 493–512.

Wallace, B. (1968) *Topics in Population Genetics*. New York: W. W. Norton.

Wallace, B. J. (1970) *Hill and Valley Farmers: Socio-Economic Change among a Philippine People*. Cambridge, MA: Schenkman.

Wandel, M., Holmboe-Ottesen, G. and Manu, A. (1992) Seasonal work, energy intake and nutritional stress: A case study from Tanzania. *Nutrition Research*, 12, 1–16.

Ward, A. D. and Trimble, S. W. (2003) *Environmental Hydrology*, 2nd edn. Boca Raton, FL: CRC Press.

Watabe, T. (1981) *Report of the Scientific Survey on Traditional Cropping Systems in Tropical Asia: Part 1 (India and Sri Lanka), Part 2 (Indonesia)*. Kyoto: Kyoto University Press.

Waterlow, J. C. (1992) *Protein-Energy Malnutrition*. London: Edward Arnold.

Watkins, S. C. and Menken, J. A. (1985) Famines in historical perspective. *Population and Development Review*, 11, 647–75.

Watkins, S. C. and van de Walle, E. (1983) Nutrition, mortality, and population size: Malthus' court of last resort. *Journal of Interdisciplinary History*, 14, 205–26.

Watson, E. E., Adams, W. M. and Mutiso, S. K. (1998) Indigenous irrigation, agriculture and development, Marakwet, Kenya. *The Geographical Journal*, 164, 67–84.

Watson, P. J. (1979) *Archaeological Ethnography in Western Iran*. Tucson, AZ: The University of Arizona Press.

Watters, R. F. (1971) *Shifting Cultivation in Latin America*. Rome: Food and Agriculture Organization of the United Nations.

Weil, P. M. (1970) The introduction of the ox plow in central Gambia. In *African Food Production Systems: Cases and Theory*, ed. P. F. M. McLoughlin. Baltimore: Johns Hopkins University Press, pp. 229–63.

Wercshler, T. and Halli, S. (1992) The seasonality of births in Canada: A comparison with the northern United States. *Population and Environment*, 14, 85–94.

West, C. T. (2009) Domestic transitions, desiccation, agricultural intensification, and livelihood diversification among rural households on the Central Plateau, Burkina Faso. *American Anthropologist*, 111, 275–88.

West, C. T. (2010) Household extension and fragmentation: Investigating the socio-environmental dynamics of Mossi domestic transitions. *Human Ecology*, 38, 363–76.

West, R. C. (1957) *The Pacific Lowlands of Colombia: A Negroid Area of the American Tropics*. Baton Rouge, LA: Louisiana State University Press.

Westphal, E. (1975) *Agricultural Systems in Ethiopia*. Wageningen: Centre for Agricultural Publishing and Documentation.

Wharton, C. R., ed. (1969) *Subsistence Agriculture and Economic Development*. Chicago: Aldine.

Wheeler, E. F. and Abdullah, M. (1988) Food allocation within the family: Response to fluctuating food supply and food needs. In *Coping with Uncertainty in Food Supply*, ed. I. deGarine and G. A. Harrison. Oxford: Oxford University Press, pp. 437–51.

White, B. (1973) Demand for labor and population growth in colonial Java. *Human Ecology*, 1, 217–36.

White, B. (1983) "Agricultural involution" and its critics: Twenty years after. *Bulletin of Concerned Asian Scholars*, 15, 18–23.

White, D. R., Burton, M. L. and Dow, M. M. (1981) Sexual division of labor in African agriculture: A network autocorrelation analysis. *American Anthropologist*, 83, 824–49.

White, G. F., Bradley, D. J. and White, A. U. (1972) *Drawers of Water: Domestic Water Use in East Africa*. Chicago: University of Chicago Press.

White, L. (1962) *Medieval Technology and Social Change*. Oxford: Oxford University Press.

Whitmore, T. M. and Turner, B. L. (2001) *Cultivated Landscapes of Middle America on the Eve of Conquest*. Oxford: Oxford University Press.

Whitmore, T. M., Turner, B. L., Johnson, D. L., Kates, R. W. and Gottschang, T. R. (1993) Long-term population growth. In *The Earth as Transformed by Human Action: Global and Regional Changes in the Biosphere over the Past 300 Years*, ed. B. L. Turner, W. C. Clark, R. W. Kates and J. F. Richards. Cambridge: Cambridge University Press, pp. 25–39.

Whittlesey, D. (1937a) Shifting cultivation. *Economic Geography*, 13, 35–52.

Whittlesey, D. (1937b) Fixation of shifting cultivation. *Economic Geography*, 13, 139–54.

Whyte, R. O. (1974) *Rural Nutrition in Monsoon Asia*. Kuala Lumpur: Oxford University Press.

Wiber, M. G. (1985) Dynamics of the peasant household economy: Labor recruitment and allocation in an upland Philippine community. *Journal of Anthropological Research*, 41, 427–41.

Widdowson, E. M. (1976) Changes in the body and its organs during lactation: Nutritional implications. In *Breast-feeding and the Mother*. CIBA Foundation Symposium 45 (new series). Amsterdam: Elsevier North-Holland, pp. 103–18.

Widgren, M. (2004) Towards a historical geography of intensive farming in Eastern Africa. In *Islands of Intensive Agriculture in Eastern Africa: Past and Present*, ed. M. Widgren and J. E. G. Sutton. Oxford: James Currey, pp. 1–18.

Widgren, M. (2007) Pre-colonial landesque capital: A global perspective. In *Rethinking Environmental History: World-System History and Global Environmental Change*, ed. A. Hornborg, J. Marinez-Alier and J. R. McNeil. Walnut Creek, CA: AltaMira Press, pp. 61–77.

Widgren, M. and Sutton, J. E. G., eds. (2004) *Islands of Intensive Agriculture in Eastern Africa: Past and Present*. Oxford: James Currey.

Wiggins, S. (1995) Change in African farming systems between the mid-1970s and the mid-1980s. *Journal of International Development*, 7, 807–48.

Wijsman, E. M. and Cavalli-Sforza, L. L. (1984) Migration and genetic population structure with special reference to humans. *Annual Review of Ecology and Systematics*, 15, 279–301.

Wilhusen, R. H. and Stone, G. D. (1990) An ethnoarchaeological perspective on soils. *World Archaeology*, 22, 104–14.

Wilk, R. R. (1989a) Decision-making and resource flows within the household: Beyond the black box. In *The Household Economy: Reconsidering the Domestic Mode of Production*, ed. R. R. Wilk. Boulder, CO: Westview, pp. 23–52.

Wilk, R. R., ed. (1989b) *The Household Economy: Reconsidering the Domestic Mode of Production*. Boulder, CO: Westview.

Wilk, R. R. (1991) *Household Ecology: Economic Change and Domestic Life Among the Kekchi Maya in Belize*. Tucson, AZ: University of Arizona Press.

Wilk, R. R. and Netting, R. M. (1984) Households: Changing forms and functions. In *Households: Comparative and Historical Studies of the Domestic Group*, ed. R. M. Netting, R. R. Wilk and E. J. Arnould. Berkeley: University of California Press, pp. 1–28.

Wilken, G. C. (1969) Drained-field agriculture: An intensive farming system in Tlaxcala, Mexico. *Geographical Review*, 59, 215–41.

Wilken, G. C. (1970) The ecology of gathering in a Mexican farming region. *Economic Botany*, 24, 286–95.

Wilken, G. C. (1972) Microclimate management by traditional farmers. *Geographical Review*, 62, 554–60.

Wilken, G. C. (1977) Manual irrigation in Middle America. *Agricultural Water Management*, 1, 155–65.

Wilken, G. C. (1979) Traditional slope management: An analytical approach. In *Hill Lands: Proceedings of an International Symposium*. Morgantown, WV: West Virginia University Books, pp. 416–22.

Wilken, G. C. (1987) *Good Farmers: Traditional Agricultural Resource Management in Mexico and Central America*. Berkeley, CA: University of California Press.

Wilkinson, J. C. (1977) *Water and Tribal Settlement in South-East Arabia: A Study of the Aflāj of Oman*. Oxford: Clarendon Press.

Wilkinson, T. (2006) From highland to desert: The organization of landscape and irrigation in Southern Arabia. In *Agricultural Strategies*, ed. J. Marcus and C. Stanish. Los Angeles: Cotsen Institute of Archaeology, University of California at Los Angeles, pp. 38–88.

Willekins, F. (1988) A life course perspective on household dynamics. In *Modeling Household Formation and Dissolution*, ed. N. Keilman, A. Kuijsten and A. D. Vossen. Oxford: Oxford University Press, pp. 87–107.

Williams, G. C. (1972) *Adaptation and Natural Selection: A Critique of Some Current Evolutionary Thought*. Princeton, NJ: Princeton University Press.

Wilson, D. S. (1987) Altruism in Mendelian populations derived from sibling groups: The haystack model revisited. *Evolution*, 41, 1059–70.

Wilson, D. S. and Wilson, E. O. (2008) Evolution "for the good of the group". *The American Scientist*, 96, 380–9.

Wilson, G. L. (1917) *Agriculture of the Hidatsa Indians: An Indian Interpretation*. Minneapolis, MN: University of Minnesota Press.

Wilson, W. M. and Dufour, D. L. (2002) Why "bitter" cassava? Productivity of "bitter" and "sweet" cassava in a Tukanoan Indian settlement in the northwest Amazon. *Economic Botany*, 56, 49–57.

Winch, D. (1992) *Malthus: 'An Essay on the Principle of Population.'* Cambridge: Cambridge University Press.

Winterhalder, B. (1990) Open field, common pot: Harvest variability and risk avoidance in agricultural and foraging societies. In *Risk and Uncertainty in Tribal and Peasant Economies*, ed. E. Cashdan. Boulder, CO: Westview, pp. 67–87.

Winterhalder, B., Larsen, R. and Thomas, R. B. (1974) Dung as an essential resource in a highland Peruvian community. *Human Ecology*, 2, 89–104.

Wittfogel, K. (1964) *Oriental Despotism: A Comparative Study of Total Power*. New Haven, CT: Yale University Press.

Wood, J. W. (1980) *Mechanisms of Demographic Equilibrium in a Small Human Population, the Gainj of Papua New Guinea*. PhD dissertation, Department of Anthropology, University of Michigan, Ann Arbor, MI.

Wood, J. W. (1987) The genetic demography of the Gainj of Papua New Guinea. 2. Determinants of effective population size. *The American Naturalist*, 129, 165–87.

Wood, J. W. (1994a) *Dynamics of Human Reproduction: Biology, Biometry, Demography*. Hawthorne, NY: Aldine de Gruyter.

Wood, J. W. (1994b) Maternal nutrition and reproduction: Why demographers and physiologists disagree about a fundamental relationship. *Annals of the New York Academy of Sciences*, 709, 101–16.

Wood, J. W. (1998) A theory of preindustrial population dynamics: Demography, economy, and well-being in Malthusian systems. *Current Anthropology*, 39, 99–135.

Wood, J. W., Holman, D. J., Weiss, K. M., Buchanan, A. V. and LeFor, B. (1992a) Hazards models for human population biology. *Yearbook of Physical Anthropology*, 35, 43–87.

Wood, J. W., Johnson, P. L. and Campbell, K. L. (1985a) Demographic and endocrinological aspects of low natural fertility in highland New Guinea. *Journal of Biosocial Science*, 17, 57–79.

Wood, J. W., Lai, D., Johnson, P. L., Campbell, K. L. and Maslar, I. A. (1985b) Lactation and birth-spacing in highland New Guinea. *Journal of Biosocial Science*, Supplement 9, 159–73.

Wood, J. W., Milner, G. A., Harpending, H. C. and Weiss, K. M. (1992b) The osteological paradox: Problems of inferring prehistoric health from skeletal samples. *Current Anthropology*, 33, 343–70.

Wood, J. W. and Smouse, P. E. (1982) A method of analyzing density-dependent vital rates, with an application to the Gainj of Papua New Guinea. *American Journal of Physical Anthropology*, **58**, 403–11.

Wood, J. W. and Smouse, P. E. (1983) Population regulation and stable limit cycles in highland New Guinea. Paper presented at the Human Biology Council meetings.

Wood, J. W., Smouse, P. E. and Long, J. C. (1985c) Sex-specific dispersal patterns in two human populations of highland New Guinea. *The American Naturalist*, **125**, 747–68.

Woods, R. I., Watterson, P. A. and Woodward, J. H. (1988) The causes of rapid infant mortality decline in England and Wales, 1861–1921. *Population Studies*, **42**, 343–66.

Woodward, B. (1998) Protein, calories and immune defenses. *Nutrition Reviews*, **56**, S84–S92.

Woolf, L. (1913) *The Village in the Jungle*. London: Edward Arnold.

Worthington-Roberts, B. S., Vermeersch, J. and Williams, S. R. (1985) *Nutrition in Pregnancy and Lactation*, 3rd edn. St. Louis, MO: Times Mirror/Mosby College Publishing.

Wrigley, E. A. (1981) The prospects for population history. *Journal of Interdisciplinary History*, **12**, 207-26.

Wrigley, E. A. (1986) Elegance and experience: Malthus at the bar of history. In *The State of Population Theory: Forward from Malthus*, ed. D. Coleman and R. S. Schofield. Oxford: Blackwell, pp. 46-64.

Wrigley, E. A. (1988) *Continuity, Chance and Change: The Character of the Industrial Revolution in England*. Cambridge: Cambridge University Press.

Wrigley, E. A. (1991a) Energy availability and agricultural productivity. In *Land, Labour and Livestock: Historical Studies in European Agricultural Productivity*, ed. B. M. S. Campbell and M. Overton. Manchester: Manchester University Press, pp. 323-9.

Wrigley, E. A. (1991b) Why poverty was inevitable in traditional societies. In *Transition to Modernity: Essays on Power, Wealth and Belief*, ed. J. A. Hall and I. C. Jarvie. Cambridge: Cambridge University Press, pp. 91–110.

Wrigley, E. A. and Schofield, R. S. (1981) *The Population History of England 1541–1871: A Reconstruction*. Cambridge: Cambridge University Press.

Wynne-Edwards, V. C. (1962) *Animal Dispersion in Relation to Social Behaviour*. Edinburgh: Oliver and Boyd.

Wyon, J. B. and Gordon, J. E. (1971) *The Khanna Study: Population Problems in the Rural Punjab*. Cambridge, MA: Harvard University Press.

Xu, G. and Peel, L. J., eds. (1991) *The Agriculture of China*. Oxford: Oxford University Press.

Xu, J., Yang, Y., Pu, Y., Ayad, W. G. and Eyzaguirre, P. B. (2001) Genetic diversity in taro (*Colocasia esculenta* Schott, Araceae) in China: An ethnobotanical and genetic approach. *Economic Botany*, **55**, 14–31.

Yanagisako, S. J. (1979) Family and household: The analysis of domestic groups. *Annual Review of Anthropology*, **8**, 161–205.

Yang, M. C. (1945) *A Chinese Village: Taitou, Shantung Province*. New York: Columbia University Press.

Yen, D. E. and Mummery, J. M. J., eds. (1990) *Pacific Production Systems: Approaches to Economic Prehistory*. Canberra: Research School of Pacific Studies, Australian National University.

Yentsch, A. (1990) Minimum vessel lists as evidence of change in folk and courtly traditions of food use. *Historical Archaeology*, **24**, 24–53.

Yin, S. (2001) *People and Forests: Yunnan Swidden Agriculture in Human-Ecological Perspective*. Kunming, China: Yunnan Education Publishing House.

Yule, G. U. (1926) Why do we sometimes get nonsense correlations between time-series? A study in sampling and the nature of time-series. *Journal of the Royal Statistical Society*, **89**, 1–63.

Zeven, A. C. (1998) Landraces: A review of definitions and classifications. *Euphytica*, **104**, 127–39.

Zimmerer, K. S. (1991) Labor shortages and crop diversity in the southern Peruvian sierra. *Geographical Review*, **81**, 415–32.

Zimmerer, K. S. (1994) Local soil knowledge: Answering basic questions in highland Bolivia. *Journal of Soil and Water Management*, **49**, 29–34.

Zimmerer, K. S. (1996) *Changing Fortunes: Biodiversity and Peasant Livelihood in the Peruvian Andes*. Berkeley, CA: University of California Press.

Zipf, G. K. (1949) *Human Behavior and the Principle of Least Effort: An Introduction to Human Ecology.* Cambridge, MA: Addison-Wesley.

Zolitschka, B., Behre, K.-E. and Schneider, J. (2003) Human and climatic impact on the environment as derived from colluvial, fluvial and lacustrine archives: Examples from the Bronze Age to the Migration Period, Germany. *Quaternary Science Reviews*, 22, 81–100.

Zong, G. (1982) The mulberry dike-fish pond complex: A Chinese ecosystem of land-water interaction on the Pearl River delta. *Human Ecology*, 10, 191–202.

Index